W9-AZZ-552

CULTURAL STUDIES
An Introduction to
GLOBAL AWARENESS

"CUSTOM EDITION FOR THE US ARMY, MARINE CORPS, NAVY, AND AIR FORCE JUNIOR ROTC PROGRAMS"

JONES AND BARTLETT PUBLISHERS
Sudbury, Massachusetts
BOSTON TORONTO LONDON SINGAPORE

World Headquarters
Jones and Bartlett Publishers
40 Tall Pine Drive
Sudbury, MA 01776
978-443-5000
info@jbpub.com
www.jbpub.com

Jones and Bartlett Publishers Canada
6339 Ormindale Way
Mississauga, Ontario L5V 1J2
Canada

Jones and Bartlett Publishers International
Barb House, Barb Mews
London W6 7PA
United Kingdom

Jones and Bartlett's books and products are available through most bookstores and online booksellers. To contact Jones and Bartlett Publishers directly, call 800-832-0034, fax 978-443-8000, or visit our website www.jbpub.com.

Substantial discounts on bulk quantities of Jones and Bartlett's publications are available to corporations, professional associations, and other qualified organizations. For details and specific discount information, contact the special sales department at Jones and Bartlett via the above contact information or send an email to specialsales@jbpub.com.

Editorial Credits
High Stakes Writing, LLC, Editor and Publisher: Lawrence J. Goodrich
Department of the Air Force Editor: Linda F. Sackie
Primary writer: Ruth Walker
Editor: Katherine Dillin
Photo Research: Sarah Beth Glicksteen

Production Credits
Chief Executive Officer: Clayton Jones
Chief Operating Officer: Don W. Jones, Jr.
President, Higher Education and Professional Publishing: Robert W. Holland, Jr.
V.P., Professional Sales and Business Development: Christopher Will
V.P., Design and Production: Anne Spencer
V.P., Manufacturing and Inventory Control: Therese Connell
Publisher: Kimberly Brophy
Editor: Jennifer Kling
Production Editor: Wendy Swanson
Photo Research and Permissions Manager: Kimberly Potvin
Text and Cover Design: Anne Spencer
Composition: Mia Saunders Design
Illustrations: Elizabeth Morales, Katrina Peterson
Cover Images: clockwise from top left: "Mount Kilimanjaro" © ShutterStock, Inc.; "Pyramids, Giza, Egypt" © ShutterStock, Inc.; "Eiffel Tower" © ShutterStock, Inc.; "St. Basil's Cathedral" © Dreamstime, LLC; "Statue of Christ the Redeemer" © ShutterStock, Inc.; "Great Wall" © ShutterStock, Inc.
Chapter Design Images: Introduction—© Neo Edmund / ShutterStock, Inc.; Chapter 2—© Vivid Pixels / ShutterStock, Inc.; Chapter 3—© AbleStock; Chapter 4—© Zastavkin / ShutterStock, Inc.; Chapter 5—© allrightimages / age fotostock; Chapter 6—© Patricia Hofmeester / ShutterStock, Inc.
Printing and Binding: Courier Companies
Cover Printing: Courier Companies

Except where otherwise noted, the photos in this book are from *The Christian Science Monitor*. The *Monitor* is renowned for its in-depth, comprehensive, and unbiased coverage of events and issues worldwide. Since its founding in 1908, the *Monitor*'s adherence to the highest standards of journalism has earned seven Pulitzer Prizes and hundreds of other awards. With a unique style of photography that expresses the *Monitor*'s mission to inform and inspire, the *Monitor* strives to cover both major news events and stories from every corner of the globe. The *Monitor* can be read on its continuously updated website, CSMonitor.com, and in its weekly print edition, which launched in 2009.

Library of Congress Cataloging-in-Publication Data
Cultural studies : an introduction to global awareness.
p. cm.
Includes bibliographical references and index.
ISBN 978-0-7637-7516-2 (hardcover : alk. paper)
1. Civilization, Modern—21st century. 2. World politics—21st century. 3. Economic history—21st century. 4. Social history—21st century. I. Jones & Bartlett Publishers.
CB428.C835 2010
909.83—dc22
2009047437

6048

Printed in the United States of America
13 12 11 10 09 10 9 8 7 6 5 4 3 2 1

Contents

CHAPTER 6 Europe 594

Preface

Cultural Studies: An Introduction to Global Awareness is a customized course about the world's cultures. The course is specifically created for the US Army, Marine Corps, Navy, and Air Force Junior ROTC programs. It is designed to introduce students to the study of world affairs, regional studies, and cultural awareness. It delves into history, geography, religions, languages, culture, political systems, economics, social issues, environmental concerns, and human rights. It looks at major events and significant figures that have shaped each region.

In this age when the Internet, trade, airplanes, satellites, and cell phones connect people everywhere, it's more important than ever to understand the world's cultures. Even if you never leave the United States, you may find yourself working with or managing people from different parts of the world. If you end up working overseas, you'll find that the more insight you have into other countries' history and customs, the more successfully you'll navigate your way around new and exciting lands.

Features in this book include detailed *topographical* (mountains, rivers, etc.) and *political maps*. Colored boxes add brief additional information about related topics, while *fastFacts* offer extra tidbits of information. The photos provide glimpses of present-day life in these lands. You will see how people dress and what their cities, cars, streets, buildings, and homes look like. While historical photos can be extremely interesting, this textbook supplies you with pictures of what these countries look like *today*.

"Chapter 1: The Middle East" reviews the region from its earliest days as the cradle of Western civilization and the birthplace of Judaism, Christianity, and Islam. It then looks at the more recent challenges of war and terrorism. It considers changes the Middle East underwent in the twentieth century and the spread of nuclear weapons there in the twenty-first. Any discussion of this region must include its most sought-after natural resource: oil.

"Chapter 2: Asia" begins with a general overview of Eastern religions and the region's peoples. You'll study Japan, Korea, and China in East Asia, as well as India, Pakistan, and Afghanistan in South Asia. The chapter looks at what unites and what divides these countries. The chapter also tackles Asia's environmental and social challenges and researches the region's impact on US security and its economy.

"Chapter 3: Africa" covers a continent subject to outside influences, from Arab merchants and Islam to European traders and Christianity. Ethnic clashes have long marred the region. Pirates patrol some areas and hinder trade. AIDS, malaria, and other diseases kill thousands each year. Yet Africa is rich with natural resources, such as oil and diamonds, and US and European development agencies are working hard to help. This chapter looks at the area's potential and what's being done to encourage it.

"Chapter 4: Russia and the Former Soviet Republics" tracks the Cold War struggle between communism and capitalism. You'll study how the Soviet Union's economy operated and why it failed. In addition, the chapter deals with Russia's relationships with Asia, Europe, America, and the United Nations. It also looks ahead to such things as the challenges to US-Russian relations.

"Chapter 5: Latin America" reviews the region's history before and after European conquest. It considers the tug-of-war between church and state, the effects of wide social and economic divisions, and struggles with weak governments and corruption. The chapter also examines the effects of poverty and population growth on the region and its flow of migrants northward.

"Chapter 6: Europe" explains how the ancient Greeks and Romans molded Europe's character. It shows how their influence eventually extended to the founding principles of the United States. The chapter also delves into Europe's colonial ambitions, the effects of new nationalism on old empires, and the effects of fascism and communism. The chapter looks in depth at the collapse of Yugoslavia into seven independent countries, and the violence involved. And you'll explore the European Union's history, including its expansion to include countries trying to leave Russia's sphere of influence.

By the time you finish this course, you will have a greater understanding of the world around you. This knowledge will help you interpret trends and events abroad. We dedicate this book to everyone in our JROTC programs and trust it will help you in any future endeavors that bring you into contact with other cultures.

Lawrence J. Goodrich and Linda Sackie

Acknowledgements

Cultural Studies: An Introduction to Global Awareness is the culmination of a collaborative effort by the Jeanne M. Holm Center for Officer Accessions and Citizen Development (Holm Center) Curriculum Directorate. The team involved in the creation of this new cultural studies course was under the direction of Charles Nath III, PhD, Director of Curriculum for the Holm Center at Maxwell Air Force Base, Alabama, and Roger Ledbetter, Chief, AFJROTC Curriculum. They facilitated an exceptional leadership team resulting in a superb product for all the JROTC programs. Special thanks go to Holm Center Curriculum's Linda Sackie, an instructional systems specialist and the primary Air Force editor, reviewer, and significant contributor for this project. We commend Linda's continued selfless dedication and outstanding efforts to produce the best academic materials possible for all JROTC units worldwide.

We are indebted to our academic consultants/reviewers who provided sustained leadership and guidance for the course: Colonel John Gurtcheff (retired), AFJROTC Unit SC-873, Crestwood HS, Sumter, South Carolina; Dr. Nath; Mr. Ledbetter; and Mr. Kevin Lynn, Curriculum Area Manager/instructor from Holm Center Curriculum's Senior ROTC and Officer Training School staff. Additionally, thanks to the following for providing their expertise: Lieutenant Colonel Valerie Lofland (retired), AFJROTC Unit CT-941, Naugatuck HS, Naugatuck, Connecticut; Colonel Ben Pittman (retired), AFJROTC Unit SC-954, Wade Hampton HS, Greenville, South Carolina; Chief Master Sergeant Howard Vosburgh (retired), AFJROTC Unit OH-941, Laurel Oaks Career Development Center, Wilmington, Ohio; Colonel Robert Penny (retired), AFJROTC Unit NC-939, Jesse O. Sanderson HS, Raleigh, North Carolina; Colonel Al Dunlap (retired), AFJROTC Unit TX-081, Abilene HS, Abilene, Texas; Major Leslie Buerki (retired), AFJROTC Unit OH-941, Laurel Oaks Career Development Center, Wilmington, Ohio; Senior Master Sergeant Mike Wetzel (retired), AFJROTC Unit CA-20052, Great Oak HS, Temecula, California; and Kimberly Combs-Hardy, PhD, Chief of Educational Technology, Holm Center Curriculum.

We would like to express our gratitude to the High Stakes Writing, LLC, team for all its hard work in publishing this new book. That team consisted of contractors at High Stakes Writing, LLC—Lawrence J. Goodrich; Katherine Dillin; Sarah Beth Glicksteen; and Ruth Walker—subcontractors from Perspectives, Inc.—Philip G. Graham, PhD; Nancy Berger, PhD; Emily Davis; Mark Davis; Mary Jean Lavery; and Suzanne M. Perry—numerous personnel from Jones and Bartlett—including Christopher Will; Anne Spencer; and Wendy Swanson—and Mia Saunders of Mia Saunders Design.

All of the people involved with this project were superbly committed to make this academic course a showcase for 21st century skills, teaching, and learning. Through their efforts, we believe this course will continue, once again, our tradition of sustaining a "world-class" academic program.

INTRODUCTION What Is Global Awareness?

Quick Write

What do you think you might be doing four years after finishing high school? Describe the cultures you might interact with and how they differ from yours.

Learn About

- how global cultures and interactions impact relationships between different cultural groups
- the significance of global economics, trade, and markets
- how the effects of global growth raises environmental concerns over natural resources
- how ethics, religion, poverty, wealth, and views of human rights influence people
- how changes in technology and education influence the competition for jobs

What will you be doing two years after you finish high school? Four years? Six years? The chances are you'll be living and working with people of varying ethnic, cultural, religious, and personal backgrounds. Events in other countries will almost surely have a direct effect on your life.

Two years after graduation, you could be a college student preparing to go overseas for a semester abroad. Or your co-worker could well be an immigrant or foreign exchange student. You might be a member of the military stationed in Europe, Asia, or the Middle East, or working overseas in construction.

Four years after graduation, you might be finishing college and entering a job market where you'll need to understand other cultures and ethnic groups. Maybe you'll be a restaurant or hotel manager working with employees whose first language isn't English. Perhaps you'll be a teacher in a school district with a large immigrant population. Maybe you'll work as a State Department employee in an embassy, dealing with diverse people both in the office and elsewhere in the host country. Or you could be an apprentice plumber polishing your skills alongside immigrant co-workers.

Six years after graduation, you might be a graduate student studying other countries or working on your degree at a foreign university. Perhaps you'll be working for the United Nations or a humanitarian relief organization or a religious group bringing medical assistance or food aid to a disaster area. Maybe you'll be an engineer for NASA collaborating with scientists from other nations. Or you might be working in a manufacturing plant that receives parts from overseas, exports products overseas, or is owned by an overseas corporation. Whether you're on the shop floor or in management, the ups and downs in foreign markets will directly affect your job.

Whatever you're doing after high school, you'll find you need to be aware of the rest of the world. Advances in transportation and communications have brought the world's peoples closer than ever. Your car may be built in the United States using parts made overseas. The fuel it runs on may come from Indonesia, Kuwait, or Nigeria. Your clothes, your food, your electronics may all be manufactured in other countries. The customers who buy the crops you grow, the steel you make, or the equipment you design may live outside the United States. As part of your job, you may talk each day with colleagues or customers in overseas offices.

The purpose of this course is to give you some basics about the history, culture, religions, and thinking of people in other countries. What you learn here will help you begin to understand why they think and act they ways they do, and how they differ from what you are used to in the United States. Wherever your future takes you, this book will help you get started.

Vocabulary

- culture
- economics
- feudalism
- mercantilism
- capitalism
- communism
- trade
- protectionism
- theory of comparative advantage
- self-determination
- outsourcing

Global Cultures, Interactions, and Relationships

You may first be aware of other cultures by contrast with your own. When you eat out, you may discover food that is much spicier—or much blander—than what you eat at home. Other peoples may enjoy different kinds of music. Different groups may dress in ways that are strange to you. But they may not be trying to stand out. They're just doing what seems normal to them.

What Culture Is and How It Affects Behavior

The *Encyclopedia Britannica* defines culture as *including language, ideas, beliefs, customs, codes, institutions, tools, techniques, works of art, rituals, and ceremonies, among other elements*. This is passed on to future generations. It binds people together but also separates them into different communities. In today's world, it's more important than ever for people to understand both similarities and differences.

Values, Norms, Customs, and Rituals

Scholars are divided as to whether to focus on the inward or the outward aspects of culture. Values, including religious beliefs, and norms are fundamental to a culture. No one would argue with that. But the physical objects people create can be easier for scientists to study once the people themselves are gone. It's easier to dig around for old pottery than it is to dig into the minds of ancient peoples.

The Erechtheion, built in the fifth century BC on the Acropolis in Athens, Greece, is one of the ancient world's finest architectural works, particularly with its famed draped maidens used in place of pillars.
Photo by Melanie Stetson Freeman / © 2007 The Christian Science Monitor

While values are fundamental to any culture, the physical objects that people create can be easier for scientists to study once the people are gone.

Dressed in colorful clothes, young Pashtun girls in Pakistan wait while their relatives do the laundry.

Photo by Robert Harbison / © 2001 The Christian Science Monitor

People's dress reflects the climate of the place they live. It also expresses wealth, their sense of modesty, their station in life, and the work they do.

Customs and rituals are other important aspects of culture. Which holidays are celebrated, and how, in a given culture? Which milestones of life are recognized with ceremonies—coming of age, graduation from school, retirement from a job?

Dress, Symbols, Food, and Festivals

People's dress reflects the climate of the place they live. But it also expresses individuals' wealth, their sense of modesty, their station in life, and the work they do. For example: From New York to Frankfurt, Germany, to Sydney, Australia, business people tend to wear dark suits. This has nothing to do with climate and everything to do with looking serious.

The symbols people honor, anything from a Christian cross on a necklace to a tattoo on an arm, are yet another part of culture.

Food is a powerful aspect of culture. Recipes and food traditions are passed down from one generation to the next. Immigrants in a new society feel "at home" when they eat familiar foods. Have you ever visited a restaurant or cultural festival to get "a taste" of an unfamiliar culture?

Styles, Roles, and Routines

Different cultures have different styles. Some emphasize long hours of hard work; others, "living well." Many Europeans, for example, value "holiday" much more than do other parts of the world. Americans take vacations, but not nearly with the fervor of Europeans. The physical places people live affect their culture, too. Compare suburbanites who drive everywhere with city-dwellers who walk.

Different cultures assign different roles to people. What is the role of women in a society? Are they included in public life—in the workplace, in government—or at home tending to the children? When do children join the adult world of work? What roles do older people fill? Are they treated with respect for their experience and wisdom—or seen as blocking the progress of younger people?

fastFACT

Scholars make a distinction between a *culture* and a *civilization*. They generally see a civilization as more advanced. Over time, a culture may develop into a civilization. But no clear line divides a civilization from a culture. And "civilization" can be a loaded term. It refers to the complexity of a society, not its quality of life or values.

Cultures vary in their sense of time. Does "10 o'clock" mean 10:00, or in reality, more like a quarter past? What is the rhythm of the workday, of the week? When do people eat meals?

Nine Influential Cultures From the Past and Present

Here are thumbnail sketches of several influential world cultures. Each has made an important contribution to the larger global culture.

Chinese

Experts divide the history of imperial China into an early period from the Qin Dynasty (221–207 BC) through the Tang Dynasty (AD 618–907), and a later period from the Song Dynasty (AD 960–1279) through the Qing Dynasty (AD 1644–1911). On the whole this period was remarkably stable. The Chinese system of governing included the concept of a meritocracy. That is, the system was open to bright newcomers who could succeed on their own merits.

China was a highly literate society, despite its complicated writing system. The Chinese excelled in technology, too. Their inventions, such as paper and porcelain (often referred to even today as "China"), have enriched the world.

Mughal Indian

The first of the Mughal emperors was Babur, a descendant of Genghis Kahn and Tamerlane. He conquered northern India in AD 1526. The reigns of his descendants, from the mid-sixteenth to the mid-seventeenth century, saw the development of a new style of art and architecture. As the Mughals pushed southward and gained control of the Deccan, the states of Central India, their wealth grew dramatically. One of the most famous Mughals was Shah Jahan, who built the Taj Mahal.

A woman walks on mosaic inlay at the base of the Taj Mahal, in Agra, India. *Photo by Robert Harbison / © 2002 The Christian Science Monitor*

Mughal emperor Shah Jahan raised the monument in the seventeenth century to immortalize his love for his favorite wife. The Mughal era saw the development of a new style of art and architecture.

Mesopotamian

Mesopotamia comes from Greek and means "between the rivers." It refers to the fertile valleys of the Tigris and Euphrates Rivers in what is today Iraq, Kuwait, and Saudi Arabia. Around 3000 BC a people called the Sumerians arose. They set up city-states governed by some sort of monarch, and established a writing system. They wrote with styluses (sharp, pointed instruments used for writing) on tablets of clay that would dry and keep indefinitely. They eventually fell to the Akkadians, who absorbed much of their culture. The *Epic of Gilgamesh*, a Sumerian-Akkadian poem, is one of the oldest known fictional works.

Egyptian

A little before 3000 BC several independent city-states merged into a single country, the ancient Egypt of the Pharaohs. Their great civilization in the Nile Valley lasted more than 3,000 years. Taking advantage of the river's annual floods, they practiced grain farming, which was the basis of Egypt's wealth. Egyptians wrote on papyrus and kept elaborate records. They may be best known for the pyramids they built. They are still standing today, and they attest to the Egyptians' skill as builders and managers.

Greek

The Greek ideal of democracy, "rule by the people," emerged in Athens around 500 BC. After driving back a Persian invasion in 480–479 BC, Greece had a golden age of drama, philosophy, literature, art, and architecture. Its effects are still evident in Western culture today. At its height under Alexander the Great, the Greek Empire stretched briefly from the western Mediterranean to India and created enormous wealth.

Roman

Tradition says Romulus, Rome's first king, founded the city in 753 BC. In 509 BC Rome became a republic ruled by the Senate (elders) and the Roman people. During its 450 years as a republic, Rome conquered the rest of Italy, then expanded into what are now France, Spain, most of Britain, Turkey, North Africa, and Greece.

The Roman Empire began with Augustus in 27 BC. Emperor Constantine moved the capital to Constantinople (present-day Istanbul) in AD 330.The western branch of the empire lasted for five centuries. The eastern branch endured until 1453 when Constantinople fell to the Turks.

Egypt's Sultan Hassan Mosque in Cairo stands as one sign of Islam's spread since the religion's birth in the seventh century.
Photo by Robert Harbison / © 1991 The Christian Science Monitor

The Arab empire grew to one-and-a-half times the size of the Roman Empire at its peak.

Arabian

Within a very short period after the birth of Islam in the seventh century, the Arabs built a vast empire that stretched from Spain and Portugal (Andalusia) in the west all the way to the Indian subcontinent in the east. Covering almost half of the old known world, the Arab empire was one-and-a-half times the size of the Roman Empire at its peak.

The period through about the thirteenth century was a golden age of Arab civilization. The Arabs excelled in medicine, astronomy, and mathematics. They brought to the West so-called Arabic numerals, much easier to work with than Roman numerals. They introduced algebra and the concept of zero. Arab scholars also kept alive the classical learning of ancient Greece and Rome during Europe's Dark Ages.

Native American

The Paleoindian tradition of North America goes back about 10,000 years to what is today New Mexico. These people were big-game hunters. They were followed by the hunters of the Archaic period, from 8000 to 1000 BC. They also exploited new plant and animal resources and developed specialized tools.

When the first Europeans arrived in the New World in the sixteenth and seventeenth centuries, there may have been as many as 12 million native inhabitants. But colonization brought disease, warfare, and eventually the near extinction of the bison on which so many native peoples depended.

Latin America was home to three great civilizations: the Aztec, the Maya, and the Inca. The Aztecs settled in the Valley of Mexico and founded their capital, Tenochtitlan, in 1345. By the beginning of the sixteenth century it was one of the largest cities in the world. The Aztecs controlled a huge empire and long-distance trading networks. They had a complex religion and tracked the dates for specific ceremonies on a detailed calendar. They practiced sculpture and other arts as well. When the Spanish explorer Hernán Cortés arrived in 1519, however, he overthrew the Aztec leader Montezuma rather easily.

The Inca citadel of Machu Picchu sits atop the Peruvian Sierra—or Andes Mountains—which separates the rain forest to the east from the Pacific coast to the west.
Photo by Alfredo Sosa / © 2002 The Christian Science Monitor

At its height, the Inca empire controlled all of western South America between Ecuador and Chile.

One of the most advanced civilizations in the Americas before the Spanish arrived was the Maya (AD 300–900). It reached from southeastern Mexico across modern-day Guatemala, Belize, and the western parts of Honduras and El Salvador. The Maya lived in about 60 separate kingdoms. Like the ancient Egyptians, the Maya built pyramids. Maya cities usually had a dramatic stepped pyramid topped by a temple sanctuary at its center. The Maya produced impressive artworks. They developed a sophisticated writing system and used an elaborate calendar system called the Long Count.

The Inca were the largest pre-Hispanic society of South America. At its height, the Inca empire controlled all of western South America between Ecuador and Chile. Estimates for the total population under Incan control range between 6 million and 9 million. The Inca were great road builders and their capital was at Cusco, Peru.

Western European

Of all civilizations, Western Europe's has most directly influenced the development of the United States. The explorers of the New World flew the flags of Western Europe—England, France, Spain, and Portugal. In Britain's North American colonies, the Industrial Revolution begun in England and Scotland continued to play out. So did the political evolutions resulting from the Enlightenment, and the Protestant Reformation and the Renaissance before that.

How Cultural Factors Affect Relationships Between People

At a personal level, it's easy to understand how shared culture affects relationships between people. In a family whose culture values education, for instance, everyone knows to keep the house quiet in the evenings so the teens can study for exams.

But cultural understanding, or lack of it, can be a big factor on a larger scale as well. One of the cultural misunderstandings between the European explorers and the native peoples they encountered in the new worlds of North America and Australia had to do with land ownership. Europeans had a concept of individuals or governments ("the crown") owning the land. The native peoples had concepts of common ownership or stewardship.

Global Economics, Trade, and Markets

People are connected by more than just cultural relationships. They're connected by money relationships, too—and by the goods and services they buy and sell.

What Economics Is and How It Affects Behavior

Economics is a social science, *the study of the production and distribution of goods and services, and their management*. Adam Smith (1723–1790), one of the founding fathers of modern economics, saw four stages of economic development:

- Hunting: At this stage, groups of people survive by hunting wild animals
- Pastoral: At this stage, people tend flocks of domesticated animals—sheep, goats, cattle, and pigs
- Agricultural: People at this stage grow crops regularly
- Industrial: Western Europe began to move into this stage in the eighteenth century. Work is based in factories rather than the home ("cottage industry") and uses machines rather than hand tools.

A vendor sells watermelons at a market in Ho Chi Minh City in Vietnam.

Photo by Melanie Stetson Freeman / © 1997 The Christian Science Monitor

People are connected not just by cultural relationships, but also by money relationships—and by the goods and services they buy and sell.

Major Economic Systems

Four major economic systems have been important from the Middle Ages onward.

Feudalism

Feudalism was *the political, economic, and social system that prevailed in medieval Europe and relied on a relationship among lords, vassals, and serfs.* It was a layered system. Serfs were at the bottom, "bound" to the land they worked. An overlord was at the top. In between were layers of vassals. They benefited from the crops grown on the land, through the work of their serfs. They rendered services to the lords above them. People knew their place but had no great incentive for individual initiative or innovation.

Mercantilism

As feudalism declined, mercantilism took its place. Mercantilism is *the doctrine that the government of a nation can strengthen its economic interests by protecting its home industries, increasing foreign trade, and ensuring that the nation exports more than it imports.* The European colonizers of the New World were mercantilists. These governments put tariffs—a kind of tax—on imported goods. This tended to shut foreign goods out of the market.

The Great Wall of China, constructed in northern China in the third century BC to guard against hostile forces, is one of the world's best-known monuments.
Photo by Peter Ford / © 2006 The Christian Science Monitor

Today, Communist China is the world's most populous nation and has turned into one of the most aggressive capitalist societies on earth.

Mercantilist governments also often set up trade monopolies. Before the Revolutionary War, for instance, the American colonies were allowed to trade only with Britain. American exports to continental Europe had to pass through British ports and be taxed there first. Governments such as those of Britain, France, and Spain saw trade as a win-lose game, and they kept score in bullion—bars of gold or silver. A nation would "win" by exporting more than it imported, and piling up the bullion to prove it.

Capitalism

The next system to develop was capitalism. Capitalism is *an economic system in which the means of production are privately owned*. A fruit orchard, a textile factory, and a printing press are all examples of "means of production." They may be owned by a single individual, or a family or other group of investors. Mercantilism focused on increasing a nation's wealth—the better to raise tax money to support the government. But capitalism is all about individuals and their freedom to pursue their dreams of making money. Capitalism is the system on which the United States economy is based.

Communism

Communism came after capitalism, but has been widely discredited as an economic system. Communism is *an economic system in which property belongs to everyone and work is organized for the benefit of everyone*. During much of the twentieth century, many countries, notably in Eastern Europe and Central Asia, lived for some decades under a form of communism. The state planned and controlled the economy and a single party held power.

The world's most populous nation, China, is still governed by the Chinese Communist Party. But an ongoing "reform" launched in the late 1970s has turned the country into one of the most aggressive capitalist societies on earth.

Trade, Protectionism, and Comparative Advantage

In today's global economy, countries are linked more tightly than ever before. But many of the issues are the same as they have always been.

Trade

Trade, or commerce, is *the buying and selling of goods and services*. In contexts like this book, trade often means trade between different countries. Some trade is barter—a direct exchange of goods or services—but most traders use money.

From earliest times, people in one primitive settlement wanted to know what others had worth exchange in neighboring settlements. Trade allows people in different places to sell what they're good at making and buy what they can't make themselves. For example, if coastal fishermen trade with inland wheat-growers, both fishers and farmers have fish and bread.

Protectionism

Trade can make people nervous. They may like to buy better or cheaper goods from outsiders, but not if those outsiders' goods undercut their own place in the market. "I really like my imported car," someone may think. "But if too many other people buy cars like mine, won't the car factory in my town have to close?"

When concern about the local car factory reaches a certain level, people may urge government to intervene.

Protectionism is *the policy or practice of restricting imports to protect home industries*. Governments may do this by imposing special taxes, known as tariffs or duties, on imported goods. Sometimes they impose quotas: for example, a limit on the number of foreign cars that may be brought in.

Sometimes protectionism is supposed to be only temporary. Its aim may be to preserve jobs, or perhaps an entire industry that has strategic significance.

The Theory of Comparative Advantage

As you learn more about economics, you will learn a lot about specialization and efficiency. The theory of comparative advantage *holds that countries should specialize in the goods and services where they have a relative edge*. This may be in lower labor costs, or better technology, or both. The theory predicts that countries following this principle will prosper from free trade, even trade with lower-wage countries.

David Ricardo and His Provocative Theory

Most people understand right away why a country that can make good watches more cheaply than anyone else, for instance, should strive to be the world's watchmaker. What the British economist David Ricardo (1772–1823) showed, though, was that two countries benefit from trade even if one country undercuts the other on wages. He looked at the trade between England and Portugal in cloth and wine. Portuguese wages were lower for both goods. But England had a *comparative advantage* in cloth. So it made sense for England to trade its cloth for wine from Portugal. It is cheaper for Portugal to buy cloth from England in exchange for surplus wine. Under the theory of comparative advantage, both sides win.

How World Trade Agreements Affect the Growth of Free Trade

History has shown how moving away from the mercantilist view, which sees trade as a win-lose game, has led to more global prosperity.

European Colonialism and the Quest for Markets

The European push to colonize the New World was motivated in part by the desire to develop new markets. Perhaps the best example of this was the British Empire. It imported raw materials from its colonies and turned them into finished goods. The colonies, under Britain's restrictive trade laws, were not only valuable sources of raw materials but also captive markets for finished goods. For example, American colonists were allowed to buy tea only from the British.

fastFACT

The World Trade Organization (WTO) is the only global organization dealing with the rules of trade between nations. At its heart are agreements signed by most of the world's trading nations and ratified in their legislatures.

World Trade Agreements, the Growth of Free Trade, and the Reaction

Particularly since World War II, economists and political leaders alike have understood the importance of trade both in helping develop poor nations and in continuing the growth of developed countries.

Free trade was a big help in rebuilding Europe after World War II. France, western Germany, and other neighboring countries were grouped into a trade organization known as the European Coal and Steel Community. It led eventually to the European Union.

Other trade blocs have developed as well in other parts of the world—such as the North American Free Trade Agreement (NAFTA), to which the United States, Canada, and Mexico are parties.

But free trade has not been without controversy. Most people enjoy the lower prices for the imported goods they buy at "big box" retailers. But many worry about jobs lost when American factories close. The early years of the twenty-first century have seen some backlash against free trade. NAFTA was ratified during Democratic President Bill Clinton's administration. But many in Congress have since become critics of the agreement.

Environmental Concerns, Natural Resources, and Global Growth

The world's economic growth has had significant side effects. In recent decades hundreds of millions of people have been lifted out of dire poverty into a form of middle-class prosperity, notably in China and India. But accompanying this prosperity have been air and water pollution, deforestation, and soil depletion.

The Growth of Environmental Consciousness

The modern environmental movement began in the 1960s. One milestone was the publication in 1962 of *The Silent Spring* by Rachel Carson. She wrote of how pesticides and other chemicals were contaminating the natural world. They were killing not only insect pests, but "good" insects, too, the ones that birds eat. With not as much bird food, there were fewer birds and less birdsong. That was the "silent spring" of her title. And she showed how this chemical pollution mattered to people as well as birds.

Her book got people's attention. In the following decade, a striking number of concrete steps were taken: the Environmental Protection Agency was established, landmark legislation was passed to control air and water pollution, and, at a popular level, the annual celebration of Earth Day began.

The ancient Egyptians erected the Great Pyramids and the Sphinx in Giza as far back as the third millennium BC.
Photo by Robert Harbison / © 1991 The Christian Science Monitor

Pollution, along with wind-blown sand and other forces, is slowly eating away these stately monuments.

The Impact of Economic Development on the Environment

Rachel Carson was a significant figure in the environmental movement. But she was hardly the first to notice the damage human activity, especially economic activity, can inflict on the natural world. As far back as 1306 King Edward III of England, concerned about foul-smelling fumes, banned the burning of "sea coal" in craftsmen's furnaces. In 1952 a five-day temperature inversion trapped deadly aerosols in the atmosphere over London. Estimates say about 4,000 people died of bronchitis, pneumonia, and other diseases.

But as new threats have developed, people and governments have taken action to correct them, often with dramatic improvements. And legislation mandating corrective action has helped create new industries in the field of environmental cleanup.

Among issues that have surfaced more recently are ozone depletion and global warming.

Ozone-Depleting Emissions

During the 1980s scientists and governments became concerned about industrial chemicals known as chlorofluorocarbons (CFCs). They found that CFCs damage the atmosphere's ozone layer. Ozone is a form of oxygen that protects Earth from the sun's ultraviolet radiation. Scientists concluded that CFCs should be phased out altogether. This led to the Montreal Protocol of 1987. If adhered to, it is expected to allow the ozone layer to recover by the year 2050.

An oil tanker unloads its cargo into underwater pipes a mile off California's coast.
Photo by Robert Harbison / © 2003 The Christian Science Monitor

One could write a whole modern history of the world from the perspective of what countries will do to secure oil supplies.

Global Warming

As global economic development has continued, the amount of so-called greenhouse gases in the atmosphere has increased—carbon dioxide, methane, and others. These gases, byproducts of industrial activity and farming, trap the sun's heat in Earth's atmosphere. They are thought to be leading to slight but significant increases in temperatures. Global warming was extremely controversial for many years. Skeptics suggested that observed changes in temperatures were within the range of normal variation over the long term. But more recently, consensus has solidified around the view that climate change is a real problem. It needs the full attention of the international community.

The Struggle Over Access to Resources

Human economic activity doesn't lead just to pollution. Lack of access to resources often leads to tensions and even war. Ideally, countries can get what they need to develop their economies through peaceful trade. But it doesn't always work out that way. One could write a whole modern history of the world from the perspective of what countries will do to secure oil supplies.

Japan's military aggression during World War II was prompted in part by its need for oil to fuel its industrialization and modernization. And throughout the twentieth century, leaders of the energy-hungry West maintained close relationships with Middle Eastern leaders whose governments were not democracies but who controlled oil resources.

Ethics, Religion, Poverty, Wealth, and Human Rights

Relationships between people as well as between countries are affected by different systems of ethics and religion. Some people have one set of rules for dealing with those in their own community versus another set for outsiders. People's wealth, or lack of it, is also a factor in their relationships. Some people have so much money they don't ever have to think about it. Other people hardly ever think of anything else. And how does someone think of strangers, outsiders, those who are "the other"? That question is essentially one of human rights.

How Worldviews Affect Attitudes

For a concrete example, picture this: A young woman dressed in jeans and a T-shirt hops into her car and drives off to work. Does that mental image give you any trouble? No? But can you imagine what might happen if she were in Saudi Arabia—where a woman isn't allowed to drive and must cover her entire body and her face? Or if she lived in an Orthodox Jewish community, and it were the Sabbath? Many such Jews walk everywhere on the Sabbath. Or if she were a member of an Amish community, which traditionally does not own cars?

A Jewish man prays at the Western Wall in Old City Jerusalem.

Photo by Robert Harbison / © 1991 The Christian Science Monitor

Orthodox Jews generally walk everywhere rather than drive on the Sabbath.

You can see how a simple set of actions can evoke different responses from people with differing systems of ethics and religion, levels of wealth, and views of human rights.

Efforts to Advance Development in Poorer Regions

"Foreign aid" is the general term for government efforts to help the poor in other countries. It's most effective when it goes to people "on the ground" rather than to governments, which may be corrupt. Many private aid organizations bypass governments altogether by working directly with the individuals they want to help. Such efforts seek to harness the entrepreneurial potential of people in poor countries, who often can start their own businesses if they get a loan as small as $100. Such loans are known as "microlending." The small businesses they fund are called "microenterprises."

The Growth of the Human Rights Movement

The human rights protections enjoyed by Americans trace back to Runnymede, in England. There, in 1215, a group of nobles forced King John to sign Magna Carta. This document limited royal powers and gave freemen some guarantees of what we now call due process of law.

Five centuries later came the Age of Enlightenment, a period in European history that celebrated reason and "the rights of man." Rights and liberties belong naturally to the people, in the Enlightenment view. They do not flow from the king or the state.

The American Revolution, with its Declaration of Independence, and the United States Constitution that followed, were part of this broader movement. So was the international effort to end African slavery, led by Quakers and other moral leaders. The Founding Fathers dodged the issue of slavery in the Constitution, which acknowledged it only obliquely in the form in which the states first ratified the document.

But the British Parliament ended the Atlantic slave trade in 1807. The US Congress banned the slave trade under legislation taking effect the following year. Slavery itself did not end until the Civil War.

The end of slavery in North America in 1865 was a forward step for individual rights. Another development was recognition of the rights of groups of people. After World War I, President Woodrow Wilson was a tireless advocate for self-determination—*the principle that the people of a particular territory should decide how it is to be governed.* At that time many people still lived in places governed from distant imperial capitals. But the war led to the breaking up of the Austro-Hungarian, German, and Ottoman (Turkish) empires. This resulted in the creation of many new independent states.

Scotland's Glasgow Cathedral, built in stages over a couple hundred years, exemplifies Gothic architecture and is still used today for Christian services.
Photo by Melanie Stetson Freeman / © 2003 The Christian Science Monitor

About the time the church's central hall, or nave, was completed in the early thirteenth century, a group of nobles forced English King John to sign Magna Carta. This document limited royal powers and gave freemen some guarantees of what we now call due process of law.

Buddhist monks take a stroll in Kampot, Cambodia.
Photo by Melanie Stetson Freeman / © 1997 The Christian Science Monitor

After World War II, the United Nations adopted the Universal Declaration of Human Rights to launch the modern human rights movement. It works to protect religious and other freedoms around the world.

After World War II, another important development was the Universal Declaration of Human Rights. This was the founding document of the modern human rights movement. Adopted by the newly formed United Nations, it was meant to embody cultural and faith traditions of the whole world, not just those of the Judeo-Christian West.

Technology, Education, and the Competition for Jobs

The ongoing technological revolution and the spread of mass higher education in much of the world have led to prosperity that earlier generations could not have imagined. Entire countries have graduated from "developing" to "developed." But this has left many businesses and individuals in North America and Europe on the defensive, as they have been forced to compete as never before for jobs and customers.

The Technology Advantage of Western Cultures

From their first encounters with native Americans, European explorers had a technological advantage with their tools and firearms. Only in the twentieth century, with the rise of Japan and the "Asian tigers" as centers of high-tech manufacturing, did the West's advantage shrink. And it still has not disappeared. For instance, much of India, for all its recent progress in technology, still lacks the basic sanitation introduced in the West a century and a half ago.

The Effects of Education on Culture and Development

For much of history, literacy was a rare privilege. Today a country's literacy rate is a good index of its overall success. Much US foreign aid goes to education, especially to teaching women and girls to read and write. Literacy gives women access to information that puts them in control of their own lives—notably their childbearing. That helps control overpopulation, improve health, build civil society, and create economic growth.

A Comparison of Literacy Rates for Men and Women

Country	Men	Women
Britain	99 percent	99 percent
China	95 percent	87 percent
Germany	99 percent	99 percent
India	73 percent	48 percent
United States	99 percent	99 percent
Afghanistan	43 percent	13 percent
Bangladesh	54 percent	32 percent
Guinea	43 percent	18 percent
Haiti	55 percent	51 percent
Somalia	48 percent	26 percent

Second-graders in Kabul, Afghanistan, must meet for their math class in a hallway because their school has more students than it can hold: 4,500 students, of which 3,000 are girls.
Photo by Melanie Stetson Freeman / © 2003 The Christian Science Monitor

Literacy gives women access to information that puts them in control of their own lives.

Workers assemble engines at a Hyundai factory in India.
Photo by Mark Sappenfield / © 2006 The Christian Science Monitor

US companies must compete for their share of world markets to grow and provide new jobs for American workers.

How Outsourcing Impacts Development

While the West supports teaching women in underdeveloped nations to read to give them greater choices in their lives, outsourcing work to these poorer countries at the possible expense of jobs at home is a touchy subject. Outsourcing is *the procurement of goods and services from an outside supplier.* A computer company, for instance, may outsource its customer support to a call center in India. Sometimes higher-level jobs are outsourced as well. Many critics worry about the loss of American jobs, but advocates say outsourcing is good for employers, gives foreigners opportunity, and enables them to buy American exports.

Outsourcing is only one of the issues in the interconnected global economy. As you read through this book, you'll get a better understanding of other countries, their pasts, and what their futures are likely to look like.

Such an understanding is more important than ever before to your security and economic well-being. You live in a global age—an age in which market conditions in China or Brazil affect the price of oil in the United States. An outbreak of disease in a remote location can quickly spread around the world if authorities don't act to control it. The US homeland is no longer automatically secure from attack by small groups of terrorists just because they live halfway around the world. US companies must compete for their share of world markets to grow and provide new jobs for American workers.

By understanding the world's different cultures, religions, and economic systems, you will be better able to make sense of what is happening around the planet and how it affects you and your loved ones. You'll be a more informed citizen and voter, better equipped to influence politicians and government officials. You'll be a more valuable employee for companies that have overseas clients. This course aims to get you started in developing that understanding.

CHECK POINTS

Introduction Review

Using complete sentences, answer the following questions on a sheet of paper.

1. What advantage do physical objects have as a source of cultural information?
2. What was the basis of Egyptian wealth?
3. How long did the western branch of the Roman Empire last? How long did the eastern branch endure?
4. What were Adam Smith's four stages of economic development?
5. What is the theory of comparative advantage?
6. What is NAFTA?
7. Why did Rachel Carson call her book *The Silent Spring*?
8. What do greenhouse gases do?
9. What guarantees did Magna Carta give freemen?
10. What is the Universal Declaration of Human Rights?
11. In which century did the West's technological advantage shrink?
12. How does literacy improve women's lives?

Applying Your Learning

13. Should companies be allowed to outsource jobs, or should government restrict this practice? Explain why.

CHAPTER 1

Since the ancient Egyptians built these pyramids at Giza, Egypt has been conquered by Greeks, Romans, Arabs, Ottoman Turks, and the British.

The Middle East

Chapter Outline

LESSON 1 The Middle East: An Introduction

LESSON 2 The Arab-Israeli Conflict

LESSON 3 The Persian Gulf Wars

LESSON 4 Islamic Fundamentalism and Terrorism

LESSON 5 US Interests and Regional Issues in the Middle East

LESSON 1 The Middle East: An Introduction

Quick Write

What powers did a sultan have that the president of the United States does not have? Was he more powerful or less? Were there any limits on his power? Explain your views.

Learn About

- why the Middle East is viewed as a cradle of Western civilization
- the characteristics of Judaism, Christianity, and Islam
- the changes in the Middle East during the twentieth century
- the different groups of people who live in the Middle East

The sultan was the man at the top of the Ottoman Turkish hierarchy. He had many roles—military, judiciary, social, and religious. He had many different titles, too. In theory, he answered only to God (whom Muslims call *Allah* or "the God") and God's law. And he was the chief executor of God's law.

The sultan made all appointments to office and created laws. He was the military commander in chief and had title—official ownership—of all land.

As the Ottomans expanded into Arabia during the early sixteenth century, Sultan Selim I took on the title of caliph. Caliph originally meant simply "successor" (to the founder of Islam). But the term came to refer to *a universal Muslim ruler.*

The sultan sounds like a powerful man, doesn't he? But in practice, it didn't work out that way. He didn't always get what he wanted. And he had to pay attention to the civil servants, the military officers, and the religious leaders around him.

Why the Middle East Is Viewed as a Cradle of Western Civilization

James Henry Breasted, an archaeologist, coined the term fertile crescent around 1900. It referred to *a crescent-shaped area reaching from the Nile Valley through the eastern shore of the Mediterranean to Mesopotamia.* This area is commonly called the Middle East.

The area was an important land bridge between Asia and Africa. Its rivers watered early settlements. The crescent was home to many plant and animal species. It was where people first learned to herd animals and grow crops. Later it was where people first organized into complex societies, complete with civil servants and official records. And spiritually, it is the home of three of the world's major religions—Judaism, Christianity, and Islam. No wonder the Middle East is known as "the cradle of civilization"!

Vocabulary 

- caliph
- fertile crescent
- autonomous
- sultan
- monotheistic
- Koran
- protectorate
- mandate
- confessionalism
- Zionism
- partition
- emigrant

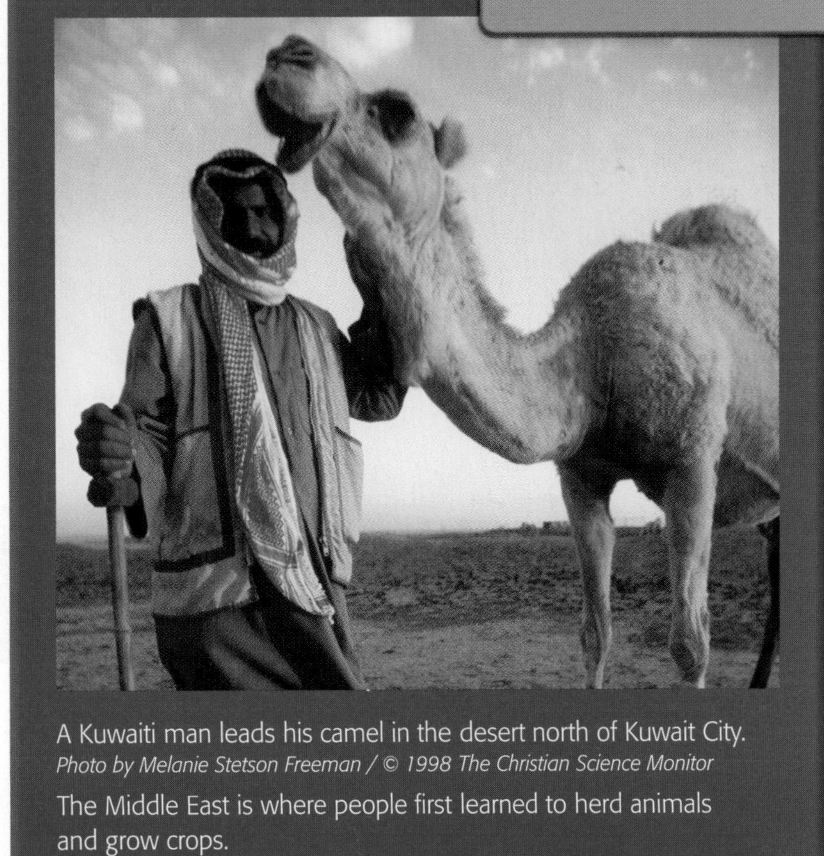

A Kuwaiti man leads his camel in the desert north of Kuwait City.
Photo by Melanie Stetson Freeman / © 1998 The Christian Science Monitor

The Middle East is where people first learned to herd animals and grow crops.

The Greek and Roman Conquests in the Ancient Middle East

You got a brief glimpse of the ancient Greek and Roman roles in the Middle East in the introductory chapter of this book. These invaders from the West played a major role in spreading ideas and religion from the Middle East into Europe and Africa.

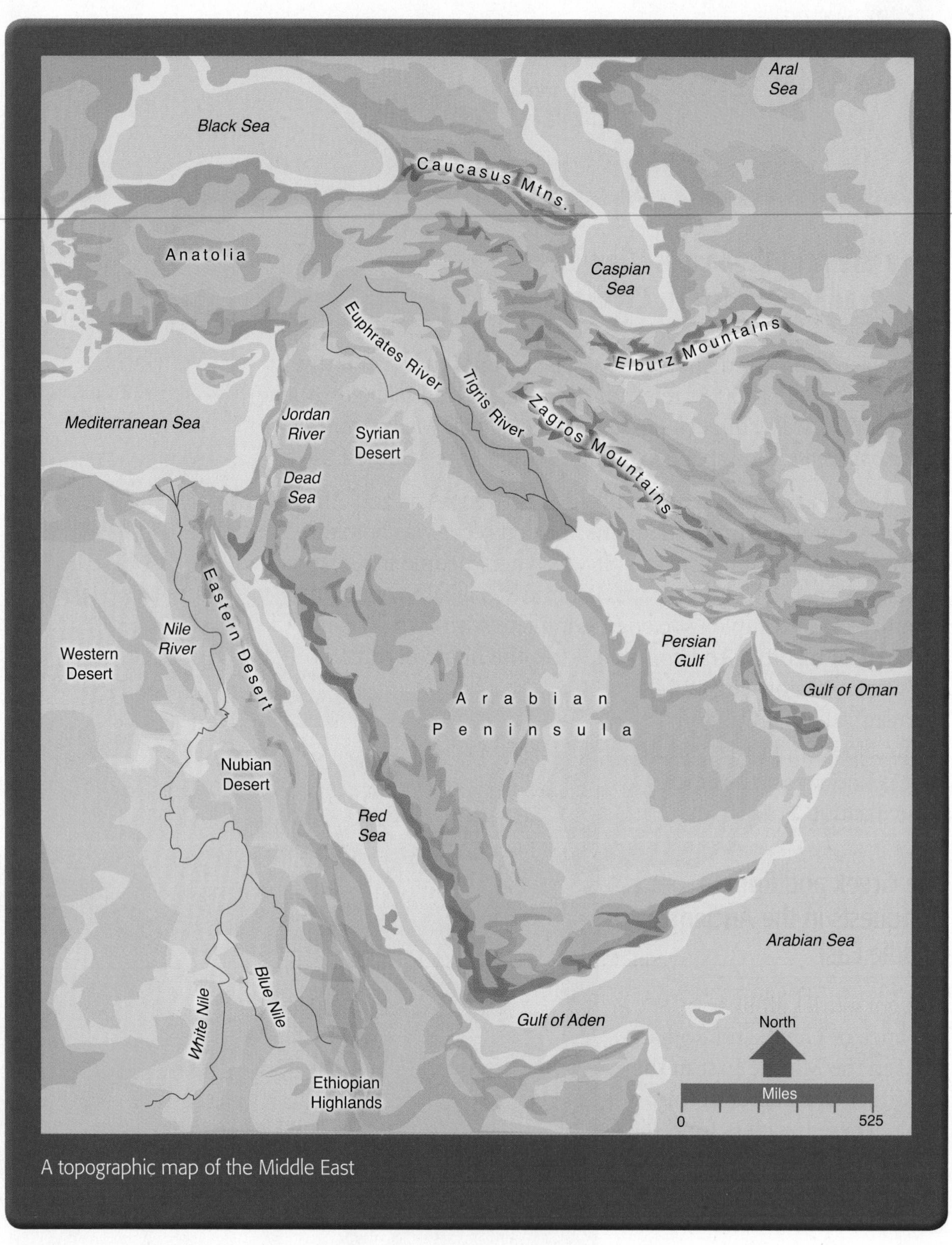

A topographic map of the Middle East

Tourists visit the Theatre of Herodes Atticus—at the foot of the Acropolis in Athens, Greece—built in AD 161.

Photo by Melanie Stetson Freeman / © 2007 The Christian Science Monitor

The Greeks and Romans played a major role in spreading ideas and religion from the Middle East into Europe and Africa.

The Greeks: Philip II of Macedon and Alexander the Great

The story of Greek conquests of the Middle East begins with Philip II of Macedon in 360 BC, and continues with his son, Alexander the Great.

Philip came to power at a time when most of his neighboring city-states were content to be autonomous—to be *independent*. They managed their own affairs, for the most part. Sometimes they got into disputes with other city-states, and then formed temporary alliances to help get them out of trouble.

Things changed, though, when Philip came to power. Within a decade, he had conquered his neighboring enemies. He defeated the Illyrians and the Paionians to the west and northwest. And he beat the Thracians to the north and northeast. He introduced reforms. He brought in new military technology—new kinds of catapults, for instance. Philip equipped each of the soldiers in his infantry units with a big pike, or spear, called a *sarissa*.

Pronunciation Guide

Boeotia – Bee-OH-shuh

Chaeronea – Kay-ROH-nee-uh

Illyrian – Ill-EER-ee-uhn

Paionian – Pay-OH-nee-uhn

Sarissa – SAH-riss-ah

After he won the battle of Chaeronea in Boeotia, in 338 BC, Philip II became the undisputed ruler of Greece. He was planning to move into Asia when an assassin killed him in 336 BC.

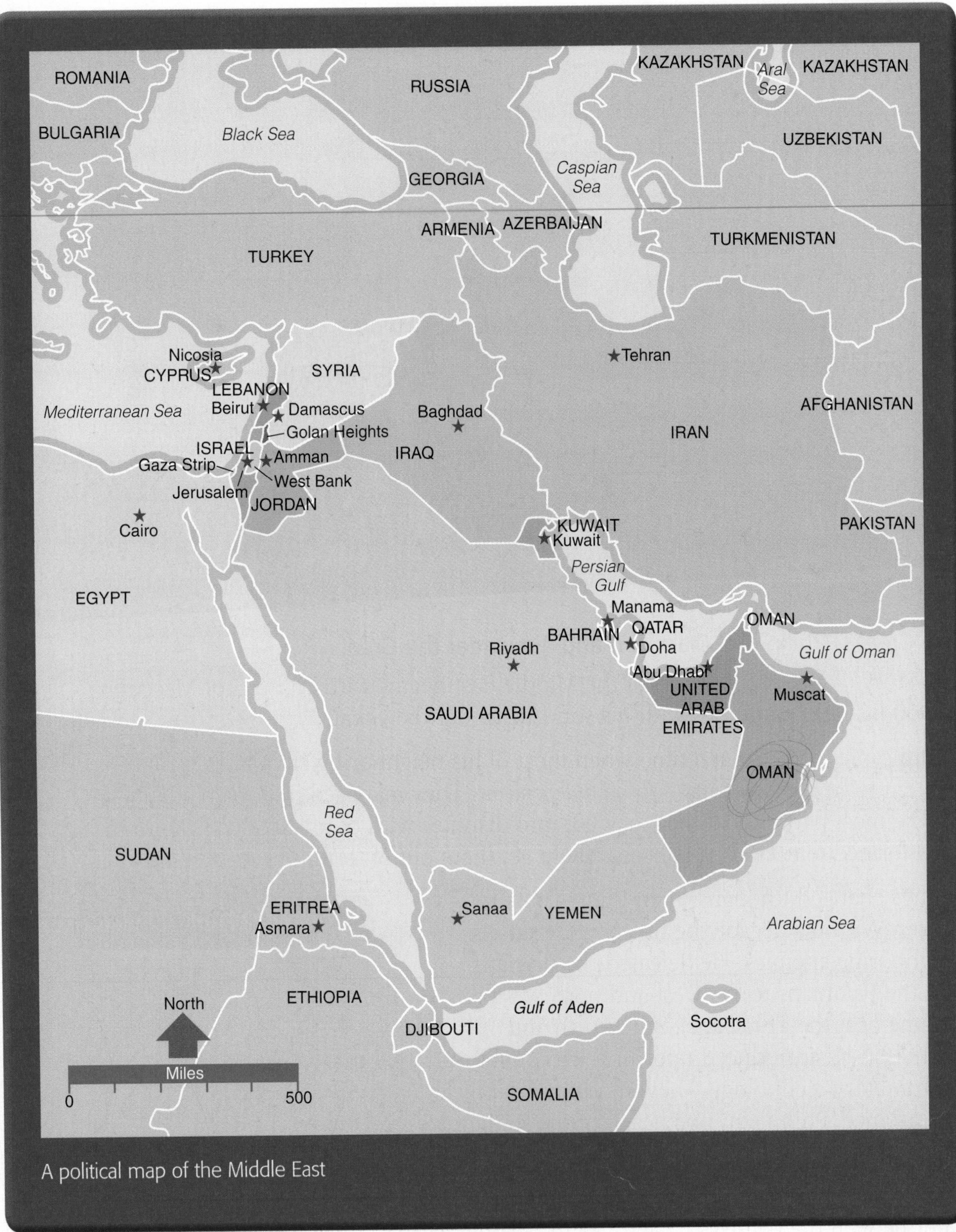

A political map of the Middle East

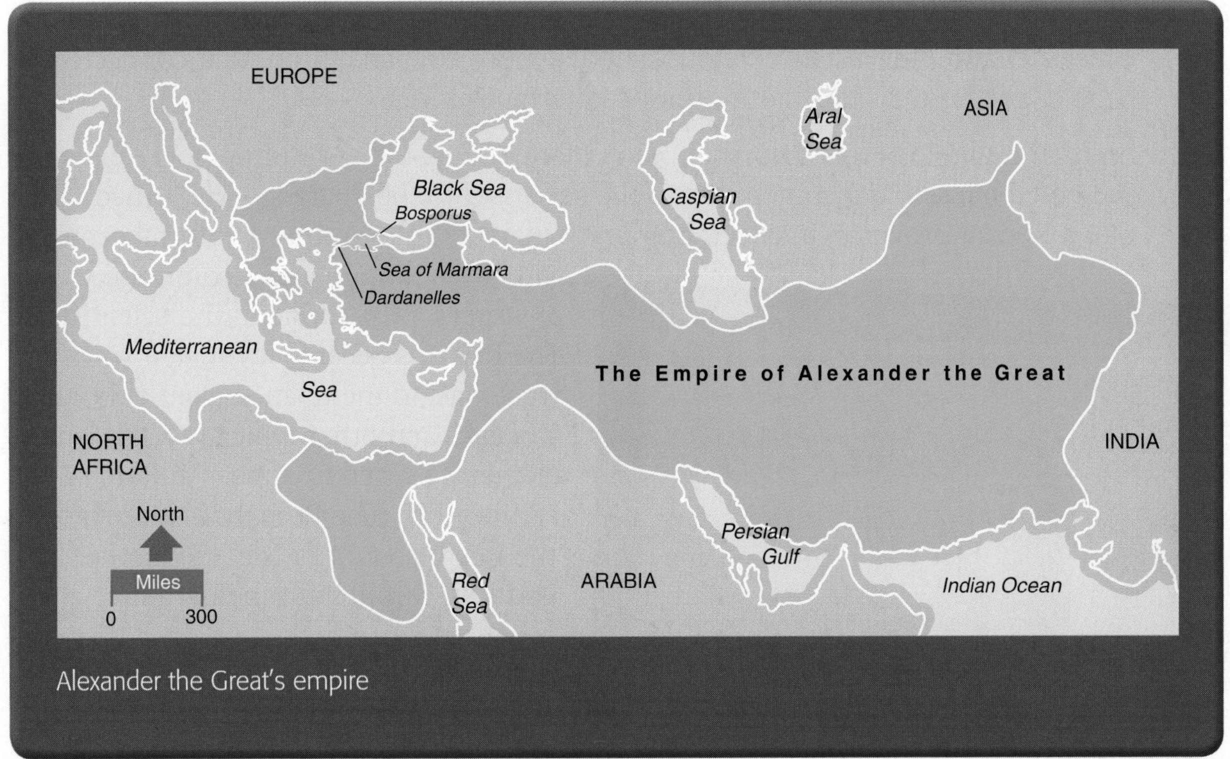

Alexander the Great's empire

But Alexander was ready to pick up where his father had left off. At age 20, he was already a charismatic and decisive leader. In 334 BC he led an army across the Hellespont into Asia. It was the biggest military force ever to come out of Greece.

His Asian campaign lasted 11 years. He conquered the Persian Empire, which spread from Egypt to western Asia. Then he pushed onward into central Asia and even as far as the Indus Valley—where India and Pakistan are today.

Finally his army insisted on turning back. Alexander died of a fever in Babylon—a city located in what is now Iraq. The lands he had conquered were divided among his generals. These political divisions became the kingdoms of the Hellenistic period (323–31 BC).

The Spread of the Roman Empire

The Roman Empire succeeded the Roman Republic and lasted for 500 years. The first emperor was Octavian, later known as Augustus. The Romans pushed eastward, as the Greeks had done, as well as west and north. By about AD 200 the Roman Empire reached from Syria to Spain and from Egypt up into the British Isles.

The Romans laid roads to connect their empire's cities. They built beautiful public buildings and constructed great aqueducts to deliver drinking water to towns.

The Romans also learned from the peoples they conquered. They absorbed the Greeks' culture, for instance, and fostered a Greco-Roman culture that connected people, goods, and ideas around the Mediterranean Sea.

Another example of this absorption took place in Egypt. Caesar (emperor) Augustus presented himself to the Egyptians as the successor to the Pharaohs. He turned Egypt into a Roman province, in effect. But Egypt included Alexandria, a cultural center with a vast library and a community of writers, philosophers, and scientists. The Romans became fascinated with what was, to them, an ancient culture. Obelisks and other typically Egyptian elements started to appear in Roman architecture. The Romans also spread the Egyptian cult of Isis, the mother goddess, throughout their empire.

Thousands of years old, these Roman ruins still stand in Samaria, north of Nablus, West Bank, Israel.
Photo by Robert Harbison / © 1991 The Christian Science Monitor

By about AD 200, the Roman Empire reached from Syria to Spain and from Egypt up into the British Isles.

The Influence of the Ottoman Turks

The first sultan, or *ruler*, of the Ottomans was Osman I. He ruled from about AD 1284 to 1324. He was the son of a tribal leader whose home was in the western part of today's Turkey. The dynasty Osman founded would stretch across six centuries and through the reign of 36 sultans. The Ottomans were strong leaders who centralized power. This helped them conquer territory. In 1354 they established a permanent foothold in Gallipoli, which is in the European region of modern Turkey.

In 1453 the Ottomans conquered Constantinople, the eastern capital of the Roman Empire. This takeover had little effect on European security. But it had huge symbolic importance. Mehmed II, the conquering sultan, renamed the city Istanbul and made it his imperial capital. It soon replaced Baghdad as a Muslim religious center.

The next couple of centuries saw Ottomans on the march in North Africa, southern and eastern Europe, and the Middle East. By the time Sultan Süleyman died in 1566, the Ottoman Empire was a world power. Mecca, Medina, Jerusalem, Damascus, Cairo, Tunis, and Baghdad—most of the great cities of Islam—were under his crescent flag.

The high-water mark of Ottoman expansion into Europe came in 1683, when the Ottoman army invaded Austria. For two months the Ottomans laid siege to Vienna, until finally the king of Poland, Jan Sobieski, pushed them back. Still, the European nations now known as Albania, Bosnia and Herzegovina, Bulgaria, Greece, Romania, and Serbia remained under Ottoman rule until the nineteenth century.

The Ottoman Empire had Turkish origins and Islamic foundations. But from the start it was a real mix of ethnic groups and religions. Non-Muslim peoples, including Greeks, Armenians, and Jews, were recognized as religious minorities with their own leaders. Such groups were allowed to operate schools, religious establishments, and courts based on their own customary law but only if they paid tithes to the sultans in exchange for these rights.

People stroll through a square in the old quarter of Istanbul, Turkey.
Photo by Robert Harbison / © 1994 The Christian Science Monitor

In 1453, after the Ottomans conquered the Roman Empire's eastern capital, Constantinople, victorious Sultan Mehmed II renamed the city Istanbul and made it his imperial capital.

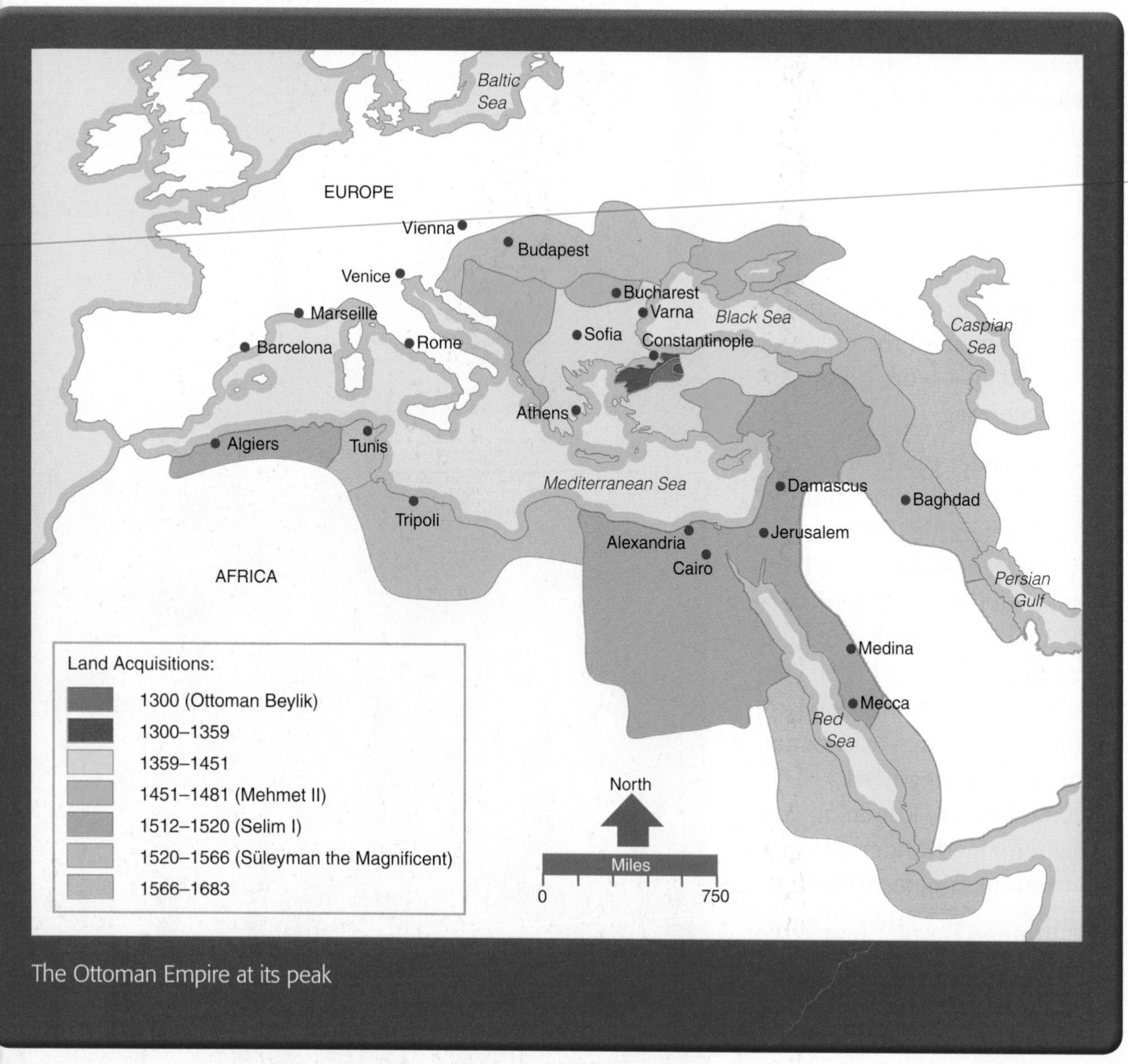

The Ottoman Empire at its peak

The Characteristics of Judaism, Christianity, and Islam

These three major world religions all have roots in the Middle East. All are monotheistic. That is, their followers *adhere to the idea of one God*. The three are known as the Abrahamic faiths of the Middle East because they claim descent from the patriarch Abraham.

Judaism

Judaism was founded more than 3,500 years ago. Jews believe that God created the universe and appointed the Jews to be his chosen people. Another interpretation views Jews as a "choosing people" for adopting monotheism. Their duties are to behave ethically and to serve as models of holiness.

Judaism teaches that every Jew can have an individual and personal relationship with God. They believe that God continues to work in the world. Jews believe they have a covenant, or treaty, relationship with God. If they follow his laws, as found in the Scripture, God protects them and makes them prosperous.

Israel was the Jews' ancient home, and the city of Jerusalem their political and religious capital. They settled there after fleeing slavery in the Exodus from Egypt, led by Moses, who gave them their laws and the Ten Commandments. The Jewish Scriptures are the Torah (the first five books of the Bible), the wisdom writings, and the writings of the prophets. The Jewish Scriptures are known by Christians as the Old Testament.

Like other world religions, Judaism has many denominations, ranging from strict religious observance to a more liberal interpretation of the faith. The largest are the Orthodox, Conservative, and Reform. Most Reform Jews live in the United States.

The essence of Judaism is summed up in the first line of the watchword of the Jewish faith, the *Shema*: "Hear O Israel, the Lord our God, the Lord is One." Devout Jews pray this prayer twice a day.

Christianity

Christianity is based on the teachings of Jesus Christ, a Jewish religious teacher who lived in the Holy Land more than 2,000 years ago. Christians believe in one God, the creator, whom they call Father. They believe that Jesus was the Son of God, and that Jesus was sent to save mankind from death and sin.

The essence of Jesus' teachings was two commands to his followers—to love God, and to love their neighbor as themselves. Christians believe Jesus' coming was foretold by the Jewish prophets. He said that he had come to fulfill God's law. The Christian Bible includes the Jewish scriptures, or Old Testament, and the New Testament, or writing about the life and works of Jesus and his early followers.

Jews pray at the Western Wall, all that remains of their ancient temple in Jerusalem.

Photo by Melanie Stetson Freeman / © 2001 The Christian Science Monitor

Also known as the Wailing Wall, it is the holiest of all Jewish sites. The essence of Judaism is summed up in the first line of the watchword of the Jewish faith, the *Shema*: 'Hear O Israel, the Lord our God, the Lord is One.'

Over the centuries, Christianity has spread worldwide but divided into three main branches: Roman Catholicism, Eastern Orthodoxy, and Protestantism. The Roman Catholic Church is a worldwide organization subject to the pope in Rome. Eastern Orthodoxy is divided into autonomous national churches all under the umbrella of the ecumenical patriarch in Constantinople (Istanbul). Protestantism is divided into hundreds of independent denominations.

Islam

The third worldwide Abrahamic religion is Islam. Islam means "submission to the will of God." Followers of Islam are known as Muslims. Islam takes many forms, but all share certain beliefs. Like Jews and Christians, Muslims believe in one God. They believe their religion was revealed more than 1,400 years ago in Mecca (today part of Saudi Arabia). They believe God sent a number of prophets to mankind to teach them how to live in accord with his law

Muslims respect Jesus, Moses, and Abraham as God's prophets. But they also believe that Muhammad was the final prophet. The **Koran** is *the holy book of Islam*. Muslims strive to follow the Sunnah, the practical example of the prophet Muhammad.

fastFACT

The word "Koran" is also spelled "Qu'ran." Many Arabic words, including names of countries, have different spellings. This is because there is no agreed upon way to write Arabic words using Roman letters.

Islam's five pillars of faith are:

- Making a declaration of faith: "There is no God but Allah, and Muhammad (peace be upon him) is his messenger"
- Praying five times a day
- Giving to charity
- Fasting (refraining from eating) at certain times
- Making a pilgrimage—the "Haj"—to Mecca at least once in a lifetime.

The two main branches of Islam are Sunni and Shia. Both agree on the fundamentals of Islam. But they have serious differences on many religious questions. These stem in part from the question of who would succeed Muhammad. When Muhammad died early in the seventh century, he left not only a religious organization but also an Islamic state consisting of about 100,000 Muslims on the Arabian Peninsula. The majority chose Abu Bakr, a close companion of the prophet, as the caliph. The caliph was understood as a social-political leader. These followers gave rise to the Sunni branch of Islam.

The minority wanted Ali, Muhammad's son-in-law and cousin, to be caliph. They believed that Muhammad had appointed him the sole interpreter of the prophet's legacy, in both political and spiritual terms. These followers gave rise to the Shia branch of Islam.

The Sunni branch is the larger of the two main branches of Islam today. Most of the major Arab countries are predominantly Sunni. The non-Arab Persians are overwhelmingly Shia. Iraq, however, is an Arab country with a strong Shia majority, and large Shia minorities exist elsewhere.

The Changes in the Middle East During the Twentieth Century

In the early years of the twentieth century, the world wasn't as neatly divided into independent countries as it is today. Empires broke up. Territories changed hands because of war. And European powers sought to control some of the less stable lands as they were going through transitions. Nowhere was all this truer than in the Middle East.

French and British Protectorates

A **protectorate** is *a relationship of protection and partial control that a superior power assumes over a dependent country or region*. The Middle East during this period was full of such relationships. In 1916, during World War I, France and Britain held a series of secret talks. These led to the Sykes-Picot Agreement, which carved up the Middle East into zones of influence. France would control Lebanon and Syria. Britain would oversee Iraq and Transjordan (today's Jordan). Palestine was to come under dual control, but the French let the British rule there, too.

After World War I, with the disintegration of the Ottoman Empire—which had controlled most of the Middle East—these arrangements became more formal. In the following sections, you'll read about how these "zones of influence" played out in different countries.

Egypt

The British role in Egypt actually goes back well before World War I. The north African country was important to Britain for two reasons: access to the Suez Canal—the main route to India—and the many British investments in Egypt. The British occupied Egypt in 1882 and made it in effect part of their own empire when disintegrating conditions within Egypt appeared to threaten both of these interests. The British had long been committed to the preservation of the Ottoman Empire, which included Egypt. But the deteriorating situation in Egypt changed their minds. When World War I broke out, they unilaterally made Egypt a protectorate. This cut it off from the Ottoman Empire.

Egyptian nationalism was a growing force during this whole period of occupation. In 1923 the British granted Egypt a limited form of independence. But not until the revolution of 1952 did Egypt win real independence under the leadership of Gamal Abdul Nasser and Anwar Sadat.

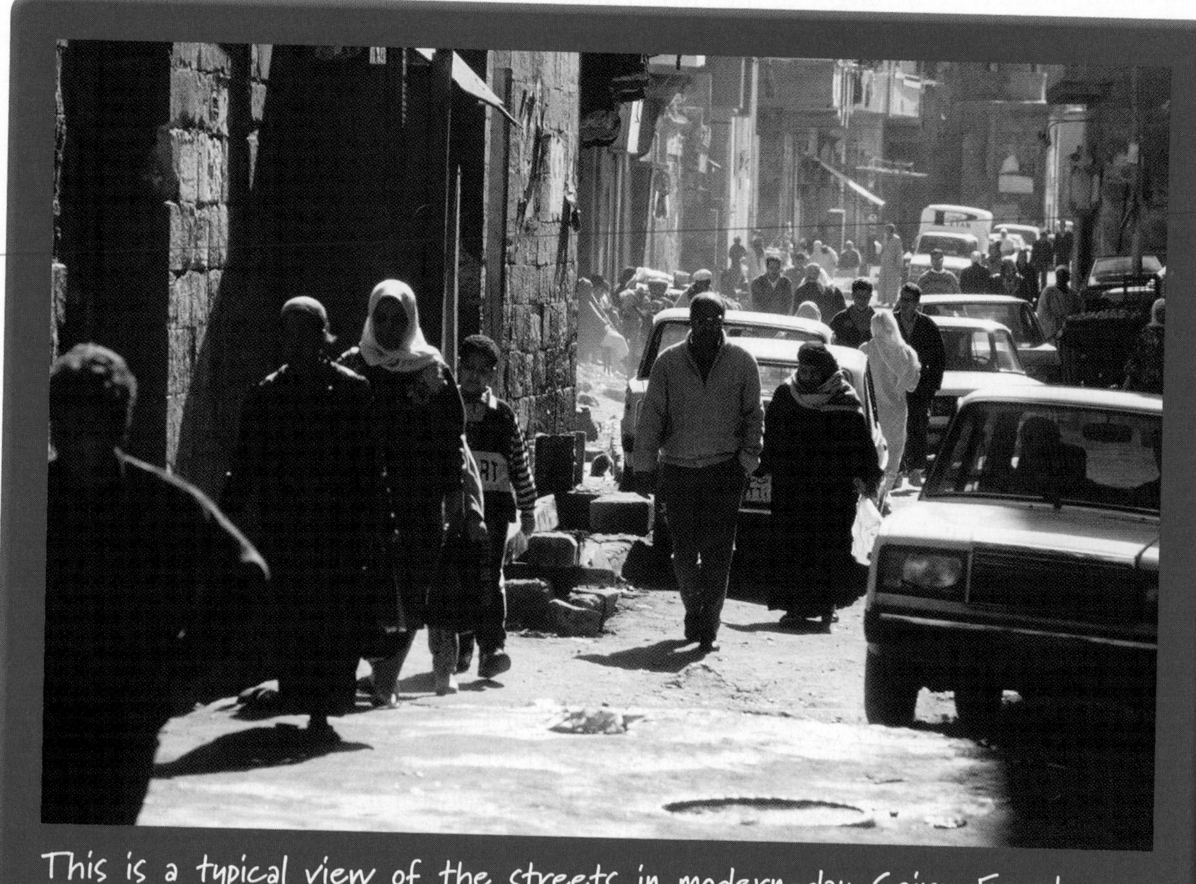

This is a typical view of the streets in modern-day Cairo, Egypt.
Photo by Melanie Stetson Freeman / © 1995 The Christian Science Monitor
Britain, which occupied Egypt in 1882, valued the country for its access to the Suez Canal, the main route to India.

Iraq

The League of Nations—the international organization that existed before the United Nations—assigned Iraq to Britain as a mandate after World War I. A mandate was *a commission, or an assignment, from the League of Nations authorizing a member nation to administer a territory.* Britain gave Iraq a constitution, a legislature, and a king, Faisal I. In 1932 Iraq became independent. Britain kept military bases there, though, and British interests explored for Iraqi oil. After the death of Faisal I, the new king, Faisal II, kept the country's pro-British stance.

But in 1958 a military revolution overthrew the king. Left-wing nationalists took over. More violence and revolution followed. In 1968 the Arab Renaissance (Ba'ath) Socialist Party seized power. Its leaders were Major General Ahmad Hassan al-Bakr and his deputy, Saddam Hussein.

Jordan

All of present-day Jordan was included in the British Mandate of Palestine. In 1921 the Emirate of Transjordan was established. It had only 400,000 inhabitants and needed financial aid from the British. Two years later, the British recognized Transjordan as a national state preparing for independence. Transjordan moved toward independence, even as the larger drama of Israel's creation on adjacent lands played out. In 1948 Transjordan became a fully sovereign state with King Abdullah at its helm. And in 1949 the country became known as Jordan.

Jordan took part with fellow Arab countries in the 1948 war against Israel. In the 1967 war with Israel, Jordan lost the land on the West Bank of the Jordan River. In the years since, it has been known as a moderate, pro-Western, Arab state.

Lebanon

Lebanon came under French mandate after World War I. It was established in 1920 as Greater Lebanon, with its present boundaries and its capital in Beirut. In 1926 it received a new constitution modeled after France's. It gained independence in 1943.

Schoolboys head home past partially destroyed buildings and an out-of-use auto causeway in Beirut, Lebanon, in 1983.

Photo by R. Norman Matheny / © 1983 The Christian Science Monitor

Lebanon has long been a troubled country. The roots of its woes lie in a peculiar constitutional system.

Lebanon has long been a troubled country. The roots of its woes lie in a peculiar constitutional system. In an attempt to keep peace among its many officially recognized religious groups, certain offices were assigned to people of certain faith. The president of the country must be a Maronite Christian. The prime minister must be a Sunni Muslim. The speaker of the Chamber of Deputies (parliament) must be a Shiite Muslim.

Confessionalism is the name for this *system of allocating offices among different religious and ethnic groups*. It was meant to give each group its fair share of power. It applies not only to the top jobs, but all the way down to the lowest ranks of the civil service. And the system hasn't changed much since it was introduced. The population, though, has changed. Most people think there are far more Muslims and relatively fewer Christians today. But here's the kicker—no one "officially" knows how the population has changed, since there hasn't been a census since 1932.

Syria

After the collapse of the Ottoman Empire, Syria had a brief period as an independent monarchy in 1920. It lasted only a few months, though. The French defeated Syrian forces, and later that year got a League of Nations mandate to govern Syria.

When France fell to Germany early in World War II, Syria came under the pro-German Vichy-French government. Then in July 1941 the British and the Free French occupied the country. Syrian nationalists forced the French out in April 1946. Since then Syria has had a republican government that developed during the mandate.

The Balfour Declaration

British Foreign Secretary Arthur James Balfour wrote a letter in 1917 to a prominent Zionist named Lord Walter Rothschild that became known as the "Balfour Declaration." In this letter Balfour indicated his government's interest in helping establish a Jewish state, long a goal of the Zionist movement. The letter said, "His Majesty's Government view with favour the establishment in Palestine of a national home for the Jewish people, and will use their best endeavours to facilitate the achievement of this object…." The letter also stressed, however, "that nothing shall be done" to limit the rights of non-Jews in Palestine, or those of Jews in other countries.

The Jewish People

The Jewish people spread far beyond Israel during the Greek and Romans eras, when they moved about within those empires. Many Jews in Israel died or were expelled after a revolt against Roman rule around AD 70. Others were killed or expelled by the Byzantines (Eastern Roman empire) around AD 628. Even so, a small remnant of Jews remained in the Holy Land throughout the centuries.

Most Jews, however, lived in Europe or in other countries of the Middle East and North Africa, such as Iran, Yemen, and Morocco. A large number settled in Spain, from which they were expelled in 1492. Many then settled in Central and Eastern Europe and Russia, where they faced periodic persecution culminating in the Holocaust of World War II, in which some 6 million died at the hands of the Nazis.

All these persecutions resulted in periodic waves of Jews returning to the Holy Land, long a dream of Jews everywhere. This movement gathered steam in the 1880s and reached its peak as those Jews who could fled the Nazi threat in Europe.

The Founding of the State of Israel

Meanwhile, Zionism—*a movement to establish a home in Palestine for the world's Jews*—was growing. Its leader was Theodore Herzl.

In 1922—some 18 years after Herzl's death—a mandate of the League of Nations gave the British formal control of Palestine (the Jewish homeland in biblical times). In the years following, Jewish immigration into Palestine increased. So did violence between the Jews and Arabs. The British tried to restrict Jewish immigration. But international support for a Jewish homeland in Palestine was on the rise. It blocked the British efforts to cut off Jewish immigration. As it became clear that the Nazi Germans had nearly wiped out European Jews, the world saw a Jewish homeland as an urgent need.

In 1947 the new United Nations made a plan to partition—to *divide*—Palestine into separate Jewish and Arab states. Jerusalem, a holy city for Jews, Christians, and Muslims, would fall under UN administration.

The British gave up control and left Palestine in 1948. Soon after, on 14 May, the State of Israel was proclaimed. Neighboring Arab states rejected the partition plan, however. Their armies immediately invaded their new neighbor.

The resulting war is known as Israel's War of Independence. It ended in cease-fires with Egypt, Jordan, Lebanon, and Syria. The fledgling state emerged with 50 percent more territory than at the start and the Arab-Israeli conflict has continued to this day.

The Different Groups of People Who Live in the Middle East

While many Americans view the Middle East as mostly Arab, it is really a collection of ethnic groups.

The Arabs

The Arabs are originally from the Arabian Peninsula but now spread across much of the Middle East and northern Africa. The League of Arab States includes 300 million people in 22 different countries.

The Arabs are defined as a people largely by their language. Classical Arabic is the language of the Koran, the Muslim holy book. Modern Standard Arabic is the language of literature, newspapers, and magazines. Arabic has many local variants used in everyday speech. Sometimes these variants are so unlike that two Arabic speakers from different countries can't understand each other. In that case, they may switch to Modern Standard Arabic to communicate.

Most but not all Arabs are Muslims. As you have read, many of them spent some time under foreign control. They have struggled for independence and self-rule. The quest for some sort of "pan-Arab" unity has been a goal for many Arab political leaders, but that goal hasn't proven practical. Another important issue is their generally hostile relationship with the State of Israel.

The Israelis

Israel has about 6.5 million people. Of these, three-fourths are counted by the state as Jewish. (Orthodox Jewish law has a narrower definition of who is a Jew than the state does.)

There are three main ethnic groups of Israeli Jews:

- Ashkenazim: They trace their ancestry to western, central, and eastern Europe. These include about a million relatively recent emigrants from the former Soviet Union. An emigrant is *someone who travels out of one place to settle in another.* Ashkenazim originally spoke Yiddish, which is mostly descended from German.
- Sephardim: Their origins were in Spain, Portugal, southern Europe, and North Africa. Their original language was Ladino, which is mostly descended from Spanish.
- Eastern or Oriental Jews: Their ancestors lived in ancient communities in Islamic lands. They originally spoke Arabic.

Jewish Israelis recreated the Hebrew language, which nobody spoke anymore except during religious rituals, and made it the everyday language of the country. Of the non-Jews in Israel, nearly 70 percent are Muslim, 9 percent are Christian, and 7 percent are Druze, whose religion is an offshoot of Islam.

A couple sits at a sidewalk café on hip Sheinkin Street in Israel's modern metropolis Tel Aviv.
Photo by Melanie Stetson Freeman / © 2001 The Christian Science Monitor

The State of Israel was founded as a homeland for the Jews after their near-extermination during World War II.

The State of Israel was founded as a homeland for the Jews after their near-extermination during World War II. The Israelis' ongoing struggle is to remain secure amid hostile neighbors. The need for peace with the Palestinians—Arabs who live in the neighboring West Bank and Gaza Strip—is especially pressing.

The Persians (Iranians)

The Persians are a proud and ancient people. They have lived in Iran since around 1500 BC. At times they have governed empires of their own, notably under Cyrus the Great. At other times they have been conquered themselves. But they have always been a distinctive people. Although they are Middle Eastern, they are not Arab. They are Muslim, but adhere mainly to the Shiite, rather than Sunni, branch of Islam. Their language, Farsi, is Indo-European. It doesn't belong to the Semitic language family as do Arabic, Hebrew, and Aramaic. Persians make up a slight majority of Iran's population of 66 million people. Azeris, people from Azerbaijan, to the north of Iran, make up about a quarter of Iran's population. This population also includes small numbers of other minority groups, including Kurds and Arabs.

In 1979 a revolutionary Shiite regime replaced the corrupt and repressive monarchy of Shah Reza Pahlavi with an Islamic Republic. This republic was based on a strict Shiite application of Islamic law as the civil law. US–Iranian relations soured at this point. Iranians were aggrieved over decades of US support for the shah and that President Jimmy Carter had allowed the ailing monarch to enter the United States for medical treatment. In November 1979 a group of student revolutionaries seized the US Embassy in Tehran. They held 52 American diplomats hostage for 444 days—until the day President Carter left office.

fastFACT

Farsi and Kurdish are Indo-European languages, as are English, French, Spanish, German, Russian, and Hindi, the most widespread language in India. Middle Easterners who speak Farsi and Kurdish are using a language directly related to yours.

Soon after its revolution, Iran fought a disastrous war against Iraq (1980–1988). The war killed hundreds of thousands on each side and cost the two countries more than $1 trillion. More recently, it has suffered from economic turmoil. Another problem is social tensions between its strict Islamist rulers and many of its Western-oriented citizens.

Commercial signs line a sidewalk in Tehran, Iran.
Photo by Robert Harbison / © 1997 The Christian Science Monitor

Social tensions are ripe in Iran between the country's strict Islamic rulers and many of its Western-oriented citizens.

A Turkish Kurd family stands on a balcony at the Bad Honnef Refugee Center in Germany.

Photo by R. Norman Matheny / © 1994 The Christian Science Monitor

The Kurds are a non-Arab, Sunni Muslim people without their own state.

The Kurds

The Kurds are a non-Arab, largely Sunni Muslim people, numbering 15 million to 20 million. They live in a rugged mountainous part of southwest Asia generally known as the Kurdistan region. It includes areas in Turkey, Iraq, Iran, Armenia, and Syria. The Kurds have their own culture and language—related to Farsi, the language of Iran.

Before World War I, Kurds were mostly nomads. They herded sheep and goats. But after the war, the Ottoman Empire was broken up. Much of its territory was turned into new nation-states. There was a plan for a new state of Kurdistan, but it never came to be. Meanwhile, the Kurds found their own movements restricted as their neighbors fenced them out.

The Kurds' story ever since has been the quest for their own state. They have tried several times to create one, but neighbors have crushed each attempt. No country wants to give away its own territory to make a country for someone else. And the world's leaders as a whole tend to like to keep things as they are—to preserve the status quo.

Since the fall of Saddam Hussein, however, Kurds have enjoyed a certain autonomy in northern Iraq. It's the closest they've come to a state of their own.

The Assyrians

Today's Assyrians are the descendants of the ancient empires of Assyria and Babylonia. The territory they governed was known as Mesopotamia. It's roughly the same as modern Iraq. Many Assyrians live outside the Middle East, however. Detroit, for instance, has a large Assyrian community.

Iraqi Assyrians are traditionally Christian rather than Muslim. They tend to belong to the Ancient Church of the East, the Syrian Orthodox Church of Antioch, and the Chaldean Catholic Church. Some Assyrians are Protestants.

Saddam Hussein's government tried to keep non-Arabs, such as the Assyrians, out of Iraq's oil-producing regions. The policy the government practiced was known as "internal deportation." This was a way to keep the country's oil wealth in the hands of Sunni Arabs.

The Turkmens

Turkmens are a small minority group in Iraq. They are predominantly but not exclusively Muslim. As their name suggests, they have close cultural and linguistic ties to Turkey. Estimates of their population in Iraq vary widely from 200,000 to 2 million. The Turkmens have clashed with Kurds and Arabs in northern Iraq. Leaders of a group known as the Iraqi Turkmen Front have called for Turkey to send troops to restore order. But the Kurds, particularly, have opposed this.

Who Speaks What? Some of the Languages of the Middle East

Group	Languages
Arabs	Arabic
Israelis	Hebrew, Arabic (especially Arab Israelis and Eastern Jews), English, Russian, and Romanian
Persians (Iranians)	Farsi (Persian)
Kurds	Kurdish (an Indo-European language, related to Farsi)
Assyrians	Neo-Aramaic
Turkmen	Turkmen (a Turkic language, related to Turkish)

Lesson 1 Review

Using complete sentences, answer the following questions on a sheet of paper.

1. Who were Philip II of Macedon and Alexander the Great?
2. How far had the Roman Empire reached by AD 200?
3. Who were the Ottomans and where did they get their start?
4. What are the three main branches of Christianity?
5. What is the origin of the split between the Sunni and Shia branches of Islam?
6. Which two European countries agreed in 1916 to carve up much of the Middle East into zones of influence?
7. What was the Balfour Declaration?
8. Which ethnic group do most Iranians belong to?
9. Which countries are home to most of the world's Kurds?

Applying Your Learning

10. Was it a good idea for the League of Nations to put Middle East lands under mandates as it did? Why or why not?

LESSON 2 The Arab-Israeli Conflict

Quick Write

What do you think went through the minds of Israeli soldiers walking through East Jerusalem for the first time during the Six-Day War? Describe how you think the Arabs of the Old City felt.

Learn About

- historical events that contributed to the founding of modern Israel
- historical events associated with the Six-Day War of 1967
- how the Yom Kippur War of 1973 affected Arab-Israeli relations
- the various attempts at lasting peace in the Middle East

On 5 June 1967 Israel staged a surprise preemptive strike against Egypt. It destroyed virtually all the aircraft in the Egyptian, Jordanian, and Syrian air forces. Most of them were destroyed while sitting on the ground.

Within three days, the Israelis had taken the Sinai Desert and reached the Suez Canal. Within six days, the Israelis had control of the West Bank, the Golan Heights, and the Gaza Strip as well.

The Israeli David had defeated the Arab Goliath. Not only Arabs and Israelis, but the whole world was stunned.

And there was more. Israeli troops were able to take East Jerusalem, site of the Western Wall of the ancient Jewish temple. To Jews, it's one of the holiest places in the world. Arabs had captured it and the rest of the old Jewish Quarter during Israel's 1948 War for Independence. And now it was back in Jewish hands.

On top of the Temple Mount stands the Dome of the Rock mosque. Muslims believe it's the spot from which the prophet Muhammad went up to heaven.

Historical Events That Contributed to the Founding of Modern Israel

In the previous lesson, you read about how the Ottoman Empire's collapse led to French and British mandates over different parts of the Middle East. These European powers controlled territories until they were either ready for independence or gained it through revolution. This process played out in British-controlled Palestine, too. But it was much more complicated than in other places because of the Jews' and Arabs' competing claims.

Vocabulary

- nascent
- white paper
- viable
- Yishuv
- clandestine
- annex
- concession
- nationalize
- Diaspora
- pogrom
- conscripts
- gross national product
- embargo
- Knesset
- intifada

The 1947 United Nations Partition Plan for Palestine

The Balfour Declaration of 1917 put the British government on record in favor of a Jewish homeland in Palestine. This statement gave the Zionists a huge boost. It showed that the government of one of the most powerful countries on earth was in favor of their cause. The institutions of the nascent—*developing*—Jewish state began to take form. Jewish immigration into Palestine increased.

A farmer walks through his pumpkin field in a kibbutz—a cooperative settlement—in Israel.

Photo by Ilene R. Prusher / © 2007 The Christian Science Monitor

The Balfour Declaration of 1917 put the British government on record in favor of a Jewish homeland in Palestine.

Israel and its Arab neighbors

The Zionist movement acquired large tracts of land in Palestine. The region lacked a clear system of private property rights, and, especially during the hard times of the 1930s, Arab landowners were willing to sell.

This led to an anti-Zionist backlash, however. Arab resistance to Jewish immigration intensified. It often led to violence. An organization called the Arab Higher Committee called a general strike and issued three demands:

- An end to further Jewish immigration
- An end to land sales to Jews
- The establishment of an Arab national government.

And so in 1939 the British government changed its policy. It issued a white paper—*a statement of government policy*—that ended its commitment to the Jews in Palestine. Instead, it called for the creation of a Palestinian (Arab) state within 10 years. The Palestinians would take over as soon as "peace and order" could be restored. This plan would severely limit Jewish immigration to 75,000 a year for five years. After that, further immigration would require the Palestinian government's consent. This policy change did not go down well with the Zionists.

The outbreak of World War II further complicated the situation. However disappointed the Jews were in the British government, they really had no choice but to support Britain in the fight against Nazi Germany, which was rounding up and murdering millions of European Jews. As David Ben-Gurion, who would eventually become Israel's first prime minister in 1948, put it, "We shall fight the war against Hitler as if there were no White Paper, and we shall fight the White Paper as if there were no war."

And so they did. Ben-Gurion played another key leadership role in Israel's founding as chairman of the Jewish Agency, which helped settle immigrants into Palestine. He held the post from 1935–1948. In 1945 the Jewish Agency joined forces with armed radical groups to form the Jewish resistance. This resistance sometimes resorted to violence in support of its goals.

By the end of World War II, the British effort to limit Jewish immigration was becoming untenable. Hundreds of thousands of Jews who had survived the Nazi Holocaust were stuck in camps for "displaced persons" in Europe. They clamored for permission to go to Palestine. They had world opinion on their side. US President Harry Truman felt morally bound to help the refugees and pushed Britain to change its policy. It was more than Britain, weakened by World War II and straining under the weight of its empire, could sustain.

On 18 February 1947 British Foreign Secretary Ernest Bevin announced that his government would hand the issue over to the United Nations. On 15 May the UN set up an 11-member Special Committee on Palestine (UNSCOP). On 31 August the committee announced a plan to divide Palestine into two states, one Jewish and the other Arab. Jerusalem would have special international status. An economic union would link the three entities.

A majority of UNSCOP's members supported the partition plan. So did the United States and the Soviet Union. The UN General Assembly adopted the plan on 29 November 1947.

The Zionist General Council thought the plan fell short of what Zionists had expected from the League of Nations mandate to Britain 25 years before. But the council was willing in principle to accept partition. On the other hand, the League of Arab States said it would do whatever was necessary to block the deal.

The US Department of State then told Truman that a Jewish state would not be viable—*able to survive*. So in January 1948 the president reversed himself. He said he could not support Israel. He agreed to postpone partition and transfer the British Mandate to a UN trusteeship council.

Young Palestinians walk down a street in Gaza City, Gaza Strip.
Photo by Melanie Stetson Freeman / © 2001 The Christian Science Monitor

After the 1948 Israeli War of Independence, only two parts of Palestine remained in Arab hands: the Gaza Strip and the West Bank.

The Arab political parties on the ground in Palestine rejected the plan as well and called for a general strike. Violence mounted between Arabs and Jews. British forces in Palestine sided with Arabs. They tried unsuccessfully to keep the Yishuv—*the Jewish community in Palestine before statehood*—from arming itself.

The Jews' first clandestine—*secret*—shipment of heavy arms arrived from Czechoslovakia in March 1948. The *Haganah*—the military arm of the Jewish Agency—went on the offensive. It set up communications links for the territory the UN plan designated as the Jewish state. Jewish forces also attacked Arabs. When the news came that they had killed 250 Arab civilians at the village of Dayr Yasin, Arabs fled from places with large Jewish populations.

Meanwhile, the US policy stance changed yet again. A Zionist leader named Chaim Weizmann persuaded Truman to pledge support for the proposed Jewish state. On 14 May 1948 Ben-Gurion proclaimed the establishment of the State of Israel. Britain gave up its mandate the next day at 6 p.m.

The Israeli War of Independence

The Zionists' dream wasn't secure, however. The day after Ben-Gurion's proclamation, Arab forces invaded the new state.

Initially these forces numbered about 25,000. They included Egyptians, Iraqis, Syrians, Transjordanians, and Lebanese, along with sprinklings of Saudi Arabians and Yemenis. On the Israeli side were the *Haganah* and irregular units, along with women's auxiliaries, totaling 35,000 or more.

By mid-October, Arab forces in the war zones rose to about 55,000, including up to 5,000 Palestine Liberation Force irregulars. With the exception of the British-trained Arab Legion of Transjordan, most of the Arab troops were ill prepared for battle. By contrast, Israeli troops grew to about 100,000, and about a quarter of these were World War II veterans. Their advantages included combat experience and good internal communications lines.

By January 1949—when hostilities ended with a set of armistice agreements—the Israelis held the area that would define their borders until June 1967. It was much more land than what the UN called for. Only two parts of Palestine remained in Arab hands: Egypt held the Gaza Strip. And the Arab Legion of Transjordan controlled the West Bank.

Jordan (formerly Transjordan) chose to annex—*take over*—the West Bank after fighting had ended. It remained under Jordanian control until 1967. But only two countries—Britain and Pakistan—officially recognized Jordanian rule there.

The Dome of the Rock (the gold-domed mosque in front) is one of the Muslim world's holiest sites.
Photo by Melanie Stetson Freeman / © 1995 The Christian Science Monitor
It sits on the site of the ancient Jewish temple. The Arabs captured the Temple Mount in 1948. Israel seized it back in 1967.

The armistice agreements settled division lines in Jerusalem as well. Jordan controlled the Old City and the Western Wall, as well as the Temple Mount. The Temple Mount is sacred to both Jews and Muslims. Solomon's Temple once stood there, and today it is the site of the mosque called the Dome of the Rock. The Israelis controlled West Jerusalem, the more modern part of the city. The situation pleased no one, but brought an end to the fighting—for the time being.

The Suez Canal

The Suez Canal is a shortcut for ships sailing between the Mediterranean Sea and the Red Sea. It was an Anglo-French project. The French designed it and provided most of the construction funding. Legions of poorly paid Egyptian laborers did most of the heavy lifting. The Europeans eventually bought out the Egyptian share of the project. And when it opened in 1869, France and Britain had a joint concession for the canal—*a contract granting the right to operate it.* It was set to expire in 1968.

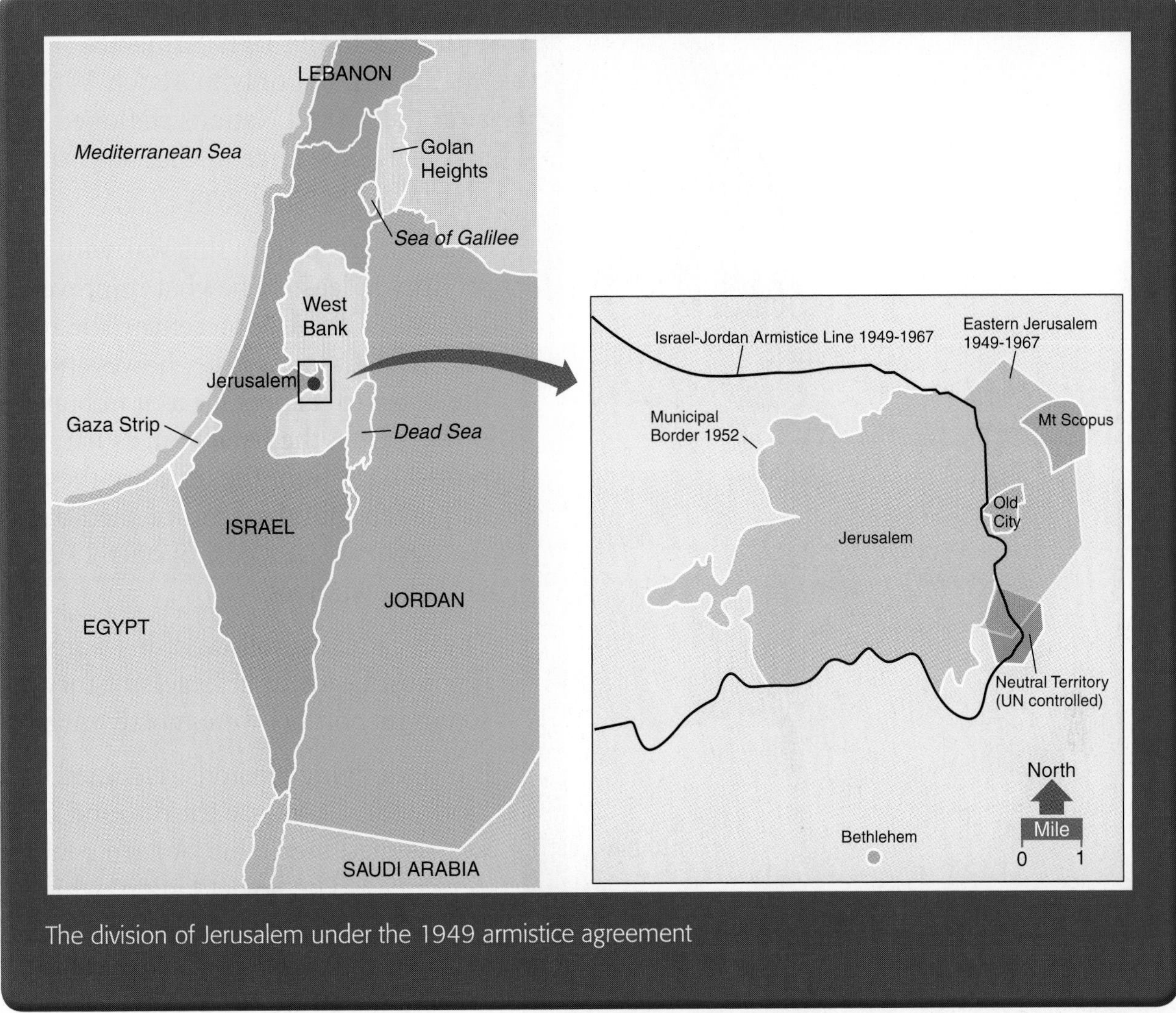

The division of Jerusalem under the 1949 armistice agreement

The Suez Conflict of 1956

The area remained relatively calm until July 1956. That's when Egypt moved to nationalize—*to put under state control*—the Suez Canal, a critical route to India. Britain and France had controlled the canal. After Egypt took it over, the two European countries worked with Israel to recapture it.

Israel took Egypt's action as a sign that it was preparing to launch another invasion. Israeli forces mobilized rapidly. Under Major General Moshe Dayan, the Israeli Defense Forces launched a preemptive strike into Sinai on 29 October. By 2 November they had cleared out the Egyptians and won control of the entire peninsula.

The French and the British, however, landed troops at Port Said and insisted that both the Egyptians and the Israelis withdraw from the canal. The UN, in turn, insisted that the French and the British pull out of Suez. They did so in December, in response to pressure from both the United States and the UN.

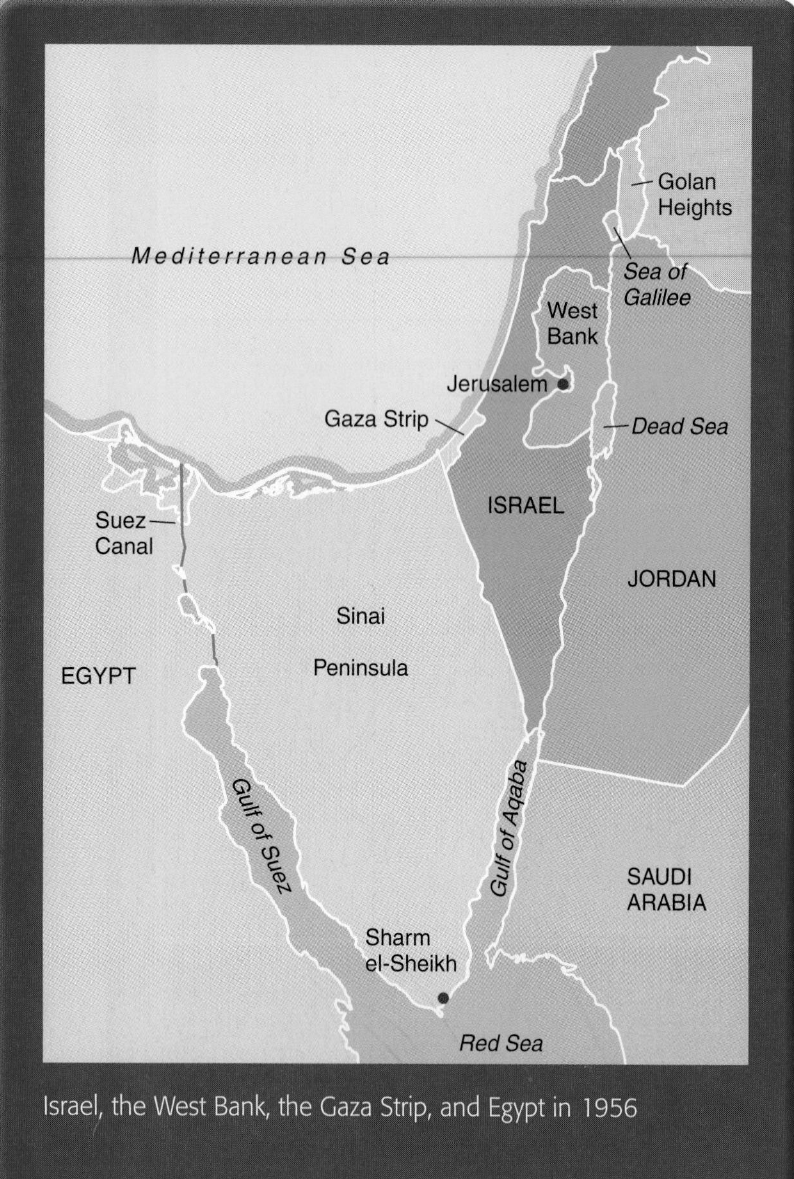

Israel, the West Bank, the Gaza Strip, and Egypt in 1956

The UN also demanded that Israel pull back to the 1949 Armistice line. It did, but only in March 1957 after the United Nations stationed an emergency force in Gaza and at Sharm el-Sheikh, Egypt.

Israel emerged from this war with its security at least somewhat improved because of the UN presence. The real benefit to the new state, however, was the boost to its prestige as a military power. True, the Israeli forces had pulled back from the territory they had taken. But they had pushed back the Egyptians at a cost of only 170 of their own lives.

The decade that followed this war was the most peaceful in Israel's history so far. Its borders were mostly quiet.

But underlying tensions remained. By the early 1960s, a third round of war seemed inevitable. An arms race developed. The Soviet Union, which had originally supported Israel, now supplied Egypt and Syria with military aid and hardware. And Israel found that the West Germans, the British, and especially the French were good sources of modern weapons.

Historical Events Associated With the Six-Day War of 1967

In June 1967 the Israeli Defense Forces (IDF) redrew the map of one of the most sensitive parts of the world in less than a week. The Six-Day War was one of the most significant since World War II. It was like an earthquake whose aftershocks still reverberate. Its still-unresolved questions—notably that of a Palestinian state—continue to drive or at least affect the political agenda of much of this region.

Arab Threats to Israel Prior to the Six-Day War

As the State of Israel neared the end of its second decade, border skirmishes, shelling, and other violence began increasing. During the 1960s, Syria repeatedly shelled Israeli border villages from the Golan Heights and by air. Most of these incidents were minor, but on 7 April 1967, Israeli fighter aircraft struck back. In the ensuing dogfight, the Syrians lost six of their Soviet-built MiG fighters. Syria began to fear an all-out attack from Israel. Egypt, an ally of Syria, began a big military buildup the next month.

Then on 18 May Egyptian President Gamal Abdul Nasser ordered UN forces out of Gaza and Sinai. UN Secretary-General U Thant agreed to pull his troops out. Four days later, Nasser announced a blockade of the Straits of Tiran. That was Israel's only outlet to the Red Sea and its markets to the east. Nasser knew that would be grounds for the Israelis to go to war. Ever since the 1956 war, Israel had stressed to the Egyptians that a blockade would be as good as a declaration of war. Soon after the Egyptian move, Jordan and Iraq joined the Syrian-Egyptian military alliance.

A Syrian minefield sits to the left of the road through the Golan Heights, which Israel took from Syria in the 1967 Six-Day War.
Photo by Melanie Stetson Freeman / © 1995 The Christian Science Monitor
During the 1960s, Syria repeatedly shelled Israeli border villages from these heights.

The Six-Day War

Moshe Dayan, hero of the 1956 war, became the Israeli minister of defense on 30 May 1967. He came to power declaring publicly that war could be avoided. But secretly, he was planning a huge preemptive strike against Arab airpower. On 5 June Israel destroyed about 370 Egyptian, Syrian, and Jordanian aircraft. Most of them were knocked out sitting on the ground.

The attack nearly eliminated Arab air forces. Next came a ground invasion of Sinai and the Gaza Strip, Jordan, and then Syria. It was a rout on all fronts for the Arab ground forces, which lacked air support.

Israel and the Occupied Territories after the Six-Day War

By the time a UN cease-fire took hold, the IDF had taken the Sinai Peninsula as far west as the Suez Canal. It had also seized the West Bank, including East Jerusalem, as well as Syria's Golan Heights. And this time, in contrast with 1956, the Israelis did not pull back once the shooting stopped.

The swift and stunning victory cost Israel 700 troops. The IDF beat back the combined Arab armies, which included far larger numbers.

Most significantly, for the first time since independence, Israel's heartland was out of its enemies' artillery range. The territory that had harbored threats to its security since 1948 was under its control.

The Issues Associated With Israeli-Occupied Territories in Palestine

From the Israeli perspective, the victories of the Six-Day War solved some major problems. But it also created new ones.

Israel might have used its captured territories to bargain for peace with its neighbors. But in the postwar euphoria, this had little appeal for the Israeli public.

An Israeli soldier guards the entrance to a Jewish hilltop settlement in Carmei Tzur, West Bank.
Photo by Melanie Stetson Freeman / © 2001 The Christian Science Monitor

Israel's persistence in building new settlements in occupied territories is one of the main issues in the Arab-Israeli conflict.

Right after the war, Israeli Prime Minister Levi Eshkol said he would negotiate "everything" for a full peace, including settlement of the refugee problem. In November 1967 he accepted UN Security Council Resolution 242. This committed Israel to "withdrawal of Israeli armed forces from territories occupied in the recent conflict." In return, Israel would get acceptance from its Arab neighbors.

But the Eshkol government also made plans to build Jewish settlements in the disputed territories. And so did Eshkol's successor, Prime Minister Golda Meir.

Israel's persistence in building new settlements in occupied territories, even as successive governments have said they are willing to negotiate land for peace, is one of the main issues in the Arab-Israeli conflict.

This Palestinian village in Jania, West Bank, shown in 2001, was all but closed down because of Israeli roadblocks meant to stop suicide bombers.
Photo by Melanie Stetson Freeman / © 2001 The Christian Science Monitor

The West Bank has provided cover and support for guerrillas since the end of the Six-Day War.

Other Political and Military Developments

The occupied territories held roughly 1 million Arabs. These provided potential cover and support for guerrillas, notably a group called Al Fatah ("the victory"). Skirmishes and sabotage continued during this period. A steady stream of men and weapons flowed into the West Bank from the end of the war until 1970. In the spring of that year, guerrillas went back to shelling Israel from Jordan and Lebanon. International terrorism intended to focus attention on Palestinian grievances also appeared after the Six-Day War.

From the Arab political perspective, the Six-Day War was not just a defeat for Egypt. It was a defeat for Nasser's goal of uniting the Arabs in one country. The Palestine Liberation Organization (PLO), led by Yasser Arafat, emerged as the political face of the Palestinian people. The Soviet Union quickly resupplied the Egyptians with weapons and became much more visible at the Suez Canal.

And fighting started again. For nearly two years, the Egyptians and Israelis waged a low-level war. The Egyptians fired missiles at Israeli positions on the east bank of the canal. The Israelis held their own and sent fighter-bombers deep into the Egyptian heartland. This was known as the War of Attrition—in other words, a war of wearing each other down.

The conflict's climax came on 30 July 1970, when Israeli fighter pilots clashed with Soviet counterparts in a dogfight near the Suez Canal. The Israelis reportedly shot down four Soviet MiGs without any losses of their own. But such a direct confrontation with a nuclear power was a frightening development. The Israelis stepped back from the brink. A new cease-fire took effect on 7 August 1970.

Jewish Military Tradition

The Jewish military tradition has ancient roots. The Bible tells, for instance, how Abraham led a force on a mission to rescue his kidnapped nephew, Lot. Joshua conquered Canaan by military might. And David, the shepherd who went on to conquer Jerusalem, was a great warrior-king.

But for the nearly 2,000 years of the Diaspora—*the scattering of Jews far from their traditional homeland*—the Jewish community lacked much of a military tradition. Many saw this as a cause of their hardships. And it was a powerful motivation for building a strong defense for Israel.

Some of the first Jews to return to Palestine were those fleeing the Russian pogroms—*organized persecutions or massacres*—of the 1880s. These settlers created self-defense units called *Shomrim*, or guardsmen. In 1909 they were formally organized and renamed *HaShomer*, or the Watchmen. There were never many of them. But they were very important to the Israeli military tradition. They set a precedent of armed self-defense of Zionism. These forces eventually led to the modern-day Israeli Defense Force (IDF).

How the Yom Kippur War of 1973 Affected Arab-Israeli Relations

Six years after the triumph of 1967, Israel found itself in another major war with its Arab neighbors. It won this one, too—but at a high price. This war almost brought the two nuclear superpowers—the United States and the Soviet Union—into direct conflict.

The Historical Events That Led Up to the War

Palestinian guerrillas continued to attack Israel through the early 1970s. But after the War of Attrition, Israel felt relatively safe. Its military intelligence thought Syria would attack only if Egypt did, too. And according to this view, Egypt wouldn't attack unless it were sure its airpower was superior to Israel's. This reasoning was known as "the concept," and it helped make Israel feel secure. Defense spending fell. Reservists served only 30 days instead of 60 each year. And by 1973, conscripts—*draftees*—served only 33 months instead of 36.

Meanwhile, Egypt was making peaceful noises. Anwar Sadat had come to power after Nasser died in September 1970. Like Nasser late in life, Sadat realized that Egypt's domestic problems were more urgent than its dispute with Israel. Peace with Israel would allow Egypt to cut its defense spending and maybe even get financial help from the United States.

And so Sadat launched a peace initiative. In 1971 he told the Egyptian parliament that "if Israel withdrew her forces in Sinai to the passes I would be willing to reopen the Suez Canal ... and to sign a peace agreement with Israel...." (The canal had been closed since the end of the Six-Day War.)

Israeli Prime Minister Golda Meir turned him down flat, however. Israel would not return to prewar borders, she said. This was the general view in Israel. The Israelis thought the neighboring Arab states were too weak to attack. The Arab world was in political disarray. Israelis were settling in the occupied territories. The Israelis saw no incentive to trade away land. And an attack on Israel seemed even less likely after Sadat expelled Soviet military advisers from Egypt in 1972.

But in fact, Meir's rejection of Sadat's peace overture convinced him he needed to try something else. He wanted to change the diplomatic status quo and to win legitimacy at home. What he needed, he concluded, was to start a war.

Traffic clogs the streets in modern-day Cairo, Egypt.

Photo by Melanie Stetson Freeman / © 1995 The Christian Science Monitor

Egyptian President Anwar Sadat realized that his country's domestic problems were more urgent than its land dispute with Israel. Even so, he went to war with Israel in 1973.

Israeli children play soccer in an Israeli hilltop settlement in the West Bank in 2001.
Photo by Melanie Stetson Freeman / © 2001 The Christian Science Monitor

Shortly before Egypt and Syria launched the 1973 Yom Kippur War, Israeli Prime Minister Golda Meir saw no incentive to trade land for peace with Israel's Arab neighbors.

The Egyptian Attack on Israel and the Israeli Counterattack

Egypt and Syria chose Yom Kippur, the Jewish Day of Atonement, to launch their surprise attack against Israel. On 6 October 1973 Egyptian infantry crossed the Suez Canal and overran Israel's defensive Bar-Lev Line. In the north, Syrian forces reached the outer edge of the Golan Heights. They greatly outnumbered the Israelis, with 1,100 tanks to 157.

Israel counterattacked, but for the first few days could make no headway. Casualties were heavy and the Israelis lost almost 150 planes as well.

On 10 October the tide turned. Israel pushed the Syrians out of all the territory they had taken since the start of the war. The next day Israeli forces got as far as 12 miles from the outskirts of Damascus, Syria's capital.

In the south, Israelis repelled the Egyptian offensive into Sinai. A force led by General Ariel Sharon crossed the Suez Canal and surrounded the Egyptian Third Army.

Russian and US Participation in the War

The Yom Kippur War, as it became known, differed from Israel's earlier wars because the world's two superpowers, the Soviet Union and the United States, quickly got involved.

A resident of Sderot, Israel, stands outside his house next to a living room wall damaged in 2006 in a Qassam rocket salvo.
Photo by Josh Mitnick / © 2006 The Christian Science Monitor

Israel has been under attack for much of its short history. In the earlier Yom Kippur War of 1973, casualties—those killed or wounded—numbered more than 6,000.

Sadat had expelled Soviet military advisers in 1972. But after Israeli forces advanced into Syria, the Soviet Union responded with huge military airlifts to Damascus and Cairo, Egypt's capital. The United States matched this move with airlifts to the Israelis.

The Soviet Union called US Secretary of State Henry Kissinger to Moscow to negotiate a cease-fire. He worked out a deal calling for a cease-fire within 12 hours. It also called for implementation of UN Resolution 242, the "land for peace" resolution. And it called for negotiation of "a just and durable peace in the Middle East."

After Kissinger returned to Washington, word came from the Soviets that the Israelis had violated the cease-fire. They had surrounded the Egyptian Third Army and were threatening to destroy it, the Soviets added. If the Israelis didn't back off, the Soviets would take action on their own.

It was everyone's nightmare scenario during the Cold War: a regional conflict that risked pulling in the superpowers as adversaries. Had the Soviets acted unilaterally, the United States would have felt a need to respond. But fortunately, Israel yielded to American pressure to let up on the Egyptians. A cease-fire took hold 25 October.

The Outcomes of the War

Israel may have "won" the Yom Kippur War, but it left the country feeling devastated. Casualties—those killed or wounded—numbered more than 6,000. The war cost the Israelis an estimated $7 billion in US dollars. This covered the loss of military equipment as well as the decline of general economic output. It was equivalent to a whole year's gross national product—*the sum total of a country's output of goods and services*.

Most important, the war shattered Israel's image of invincibility. What happened in October 1973 shook national self-confidence. Israeli citizens questioned the competence of their Labor Party government. And Defense Minister Dayan, the hero of the Sinai and the Six-Day War, drew sharp public criticism.

After the October war, Israel also became more dependent on the United States. It relied on Washington for military, economic, and diplomatic aid.

And Israel found itself in an arms race. As oil prices rose, the Arab states had the money to buy more and more advanced weapons. This, in turn, forced Israel to spend more on defense, further straining its economy.

The Arab Oil Embargo

During the Yom Kippur War, the Arab members of the Organization of Petroleum Exporting Countries (OPEC) began an oil embargo against the United States. OPEC is a group of oil-rich countries who use their collective power to set policies and prices. They do this by reducing or increasing the amount of oil they are willing to sell. An **embargo** is a *ban on trade*, or in this case, a refusal to sell oil to the United States. The Arab oil states wanted to get back at America because of its decision to resupply Israel during the war. Arab oil producers extended the embargo to other supporters of Israel. They also cut production. This drove prices up. Long lines formed at US filling stations as people waited to buy gas. The embargo came as the decades-old system of oil pricing was already breaking down for other reasons. And so the embargo was especially effective from the Arab perspective. Prices eventually quadrupled from $3 to $12 a barrel. OPEC lifted the embargo in May 1974 after progress in Arab-Israeli disengagement.

The Various Attempts at Lasting Peace in the Middle East

"Peace in the Middle East" has been on the American diplomatic agenda since at least 1948. The unresolved question of Palestinian statehood remains a sore spot in the region.

Washington's focus on the Israeli-Palestinian conflict has waxed and waned over time. But a number of attempts have been made to achieve a "just and durable peace" over the years. In the next sections you'll read about two of the most important ones.

Damascus Gate is one of the pedestrian entryways to the Arab Quarter of Jerusalem's Old City and is often crowded with vendors and shoppers.
Photo by Melanie Stetson Freeman / © 2001 The Christian Science Monitor

The unresolved questions of Palestinian statehood and Jerusalem's status remain sore spots for Arabs in the Middle East.

The Camp David Accords of 1979

When Menachem Begin came to power as Israel's prime minister in May 1977, some observers hoped he might be the leader who made peace with his country's neighbors. He was known as a real "hawk" toward the Palestinians. As a younger man, he had headed the *Irgun*, a Zionist militia trying to force the British out of Palestine.

But that might make it easier to make peace, some thought. There was no doubt he would stand up for Israel in dealings with the Arabs. And people remembered Richard Nixon's historic opening to China, just a few years before. It was precisely because he was such a well-known anticommunist that he could open dialogue with the Communists in Beijing.

In 1977, international public opinion wanted a peace conference that would lead to an overall Arab-Israeli settlement. All parties would gather in Geneva, Switzerland. The United States and the Soviet Union would oversee things. America's new president, Jimmy Carter, and Soviet leader Leonid Brezhnev issued a joint statement calling for such a conference.

But Begin had other ideas. He said that no international forum would tell him how to deal with Israeli territory. And he didn't want to attend a peace conference where he would have no allies except the United States. Within America, opposition from supporters of Israel, as well as from anti-Soviet groups who didn't want Moscow to have a bigger voice in the Middle East, also worked against an international conference.

Palestinian schoolchildren mug for the camera during a period in 2001 when roadblocks prevented many of their teachers from reaching classrooms. *Photo by Melanie Stetson Freeman / © 2001 The Christian Science Monitor*

Several attempts at lasting peace in the Middle East have been made over the years, including the Camp David and Oslo Accords.

Egyptian President Anwar Sadat also had other ideas. He feared Egypt might lose out to Syria at a Geneva conference. And what he cared most about was getting the Sinai back. At an international conference, the focus would be on a settlement for the Palestinians and the return of the Golan Heights to Syria.

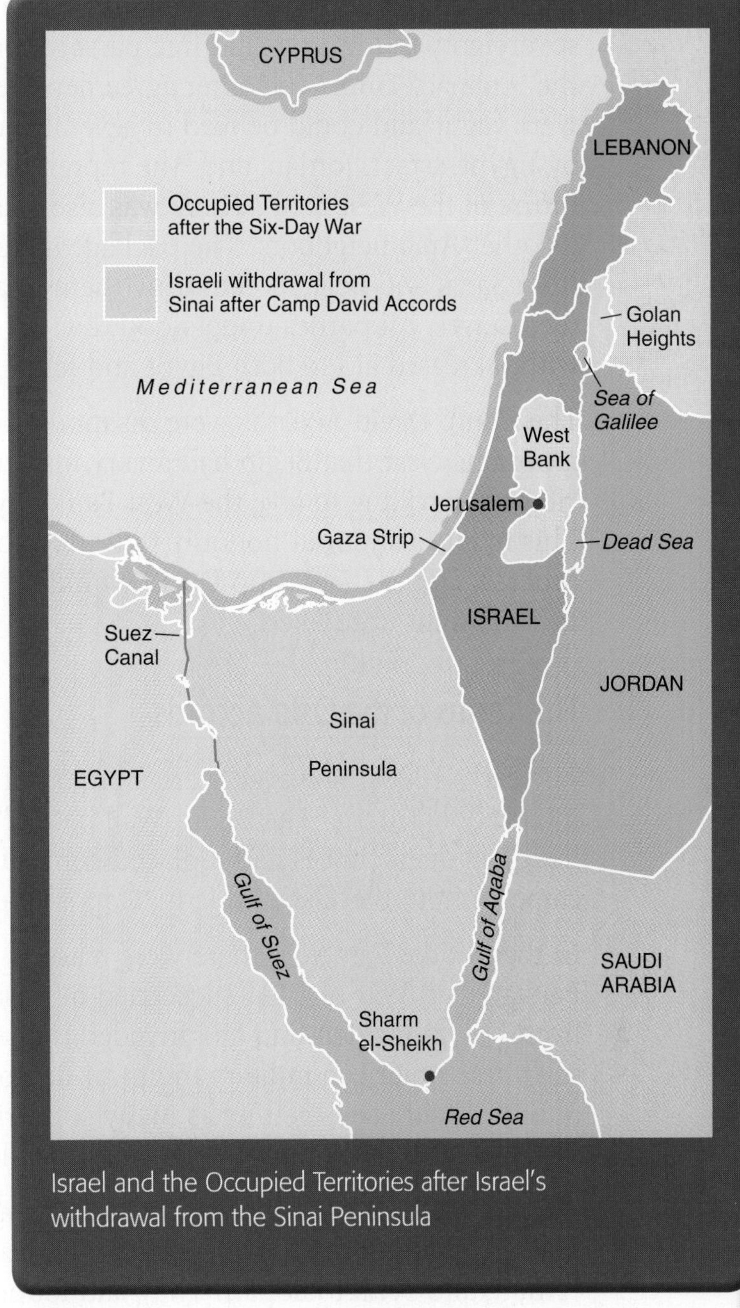

Israel and the Occupied Territories after Israel's withdrawal from the Sinai Peninsula

And so Sadat made a bold diplomatic move: his own opening to Israel. He offered to address the Knesset (kuh-NESS-it)—*the Israeli parliament*.

His November 1977 journey to Jerusalem opened a new era in Egyptian-Israeli relations. He was committed to settling the Palestinian issue, but the Sinai was his priority.

Begin responded positively. He saw Sinai as negotiable, unlike the West Bank. And peace between the two countries would remove Egypt from the Arab-Israeli military balance. It would take some of the pressure off Israel to give up any of the West Bank.

Sadat's move forced President Carter to change course and drop support for an international conference. Carter ended up playing a key role in bringing Sadat and Begin to an agreement, however.

Israeli-Egyptian negotiations began after Sadat's trip to Jerusalem, but then bogged down. After nearly a year's impasse, Carter brought Begin and Sadat to his presidential retreat at Camp David, outside Washington, for talks. Carter was putting a lot on the line for this: his own credibility and prestige.

The talks went on for two weeks, with Carter shuttling between cabins at the retreat, trying to broker an agreement. The crux of the problem was that Begin, who had opposed territorial concessions for so long, resisted dismantling settlements built in the Sinai while it was under Israel's control.

Finally he consented, and the Camp David Accords were signed 17 September 1978. The Knesset approved them the next day.

One of the two agreements dealt with Sinai. It called for restoring Egyptian sovereignty to the Sinai and free passage for Israelis through the Suez Canal and the Straits of Tiran. The other agreement dealt with the West Bank, in terms that were vague and could be read in several ways. The accord called for "negotiations" by Egypt, Israel, Jordan, and "the representatives of the Palestinian people" on the future of the West Bank. There was also a call for peace talks between Israel and its other Arab neighbors. The package included as well personal letters to Carter from Sadat and Begin committing them to actions not outlined in the agreements themselves. All parties understood that the United States would sweeten the deal with increased aid to both Egypt and Israel.

The Camp David Accords were disappointing almost from the start. Early on, it became clear that Begin had a very limited concept of Palestinian autonomy. He was unwilling to give the West Bank any real control over its own resources. This in effect shut out not only radical Arabs, but also moderates from the peace process. Hopes that Camp David would be the first of a series of Arab-Israeli accords went unfulfilled.

The Terms of the Oslo Accords

The early 1990s, however, were a period of good news and hopefulness in the international arena. The Berlin Wall had fallen. Throughout Eastern Europe, fledgling democracies had replaced communism. In most cases, the changes came without bloodshed. Many "impossible" things had come to pass.

In the Middle East, too, there were reasons for hope. The US-led coalition in the Persian Gulf War of 1991 succeeded in ousting Iraqi forces under Saddam Hussein from Kuwait, which Iraq had invaded the summer before. The victory didn't just showcase American military might. It demonstrated the value of diplomacy and of the United States getting as many countries on its "team" as it could. It made some people think "impossible" things could happen in the Middle East, too.

And so in October 1991 the United States and the Soviet Union convened the Madrid Conference in Spain. Palestinian leaders and the leaders of Israel, Lebanon, Jordan, and Syria took part. They laid foundations for negotiations to bring peace and prosperity to the region.

Within this framework, Israel and the PLO negotiated a Declaration of Principles signed 13 September 1993.

Earlier, on 14 December 1988, PLO Chairman Yasser Arafat had condemned all forms of terrorism. He'd also recognized Israel. Israel was unimpressed. But Arafat's move led President Ronald Reagan to authorize "substantive dialogue" between US diplomats and the PLO for the first time.

By signing the Declaration of Principles, Israel recognized the PLO. It also granted it limited autonomy in return for an end to Palestinian claims to Israeli land.

Pedestrians head to and from the Palestinian market in Hebron, perhaps the tensest town in the West Bank because of several Jewish settlements in the middle of the Arab city.
Photo by Melanie Stetson Freeman / © 2001 The Christian Science Monitor

Israel and the Palestine Liberation Organization signed an interim agreement in 1995, but continued violence has prevented further progress.

The declaration is known as the Oslo Accords because it was worked out in the Norwegian capital, Oslo. It set some ambitious goals for the transfer of authority from Israel to an interim Palestinian Authority. Israel and the PLO signed two other agreements the next year to prepare for a transfer of powers and responsibilities.

How the Intifada Undermined the Oslo Accords

The mid-1990s saw two more important accords signed. Israel and Jordan signed a peace treaty 26 October 1994. And on 28 September 1995 Israeli Prime Minister Yitzhak Rabin and PLO Chairman Arafat signed the Israeli-Palestinian Interim Agreement.

But just weeks later on 4 November, a right-wing Jewish radical assassinated Rabin. The murder brought to a head the bitter national debate over the peace process.

Even so, Israel continued to negotiate with the PLO. The two sides reached a number of agreements. But when President Bill Clinton hosted a summit at Camp David in July 2000 to tackle the core issues—such as Jerusalem, refugees, and Israeli settlements—the session broke down with no agreement.

Within weeks, widespread violence broke out in Israel, the West Bank, and Gaza. It started when Ariel Sharon, now the leader of Israel's right-wing opposition, visited the Temple Mount in Jerusalem. Palestinians saw the visit as a provocation. With the failed peace process as a backdrop, the episode touched off a wave of violence. By December, it had taken 300 lives.

The violence was known as the intifada, or *uprising*. (This was actually the second wave of violence to be designated this way. The first began in 1987.)

After a destructive Israeli raid in 2003 into a refugee camp in Rafah, Gaza Strip, Palestinian men use the street as their living room.

Photo by Cameron W. Barr / © 2003 The Christian Science Monitor

Six years later, in 2009, Israeli troops invaded the Gaza Strip after Hamas fired rockets into Israel.

In the final weeks of his presidency, Clinton made one more attempt at Middle East peace. He convened a summit on 17 October 2000 at Sharm el-Sheikh, Egypt, to calm the continuing violence between Palestinians and Israelis. A plan was announced. But it came unraveled almost at once.

In August 2005, after two years of diplomatic efforts, Israel began to withdraw from the Gaza Strip. In January 2006 the Palestinian terrorist group Hamas won a majority in elections to the Palestinian Legislative Council. This led to a series of armed clashes between Hamas and the PLO. In June 2007 Hamas seized control of Gaza, leaving Hamas governing it while the Palestinian Authority governed the West Bank.

Israeli troops invaded the Gaza Strip in January 2009 after Hamas fired rockets into Israel. The Israelis withdrew after three weeks of fighting, leaving the basic Palestinian-Israeli stalemate essentially unchanged. Diplomatic efforts to end the conflict continued as this book went to press.

Lesson 2 Review

Using complete sentences, answer the following questions on a sheet of paper.

1. How did the lack of a clear system of property rights in Palestine help the Zionists?
2. What important policy change did the British government announce through a white paper in 1939?
3. What actions by Egypt in May 1967 did Israel consider grounds for going to war?
4. What problems did victory in 1967 create for Israel?
5. What did Anwar Sadat conclude from Golda Meir's response to his peace initiative?
6. What were the outcomes for Israel of the 1973 war? List three.
7. What was the main result of the Camp David Accords?
8. What was the main result of the Oslo Accords?

Applying Your Learning

9. Explain what you think the United States should do to help resolve the Arab-Israeli conflict.

LESSON 3 The Persian Gulf Wars

Quick Write

If you had been secretary of State when Saddam Hussein invaded Kuwait, what course of action would you have recommended to the president? Explain your recommendation.

Learn About

- the historical situation of Iraq under the rule of Saddam Hussein
- the historical events associated with the 1991 Persian Gulf War
- events surrounding the 2003 US invasion of Iraq
- US attempts to stabilize Iraq since the 2003 invasion

Imagine yourself as the secretary of State on 2 August 1990. It's 8 o'clock in the morning, and you've just joined the president and others for a meeting of the National Security Council. The president has an important decision to make. Thirteen hours ago, forces of Iraqi President Saddam Hussein marched into Kuwait to take it over.

Now the president is asking for your recommendation–what should the United States do? Should it go to war to liberate Kuwait? Your job is to weigh the options.

Going to war means transferring hundreds of thousands of US troops halfway around the world in a short period. It will be difficult, and you'll have to get foreign governments to agree to host bases for the troops. The American people know little about Kuwait, and might not support a war to put an emir, or king, back on his throne. You hesitate to commit US troops to a war without overwhelming support. You know Iraq has a large, battle-tested army, and fear US casualties could be very high. The rest of the world might not support an invasion, leaving the US isolated. Shouldn't the US limit itself to diplomacy and economic measures? Isn't this just a fight between Arabs the United States should stay out of?

On the other hand, Kuwait is a major oil supplier to the US and its allies. Now a dictator hostile to the United States controls that oil. What if Iraq attacks Saudi Arabia next? The Saudis are an even more important supplier of oil, which the US economy needs to power factories and heat homes. You know that the Saudi armed forces would be no match for the Iraqis. And what if the United States and United Nations do nothing–won't other countries take that as a signal that they can invade their weaker neighbors and seize their natural resources? With Kuwait's oil at his disposal, Saddam Hussein can ignore diplomacy and sanctions.

The president awaits your opinion.

The Historical Situation of Iraq Under the Rule of Saddam Hussein

You read in an earlier lesson about how Saddam Hussein came to power in Iraq as deputy leader in a 1968 coup. By 1979 he had become the undisputed leader of the country.

Vocabulary

- constitutional monarchy
- coup d'état
- pan-Arabism
- status quo antebellum
- weapons of mass destruction (WMD)

The Baathist Revolution

You also read earlier that modern Iraq began as a territory under a British mandate. In 1932 it became a constitutional monarchy under the rule of the Hashemite family. The same family governed (and still governs) in Jordan. A constitutional monarchy is *government by a king or queen whose powers are limited by the constitution and laws of the country.* A constitutional monarch can't just do whatever he or she wants, in other words.

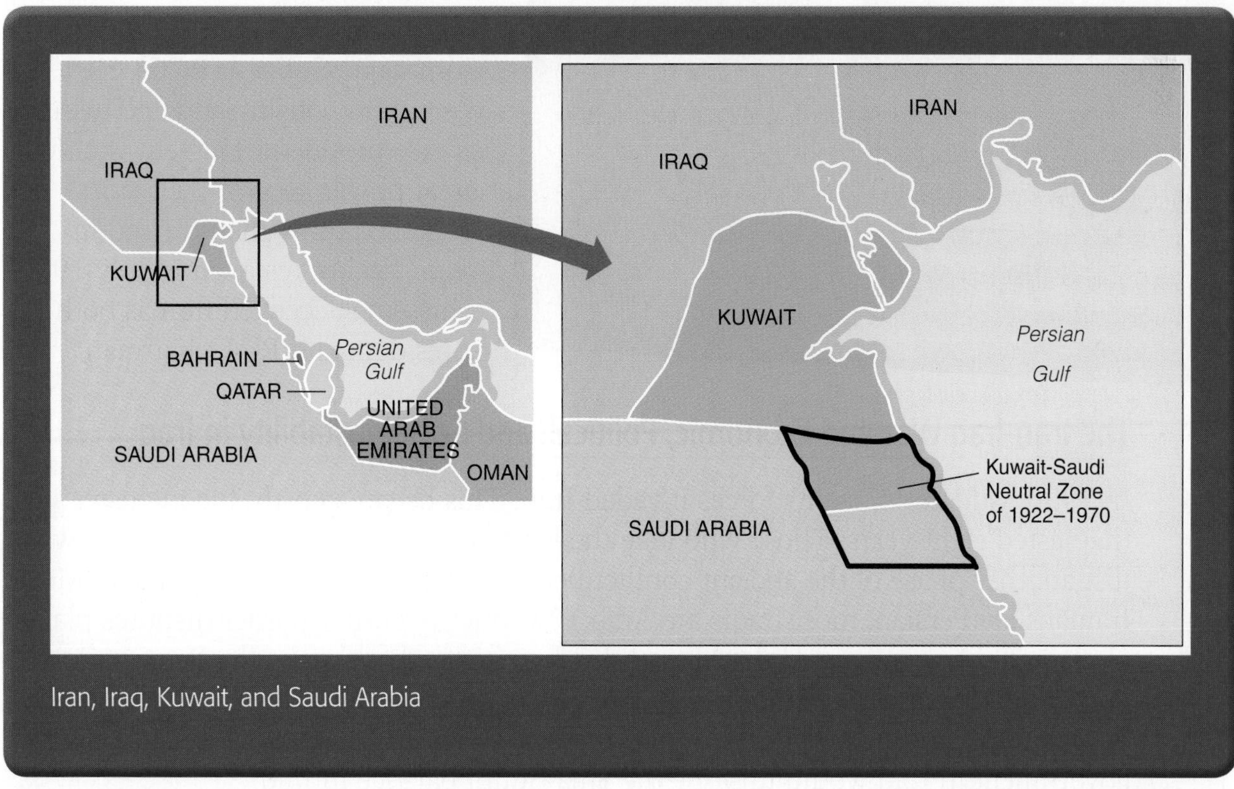

Iran, Iraq, Kuwait, and Saudi Arabia

Pictures of Iraqi President Saddam Hussein were everywhere in Baghdad before the second Gulf War.
Photo by Melanie Stetson Freeman / © 1987 The Christian Science Monitor

Hussein succeeded his cousin General Ahmad Hasan al-Bakr as Iraqi president in 1979.

In 1945 Iraq joined the newly formed United Nations. It was a founding member of the Arab League in 1945. And Iraq was also part of the 1955 Baghdad Pact, an alliance with Turkey, Iran, Pakistan, and Britain, with headquarters in Baghdad. (The alliance, also known as the Central Treaty Organization, disbanded in 1979.)

But starting in 1958, Iraq experienced a series of coups. This would lead to the Baath Revolution. A coup, or more fully a coup d'état, is *a sudden takeover of a government*, often by force and often by insiders or people already close to the center of power, such as the armed forces. In the first coup, King Faisal II and his prime minister were killed. The new leaders pulled Iraq out of the Baghdad Pact the next year.

A final coup on 17 July 1968 brought General Ahmad Hasan al-Bakr to power as president of Iraq and chairman of the Revolutionary Command Council (RCC). He named his cousin Saddam Hussein as vice president. Hussein wielded great power behind the scenes. When Bakr, by then 65 and in poor health, resigned in July 1979, Hussein succeeded him as both president and RCC chairman.

The Iran-Iraq War and Economic, Political, and Social Instability in Iraq

In 1980 Saddam Hussein's forces invaded Iran. This began a costly, inconclusive war that lasted eight years. Those who take the long view say that the Iran-Iraq war was just another phase of the ancient conflict between the Persians and the Arabs. (Most Iranians are Persian; most Iraqis are Arab.) Twentieth-century border disputes played a role, too—Iraqis worried that they didn't have enough access to the Persian Gulf. Port access is critical for shipping and receiving goods and, in short, strengthening a country's economy. Another factor was Hussein's concern that the new Shiite Islamic government in Iran would unsettle the Shia-Sunni balance in Iraq.

The Baath Party and Pan-Arabism

The Baath Party in Iraq, like its counterparts in other Arab countries, grew from a founding congress, or convention, in Damascus in 1947. The Baathists wanted to socialize the economy as well as achieve pan-Arab unity. But in Iraq, as elsewhere in the Arab world, the goal of Arab unity faded as political leaders focused on domestic problems instead.

The idea behind the Baath Party was that the separate countries carved out of the old Ottoman Empire were really parts of a whole. The Baath goal was to set up a "unified democratic socialist Arab nation." The party wanted a sort of "United Arab States," in other words. In fact, under Gamal Abdul Nasser, Egypt joined with Syria to form a union known as the United Arab Republic. Iraq considered joining as well. The idea didn't work out too well, though. One big problem was that Egypt and Syria had no common border. But the dream of pan-Arabism—*a movement for greater cooperation among Arab states*—remains important in understanding the Middle East.

The Baathists recruited urban Sunni Arabs almost exclusively. As you read in Lesson 1, Sunni is the larger of the two main branches of Islam. But Iraq has more Shiites than Sunnis. So the Baath movement recruited those who were a majority within Islam but a religious minority within Iraq. The Baath Party was a cornerstone of Saddam Hussein's power in Iraq.

When the war ended in 1988, Iraq claimed victory but didn't really get much from it. It was a return to the status quo antebellum—*the state of things before the war.* Iraq found itself with the largest military establishment in the region but huge debts as well.

The Genocide Against the Kurds and Tensions Between the Ethnic Groups Within Iraq

The Kurds, as you have read, are a distinct cultural group whose homeland stretches across several countries in the Middle East, including Iraq. After World War I, when many new countries formed, Kurds hoped for a state of their own. But they never got one.

During the Iran-Iraq War, Kurdish separatists in Iraq sided with Iran. As a result, the Hussein regime went after the Kurds with a vengeance in operations known as the *Anfal* campaign. The Iraqis attacked the Kurds with poison gas, killing as many as 180,000 of them, including women and children. Hussein put one of his closest aides—his cousin Ali Hassan al-Majid, known as "Chemical Ali"—in charge of the operation. Years later, Chemical Ali would be hanged for the crime.

Kurds in modern-day Sulaymaniya, Iraq, stroll along a street dotted with billboards and the portrait of Kurdish leader Massoud Barzani.

Photo by Howard LaFranchi / © 2003 The Christian Science Monitor

When Kurdish separatists sided with Iran during the Iran-Iraq War in the 1980s, the Hussein regime attacked the Kurds with poison gas, killing as many as 180,000 of them, including women and children.

Another major source of friction in Iraq at this time was that Sunni Muslims controlled the government, even though the country had a large Shiite majority. Yet another issue was tensions between Arabs and non-Arabs. During the 1970s, the Baath Party nationalized the country's oil industry. With oil prices rising, this led to a big boost in Iraqis' standard of living. But the Baath regime also undertook a policy of "Arabization" of its oil centers, such as the northern city of Kirkuk. Under this policy Kurds, Turkmens, and Christians who had lived there all along were expelled from the areas, and Arabs moved in.

The Historical Events Associated With the 1991 Persian Gulf War

The Persian Gulf War of 1991 shows how maps drawn in the early years of the twentieth century are revisited later on. In this case, the country at the center of the dispute was Kuwait.

The Iraqi Invasion of Kuwait

Kuwait's modern history goes back to the eighteenth century. That's when the Uteiba tribe founded the city of Kuwait. They were part of the Anaiza tribe and historians think they traveled north from Qatar. By the end of the nineteenth century, Kuwait felt threatened by the Ottoman Turks as well as powerful groups from the Arabian Peninsula. So Kuwait sought British protection, as other small states in the region had done.

In January 1899 Sheikh Mubarak al-Sabah signed an agreement with the British government. The Kuwaiti leader pledged that he and successors would never give up territory nor receive any agents or representative of a foreign power without British consent. In exchange, the British provided protection and financial support.

Sheikh Mubarak's descendants continue to rule Kuwait. During the twentieth century's early decades, two things occurred in Kuwait that you have read about in other parts of the Middle East: the discovery of oil and the redrawing of borders. The two were related.

In Sheikh Mubarak's day, Kuwait had about 35,000 people. They built ships out of wood brought in from India and they dived for pearls. But oil changed everything.

The 1922 Treaty of Uqair set the border between Kuwait and Saudi Arabia. It also established an area known as the Kuwait–Saudi Arabia Neutral Zone adjacent to Kuwait's southern border. Before then there had been no internationally accepted borders. But when oil was discovered in the 1930s, it suddenly became important to know just where Saudi Arabia left off and Kuwait began.

In 1961 Britain granted Kuwait independence. The new country enjoyed great prosperity under Amir Sabah al-Salim al-Sabah. Kuwait became a sophisticated modern state with a free-market economy. The Kuwaitis and the Saudis worked out some new borders and figured out how to share the oil wealth from their Neutral Zone, renamed the Divided Zone.

The Kuwait Towers, water towers designed by Swedes and built by Yugoslavs in 1975, are a major tourist attraction in Kuwait City.
Photo by Robert Harbison / © 1991 The Christian Science Monitor

After gaining its independence from Britain in 1961, Kuwait became a sophisticated modern state with a free-market economy.

But along Kuwait's northern border, things were less friendly. That border dated from an agreement made in 1913 with Turkey—with the Ottomans, in other words, in the last days of their empire. When Iraq became an independent monarchy in 1932, it accepted this border. At that point, Kuwait was still under British protection, while Iraq was just getting its independence from Britain.

The discovery of oil in Kuwait later on in the 1930s, though, made it hard for Iraqis to let go of their claim on this potentially very rich "province." Iraq also wanted more than just its one port on the Persian Gulf, Basra.

When the British granted independence to Kuwait in 1961, Iraq claimed the new country as its own territory. After all, Baghdad argued, Kuwait had been under Iraqi authority when both countries were part of the Ottoman Empire. Not so, the Kuwaitis argued back. Yes, their country had been part of the empire, but never directly under Iraqi control.

British forces, as well as a force from the Arab League, showed up to protect Kuwait. Iraq eventually backed down in 1963, when a new government, more willing to get along with its neighbors, came to power in Baghdad. Iraq reaffirmed the boundary it had accepted twice before already. Iraq also dropped its objection to Kuwait joining both the United Nations and the Arab League.

Tensions over the issue remained, however, during the 1960s and 1970s. They eased during the 1980s when Iraq was preoccupied with its war with Iran. And Kuwait was a helpful ally to Baghdad, loaning money and allowing the use of its port facilities on the Persian Gulf. But after the war's end, the issue came back to a boil.

The wreckage of a communications tower destroyed during the 1991 Gulf War frames oil facilities in Kuwait's northern desert.
Photo by Melanie Stetson Freeman / © 1998 The Christian Science Monitor

On 2 August 1990 Iraq invaded Kuwait for its oil fields.

The reasons for this were complex:

- Iraq was having trouble repaying its debt to Kuwait
- It accused Kuwait of "slant drilling"—drilling for oil at an angle across the border into Iraq's own territory and taking oil that was rightfully Iraq's
- Iraq also accused Kuwait of manipulating the price of oil to limit Iraq's oil earnings
- Iraq wanted Kuwait's oil fields for itself.

On 2 August 1990 Iraq attacked and invaded Kuwait, claiming it as a nineteenth province. It took Saddam Hussein's 120,000 troops just two days to overrun Kuwait.

The United Nations and US Reaction to the Iraqi Invasion of Kuwait

Many world leaders condemned the move at once. British Prime Minister Margaret Thatcher called it "absolutely unacceptable." US President George H. W. Bush called the invasion "a naked act of aggression." The United Nations Security Council went into an emergency session. It called for the "immediate and unconditional" pullout of Iraqi forces. On 9 August the council voted 15-0 to declare Iraq's annexation of Kuwait "null and void." The Soviet Union, Iraq's main arms supplier, stopped shipments of all military aid.

No Arab state condemned the invasion, however. And at first, there was no suggestion of Western military action.

Operations Desert Shield and Desert Storm

Over the following months, the crisis grew more intense. Early on, Iraq marched 20,000 troops to the Kuwaiti-Saudi border. Some feared this was preparation for an Iraqi attack on Saudi oil fields through Kuwait. Officials in Washington worried that such an attack might distract Saudi Arabia and other countries from Kuwait's plight. If Saudi oil fields were left alone, the world might just accept the Iraqi takeover of Kuwait.

On the other hand, many people around the world doubted that President Bush would actually lead the United States to war to liberate Kuwait. But he insisted, "This will not stand." He continued to pursue diplomatic options. He hoped that Saddam Hussein could be persuaded to withdraw from Kuwait. He tried to find a way to let the Iraqi leader pull out and still save face. But Bush also continued to insist that his options were "wide open." And so he worked to line up an international coalition that would oust Iraq from Kuwait, by armed force if necessary.

The American perspective held to two important principles here. One was the US national interest in keeping the Gulf region's oil lanes open. President Carter stated in 1980 that this was an interest the United States would defend at all costs, including military force.

fastFACT

NATO is the North Atlantic Treaty Organization, created in 1949 by the United States, Canada, and their European allies. Current members include:

- Albania
- Belgium
- Britain (the United Kingdom)
- Bulgaria
- Canada
- Croatia
- the Czech Republic
- Denmark
- Estonia
- France
- Germany
- Greece
- Hungary
- Iceland
- Italy
- Latvia
- Lithuania
- Luxembourg
- the Netherlands
- Norway
- Poland
- Portugal
- Romania
- Slovakia
- Slovenia
- Spain
- Turkey
- the United States.

The other was political stability and the rule of law. States need to keep their promises, just as people do. Iraq had officially accepted its border with Kuwait. The world needed to hold Iraq to that commitment.

Arab engagement in the coalition against Iraq was crucial. As a practical matter, in case of war, the coalition would need to use bases in Saudi Arabia. And as a former diplomat, Bush knew that a war against Iraq would have more legitimacy if it had the support of its neighbors, and not just of the West.

Eventually he built a coalition of dozens of countries, including not only North Atlantic Treaty Organization (NATO) allies like Britain and Canada, but Muslim and Arab countries such as Egypt, Saudi Arabia, Syria, and Turkey. The coalition also included Poland and Czechoslovakia, longtime Soviet allies.

A service member aboard the USS *Saratoga* arms a missile before the outbreak of the 1991 Gulf War.

Photo by Peter Main / © 1991 The Christian Science Monitor

President George H. W. Bush worked to line up an international coalition that would oust Iraq from Kuwait.

The USS *Saratoga* readies to support land forces during the first Gulf War.
Photo by Peter Main / © 1991 The Christian Science Monitor

On 24 February 1991, after more than a month of air bombardment against Iraqi forces, the ground war began.

The Bush administration also sought to work through the United Nations. During this time, the UN Security Council passed a series of resolutions calling on Iraq to leave Kuwait. One of the most important, Resolution 678, gave Iraq until 15 January 1991 to withdraw. It also authorized use of "all necessary means" to enforce an earlier resolution. In other words, it authorized war.

More than half a million troops deployed to the region. The US part of this effort was known as Operation Desert Shield. On 17 January 1991 Baghdad time, after Saddam Hussein had made clear he would not withdraw, the coalition began bombing the Iraqis.

On 24 February, after more than a month of air bombardment, the ground war began. The coalition routed Iraqi forces in what has been called the "100-hour war." US General Norman Schwarzkopf launched an "end run" around Iraqi forces in Kuwait, cutting them off from Iraq. Coalition control of the air meant that Iraqi forces could not see where coalition troops were moving. After just 100 hours of ground fighting, President Bush declared Kuwait liberated.

The Repression of the Shia and Kurdish Uprisings in Iraq

The war to liberate Kuwait released tensions in Iraq. The very next month, the regime in Baghdad had two rebellions on its hands, by Kurds in the north and by Shia Muslims in the south.

During the war, President Bush had called repeatedly for the Iraqi people to overthrow their government. Within days of the cease-fire, Shia Muslims in the south of Iraq took up arms against Saddam. For a few days, they controlled the streets.

But the Baghdad regime quickly moved against them. Postwar peace negotiations had allowed the Hussein regime to keep its helicopters. The Iraqis said they needed them because coalition bombing had destroyed so many of their roads. But the regime soon turned those aircraft on the Shiite rebels, killing tens of thousands, by some estimates. US troops were within sight of the fighting but Washington decided not to intervene.

A British Royal Marines Military Policeman conducts a security search in March 2003 near Basra in southern Iraq.
Photo by Andy Nelson / © 2003 The Christian Science Monitor

Coalition forces encountered little trouble in the south, home to Shia Muslims. Shortly after the 1991 Gulf War, Saddam Hussein's Sunni regime turned its aircraft on Shiite rebels, killing tens of thousands by some estimates.

Then in the north of Iraq, a Kurdish rebellion broke out. Unlike the Shiites, who rose up more or less spontaneously, the Kurds had an organized political leadership. Kurdish exiles returned from abroad, hoping for a coup that would topple Saddam Hussein and replace him with new leadership that would grant Kurds some autonomy.

Hussein's forces soon attacked the Kurds. Kurdish cities emptied out. A million refugees headed to the mountains in search of safety in Turkey or Iran. When Turkey refused to admit the refugees, hundreds of thousands were stranded in the mountains without food, water, or medical supplies. Hundreds began dying each week.

Although the United States was reluctant to support an independent Kurdistan, UN Security Council Resolution 688 established a "safe haven" for Kurds in the northern part of Iraq. At this point, President Bush ordered US forces to provide relief and protection. Together with other coalition forces, they provided humanitarian supplies and established a demilitarized zone to protect the Kurds. It included much though not all of the traditional Kurdish areas. US and British airpower protected the area in an action known as Operation Provide Comfort.

In 1970 the Baath government had set up an autonomous region for the Kurds, but its governing council was under the control of the Baghdad regime. This time, the safe haven gave the Kurds some real independence. Iraqi forces pulled out of the region in October 1991. Liberty came at a price, though, because Baghdad then imposed an embargo on the Kurds. This was a double blow for the Kurds, since they also came under sanctions aimed at Iraq as a whole. By 1996 the situation improved as the autonomous Kurds were receiving a share of Iraq's oil wealth, and that gave them a measure of prosperity.

Events Surrounding the 2003 US Invasion of Iraq

The coalition won Kuwait's freedom back with far fewer casualties, among its own forces at least, than expected. Hussein's forces largely just crumpled under the coalition's assault.

But for all its condemnation of Hussein, the administration in Washington stopped short of actually overthrowing him. The president wanted to stay within the limits of the UN mandate, for one thing. And continued war would surely cost more American lives. The administration didn't think the public would accept this. Besides, Washington hesitated to see Iraq break up altogether. Supporting Kurdish rebels, in particular, could make that happen. After all, the United States had just gone to war—its biggest deployment since Vietnam—in part over the principle that the lines on the map should stay where they are. Many people, however, saw Saddam Hussein's remaining in power as an item of unfinished business on the American foreign policy agenda.

The Cease-Fire Violations and No-Fly Zones

United Nations Security Council Resolution 687 set out the terms of the cease-fire after the war. Iraq had to destroy its nuclear, biological, and chemical weapons. It also had to get rid of its ballistic missiles with a range greater than 150 km (93 miles). The resolution required Iraq to honor its foreign debts and pay damages to Kuwait.

But almost from the start, the United States and its allies doubted whether the Iraqis would keep their word. Iraq's nuclear activities were a particular concern. Just a few months after the war's end, the US ambassador to the United Nations told Congress how Baghdad was falling short: The regime had a secret uranium enrichment program. It was blocking UN weapons inspectors. Many of its missiles were unaccounted for. The list went on.

Another development at this time was the establishment of no-fly zones in both southern and northern Iraq. The United States, Britain, and France drew lines north and south of which Iraqi military aircraft were simply not allowed to fly. Coalition aircraft enforced these boundaries. The coalition also set up a "no drive" zone in southern Iraq to keep Hussein from massing forces to invade Kuwait again.

In addition to its attacks on Kurds and Shiites, the Baghdad regime went after the "marsh Arabs" living in southern Iraq by draining the wetlands in which they lived. It was not only a human rights offense, in that it deprived this people of their homeland and way of life, but it was an environmental policy disaster as well.

Saddam Hussein's Quest for Weapons of Mass Destruction (WMD)

Even more troublesome than Hussein's treatment of the Kurds, Shiites, and "marsh Arabs" was his potential to harm the wider world. What most worried the United States and its allies about Saddam Hussein was his possible continuing development of weapons of mass destruction (WMD). WMDs are *chemical, biological, or nuclear weapons that can kill large numbers of people in one use*. If there were a case to make for invading Iraq again to oust Hussein, it was over WMD.

Hussein's regime had used poison gas on numerous occasions in the past. He had long been suspected of developing nuclear weapons. In 1981 Israeli F-15s and F-16s bombed a nuclear plant under construction at Osirak outside Baghdad. The Israeli government said the plant was meant to make nuclear weapons to destroy Israel. Iraq denied this.

fastFACT

"Weapons of mass destruction" (WMDs) refers to weapons that produce devastating results in one strike. A nuclear bomb would be an example of WMD. So would the chemical weapons (poison gases) Saddam Hussein used against the Kurds. Biological weapons—germ warfare on a large scale, for instance—are the third major kind of WMD. These three categories are sometimes referred to as a group—"NBC" (nuclear, biological, and chemical).

Boys play soccer in the streets of Sadr City, a Shiite slum in Baghdad.

Photo by Howard LaFranchi / © 2008 The Christian Science Monitor

In the years before the 2003 US-led invasion of Iraq, the Baghdad regime not only oppressed Shiites and Kurds—many in the international community worried that Saddam Hussein was continuing to develop weapons of mass destruction.

Hussein also had a strong interest in biological weapons. Richard Butler, the Australian who chaired the United Nations commission set up to find and dismantle Iraq's WMD after the 1991 war, said Hussein was "addicted" to WMD. He cared most about biological weapons, particularly anthrax, Butler said in a 2001 interview. "I had in my own hand pieces of a destroyed missile warhead that we swabbed and it had anthrax residue in it. It was a serious program."

But what wasn't clear was the state of those programs. Were they still active? Spy agencies in the United States, Britain, and elsewhere produced intelligence that appeared to indicate they were. UN weapons inspectors found no "smoking gun," or inescapable evidence of WMD programs. But they didn't exactly rule them out either.

As President George W. Bush's National Security Adviser Condoleezza Rice said, "There will always be some uncertainty about how quickly [Hussein] can acquire nuclear weapons. But we don't want the smoking gun to be a mushroom cloud."

The Coalition Forces' Invasion of Iraq

In 1998 the US Congress passed the Iraq Liberation Act. The law said, "It should be the policy of the United States to support efforts to remove the regime headed by Saddam Hussein from power in Iraq."

In October 2002 Congress passed the Iraq War Resolution. This authorized the president to commit US forces to protect the United States from the threat posed by Iraq. It also called on him to enforce the relevant UN Security Council resolutions regarding Iraq.

The next month, the council found Iraq to be "in material breach" of those resolutions. The UN gave Iraq until 8 December 2002 to comply. It also demanded that Iraq give a full accounting of its weapons programs and cooperate with UN weapons inspectors.

On 17 March 2003 President George W. Bush gave Saddam Hussein and his sons 48 hours to leave Iraq or face "military conflict commenced at a time of our choosing." On 19 March the US armed forces began their assault. They were backed up by Britain, plus contingents from Australia, Spain, Poland, and Denmark.

US Marines relax on the front porch of one of Saddam Hussein's palaces in Baghdad in April 2003.

Photo by Andy Nelson / © 2003 The Christian Science Monitor

Only a month before, President George W. Bush had given Hussein and his sons 48 hours to leave Iraq or face military conflict. The photographer who took these and the following Iraq photos was embedded with a Marine unit as it entered Baghdad.

Iraqis greet US Marine assault amphibious vehicles in southeastern Baghdad on 8 April 2003.
Photo by Andy Nelson / © 2003 The Christian Science Monitor

The toppling of the Baghdad regime ended a dozen years of Iraqi defiance of the United Nations, but led to years of insurgency.

Baghdad fell in April. Saddam Hussein went into hiding and would not be captured until December 2003. But despite searching everywhere, coalition forces found no WMD in Iraq. The intelligence reports were from dubious sources, doctored, or just plain wrong. The failure to find these weapons set off an intense political debate in the United States and Europe. However, on 2 May 2003, President Bush announced in a nationally televised address that "major combat operations in Iraq have ended."

US Attempts to Stabilize Iraq Since the 2003 Invasion

It turned out to be not quite that easy. The military victory came swiftly. The toppling of the Baghdad regime ended a dozen years of Iraqi defiance of the United Nations. But it was soon clear that winning the war would prove much easier than winning the peace.

The Coalition Provisional Authority provided a transitional government for Iraq until 28 June 2004. At that point it disbanded in favor of the Iraqi Interim Government. That government ruled until elections took place 30 January 2005.

The Activities of Insurgents and al-Qaeda After the War

When President Bush spoke on 2 May 2003, he stood before a banner reading "Mission Accomplished." He would later call this one of his mistakes in office. Major combat was over. But the insurgency was just beginning. In May 2003 the United Nations lifted sanctions against Iraq and backed the US-led administration there. The United States abolished the Baath Party and its institutions. By July the commander of US forces acknowledged that his troops faced low-level guerrilla warfare.

A US Marine signals an Iraqi girl to come out of the street while he directs traffic in the heart of Baghdad in April 2003.
Photo by Andy Nelson / © 2003 The Christian Science Monitor

By July, the commander of the US forces acknowledged that his troops faced low-level guerrilla warfare, including attacks using car bombs and roadside bombs.

Car bombs and roadside bombs—known in military jargon as improvised explosive devices (IEDs)—were frequent. So were suicide bombings, sometimes carried out by women. Casualties from such attacks often numbered in the dozens and sometimes exceeded 100.

One of the controversies over the war's launch was whether Saddam Hussein had supported al-Qaeda, the group behind the terrorist attacks of 11 September 2001. Although he hadn't, polls showed that many Americans believed he had.

By 2004 Americans were hearing about a mysterious but deadly new group known as "al-Qaeda in Iraq." Its origins were unclear. Foreigners led it, but its members were mostly Sunni Iraqis who felt they were losing the privileged position they held under Hussein. Many bombings and other attacks were blamed on the group.

A key strike during this period was the bombing of the historic Shiite Golden Mosque in Samarra on 22 February 2006 by insurgents. This triggered a wave of unprecedented violence in Iraq between Shiites and Sunnis.

The "Surge" and Current Iraqi Politics

From the beginning of the Iraq war, people disagreed over how many US troops would be needed to fight it. Defense Secretary Donald Rumsfeld believed in smaller, lighter, more "nimble" forces. He thought only 135,000 troops were necessary. Others, such as General Eric Shinseki, the Army chief of staff, called for a larger American force. Rumsfeld prevailed, though. US forces went into Iraq in the smaller numbers he advocated.

In late 2006 Rumsfeld resigned amid escalating violence in Iraq. Robert Gates, a former director of the Central Intelligence Agency, took his place, and in early 2007 the United States implemented a new approach in Iraq referred to as a troop "surge." This meant sending in 30,000 more troops for a time to help stabilize Iraq.

The new plan also called for troops to be out among the people, and not barricaded in their bases. It also called for working with Sunni tribal leaders and militias to isolate al Qaeda in Iraq. The terrorist group's violence and extreme religious views had lost it support among these groups.

By September 2007 General David Petraeus, the top American commander in Iraq, told Congress that the surge was working. Sectarian violence was still at "troubling levels," he said, and that achieving US goals would be neither quick nor easy. But violence was coming down, and Iraqi forces were able to assume responsibility for their own security. The number of American casualties fell dramatically.

By 2008 the first US troop drawdowns had begun. By the time the fall election campaign was in high gear in the United States, the war in Iraq had faded as an issue for American voters.

The Golden Mosque in Samarra, Iraq, before it was bombed.
© age fotostock

US Marines have their photo taken with members of the Baghdad Police Department in April 2003.
Photo by Andy Nelson / © 2003 The Christian Science Monitor

As the US approach to Iraq has evolved after 2003, the military plan called for troops to be out among the people, and not barricaded in their bases.

On 31 January 2009 Iraqis went to the polls for provincial elections. One of the most noticeable results was how smoothly the voting went. There was relatively little violence, and a high level of participation by Sunnis, who had boycotted the last provincial elections in 2005. Prime Minister Nouri al-Maliki's party came out ahead. This seemed to signal voters' approval of the reduced violence and his party's secular, rather than religious, approach to governing.

While the situation in Iraq continued to improve, and new US President Barack Obama hoped to withdraw American forces as soon as practical, it appeared likely that challenges would continue in Iraq for some time to come.

Lesson 3 Review

Using complete sentences, answer the following questions on a sheet of paper.

1. What were the Baath Party's goals?
2. Who was affected by the "Arabization" program in northern Iraq?
3. What was behind the Iraqi invasion of Kuwait? List two reasons.
4. How did Saddam Hussein respond to the Shia uprising?
5. What were no-fly zones?
6. What are WMDs?
7. What happened to the Golden Mosque in Samarra in February 2006?
8. What was the "surge" of early 2007?

Applying Your Learning

9. One of the threads through this lesson has been international boundaries and whether they should be redrawn or left as they are. Do you think it's sometimes a good idea to change the map? Why or why not?

LESSON 4 Islamic Fundamentalism and Terrorism

Quick Write

Do you think the airline acted properly in taking these families off the plane? Explain whether you think it's OK to suspect people based on their religion and ethnic origin.

Learn About

- the general impact of terrorism in the world
- how radical Islamist beliefs contribute to terrorism
- the events associated with the 9/11 attacks and the global war on terror

Two Muslim families of Middle Eastern origin were walking through a Washington, D.C., airport to board their plane. As they walked, they began discussing among themselves the safest place to sit on a plane.

Another passenger on the plane, who overheard the families talking, reported a "suspicious" conversation to a flight attendant. The pilot called in the authorities, who removed the families from the plane. The FBI interviewed the families. The agents determined the families posed no threat to the flight, and asked the airline to reboard them. The airline refused and the FBI was forced to help the families book tickets on another airline.

The next day, the first airline issued an apology to the families, refunded their money, and offered to fly them home free.

The General Impact of Terrorism in the World

- terrorism
- international terrorism
- terrorist group
- agenda
- figurehead
- proxy
- sharia
- Wahhabism
- caliphate
- insurgency
- transnational
- reactionary
- safe haven

If you travel by air, you've come face to face with terrorism's aftershocks. After check-in, you have to take off your shoes and empty your pockets. You must walk through metal detectors and send your luggage through X-ray machines.

You may have also noticed metal detectors at government buildings such as courthouses. Other large buildings, such as corporate offices, often have concrete barriers out front to protect against car bombs.

Transportation Security Administration employees screen passengers heading to their gates at Boston's Logan Airport.
Photo by Melanie Stetson Freeman / © 2006 The Christian Science Monitor

If you've traveled by air since 9/11, you've likely had to take off your shoes, empty your pockets, and walk through metal detectors before boarding your plane.

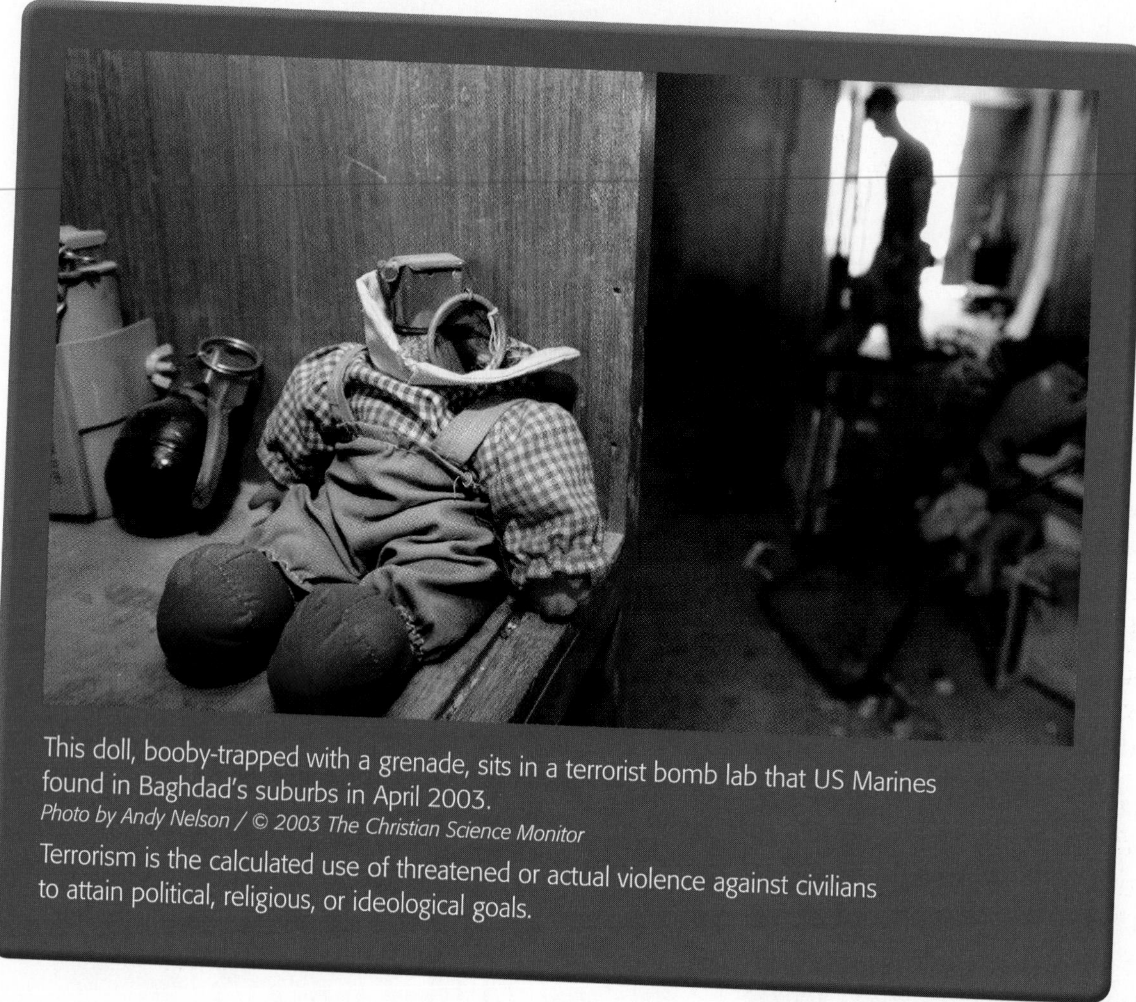

This doll, booby-trapped with a grenade, sits in a terrorist bomb lab that US Marines found in Baghdad's suburbs in April 2003.
Photo by Andy Nelson / © 2003 The Christian Science Monitor

Terrorism is the calculated use of threatened or actual violence against civilians to attain political, religious, or ideological goals.

Outside the United States and other countries like Canada and Britain, the threat of terrorism affects people's daily lives far more strongly. Many developing countries with lots of sunshine and beaches depend on foreign tourists for much of their national income. But those tourists will change their travel plans in a minute if they have to worry about a bomb at their hotel.

The terrorist threat often keeps foreign investors away from a country. And at its worst, terrorism can shut down a society. It can make it impossible for someone to go out and buy milk and diapers, for instance. And it can make it impossible to establish a government in which the people have confidence.

Defining Terrorism

US law defines terrorism as *premeditated, politically motivated violence against noncombatants by subnational groups or clandestine agents, generally to influence an audience.*

A more general definition of terrorism is the calculated use of threatened or actual violence against civilians to attain political, religious, or ideological goals. Terrorists do this through intimidation or fear.

For instance, terrorists trying to overthrow their national government might bomb a foreign-owned factory in their country. The victims of the attack would be largely ordinary local factory workers. The "audience" for the attack would be the factory's foreign owners, including stockholders. The terrorists' immediate goal would be to get the foreign company to leave the country. Their larger goal would be to drive out all foreign investment. That would cause people to lose their jobs, hurt the local economy, and put pressure on the government they want to overthrow.

International terrorism is *terrorism that involves the citizens or territory of more than one country*. The US government defines a terrorist group as *any group that practices terrorism or has a subgroup that does*.

Terrorist Groups and Their Activities Through the Ages

Terrorism is nothing new. During the Crusades in the thirteenth century, Hasan ibu-al-Sabbah, known as the "Old Man of the Mountains," led a fanatical Muslim sect. His followers were known in Arabic as *hashishiyyin*, or "hashish users." They would get high on the drug hashish and then murder their opponents. The English word *assassin* comes from these early "terrorists."

Later on, the French Revolution went through a phase (1793–1794) known as "the Reign of Terror." The new government that had overthrown King Louis XVI turned on the French people. It killed thousands of innocent men and women. The violence appalled outside observers, notably in Britain and the United States. It gave some folks second thoughts about whether rule by the people was such a good idea after all.

But the French terror had a national government behind it. More recently, terrorist groups have generally been people outside the national government trying to overthrow it. They tend to have a specific agenda, *a set of goals to achieve*. Sometimes they are willing to give up violence in favor of politics if they get an opportunity to do so.

During the twentieth century's final decades, a number of guerrilla groups gave up terrorism for politics. They traded bullets for ballots, as the saying goes, in Zimbabwe, South Africa, and Northern Ireland. Hamas in Palestine and Hezbullah in Lebanon, on the other hand, continue to fire rockets at Israel and spread other havoc in the Middle East despite their governmental roles.

During this same period, however, another more sinister terrorist movement was developing. This one was international, more loosely organized, and less clear in its goals. And it was aimed at the United States and its friends around the world. It calls itself *al-Qaeda* (in English, the Base).

Current Terrorist Threats

Al-Qaeda and allied groups have been the greatest terror threat to the United States and its partners since the 1993 World Trade Center bombing. Its story begins with the Soviet invasion of Afghanistan in 1979. The Soviets were trying to prop up a Communist government.

Young Muslim men from around the world flocked to Afghanistan to help fight the Soviets. Many of these men came from the Middle East. Among them was Osama bin Laden, the son of a wealthy Saudi family. Bin Laden, who had access to family money, helped fund the anti-Soviet resistance. He set up a worldwide network to support the effort. When the war ended in 1989 and the Soviets withdrew, this network became al-Qaeda.

Bin Laden returned to Saudi Arabia, but left for Sudan in 1991. In 1992 he first declared war on the United States. He returned to Afghanistan in 1996, protected by the fundamentalist Taliban regime that had taken power there. When the United States and its Afghan allies defeated the Taliban in 2001, Bin Laden and others fled into the mountainous border area between Afghanistan and Pakistan.

The Pakistani government doesn't really control all of its territory, and al-Qaeda has taken advantage of this. It uses Pakistan's "tribal areas" in the northwestern region of the country to build bases and training camps. Osama bin Laden remains the al-Qaeda figurehead. That is, he's *the one supposedly in charge*. But Egyptian Ayman al-Zawahiri has emerged as the group's intellectual leader.

In Afghanistan itself, remnants of the Taliban remain al-Qaeda allies, and they remain a threat. They, too, exploit the Pakistani government's weakness in the border regions. They murder local Afghan officials as well as attack government outposts and NATO forces helping the government.

fastFACT

The Maghreb is a region of northwest Africa made up of the coastlands and the Atlas Mountains of Morocco, Algeria, and Tunisia.

One troubling trend is that regional terrorist groups are developing ties to al-Qaeda. In 2007, for instance, an Algerian group mostly focused on issues in its own country merged with al-Qaeda. It has taken the new name *al-Qaeda in the Islamic Maghreb*, or AQIM.

Elsewhere, Iran remains a threat as a state sponsor of terrorism because of its support for Hezbullah in Lebanon. The US government considers the Shiite Hezbullah a foreign terrorist organization. The United States also regards Hezbullah as a proxy—a *stand-in*—for Iran. In other words, Hezbullah does some of the work Iran doesn't want to be seen doing. This includes destabilizing the governments of Lebanon and Iraq.

Syria is another bad actor in the region. It freely allows troublemakers to pass through its borders to and from Iraq.

Men attend a rally in Peshawar, Pakistan, in October 2001 denouncing US plans to attack Afghanistan for harboring Osama bin Laden. *Photo by Robert Harbison / © 2001 The Christian Science Monitor*

When the United States and its Afghan allies defeated the Taliban later that year, Bin Laden fled into the mountainous border area between Afghanistan and Pakistan.

How Radical Islamist Beliefs Contribute to Terrorism

You read in Lesson 1 about the core beliefs of Islam. Now you will read about some interpretations of Islam adopted by sworn enemies of the United States. They are relevant because they form the basis of those enemies' agenda and actions. But the United States has no quarrel with the Muslim faith. About 2 million to 3 million Americans practice it. And many Muslims who have immigrated to the United States freely practice their religion here. What's more, the United States has many friends among Muslim countries.

Islamic Fundamentalism and Its Impact on the Middle East

In the early twentieth century, Middle Eastern peoples shared their grievances against the ruling colonial powers through Muslim religious leaders. But the new independent states that emerged as Europe released or lost its colonies had mostly secular—nonreligious—leadership. Western-educated lawyers, politicians, and soldiers were in charge. Many people turned their backs on religion and traditional culture in favor of modernization.

What eventually came, however, were ruling families and nationalist revolutionaries unwilling to suffer any opposition to their hold on power. By the late 1970s no one could challenge the government in many Middle Eastern countries.

Consequently, grievances built up again. Many Muslim peoples of the Middle East became a ready audience for calls to reject modernization, purify their society, and adhere strictly to sharia—*Islamic religious law*. Islamic fundamentalists offered these ideas as the answer to serious problems many Muslim societies faced.

Iranian women, dressed in full-length clothing and head coverings according to Iran's interpretation of Islamic law, walk in front of a towering mural of religious leader Ayatollah Khomeini in Tehran, Iran.
Photo by Robert Harbison / © 1997 The Christian Science Monitor

In 1979 Khomeini's followers overthrew Iran's corrupt monarch, Shah Reza Pahlavi, and created the Islamic Republic of Iran.

Saudi Wahhabism

In 1979 Iran gave the Muslim world another model of political Islam: revolution. That February, the religious leader Ayatollah Ruhollah Khomeini's followers overthrew the corrupt monarch Shah Reza Pahlavi and created the Islamic Republic of Iran.

The Iranians were Shiites. But their success at installing a religious, clergy-run state became a model for Sunni Muslim fundamentalists to follow.

Like Iran, Saudi Arabia is awash in oil wealth. Saudi Arabia is also home to Islam's holiest sites—Mecca and Medina—a fact that places heavy additional responsibilities on Saudi Arabia's ruling royal family.

Many in the Saudi royal family live a lifestyle that's not always in keeping with Islamic religious beliefs. To stay in power, the family supports a fundamentalist sect of Islam called Wahhabism. Wahhabism is *an austere form of Sunni Islam, a so-called reform movement that began 200 years ago to rid Islamic societies of practices and teaching acquired over the centuries*. Muhammad ibn Abd al Wahhab founded Wahhabism in the eighteenth century. Most Wahhabis live in Saudi Arabia, and almost all Mecca's and Medina's residents are Wahhabis.

As part of their campaign to promote Wahhabism, the Saudi royals raise funds through oil sales or from wealthy donors in the kingdom and other Persian Gulf states. They use them to build mosques and schools around the world, including in the United States, that spread Wahhabi ideas. Appeasing the Wahhabis in this manner helps the royals to cling to power.

A central idea of Wahhab's message was the essential oneness of God. His basic text was *Kitab at-tawhid*, or "The Book of Unity." He was troubled by the religious practices he saw around him, such as pilgrimages to shrines. He also believed many fellow Muslims worshipped the prophet Muhammad rather than God.

This led him to preach the simplicity of early Islam as he understood it, founded on the Koran and Sunna (i.e., Muhammad's manner of life). Many of the practices that Wahhab condemned were specifically Shiite. That gave, and still gives, his teachings a political edge within the Muslim world—especially in countries with large Shiite minorities.

The Beliefs of Osama bin Laden and al-Qaeda

Bin Laden, who orchestrated the 9/11 attacks on the United States, claims universal leadership within Islam. But he offers an extreme view of Islamic history. It's designed to appeal mainly to Arabs and Sunnis.

Bin Laden calls on his followers to embrace violence and martyrdom, that is, to sacrifice and suffer in order to further a cause. He tells his followers that the **caliphate**—*the Arab political unity of Islam's golden age, centered in Baghdad*—collapsed because its leaders strayed from true religion. He aims to replace Arab governments and re-create the caliphate.

Bin Laden also draws heavily on the Egyptian writer Sayyid Qutb. Based on Qutb's teachings, Bin Laden and his followers justify mass murder. They say it's acceptable to defend their embattled faith.

Bin Laden explains that al-Qaeda hates the United States because America has attacked or insulted Islam. For instance, many Muslims deeply resent the fact that the Saudi ruling family permits US military bases in Saudi Arabia. That's because it is the home of the prophet's birth and gravesites in Mecca and Medina. He blames America for all conflicts involving Muslims anywhere.

Unfortunately, many Muslims and Arabs have long been at odds with the United States over some of these conflicts. The Israel-Arab conflict is one example. And so Bin Laden's blasts against Americans strike a chord with millions. Bin Laden's agents have said that only by leaving the Middle East, converting to Islam, and ending what he calls its "immorality" and "godlessness" can America ever put an end to al-Qaeda attacks.

Sayyid Qutb (1906–1966)

Egyptian writer Sayyid Qutb's works have strongly influenced Osama bin Laden and his followers. Qutb combined Islamic scholarship with a loathing of the West. The Egyptian government sent him to study in the United States in the 1940s. He returned with the feeling that Western achievements had no real substance.

Three themes emerge from Qutb's writings:

- The world is beset with *jahiliyya*, a condition of barbarism, evil living, and unbelief in God. Everyone must choose between this state and Islam.
- More people are attracted to *jahiliyya* and material comfort than to Islam; this is true even of Muslims.
- There is no middle ground in the struggle between God and Satan. Therefore, all Muslims, as Qutb defines them, must take up the fight. Muslims who do not are no better than infidels (nonbelievers).

Qutb was a member of the Muslim Brotherhood organization. He was hanged on charges of trying to overthrow the Egyptian government, and thus became a martyr in the eyes of Bin Laden and others.

An Osama bin Laden poster shares space with a Nike logo on a truck in Rawalpindi, Pakistan. *Photo by Robert Harbison / © 2001 The Christian Science Monitor*

Bin Laden blames America for all conflicts involving Muslims anywhere. He aims to re-create Islam's golden age.

The Events Associated With the 9/11 Attacks and the Global War on Terror

Until the final years of the twentieth century, terrorism for most Americans was something that happened elsewhere. But many countries, including close US allies, faced terrorist campaigns of one kind or another. In Northern Ireland, the Irish Republican Army used terrorism to try to force the British out. Leftist terrorists fought against the state in Germany and Italy. Basque separatists used terrorism to fight for their own homeland in Spain. And Americans sometimes fell victim to terrorism when they traveled.

By the 1990s, however, the threat had come closer to home. In 1993 terrorists thought to be linked to al-Qaeda set off a truck bomb in the garage of New York's World Trade Center, trying to destroy it. Six people died and 100 were injured. Then in 1995 an American terrorist, Timothy McVeigh, bombed the federal building in Oklahoma City. The bombing killed 168 people and injured 800. (Two other men were also sentenced for their roles in planning the attack.)

In 1996 terrorists blew up the Khobar Towers in Dhahran, Saudi Arabia, which housed the US Air Force 4404th Wing (Provisional). At least 19 US service members were killed and as many as 500 wounded. Two years later, under Bin Laden's direct supervision, al-Qaeda terrorists bombed the US Embassy in Nairobi, Kenya, killing 12 Americans and 201 others, mostly Kenyans. Some 5,000 other people were wounded. On the same day, an al-Qaeda bomb killed 11 more people at the US Embassy in Dar es Salaam, Tanzania. Then in 2000 al-Qaeda struck again when terrorists in a small boat filled with explosives attacked the USS *Cole*, a Navy destroyer. The blast killed 17 members of the ship's crew and injured another 40.

How the 9/11 Attacks Were Carried Out

Tuesday, 11 September 2001, dawned a beautiful clear morning along the East Coast of the United States. But it would end a very dark day.

At three airports—Boston; Newark, New Jersey; and Dulles, outside Washington, D.C.—four teams of al-Qaeda hijackers boarded westbound flights. They would soon turn those aircraft into weapons. They would strike some of the most powerful structural symbols of American might: the World Trade Center's Twin Towers in New York, and the US Defense Department's headquarters at the Pentagon outside Washington.

For years some security experts had warned of such a possibility, especially after the 1993 attack. And during the summer of 2001 intelligence services worried that another attack was imminent.

The 9/11 operation had been years in the planning. Its estimated cost was $500,000. The 19 hijackers established residence in the United States, took flying lessons, and made other preparations.

Three days after the 9/11 attacks, a man holds an American flag aloft during a prayer vigil outside the damaged Pentagon building in Arlington, Virginia.
Photo by Andy Nelson / © 2001 The Christian Science Monitor

Four teams of al-Qaeda hijackers struck some of the most powerful structural symbols of American might on 11 September: the World Trade Center's Twin Towers in New York, and the US Defense Department's headquarters at the Pentagon.

The hijackers picked planes just starting westward on transcontinental flights—big aircraft with lots of fuel in them. The 19 men were armed with box-cutters—considered tools rather than weapons, and so not hard to get past airport security.

Soon after takeoff they overpowered the flight crews and took the planes' controls. They flew two of the aircraft into the Twin Towers. Both buildings collapsed. A third flight struck the Pentagon, causing significant damage. Investigators believe the hijackers planned to crash the fourth jet into another target in Washington—possibly the Capitol Building or the White House. But passengers on that flight, warned by phone of the other attacks, tried to wrest control of the plane from the hijackers, who crashed it into a Pennsylvania field.

Not since the Japanese attack on Pearl Harbor had Americans been hit on their own soil. About 3,000 people died in the attacks, most of them in New York. It wasn't an attack just on Americans, though. Ninety countries around the world lost sons and daughters as the Twin Towers came down.

In 1941 the US Congress answered the attack on Pearl Harbor with a declaration of war on Japan. Sixty years later, the country answered the 9/11 attacks with the global war on terror.

The US Invades Afghanistan

It didn't take long for the US government to determine that al-Qaeda was the power behind the spectacular 9/11 attacks. At that point, al-Qaeda's base was in Afghanistan.

The Bush administration in Washington quickly decided that the terror attacks had to be answered with force. But it wasn't as straightforward as declaring war on Japan after Pearl Harbor. Al-Qaeda wasn't a state. So there wasn't a real government on which to declare war, as Congress had done in 1941.

Yet the 9/11 attacks were seen as more than an act of terrorism; they were seen as an act of war. Many in and out of government believed the United States needed to respond with military force—a different response from those that followed previous terror attacks.

The Bush administration demanded that the Taliban surrender al-Qaeda's leader, Bin Laden. He was already wanted in connection with the 1998 bombings of two US embassies in Africa. But the Taliban failed to respond.

On 7 October 2001, less than a month after the attacks on New York and Washington, the United States and its allies invaded Afghanistan. The opposition Afghan Northern Alliance provided a majority of the troops. Britain, Canada, Australia, France, New Zealand, Italy, and Germany also supported the operation.

Fighting raged for several bloody weeks. But on 12 November Kabul, the Afghan capital, fell. By the end of November the Taliban forces had surrendered or fled into hiding.

Special Forces conduct a roadblock in Kunar, Afghanistan, to check for firearms.

Photo by Robert Harbison / © 2002 The Christian Science Monitor

Many in and out of government believed in the wake of 9/11 that the United States needed to respond to the attacks with military force—a different response from those that followed previous terror attacks.

Passengers wait to board a London Underground (subway) train.
Photo by Alfredo Sosa / © 2006 The Christian Science Monitor

While al-Qaeda has not attacked the United States on its own soil since 2001, it has targeted American allies in recent years. On 7 July 2005, 56 people died when four suicide bombers attacked London's transport system during the morning rush hour.

This wasn't the end of either the Taliban or al-Qaeda, however. The allies hadn't captured Osama bin Laden, who reportedly escaped to Pakistan. As this book was published, the hunt for Bin Laden and the fight with elements of the Taliban and al-Qaeda continued. And so did the Western effort to help the new leaders of Afghanistan create a stable government that does not foster terrorists.

Al-Qaeda Attacks Since 9/11

As of this writing, al-Qaeda had not attacked the United States on its own soil since 2001. Nor has there been any other attack anywhere on the scale of 9/11. But al-Qaeda and its allies around the world are known or believed to have attacked American allies and sites Westerners visit in several countries in recent years.

- On 12 October 2002 an attack on the Indonesian island of Bali killed 202, including 88 Australians, and hurt 300. Nearly three years later there was another attack in the same area. Three suicide bombers killed 26 people and injured more than 100. Al-Qaeda affiliates are thought to be behind both attacks.
- On 13 May 2003 in Saudi Arabia, four suicide bombs went off almost simultaneously. Three exploded at residential compounds housing Westerners and a fourth at the headquarters of the Saudi Maintenance Co., co-owned by American and Saudi partners. Fatalities numbered 34; an additional 60 were injured. On 8 November a car bomb detonated, killing 17 and injuring 120. US and Saudi officials said it resembled the May bombing and linked both to al-Qaeda.

- In November 2003 two separate incidents just a few days apart claimed 53 lives in Istanbul, Turkey. Another 750 people sustained injuries. It's not certain who was behind the attacks, but investigators strongly suspect al-Qaeda allies.
- On 11 March 2004, 10 bombs went off in four locations in Madrid's transport system. Fatalities totaled 191. More than 600 people were injured. An al-Qaeda branch claimed responsibility.
- On 7 July 2005, 56 people died when four suicide bombers attacked London's transport system during the morning rush hour. Another 700 were hurt. A group calling itself "the Secret Organization of al-Qaeda in Europe" was among several organizations claiming responsibility for the attack.

US Activities in the Global War on Terror

Some experts describe the al-Qaeda network as a "globalized insurgency." An **insurgency** is *an organized rebellion trying to overthrow a government*. A globalized insurgency would seek to overthrow the whole world order—not just individual countries but international institutions as well.

Al-Qaeda seeks weapons of mass destruction—nuclear, chemical, and biological weapons that can kill thousands of people at once. It also seeks to replace the current international system with a transnational entity. An entity that's **transnational** is one that is *active across international borders*.

A US Border Patrol agent in Douglas, Arizona, interviews a man who illegally crossed the US–Mexico border.
Photo by Melanie Stetson Freeman / © 2000 The Christian Science Monitor

In the post–9/11 world, the Border Patrol must watch carefully, not only for illegal immigrants, but also for al-Qaeda and other terrorists trying to sneak across US borders. Al-Qaeda seeks to use weapons of mass destruction—nuclear, chemical, and biological weapons that can kill thousands of people at once.

A small floral memorial is tacked to a post overlooking the pit at Ground Zero in New York City during clean-up operations six months after the attack on the World Trade Center.

Photo by Andy Nelson / © 2002 The Christian Science Monitor

Experts say that the threat al-Qaeda poses will last a long time: not years, but decades.

Al-Qaeda is reactionary—*opposed to progress*. It wants to force its brand of Islam—a brand most Muslims reject—on the world. It wants to outlaw many books, movies, and television programs and implement its interpretation of Islamic law (sharia) as criminal law. It would take from women the rights they enjoy in Western and many other countries—such as the right to vote, to own property, to have a job, or to drive a car. Experts say that the threat al-Qaeda poses will last a long time: not years, but decades. It will demand that the United States and its allies respond with a global strategy.

As noted earlier, al-Qaeda has extended its reach by seeking local allies in different parts of the world. These alliances include local issues into the terrorists' worldwide, anti-Western agenda. Al-Qaeda connections also give local actions more impact.

Therefore, the United States and its allies try to break links among terror groups. This divides and isolates them, and so reduces their threat. It gets them down to a size where local governments can deal with them. The Western countries also try to intercept terrorists' money moving through different nations' banks, thus preventing one group from financing another.

A Threefold Threat

The US government describes the enemy in the war on terror as a "threefold threat complex." It attacks the enemy at all three of these levels—*leaders*, *safe havens*, and *underlying conditions*.

Leaders

So-called *global actors* are people who can mount attacks anywhere around the world. They give terrorists leadership, resources (including money and know-how), ideas, and guidance. And as noted previously, they can recruit local terror groups by making their issues part of a worldwide agenda.

Safe Havens

This sounds like a positive term. But actually it refers to lawless places where evildoers are free to hatch their schemes and plan their operations. When it comes to terrorism, a safe haven is *a space that provides a secure base for extremist action.* The concept is used at three different levels.

- *Physical Space*. In some countries, the government has broken down so completely that the country is referred to as a "failed state." This often happens because of civil war. The African nation of Somalia is a good example of this category. In other places, such as Afghanistan and Pakistan, the government functions but does not have complete control of all the territory within its borders. Often this is because of difficult terrain, with few roads, and strong traditions of tribal control. The central government's representatives can't or don't go there.

  Either kind of place is likely to become a place where terror groups gather. They can establish training camps, for instance, and no one will bother them. A failed or failing state can be a dangerous vacuum.

  You may have seen this principle at work in your own community. Neighbors on a street are always keen to see every house occupied, for instance. If a house is being sold, they at least want someone to mow the lawn and take other actions that show that someone is in charge. An abandoned home invites crime; a failed state invites terrorists.

- *Cyberspace*. Many terror groups use the Internet and e-mail to communicate among themselves, to recruit, to spread their message via "news and information" sites, and to raise money.

- *Ideological Space*. Freedom of thought, belief, and expression are fundamental to the US constitutional system. So it goes against the grain for Americans to identify some ideas as "bad."

  But some ideologies based on hatred and ignorance feed terrorism. Racism feeds terrorism, too. So do different kinds of identity politics—movements that encourage people to see themselves as oppressed racial or religious minorities, or encourage hatred or contempt for "infidels" of other faiths.

  In some places, the political culture itself is a problem. Freedom of speech and expression are underdeveloped, and people don't know how to disagree with each other without throwing bombs.

Underlying Conditions

Terrorists exploit all kinds of political and social problems. The failure to establish an independent state for the Palestinian people, for instance, has been an open wound for decades.

Mature democracies know how to resolve problems through political processes, however long it takes. Extremists, especially in places without much democratic tradition, are quick to seek other means. The issues they exploit, such as Palestinian statehood, are often just excuses. But resolving such longstanding issues is a way to fight terrorism. Some people say it is the most effective way.

The Coast Guard patrols Boston Harbor with a 25-foot Defender Class Homeland Security boat armed with an M60 machine gun.
Photo by John Nordell / © 2004 The Christian Science Monitor

The Department of Homeland Security, of which the Coast Guard is a part, has more than 200,000 employees.

fastFACT

The Global War on Terror has many fronts. On the home front, Congress passed a law in 2002 to create the Department of Homeland Security (DHS). It's part of the executive branch of the federal government. DHS includes many agencies charged with protecting the United States. The Transportation Security Administration is one of these. So are US Immigration and Customs Enforcement and the Coast Guard.

Unlike the Defense Department, DHS works in the civilian sphere. With 200,000 employees, it's one of the largest entities in the federal government. Only the Departments of Defense and Veterans Affairs have more employees.

Lesson 4 Review

Using complete sentences, answer the following questions on a sheet of paper.

1. What is terrorism?
2. What's an example of terrorism in earlier times?
3. What problem does Pakistan pose to US interests?
4. What is Wahhabism?
5. What are Osama bin Laden's aims?
6. What happened during the 9/11 attacks?
7. What are the elements of the "threefold threat complex"?
8. What are the three kinds of "spaces" where terrorists find safe havens?

Applying Your Learning

9. Which element of the "threefold threat complex" do you think needs the most attention? Why?

LESSON 5 US Interests and Regional Issues in the Middle East

Quick Write

How do you think the United States should treat Saudi Arabia? As a friend whose shortcomings are to be overlooked because of its oil? As an ally that needs to do better on human rights? Or as a country the United States does business with because it has to? Explain why you feel that way.

Learn About

- the importance of the production and distribution of oil and energy
- the clash between Middle Eastern and Western cultures
- the importance of nuclear nonproliferation and the Iranian issue for the United States
- the importance of the water problem in the Middle East

Imagine this scenario: You're an aide to a member of Congress. Your boss has been hearing a lot lately from a group of voters in the college town in his district. They want to see a change in US policy toward Saudi Arabia. Before he responds to them, he asks you to research the issue and write him a memo with some advice.

Here's what you find out:

Saudi Arabia is a human rights disaster. Whatever individual liberties there are apply only to Sunni Muslim males. The country has never signed onto the United Nations' basic document on human rights. The Saudis have something known as the Commission to Promote Virtue and Prevent Vice. It runs the religious police, or *mutawaa*. They exercise largely unchecked power to curtail rights. The Saudi courts do not offer due process protecting the individual. Nor do they offer effective remedies for violations of those rights. Saudi Arabia doesn't even allow women to drive cars. The US Commission on International Religious Freedom has recommended that the State Department label Saudi Arabia a "country of particular concern."

On the other hand, Saudi Arabia is the United States' second leading oil supplier, behind Canada. Within the oil exporters' group, the Saudis are a moderating influence. They often get lower oil prices for the United States. Saudi Arabia, at times, supports US foreign policy goals. During the Persian Gulf War of 1991, Saudi Arabia was a big help. It allowed the United States and its allies to use bases on Saudi soil as a staging ground. It did this despite criticism from other Muslim countries. Use of Saudi bases made it much easier to free Kuwait from the Iraqi invaders.

What do you recommend?

The Importance of the Production and Distribution of Oil and Energy

Vocabulary

- crude
- oil reserves
- cartel
- quotas
- burqa
- nuclear nonproliferation
- superpowers

At the beginning of the twentieth century, geologists made a discovery that would change the Middle East forever: oil.

It happened first in Iran. By 1911 the Anglo-Persian Oil Company, a British firm, was producing oil in Iran. British geologists found oil in Iraq in 1927. Standard Oil Company of California started exploring the region in the 1930s. In 1938 the company found crude—*another name for oil, especially in its raw or unprocessed state*—in Saudi Arabia. Saudi Arabia, Iraq, and Iran are among the world's leaders in known oil reserves, *the supply of crude oil that a country can retrieve*. Saudi Arabia is the world's leading oil exporter.

A tanker unloads oil at the Port of Los Angeles, the busiest port in the United States.
Photo by Robert Harbison / © 1999 The Christian Science Monitor

The United States imports well more than half the oil it uses.

The Carter Doctrine

"An attempt by any outside force to gain control of the Persian Gulf region will be regarded as an assault on the vital interests of the United States of America, and such an assault will be repelled by any means necessary, including military force."

—From the State of the Union Address, 1980

The oil fields took time to develop. But as the West rebounded after World War II, it thirsted for oil. Billions of dollars flowed into the Middle East and funded waves of economic development.

Political development, however, was another thing. The Middle Eastern states that emerged in the early twentieth century struggled with concepts of legitimacy and democracy. More often than not, oppressive rulers governed them.

Despite the Middle East's general lack of freedom, the United States' need for oil then and now colors its relations in this part of the world. In 1945, for example, President Franklin Roosevelt agreed to protect the Saudi royal family in return for access to their oil. This policy continues today.

Later presidents followed similar policies—even Jimmy Carter, known for his idealism and focus on human rights. In 1980 he called Persian Gulf oil a vital US interest to be defended "by any means necessary." This policy is known as the *Carter Doctrine*.

US Dependence on Foreign Oil Supplies

The United States imports well more than half of the oil it uses. This dependence on imports will only grow as domestic oil reserves run out. Most of the world's oil reserves are in the Middle East. OPEC—the Organization of Petroleum Exporting Countries, which you will read about later in this section—controls about two-thirds of the world's reserves.

fastFACT

The world's top five crude-oil–producing countries are:

- Saudi Arabia
- Russia
- the United States
- Iran
- China.

This group has pricing power in world energy markets. That is, it is able to manipulate prices by setting production levels. When OPEC produces more oil, the price falls. When OPEC tightens the spigot, less oil is available and the price goes up. These changes sometimes lead to "oil shocks." Such shocks in turn can trigger significant recessions.

The United States also gets its oil from sources closer to home. Canada is a reliable trade partner. Mexico also regularly ships supplies to the United States. The US relationship with Venezuela (an OPEC member) is troubled as of this writing, but nonetheless, the United States receives a steady flow of oil from that Latin American nation as well.

The Production and Shipping of Oil

Many of the places where oil is found are hot and dry. But oil deposits begin in watery places that scientists call marine environments. When plants and animals died millions of years ago, water and layers of mud oozed over their remains. Heat and pressure, acting over a very long time, melted all these ingredients together to make crude oil. *Petroleum* is yet another name for oil. It means "rock oil," or "oil from the earth."

Crude oil is a smelly liquid. Its color can range from yellow to black, and it's usually found in underground pools known as *reservoirs*. Sometimes people come across oil just bubbling out of the ground. But with so much oil already pumped out of the ground, the easy reserves have already been found. Today, scientists and engineers study rock samples and conduct tests before they start drilling. Once they hit "black gold," as it's often called, the drilled well will bring the oil to the surface in a steady flow.

*fast*FACT

The top five crude-oil–producing states in the United States are:

- Texas
- Alaska
- California
- Louisiana
- Oklahoma.

The amount of oil produced in the United States gets smaller each year. US domestic reserves are running out, yet the population and the economy continue to grow and more oil is needed. More people are driving cars and making more petroleum-based goods to sell.

The United States uses about 21 million barrels of petroleum products a day. Almost half of that is in the form of gasoline. More than 210 million motor vehicles in the country drive 7 billion miles a day. The rest of those 21 million barrels go to other kinds of fuels—jet fuel, diesel, heating oil—and to the manufacture of plastics.

Refining is the process that turns crude oil into a fuel that powers your car. While the United States imports a majority of its oil, it refines most of its fuel here at home. The gasoline travels from the refinery by pipeline to a storage depot near its final destination—Los Angeles, for instance. The gasoline is then loaded into trucks for delivery to individual stations.

OPEC and the Politics of Oil

In 1960 five countries with vast amounts of oil—Iran, Iraq, Kuwait, Saudi Arabia, and Venezuela—banded together to form OPEC. Their goal was to stand up to the Western firms that, at that point, controlled the world oil industry. Until then, production, distribution, and pricing were in the hands of a group of Western oil companies known as "the Seven Sisters." These were the companies that first explored the Middle Eastern oil fields.

In its first years, OPEC members moved to nationalize some of the Western oil companies operating on their territory. They struck deals that gave host countries more control over oil prices. OPEC functions as a cartel—*a group of independent entities that band together to control the price of a commodity.*

The original OPEC five expanded over time. (They also moved their headquarters from Geneva, Switzerland, to Vienna, Austria.) The organization now includes Qatar, Libya, the United Arab Emirates, Algeria, Nigeria, Ecuador, and Angola. Some countries have joined and then withdrawn. Indonesia, which signed up in 1962, suspended its membership in early 2009.

OPEC's big year was 1973. That was when its members finally wrested control of oil prices from the multinational companies. And as you read in Lesson 2, during the Yom Kippur War of October 1973, Arab oil producers within OPEC began an embargo against the United States to protest its support of Israel during the war. The Arabs extended the embargo to other supporters of Israel as well. At the same time, OPEC engineered an oil price hike that led to a quadrupling of oil prices.

Prices eventually eased somewhat. But then again in 1979, oil markets faced another major disruption. The Islamic Revolution in Iran interrupted oil production. With less oil coming onto the market, prices spiked.

When people speak of "the oil shocks" they generally are referring to the price hikes of 1973 and 1979. But from OPEC's perspective, the 1980s brought oil shocks of another kind—a collapse in prices.

What happened then was a classic example of a basic economic principle. If the price of something goes up, two things will happen: Some customers will leave the market, and more suppliers will enter it. Both will work to pull prices back down. The oil-price shocks of the 1970s led more people to buy smaller cars, to drive less, and to conserve energy generally. Ultimately, they bought less oil. And new suppliers entered the market. Britain and Norway worked to develop their offshore oil reserves in the North Sea, for example. That oil was more expensive to produce. But at the new higher prices, it was worth it. The result of all this: In 1986 oil plummeted from $27 to $9 a barrel.

Oil prices have risen and fallen in the years since. The classic law of supply and demand continues to work to keep the market more or less in balance. As a cartel, OPEC controls prices by assigning strict production quotas—*limits*—to its members. But it's not always easy for OPEC to enforce its policies and quotas. Its members are sovereign states, with different political concerns and different amounts of oil. Sometimes they cheat on their quotas. Saudi Arabia, generally a friend of the United States, has enough reserves to exercise a leadership role within OPEC.

Many Americans are uneasy about the nation's reliance on oil imported largely from such a troubled part of the world. They realize that a good part of the US defense budget goes to protect oil supplies. Especially during times of recession or conflict, many Americans call for energy independence. But for the foreseeable future, imported oil seems destined to play a major role in the US and global economy.

The Clash Between Middle Eastern and Western Cultures

In the Introduction, you read about culture as *including language, ideas, beliefs, customs, codes, institutions, tools, techniques, works of art, rituals, and ceremonies, among other elements*. In this section you will read about ideas and behavior that seem very different from what is familiar to you as an American. It's important to understand these differences, since they affect relationships between peoples and nations.

Some differences are rooted in religion; others in a country's customs and traditions. All shape a person's beliefs and attitudes and, consequently, the way that person behaves or acts. Just as people interpret Christianity in numerous ways—think of the range of Protestant churches in America—people interpret and practice Islam in a wide variety of ways—think of the Sunnis and Shias. These different beliefs also affect the way a government behaves.

Men pray at a mosque in Islamabad, Pakistan.

Photo by Robert Harbison / © 2001 The Christian Science Monitor

Some cultural differences are rooted in religion, others in a country's customs and traditions. All shape a person's beliefs and attitudes.

Western and Middle Eastern Views of Government

The United States firmly believes in the separation of church and state. In fact, this is law as spelled out in the First Amendment to the US Constitution. Government and religion don't mix. Government doesn't interfere in religious matters, and religious institutions don't run the government.

Many people in the Middle East hold different views on the relationship between religion and government. Muslims remember that Muhammad was both a spiritual and a political leader. He founded a religion. But he led armies, too. And his successor, the caliph, was also to be both a civil (political) and religious leader.

The Old City in Jerusalem, Israel, is home to the Dome of the Rock, one of Islam's most ancient shrines.
Photo by Robert Harbison / © 1991 The Christian Science Monitor

In response to a 2002 survey, majorities of Muslims in countries with large Islamic populations agreed that religion and government should be kept separate.

However, Muslims around the world live in countries with many different constitutional systems. Some are Islamic republics, where Islam is the official state religion. Some, such as Turkey, are secular states with strict separation of religion and state. Even some countries with Islam as the state religion, such as Algeria and Bangladesh, provide guarantees of freedom of religion and expression. Some of these guarantees "compare favorably" with international standards, says a study by a US government advisory commission.

Moreover, recent research shows many Muslims support separation of religion and state. In 2002 the Pew Research Center surveyed public opinion in 44 different countries. It found that in all the countries with large Muslim populations, majorities of Muslims agree with this statement: "Religion is a matter of personal faith and should be kept separate from government policy." This feeling was especially strong in Turkey and in several African countries. But many Muslims also back the idea of religious leaders playing a bigger role in politics.

The Dancer Who Ran Afoul of the Iranian Religious Police

Mohammed Khordadian's story shows the control the religious police exercise in Iran. In the early 1980s he left his native Iran for Los Angeles to teach and perform traditional Iranian dance. California has a large Iranian community familiar with this dance form. Khordadian had a lot of fans. Television stations run by Iranian exiles beamed some of his performances into Iran. And some of his videos made their way to Iran, too. He became well-known, and was quite popular with young people, especially young girls.

After many years, he heard that his mother had died, and he went back to Iran to visit his family for a few months. But when he was ready to return to California, he was arrested at the airport. The charge: enticing and inciting the nation's youth to corruption. After several months in jail in 2002, officials finally released him, but not before a Tehran court found him guilty as charged and told him he would not be allowed to leave the country for another 10 years.

Many Iranians enjoy dancing at private parties. But Iran's religious rulers frown on dancing, especially when men and woman dance together. In Iran it is against the law for an unwed couple to go out in public. The law is not always enforced, though. At the time of Khordadian's sentence, young Iranians noticed stepped-up street patrols by the religious police.

Iran's Persecution of the Baha'i Faith

In 2008 the Iranian government arrested seven members of the Baha'i faith in their country, including two women. It accused them of spying, and held them without counsel. The government didn't make public any of the evidence used against them. In February 2009 the US State Department protested this as "part of the ongoing persecution of Baha'i in Iran." It noted that 30 other Baha'is were also political prisoners.

Persecution of the Baha'i is not new. It goes back to the nineteenth century. That's well before the Islamic Republic began. But this treatment of a religious minority is notable because Baha'i developed within Iran. It is not a "foreign" religion. But Iran's Islamic leaders consider the Baha'i faith to be a heresy—a doctrine that departs from a religion's traditional teaching. They have even executed Baha'is in the past.

Freedom to practice their religion is also important to Muslims. Pew found large majorities calling it "very important" to them to live where they can practice their religion freely.

Human Rights in the West and Middle East

The Middle Eastern tendency to see the spiritual and political realms as one affects views of human rights, too. "When we want to find out what is right and what is wrong," one Iranian leader said, "we do not go to the United Nations; we go to the Holy Koran."

Meanwhile, the United Nations' Universal Declaration of Human Rights (UDHR) is a basic statement of international law. It doesn't mention religion, or describe human rights as "God-given." But its authors meant it to reflect the world's spiritual and religious traditions.

Most Middle Eastern nations have signed the Universal Declaration of Human Rights. But some of them have since changed their stance. The Pakistani Islamic scholar Abul Ala Mawdudi, for instance, saw a conflict between women's rights, as enshrined in the UDHR, and what he saw as the need to protect and preserve the chastity of women.

Concerns about such conflict have led some scholars to come up with Islamic statements of human rights. Others have tried to show that Islamic law is not at odds with international norms. In 1981 a group of eminent scholars produced the Universal Islamic Declaration of Human Rights. They based it on the Koran and the Sunna. Critics, however, say it falls short in many ways. For instance, it doesn't ban discrimination against women, religious minorities, and nonbelievers in God.

The Pew research, however, suggests that average Muslims are at least somewhat attuned to global norms: "Majorities of Muslims in every country surveyed also say it is at least somewhat important to them to live in a country that has freedom of speech, freedom of the press, an impartial judiciary and honest elections where voters have the choice of at least two political parties." Freedom to practice their religion does seem, though, to be the most important civil liberty for those Pew talked with.

The Role of Women in the West and Middle East

Moroccan scholar Muhammed Naceri said, "The Universal Declaration of Human Rights was for complete equality for man and women. For us, women are equal to men in law, but they are not the same as men, and they can't be allowed to wander around freely in the streets like some kind of animal."

Equality of the sexes in the West is certainly not an absolute. Nor has it been fully achieved. Many people feel traditional roles have changed too much, too fast. But equality of the sexes is one of the principles on which Western society is built. In the West, women are present in the workplace and elsewhere in public life. They are present in the news media, in political and religious life, in law enforcement, and in the military.

Women in the Middle East tend to have far fewer opportunities, although this is changing. Many countries require them to wear head scarves, veils, or even the **burqa**—*a full-body covering for women* that is hard to see out of or walk in comfortably.

But again, the Middle East is not all the same. Pew research suggests relatively high levels of support for providing freedom and opportunity for women. Asked whether women should have the right to decide whether to wear a veil, majorities of Muslims in every country surveyed said yes, except for Nigeria and Uganda. In Lebanon and Turkey, 3 Muslims out of 4 endorsed this view.

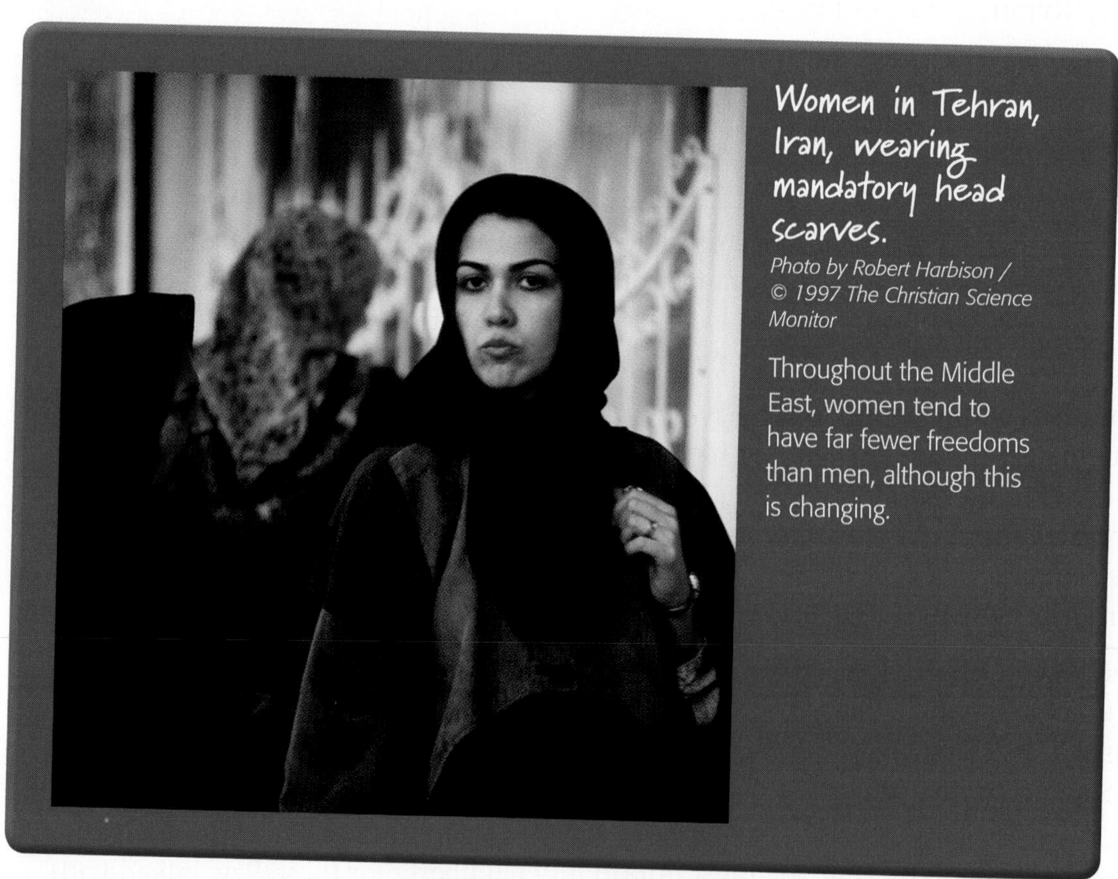

Women in Tehran, Iran, wearing mandatory head scarves.

Photo by Robert Harbison / © 1997 The Christian Science Monitor

Throughout the Middle East, women tend to have far fewer freedoms than men, although this is changing.

Majorities of Muslims in every country surveyed favored letting women work outside the home. This view was especially strong in Lebanon and Turkey. However, some Muslims in countries such as Jordan supported restrictions on men and women being together in the workplace.

Pew asked Muslims in all 44 countries it surveyed whether they preferred (a) a marriage where the husband provides for the family and the wife stays home, or (b) one where both partners have jobs and care for the home and family. In four countries, including Egypt and Jordan, at least half the Muslims surveyed preferred option (a). By contrast, the majority preference in Europe, Africa, and the Americas was option (b).

Women and children rest outside the Sultan Hassan Mosque—built in the fourteenth century as an Islamic school—in Cairo, Egypt.
Photo by Robert Harbison / © 1991 The Christian Science Monitor

According to one survey, Muslims in Egypt and other Middle Eastern countries prefer that husbands provide for the family and the wife stay at home rather than both partners work and care for the home and family together.

Study Shows Women's Rights Gain

A study released in February 2009 by Freedom House, a human rights group in Washington, found women's rights on the upswing in the Gulf states. The project director went so far as to call it a "seismic shift" over the previous five years. The study confirmed that women with paid jobs can make some positive changes in their lives. Even so, without certain civil liberties, including freedom of speech and assembly, women can progress only so far.

Beyond paid jobs, another key development for women in the Middle East took place in the courts in Oman, a small Arab country. In many Arab countries, a woman's testimony in court gets only half the weight of a man's. The new law in Oman makes a woman's testimony equal to a man's in most cases.

Even in a strict Islamic country like Saudi Arabia, women's rights are on the rise, Freedom House reported. Saudi women can now study law, obtain their own identity cards, and check into hotels alone. And they can register a business without having to hire a male manager first. "Their overall degree of freedom, however, remains among the most restricted in the world," the study says.

The Importance of Nuclear Nonproliferation and the Iranian Issue for the United States

In August 1945 the United States dropped two nuclear bombs on Japan, killing about 200,000 people. They were the first, and so far, only nuclear attacks in the history of warfare. Within days, Japan surrendered unconditionally to the United States. World War II, the deadliest conflict in human history, was over.

The nuclear age had just begun, however. These new weapons were like nothing anyone had ever seen before. Efforts to control their spread began within months. On 15 November 1945 the United States, Britain, and Canada proposed a UN Atomic Energy Commission for the purpose of "entirely eliminating the use of atomic energy for destructive purposes."

The following year the United States offered a plan to put all nuclear resources under international control. It didn't work, however. Within 20 years, the "club" of nations with nuclear weapons grew from one member (the United States) to five.

This spread of nuclear arms is known as *proliferation*. It has been an important US foreign policy concern since that first proposal in November 1945. It took many years, though, to find the right instrument to deal with this matter.

Nuclear Nonproliferation

Nuclear nonproliferation is *preventing the spread and increase of nuclear weapons.* As the nuclear "club" expanded, it became clear that materials for a nuclear bomb weren't all that scarce. And such bombs turned out to be relatively easy to make.

Besides, by the early 1960s, several countries were turning to nuclear energy to make electricity. By 1985, experts predicted, there would be more than 300 nuclear reactors in operation, under construction, or on order. These reactors would produce not only power, but plutonium as well, as a byproduct. Plutonium is a *fissionable* material—its atoms can be split. And it can be used to make nuclear weapons. There would be enough of it by 1985, experts said, to make 15 to 20 bombs a day.

It all added up to a grave new threat. Policymakers didn't have to worry just about enemy states (such as the Soviet Union) having bombs. They had to think about nuclear materials possibly being diverted (stolen) from power plants and made into bombs. And they had to worry about bombs falling into the hands of unstable countries that might be tempted to use them, rather than keep them as a deterrent—a way of discouraging an enemy attack by threatening to retaliate. Today, this danger is even greater as non-state actors such as terrorists try to lay their hands on nuclear weapons as well.

The Nuclear Club After World War II

These countries first followed the United States into the nuclear "club," with the dates of their first bomb tests:

1. The Soviet Union: 1949
2. Britain: 1952
3. France: 1960
4. China: 1964.

France generates energy at the Saint-Laurent Nuclear Power Plant on the banks of the Loire River.
Photo by R. Norman Matheny / © 1992 The Christian Science Monitor

As early as the 1960s several countries were turning to nuclear energy to make electricity. But policymakers have long worried that nuclear materials could be stolen from power plants and made into bombs.

The Nuclear Non-Proliferation Treaty

The Nuclear Non-Proliferation Treaty (NPT), created in the United Nations and signed on 1 July 1968, entered into force on 5 March 1970. This occurred during the period of history known as the Cold War (1948–89) when the United States and the Soviet Union faced off against one another. The United States and the Soviet Union were the world's two superpowers, *militarily superior countries*. Each superpower had a vast nuclear arsenal with missiles aimed at the other's cities. Each knew that a nuclear attack on the other would mean instant retaliation. The system was called *mutual assured destruction*, or "MAD." And in a crazy way, it worked. It was stable.

But from the beginning of the nuclear age, people felt that these new weapons needed to be controlled. It wasn't easy to develop a treaty that would do the job, but the superpowers both wanted one. So did non-nuclear powers, such as Africa's developing countries. They wanted access to this promising new technology for their energy needs.

The gist of the NPT is that it seeks to confine nuclear weapons to the countries that already had them when the treaty was negotiated. And it sought to reward countries that renounce nuclear arms by supporting their peaceful nuclear activities, such as producing electricity.

The NPT in a Nutshell

Here are the main aims of the Nuclear Non-Proliferation Treaty (NPT):

- To prevent the spread of nuclear weapons
- To keep states without nuclear weapons from making them with materials diverted from their nuclear power plants
- To promote the peaceful use of nuclear energy (to make electricity) as much as possible
- To support arms control and nuclear disarmament.

How the UN Enforces the Treaty

The NPT tasked the International Atomic Energy Agency (IAEA) with enforcing the treaty. The agency, part of the United Nations, does this by inspecting nuclear facilities. IAEA inspectors make sure that countries are using their reactors for peaceful purposes, such as generating electricity or conducting research in nuclear medicine.

A review conference held every five years also enforces the treaty. It ensures that the treaty is fulfilling its purposes. On 11 May 1995 representatives of more than 170 countries at the NPT Review Conference in New York decided to extend the treaty indefinitely and without conditions.

The NPT is the cornerstone of the global effort to halt the spread of nuclear weapons. More than 180 countries have signed on. No other arms control agreement in history has been so widely adhered to. And its list of signers continues to grow. This shows wide support around the world for nonproliferation.

Despite the NPT's popularity, however, the situation grows more complex with each passing year. Back in 1974 India carried out its first nuclear test. In 1998 India's regional rival Pakistan conducted its first nuclear test. More recently, in 2006, North Korea conducted its first nuclear test. All three of these are declared nuclear powers that operate outside the NPT. Israel is also widely understood to have a small nuclear arsenal.

On the other hand, since 1995 a number of states have given up nuclear weapons to sign the NPT. South Africa is one. It had a small nuclear weapons program but dismantled it before signing the NPT in 1991. Also, three of the countries that became independent at the Soviet Union's breakup gave up their nuclear weapons. Belarus, Kazakhstan, and Ukraine all "inherited" nuclear arms that Moscow had put on their soil when they were Soviet republics. But when each decided to sign the NPT, they returned the nuclear weapons to Russia, the successor state to the old Soviet Union.

Why Iran's Nuclear Program Concerns the United States

In November 2003 the IAEA issued a troubling report. It said that Iran had been carrying on secret nuclear activities for 18 years. This violated Iran's international agreements. After all, it had signed the NPT, which forbids such activities.

The report got the international community's attention. A few weeks later, on 18 December 2003, Iran signed another agreement, the Additional Protocol to the Safeguards Agreement. In this document, Iran agreed to suspend all uranium enrichment and reprocessing. Iran also swore to cooperate fully with the IAEA to answer questions.

Six months later, though, Iran still hadn't opened up. It got another rebuke from the IAEA. Then in November 2004 Iran made a deal with the European Union. Iran promised to suspend most of its uranium enrichment. But the government in Tehran didn't keep its word then, either. Concerns about Iran's nuclear activities have grown ever since.

On 6 June 2006 China, France, Germany, Russia, the United States, and Britain offered Iran a big aid package. This depended, however, on Tehran's falling into line with IAEA guidelines. It needed to stop enriching uranium. Iran was also to stop other nuclear activities, including research and development.

But the regime in Tehran defied a string of deadlines. This led in turn to a series of UN Security Council resolutions. The Iranians insist that their nuclear efforts are for peaceful purposes. But outside observers express skepticism that a country with so much oil needs electricity from nuclear sources. They also note that Iran has been trying to rebuild its military forces since its disastrous war with Iraq during the 1980s. Iran is also trying to build ballistic (long-range) missiles. In fact, in early 2009 Iran sent a satellite into space with an Iranian-made rocket. This puts the country that much closer to assembling a successful long-range missile that could target Israel with nuclear weapons.

All of this would be a concern in and of itself. But there are other reasons to worry. The United States considers Iran a state sponsor of terrorism. That is, it aids groups that use terrorism against other countries. Iran aids Hizballah, which makes trouble for Lebanon and Israel. Furthermore, Iran opposes efforts to make peace between Israel and the Palestinians. And Iranian leaders continually call for Israel's destruction.

Iran doesn't get on well with its Arab neighbors, either. One reason is that Iranians and Arabs belong to very different ethnic groups. Another is that, as you read in Lesson 1, Iran follows Shiite Islam while most of its Arab neighbors are Sunni Muslims. This makes for religious tensions. One irony about Iran's war with Iraq in the 1980s was that Iraq is really a Shia majority country. In theory, Iran and Iraq should have been great allies. However, the Sunni Muslims under Saddam Hussein ruled Iraq. Now that Hussein is dead, however, Iran continues meddling in Iraq's politics in hopes of making use of potential Shia allies.

Iran's human rights record is dismal as well. It punishes criminals by cutting off their hands or stoning them. Its judges are not independent. The Tehran government severely limits freedom of speech, of the press, and of assembly. Women and minority groups suffer discrimination and often actual violence.

The UN General Assembly has passed several resolutions expressing "deep concern at ongoing systematic violations of human rights" in Iran. But the Iranians have shown little regard for the UN's views on nonproliferation or human rights. Iran remains one of the US government's most serious foreign policy challenges.

The Importance of the Water Problem in the Middle East

Water may cover the world, but most of it is salty. Only 2.5 percent of it is fresh water. Two-thirds of that is frozen, locked up in polar ice caps and glaciers. Of the remaining third, much is in remote areas where people can't use it. Or it arrives in floods and monsoons, which amounts to the same thing. The bottom line: Only 0.08 percent of Earth's water is available to drink.

Is it any wonder that in 1999, United Nations Environment Program scientists named water shortage, along with global warming, as one of the new century's two most worrying problems?

The situation starts to sound even more serious when you focus on the Middle East. According to the UN Food and Agriculture Organization, the region it calls the Near East (running from northern Africa to Central Asia) has only 2 percent of the world's total renewable water resources. It has, however, 14 percent of the world's total land area and 10 percent of its population.

Water supplies vary widely within the region, however. The Arabian Peninsula and the Maghreb (northern Africa) have very little water. On the other hand, places such as Turkey and parts of Central Asia have more reliable water supplies.

Water and the Arab-Israeli Conflict

One way to understand the deep impact water supply can have on relations between nations is to look at the Arabs' and Israelis' contentious history. Competition for water from the Jordan River helped cause their 1967 Six-Day War, though it was not the war's only cause.

The Litani River is another source of concern in the Arab-Israeli conflict. It's a Lebanese river. It originates in Lebanon and flows into the Mediterranean. It provides water for much of southern Lebanon. But it was under Israeli control from 1982 to 2000. The Lebanese accuse the Israelis of wanting to take it back.

Water also plays a role in Israel's occupation of the Golan Heights. The heights provide about one-third of Israel's water. If Israel withdrew to pre-1967 borders, it would have to contend with a significant loss of water. But it would also face the prospect of up to half a million Syrians moving into the region, with environmental strain on the Sea of Galilee as a result.

Water is also a direct source of tension between Israelis and Palestinians. Israelis use four times as much water per capita as their Palestinian neighbors. Some of this may be for cultural reasons. Many Jewish immigrants move from Britain and the United States to new settlements in the West Bank. They often want the green lawns and swimming pools they grew up with. Palestinians, meanwhile, have access to only about 2 percent as much water per capita as most Americans take for granted.

Around the world, 70 percent of water use goes to farming. In Israel, farming drinks up a lot of water, too. Food self-sufficiency is important to many Israelis—important enough to justify their farmers' growing such water-intensive crops as rice and citrus. Palestinians have called on Israel to change these practices.

What the Future May Hold

Many observers and political leaders predict that tension over water resources could lead to war between Israel and its neighbors. The Nile, in Egypt, at one point seemed as if it might figure into a peace deal with Israel. During the 1970s Israeli water planners were scouting water resources outside their borders. And during the late 1970s Egyptian President Anwar Sadat was willing to share some of his country's water in exchange for concessions from the Israelis on Jerusalem.

The famed Nile River of Egypt slips past Cairo and the great pyramids, seen in the distance.

Photo by Robert Harbison / © 1991 The Christian Science Monitor

During the late 1970s Egyptian President Anwar Sadat was willing to share some of his country's water in exchange for concessions from the Israelis on Jerusalem.

Tension among Turkey, Syria, and Iraq over the allocation of waters from the Tigris and Euphrates rivers goes back to the 1960s. At issue were two dams, one built by Turkey and one by Syria in the early 1970s. These cut the flow of water into Iraq significantly. In 1975 Syria and Iraq nearly went to war over this. Saudi Arabian mediation averted war and restored much of Iraq's water. But the sides never came to a final agreement. International talks among the three states continued inconclusively for years. After coalition forces overthrew Saddam Hussein in Iraq, the country's new leadership stated its intention to renew negotiations.

In 2008 Turkey, Syria, and Iraq announced their intent to form a joint institute to study and map water resources. The institute will also try to resolve water allocation issues.

There can be no doubt that water is a serious issue in the Middle East. But some observers like to say that, even so, no one has gone to war there simply over water.

"Miraculously, and above all silently, Middle East governments have been able to avoid the apparently inevitable consequences of their inherited water deficits," Tony Allan of the University of London wrote in 1998. He further emphasized, "This is a life-and-death economic issue for them and their peoples."

And how have they managed? By making use of an important resource: "virtual water." By this Allan meant the water in imported food. It takes 1,000 cubic meters of water to grow the food a person eats in a year. (By contrast, a person needs only about one cubic meter of drinking water in a year.) If that person can afford to buy food on the open market, the food can be produced where the water is more readily available. Middle Eastern governments have avoided wrangling over local water by importing food in large amounts.

A US Marine rinses his socks along the banks of the Tigris River in Baghdad.
Photo by Andy Nelson / © 2003 The Christian Science Monitor

Tension among Turkey, Syria, and Iraq over the allocation of waters from the Tigris and Euphrates rivers goes back to the 1960s.

Lesson 5 Review

Using complete sentences, answer the following questions on a sheet of paper.

1. How much of its oil does the United States import?
2. What is the Carter Doctrine?
3. What is OPEC?
4. In Islam, what is the caliph's dual role?
5. What does Oman's new law on courtroom testimony say?
6. What is nuclear nonproliferation?
7. What does the Nuclear Non-Proliferation Treaty promise countries that choose not to pursue nuclear weapons?
8. What is the importance of the Golan Heights to the water problem in the Middle East?
9. What is virtual water?

Applying Your Learning

10. Which individual liberty—for example, freedom of religion, freedom of the press, more rights for women, freedom of assembly—would do the most to change the Middle East, and why?

CHAPTER 2

The Great Wall testifies that China was for centuries a leading civilization in the world, ahead of others in arts and sciences. Chinese culture has influenced many other Asian countries.

© Fisherss/ShutterStock, Inc.

Asia

Chapter Outline

LESSON 1 Asia: An Introduction

Quick Write

Think about some of the favorite foods at your home, or in your community. Where do they come from? How many different parts of the world are represented in all the foods you eat in a week?

Learn About

- the geographic locations of Japan, Korea, China, India, Pakistan, and Afghanistan
- the major religions of Asia
- the main ethnic groups of Asia

Everybody knows that pasta comes from Italy, right? But did you know that the Italian traveler Marco Polo reported eating noodles on his travels to China in the thirteenth century? The idea that he "brought pasta back" to Europe from China is considered a myth. But it's clear that he ate some kind of noodles in Asia.

A few centuries later, European explorers—looking for a faster way to the East than the dangerous overland route Marco Polo followed—discovered the new world of the Americas. They were looking for gold and silver, and they found them. But they also brought back new foods—corn, potatoes, sweet potatoes, tomatoes, avocados, and chocolate.

And the food transfers didn't go just one way. Europeans brought crops such as wheat and barley to the New World. More recently, the people of the small island nation of Papua New Guinea (PNG), long dependent on the starchy taro as a primary food source, have shifted to the sweet potato. It grows faster and produces bigger yields.

No one knows for certain just how the sweet potato came to PNG in the first place. It's clear that it originated in South America, though. Scientists keep making new discoveries about the movements of different peoples (and their foods), and the connections among them. Maybe someday there will be a clear answer to the mystery of the sweet potato.

A Geographical Overview

Asia includes everything in Eurasia—*the land mass that includes Europe and Asia*—east of the Ural Mountains. These mountains separate Russia from Siberia. The Middle Eastern countries,

Vocabulary

- Eurasia
- analects
- transcendental
- karma
- guru
- homogeneous
- archipelago
- lingua franca

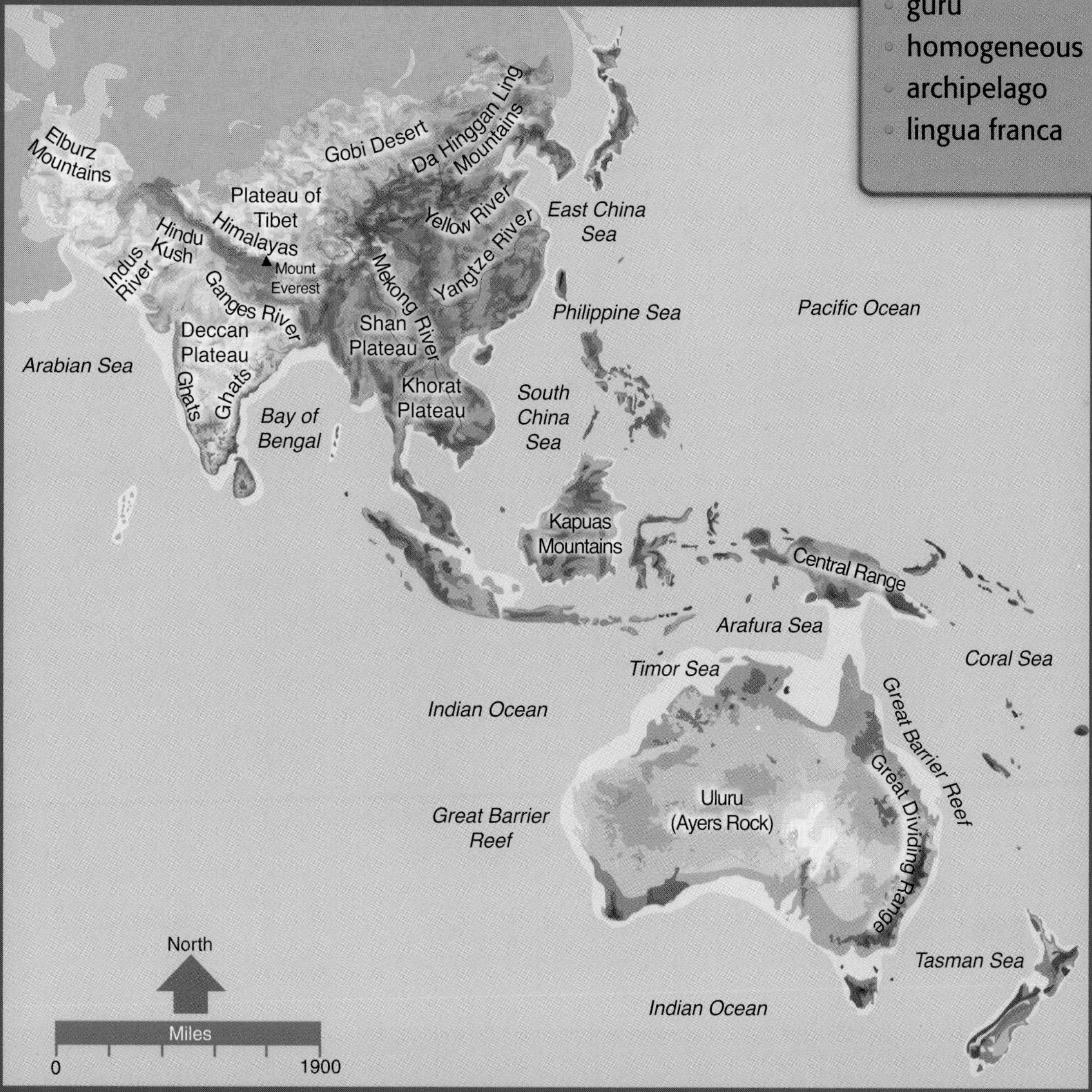

A topographic map of East and South Asia

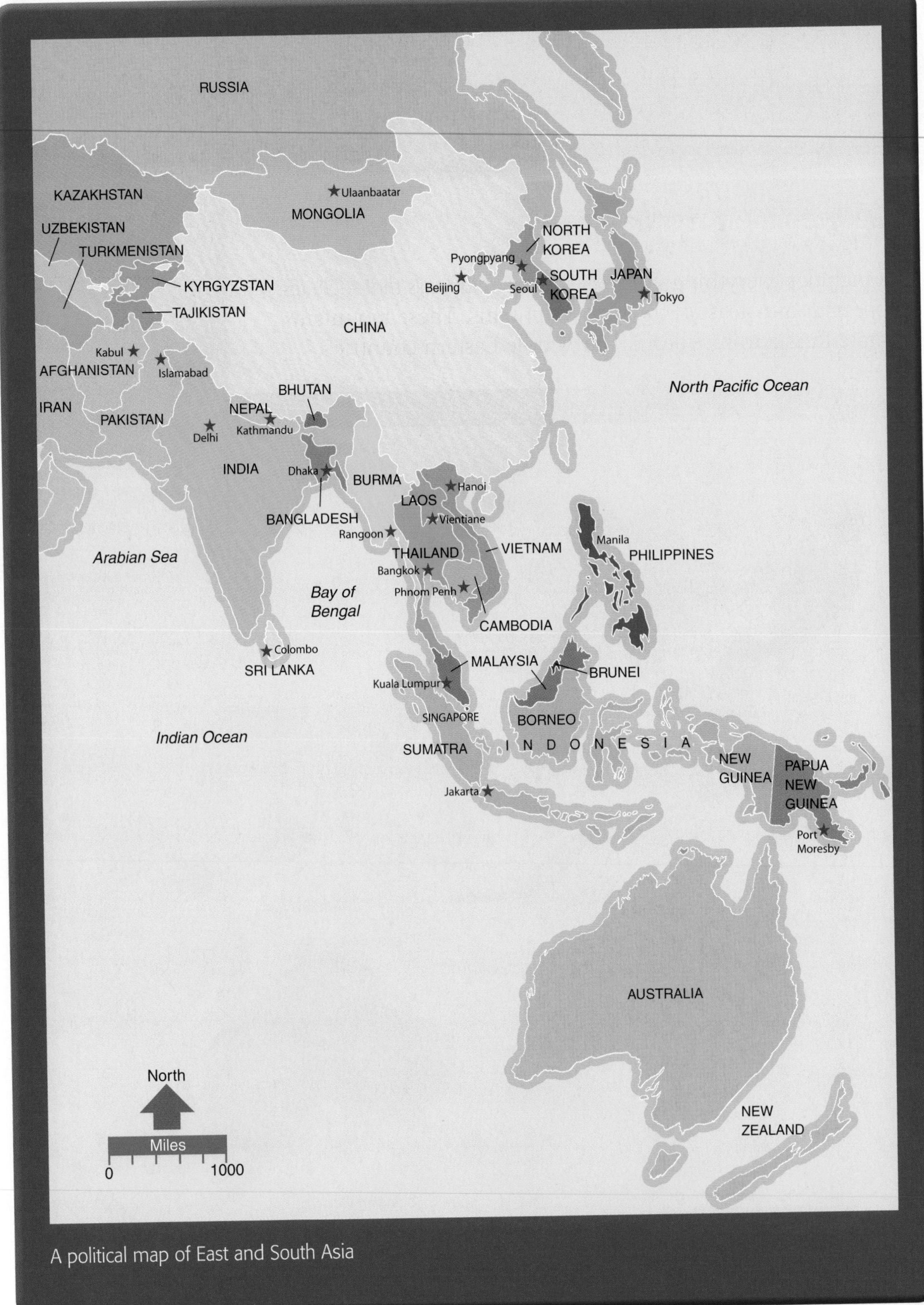

A political map of East and South Asia

Siberia, and many of the former Soviet republics are part of Asia. This chapter, however, will focus on two specific parts of the continent:

- East Asia, which includes China, Mongolia, Japan, the two Koreas, and the countries and islands of Southeast Asia. This area stretches from Siberia in the north to Australia in the south.
- South Asia, which includes Afghanistan, Bangladesh, Bhutan, India, Nepal, Pakistan, and Sri Lanka. This area lies between Iran in the west, Burma in the east, and East Asia to the north.

This vast region contains several mountain ranges. The most important is the Himalayas, which lie between East and South Asia. The world's highest mountain, Mt. Everest—29,035 feet high—is located here. Of the many rivers that flow through East Asia, China's Yangtze and Yellow are the most important. The Mekong River flows from southern China through Southeast Asia. South Asia's major rivers include the Indus and the Ganges. The last is considered holy by members of the Hindu religion.

An Indonesian <u>becak</u> (pedicab) driver loads tuna into baskets from a dock for distribution in the nearby town of Banda Aceh.

Photo by Andy Nelson / © 2005 The Christian Science Monitor

Indonesia is a huge country, made up of thousands of islands in Southeast Asia.

The Major Religions of Asia

Even if you've never traveled to Asia, you're likely to have had some exposure to one or more Asian religions. They range from Shinto, widely practiced in Japan; to Confucianism; to Taoism (DOW-ism) and Buddhism, which have influenced American popular culture; to Hinduism; to the lesser-known monotheistic faiths—faiths that worship one God—of Sikhism and Zoroastrianism.

Confucianism

Confucius (551–479 BC) was a Chinese philosopher. While Confucius is a well-known name, his fellow countrymen more commonly called him *Kongzi* ("Master Kong"). His teachings have long held immense influence in China as well as in Japan, Korea, and Vietnam.

His reputation has risen and fallen over the years, both in Asia and outside it. In Communist China's early years, for instance, the people rejected him as part of the old order. More recently, as the Chinese people have tried to reconnect with their spiritual traditions, Confucius has come back into favor.

The religious tradition that bears his name, Confucianism, goes back to the sayings and fragments written down in a text known as the Analects. Analects are *fragments or literary excerpts*. So you might think of the Analects, in other words, as a sort of scrapbook. Scholars disagree about many aspects of the Analects. But they remain the traditional source for information about the life and teachings of Confucius.

Confucius claimed that *Tian* (heaven) is aligned with moral order but depends on human beings to carry it out. He believed in *li*, ritual propriety—or in other words, performing rituals precisely and with respect—as the way the family, the state, and the world come into alignment with Tian.

Confucius also believed that moral force (*de*) was "contagious"—easily spread from one person to another. Thus moral rulers could spread their morality to their subjects, parents could rear their children to be moral, and so on.

Taoism

Taoism began in China about 2,000 years ago. It is rooted in Chinese customs and the Chinese outlook on the world. You may have seen Taoism in action if you've ever spotted a group of people exercising together in a park early in the morning, going through slow stately motions. This is called *tai chi*. Taoism teaches a connection between physical actions and spiritual effects. It values exercises such as *tai chi chuan* and *qigong* (CHEE-gong), along with yoga, meditation, and martial arts. Many Westerners and others outside Chinese culture learn something about Taoist ideas when they take up these practices.

fastFACT

Taoism is also known as Daoism. The second spelling comes closer to the sound of the Chinese word.

People in China jumpstart their day with *tai chi*, a slow stately exercise that is part of a Chinese religion known as Taoism.
Photo by R. Norman Matheny / © 1990 The Christian Science Monitor
Taoism teaches a connection between physical actions and spiritual effects.

Taoism is about the *Tao*, or *Dao* ("the way"), the creative principle of the universe. The Tao unifies and connects all things. Taoism teaches the principle of Yin and Yang, of complementary forces—male and female, light and dark, hot and cold. The Tao is not God and is not worshipped, although Taoism has many deities—gods—whom people worship in temples.

One key concept in Taoism is *tzu jan*. This is usually translated "naturalness" or "spontaneity." But this is misleading. A better translation might be, "that which is naturally so." This refers to the state something will be in if it is permitted to "exist and develop naturally and without interference or conflict." The Taoist ideal is to fulfill "that which is naturally so."

Shintoism

Shinto is a Japanese religion, but its name comes from Chinese characters: *shen*, meaning "divine being," and *tao*, which as you just read, means "way." In other words, it's "the way of the spirits." Its essence is devotion to invisible spiritual beings and powers called *kami*, to shrines, and to certain rituals.

Shinto doesn't "explain the world." Rather, it teaches rituals that let people communicate with *kami*. The *kami* are not gods. They are spirits that want people to be happy. If people treat them well, the spirits intervene to bring people health and success.

Young escorts follow a wedding party at the Meiji Shrine—a Shinto shrine—in Tokyo.

Photo by Andy Nelson / © 2008 The Christian Science Monitor

To many Japanese, Shintoism is more an aspect of Japanese cultural life than a religion.

Visiting shrines is an important aspect of Shinto. Many shrines are strictly local, and many Japanese homes include their own shrine altar. But some shrines draw visitors from a considerable distance, especially at the New Year. Festivals around shrines are important bonding experiences for Japanese communities.

Because Shinto is essentially an ethnic religion, there is little effort to convert others. To many Japanese it is more an aspect of Japanese cultural life rather than a religion. And it doesn't demand exclusivity; that is, a person can practice Shintoism along with other beliefs. Therefore Shinto has coexisted in Japan with Buddhism for centuries.

Shinto sees people as basically good. Shinto teaches ethical principles but has no commandments. It has no concept of a transcendental world—*a supernatural world beyond the human "here and now."*

Hinduism

Hinduism originated in the Indus Valley, in what is today Pakistan. It goes back before 3000 BC. Today Hinduism has more than 900 million adherents, including about 80 percent of India's population.

Hinduism has no single doctrine, nor was there a single founder or teacher. Hindus embrace the concept of *Brahman*, a universal eternal soul, who created all and is present everywhere.

Hindus worship other deities as well, including Ram, Shiva, Lakshmi, and Hanuman. They believe these deities have different attributes of Brahman in them. Hindus believe in a cycle of birth, death, and rebirth. Karma—*the total effect of someone's actions and conduct throughout his or her life*—governs this cycle. Hindus believe karma determines a person's destiny. The soul passes through a cycle of successive lives. The next incarnation always depends on how a person lived his or her previous life.

The Hindus' most ancient religious text is the Vedas. Hindus believe that scholars received these sacred texts directly from God and passed them down by word of mouth. Diwali, the Festival of Lights, is the best known Hindu holy day.

Buddhism

Buddhism focuses on personal spiritual development. It encourages attainment of deep insights into the true nature of life. Buddhism teaches that all life is interconnected. This means that compassion is important and natural.

Buddhism is 2,500 years old. It grew out of Siddhartha Gautama's quest for "enlightenment" around the sixth century before Christ. (Gautama was born in South Asia in what is now the country of Nepal.) Today Buddhism has more than 375 million followers around the world, including in Japan, China, and North and South Korea.

Hindus parade a cow—a sacred animal in their religion—around a temple in Bali, Indonesia, for a wedding celebration.
Photo by Melanie Stetson Freeman / © 1998 The Christian Science Monitor

Hindus embrace the concept of *Brahman*, a universal eternal soul, who created all and is present everywhere.

The two main Buddhist sects are Theravada ("Teachings of the Elders") Buddhism and Mahayana ("Great Vehicle") Buddhism, but there are many others as well. Theravada Buddhists—who live mainly in Sri Lanka, Bangladesh, Burma, Laos, Cambodia, and Thailand—believe their school of Buddhism has remained closest to Buddha's original teachings. Mahayana Buddhists, who live mainly in China, Japan, the Koreas, Mongolia, Tibet, Nepal, Vietnam, and Indonesia, have taken on many local influences, and have different views about the nature of Buddhahood.

Buddhist worship can take place at home or at a temple. Buddhists celebrate many festivals throughout the year as well.

Buddhism accepts the doctrines of karma and reincarnation. It teaches that change is always possible because nothing is fixed or permanent. The path to enlightenment is through morality, meditation, and wisdom. The core of Buddhism is the Four Noble Truths:

1. All existence is suffering
2. Suffering results from desire—craving or clinging to the wrong things
3. It is possible to find an end to suffering—this end is called *nirvana*
4. The solution to suffering is the Noble Eightfold Path: right seeing, right thought, right speech, right action, right livelihood, right effort, right mindfulness, and right contemplation.

Young Buddhists from Tibet practice their religion at the Padmasambhava Temple in India, where many Tibetan Buddhists seek safety from Chinese Communist rule in their home country.
Photo by Robert Harbison / © 2002 The Christian Science Monitor

Buddhists believe the path to enlightenment is through morality, meditation, and wisdom.

Zoroastrianism

The Iranian prophet Zoroaster, or Zarathustra, founded Zoroastrianism about 3,500 years ago in ancient Iran. It is a monotheistic religion. It was the religion of the ancient Persian Empire from 600 BC to AD 650. Now it's one of the world's smallest major religions, with around a quarter-million followers.

Zoroastrians believe in one God, *Ahura Mazda* (Wise Lord). He created the world. They also believe that fire represents God's light or wisdom. Fire is also seen as the supreme symbol of purity. Zoroastrians worship in structures known as fire temples, where a sacred fire is always present. Zoroastrians do not, however, worship fire itself.

Zoroastrians stress purification in their rituals. Believers focus on keeping their minds, bodies, and surroundings pure in the quest to defeat evil. Zoroaster himself focused less on ritual worship and more on "Good Words, Good Thoughts, and Good Deeds."

Zoroastrians traditionally pray several times a day. Sometimes they wear a cord with three knots in it to remind themselves of the "Good Words, Good Thoughts, and Good Deeds" maxim. They wrap the *kusti*, as the cord is known, around a long white cotton shirt known as a *sudreh*. After they wash their hands as a purification ritual, they may untie and retie the *kusti* while saying their prayers. They typically do this facing the sun, a fire, or other source of light.

The Zoroastrians' holy scriptures are known as the Avesta. It comes in two parts: the Avesta and the Younger Avesta. The Avesta itself includes 17 hymns thought to be composed by the prophet Zoroaster himself. The Younger Avesta contains commentaries, myths, stories, and details of ritual observances.

While there are still about 40,000 Zoroastrians in Iran, nowadays most live near Mumbai (Bombay), India, where they are known as *Parsis*.

Sikhism

Sikhism has 20 million followers around the world, most of them in the Indian state of Punjab. Guru Nanak (1469–1539), born in what is today the Pakistani province of Punjab, founded Sikhism in the sixteenth century.

Guru comes from Hindi and means *teacher or priest*. Guru Nanak is regarded as a great religious innovator. His ideas drew on Hinduism and Islam. But he wasn't just combining ideas. He was an original thinker whose poetry forms the basis of Sikh scripture.

What's known about him comes mostly from tradition rather than historical documentary evidence. But these much-loved traditions teach that even when he was just a boy, "God had marked him out for something special and was keeping an eye on him."

Many Sikhs, like this rickshaw driver and guide in India, wear turbans.
Photo by Robert Harbison / © 2001 The Christian Science Monitor
Sikhism stresses good actions rather than rituals.

One famous story about him tells how he rebelled at age 11. He came from a high-caste Hindu family. By age 11, boys like him would start to wear the "sacred thread" that shows their status. But Nanak refused. He said that people should be marked by their action and their character, rather than just by a thread.

Sikhism is a monotheistic religion. It focuses more than anything else on an individual's internal religious state. It stresses good actions rather than rituals. Nine other Sikh gurus followed Guru Nanak. Their teachings also form the basis of Sikhism.

The Sikh scriptures are a book called the *Guru Granth Sahib*. The tenth Sikh Guru, Guru Gobind Singh, ruled that after his death, the Sikhs should rely on their scriptures as their spiritual guide. This means the book itself has the status of a guru.

Religion and Geography

Confucianism has a strong religious influence throughout East Asia. So have Buddhism and Taoism. Hinduism has some influence. Christianity has gained in the postcolonial period, especially in South Korea. Christianity has also grown somewhat in China during the latest economic boom there.

In South Asia, the major religions are Hinduism, Islam, Christianity, and Sikhism. Only the island of Sri Lanka is majority Buddhist.

Everywhere in Asia—as in much of the world outside North America—a person's religion usually depends on the ethnic group he or she is born into. Now that you've read about Asia's faiths, it's time to study the region's people.

The Main Ethnic Groups of Asia

How do the different branches of the human family relate to one another? New research has changed scientists' minds about how to classify and understand the world's peoples. As you read about some of the main ethnic groups of Asia, you may be surprised at some of the connections among them—and some of the distinctions.

Asia's ethnic groups

East Asians

The dominant culture of this region is Chinese. Its writing system influenced those of Japan and Korea, which both built on Chinese characters, although in different ways. The largest East Asian ethnic groups are the Chinese, Japanese, Koreans, and Vietnamese.

The Chinese

China was a leading civilization for centuries, ahead of the rest of the world, particularly in the arts and sciences. But in the nineteenth and twentieth centuries, that changed. The Middle Kingdom, as China is often known, went through a difficult period: civil unrest, major famine, military defeat, and even foreign occupation.

In 1949, following years of civil war and a brutal Japanese occupation of eastern China, Mao Zedong established the People's Republic of China, a Communist government. This move ensured Chinese sovereignty—but at a price. Chinese people had to endure strict controls on all aspects of daily life, including a program of birth control put into practice to limit China's exploding population.

Mao died in 1976 and, two years later, his successor, Deng Xiaoping introduced market-oriented economic development. By 2000 Chinese output had doubled. Living standards improved dramatically. People had much greater freedom of choice—in the economic sphere. In the political sphere, controls remained very tight, as they are today.

A bride, dressed in traditional red, smiles with her family at her wedding in Hubei, China.
Photo by Robert Harbison / © 1994 The Christian Science Monitor

Chinese is the dominant culture of East Asia.

Meanwhile the Nationalist Party government that Mao defeated established itself on the island of Taiwan, which has grown into a thriving economic powerhouse. The residents of Taiwan enjoy far more political and other freedoms than those on the mainland.

The mainland government continues to insist that Taiwan is a province of China. Low-level friction has replaced the outright hostility of previous decades, however. Trade between the two has mushroomed, and an official dialogue has developed in recent years.

The other majority-Chinese nation is the island of Singapore. Important Chinese minorities live in many other countries, particularly Malaysia, Indonesia, Vietnam, and Brunei.

Three fashionable Japanese teens hang out and shop along trendy Takeshita Street in Tokyo.

Photo by Melanie Stetson Freeman / © 2002 The Christian Science Monitor

Japan, with only a tenth of China's population, is the world's second-largest economy.

The Japanese

Japan is one of the most homogeneous countries in the world. Homogeneous means *to be of one kind, to be similar*, in this case, of one ethnicity. Some 98.5 percent of its people are ethnic Japanese. People of Chinese, Korean, and "other" heritage account for about half a percent each of the population. Japan also has up to 230,000 Brazilians of Japanese origin. They came to Japan in the 1990s to work in industries. In more recent years many of them have returned to Brazil, however. About 84 percent of the people of Japan practice both Buddhism and Shintoism.

Japan has not had the same long history of cultural self-confidence as China. For 200 years, until the middle of the nineteenth century, almost all foreigners were barred from the country. But Japan, with only a tenth of China's population, is now the world's second-largest economy. A ruthless imperial power allied with Nazi Germany during World War II, Japan nonetheless rebuilt itself from the ashes of defeat. And it did so fast enough to be a top-tier economic power for much of the twentieth century.

China, meanwhile, was still very poor. It was very much a developing country. It went through one major upheaval after another—one at the hands of the Japanese in World War II; another in its Communist revolution in 1949. Japan's behavior during World War II and its economic dominance since mean that Asians tend to be warier of Japan than of China. However, China's giant economy and growing military might are beginning to worry its neighbors as well.

The Japanese have shown themselves very skilled at adapting foreign ideas and technology and making them their own. They've displayed this talent in their writing system, which is largely derived from Chinese. After World War II, they adopted two important ideas from the United States—American management and production systems, and baseball. The Japanese, in turn, have shared pop culture inventions such as karaoke and *anime*—a style of cartoon and animation—with the rest of the world.

The Koreans

Korea was an independent country for thousands of years. Then, as in many other places, things changed in the twentieth century. In 1905 Japan occupied Korea. Ten years later it annexed the whole Korean Peninsula. After the Allies defeated Japan in World War II, they divided and then occupied Korea. The North was under the Soviet Union's control, and the United States occupied South Korea.

Koreans, like these farmers in Ulsan in the South, live in an ethnically homogenous country.
Photo by Robert Harbison / © 1989 The Christian Science Monitor

Korea was an independent country for thousands of years until Japan occupied it during the first half of the twentieth century.

Today it's hard to imagine two countries much more unlike each other. In the 1960s South Korea was genuinely poor, on a par with a developing country. But its people have worked and studied hard. Today their standard of living resembles that of Czechs or New Zealanders.

Meanwhile, North Korea has been in the grip of a hard-core Communist dictatorship extreme even by Cold War standards. Its leaders have said they are practicing "self-reliance" to protect against outside influences. They have demonized the United States—tried to blame it for their own problems.

A Vietnamese family gathers to watch TV in their rural farmhouse north of Hanoi.
Photo by Melanie Stetson Freeman / © 1997 The Christian Science Monitor

Vietnamese, the country's official language, uses the Roman alphabet but has many words borrowed from Chinese, especially to express abstract concepts.

Both Koreas are ethnically homogeneous. The overwhelming majority of their people are ethnic Koreans. North Korea has a small Chinese community and a few ethnic Japanese. South Korea likewise has about 20,000 ethnic Chinese citizens. The 1995 census showed that South Korea has more Christians (26.3 percent of the population) than Buddhists (23.2 percent). On the other hand, 49.3 percent listed their religion as "none." North Korea is traditionally mostly Buddhist and Confucianist. Independent religious activity is almost nonexistent. Government-sponsored groups exist only to give the impression of religious freedom.

The Korean language, spoken in both the North and the South, is thought by some scholars to be distantly related to the Turkic languages and more closely to Japanese. Other scholars think it may be just an "orphan" with no real relatives. Korean uses a writing system developed in the fifteenth century, built on Chinese characters.

The Vietnamese

Vietnam's 86 million people are mostly of the Kinh, or Viet, ethnic group. No other ethnic group accounts for even 2 percent of the population. The religious preference of more than 80 percent of the population is "none." Buddhism and Roman Catholicism are in second and third place, respectively, but both are in the single digits. There are also a few Protestant groups.

Vietnamese is the country's official language, but it has not always been so. For most of its history, the rulers of present-day Vietnam used classical Chinese as their language for governing. The Vietnamese language uses the Roman alphabet, as English does. But it has many words borrowed from Chinese, especially to express abstract concepts. (In a similar way, English often uses words borrowed from Greek and Latin.) English is on the rise as a second language in Vietnam. Some people in Vietnam speak French, a legacy of French rule in the nineteenth and twentieth centuries. Some speak Chinese as well—a testament to the Chinese cultural influence mentioned earlier, as well as to an influential ethnic Chinese minority.

Indo-Europeans and Dravidians

Broadly speaking, the peoples of India, Pakistan, Bangladesh, and parts of Afghanistan are Indo-Europeans. These peoples use other alphabets than the Roman letters so familiar to you. Their skins are often much darker than those of Europeans. And they live in Asia. But they are more closely related to Europeans than to the East Asians of China and Japan. And their languages—Hindi, for example, spoken in India—are related to groups like the Latin or Germanic or Slavic languages of Europe. These languages are not related to Chinese or Japanese, for instance.

Shoppers buzz in this busy market in Delhi, India, where they can buy food like *jalebis*—fried dough soaked in honey.
Photo by Melanie Stetson Freeman / © 2003 The Christian Science Monitor

While India is in Asia, its people are more closely related to Europeans, and many Indian languages are related to those of Europe.

Women cultivate rice by hand on a one-acre plot in central-southeastern India.

Photo by Andy Nelson / © 2006 The Christian Science Monitor

Dravidians live in this region of India and are widely thought to be the earliest inhabitants of India.

This is one of those parts of the world, by the way, where countries' names don't always match the names of the ethnic groups who live there. Most people in Japan are Japanese. But Afghanistan has, among other groups, Pashtuns, Tajiks, and Hazaras. The homelands of some of these peoples straddle political boundaries. Punjabis, for instance, live in the Indian state of Punjab and the Pakistani province of Punjab. Until 1947, when the British withdrew from the region and the two countries separated, it was all just "Punjab," a district within what was known as British India.

The Sindhis are another distinct people who have developed under the influence of many different neighbors—and sometimes even invaders. They now live mostly in Pakistan. They are Muslim and they eat meat, unlike many of their Indian neighbors. They have been influenced by Iranians and by Turkic peoples, as well as Arabs.

Another group of people in South Asia—or the Indian subcontinent, as it is sometimes known—is the Dravidians. These peoples range across central and especially southern India and Sri Lanka. They also live in parts of Afghanistan, Pakistan, Iran, and Bangladesh. The Dravidians are widely thought to be the earliest inhabitants of India. The Indo-Europeans came later. The Dravidian languages include 200 million speakers.

The Turkic Peoples

The Turkic peoples live in northern, central, and western parts of Eurasia. Besides the Turks of Turkey, they include the Azerbaijanis, the Kazakhs, the Kyrgyz, the Uzbeks of Uzbekistan and Afghanistan, the Uighurs of western China, and Turkmens.

The Silk Road

The homes of the Turkic peoples spread along an important main street across Asia: the Silk Road. It wasn't really one road. And it wasn't built just to make it easy for merchants to trade in silk. In fact, it was hardly "built" in any sense that you would recognize today. But the Silk Road was an important network of primitive roads connecting Europe and Asia beginning about the first century BC. It started in the Chinese city of Xian and stretched westward through places like today's Turkmenistan, Uzbekistan, and Iran, and on to Byzantium (today's Istanbul, Turkey) and Rome.

Marco Polo followed the Silk Road from Italy to China in the thirteenth century. It carried Chinese silk to Rome. And it carried Buddhism from India to China. Trade along the Silk Road helped develop the great civilizations of China, India, Egypt, Persia, Arabia, and Rome. You might say that the Silk Road was the Internet of its day.

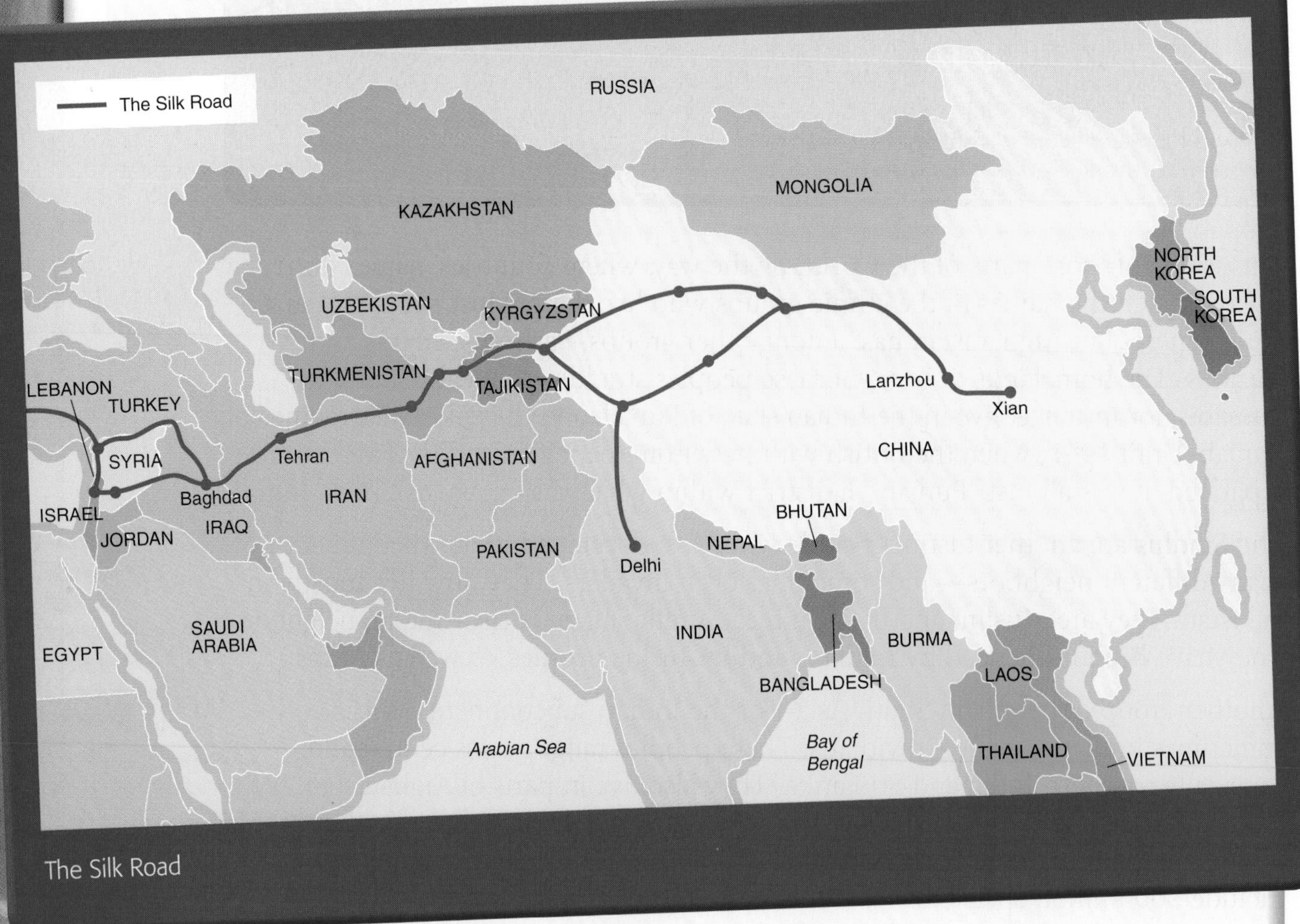

The Silk Road

The Turkic peoples speak about 30 languages. They have, all together, about 180 million native speakers. Another 20 million people speak some form of Turkic as a second language. The most widely spoken language is Turkish, sometimes called Anatolian Turkish. It has about 60 million native speakers in Turkey. Most Turkic peoples are Muslims.

The Malay-Speaking Peoples

An archipelago is *a large group of islands spread across the sea*. The largest one in the world, in terms of area, is the Malay Archipelago. It stretches between the Asian mainland and Australia. It includes the Philippines, Indonesia, Malaysia, Singapore, and Brunei. Among its peoples are the Malays, Indonesians, Filipinos, and other islanders.

The Malay language has about 33 million native speakers. Long before Europeans first arrived in the area, Malay speakers ranged on either side of the Strait of Malacca. It was a crucial trade route between India and China. Because they were on both sides of the strait, Malays were drawn into international trade early on. This, in turn, meant that Malay became a lingua franca—*a common language used by the speakers of other languages*—in the area's ports.

The oldest Malay texts go back to the seventh century. But a continuous Malay literary tradition began only in the fourteenth century, with the arrival of Islam on the Malay Peninsula.

In the twentieth century, the new nation state of Indonesia adopted a form of Malay, written in Roman letters, as its new national language. Malaysia and Brunei did much the same thing for their national languages.

Beyond Malay itself, the Malayo-Polynesian family of languages includes about 1,200 tongues with about 200 million native speakers in Indonesia, the Philippines, Madagascar, and the central and southern Pacific island groups.

Another language spoken in the archipelago is Tamil—reflecting the spread of the Dravidians. Some people in the region speak Dutch and English, the languages of European colonizers. Chinese is also spoken, especially by the ethnic Chinese business classes.

Children play near a canal in Manila, the Philippines.
Photo by Robert Harbison / © 1995 The Christian Science Monitor

The Philippines are part of the Malay Archipelago—the world's largest group of islands.

Indonesia is mostly Muslim—the world's most populous Muslim country, in fact. Malaysia, too, is largely Muslim. Buddhism and Hinduism have adherents in the region. The Philippines is mostly Roman Catholic, with some Protestants and a small Muslim minority. It and tiny East Timor are the only two majority-Christian states in Asia.

The People of Papua New Guinea

On the eastern half of the island of New Guinea, hundreds of different ethnic groups make up the people of Papua New Guinea, or PNG. Various countries—Germany, Britain, and finally Australia—controlled PNG beginning in 1885. But Australia granted the constitutional monarchy its independence in 1975. New Guinea is geologically part of Australia, rather than Asia. Its people, mostly Christian, number only 6.3 million but belong to hundreds of different ethnic groups. PNG is one of the world's most rural countries. Many of its people live in traditional societies. They speak more than 820 languages, which is more than a tenth of all the languages in the world today. You might call PNG a real hot spot of cultural diversity.

The countries of East and South Asia contain about half the world's population. They are home to several of its most important religions. Twelve of the world's Top 20 languages—measured by number of native speakers—are based there. Two of the most ancient and influential cultures—the Chinese and the Indian—were born there. And the economic potential of both is already influencing life in the United States.

The cultural exchange between Americans and the peoples of East and South Asia has been steadily growing for the last 150 years. This growth will likely speed up in the decades ahead.

Some Language Families Found in East and South Asia

Family	Languages
Austro-Asiatic	Khmer, Vietnamese
Dravidian	Kannada, Malayalam, Tami, Telugu
Indo-European	Assamese, Balochi, Bengali, Dutch, English, French, Gujarati, Hindi, Urdu, Marathi, Kashmiri, Maithili, Nepali, Oriya, Pashtu, Punjabi, Sindhi, Sinhalese, Tajik
Japonic	Japanese
Korean	Korean
Kradai	Lao, Thai
Malayo-Polynesian	Indonesian, Javanese, Malay, Tagalog (Pilipino)
Mongolic	Buryat, Mongolian
Sino-Tibetan	Burmese, Chinese (several languages), Karen, Tibetan
Turkic	Uighur, Uzbek

Lesson 1 Review

Using complete sentences, answer the following questions on a sheet of paper.

1. What are the two major rivers of East Asia and the two of South Asia?
2. What are the Analects of Confucius?
3. What is the Taoist concept of *tzu jan*?
4. Why is fire important to the Zoroastrians?
5. Who was Guru Nanak?
6. What language did the rulers of present-day Vietnam use for governing for most of their history?
7. Who are the Dravidians?
8. What was the Silk Road?

Applying Your Learning

9. Of all the religious concepts mentioned in this lesson, pick one that has struck you for some reason and write a few sentences about it. Explain why it caught your attention. Was it because it was different from your own religious ideas—or close to them?

LESSON 2 Japan, Korea, and China

Quick Write

If you had been Lord Macartney, would you have *kowtowed*? Was Emperor Qian Long's attitude justified?

Learn About

- the history of unitary government and the rule of warlords in China
- causes of the shift from isolation to openness in Japan
- the impact of domination and division on Korea
- the political and economic impact of World War II on China and Japan
- Japan, South Korea, and China as economic powerhouses

In 1793 a British diplomat named Lord George Macartney arrived in China on a mission. He wanted to open China as a market for British goods. But the Chinese didn't see trade the way the British did, as a simple, natural buying and selling of goods. Rather, the Chinese imperial court insisted that foreign trade had to go through the emperor. Instead of being a matter of "just business," trade was seen as an elaborate exchange of gifts. One paid "tribute"—something almost like a bribe—and then hoped to get something in return.

Another custom that Europeans disliked was performing the *kowtow* before the emperor. To do it someone would kneel three times and, at each kneeling, bow so deeply that his head touched the floor. It was a way of signifying that the emperor was a god. Lord Macartney's mission was the first official contact between a British king and a Chinese emperor. He told the Chinese courtiers that he would *kowtow* only if one of them would *kowtow* before a picture of George III.

Finally a deal was struck. The emperor agreed to receive Macartney in a less formal setting, outside the capital, and there he allowed Macartney merely to bend his knee, as he would have done before his own king.

The diplomat was not successful in opening China to trade, however. The letter the emperor wrote to King George sheds light on the Chinese perspective:

"Our dynasty's majestic virtue has penetrated unto every country under Heaven, and Kings of all nations have offered their costly tribute by land and sea. As your Ambassador can see for himself, we possess all things. I set no value on objects strange or ingenious, and have no use for your country's manufactures."

The History of Unitary Government and the Rule of Warlords in China

- ideology
- civil service
- edicts
- concession
- republic
- provisional
- warlords
- shoguns
- samurai
- gunboat diplomacy
- trusteeship
- martial law
- communal
- anarchy
- arable

China is the oldest continuous major civilization in the world. Some of its records go back 3,500 years. The Chinese practiced farming, which meant they were more stable as a people than some of their nomadic neighbors.

A Chinese university professor takes his child sledding along a canal on campus.

Photo by Kevin Platt / © 1997 The Christian Science Monitor

China is the oldest continuous major civilization in the world, with some records going back 3,500 years.

Although it has had several long periods of disunity, China had a unified government at a time Europeans were divided into many small political units ruled by a prince or a duke. Confucius' teachings gave China a state ideology, *a core shared belief*. A common written language meant that the Chinese could communicate with one another over great distances. And the civil service—*government employees and institutions*—kept the government running smoothly. Even when China's enemies arrived as "conquerors"—as the Mongols did in the thirteenth century—they tended to adopt China's more civilized ways.

But by the nineteenth century, China had hit some rough patches. The country had more than 300 million people and not enough work for them all. The wheels of China's economy were simply not turning very fast. What's more, out in the countryside, a shortage of land led to a breakdown of law and order.

China's imperial rulers had long presided over a peaceful and prosperous country. They had grown complacent—"fat and happy," you might say. The ruling classes remained convinced of their cultural superiority over the West. They clung to this attitude despite Western progress. The Chinese remained unwilling to adopt "foreign" ideas or even to try to innovate on their own.

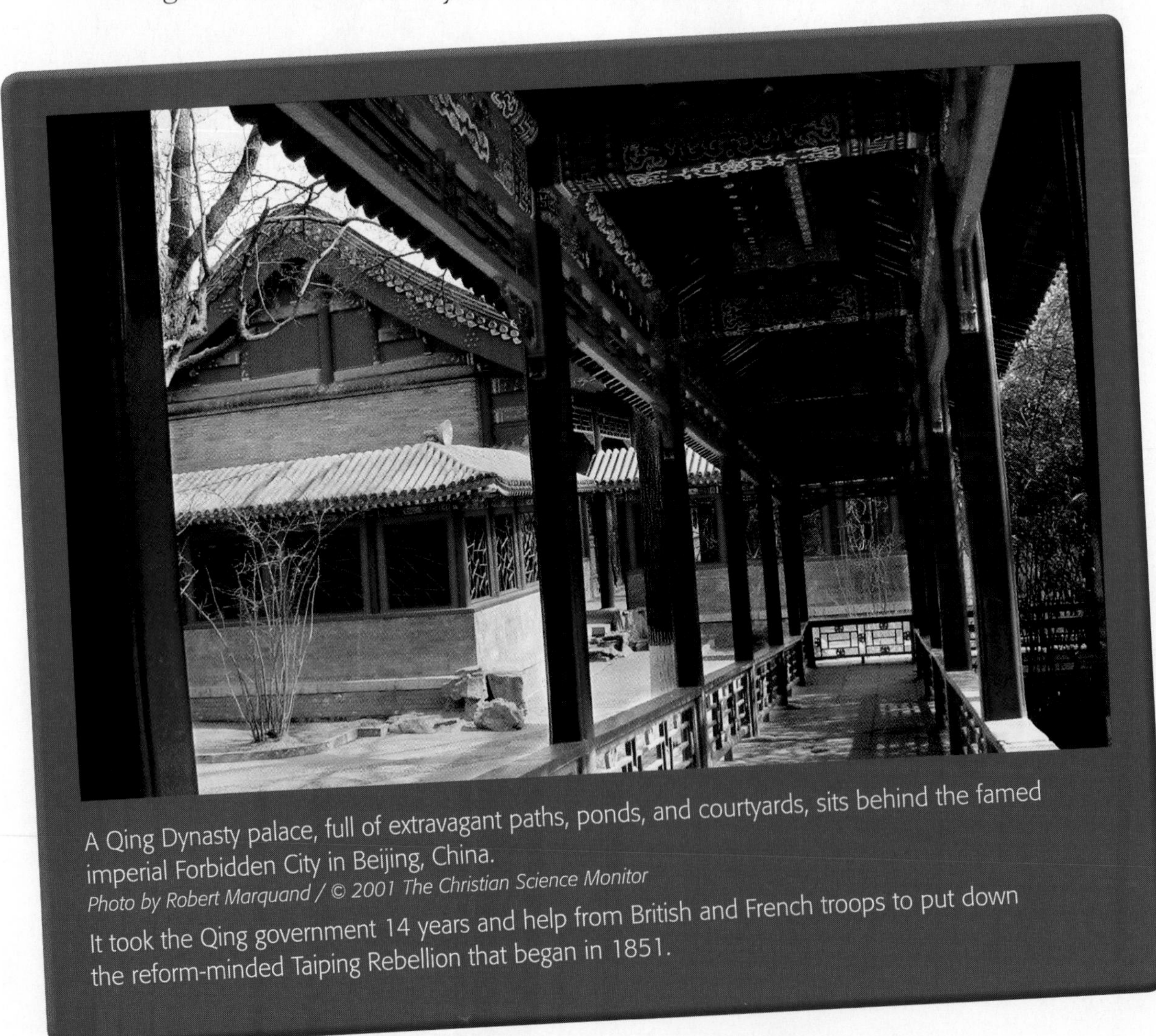

A Qing Dynasty palace, full of extravagant paths, ponds, and courtyards, sits behind the famed imperial Forbidden City in Beijing, China.
Photo by Robert Marquand / © 2001 The Christian Science Monitor

It took the Qing government 14 years and help from British and French troops to put down the reform-minded Taiping Rebellion that began in 1851.

Meanwhile, Europeans were knocking at China's gates. Many of them had read Adam Smith, David Ricardo, and other economists and thinkers you read about in the Introduction. They had their own ideas about what would solve China's problems: trade with the West. The Portuguese arrived first, establishing themselves in Macau. Then came the Spanish, followed by the French and the British.

The many changes led to the Taiping Rebellion in 1851. The rebels, some influenced by Protestant Christian ideals, opposed Confucianism and the central government, or Qing (pronounced CHING) Dynasty. The Qing government was run by Manchus, a non-Chinese ethnic group from Northern China. The rebels were strongest among ethnic Chinese in the south. But their ideas for reform were too radical for many Chinese. It took the Qing government 14 years and help from British and French troops to put down the rebellion. By then, about 30 million people had died.

These economic and social pressures led China's rulers to introduce something called "the Self-Strengthening Movement." From 1861 to 1894, a group of scholar-generals who had become leaders in the government tried to modernize China. They attempted to set up industries and improve transportation and communication. But they didn't grasp the role of political institutions, such as parliaments, in fostering progress. They didn't see the importance of individual liberty and social progress. And so their movement did not succeed.

fastFACT

What Westerners call the Chinese language is really a group of several related languages. People who speak one often can't understand those who speak another. But they can all communicate in writing because they all use the same written symbols to represent the same objects and ideas.

In Chinese writing, each word has its own symbol. There are up to 56,000 of them, but many are rarely used. An educated Chinese person recognizes about 6,000 to 7,000 of these symbols; you need to know 3,000 to read a mainland Chinese newspaper.

The Boxer Rebellion and the Invasion of the Eight-Nation Alliance in 1900

Some of the most progressive thinkers suggested that China needed more than "self-strengthening." And so in the summer of 1898, the Qing emperor, Guangxu, under the influence of these progressives, ordered a more sweeping set of reforms. They addressed not just technical innovation but institutional and ideological change.

The emperor's reform edicts—*proclamations or commands*—sought to stamp out corruption. They called for reform of the academic and civil-service exam systems, as well as the legal system and the post office. Other fields targeted for reform were agriculture, medicine, and mining. The emperor wanted students to focus less on what Confucius said and more on practical topics. He also planned to send students abroad to see the world for themselves.

Conservatives weren't happy, however. They fervently opposed the reforms. At first they just called for a go-slow approach. Then the Empress Dowager Ci Xi staged a coup. She had a fancy title, and she wielded a lot of power. But she was really just the girlfriend of the former emperor, Guangxu's uncle. She put the young reformer under house arrest and ran the country herself. The new government halted the reforms and executed six of their advocates.

The conservatives also quietly backed a movement of secret societies known as Yihetuan—the Society of Righteousness and Harmony. They're better known in the West as the Boxers. They were opposed to foreigners and to Christians. In 1900 bands of Boxers swarmed over the north China countryside. They burned missionaries' churches and killed Chinese Christians. Then they laid siege to the concessions in Beijing and Tianjin. In this context, a concession is *a land area under the control of a foreign power*. (As Europeans forced their way into China to trade, they brought their own armed troops to protect the railways and other facilities they were building.)

Chinese tourists pose in front of the Gate of Heavenly Peace, which dates from the seventeenth century and stands in Tiananmen Square in Beijing.
Photo by Andy Nelson / © 2005 The Christian Science Monitor

Although reformers tried to change China beginning in the nineteenth century, other groups like the Boxers were opposed to foreigners and to Christians—to anything that represented the influence of the outside world.

The Boxers' attacks on the concessions prompted the foreign powers to respond with what is known as the invasion of the Eight-Nation Alliance. All eight of the foreign powers present in China—the United States, along with Austro-Hungary, Britain, France, Germany, Italy, Japan, and Russia—took part.

The Qing declared war on the foreigners, but the eight responded forcefully. In the end, the Qing had to accept the Boxer Protocol, a treaty framed by the Eight-Nation Alliance. It stipulated the execution of certain high officials, the imprisonment of others, the stationing of foreign troops in China, and the razing of some Chinese military fortifications.

After all this, the court actually introduced some reforms. It abolished exams based on Confucius' teachings, for instance. China also modernized its schools and the military, as the Japanese had done. The nation even experimented with constitutional government. But things really did move too fast for many Chinese. A backlash followed. So did the establishment of new armies. And that, in turn, gave rise to warlordism.

The Warlord Period of Chinese History Between 1911 and 1928

After the reform movement's failure and the Boxer Rebellion fiasco, many Chinese felt they needed more than change. They wanted a revolution. They found a revolutionary leader in Sun Yat-sen. He was a republican activist who had a great following among overseas Chinese. His movement gained support, including from some military officers.

Sun's idea was the "Three Principles of the People"—nationalism, democracy, and people's livelihood. He wanted to end foreign domination over China. He wanted a republic—*a form of government run by the people generally through elected representatives*—not a monarchy. And he wanted to help the people prosper by regulating land ownership and the means of production, such as farms or factories. In other words, his idea of "the people's livelihood" was a form of socialism.

The Republican Revolution of 1911 broke out 10 October in Hubei Provence, and quickly spread throughout the country. On 1 January 1912, in Nanjing, Sun became the provisional—*temporary*—president of the new Chinese republic. But back in Beijing, the commander in chief of the imperial army, Yuan Shikai, had taken control. He was the strongest regional military leader at the time. He demanded that China be united under a government based in Beijing, with him in charge. This would keep the infant republic from breaking down in civil war, or falling under foreign rule, he argued. Sun assented. And so on 10 March 1912 Yuan Shikai became provisional president of the Republic of China.

He didn't share Sun Yat-sen's ideas about democracy, though, and tried to name himself emperor. Yuan Shikai's plan didn't work, however. And after he died in 1916, he left the republican government in tatters. This led to an era of warlords—*rulers who exercise both military and civil authority in the absence of a strong central government*. China had a very hard time under these brutal rulers, who were continually forming and re-forming alliances.

Tourists visit the defensive 4,000-mile-long Great Wall of China at Si Ma Tai, a section of the wall 100 miles northeast of Beijing.

Photo by R. Norman Matheny / © 1990 The Christian Science Monitor

The ancient wall was aimed at foreigners from the west, but in the twentieth century, the threat to China came from the Japanese in the east.

The Development of the People's Republic of China Under Mao Zedong

By the 1920s Sun Yat-sen was attempting another revolution. He established a base in the south of China and tried to put the pieces of the broken country back together again. He organized the Kuomintang (KMT) (also spelled Guomindang), the Chinese Nationalist People's Party. In addition, he formed an alliance with the Chinese Communist Party. When he died in 1925, Chiang Kai-shek took over the KMT. He brought most of south and central China under its control.

In 1927 Chiang Kai-shek turned on his Communist allies. He executed many of their leaders and drove the rest into the mountains of eastern China. Then in 1934 the KMT drove the Communists even out of their mountain bases.

And so the Communists began what's known as their "Long March" to the northwestern province of Shansi. There they established a guerrilla base at Yanan. Mao Zedong came to power during this period. The two parties—the Communists and the KMT—struggled for years, either openly or secretly. This continued even during Japan's 14-year invasion of China (1931–1945). During this time, the two rival parties were supposedly allies. After Japan's defeat during World War II, open warfare between the Communists and Nationalists resumed.

By 1949 the Communists occupied most of the country. Chiang fled with the remnants of his forces to Taiwan. There he proclaimed the city of Taipei to be China's "provisional capital." He vowed to reconquer the mainland. To this day, Taiwan refers to itself as the Republic of China.

fastFACT

You may have seen Mao Zedong's name spelled as "Mao Tse-tung." That's because, as with Arabic, there are different systems for spelling Chinese words in English. The most commonly accepted system today is called *pinyin*. Here are some old spellings, for example, together with the newer, *pinyin* spelling:

Peking–Beijing
Nanking–Nanjing
Teng Hsiao-peng–Deng Xioping
Kung Fu-tsu (Confucius)–Kung Fu Zi
Ching Dynasty–Qing Dynasty
Kuomintang–Guomindang

On 1 October 1949 Mao proclaimed the founding of the People's Republic of China (PRC). The country was exhausted by decades of war and upheaval. Its economy was in shambles and its transport links disrupted. Chairman Mao swiftly introduced a new political and economic order, based on those of the Soviet Union. The Communist state he founded created the China of today.

Causes of the Shift From Isolation to Openness in Japan

Legend traces Japan's founding back to 600 BC and the Emperor Jimmu. According to legend, he was a descendant of the sun goddess and an ancestor of the current imperial family of Japan.

Early in the fifth century, the Japanese court officially adopted the Chinese writing system. In the following century, the Japanese adopted Buddhism. These two events transformed Japanese culture. They marked the beginning of a long period of Chinese influence.

Like China, Japan has gone through some profound changes in its relations with the West over the past few centuries. In fact, the story of Japan's first contact with the West begins with a ship en route to China.

Reasons for Japan's Isolation During the Edo Period

Japan's first recorded dealings with the West occurred in 1542. A Portuguese ship headed for China blew off course and landed in Japan instead. For the next hundred years, traders from Portugal, the Netherlands, England, and Spain came to Japan. So did a stream of Roman Catholic missionaries. At this time, real power in Japan was in the hands of shoguns, or *military governors*. They worried that the traders and missionaries were a sort of advance team for a European invasion. And so the shoguns started to restrict the movements of foreigners. They liked foreign trade but did not trust outsiders or Christianity.

By 1612 the shogun in power at that time insisted that anyone working for him or living on land he owned had to promise not to become Christian. A few years later, he restricted foreign trade to Nagasaki and Hirado, two cities on Kyushu, the southernmost of Japan's four main islands. The idea was to keep foreign trade as far away as possible from Japan's main cities.

Then came actions against Christians. In 1622 the shogun ordered the execution of 120 missionaries and converts. He forced out the Spanish in 1624. And he executed thousands more Christians in 1629.

Then in 1635 an edict banned any Japanese from traveling outside Japan. Any who left were forbidden to return. In 1636 Japan restricted the Portuguese to a man-made island called Deshima in Nagasaki's harbor.

It got worse. In 1637–38 unhappy Christian aristocrats and peasants rebelled against the *bakufu*—the shogun's officials. The government called in Dutch ships to bombard the rebel stronghold, and that was the end of the rebellion. Japan also permanently threw out the Portuguese and executed their diplomats. Furthermore, the government ordered all Japanese to register at a Buddhist or Shinto temple. And the country restricted the Dutch to Deshima and confined the Chinese to one section in Nagasaki.

By 1641 except for these provisions for foreigners, and a little trade with Korea and some nearby islands, Japan had shut its gates to the outside world. Scholars refer to this time of isolation from the West, from 1603 to 1868, as the Edo period. Edo was an earlier name for Tokyo.

For all its inwardness, it was in many ways a culturally rich period. In addition to *bushido*, "the way of the warrior," the Japanese began to cultivate the ideal of *chonindo*, "the way of the townspeople." It was a time when people studied mathematics, astronomy, engineering, and medicine. People strove for quality of workmanship, especially in the arts. For the first time, city-dwellers could afford mass culture and popular entertainment. They enjoyed beautiful woodblock prints, music, poetry and other literature, Kabuki theater, and other forms of the arts.

Confucian ideas about social order also influenced Japanese society during this period. The imperial court families at Kyoto, then the capital of Japan, were at the top of the hierarchy. But the samurai—*the warrior aristocrats of Japan*—held the real political power. Below them were farmers and then city-dwellers. The individual had no legal rights at this period. The family was the smallest legal unit. Maintaining family status and privilege mattered deeply to Japanese at all levels of society.

A Japanese national treasure, the bronze Great Buddha—dating from 1252 AD—watches over Kamakura, Japan.

Photo by Gloria Goodale / © 2006 The Christian Science Monitor

The Japanese, who adopted Buddhism from China in the sixth century AD, shut their gates to the outside world several centuries later in a phase known as the Edo period.

Gunboat Diplomacy and the Opening of Japan to Trade With the West

President Theodore Roosevelt had an ideal of foreign policy: "Speak softly and carry a big stick." By this he referred to negotiations ("speak softly") backed up by the threat of force ("big stick"). Sometimes the threat of force, not force itself, is all that's needed.

That's the idea behind "gunboat diplomacy," a term referring to *the threat, or limited use, of naval force to reach a foreign policy goal*. It's a term rooted in the eighteenth, nineteenth, and early twentieth centuries. That's when Europeans, and later Americans, often relied on sea power to "send a message" to another country. Today, airpower is used for the same purpose, and people speak of "power projection." But whichever term you prefer, the opening of Japan to trade with the West is a classic example.

Commodore Matthew Perry's Role in Ending Japanese Isolation

On 8 July 1853 four giant dragons puffing smoke swam into Tokyo Bay and then came to a halt—like ships at anchor. Could they be some kind of ships? the Japanese wondered. They had never seen anything like them. They didn't know such things even existed. Then when they got a closer look, they could see enormous guns, and lots of them. Each of the smoking dragon ships flew a flag—red and white stripes, and stars in a field of blue.

The "dragons" were US Navy steamships under Commodore Matthew Calbraith Perry's command. His mission wasn't to invade Japan. In one sense, you might say he was just there to deliver a letter—from President Millard Fillmore to the emperor of Japan. Perry's mission was to negotiate a trade agreement between the two countries. But he had brought his big guns along to be sure he got Japan's attention.

The United States wanted Japan to open certain ports to American ships for trade. American vessels also needed a "pit stop" in Asia—a place for commercial whaling ships to load up on coal and other supplies.

Courtiers and other imperial staff members showed up to talk with Perry. But he brushed them off and held firm. He had come to Japan to negotiate with the emperor and his top-level aides, not with underlings.

The Japanese eventually realized that they could not defend themselves against a foreign power and that to continue to try to shut out foreign traders would be to risk war. They began to negotiate.

On 31 March 1854, more than nine months after the arrival of the "black ships," representatives of the two countries signed the treaty that opened Japan. The treaty, officially known as the Convention of Kanagawa, called for:

- Peace and friendship between the United States and Japan
- The opening of two ports to American ships
- Help for shipwrecked American persons and vessels
- Permission for American ships to buy supplies in Japanese ports.

Women harvest rice on a farm in twenty-first-century Japan.
Photo by Marjorie Coeyman / © 2002 The Christian Science Monitor

Renewed contact with the West—starting with Commodore Matthew Perry's arrival in Tokyo Bay in 1853—began to transform Japanese society, leading to the end of its feudal system.

Commodore Perry

Commodore Matthew Calbraith Perry was 60 years old when he arrived in Tokyo. ("Commodore" is a Navy rank no longer in use. It was something between a captain and a rear admiral.) He had spent a long and distinguished career, but he knew this was his biggest assignment. He had three roles to fill: Navy officer, diplomat, and cultural ambassador.

After they signed the treaty, the Japanese invited the Americans to dinner to celebrate. The Americans had an opportunity to admire their hosts' courtesy and the rich Japanese culture. And the Japanese must have realized that Perry's mission had broken down barriers separating them from the rest of the world.

Today the Japanese celebrate Perry's mission with "black ship festivals" every year. And Perry's hometown, Newport, Rhode Island, is sister city to Shimoda, one of the Japanese ports Perry's treaty opened.

Soon renewed contact with the West began to transform Japanese society. The *shogunate*—the military governors—resigned. The emperor regained real political power, in what's known as the "Meiji restoration." The feudal system was abolished, and many Western ideas came in instead, including Western-style legal and education systems.

The Impact of Domination and Division on Korea

Korea's neighbors have invaded it and fought over it and influenced it for centuries. But it's held its own for much of the time, culturally, at least. In the face of "gunboat diplomacy" from the West in the middle of the nineteenth century, Korea kept its door shut and earned the nickname "Hermit Kingdom."

The Chinese and Japanese Domination of Korea Prior to 1945

While keeping the West at arm's length, Korea accepted Chinese control in East Asia. The Chinese, on the other hand, worried about Japan's growing influence in Korea in the late nineteenth century. Meanwhile, the Russians were pushing for more trading opportunities in Korea. These pressures led to two wars: the Sino-Japanese War of 1894–95, between China and Japan, and then the Russo-Japanese War of 1904–05, between Russia and Japan. Japan won both. From 1905 it occupied Korea, and then in 1910, annexed it. Korea thus became part of the Japanese Empire. Japanese rule meant tight control from Tokyo. It also meant relentless efforts to suppress the Korean language and culture. Some Koreans tried to resist, but their efforts generally failed. Japan remained firmly in charge on the Korean Peninsula until August 1945, when World War II ended with Japan's surrender to the Allies.

The Division of Korea After World War II

Even with Japan's defeat, Korea didn't regain its independence. In August 1945 the Allies split Korea in two for purposes of accepting the surrender of Japanese troops stationed there. The Soviet Union dealt with those north of the 38th parallel. The United States accepted the surrender of those south of that line. The division of Korea began as a necessity of military procedure. But it soon became clear that it would last for some time.

Initially, the division was to last until the United States, the Soviet Union, China, and Britain could arrange some sort of trusteeship for Korea. A trusteeship is *an arrangement for one country to govern another under international control*. It's a setup much like the mandates in the Middle East under the old League of Nations.

Right after the end of World War II, countries that had been allies in the fight against Hitler began to look at each other anew. The Soviets seemed eager to claim as much territory as they could, both in Eastern Europe and in Asia. And the Chinese, as you've just read, were about to go through a revolution that would put them on the Soviet Union's side. This was the start of the Cold War.

The United States and the Soviet Union set up a joint commission on the Korean question. It met off and on but soon deadlocked over the issue of a national government for Korea. In September 1947 the United States submitted the Korean question to the new United Nations General Assembly. Cold War politics, plus opposition from the Koreans themselves to a trusteeship, shattered hopes of a unified independent Korea.

And so 1948 saw the launch of two Koreas. Their political, economic, and social systems could not be more different. On 15 August the nationalist leader Syngman Rhee became president of the Republic of Korea in the south. In the north, Kim Il-sung, the Soviets' favored candidate, became premier of the Democratic People's Republic of Korea.

In 1950 North Korea invaded South Korea. US and other troops, operating under the United Nations flag, turned back the invasion, and in turn entered the north. Fighting raged up and down the peninsula, with Communist Chinese forces joining the war on North Korea's side. A cease-fire agreed to in 1953 set the border in its present location, not far from the 38th parallel. The cease fire, or armistice, remains in effect to this day. The countries are technically still at war.

The Difference in the Politics and Economics of North and South Korea

"Hermit Kingdom" used to apply to Korea as a whole. But nowadays it's used to refer to North Korea alone. This Communist country is one of the most closed societies in the world. It has a rigid centralized government under the Korean Workers' Party (a Communist party). From 1948 until his death in 1994, Kim Il-sung ruled as head of the party and president of North Korea. His son, Kim Jong-il, inherited supreme power from his father.

Two women do business at an outdoor market in Ulsan, South Korea.
Photo by Robert Harbison / © 1989 The Christian Science Monitor

While North Korea's economy declined during the 1990s, the South's economic growth over the last few decades has been spectacular.

North Korea has a formal written constitution, but not much is known about actual lines of power and authority there. In recent years outside observers have speculated about Kim Jong-il's health. He may have suffered a stroke and be fighting cancer. And in a country where so much power is—apparently—in the hands of one man, those are important questions.

The end of Soviet communism in 1991—which you'll read more about in Chapter 4—hit North Korea hard. Under the old Soviet trading system, Communist countries had to trade with one another. This benefited North Korea. Most of those countries now have market economies and can sell their goods elsewhere. North Korea no longer gets the bargains it once did. And its goods cannot compete on the world market—their quality and technology are not up to world standards.

Outside experts think that between 1990 and 2002, gross national income per capita, an important measure of a country's wealth, fell by a third in North Korea. Between 2 million and 3 million people starved to death in the mid-1990s. The situation has improved somewhat since then. The regime has introduced some market reforms. But the Communist regime hangs on. It devotes a huge share of the economy to defense, and still practices food rationing.

The South

In South Korea, the story is very different. Its economic growth over the past several decades has been spectacular; in 2008 the US State Department ranked South Korea as the thirteenth-largest economy in the world, and the United States' seventh-largest trading partner.

In the early 1960s South Koreans produced about $100 per person every year. Then the government began to stress exports and labor-intensive light industries. This put people to work, making things to sell abroad. This in turn expanded the industrial sector. Over the years, the government introduced wave after wave of reform, moving the economy into heavier industry. Koreans began to make consumer electronics and cars.

The government also moved away from central planning to free-market capitalism. That is, rather than regulating or trying to control every aspect of the economy, the government lets the natural flow of the supply of goods and the demand for those goods determine how much or how little business produces and charges for its merchandise. This helped South Korea bounce back well from the Asian financial crisis of 1997. The country still has room for improvement, especially as it has become wealthier and now faces competition from lower-wage countries. It remains an economic powerhouse, however.

South Korean politics, on the other hand, have been much more tumultuous. Its story has been one of democratic activism defeating military rule. Its first president, Rhee, resigned in the face of a student uprising in 1960. Major General Park Chung-hee led a coup against Rhee's successor soon after that. Under Park, the economy grew but political freedom shrank. After his assassination in 1979, a group of military officers led by Chun Doo Hwan declared martial law—*military rule*—and took power.

Workers manufacture cars at a Hyundai car plant in Ulsan, South Korea.

Photo by Robert Harbison / © 1989 The Christian Science Monitor

In 2008 the US State Department ranked South Korea as the thirteenth-largest economy in the world.

Even under martial law, however, South Korea developed a strong civil society. Students and labor unionists protested strongly against authoritarian rule and, especially, the 1979 coup. After 200 civilians died in a confrontation in Gwangju in 1980, the democracy movement grew even more intense.

Faced with overwhelming opposition, the government had to yield to the activists in 1987. They won the right to have direct presidential elections. A vote that year brought Roh Tae-woo, another former general, to power. But democratic advances continued. These led in 1992 to the election of Kim Young-sam. He was the first civilian elected president in 32 years. Korean democracy passed yet another milestone in 1997, when Kim Dae-jung, a lifelong human rights activist, won election as president from a major opposition party.

The Political and Economic Impact of World War II on China and Japan

For the Chinese, World War II began in 1937, when Japan invaded, seizing some of China's most important cities, such as Peking (Beijing), Nanking (Nanjing) and Shanghai. The Japanese conquest and occupation were brutal: Japanese troops murdered millions of Chinese civilians.

China was in the midst of civil war between Nationalists and Communists even as it fought on the Allied side during World War II. China ended the war on the brink of revolution.

Japan, on the other hand, ended World War II in utter defeat and ruin, after the United States carried out a major aerial bombing campaign that ended in the atomic bombing of two Japanese cities, Hiroshima and Nagasaki.

International Control of Japan After World War II

After these atomic attacks, Emperor Hirohito asked that his people bring peace to Japan. By this he meant that he wanted Japan to surrender to the Allied powers. And so Japanese officials signed documents of surrender aboard the USS *Missouri* on 2 September 1945.

Under its agreement with the Allies, Japan had to:

- Consent to occupation by Allied forces
- Promise never again to go to war
- Give up any claim of sovereignty beyond Japan's four main islands "and such minor islands as may be determined"
- Give up its colonial holdings, such as Korea.

With this a period of demilitarization and democratization began. Special tribunals found 4,200 Japanese officials guilty of war crimes. Of these, 700 were executed. Another 186,000 people were banned from public life and politics. Shinto lost its role as the established (that is, state supported) religion. And on New Year's Day 1946 Emperor Hirohito repudiated his claim to divinity. He stated that he no longer saw himself as a god, in other words.

The Role of General Douglas MacArthur in Japan After World War II

Japan's 1947 Constitution is sometimes known as "the MacArthur Constitution." That highlights General Douglas MacArthur's importance in postwar Japan.

His title was Supreme Commander for the Allied Powers, or SCAP. During his tenure, Japan abolished its army and naval ministries and converted war industries to civilian use. He pushed the government to amend its 1889 Meiji Constitution, and it did so. The new one came into force on 3 May 1947.

During this period Japan introduced economic reforms as well. It redistributed ownership of farmland, reestablished trade unions, and limited the *zaibatsu*, or diversified business corporations, that had been such a feature of the Japanese economy.

The war had erased many of the gains Japan had made since its big wave of modernization that started in 1868. Allied attacks had wiped out about 40 percent of its industrial capacity—factories and the like. The shock of this made people swing into action. They rebuilt and soon had more modern factories than the countries that had defeated them.

A strong education system was a big help in modernizing after the war. Japan had the highest literacy rate in the world. The schools also encouraged discipline, which helped develop a strong work force.

All in all, Japan rebounded quickly. Soon the SCAP began to relax some of the restrictions, including press censorship. Restrictions on the *zaibatsu* and on foreign trade eased as well.

In 1951 Japan signed a treaty formally known as the Treaty of Peace. In it Japan gave up its claims to Korea, Taiwan, and a number of islands. It agreed to settle disputes peacefully, under the United Nations Charter. The treaty acknowledged Japan's right to self-defense. In 1952 Japan signed an accord with the United States that ensured it would have a strong defense. With these steps, Japan was back in the family of nations.

The Rise of the Communist System of Government and Economics in China

In the early 1950s the new Communist leaders under Mao Zedong launched a major program of economic and social rebuilding. They won popular support by curbing inflation, getting the economy going again, and repairing factories damaged by war.

China called this period its "transition to socialism." It had its first Five-Year Plan from 1953 through 1957. Industrialization was one of its goals—making more things with machines in factories, instead of by hand in workshops.

Collectivization of agriculture was another goal. This meant converting farms from individual or family ownership to ownership by a group, often known as a collective. The idea of communal, or *shared*, ownership of means of production was essential to communism. China's leaders thought this approach to agriculture would help the country feed its people.

A third major goal of this time was political centralization. Following the Soviet model, the Communist Party soon had a finger in every pie. Large politically loyal armed forces and secret police helped keep the party in power. Government agencies took their cues from the party. And party members became leaders of labor unions, women's groups, and other mass organizations.

To meet their industrialization goals, the Chinese worked with the Soviets, who provided economic and technical help. During this period, China nationalized banking, industry, and trade. Soon China had virtually no private enterprise.

Tokyo's Shibuya shopping district bustles day and night with activity.
Photo by Melanie Stetson Freeman / © 2002 The Christian Science Monitor

Allied attacks wiped out about 40 percent of Japan's industrial capacity during World War II, but in the war's aftermath the Japanese people swung into action and rebuilt.

China conducted its first real census at this time, too. The new People's Republic found out it had 583 million people. That was far more than anyone expected and explained the need for more food.

Chinese walk near the Forbidden City under Chairman Mao Zedong's gaze.
Photo by Robert Harbison / © 1994 The Christian Science Monitor

Under Mao, China had virtually no private enterprise—a result of the first Five-Year Plan—and during his Great Leap Forward, an estimated 15 million to 36 million people died of starvation.

The Role of Mao Zedong in China After World War II

By the end of the first Five-Year Plan, Mao Zedong broke with the Soviet model. He was ready to try something else that would help China develop faster. In addition, relations with the Soviet Union were growing worse. China would make what he called a Great Leap Forward.

The goal of the Great Leap Forward was to raise both farm and factory production. Under Mao's direction, China worked on both large and small scales. Farms merged into giant enterprises known as cooperatives or communes. And little "backyard factories" were everywhere.

The new approach was a disaster. People soon found they were exhausting themselves to produce goods no one would buy. Farm production fell behind, too. Within a year, people were starving in prime farming areas. Poor planning and bad weather combined in 1960-61 to produce one of the deadliest famines in human history. An estimated 15 million to 36 million people died.

About the same time, China's ties with the Soviets were souring. The Russians stopped sharing scientific information with the Chinese, and in August 1960 they pulled all their people out of China. What's more, the two former allies were willing to disagree in public.

The Cultural Revolution

Mao began to face a couple of challengers. State President Liu Shaoqi and his protégé, Party General Secretary Deng Xiaoping, started to follow more practical policies. These were at odds with Mao's revolutionary vision, however. He was not happy. He wanted to remain in charge. And so in the spring of 1966, he launched a huge political attack on his challengers and their allies.

He called his new movement "the Great Proletarian Cultural Revolution." There had been nothing like it in Communist history. That's saying a lot because communism has included some pretty rough fellows. For the first time, part of the Chinese Communist leadership was trying to get the people to rally against another part of the leadership. Mao accused Liu, Deng, and others of trying to drag China back into capitalism. The resulting strife set China on a frightening course of political and social anarchy—*a situation that's out of control with, in effect, no one in charge*—that lasted for most of the next 10 years.

Gradually things calmed down. The political situation stabilized. Then in September 1971 Defense Minister Lin Biao reportedly tried to stage a coup against Mao. This was all the more shocking, since he had been a close ally of Mao. Lin later died, allegedly in a plane crash in Mongolia.

In the incident's aftermath, many of the officials dismissed earlier returned to power. Chief among these was Deng Xiaoping, who stepped into several important posts. One of China's themes until around the time of Mao's death in 1976 was the struggle between pragmatists and radicals. In general, the pragmatists wanted to introduce capitalist-style reforms into the economy. The radicals opposed this. Soon after Mao's death, Deng's ascent indicated that the pragmatists were gaining the upper hand.

Japan, South Korea, and China as Economic Powerhouses

Japan and China are two of the world's three largest economies. (The United States is in first place.) And South Korea, with a population of less than 50 million, is well ahead of other countries with far more people and resources.

The Role and Impact of Japan on the Global Economy

Japan has an industrialized free-market economy that is still the second largest in the world. This is despite its dramatic slowdown of the 1990s, sometimes called its "lost decade." Japanese companies that must compete internationally do very well. Japanese producers who are protected from competition, such as farmers, are less efficient.

Among Japan's economic strengths are:

- A strong industrial culture, with a broad knowledge base
- An educated workforce
- A strong work ethic
- High savings and investment rates
- Openness to trade.

A worker assembles a copier at a Fuji Xerox plant of Shenzhen in China.
Photo by Andy Nelson / © 2009 The Christian Science Monitor

China's economy has grown an average of 9.5 percent per year for more than a quarter-century, and the country now boasts one of the world's three largest economies.

Japan has few natural resources. Only 15 percent of its land is arable—*able to be farmed*. It tries to grow as much of its own food as possible, but it's the biggest market for American agricultural exports. It has little in the way of energy resources. Since the oil shocks of the 1970s, it has reduced its dependence on imported oil from 75 percent of its energy needs to only 52 percent. It is one of the most energy-efficient developed economies in the world. Japan must import many of the mineral resources it needs, as well as many forest products.

The Role and Impact of South Korea on the Global Economy

For all its strong performance, South Korea has critics who point out how it could do better. Since South Korea is an export-oriented economy, the economic downturn of 2007–09 hit the country hard. It remains an important trade partner of the United States and Japan. It serves somewhat to counterbalance China's rising economic strength.

Economists fret about South Korea's aging population and structural problems, such as its rigid labor regulations. Labor-management relations should be better, too, they say. And the country would benefit from better, more transparent financial regulation.

In December 2007 Koreans elected Lee Myung-bak as their president. He campaigned on a platform calling for deregulation, tax reform, more foreign direct investment, labor reform, and free-trade agreements with major partners.

One final point: South Koreans worry that if North Korea collapses, they will have to absorb it into their own country just as West Germany absorbed East Germany. But West Germany was much richer than South Korea is. Besides, West Germany was bigger in proportion to East Germany than South Korea is to North Korea. Moreover, even as it was crumbling, East Germany was in better shape than North Korea is.

The Role and Impact of China on the Global Economy

Since 1979 China has opened and reformed its economy. It has grown an average of 9.5 percent per year for more than a quarter-century. It's been a victory for Deng Xiaoping and his pragmatist allies and heirs. Free-market reforms have unleashed immense individual initiative. This has led to the largest reduction of poverty and one of the fastest rises in income levels ever seen.

Today's China can feed itself. It still has 40 percent of its workforce engaged in farming, a huge share by the standards of developed countries. It has only 75 percent as much farmland as the United States. But by practicing intensive agriculture, it outproduces the United States in crops and livestock by about 30 percent. And Chinese experts see more room to improve, as they turn to better plant stocks, more fertilizer, and other technology. Better port facilities, warehouses, and cold storage would help Chinese agriculture, too. Land ownership remains a problem, however. Farmers do not own, and cannot buy or sell, their land, since all land in China is leased from a rural cooperative or the state. The government was considering a land-reform law as this book went to print.

Employees make shoes at a family-owned factory in China.
Photo by Robert Marquand / © 2003 The Christian Science Monitor

The giant country has become the world's factory: Look carefully at the labels on your computer, your clothes, or any number of items at home, and you are likely to see a 'Made in China' label.

China has become the world's factory. Look carefully at the labels on your computer, your clothes, or any number of items at home, and you are likely to see a "Made in China" label. The safety standards for consumer products in China lag behind those in the West, however. Scandals over tainted milk and lead paint on children's toys have given China's trade partners pause. They have also had repercussions in China.

As it has grown, China has become a competitor with the United States and other countries. China's construction boom has driven up prices for products like concrete. The country has become a factor in world oil markets, as it must import more and more oil. China's growth has also come at the price of environmental degradation—filthy air and sullied waters.

China belongs to the World Trade Organization. As a member, it has opened up sectors of its economy that were previously closed. China has surpassed Japan and has the largest reserves of foreign currency and gold in the world. China also loans money to the United States government by buying US Treasury bonds when Washington spends more money than it collects in taxes. This can create challenges for both sides. If China loans too much to the United States, it could try to influence US policies. At the same time, however, it could become overly dependent on the health of the US economy and the strength of the US dollar.

The Chinese Languages

The Chinese languages are *tonal*—that is, the same word pronounced with a different tone, has different meaning. Standard Mandarin has five tones, while Standard Cantonese, spoken in southern China, has nine.

Here's an example of how these tones work:

The Mandarin word *ma* pronounced in a high tone means "mother."

Pronounced in a high and rising tone, it means "hemp" or "torpid."

Pronounced in a low falling, then rising tone, it means "horse."

Pronounced in a high falling tone, it means "scold."

Pronounced in a neutral tone, it indicates you are asking a question.

Lesson 2 Review

Using complete sentences, answer the following questions on a sheet of paper.

1. Who were the Boxers?
2. Who was Sun Yat-sen and what were his three principles?
3. What, and when, was the Edo Period?
4. How did Commodore Perry end Japan's isolation?
5. How did the division of Korea occur?
6. How do the politics and economics of North Korea differ from those of South Korea?
7. Who was General Douglas MacArthur and what was his role in postwar Japan?
8. What was the Great Leap Forward?
9. Why did Japan become more energy-efficient?
10. How has China affected the price of concrete?

Applying Your Learning

11. Is China's economic growth a good thing for Americans? Why or why not?

LESSON 3 India, Pakistan, and Afghanistan

Quick Write

What approach should British India have taken to independence? Why?

Learn About

- the precolonial history of the Mughals in the Indian subcontinent
- the encounter with Europe and the colonial period in the region
- the history of the struggle for independence in South Asia
- what caused the partition and war between India and Pakistan
- how Muslim-Hindu strife affects the politics and economics of South Asia
- which groups have struggled for control in Afghanistan and why

Imagine this: The year is 1921, and you're a teenager in school in India. Your land has been under British rule for as long as anyone can remember. You're starting to hear about independence for India, though, and it sounds like an exciting idea. But what kind of independence? Self-rule within the British Empire? Or complete independence, like what the Americans got after 1776?

India is a vast country—Hindus and Muslims are only two of its mixture of religious and ethnic groups. Could one country possibly be big enough to include everybody? Won't some groups get lost? Should certain groups be guaranteed a share of seats in Parliament? Maybe two or more smaller countries would make more sense. British India could draw the map so that each territory was pretty clearly Hindu or Muslim and everybody spoke the same language. What do you think is best, and why?

The Precolonial History of the Mughals in the Indian Subcontinent

Vocabulary

- Indian subcontinent
- aristocrat
- caste
- British raj
- interim
- de facto
- infrastructure
- Taliban
- madrassa

You read briefly in the Introduction about the Mughal Empire in the Indian subcontinent. Indian subcontinent is *a term used to refer to India, Pakistan, Bangladesh, and Sri Lanka.* These countries spent many years under British rule, and so the term "British India" is used to refer to them during that time.

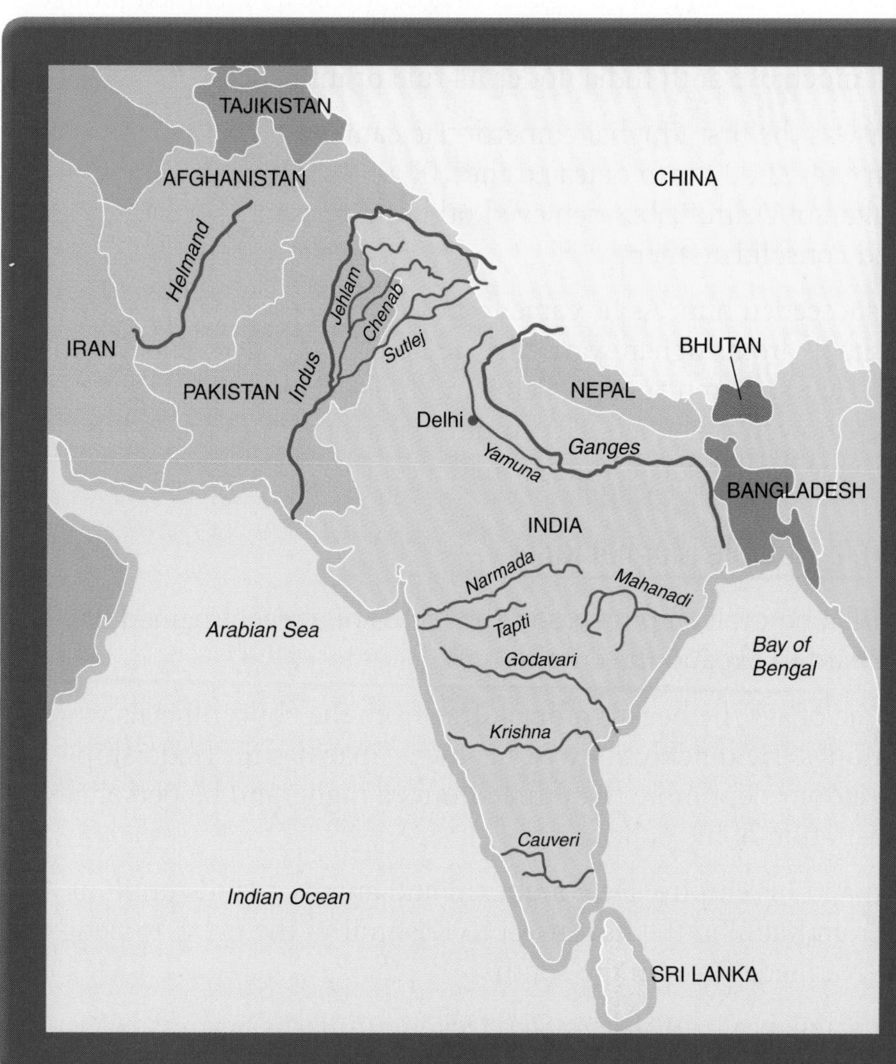

The Indian subcontinent and Afghanistan

People have lived in this part of the world—also called South Asia—for more than 4,000 years. Around 2500 BC people living in the Indus River valley built an urban culture based on farming and trade. After about a thousand years, this group declined. Then Aryan-speaking—early Indo-European—pastoral tribes moved in from the northwest. (Pastoral peoples are those who tend sheep and cattle.) They settled in the Ganges River valley and mixed with the people already there.

The Gupta Dynasty unified northern India during the fourth and fifth centuries. It was a golden age of Hindu culture. But then in the eighth century, Muslim traders began to arrive in Sindh, which is today part of Pakistan.

The Rule of Islamic Mughal Emperors in Northern India

Islam spread across the subcontinent during 700 years. In the tenth and eleventh centuries, Turks and Afghans invaded. They set up sultanates in Delhi, near India's modern-day capital.

Then in the early sixteenth century, the Mughals, whose forebears included Mongols, Turks, Iranians, and Afghans, invaded India. Their dynasty lasted 200 years and eventually included much of South India under its rule or influence.

Zahir-ud-Din Babur was the first Mughal emperor. He came to power when his well-disciplined force of 12,000 men defeated the 100,000 disorganized troops of Ibrahim Lodi, sultan of Delhi. Babur achieved other military gains as well but died before he could consolidate them.

His son Humayun succeeded him. As he came to power, he faced challenges to his rule in Delhi, notably from Afghan warlords. He fled to Persia and hid out there for almost 10 years. He finally returned to Delhi and took control in 1555. Just a year after this victory, however, he died. His empire passed to his 13-year-old son Jalal-ud-Din Akbar, who would rule for nearly half a century.

Akbar (1556–1605), a Notable Mughal Ruler

While Akbar was still a boy, the empire was in the hands of a regent named Bayram Khan, who pushed hard to expand the empire.

But when Akbar came of age, he began to break free from the court officials who had been running things. He quickly showed his own capacities for leadership and judgment. He seldom slept more than three hours a night, and he personally oversaw the administration of his policies.

He continued to expand his empire. He conquered and annexed lands until his territory stretched from Kabul in the northwest to Kashmir in the north to Bengal in the east, and the Narmada River in the south.

Akbar built a walled capital called *Fatehpur Sikri* (Fatehpur means Fortress of Victory) near Agra, starting in 1571. He kept moving his capital, however; whether for lack of water, or because he had to attend to the far reaches of his empire, is unknown.

Historians consider Akbar a good manager. He kept track of a vast territory filled with many different ethnic groups. In 1580 he collected revenue records going back 10 years. He and his aides figured out how good each year's harvest had been, and the related crop prices. He used this information to figure out how much tax the farmers could pay without hardship. He wanted to bring in as much tax revenue as possible, but he knew it wouldn't be wise to demand more than farmers could comfortably pay. He relied on *zamindars*, or local revenue agents, to bring in money and deliver it to the treasury.

He also organized the warrior class, the *mansabars*, into an orderly system of ranks. Different ranks were associated with different numbers of troops, amounts of pay, and so on.

Akbar also possessed good people skills. He encouraged good relations with Hindus, who made up most of the population. He recruited Hindu chiefs for top posts in government. He encouraged intermarriage between the aristocrats—*the nobles or "top class"*—of the Mughals and Hindus. He practiced this policy personally, in fact. Maryam al-Zamani, the mother of his son and heir, Jahangir, was a Hindu *Rajput*—a member of the dominant military caste, or *hereditary social class.*

In 1565 Mughal ruler Jalal-ud-Din Akbar began building the Agra Fort in Agra, India.
Photo by Melanie Stetson Freeman / © 2003 The Christian Science Monitor

Historians consider Akbar a good manager, who kept track of a vast territory filled with many different ethnic groups.

Even before Akbar, Muslim sultans in India offered their Hindu subjects some religious freedom. If they paid a special head tax for "peoples of the book," on the basis of their own Scriptures, Hindus, like Christians and Jews, counted as more than "infidels" and retained the right to practice their own religion.

But Akbar went beyond this. He personally celebrated *Diwali*, the Indian Festival of Lights, and even abolished the tax imposed on non-Muslims. In addition, he came up with his own religion, Din-i-Ilahi (Divine Faith), which incorporated the idea of acceptance of all religions.

He also advanced women's rights. He encouraged widows to remarry, discouraged child marriages, and banned *sati*, the traditional Hindu practice of *suttee*. This practice called for a widow to throw herself onto her husband's funeral pyre to be cremated with him. Akbar also persuaded merchants to set up special market days for women only, so that they could get out and about occasionally. His reign ended with his death in 1605.

Efforts to Encourage Artistry

As the Mughals continued their rule, under Jahangir (1605–27) and later Shah Jahan (1628–1658), they provided political stability and good economic conditions. This gave the arts room to flower. Painting flourished. Writers and artists produced books. Architects designed and erected monumental buildings. Jahangir married a Persian princess whom he renamed Nur Jahan (Light of the World). She became the most powerful person at court, after the emperor himself. She attracted a number of notable Persians—artists, scholars, and military officers—to the imperial court.

Nur Jahan constructed an elaborate family tomb—named Itmad-ud-Daulah—for her father.
Photo by Robert Harbison / © 2002 The Christian Science Monitor

Her husband, Mughal ruler Jahangir, gave the arts room to flower as shown by this colorful inlay at the tomb.

The Taj Mahal is the crowning achievement of Mughal architecture.

Photo by Melanie Stetson Freeman / © 2003 The Christian Science Monitor

One writer called it a "tear on the face of eternity."

Even as far back as Akbar, the imperial courts supported the arts. Although experts believe Akbar couldn't read, he commissioned a book called the *Hamzanama*, which the Smithsonian Institution calls "one of the most unusual and important manuscripts made during the Mughal dynasty (1526–1858). . . ." This book followed the adventures of the Prophet Muhammad's uncle Hamza with text and colorful illustrations. Akbar's successors also paid artists to create illustrated books.

In addition, the Mughal rulers backed painters, who came from around India and Iran. Like the manuscripts, the paintings came in bright colors. Subject matter ranged from plants and animals to court scenes and portraits. The arts came to an abrupt end under Shah Jahan's son, Aurangzeb, who outlawed paintings and music.

The Taj Mahal

If there's one Mughal Dynasty achievement you might have heard of before opening this book, it's probably the Taj Mahal. This beautiful building is the crowning achievement of Mughal architecture. Shah Jahan ordered it built in Agra as a tomb for his beloved wife Mumtaz Mahal. The writer Rabindranath Tagore (1861–1941) called it "a tear on the face of eternity."

The tomb, higher than a modern 20-story building, was the work of 20,000 laborers. They spent 22 years completing it—longer than Shah Jahan and Mumtaz Mahal were married. Craftsmen came from as far away as Turkey to work on the edifice. The marble came from 300 miles away. To get material up to the level of the dome, the engineers built a two-mile ramp.

The white marble takes on different colors at different times of day. Early in the morning, it has a soft, dreamy look. It dazzles white at midday. By moonlight, the dome looks like a giant pearl. No wonder people around the world think of the Taj as the ultimate labor of love.

The Encounter With Europe and the Colonial Period in the Region

The Portuguese explorer Vasco da Gama opened a new chapter in India's history in 1498. That's when he arrived in Calicut, today known as Kozhikode, on India's west coast. The Portuguese were after spices and Christian converts, and they were ready to challenge Arab supremacy in the Indian Ocean. Other Europeans came along soon after.

The Role of the East India Company as the First British Outpost in India in 1619

The British, the Dutch, and the French wanted to trade with India, too. So these countries set up trading companies. The first of these was the British East India Company, set up in 1600 with a royal charter. It was a joint-stock company. People could buy shares of stock in it and became part-owners, as investors do today.

The Dutch founded their trading company in 1602. They had lots of money and government support, and they soon managed to shut the British out of the heart of the trade, the area that is today Indonesia. But both companies managed to set up "trading factories" (really warehouses) on the Indian coast. Indian rulers welcomed the newcomers. They saw an opportunity to give the Portuguese some competition and get better deals for themselves.

A key date was 1619. That's when Jahangir, one of the Mughal emperors you just read about, granted the British permission to trade in his territories. Soon the British had several different hubs of trade in the important goods of the day: spices, cotton, sugar, raw silk, saltpeter (for explosives), calico, and indigo (a dye).

The Effect of British Rule on South Asian Economic and Political Systems

British agents in India learned the local customs and languages, including Persian, the Mughals' official language. Many of the agents lived like Indians and never returned to England. All this gave the British East India Company an edge over its European rivals.

British trading privileges, meanwhile, kept expanding. By the early eighteenth century the Mughal emperor acknowledged that the East India Company helped keep the wheels of local commerce turning. The British trained Indians to serve as soldiers known as *sepoys*. With these troops protecting property, the British were able to treat parts of India as if they were in England. British law prevailed, and the British were able to offer jobs to foreigners and Indians alike.

The British had three main motives in India. They wanted to trade, to maintain their security, and to "uplift" the Indian people. They kept annexing more territory, in some cases by military conquest. This expansion continued into the middle of the nineteenth century.

British attitudes toward India changed over this period. At first, they were great admirers of Indian culture. But eventually they became sharply critical. British intellectuals, including Christian missionaries, felt a need to "civilize" India with Western religion and technology. The missionaries made relatively few converts. The Indians didn't feel they had any need of "civilizing." But the missionaries had an unmistakable impact on the country by setting up schools, orphanages, hospitals, and clinics, as well as publishing organizations.

Hyderabad, India, hums with motorized rickshaws, pedestrians, and cars as well as high-tech industry alongside vast swaths of poverty.
Photo by Andy Nelson / © 2006 The Christian Science Monitor

Three "engines of social improvement" began arriving in India back in the 1850s: railroads, the telegraph, and the uniform postal service.

In 1813 the British Parliament passed the Charter Act, which introduced just and humane laws in India. It also banned a number of traditional practices, such as *suttee*. The expansion of British law in India had other effects as well. It provided professional opportunities for many talented Indians. Education improved, too. English finally replaced Persian as the language of instruction.

The 1850s saw the coming of three "engines of social improvement" to India: railroads, the telegraph, and the uniform postal service. Improved communications helped tie a vast country together. And the railroads moved goods much more easily and faster. But as a means of personal transportation, the railroads tended to divide people by class. The wealthy would travel in separate compartments from the masses.

The Sepoy Rebellion

On 10 May 1857 a group of mostly Muslim soldiers at a British Indian Army base called Meerut mutinied. They didn't want to fight for the British anymore. They marched 50 miles to Delhi, the capital, to offer their services to the Mughal emperor. Soon much of north and central India was caught up in a yearlong insurrection. The Sepoy Rebellion released decades of Indian resentment at the British. The British won in the end, but not before each side had tasted both triumph and humiliation.

This civil war was a major turning point. In May 1858 the British exiled Bahadur Shah II to Burma. That was the end of the Mughal Empire. It was also the end of the East India Company. The British crown abolished it and began to rule India directly.

The History of the Struggle for Independence in South Asia

The Sepoy Rebellion seriously threatened the British raj—*British rule in India*. The conflict goes by many different names, including the Great Mutiny and the Revolt of 1857. But many in South Asia call it India's first war of independence.

A woman shops in Islamabad, the capital of Pakistan.

Photo by Robert Harbison / © 2001 The Christian Science Monitor

India's road to independence would eventually come to a fork: One branch would lead to a new India, and the other to a new state called Pakistan.

Mohandas Gandhi

Gandhi was born in 1869 in Gujarat, a state on the western "arm" of today's India. Schooled in England, he became a lawyer but not a successful one. In 1893 he traveled to South Africa to represent Indian laborers there. He had a year's contract, but ended up staying for more than 20 years. He emerged as a powerful voice against racial discrimination in South Africa, which was at that time under white-minority rule. He returned to India in 1915, unknown but "fired with a religious vision of a new India," as the historian Judith M. Brown has written. His goal was *swaraj*, self-rule. And he would reach it through nonviolence.

Mohandas Gandhi
© Dinodia Images / Alamy Images

Gandhi and Jinnah Lead India and Pakistan to Independence

The decades after the Sepoy Rebellion were a time of growing political awareness for Indians. They began to think of themselves as "a nation," despite their differences in language, culture, and religion. They started expressing their political opinions. And many of them began to worry about their future. Every year, more and more Western-educated Indians prepared to enter the workforce. But they couldn't be sure just what opportunities lay in store for them in British-controlled India.

And so in 1885 a group of 73 Indians met in Bombay (now Mumbai) to launch the Indian National Congress. Its members were mostly Western educated. They were lawyers, journalists, and teachers. The Congress began to meet annually. It passed resolutions on issues of the day, never anything too sensitive, and then forwarded them to the colonial government.

At the start, most members of the Congress were city-dwellers. But they claimed to represent "all India." And by 1900, as more rural members joined the Congress, that claim became more valid. Congress's weakness, though, was that it failed to attract Muslims. By this time, Muslims had come to see that they were underrepresented in government service and less educated than the Hindus. But they weren't sure how best to advance their rights. Many felt they would be better off under British rule than in an independent country dominated by Hindus.

Mohammad Ali Jinnah

Like Gandhi, Jinnah studied law in England. And like Gandhi, he was a member of the Congress—one of relatively few Muslims to join. In 1913 he joined the Muslim League as well. For a time he was a member of both organizations. He gained a reputation as an "ambassador of Hindu-Muslim unity."

But Jinnah disagreed with Gandhi on many points. He didn't think much of nonviolent resistance, for one thing. He believed constitutional change was needed instead.

In 1929 Jinnah drafted a statement of principles that he said would satisfy Muslims' concerns about preserving their rights within a self-governing India. These became known as "the 14 Points of Mr. Jinnah." The Congress and other parties rejected them, however. And after that, Hindu-Muslim political cooperation was rare. The people of India and Pakistan are still paying the price.

India's road to independence would eventually come to a fork. One branch would lead to a new India, and the other to a new state called Pakistan. Mohandas K. Gandhi would lead Hindus along the path to an independent country known as India. And Mohammad Ali Jinnah would be known as the "Father of Pakistan," a Muslim-majority country carved out of British India.

In 1906 a group of anticolonial Muslims formed the All-India Muslim League. At first, it had the same goal as the Congress: self-government for India within the British Empire. But the two organizations couldn't agree on a formula to ensure Muslims' religious, economic, and political rights.

The Role of the Indian National Congress in the Mass Movement Against British Colonial Rule

The Indian National Congress began as a debating society for the educated elite. But starting in 1920 Gandhi transformed it into a mass movement. He reorganized it and opened it to anyone who would pay a token membership fee.

The party used nonviolent resistance and noncooperation as ways to win independence. One of Gandhi's targets was the salt tax. Under British law, salt was a British government monopoly. Everyone had to pay a tax on it. Anyone evading the tax, even if he made his own salt from seawater, was subject to prosecution. Salt is a basic commodity. But it's especially important in a hot climate where people sweat heavily and need salt to maintain their health.

On 12 March 1930 Gandhi started with about 80 people on a 200-plus-mile march to the seacoast town of Dandi where he would lead his followers in making salt from seawater. Many thousands joined him along his journey; they reached Dandi in April.

In early May, police arrested Gandhi and thousands of other protesters around the country. But the pressure from Gandhi's nonviolent movement began to affect the colonial government. In 1931 the British government released Gandhi from custody and allowed Indians to make their own salt.

What Caused the Partition and War Between India and Pakistan

Many Indians served with distinction in the British forces during World War II. But by the war's end, Indians were united in the desire for independence. Britain, exhausted by war, was ready to let them go. British Prime Minister Clement Attlee's government started to prepare in earnest for independence.

How Tensions Between Hindus and Muslims Led to Partition Into Two Separate States

The idea of a Muslim state in British India first surfaced in the 1930s. On 23 March 1940 the Muslim League's Jinnah endorsed the Lahore Resolution. It called for the creation of an independent state in areas where Muslims were a majority.

But the Congress Party and the Muslim League, the two parties who between them spoke for the vast majority of Indians, couldn't come to terms. They disagreed about a Constitution and an interim—*temporary*—government. The Muslims didn't want to be swallowed up in a majority Hindu state. And so in June 1947 the British Government said it would create two states—India and, in Muslim-majority areas, Pakistan.

How India Became a Dominion Within the British Commonwealth

On 14 August 1947 the Dominion of Pakistan won independence. Later it became the Islamic Republic of Pakistan. On 15 August 1947 India became a dominion within the British Commonwealth. Jawaharlal Nehru was India's new prime minister. On 26 January 1950 India put into effect a new constitution that made the country a republic. But India has remained within the British Commonwealth, now known as the Commonwealth of Nations.

This partition of British India into India and Pakistan unleashed untold misery. Millions of Hindu and Muslim refugees fled from one new country to the other. Hundreds of thousands died. Both new states struggled to allocate assets, draw boundaries, and figure out how to share water. All this was on top of the many challenges of national integration that any new country faces.

Conflict in Jammu and Kashmir

Then there was the question of Jammu and Kashmir, often called simply "Kashmir." It was one of India's 562 independent princely states. All of these independent states were under British control. But they weren't organized like the other parts of India. As the British were leaving, they let these states choose whether to join India or Pakistan. A few went to Pakistan; most went to India. India annexed Hyderabad, the largest one, with 14 million people, and Junagadh, with half a million. These moves required "police actions" and promises of favors for the rulers. But those annexations went smoothly—Kashmir was another story.

The state was largely Muslim, but had a Hindu ruler—a *maharajah*. He was uncommitted. After Pakistani troops and armed tribesmen moved into his territory, he signed the Instrument of Accession to India on 27 October 1947. Pakistan challenged the agreement and war broke out.

This first Indo-Pakistani war ended 1 January 1949 with a UN-imposed cease-fire. The cease-fire line reflected the positions of troops on the ground. It has since become a de facto—*accepted as fact even if not based on law*—line of partition between the two parts of Kashmir. One is under Pakistani control and the other, under Indian control. The war cost 1,500 lives on both sides.

War broke out again between the two countries in 1965. Unhappy with the course of negotiations, Pakistan tried to grab control of Kashmir. But India held its ground. This second war lasted less than two months. But it was much deadlier. The two countries had more firepower this time around, and the struggle cost more than 6,000 lives.

In 2002 tensions over Kashmir peaked again. By that time, both countries had acquired nuclear weapons. The Kashmir issue remains unresolved at this writing. Several Pakistani groups have committed acts of terrorism in attempts to force the issue and drive the Indians out.

India and Its Hindu Majority

Hindus make up more than 80 percent of India's 1.14 billion people. Its Muslim population is only 12.4 percent. But in such a big country, that 12.4 percent is one of the largest Muslim populations in the world. Hindu-Muslim strife has been a recurring theme in Indian history. A Hindu radical murdered Gandhi in New Delhi less than a year after Indian independence. Hindus often criticized Gandhi for being too conciliatory to Muslims.

India's first prime minister, Jawaharlal Nehru, once said, "The danger to India, mark you, is not communism. It is Hindu right-wing communalism." In other words, Nehru was warning his country against a protective, "my tribe first" attitude.

Recent years have seen a resurgence of Hindu terrorism against Muslims and also Christians, who make up about 2 percent of India's population. In 2002 as many as 2,000 people died and another 150,000 were displaced from their homes during rioting in Gujarat that broke out between Hindus and Muslims after Muslims burned 58 Hindu pilgrims alive in a train in Godhra, India.

Pakistan and Its Muslim Majority

Pakistan's Muslims are mostly Sunni, but its large Shia minority faces attacks, perhaps aided by national security forces. In February 2009, for instance, a suicide bomb attack on the funeral of a Shia leader killed 28 and triggered rioting.

Many observers believe Pakistan has been behind attacks on India and Hindus generally. The November 2008 attacks on Mumbai, India, for instance, which lasted two and a half days and left 163 dead, prompted the Indian foreign minister to describe Pakistan as "the epicenter of terror attacks against India."

In addition, Pakistan fostered the development of the Afghan fundamentalist militia. It also in effect banned the Ahmadi sect in 1984. Its members consider themselves Muslims but Pakistani law does not, leading to serious acts of persecution.

Pakistanis tend to their daily errands near a bus stop in Islamabad.

Photo by Robert Harbison / © 2001 The Christian Science Monitor

The partition of British India into India and Pakistan unleashed untold misery as millions of Hindu and Muslim refugees fled from one new country to the other.

The Division of Pakistan

At independence, Pakistan was made up of two pieces of land—so-called West Pakistan and East Pakistan. Geographically, India stood between them. Almost from the start, Pakistan's two "wings" had trouble getting along. After all, they were more than 1,000 miles apart. West Pakistan dominated the central government. True, the two parts of the country were both largely Muslim. But they spoke different languages and came from different ethnic groups, too.

A political party known as the Awami League formed to promote Bengali interests. (The Bengalis lived in East Pakistan.) In the 1970–71 national elections, the league won almost all the East Pakistani seats. This led to negotiations to redistribute power between the central government and the provinces. These talks soon broke down, however.

That led to civil disobedience in the East, and then a crackdown by the Pakistani Army. Many Bengali leaders fled to India. There they set up a provisional government while fighting continued. In November, India entered the war on the East Pakistani side. On 16 December 1971 Pakistani forces gave up. The independent state of Bangladesh—which means "Bengal country"—was born.

Democracy has run smoothly in neither Pakistan nor Bangladesh. Both countries have known military rule, political murder, and, more recently, Islamist extremism.

How Muslim-Hindu Strife Affects the Politics and Economics of South Asia

The long-standing hostility between Muslims and Hindus in South Asia moved Britain to split India into two states once they granted the people their independence.

That said, the lines that a British civil servant named Sir Cyril Radcliffe drew on the map of India—during his one visit to the country—only made things worse. These borders have led to three wars so far. And Kashmir remains one of the flash points where a nuclear war could start.

The Impact of Cultural Identities on South Asian Economics

As a social hierarchy that limits people's economic potential, there is nothing else on earth quite like India's caste system. People's caste status, which they are born into, affects their economic status. Many castes are associated with occupations, from the high-ranking Brahmans to the mid-ranking farmers and skilled tradespeople down to the low-ranking "untouchables." This last group does the jobs that put them in touch with death and decay, so to speak. They clean latrines because India largely lacks modern sanitation. They are also leatherworkers, butchers, and even launderers. High-caste people, unsurprisingly, tend to be well off. Lower-caste people tend to live in poverty and at a social disadvantage.

Men separate rice from stems with sifters in India.
Photo by Andy Nelson / © 2006 The Christian Science Monitor

Many castes in India are associated with occupations, from the high-ranking Brahmans to the mid-ranking farmers and skilled tradespeople down to the low-ranking "untouchables."

Efforts to help the lower castes, especially the "untouchables," go back to Gandhi's day. He called them *"Harijan,"* children of light. Today they are known as *dalits* (dah-LEETS). Much remains to be done to bring them up the economic ladder. But, as a US government report puts it, "a quiet social transformation in this area" has begun.

The Impact of Caste and Religion on South Asian Politics

Hindu-Muslim tensions worsened during the 1990s. This likely had less to do with ancient hatreds and religious beliefs than with economic upheaval. As more people left the farm for work in the cities, they found themselves competing for jobs and places to live. Even high-caste Hindus often had to do work they considered beneath them. Hindu anger and frustration often turned against successful Muslim merchants. It also turned against those returning from well-paying jobs in the oil-rich Persian Gulf states. These workers tended to be Muslim. All these developments led some Hindus, especially those of the higher castes, to join militant or even terrorist groups.

Politicians have helped increase Hindu-Muslim tensions as well. Some observers point to Shah Bano's case in 1985. She was a 73-year-old Muslim who sought alimony after her husband divorced her according to Muslim law after 43 years of marriage. India is a secular state. But Shah Bano's case brought the question of the state and religion to the top of the political agenda. When the Supreme Court awarded her alimony, many Muslims were outraged. Sharia, Islamic law, does not allow for alimony in case of divorce, they insisted. They felt the court's ruling disrespected Islam.

At this point, Prime Minister Rajiv Gandhi apparently felt he was in danger of losing support from a key voting bloc. So he pushed through legislation that moved Muslim divorce cases from India's civil law to the jurisdiction of Islamic sharia courts. This, in turn, enraged many Hindus, many of whom submit to orders from civil court judges to pay alimony to wives they divorce.

Political and Economic Growth in India and Pakistan Since Independence

India

In India, Congress, the organization that won independence from Britain, continues to rule today. A secular, left-of-center party, Congress at this writing leads a coalition in the Lok Sabha, the lower house of Parliament. Its support declined for several years, during which other parties sometimes formed the government. But it bounced back in the 2004 elections after reaching out to many poor, rural, and Muslim voters.

India's economy, the world's 12th largest as of the end of 2007, has a gross domestic product of more than $1 trillion. Its annual growth, while not as strong as China's, has still been more than 9 percent in recent years. Hundreds of millions of Indians live on $2 per day or less. But the country also has a growing middle class. It's expected to number 500 million by 2025.

The downside is that India has been slow to move to free-market reforms. In other words, government imposed many regulations on business. That has changed in recent years. But experts see India still held back by lack of good infrastructure—*roads, rail lines, power lines, communications cables, and water and sewer lines*. Other problems include bureaucracy, corruption, and too-rigid controls on foreign investment. Outside experts see Indian labor regulations as inflexible, too. India also has high fiscal deficits. In other words, its government spends more than it collects in taxes.

Pakistan

Pakistan has spent much of its history under military rule. Most of the exceptions have been periods dominated by the Bhutto family. Zulfikar Ali Bhutto served as prime minister during the 1970s but was eventually hanged on charges of conspiracy to murder. His daughter Benazir Bhutto was prime minister at different times during the 1980s and 1990s. She was assassinated in 2007 shortly after her return from a period of exile. Her political opponent Muhammad Nawaz Sharif has also been prime minister. He was in office in 1999 when General Pervez Musharraf took over in a bloodless coup.

After the 9/11 terror attacks, Musharraf allied Pakistan with the United States in its global war on terror. Pakistan's location, next to Afghanistan, which had harbored al-Qaeda, has made Pakistan a frontline state in the fight against terrorism. Musharraf has since been replaced as president of Pakistan by Asif Ali Zardari, Benazir Bhutto's widower.

Pakistan's economic story is more troubled than India's. Its population and economy are both about one-seventh that of its larger neighbor. Its exports are largely agricultural products and textiles. International sanctions slapped on Pakistan after its first nuclear test in 1998 limited economic growth. In more recent years, though, cooperation with the United States has won it international aid.

A large section of Pakistan along the border with Afghanistan makes up the "Federally Administered Tribal Areas." The Pakistani government exercises control over these economically undeveloped areas in name only. Their residents are the same Pashtun tribesmen who live on the other side of the border in Afghanistan. From this region, where some believe al-Qaeda's Osama bin Laden is hiding, emanates much of the terrorism that bedevils both nations.

Pakistan is a good example of how political instability interferes with economic development—which then fosters more political instability.

Which Groups Have Struggled for Control in Afghanistan and Why

Afghanistan is a good place to remember why people say "geography is destiny." A look at the map will give you some clues about why Afghanistan has been hard to control. It is mountainous and landlocked, with few roads even today.

Afghanistan isn't just a political nowheresville, though. True, much of its terrain is of the type best traveled on horseback. And yet Afghanistan is on the historic trade and invasion routes from Central Asia into South and Southwest Asia. It's been an important piece of real estate for a long time.

Children watch goats pass their walled home compound in Marouf, Afghanistan, a village near the border with Pakistan.

Photo by Robert Harbison / © 2001 The Christian Science Monitor

Afghanistan is on the historic trade and invasion routes from Central Asia into South and Southwest Asia.

Afghanistan as a Crossroads Over the Centuries

Afghanistan has been known as the crossroads of Central Asia. It was under Persian rule when Alexander the Great arrived in 328 BC to set up a Hellenistic (Greek) state. Scythians, White Huns, and Turks invaded over the next few centuries. In the seventh century, the Arabs arrived and brought Islam. More invaders and conquerors came and went, including Genghis Khan and Tamerlane, forebear of the Mughals.

But the founder of today's Afghanistan was Ahmad Shah Durrani. A tribal council elected him king in 1747. He managed to weld a group of disparate provinces and fiefdoms into one country.

During the nineteenth century, as the British were expanding their empire in the Indian subcontinent, they worried about czarist Russian advances in Central Asia and Persia. You might say the two empires "met in the middle," and that middle was Afghanistan.

The British fought two wars there. In the first Anglo-Afghan war, in 1839, they lost an army. After the second, Amir Abdur Rahman came to the Afghan throne. He reigned from 1880 to 1901, and during that time, the British and the Russians managed to agree on the boundaries of modern Afghanistan. The British didn't exactly control Afghanistan at this point, but they controlled Kabul's foreign affairs. That is, they did until 1919 when they signed this authority away in the Treaty of Rawalpindi.

During much of the twentieth century, Afghanistan was a constitutional monarchy. It became less isolated. Its rulers experimented with social reforms such as education for women. (This didn't sit well with tribal leaders.) And while the king was focused on other things, extreme political parties developed. One was a Communist Party allied with the Soviet Union.

In 1973 Sardar Mohammad Daoud, the king's cousin and prime minister, staged a coup. He set himself up as president and prime minister of a reformist republic. That didn't go well, and in April 1978 the Communists staged a bloody coup. Opposition to their brutal rule emerged almost at once. The Communists' Marxist "reforms" ran counter to Afghan traditions.

More coups and rebellions followed, and then on Christmas Eve 1979, Soviet aircraft started delivering troops to Kabul to "support" the regime of Afghan leader Babrak Karmal. Despite their 120,000 troops, however, the Soviets couldn't control much of the country beyond Kabul. Afghan freedom fighters (*mujahideen*) kept the Soviets confined largely to the capital. The resistance grew, in part with covert financial support from the United States.

It was a long, hard slog for the Russians, and they never succeeded in winning over the Afghan people. Moreover, the occupation was souring Soviet relations in much of the West as well as the Islamic world.

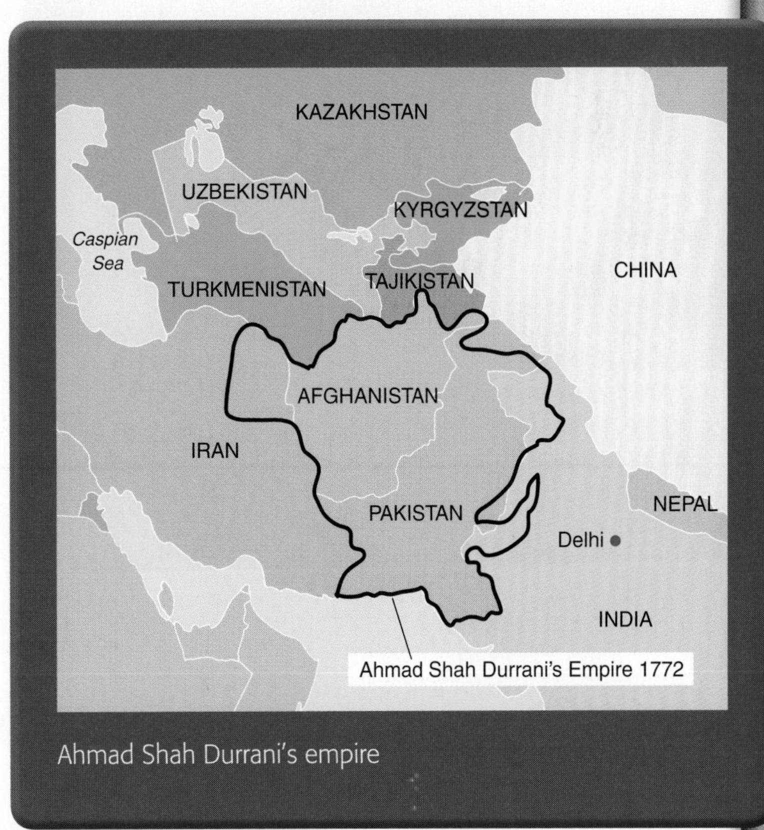

Ahmad Shah Durrani's empire

The Russians finally signed an accord in Geneva that committed them to leave Afghanistan in 1989. But significantly, the *mujahideen* were not party to the deal. This meant that the civil war going on in Afghanistan would not end just because the Soviets were pulling out. This imperfect solution to one problem in Afghanistan sowed the seeds of another.

Mud-brick homes look out over one of the busiest squares in Kabul, Afghanistan.
Photo by Robert Harbison / © 2002 The Christian Science Monitor
Afghanistan is an Islamic country—80 percent of Afghans are Sunni Muslims.

Afghanistan's Ethnic Groups

The same factors that have made Afghanistan hard to govern also make it a hard place to take a census. Pashtuns are the largest ethnic group there. They make up 38 percent to 44 percent of the population. The estimate for Tajiks, the second-largest group, is 25 percent. Next come Hazaras, about 10 percent, and Uzbeks, 6 percent to 8 percent. A number of other small groups make up the rest of the population.

Dari (Afghan Farsi, or Persian) and Pashto are the official languages. A third of Afghans speak Dari as a first language, and it's a common language for most of the country. Pashto is spoken in the east and south. People in the north speak Tajik and Turkic languages. More than 70 smaller groups have their own languages as well.

Afghanistan is an Islamic country—80 percent of Afghans are Sunni, and the rest, primarily the Hazara, are mostly Shia.

Culture and Politics Until the Taliban Era

Experts describe Afghanistan's culture as an ethnic mosaic. But it's a mosaic in which the tiles tend to overlap with one another. There isn't a homogeneous national culture. Most of Afghanistan's ethnic groups have come from someplace else—the legacy of centuries of invasion. And few of its groups are racially homogeneous. The overlapping between groups has only increased as roads have improved (somewhat) and people have had more opportunity for schooling.

Ethnic differences have played a role in Afghan politics, which have traditionally favored the Pashtuns. But interethnic tensions tend to be based on some particular issue. If there's a grievance, there's a reason for it, in other words. Afghans tend not to distrust members of another group just because they're "different," for instance.

Afghan ethnicities became more apparent during the Soviet-Afghan war. The appeal of the *mujahideen* related to Afghan traditions of religion, family, tribe, and ethnic group. It was a stark contrast with the culture of the atheist-Communist Soviet invaders, who seemed so foreign.

Perhaps the most important legacy of the many invasions was Islam. The Arabs brought it to Afghanistan as part of their seventh-century sweep across Africa and Asia. During the decade of Soviet domination, Islam became important not just as a religion but as a form of cultural expression. It was a way for Afghans to push back against the Soviets.

The Taliban Era

The withdrawal of Soviet forces from Afghanistan in 1989 left a vacuum. The Taliban arose to fill it. The **Taliban** are *an Islamic fundamentalist militia that governed Afghanistan for several years*. The name comes from *talib*, an Arabic word meaning "student." Many of them had studied in **madrassas**—*religious schools*—in Pakistan. They captured Kandahar from a local warlord in 1994. Two years later they had control of Kabul, the capital. By the end of 1998 they occupied about 90 percent of the country.

The Taliban introduced an extremely strict version of Islam. It was based on the tribal code of their rural Pashtun stomping ground. The Taliban violated the human rights of women and girls. They also committed atrocities against minority groups, such as the Hazaras. And from the mid-1990s they sheltered 9/11 mastermind Osama bin Laden and provided al-Qaeda a base of operations for terrorism. Bin Laden, as you read in Chapter 1, Lesson 4, was a Saudi national who fought the Soviets as part of the Afghan resistance. In exchange for being left alone, he gave the Taliban financial and political support.

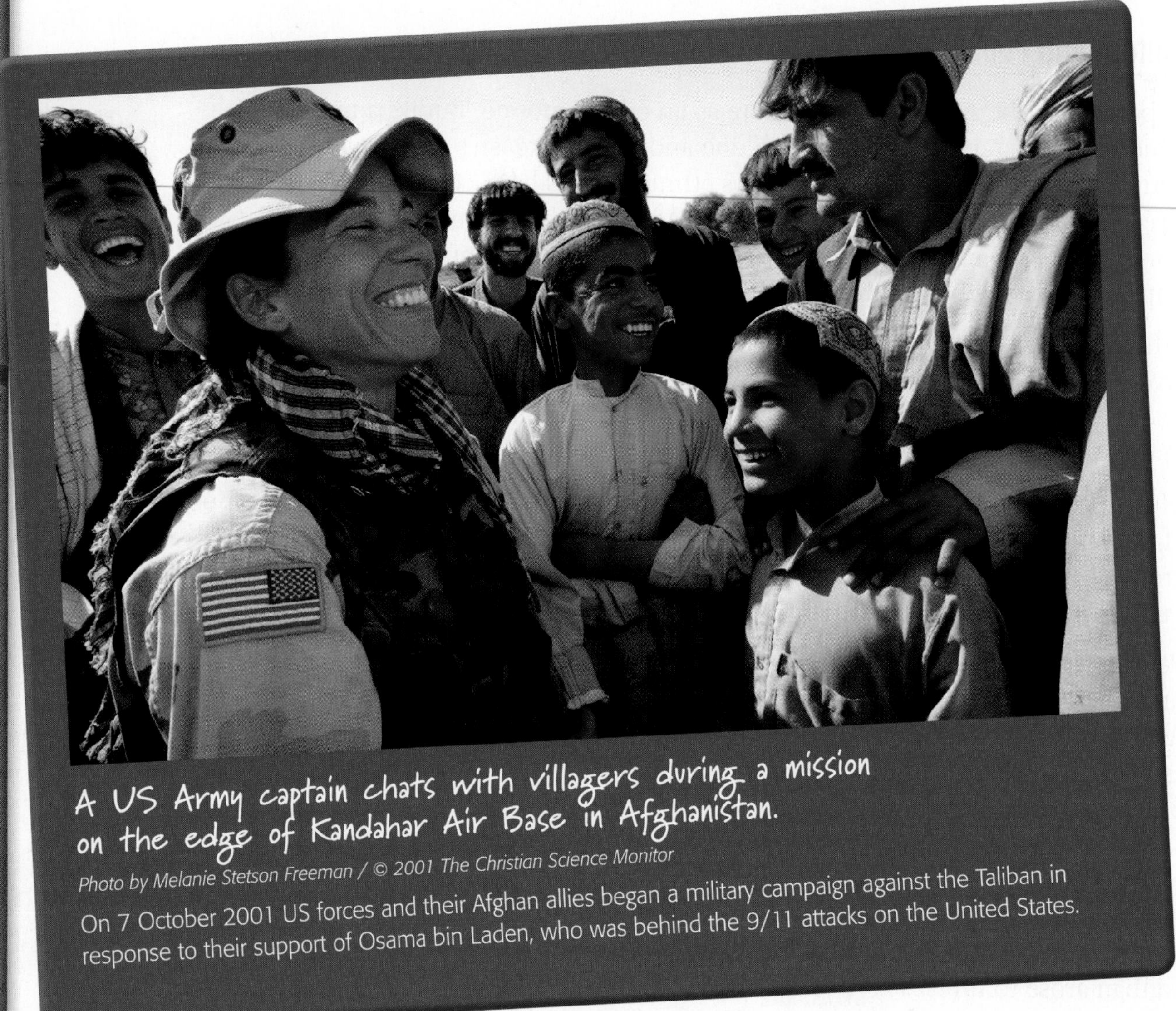

A US Army captain chats with villagers during a mission on the edge of Kandahar Air Base in Afghanistan.

Photo by Melanie Stetson Freeman / © 2001 The Christian Science Monitor

On 7 October 2001 US forces and their Afghan allies began a military campaign against the Taliban in response to their support of Osama bin Laden, who was behind the 9/11 attacks on the United States.

During this time, al-Qaeda is believed to have bombed two US embassies in Africa in 1998 and the USS *Cole* in 2000. And on 11 September 2001 it launched the attacks on the World Trade Center and the Pentagon.

Afterward, the United States demanded the Taliban hand over Bin Laden. But they refused—repeatedly. And so on 7 October 2001 US forces and their Afghan allies began a military campaign against the Taliban. The Taliban fell apart quickly. Kabul was in US hands by 13 November.

But the Taliban did not go away. The new Afghan government under President Hamid Karzai has struggled in its efforts to control the country, end corruption, and develop the economy. The Taliban have made a comeback—not surprisingly, in ethnically Pashtun areas. The resulting low-level conflict continues to challenge the United States and its NATO allies in their support of the government in Kabul.

Lesson 3 Review

Using complete sentences, answer the following questions on a sheet of paper.

1. Who were the forebears of the Mughals?
2. What is the Taj Mahal and why is it important?
3. What was the British East India Company?
4. What was the Sepoy Rebellion?
5. Who was Mohandas K. Gandhi?
6. Who was Mohammad Ali Jinnah?
7. What was the partition of British India?
8. What is the significance of Kashmir?
9. Who are India's "untouchables"? What is a better name for them today?
10. Identify the Bhutto family.
11. Which European power left Afghanistan in defeat in 1839? In 1989?
12. Who are the Taliban and why did the United States attack them?

Applying Your Learning

13. Identify something in what you have read about Afghanistan that you think might apply to what's happening there now. Why do you think it's relevant?

LESSON 4 Environmental and Social Issues in Asia

Quick Write

What lesson or lessons can you draw from China's challenge with air quality during the 2008 Olympics?

Learn About

- the impacts of industrialization and pollution in China and India
- the interactions between Asia's rich cities and its poor rural areas
- the role of women in India, Pakistan, and Afghanistan
- China's one-child policy
- the challenges of human trafficking and sex tourism in Asia

Three days before the start of the Beijing Olympics in August 2008, a gray-yellow haze hung over the city. An International Olympic Committee senior official said it was no problem; it was just "mist." But even local people were worried. Pictures of American athletes wearing face masks to protect against air pollution started to appear on television and in newspapers. Some officials wondered whether they would have to move events like the marathon out of Beijing to where the air would be cleaner.

It would be hard to overestimate the importance to Beijing of having the Olympics go smoothly. An air-quality crisis would be a great blow to national prestige. Fortunately, it didn't happen. The air cleared enough that the marathon could be run outdoors.

Six months later, the United Nations Environment Program gave the Beijing Olympics a good report card. Beijing had met if not exceeded its environmental goals for the Games. The Chinese government could have done more, the agency stressed. But overall the Beijing Games "raised the environmental bar."

The Impacts of Industrialization and Pollution in China and India

On 3 December 1984 a poisonous gas leaked from a pesticide plant in Bhopal, India. Half a million people were exposed, the government reported later. At least 3,800 people died at once. Up to 20,000 are thought to have later died prematurely because of their exposure.

Observers have called it the worst industrial accident in history. The company involved—the Indian subsidiary of US-based chemical giant Union Carbide—initially tried to duck responsibility. Eventually it came to terms with the Indian government and paid some compensation.

The disaster showed the need for safety standards with real "teeth." At the time of the accident, the plant had become unprofitable. Its owners were trying to sell it. What's more, the plant had safety problems. Local officials knew about them. But they were afraid to push the company to correct them. They didn't want their city to lose a major employer.

In the years since, India has industrialized rapidly. To industrialize means *to develop and build a modern manufacturing base (factories) in a country or region*. Safety practices have improved somewhat. But major dangers remain. Twenty years after the accident, a US government publication reported, "Widespread environmental degradation with significant adverse human health consequences continues to occur throughout India."

Vocabulary

- industrialize
- urbanization
- affirmative action
- purdah
- contraceptives
- human trafficking
- defraud

This widow from Bhopal, India, lost her husband, two daughters, and a son in the 1984 Union Carbide poisonous gas leak.
Photo by Scott Baldauf / © 2004 The Christian Science Monitor

The disaster that killed thousands showed the need for safety standards with real "teeth."

If Bhopal represents developing Asia's disastrous recent past, the Three Gorges Dam represents its controversial imminent future. People call it the biggest construction project in China since the Great Wall. It will create clean hydroelectric power, and that's a good thing. China currently gets much of its electricity from dirty coal-fired power plants. The dam will create a reservoir big enough for ocean-going ships. That will open the area to new development. And finally, the dam will tame the Yangtze River. Its floods have taken a million human lives over the past century.

It all sounds pretty good, doesn't it? Ah, not so fast, critics say. They argue that officials have ignored the river's ecology. They worry that, without water treatment, the reservoir will be a catch basin for all sorts of pollution. They aren't sure the power plant will produce as much electricity as its builders claim. And some even question the quality of the concrete the builders used.

Drill-rig workers take a break from the Three Gorges Dam Project along the Yangtze River in Hubei Province, China.

Photo by Robert Harbison / © 1994 The Christian Science Monitor

People call the controversial dam the biggest construction project in China since the Great Wall.

How China and India Have Attracted Global Manufacturing Facilities

In many respects, China has become the world's factory. It makes half the world's cameras. It turns out 30 percent of the world's suitcases, and one-quarter of its washing machines. Chinese factories crank out everything from computers and pharmaceuticals to children's toys. Because of China's large pool of low-cost labor and its favorable trade regulations, foreign companies have invested more than half a trillion dollars in China over the past 20 years. China is on track to replace the United States as the world's leading manufacturing nation.

If China has become the world's factory, India has become its call center. Since opening its markets in 1991, India has benefited from having many well-educated English speakers willing to work for relatively low wages. Many Western companies, especially in technology and software, have set up customer-service operations in India. They like the low cost of doing business there, and the high level of talent.

Pollution leaves a haze over Guangzhou, China.
Photo by Robert Harbison / © 1994 The Christian Science Monitor

Economic growth has come at a great cost to China's natural environment.

Rapid Industrialization, Lax Regulation, and Pollution

The Bhopal disaster may be the extreme example of industrialization without adequate safety and environmental regulation. The plant was in some ways fairly advanced technically. But it wasn't run in accord with the standards in place at a West Virginia plant owned by the same company.

China, in particular among developing countries, has grown so fast in recent years that it has lifted many of its people out of poverty. But growth has come at a great cost to China's natural environment and its resource base. Experts say this will have long-term consequences for both the health of the Chinese people and their continuing economic growth.

Women wash clothes in a canal in India, which faces what the World Bank calls "a turbulent water future."
Photo by Andy Nelson / © 2006 The Christian Science Monitor

For instance, the country's water infrastructure is crumbling and urgently needs replacing.

China has introduced a great many environmental laws in recent years. The real problem, some say, is the lack of enforcement and of meaningful penalties for offenders. Businesses often find it easier to pay fines than to obey the law.

The World Bank—which loans money to developing countries—is working with the Chinese to help them understand environmental health risks and the links between poverty and environment. The bank is also helping China implement pollution control. One of the challenges is that China's economy is simply growing so fast that it has been hard to balance the need to cut emissions against the need to keep making more goods, right away.

The fastest "urban growth" in China now is in places you would probably think of as small towns, with 5,000 to 10,000 people. These communities don't monitor their own pollution very well. And their development plans don't include much provision for controlling it, either.

Problems Tied to Polluted Water Supplies in China and India

Industrialization and rapid economic growth are also causing water problems in China. According to the World Bank, China doesn't have enough water, and what it has isn't clean enough.

The bank has helped China build a number of big water projects: sewerage, drainage, and wastewater treatment. Still, some 320 million Chinese lack access to clean drinking water. And more than 70 percent of China's lakes and rivers are polluted. The World Health Organization estimates that diseases caused by pollution kill nearly 100,000 people in China annually.

India also faces what the World Bank calls "a turbulent water future." Since independence, India has invested heavily in water infrastructure. The results have been "spectacular," according to the bank. Many Indians now have enough to eat and have risen out of poverty. But much of that infrastructure is now crumbling and urgently needs replacing.

Another problem in India is the lack of a system for sharing water rights across state lines. This means that it's not clear who gets how much of a given river's water. India is facing water shortages severe enough to lead to conflict.

And finally, India lacks sanitation. The country has a blossoming middle class. But three-quarters of the population lack access to toilets. Many cities and towns simply dump untreated sewage into their rivers. The results are easy to imagine. Diseases linked to poor sanitation kill nearly 600,000 children in India every year.

The sanitation problem has another aspect: jobs. India has many low-caste workers known as scavengers. Every day, all over the country, they carry human waste away in buckets from the homes of the wealthy. Reformers want to introduce inexpensive toilets. But that would put the scavengers out of work. So reformers also want to train the scavengers for more productive careers.

The Interactions Between Asia's Rich Cities and Its Poor Rural Areas

One of the great trends around the world is urbanization—*the movement of population from rural areas into cities*. People are leaving farms to seek work in urban areas. China, for instance, had 430 million people in its cities in 2001. Estimates are that by 2015, 850 million Chinese will live there. The number of cities themselves is increasing, too. In 2001 China had 630 cities with more than 100,000 people in each. By 2015, experts predict, it will have more than 1,000 cities that size.

In a scene typical of a rural Chinese village, people gather in the street—even in winter—to socialize.
Photo by Robert Harbison / © 1994 The Christian Science Monitor

The fastest "urban growth" in China now is in towns of 5,000 to 10,000 people.

The World's Most Populous Metropolitan Areas

Rank	Metropolitan area	Country	Population
1	Tokyo	Japan	32,450,000
2	Seoul	South Korea	20,550,000
3	Mexico City	Mexico	20,450,000
4	New York City	United States	19,750,000
5	Mumbai	India	19,200,000
6	Jakarta	Indonesia	18,900,000
7	São Paolo	Brazil	18,850,000
8	Delhi	India	18,600,000
9	Osaka–Kobe–Kyoto	Japan	17,375,000
10	Shanghai	People's Republic of China	16,650,000
11	Metro Manila	Philippines	16,300,000
12	Hong Kong–Shenzhen	People's Republic of China	15,800,000
13	Los Angeles	United States	15,250,000
14	Calcutta	India	15,100,000
15	Moscow	Russia	15,000,000
16	Cairo	Egypt	14,450,000
17	Buenos Aires	Argentina	13,170,000
18	London	United Kingdom	12,875,000
19	Beijing	People's Republic of China	12,500,000
20	Karachi	Pakistan	11,800,000

Of the world's 20 most populous metropolitan areas in 2003, 12 were in Asia.

Cities offer people opportunity to do work that creates more value than they could simply working the land. They can make more money in town. That's the "pull" of cities. Meanwhile, the use of tractors and other farm machinery—along with improved seeds, fertilizers, and pesticides—means that it takes fewer farmers to feed people than it used to. That's the "push" from the countryside.

When people go to the big cities, they don't necessarily forget where they came from. The connections between the cities and the rural areas are still important. At a personal level, people keep in touch with their home villages and their relatives who still live there. The bigger picture is that the cities rely on the countryside to supply food.

The Difficulty of Securing Basic Resources in Rural Asia

Asia has made great economic strides over the past few decades. The region has benefited from the Green Revolution, a movement to improve food yields beginning in the 1960s. Millions of people in Asia are eating better than they used to. The number of calories the average person ate every day rose 20 percent between 1970 and 1995, for instance. Between 1975 and 1995 the share of all Asians living in poverty fell from 1 in 2 to only 1 in 4. During that same period, the share of rural Asians living in poverty fell from 1 in 2 to 1 in 3.

But a report in 2001 by the International Food Policy Research Institute (IFPRI) called Asia's progress an "unfinished revolution." It found that 670 million rural Asians still live in poverty. They tend to be less healthy and less educated than their counterparts in the cities. Most of these rural people rely, directly or indirectly, on farming, forestry, or fishing for their living. This puts great pressure on natural resources. Too many farmers planting too many crops may "exhaust" farmland. Too many woodcutters may chop down all the trees. Fish may disappear if too many fishermen go after them. This isn't just bad for the soil, the trees, and the fish, but for the people as well. Degradation of the natural environment may lead to social conflict, experts warn.

A man collects water from a local pond in India.

Photo by Mark Sappenfield / © 2007 The Christian Science Monitor

Most rural Asians rely on farming, forestry, or fishing for their living.

Another issue is the shift to the market economy. This is one in which people work for money and use it to buy what they need. In rural areas, many people raise their own food by planting gardens and small farm plots and by tending livestock. People who don't earn much in the cash economy need this to survive. Experts don't want to see rural people give up their gardens.

fastFACT

The Green Revolution that took place during the 1960s and '70s was a significant increase in agricultural productivity. It came about after experts brought in new high-yield grains, showed farmers how to use pesticides, and taught them better management techniques.

Water scarcity is another issue the IFPRI report touched on. It called water scarcity and quality "probably the most severe challenges facing developing Asia." They will reach crisis levels by 2020, the report said. Demand for water is growing from agriculture, industry, and households. But the potential for expanding the water supply is diminishing. And that could spell trouble.

Social and Economic Problems Tied to India's Caste System

In this lesson, you have read about a low-status group, the scavengers, stuck doing some very dirty work. Their plight shows how the caste system overshadows India's society and economy. A job associated with low-caste workers has hindered Indians from getting modern sanitation. The system doesn't hurt just the people at the bottom. It hurts everyone.

It is officially illegal in India to discriminate against someone based on caste. But such discrimination does take place, and it is accepted. It's prevalent, in fact, especially in the countryside. Sometimes the resistance to change results in violence.

The caste system has four major categories:

- Priests (*Brahmin*)
- Warriors (*Kshatriya*)
- Traders/artisans (*Vaishya*)
- Farmers/laborers (*Shudra*).

Tribal people and the dalits, or "untouchables," are a fifth broad category. In addition to these, there are thousands of *jatis*. These are local groups, based on occupations. Their members intermarry. All these groups are organized in a rank order in accord with complex ideas of purity and pollution.

However, the government has worked hard to make caste status less important. In rural areas, especially, it's tried to make information, communication, transport, and credit more available. This has helped soften the harshest aspects of the caste system. The government has also introduced forms of affirmative action—*a government policy that enforces hiring and other goals to combat discrimination*—and other social policies. And in India's bustling, prosperous cities, caste becomes much less visible.

Neon signs in Chinese and English hang along a busy street in Hong Kong, China.
Photo by Melanie Stetson Freeman / © 1996 The Christian Science Monitor

Cities draw more investment than rural areas because investors like to put money into places where people are better educated.

The Widening Gap Between Urban Wealth and Rural Poverty in Asia

As Asia's economies have boomed in recent years, gaps between rich and poor have widened sharply. The rich people tend to be in the cities, and the poor are out in the country. This is especially true in China, but also in India, Cambodia, and Sri Lanka.

According to the Asian Development Bank, the problem is that the cities draw more investment than rural areas. Investors like to put money into places where people are better educated. On the other hand, government policies often keep private investors from putting money into rural Asia, which needs so much new infrastructure.

It's not unusual for growing economies to have differences in incomes between the rich and the poor. But extreme differences are not healthy, experts say. They can weaken national unity and lead to civil unrest.

Growth in China and India's big cities has already caused problems. Economic booms have even more people moving to cities that are already overcrowded. Meanwhile, more isolated areas lack foreign investment and other opportunities. In a 2007 report, the Asian Development Bank called for efforts to provide better nutrition, education, and health care in rural Asia.

The Role of Women in India, Pakistan, and Afghanistan

You can tell a lot about a society by looking at the roles women fill. India and Pakistan have both had women leaders. Indira Gandhi in India and Benazir Bhutto in Pakistan each followed in her father's footsteps to go into politics. Each eventually became her country's prime minister. In 2007 Indians elected Pratibha Patil as their first female president. It's a largely ceremonial post—the prime minister has the real power in India. But it's still a significant position.

Even in Afghanistan, the picture for women is slightly improved. At different times, it has allowed women to go without the traditional Muslim veil and opened some coeducational schools. And the 2004 Constitution reserved 25 percent of seats in the parliament's lower house for women.

A woman steps out in public at a local market in Kabul, Afghanistan, with her face uncovered, a punishable offense during the Taliban's rule.
Photo by Robert Harbison / © 2002 The Christian Science Monitor

Once the United States drove the Taliban out of power in the weeks after 9/11, the picture for women in Afghanistan was slightly improved.

Despite such gains, however, all three of these countries severely limit women's roles in other ways. All three practice some form of purdah, at least in some places. Literally a "curtain," purdah is *the veiling and seclusion of married women*. Those who follow this practice believe that it protects family honor. Allowing women to leave home—to go to a job or even to go out shopping—could endanger the family honor, in this tradition. Purdah is certainly not universal. But it is widespread across all these countries.

India

Purdah is particularly common in northern and central India, among both Hindu and Muslim women. The rules differ between the two communities. But in general purdah is part of a hierarchical society with elaborate rules of deference, or submission. Older people have authority over younger ones and men over women.

The US State Department, in a recent Human Rights Report, found several gross violations of women's human rights in India. It labeled these violations as "serious problems." They are:

- ***Domestic violence***: This is a broad term for assaults and other physical attacks within the home. It generally refers to actions by men who beat up their wives and, less often, to actions by women.
- ***Dowry deaths***: A common practice in many cultures over the centuries has been for a woman's parents to provide a dowry—property or an amount of money—to her bridegroom at their marriage. But it is a tradition open to abuse. Since 1961 it has been illegal in India for a man to demand a dowry. The practice continues, however. Many men agree to a "bride price" and then demand more money. In extreme cases, a man kills his wife if her family can't bring him enough. Official statistics show that husbands and in-laws killed nearly 7,000 women in 2001 over inadequate dowries.

One writer describes purdah in India this way: "The importance of purdah is not limited to family life; rather, these practices all involve restrictions on female activity and access to power and the control of vital resources in a male-dominated society. Restriction and restraint for women in virtually every aspect of life are the basic essentials of purdah."

- ***Honor crimes***: This refers to cases when a father, brother, or husband kills his daughter, sister, or wife because he believes she has brought dishonor to the family. This may occur if she is seen in public with a man she is not related to, or even if she is raped.
- ***Female infanticide***: This is the killing of baby girls.
- ***Female feticide***: This occurs when expectant parents abort a fetus because it is female.

As is often the case in developing countries, female literacy rates in India lag behind those of men—54 percent compared with 75 percent, according to India's 2001 census. Too few girls are enrolled in school in the first place, and too many drop out or are forced into domestic service.

Pakistan

In 1944 Mohammad Ali Jinnah, the Father of Pakistan, made a powerful statement against purdah: "No nation can rise to the height of glory unless your women are side by side with you; we are victims of evil customs. It is a crime against humanity that our women are shut up within the four walls of the houses as prisoners."

Unfortunately, Pakistan has not realized that progressive vision. Traditional ideas persist about keeping women at home and keeping them out of the workforce. When women do paid work, it tends to be piecework done at home. Often women's earnings are credited to their husbands.

This is changing, though. The 1981 census reported that 5.6 percent of all women did paid work, compared with 72.4 percent of men. By 1988 the number had risen to 10.2 percent. By 2005, 28 percent of women were in the labor force in some way.

The traditional preference for sons in Pakistan disadvantages girls and women at all levels. Girls have lower school-enrollment rates than boys even in the early grades. Girls have higher dropout rates, too. Female literacy is lower than for males. In some parts of the country, only 1 percent of women know how to read. Families with limited health-care resources tend to deprive their daughters to ensure care for their sons. This leads to poorer health for women.

Pakistan is not a rich country. But research by organizations like the United Nations Development Program suggests that Pakistan could do better with the resources it has if it could address inequality between the sexes in education and health care.

Afghanistan

Even as Afghanistan stabilized after the Taliban government's ouster in 2001, women and children there faced an "acute emergency." Public health is a particular concern. Afghanistan has extremely high maternal mortality rates and infant and child mortality rates. In other words, just giving birth is a very dangerous event for Afghan women. One Afghan child in five dies before his or her fifth birthday. A visiting United Nations official reported in 2005 that girls were "particularly vulnerable" in this situation.

Fourth-grade schoolgirls eagerly participate in class in Jalalabad, Afghanistan.

Photo by Robert Harbison / © 2001 The Christian Science Monitor

School enrollment for young girls in Afghanistan is among the lowest in the world.

Afghan girls and women have little opportunity for schooling. A United Nations report in 2005 said that only about 15 percent of them can read. School enrollment for young girls in Afghanistan is among the lowest in the world. Afghan girls' enrollment in secondary schools was less than 10 percent.

The human rights picture for Afghan women is also grim. According to the US State Department, police often detain women at the request of the woman's own family for *zina*. This term covers any action that defies family wishes. A woman who chooses for herself the man she wants to marry, or who runs away from home, or who leaves a husband who beats her, would be accused of *zina*. So would a woman who has sex with a man she's not married to.

Afghan police sometimes jail women who report crimes against themselves. And some women are forced to serve sentences when their husbands are convicted of crimes. And finally, the State Department found that Afghan police sometimes take women into custody to protect them from violent retaliation by their own families.

China's One-Child Policy

One of China's more prominent issues is population size. China has more people than any other country on earth. By July 2007 it had 1.3 billion, according to the US State Department. In the 1950s the leaders of the People's Republic of China thought a large population was a good thing. It didn't take long for them to change their minds, however. The ever-growing population was adversely affecting quality of life, everything from education to housing to clean air.

"It is important to keep in mind that population stresses are everywhere apparent in China, and no more so than in its overcrowded cities where air pollution far exceeds levels permitted in [America]," said Marshall Green, former assistant secretary of State for East Asian Affairs, in a 1986 column for *The New York Times*. And as recently as early 2009, the US State Department reported that the World Health Organization found that China was home to "seven of the world's 10 most polluted cities. . . ."

These kinds of negative impacts from population growth led to a series of campaigns starting decades ago to encourage birth control. Some were more successful than others. By the early 1970s Chairman Mao became personally involved. A special group in China's State Council had charge of birth control activities around the country. Committees were set up to monitor the family status of laborers in factories and other workplaces. So-called "barefoot doctors" distributed information and contraceptives—*birth control pills and devices*—in the countryside.

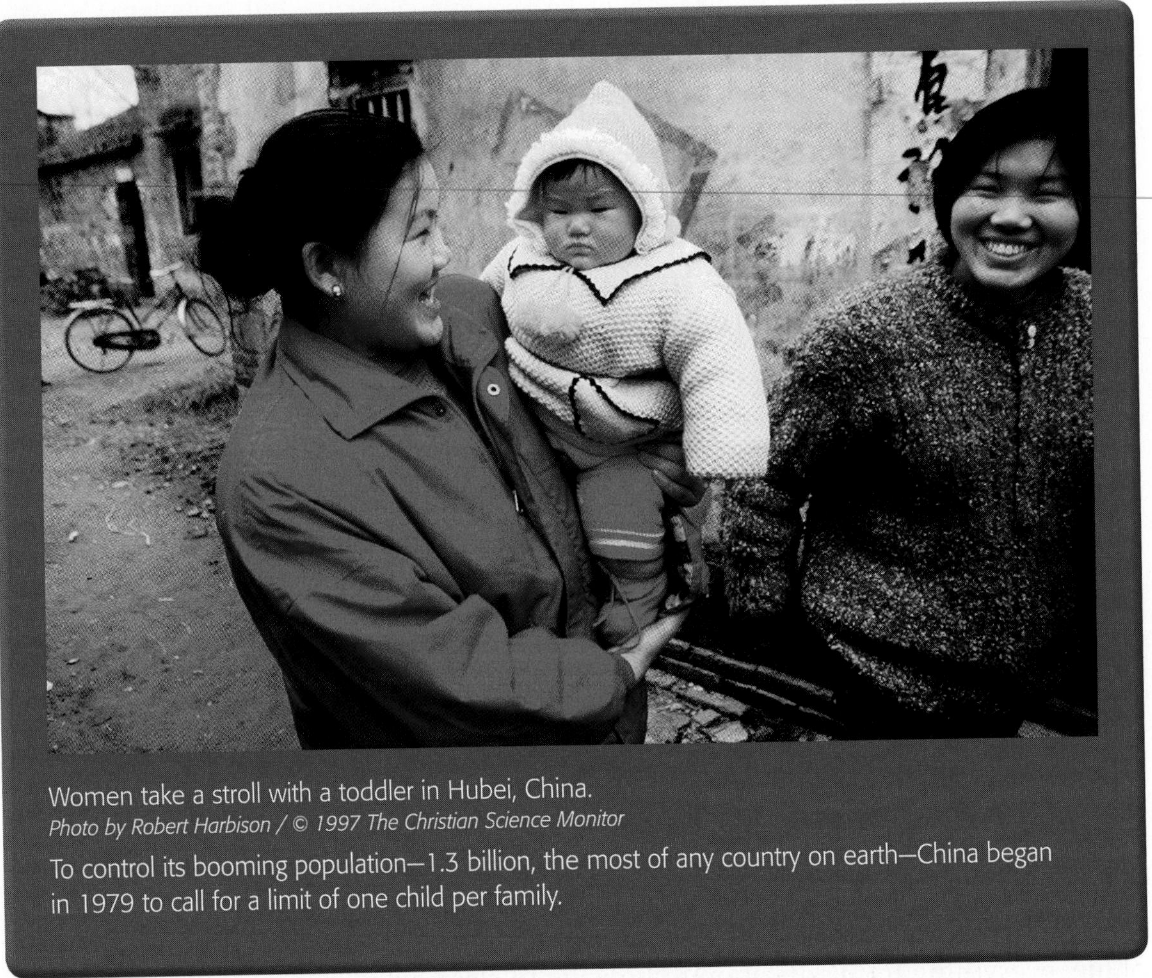

Women take a stroll with a toddler in Hubei, China.
Photo by Robert Harbison / © 1997 The Christian Science Monitor

To control its booming population—1.3 billion, the most of any country on earth—China began in 1979 to call for a limit of one child per family.

Through the mid-1970s the goal was two children per family. In 1979 the government began to call for a limit of one child per family. Those who observed the policy got special rewards. Those who didn't were penalized. In the countryside, where extra children mean extra help on the farm, officials visited households regularly to collect information on who was using which contraceptives. Officials urged those with one or more children to be sterilized.

The 2002 Population and Family Planning Law

China's 2002 Population and Family Planning Law enshrined the one-child policy in law. But the government makes exceptions. In some cases, especially in rural areas, couples may be allowed to have a second child. For instance, parents who lost children in the 2008 Sichuan earthquake won permission to try to have additional children. And the guidelines are looser for minority ethnic groups with fewer people.

The government enforces the policy largely with "social compensation fees"—heavy fines that may amount to a year's income. Forced abortion and sterilization are illegal under the new law. But reports say they widely occur.

The one-child policy has intensified the traditional Chinese preference for sons. The use of sex selection technology, used to detect and abort females, is illegal in China. But many more boys than girls are born in China anyway. Experts worry about what it will mean for social stability in China for so many young men to be unable to find wives and start families of their own. Another concern is how single children will be able to care for their elderly parents and grandparents. And some wonder whether it's a good idea for a whole country to be full of "only children."

The government's goal is to stabilize the population by the middle of the twenty-first century. Currently, experts say China's population will peak at 1.6 billion by 2050.

The Challenges of Human Trafficking and Sex Tourism in Asia

Western countries abolished the transatlantic slave trade 200 years ago, but slavery didn't end everywhere around the world. In many places, it just took on new forms. Today people speak of "human trafficking," or "trafficking in persons." It's a particular problem in Asia. As you have read in this lesson, this is a time of great growth and change for Asia. Its booming cities have drawn millions from the countryside. But not everyone ends up with the kind of work he or she was looking for. And desperate poverty persists, especially in the countryside.

In 2001 the US State Department established the Office to Monitor and Combat Trafficking in Persons to fight this new-old form of slavery. Human trafficking ensnares women and young people, but grown men as well. Some of them end up as prostitutes. Others end up doing forced labor. In every case, the State Department finds, the ordeal begins with someone's search for "economic alternatives"—the search for a better life.

What Is Meant by 'Human Trafficking'

Human trafficking means *forcing, defrauding, or coercing someone into labor or sexual exploitation*. The force involved is often physical force. To defraud is *to deprive someone of something by lying or cheating*. For example, a young woman from a rural village may be promised a respectable, well-paying job at a seacoast resort. Then when she gets there she finds she has to work as a prostitute. The work isn't what she was promised. Someone has lied to her.

US government research estimates that about 800,000 people are trafficked across national borders each year. Millions more are trafficked within their own countries as well. Of those taken across borders, about 80 percent are women and girls. Up to half are minors. Most of the transnational victims end up in forms of prostitution—selling sex. The majority of those trafficked within their borders are ensnared in forced or bonded labor.

Forced labor can be anything from factory work to household help. Forced laborers work at jobs they can never leave. They may be locked in a factory or dormitory. *Bonded labor* is another form of modern slavery. A man or woman may be forced to work off a debt. Perhaps the employer paid the worker's way from the countryside. But such laborers often find that however long they work, the balance owed never gets smaller.

Migrant workers—cut off from the support of family and friends in their native villages—are particularly vulnerable to being caught in both forced and bonded labor. Trafficked children are at risk of ending up in involuntary domestic servitude (as household slaves), in forced labor in factories, or as child soldiers.

How Human Trafficking Hurts

Human trafficking deprives people of the most elemental human rights—personal freedom of movement and control over their bodies. Trafficking also creates global health risks.

Prostitution always carries dangers of sexually transmitted and other diseases. But beyond that, any group of people "in the shadows" anywhere is at risk. If people aren't living openly, freely, in communities where they are entitled to be, they may lose access to health care and protection from the police. They may not be able to report or receive protection from crime, fire and safety hazards, or threats to public health, including sanitation problems.

Human trafficking also drives the growth of organized crime. Traffickers can themselves be big employers. They may co-opt, or corrupt, local law enforcement. They may smuggle people against their will from one location to the next. Yet they may also own some legitimate businesses as cover. Again, part of the problem is people living in the shadows. They are vulnerable to extortion. They have less access to legal alternatives for places to live or shop or borrow money.

The Nature and Extent of Human Trafficking and Sex Tourism in Asia

The US State Department monitors governments' efforts around the world to control trafficking in persons. It groups countries into three "tiers." Tier 1 countries are doing the best job of controlling the problem. Tier 3 countries may face sanctions. Tier 2 is in the middle. The State Department also has a group called the Tier 2 Watch List, consisting of countries whose status is under scrutiny. Both China and India have spent several years on the Tier 2 Watch List. The State Department calls their governments' efforts to control human trafficking extensive, but still not enough.

China

Forced labor, including of children, is a big problem in China. Reports allege that children as young as 12 are put to work in factories under the guise of "work and study" programs. There they face long hours, mandatory overtime, dangerous conditions, low pay, and involuntary pay deductions. A Guangdong factory licensed to make Olympic logo merchandise admitted to hiring 12-year-olds under such conditions.

Uighur children from western China have been abducted and forced to beg and work as street thieves in Chinese cities. Another problem in China, as young men outnumber young women to the point that many men can't find anyone to marry, is young women abducted as brides.

India

Internal forced labor seems to be the biggest trafficking problem in India. Those who peddle in human trade hold men, women, and children in debt bondage. They force them to work in brick kilns and rice mills, on farms and in embroidery factories. Aid organizations estimate that as many as 65 million people may be caught up in this work. Criminals traffic in women and girls within India for prostitution and forced marriage. They force children to work in factories, as domestic servants, beggars, and farmhands. Terrorist and insurgent groups arm children and deploy them in combat. The US government calls the Indian government's efforts to correct these problems "uneven."

These 5- and 6-year-old brothers from Mumbai, India, do not go to school but instead work all day from 6:00 a.m. to 6:00 p.m. collecting cardboard trash to earn together a total of $3 a day.
Photo by Melanie Stetson Freeman / © 1999 The Christian Science Monitor

Child labor is a problem in many countries, including India and China.

Sex Tourism

Sex tourism involves travelers, usually from wealthier countries, visiting other countries for the purposes of having sex with prostitutes. From a strictly economic perspective, it's not unlike other kinds of tourism. Like travelers who visit to see temples and museums, sex tourists buy airline tickets, book hotel rooms, and eat in restaurants. So some observers insist that as long as the paid sex is between consenting adults, there's no real problem. But for people caught in human trafficking, there is no meaningful "consent."

In 1998 the International Labor Organization reported that 2 percent to 14 percent of the gross domestic product of Indonesia, Malaysia, the Philippines, and Thailand came from sex tourism. The gross domestic product is the market value of the goods and services a country produces.

Perhaps the most abhorrent form of sex tourism involves children. Being caught up in such exploitation can be devastating for children. Effects include physical and psychological trauma, disease (including HIV/AIDS), unwanted pregnancy, malnutrition, social ostracism, and even death. Countries with a lot of child sex tourism typically have weak law enforcement, corruption, and poverty.

To fight this exploitation of children, the US Congress passed a law in 1994 making it illegal for Americans to travel abroad to engage in illegal sex with a minor. But the countries in which sex tourism takes place must do more to protect their most vulnerable citizens.

Lesson 4 Review

Using complete sentences, answer the following questions on a sheet of paper.

1. What are the advantages and disadvantages of the Three Gorges Dam?
2. What advantage does India have as a location for call centers?
3. Why do people move to cities from the country?
4. What was the Green Revolution?
5. What is purdah?
6. What public health challenges do Afghan women and children face?
7. What policy did China's 2002 Population and Family Planning Law enshrine?
8. When, and at what number, is China's population expected to stabilize?
9. What is human trafficking?
10. What is bonded labor?

Applying Your Learning

11. What, if anything, do you think should be done to close the gap between Asia's rich cities and its poorer countryside? Explain your answer.

LESSON 5 US Interests and Regional Issues in Asia

Quick Write

How do you think you would react to India's 1998 nuclear tests if you were Indian? If you were Pakistani? If you were an American diplomat at the US embassy in New Delhi?

Learn About

- the dilemma that North Korea creates for the United States
- important issues of nuclear nonproliferation in India and Pakistan
- the impacts of global wages, labor, outsourcing, and offshoring in the United States
- why Asia represents a new target market for US corporations
- the effects of Asian imports on the US market and economy
- human rights issues in various Asian nations

Imagine this scenario: It's the spring of 1998. India has a new government. It's led by the Hindu nationalist Bharatiya Janata Party. It has said for years—decades, really—that India needs nuclear weapons to be secure. China is the big worry, some say. But things haven't been too smooth with Pakistan lately either. Is the new prime minister serious about nukes? India tested a device in 1974. But the government has always called it a "peaceful nuclear explosion."

Then one morning in May you read in the paper that India has just tested three nuclear devices in its northern desert. The world is stunned. For some, though, the tests confirm what they have long suspected. India has secretly been working on nuclear bombs for years—since well before 1974.

The Dilemma That North Korea Creates for the United States

Vocabulary

- hard currency
- plebiscite
- doctrine
- dual-use technology
- offshoring
- capital
- market share
- renounce

Nuclear weapons are one of the main US concerns over North Korea. As you may have gathered from what you've read so far in this chapter, North Korea is a strange place. To call it a closed society is an understatement. Even by the standards of the old Communist bloc, it is a repressive, authoritarian state. It's also isolated. It doesn't have many friends within the family of nations. And for more than half a century, it has been—technically—at war with its prosperous neighbor to the south.

North Korea regularly holds large, state-planned shows in honor of its leader Kim Il-sung.
Photo by Clayton Jones / © 1992 The Christian Science Monitor

To call North Korea a closed society is an understatement. Even by the standards of the old Communist bloc, it is a repressive, authoritarian state.

The United States has to pay attention to North Korea—officially the Democratic People's Republic of Korea. The "Hermit Kingdom" is bent on developing nuclear weapons and the missiles to deliver them. A main focus of US foreign policy in Asia is finding a way to keep North Korea from going any further down the nuclear path, and bring it back within the limits of the Nuclear Non-Proliferation Treaty (NPT). You read about this treaty in Chapter 1, Lesson 5.

Any country's acquisition of nuclear weapons changes the game. The United States doesn't want to see any more countries building nuclear weapons. But the idea of a nuclear-armed North Korea is a terrifying scenario for American policymakers—and their South Korean and Japanese allies. A related issue is the possibility that North Korea would sell advanced weapons technology to a terrorist group. The country is in desperate economic straits, and building weapons is the one thing it does relatively well.

North Korea's Withdrawal From the Nuclear Non-Proliferation Treaty (NPT) in 2002

North Korea joined the NPT in 1985 as a nonnuclear weapons state. In 1992 the two Koreas agreed to keep the Korean Peninsula free of nuclear weapons. But North Korea broke its promises. The International Atomic Energy Agency (IAEA) faulted it for failing to let inspectors visit its nuclear facilities. In March 1993 North Korea said it would withdraw from the treaty.

North Koreans emerge from a pedestrian underpass beneath a wide street in Pyongyang.
Photo by Clayton Jones / © 1992 The Christian Science Monitor

A main focus of US foreign policy is finding a way to keep North Korea from developing nuclear weapons.

Soon after, the United States opened talks with the North Koreans. In October 1994 it announced a plan known as the Agreed Framework. If carried out, this plan would result in a nuclear-free peninsula. The North Koreans took steps to implement the agreement. But the United States wasn't sure they were playing by the rules. In 1998 US intelligence identified a site that appeared related to the nuclear program.

By October 2002 a visiting American delegation said it believed the North Koreans were enriching uranium. This was against the rules of the Agreed Framework. Enriched uranium can be used to make nuclear weapons. The North Koreans at first admitted the existence of the enrichment program, then denied it. But after the US delegation's visit, the North kicked out the IAEA inspectors, announced their withdrawal (again) from the NPT, and said they were going to make plutonium for weapons.

By mid-2003 the North Koreans were making claims about their "nuclear deterrent force," but it wasn't clear they were telling the truth. In August of that year, talks on North Korea's nuclear program got under way in Beijing, China. They included China, Japan, Russia, and South Korea, as well as the United States and North Korea. These so-called Six-Party Talks have been an off-again, on-again process. In March 2005 North Korea declared itself a "nuclear weapons state." On 9 October 2006 it announced the successful test of a nuclear explosive device. The United States verified this two days later.

The Six-Party Talks resumed in December of that year but North Korea called an end to them in July 2009. Even so, the United States continues to work with its partners in these talks for a nonnuclear North Korea.

Why the US Secretary of State Designated North Korea a Sponsor of Terrorism

On 29 November 1987 a South Korean jetliner en route from Abu Dhabi, United Arab Emirates, to Bangkok, Thailand, blew up over the Indian Ocean. All 115 people aboard perished. The subsequent investigation led to two North Korean agents. The US government considers the episode a terrorist attack and holds the North Korean government responsible. For this, the United States designated North Korea as a state sponsor of terrorism in 1988.

The Pyongyang regime is not known to have sponsored any other such attacks since then, however. As a result of this more recent clean record and a deal made between the United States and North Korea in 2008, former US Secretary of State Condoleezza Rice lifted the sponsor-of-terrorism label from North Korea on 11 October 2008.

How the North Korean Government's Economic Policies Have Led to Widespread Famine

North Korea is a largely mountainous country. Much of its land is not farmable. Its winters are long, cold, and dry, and its summers are short, hot, and humid. But the North Korean government cares passionately about "food security," growing its own grains without reliance on imports. This concern is an aspect of the government's policy of self-reliance, or *juche*, in Korean.

North Korea's agricultural strategy has a flaw, however. It's built on assumptions of cheap energy—assumptions that are no longer true. North Korean farms are, by Asian standards, highly mechanized. Farmers plow with tractors, rather than oxen, for instance. And tractors run on gasoline. North Koreans are also among the world's biggest users of chemical fertilizers, which are made from petroleum. When oil prices went up, starting in the mid-1990s and more recently again in 2007, North Korean farmers really felt the pinch.

As you read in Chapter 2, Lesson 2, the collapse of the old Soviet trading system hit the North Koreans hard. Many of their longtime trading partners were suddenly free to trade with the West. What's more, Russia and China started demanding payment for oil in hard currency—*money that can be converted to other currencies.* They wanted "real money," in other words, dollars or yen, for instance, not Soviet-bloc "play money" valid in only a few countries.

Meanwhile, North Koreans had exhausted the land with their intensive farming techniques. They had chopped down most of the trees. Crop yields began to fall, and a string of natural disasters hit as well. By the mid-1990s North Korea went spinning into a major food crisis. Famine killed about 1 million people, including soldiers.

International humanitarian aid brought the country back from the brink. But North Korea has still not addressed the fundamental problems of its agricultural sector. Many foods remain too expensive for the average person to buy. To highlight this point, a *Los Angeles Times* article in 2008 reported that many North Korean adults were cutting back to only two meals a day, and the reporter found people plucking grasses and weeds to eat.

As long as North Korea's leaders continue the policies of the past six decades, North Korea will continue to be a serious problem for its neighbors and the United States.

Important Issues of Nuclear Nonproliferation in India and Pakistan

North Korea is not the only country in Asia with a nuclear program outside the NPT. India and Pakistan are two other countries with nuclear weapons outside the treaty. The two have been rivals, often tense ones, ever since they emerged from British India in August 1947. Their relationship has tended to move one step backward for every two steps, or even one step, forward.

The Political, Economic, and Military Tensions Between India and Pakistan

The principal issue between these countries has been the disputed territory of Kashmir. As you read in Chapter 2, Lesson 3, Kashmir and Jammu was a largely Muslim state with a Hindu ruler. He chose to join Kashmir to India rather than Pakistan. The two countries have waged two all-out wars over Kashmir, in 1947 and 1965. They came dangerously close to war in 1999 and 2002 as well.

Indian paramilitary troops patrol Kashmir's capital after terrorist attacks on trains in faraway Mumbai, India.

Photo by Scott Baldauf / © 2006 The Christian Science Monitor

Muslims and Hindus have warred over Kashmir since 1947 when the state's Hindu ruler pledged to join India rather than Pakistan.

The original 1949 cease-fire deal called for a UN–supervised plebiscite—*a direct vote of the entire electorate*—to determine which country Kashmir should be part of. But that vote never took place. Under the agreement's terms, both India and Pakistan must pull their troops out of Kashmir before the balloting. And that has never happened.

The two countries also went to war in 1971 after a crisis in what was then East Pakistan. This led to the creation of a third country, Bangladesh. Since this conflict, India and Pakistan have progressed—slowly—toward more normal relations.

The Soviet invasion of Afghanistan in 1979 strained relations between India and Pakistan. Pakistan supported the Afghan resistance. The Indians tended to side with the Soviet Union.

India and Pakistan's Pursuit of Nuclear Weapons

India conducted its first nuclear test in 1974. But Pakistan wanted nuclear weapons, too. Each side knew the other had a weapons program under way. To ease tensions, in 1988 their two prime ministers, Rajiv Gandhi of India and Benazir Bhutto of Pakistan, signed a pact not to attack each other's nuclear facilities. This was a step forward.

They took a step back in 1997 when talks on the Kashmir issue broke down. On 28 May 1998 India conducted its second nuclear test. A few weeks later, Pakistan tested five nuclear devices.

Dialogue started up again in 1999 but then broke down after fighting near Kargil, Kashmir, in May 1999. Then in October 1999 a military coup ousted Pakistan's civilian government. That unsettled things further. In December 2001 came a terrorist attack on the Indian Parliament. India accused Pakistan of involvement. That led in early 2002 to a troop buildup on both sides of the Line of Control in Kashmir. The Line of Control, created in 1972, splits Kashmir between India and Pakistan. India controls the region south of the line and Pakistan the land north of it. More recently, India has accused Pakistan of a role in two sets of terrorist attacks in Mumbai (Bombay), one in July 2006 and the other in November 2008.

But Pakistan continues to feel itself under threat from India. This is a big challenge in the region for the United States. It wants Pakistani help in the fight against al-Qaeda, whose leaders may be hiding in Pakistan's mountains. Many Pakistanis are so focused on India, however, that they don't feel al-Qaeda is such a threat.

India and Pakistan trade very little. In recent years they had made efforts to develop trade further. For instance, India planned to set up border posts to help move goods and people to and from Pakistan. But the plan was dropped after the November 2008 attacks. It's a sign of how security issues overwhelm economic and social ties between these two rivals who once made up one country.

In 1999, a year after its second nuclear test, India released a draft "nuclear doctrine." A doctrine in this sense is *a body of principles*. It is a statement of how the Indian government thinks about nuclear weapons, why it wants them, and what it intends to do with them.

This doctrine said that India's nuclear weapons weren't aimed at any one country. India saw having nuclear weapons as a good way to keep from being pushed around—especially by other countries with bombs of their own. Another part of India's doctrine is "no first use." India says it won't use its nuclear arms unless others attack it first.

Not surprisingly, Pakistan's doctrine is different. It is willing to adopt a "no first use" policy for nuclear arms, but only if India agrees to a "South Asian Non-Nuclear Treaty." India proposed a "no first use" treaty to Pakistan soon after the 1998 tests. Pakistan rejected this idea, saying that its nuclear program was indeed aimed at India. Pakistani officials said they wanted to keep their options open.

The Environmental and Social Implications of the Proliferation of Nuclear Weapons

For those who believe in the NPT as the way to control the nuclear threat, both India and Pakistan offer reason to worry. On 1 October 2008 the US Congress gave final approval to a deal that allows the United States to share nuclear technology with India. It was controversial for the United States because it was a step outside the NPT's limits—India is not a party to the treaty. The deal overturned a three-decade-old ban on nuclear trade with India.

The deal's supporters point out that it focuses on civilian technology. The United States is not building India's nuclear arsenal. They further argue that the deal strengthens US relations with India. And besides, India is the world's largest democracy. It's not a rogue nation. It can be trusted with nuclear technology. And even though India is not a party to the NPT, the new deal commits it to allowing international inspectors into its nuclear facilities.

But critics counter that it's not good for the United States to set aside NPT rules. It doesn't look good when America acts inconsistently. Besides, some of what the deal gives India is dual-use technology—*technology that can be used for civilian or military purposes*.

The story of what happened in Pakistan is far more troubling. Politically, Pakistan is much less stable than India. Furthermore, the country doesn't hold tight enough controls over its nuclear technology program. This lack of strict controls helped lead to a marketplace in which anyone—including terrorists—could buy dangerous nuclear materials and technology. It's every arms control expert's worst nightmare.

Dr. A. Q. Khan is a Pakistani nuclear scientist who helped his country smuggle in materials to develop its nuclear arsenal. For arms control experts who don't want to see the "nuclear club" get any bigger, that's bad enough. But it gets worse. His global network provided "one stop shopping" for any country wanting nuclear weapons. His customers included Iran, Libya, and North Korea. These are some of the last countries that the United States would want to see equipped with nuclear weapons. (In 2004, however, Libya gave up its attempts to develop weapons.)

The US government believes the Khan network has been shut down. Many of its operatives are either already in prison or are in custody awaiting trial or being tried. Khan acknowledged his own role in the network in 2004. He was freed from prison in 2009 and has since been at liberty in Pakistan.

As long as Pakistan remains unstable and Indian-Pakistani relations remain poor, the nuclear issue in South Asia will continue to trouble American and world leaders.

The Impacts of Global Wages, Labor, Outsourcing, and Offshoring in the United States

Asian countries also pose serious economic challenges to Americans. Shortly after World War II, more than half of the world's gross production was in the United States. This meant more than half of all the "stuff" in the world that people produce, on farms, and in factories was made in America. This was partly because the United States was then, as it is now, a great country with an advanced economy.

Vietnamese construction workers have some laughs during a break on Hanoi's streets.

Photo by Melanie Stetson Freeman / © 1997 The Christian Science Monitor

Asian countries like Vietnam pose serious economic challenges to Americans.

Textile workers in China stitch clothing for high-end American women's shops.
Photo by Robert Marquand / © 2003 The Christian Science Monitor
Businesses will move production to wherever they can get the work done most efficiently.

But it was also partly because many of the world's great industrial economies were in ruins after years of war. Many other places were still underdeveloped—without electricity or roads, without labor forces trained for modern workplaces.

But all that has changed. Those war-damaged economies in Europe and Japan have long since rebuilt. And the underdeveloped ones have grown up. Countries like South Korea, Brazil, and Mexico have vaulted into the top ranks in the world.

This matters for Americans. They now have to compete in a global marketplace. Capital moves to wherever it gets the best return. Investors will put money into companies that produce the most profit. That means businesses will move production—jobs and factories—to wherever they can get the work done most efficiently. That doesn't necessarily mean most cheaply. Highly skilled workers may command high wages if they do a good job making a product that can be sold at a high price.

What Pushes Jobs to Asia and What Pulls Them There

As you read in Chapter 2, Lesson 4, Asia's two big economies, China and India, have different strengths. China makes things. India provides services. That analysis oversimplifies but is largely true. Other Asian countries fulfill one role or the other, or some combination of both.

Some kinds of work can be sent abroad more readily than others. Chinese factories can make toys or clothes for Americans. But if you want fresh bread, it's much better from a local bakery.

Still, many changes in the world have made it easier for work to "travel." A country's political stability, for one thing, is important. That doesn't mean full-blown democracy. But foreign investors want to be sure their factories won't be overrun by angry mobs or seized by the government.

Faster and more reliable transportation and communications matter, too. Mass literacy means that large populations of workers are available to hire for jobs in factories and other workplaces.

High costs may push jobs out of the United States. This includes labor costs—some workers may price themselves out of the market. But it also includes the cost and availability of land for factories, the cost of construction, and the cost of federal, state, and local regulations. Even the cost of allowing public input at local planning board meetings is a factor. It may be hard to measure, but it's real.

All this can be very sensitive politically. Trade unions don't like to hear that their wage and benefit demands are causing their members to lose jobs. Businesses don't want to say they're locating smelly, dangerous factories in places with looser rules about clean air and worker safety. Environmentalists don't like to think that their work on behalf of pollution controls merely leads to industry taking its pollution elsewhere.

In addition to these "push" factors, many factors have "pulled" jobs to Asia from the United States and other Western countries. Asia has productive, well-educated workers, many fluent in English—especially in India, Singapore, and Hong Kong. Another plus is that some parts of Asia use accounting and legal systems that are familiar to American businesses.

In certain industries that need to function around the clock, locations in Asia offer a time-zone advantage: A New Yorker who needs tech support for his computer at 2 o'clock in the morning can get help from a call center in Bangalore, India, where it's 11:30 a.m.

The Number of US Jobs Being Outsourced to Firms in Asia

"Everyone knows" that American jobs are moving to Asia. But nobody knows just how many.

You read in the Introduction that outsourcing is the procurement of goods and services from an outside source. Sometimes this outside source is in another country. This is an extremely controversial question within the United States because of how it may affect the domestic economy. And it's only gotten more so as it has grown beyond call centers and reached into the ranks of white-collar professionals. Even accountants and software engineers have felt the pinch. One University of California study found that 14 million additional American jobs could be at risk of outsourcing overseas.

Others aren't so sure. A 2005 study by the Federal Reserve Bank of New York concluded that offshoring—*moving factories or work from the United States to other countries*—has not been all that widespread. And it has contributed "only marginally" to the labor market's recent weak performance.

Another school of thought attributes weak job creation to productivity. American workers are getting more productive all the time, they say. And productivity is a "job killer," as one analysis put it. Every percentage point of increase in annual productivity growth costs 1.3 million jobs, in other words.

The Significant Impacts of Offshoring on the US Economy and Labor Force

One kind of job that has held its own in recent years is the service job—especially health-care service and other jobs tied to a specific location. A nurse needs to tend patients where they are, for example.

US employees used to be protected from competition from low-wage foreign workers. American companies had more capital (*money and resources available to invest*) and better technology—the latest tools and state-of-the-art factories. And American workers' productivity justified their higher wages.

A Chinese man reads newspapers posted in kiosks in Beijing, China.

Photo by Andy Nelson / © 2005 The Christian Science Monitor

Foreign businesses placing their factories and labs overseas look for, among other things, mass literacy in the local populations.

But now, more and more Americans compete against foreign workers, many of them in Asia. The Asian workers may have received better math scores in school. They receive good wages compared with others in their countries—although they are modest compared with wages paid in industrialized countries.

A company may choose to place—to offshore—its state-of-the-art factory in Asia rather than an American town for any number of reasons. The Asian location may have lower wages, lax environmental laws and other regulations, a desire to sell to the market where the factory is, availability of English-speaking employees abroad, or a bigger profit for the company when it ships the goods back home. The list goes on.

Critics of this transfer of factories from America to Asia point to World War II. American factories—also referred to as the manufacturing base or industrial base—were crucial to defeating Germany and Japan. Without it, they note, the Allies would have been hard put to crush the Axis Powers. For instance, the United States took its auto factories and transformed them quickly and efficiently into assembly lines that churned out tanks, aircraft, and munitions for the troops at the front.

These critics argue that by losing manufacturing to Asia, the United States faces not only job loss, but also national security risks. Supporters of free trade respond, however, that while the United States was totally unprepared for war in 1941, that is not the case now. And so the controversy continues.

Why Asia Represents a New Target Market for US Corporations

The more than 4 billion Asians in the world represent new economic competition for Americans. But they also represent economic opportunity.

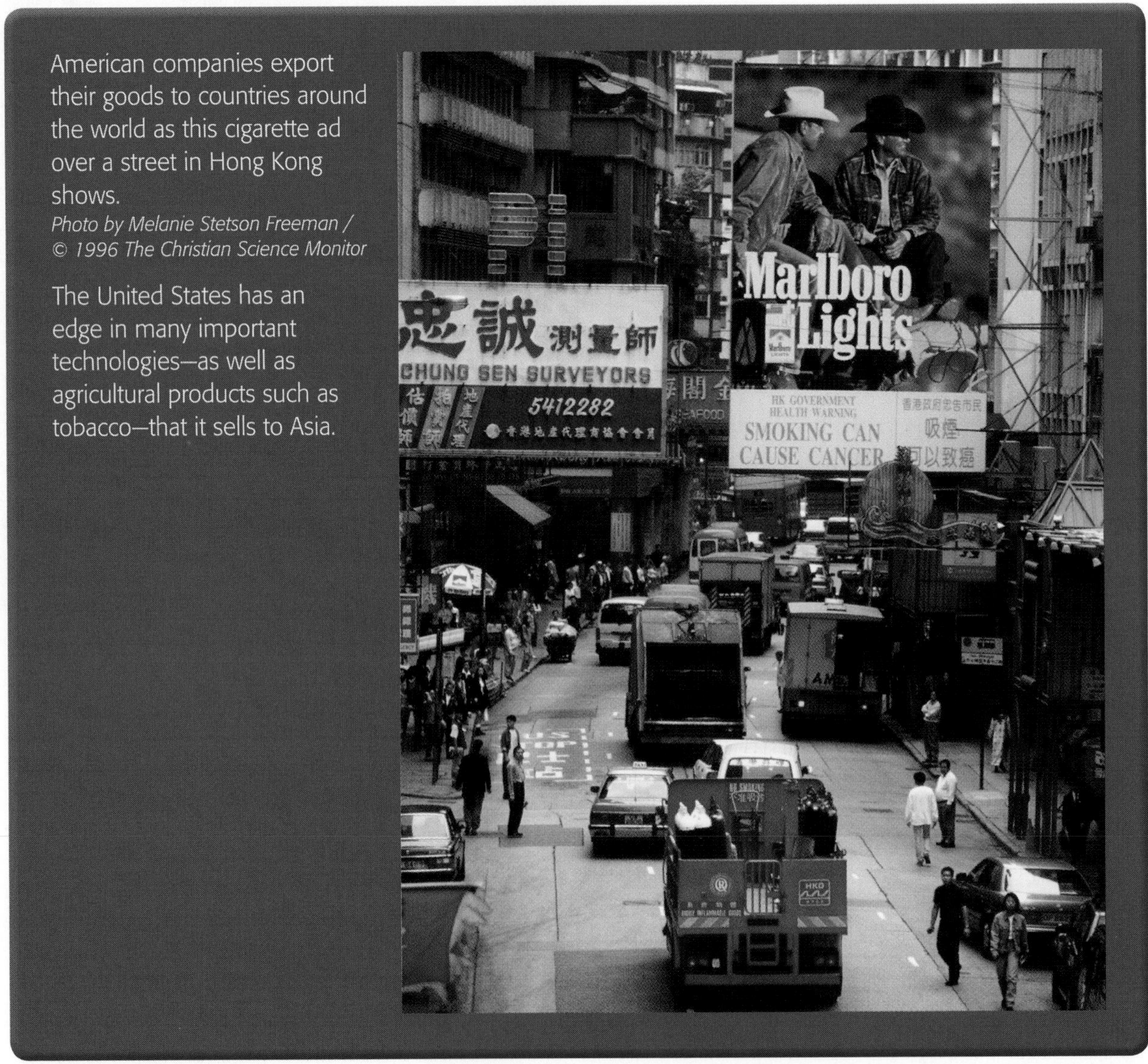

American companies export their goods to countries around the world as this cigarette ad over a street in Hong Kong shows.
Photo by Melanie Stetson Freeman / © 1996 The Christian Science Monitor

The United States has an edge in many important technologies—as well as agricultural products such as tobacco—that it sells to Asia.

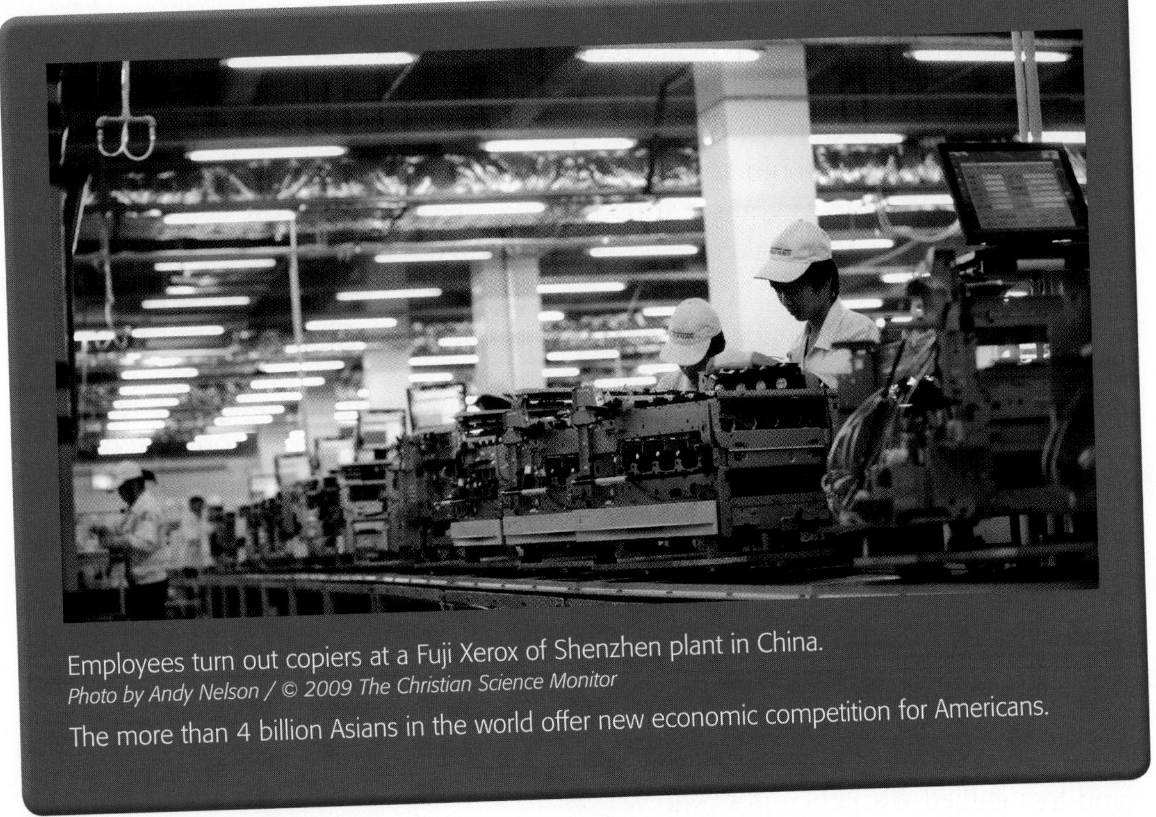

Employees turn out copiers at a Fuji Xerox of Shenzhen plant in China.
Photo by Andy Nelson / © 2009 The Christian Science Monitor
The more than 4 billion Asians in the world offer new economic competition for Americans.

The Significance of Technology in Expanding Potential Target Markets

The United States still has an edge in many important technologies. This edge, along with agricultural products, is what it sells to Asia. A little research into American companies expanding into Asia suggests that they tend to offer products with a technology edge to expanding consumer markets.

In 2003 a New Jersey firm announced a deal to sell a new wireless technology to, among others, three South Korean wireless telecommunications firms. The new technology is said to provide mobile wireless service better than Wi-Fi but much cheaper. In 2008 a Massachusetts maker of solar energy equipment announced a deal to partner with a Singapore firm to sell its products in the high-growth markets of Singapore, Malaysia, Thailand, the Philippines, and Indonesia.

In 2007 another Massachusetts firm, this one a maker of data-storage devices, announced a plan to build a development lab in Singapore. It was the company's first such facility outside the United States. The announcement illustrates a company moving to where its growing markets are.

It also shows how Asia's technological base has broadened. A lab is higher up the ladder than just a factory. Its work is of greater value. To run a lab, a company needs creative thinkers, not just people pushing buttons. The lab and the technical labor pool reinforce each other. The labor pool had to be there in the first place for the company to want to build the lab there. But once the lab is there, it continues to strengthen the labor pool. It does this by giving workers higher-value opportunities than a factory would.

Europe and North America are what economists call "mature" markets. They're affluent areas whose residents already have most of the "stuff" they need. They buy new washing machines when their old ones give out, for instance. Asia, on the other hand, is full of people with no washing machines at all. But that is changing, rapidly. And as you see from the previous examples, the technologies they're buying are much higher-tech than washing machines.

The Emergence of Asian Nations as Participants in the Global Economy

Asia has emerged as the world's supplier of electronics and manufactured goods. China, Japan, South Korea, and, to a lesser extent, India are major producers of electronics. Hong Kong, Taiwan, and Singapore are also strong in electronics. But they excel in financial services, too.

These countries combine high levels of technical knowledge among the population and relatively low labor costs.

Meanwhile, Bangladesh, Cambodia, Indonesia, Vietnam, and the Philippines export textiles. The textile industry doesn't demand such high technical skills as electronics. It therefore tends to migrate to places with even lower labor costs and less-skilled workers.

Malaysia and Indonesia are Asia's energy exporters. They produce oil, gas, and biofuels. Bangladesh, China, India, and Pakistan supply rice and other grains. All these export roles mean that Asia is well integrated into the global economy.

Selected Asian Countries' Exports to the United States, 2008

Country	Exports
China	$338 billion
Japan	$139 billion
South Korea	$ 48 billion
Taiwan	$ 36 billion
Malaysia	$ 31 billion
India	$ 26 billion
Indonesia	$ 16 billion
Vietnam	$ 13 billion
Philippines	$ 9 billion
Bangladesh	$ 4 billion
Pakistan	$ 4 billion

Source: US Census Bureau, Foreign Trade Statistics

These Toyota Motor workers in Japan assemble 852 vehicles, such as the Prius and Corolla, on their line each day.
Photo by Andy Nelson / © 2008 The Christian Science Monitor

While Japanese automakers have many of their plants in their home country, these companies also have factories in the United States that built 3.5 million cars in 2005 alone.

The Effects of Asian Imports on the US Market and Economy

In the Introduction you read about David Ricardo's idea of comparative advantage. He argued that countries should focus on what they do best and get the other things they need through trade. Furthermore, he argued that everyone would be better off this way. The question of competition from Asia brings Ricardo's ideas into focus.

The Impact of Japanese and Korean Automakers on the US Auto Industry

In the 1960s the American automaker General Motors had a market share of about 60 percent. Market share is *the percentage, or amount, of overall sales of any particular product a company controls*. Chevys, Buicks, Pontiacs, Oldsmobiles, and even Cadillacs accounted for 3 out of every 5 cars on the road.

By February 2009 GM was still the leader. But its share was less than a third of what it was before, and the company faced possible bankruptcy. Toyota, a Japanese carmaker, was in the No. 2 spot, ahead of Ford and Chrysler. Except for Volkswagen of Germany, the rest of the top 10 are Japanese or Korean. Many of these firms weren't even making cars back in the days when GM had such a commanding share of the market.

It wouldn't be quite right to call these Japanese or Korean vehicles "foreign," however. Many Japanese cars are made in the United States. This has created more than 60,000 factory jobs. In 2005 these plants built about 3.5 million cars. Car dealerships selling Japanese cars employ about 400,000 Americans. Korean carmaker Hyundai has joined the trend of making cars near the customer, too, operating a factory in Montgomery, Alabama.

Top 10 US Auto Market Shares, February 2009

Company	Market share
GM	18.2 percent
Toyota	15.9 percent
Ford	13.9 percent
Chrysler	12.2 percent
Honda	10.4 percent
Nissan	7.9 percent
Hyundai	4.4 percent
Volkswagen	3.7 percent
Kia	2.9 percent
Mazda	2.4 percent

The Impact of Electronic Products Manufactured in Asia on the US Market

Very little in the way of consumer electronics is made in the United States today. Televisions sets, for instance, are all made abroad—even those with an American name on them. Some people think it's a bad thing for the US economy to lose any sector.

When a factory closes, the town around it can be deeply affected. People lose their jobs. Family members move away to find work. The effects ripple through the local economy. Local stores and businesses that sold to the factory or its workers may close, too. The local economy that remains may be a shadow of its former self.

But economists who support trade recall Ricardo's idea of comparative advantage. Every national economy, and every firm, always needs to be looking for things it can do better than anyone else. There's no use hanging on to business that others can pursue more profitably, in this view. That only gets in the way of new opportunities. After all, the US economy has expanded enormously since the last television set made in America left the factory.

As Asian and other markets grow, Americans will continue to wrestle with these issues.

How Increased Oil Consumption in India and China Affects Supplies and Prices

The growing economies of Asia have other effects, as well. Whenever more buyers enter a market for a certain good—oil, to take a not-so-random example—the price goes up. That's how the law of supply and demand applies to China and India and their effect on world oil prices. As millions of Chinese and Indians trade in their bicycles and scooters for cars, world demand for oil surges. Building cities, roads, subways, airports, housing, office towers, all creates enormous demands on world oil supplies.

Of course, world oil markets are complex. Many different factors affect prices. An economic slump may make energy demand soften, and thus lead to lower prices. War damage to oil-field production facilities may limit supply and therefore push oil prices higher. But, all other things being equal, 2.5 billion Chinese and Indians becoming more prosperous and demanding more oil means that supplies will tighten and prices will rise.

Human Rights Issues in Various Asian Nations

The United States has another important interest in Asian countries—human rights. Every year, the US State Department reviews the state of human rights around the world. As of early 2009 several Asian nations—including China, North Korea, India, Pakistan, Afghanistan, Vietnam, and Burma—figure among the top-tier areas of concern.

The Universal Declaration of Human Rights

On 10 December 1948 the General Assembly of the United Nations adopted and proclaimed the Universal Declaration of Human Rights—one of the foundation documents of international law. Afterward, the Assembly called on member nations to publicize this important statement. The delegates were especially keen to have students in schools and colleges understand it. You can help to fulfill that desire by reading about the declaration at **http://www.un.org/en/documents/udhr/**. The State Department's annual review keeps tabs on progress toward meeting its standards.

The United Nations building sits on the East River's banks in New York City.

Photo by Bill Grant / © 1991 The Christian Science Monitor

In 1948 the General Assembly of the United Nations adopted and proclaimed the Universal Declaration of Rights.

The US Commitment to Protect Human Rights

Some terms in the Declaration above may remind you of the US Declaration of Independence or the Constitution. This is no coincidence. The United States rests on a foundation of human rights. Promoting human rights around the world is central to US foreign policy. Human rights help secure the peace. They deter aggression and crime. They promote the rule of law. Strong traditions of human rights and civil order help prevent disasters such as famine. They speed recovery when these occur.

Religious and Social Freedoms in China, Japan, and Korea

One important human right is religious freedom. The government-funded United States Commission on International Religious Freedom (USCIRF) has recommended China be named a "country of particular concern (CPC)." The State Department has done so. China restricts religious liberty. It treats minority faiths and the Falun Gong spiritual movement badly. It restricts Tibet's freedom.

Japan's constitution guarantees freedom of religion. So does South Korea's. North Korea, however, is a very different story. As USCIRF reports, "Religious freedom is essentially absent in North Korea." The government sharply restricts public and private worship. It actively discriminates against believers. It has reportedly jailed, tortured, and even executed North Koreans with ties to evangelical Christians in China. Those engaged in other religious activities, too may have met similar punishments.

A wealthy local businessman is building the Islamic Culture City in Yinchuan, China, to celebrate the region's Muslim culture. *Photo by Peter Ford / © 2008 The Christian Science Monitor*

In general, China restricts religious liberty, and a US government commission has recommended that China be named a "country of particular concern."

The Pyongyang government has set up fake religious organizations. It uses them to fool people into thinking it allows religious freedom. Apparently some foreign residents have attended services at these "pretend" churches without realizing they are just for show.

North Korea arrests people found carrying Bibles in public. Exact numbers are hard to come by, but a press report in 2001 estimated that 6,000 Christians were in prison. The State Department has named North Korea a CPC, too.

fastFACT

Under the law, USCIRF can recommend a country be named a CPC, but only the State Department can name it one. The two don't always agree.

Once the State Department names a country a CPC, it can impose sanctions against it or grant a waiver of sanctions.

Challenges to Freedom in India, Pakistan, and Afghanistan

India earned a dubious honor in 2004. The state of religious freedom there prompted the USCIRF to recommend the State Department name India a CPC. This may be surprising. After all, India is a democracy. It's under the rule of law. It has a long tradition of secular governance. That is, it separates religion and state.

Even so, religious minorities in India are still subject to violent attacks. Sometimes these are fatal. Those responsible are seldom punished. They attack with impunity, in other words. This violence spiked as a Hindu nationalist political party came to power in 1998. It lessened somewhat once the Congress Party returned to power, though. In this case, the State Department did not name India a CPC, and USCIRF has since lifted its recommendation.

In the wake of the December 2007 assassination of former Prime Minister Benazir Bhutto, human rights and religious freedom in Pakistan appeared to be under threat, the USCIRF reported. It cited "disturbing" reports of thugs harassing human rights defenders. Gun-wielding men reportedly threatened the leader of the Human Rights Commission of Pakistan. The Human Rights Commission said that local officials, including a couple of police officers in uniform, backed the harassers. USCIRF has recommended Pakistan as a CPC, but the State Department has not declared it one.

As Afghanistan struggles to rebuild after Taliban rule, the human rights picture there is better than some feared but not as good as they hoped. Under the new constitution, Afghanistan is an Islamic republic. All laws must be compatible with Islam, in other words. But the new constitution guarantees equal rights for women and men. It also protects the right to practice minority religions, too. However, human rights advocates say they don't see good legal means to protect these and other rights. The country lacks a real working legal system. There is also serious resistance to the idea of equal rights for women.

Indonesian women pray at a mosque in Banda Aceh during ceremonies marking an Islamic holiday called Idul Adha.

Photo by Andy Nelson / © 2005 The Christian Science Monitor

Officially recognized religions, such as Islam, operate fairly freely in Indonesia, while minority faiths face some discrimination.

Challenges to Freedom in Southeast Asia

After more than 30 years of strongman rule, Indonesia became a democracy in 1998. This change has been good for human rights. People have somewhat more freedom than before. Officially recognized religions operate fairly freely. Minority faiths do face some discrimination, though. And communal violence has taken place, as in India. During 1999–2000, for instance, more than 3,000 people reportedly died in Christian-Muslim clashes in the Maluku Islands.

Communal violence has also been an issue in Malaysia. In late 2007, for instance, police used tear gas and water cannons against 10,000 ethnic Indian Hindus. They were just demonstrating peacefully against religious discrimination, including the destruction of their temples and shrines.

Vietnam

USCIRF has recommended that two Southeast Asian countries, Vietnam and Burma, be named "countries of particular concern." Vietnam's state of religious liberty has long been poor. It has worsened in recent years. Some key religious dissidents have gone to jail. Others have been put under house arrest. Meanwhile, the government harasses religious minorities. Agents sometimes put them under surveillance. The regime has forced churches to close. It has also forced people to renounce their faith—*to give up or turn away from it*. Moreover, high-level government officials have approved these actions.

The Unified Buddhist Church of Vietnam is under attack. Many of its leaders are under house arrest or in prison. The Vietnamese government also harasses Christians among its ethnic minorities. Christians who refuse to renounce their faith are often beaten. The State Department once designated Vietnam as a CPC, but lifted that designation in 2006, despite USCIRF's recommendation that it remain one.

The Vietnam War

Some human rights violations in Vietnam stem from the government's distrust of groups that supported the South Vietnamese government and its US ally during the Vietnam War. The causes of that war were very complex and remain controversial to this day.

The 1954 treaty that ended Vietnam's war for independence from France divided the country temporarily into a Communist Party-controlled north and a noncommunist south. The agreement called for elections in both parts of the country for a unified government. But the southern government refused to hold elections and declared an independent South Vietnam (Republic of Vietnam) in 1955. At the same time, the Communist government in the north instituted harsh economic and social policies that sent some 450,000 refugees fleeing to the south. Many of these were Vietnamese Roman Catholics. A smaller number of people moved north.

In the late 1950s North Vietnam organized a guerrilla war against the south. The United States came to the south's aid. Seeing the situation primarily as a front in the Cold War struggle against communism, President John Kennedy sent military advisers to help the South Vietnamese government. Then, in 1965, President Lyndon Johnson sent in regular US forces. The number of American Soldiers, Airmen, Sailors, and Marines fighting in the war grew until half a million Americans were stationed there. North Vietnam eventually sent its own regular forces into the south to reunify the country under its control.

US and South Vietnamese forces kept the northern troops at bay for several years. They beat back a determined North Vietnamese attack during the Lunar New Year (Tet) in 1968. But the American people tired of the war and its large number of casualties. President Richard Nixon eventually began withdrawing American troops in the early 1970s.

In 1973 the warring parties negotiated the Paris Peace Accords, which led to a cease-fire. North Vietnam violated the accords in 1975 with an all-out attack on southern-held territory. The US Congress had banned further aid to the South Vietnamese government, which fell in April 1975.

Between 3 million and 4 million Vietnamese on both sides died in the war, along with almost 60,000 Americans, 5,000 South Koreans, and 520 Australians. The last two countries had also sent troops to help the south.

In the years after the war, hundreds of thousands of former South Vietnamese citizens fled the country. Many emigrated to the United States. The United States and Vietnam restored diplomatic relations in 1995, and ties have grown deeper since then. But the United States has not dropped its concerns about human rights in Vietnam.

Buddhist monks rest at Saigon's oldest pagoda, Giac Lam Pagoda, built in 1744.
Photo by Melanie Stetson Freeman / © 1997 The Christian Science Monitor

Generally, the more democratic a country is, the greater the respect for human rights. The less democratic it is, the less respect there is for human rights..

Burma

In Burma, the military regime widely represses all human rights. This includes "severe violations" of religious freedom, according to USCIRF. In some places, the regime promotes Buddhism over other religions. Sometimes it has pushed Buddhists to attack Christians and Muslims. But the government is "suspicious" of all independent religious activity, the USCIRF says, even Buddhism. This is because both Buddhists and followers of minority faiths have actively opposed the military regime.

Burmese officials have forced Christians to destroy churches and cemeteries to make room for military camps. Christians, Muslims, and even Buddhists have been made to build and maintain Buddhist pagodas and monasteries—for no pay. Sometimes officials take Christian children away from their parents without consent to teach them about Buddhism. The State Department has agreed with the recommendation and named Burma a CPC.

So the human rights picture in Asia varies greatly. Generally, the more democratic a country is, the greater the respect for human rights. The less democratic it is, the less respect there is for human rights. That's why the United States tries to promote democracy in Asia and elsewhere.

Lesson 5 Review

Using complete sentences, answer the following questions on a sheet of paper.

1. American policymakers don't want to see North Korea have nuclear weapons, but there's a related issue that also has them concerned. What is it?
2. After the end of the communist trading system, Russia and China demanded payment for their oil in hard currency. Why did this lead to famine in North Korea?
3. What is the main point of contention between India and Pakistan? Explain briefly.
4. How does Pakistan's nuclear doctrine differ from India's?
5. What are some of the "push" and "pull" factors that move jobs from the United States to Asia?
6. How many American jobs are at risk of outsourcing overseas?
7. What do American companies expanding into Asia tend to offer?
8. How do the Asian countries that produce electronics compare with the ones that produce mostly textiles?
9. How have automakers' shares of the US market changed since the 1960s?
10. How is oil consumption by China and India expected to affect world oil prices?
11. Why is defense of human rights important to US foreign policy? Explain briefly.
12. Why is China a "country of particular concern" in the eyes of the United States Commission on International Religious Freedom and the State Department?

Applying Your Learning

13. Visit the United Nations' website and read The Universal Declaration of Human Rights (**http://www.un.org/en/documents/udhr/**). Which words or phrases in the Universal Declaration of Human Rights remind you of the Declaration of Independence or the US Constitution?

CHAPTER 3

Mt. Kilimanjaro, Africa's highest peak, rises in Eastern Africa. In the same region lie the Great Lakes and the Great Rift Valley, where scientists believe the ancestors of all human beings originally lived.

Africa

Chapter Outline

LESSON 1 Africa: An Introduction

Quick Write

How do you think this knowledge about the origins of modern humans affects the way most people think about Africa? How does it make you think about Africa?

Learn About

- the five major regions of Africa
- the natural resources of Africa
- the distinctive characteristics of African culture
- the main ethno-linguistic groups in Africa
- the main language groups in Africa
- how Islam, Christianity, and indigenous religions influence Africa

In this lesson you will read about Africa's tradition of extended families. But before you do, take a few moments to think about the biggest extended family of all—the human race.

In 1925 a scientist named Raymond Dart found a fossil in a cave in South Africa. The fossil was what remained of the skull of a six-year-old creature. It looked like an ape but had some human characteristics. It had lived millions of years before.

Scientists have been hot on the trail of human evolution ever since. Many of their most significant finds have been in the Great Rift Valley of Eastern and Southern Africa.

That's where modern human beings evolved, somewhere between 90,000 and 130,000 years ago. These people belonged to the Early Stone Age. But they had the same capacity to think as people today do. They were the fathers and mothers of all humanity.

"There is no question that Africans contributed towards the development of human beings as we know them today," George Abungu, of the National Museums of Kenya, told the British Broadcasting Corporation (BBC). "They were the first to use their physical capabilities to enlarge their brains."

"They were able to develop the technology of stone tools. They were the first ones to move out of trees and walk upright and they were the first ones to explore crossing the seas and going out to Asia and Europe . . . and to me this is the greatest achievement that humanity has ever done."

The Five Major Regions of Africa

Africa is the world's second-largest and second-most populous continent. Only Asia is bigger and has more people. The United Nations divides Africa into five major regions: North, West, Central, Eastern, and Southern.

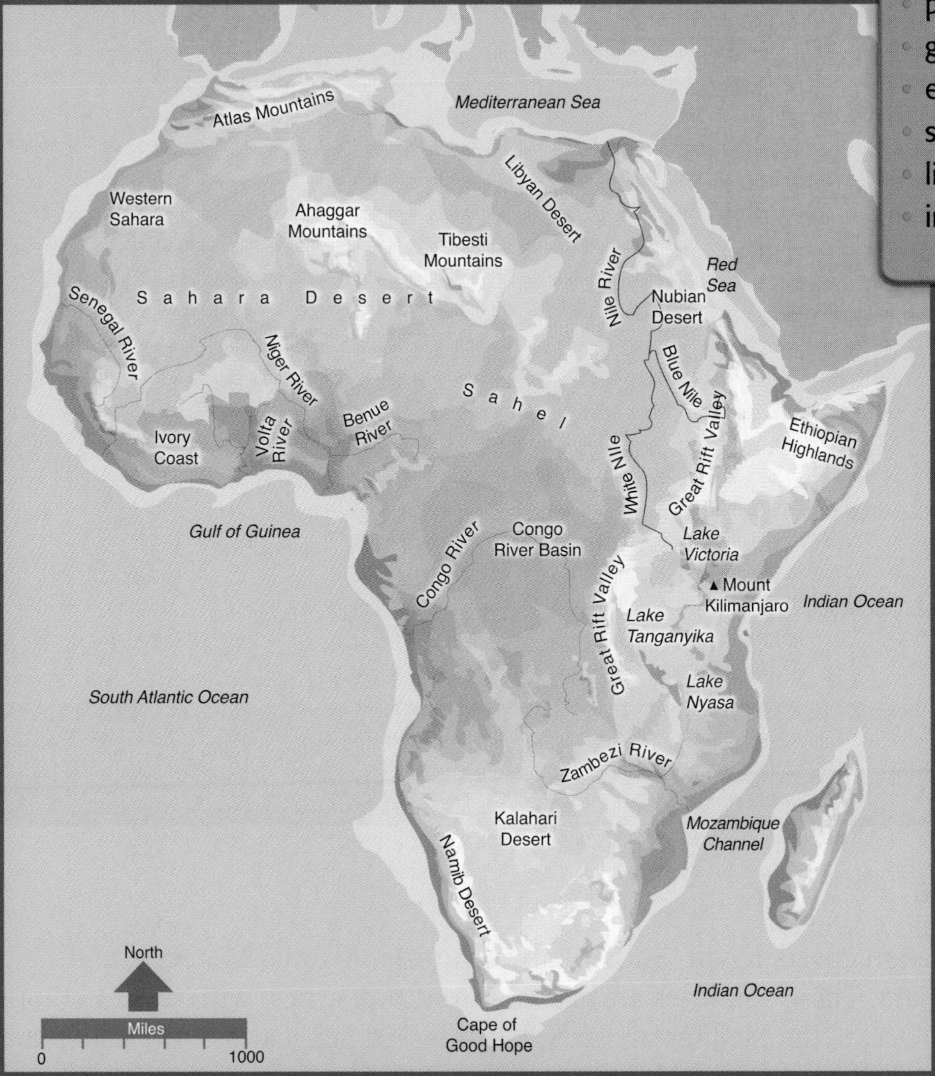

A topographical map of Africa

Vocabulary

- equatorial
- savanna
- fissionable
- irrigate
- faction
- polygamy
- griot
- ethno-linguistic group
- sub-Saharan Africa
- linguist
- indigenous

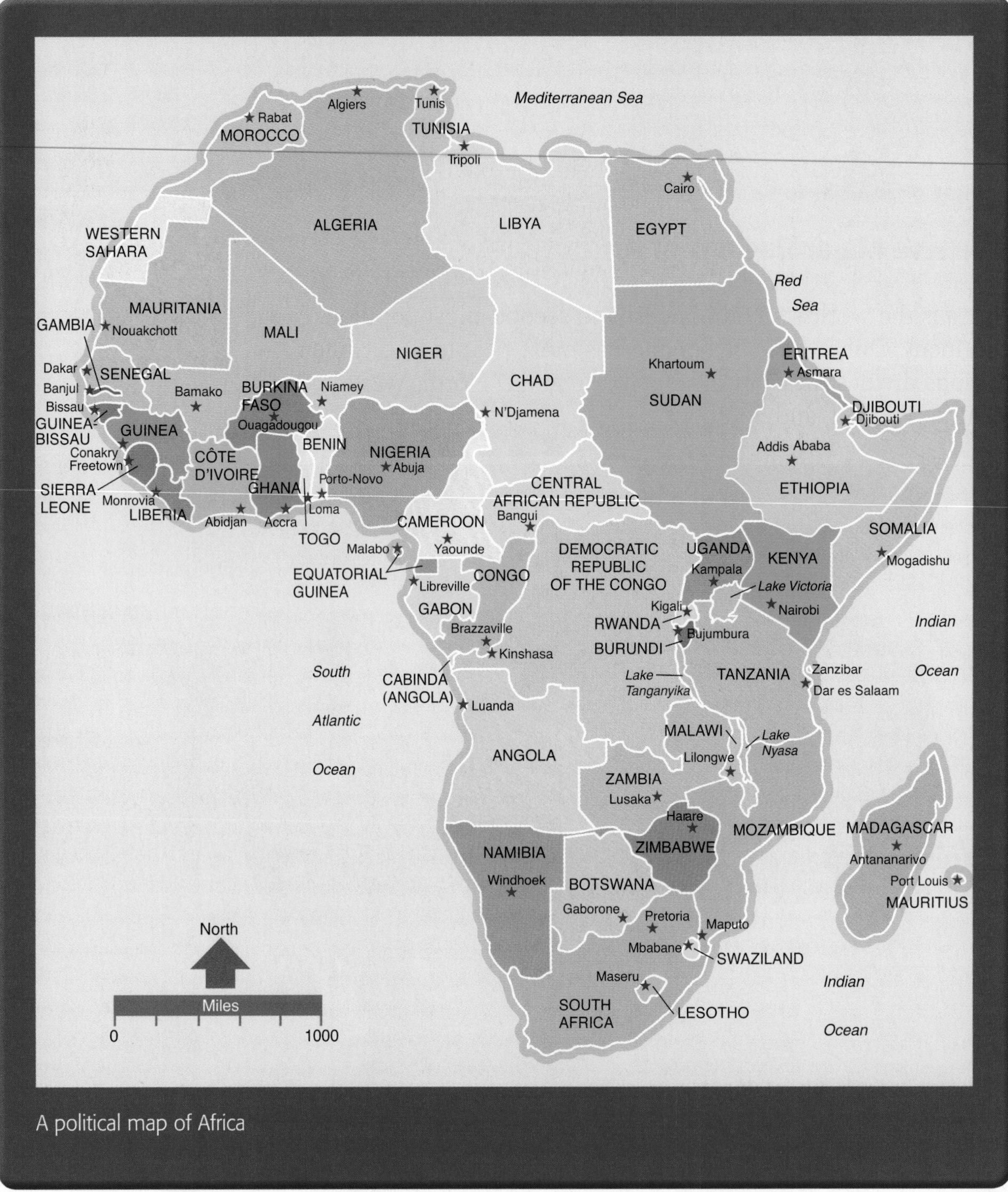

A political map of Africa

North Africa

This designation covers Egypt, Sudan, Libya, Tunisia, Algeria, Morocco, and Western Sahara. These countries are all waterfront properties, with seacoast along the Atlantic Ocean, the Mediterranean Sea, or the Red Sea. Parts of the region are quite mountainous. The Atlas Mountains follow Africa's northwestern "shoulder." But if you think of the area as a whole as largely desert, you'd be correct, too.

Except for areas right on the coasts, almost all of North Africa is desert: the Sahara Desert is the largest hot desert in the world.

West Africa

West Africa consists of Benin, Burkina Faso, Côte d'Ivoire, the Gambia, Ghana, Guinea, Guinea-Bissau, Liberia, Mali, Mauritania, Niger, Nigeria, Senegal, Sierra Leone, and Togo, plus the island nation of Cape Verde. These countries are largely equatorial jungle. Equatorial means *set along the equator*. The Senegal and the Niger are this area's important rivers.

Central Africa

Equatorial jungle also describes the countries of Central Africa. They are Angola, Cameroon, the Central African Republic, Chad, Congo, the Democratic Republic of the Congo (DRC), and Gabon. Two other island nations belong to Central Africa: Equatorial Guinea plus Sao Tome and Principe. The latter are two islands in the Gulf of Guinea. Together they make up one country. The Congo is Central Africa's main river.

Mikeno Mountain (on the right) looks out over Virunga National Park, home to about 200 gorillas in the Democratic Republic of the Congo.
Photo by Mary Knox Merrill / © 2009 The Christian Science Monitor
Jungles flourish in West Africa, Central Africa, and Eastern Africa.

Eastern Africa

The countries of the Eastern African mainland are Burundi, Djibouti, Eritrea, Ethiopia, Kenya, Malawi, Mauritius, Mozambique, Rwanda, Somalia, Uganda, Tanzania, Zambia, and Zimbabwe. The big island of Madagascar is also part of Eastern Africa, as are two island chains, the Comoros and Seychelles.

Much of Eastern Africa is highlands. This area is also Africa's "Great Lakes" region. Lake Victoria, Lake Tanganyika, and Lake Nyasa are all here. The mighty Nile has its source in Eastern Africa. It flows north from here to Egypt and the Mediterranean. The Zambezi River, in Mozambique, is another important river of this region. Mt. Kilimanjaro, Africa's highest peak at 19,330 feet, is in Tanzania. This region's lowlands are largely jungle.

Southern Africa

Southern Africa consists of Botswana, Lesotho, Namibia, South Africa, and Swaziland. Its typical landscape is the savanna—*a flat grassland of tropical or subtropical regions*. The region has some mountain ranges and is also home to the Kalahari Desert.

The Natural Resources of Africa

Africa has many significant minerals. But sometimes, as you will read below, they have led to conflict rather than wealth. African farmers, meanwhile, face enormous challenges. Experts believe that better farming practices will lead to more prosperity in Africa.

Mineral Resources

Africa accounted for 53 percent of the world's diamond production in 2006. Botswana, the Democratic Republic of the Congo (DRC), South Africa, and Angola were the top four producers.

Africa is also a big gold producer. It accounted for 21 percent of world production in 2006. South Africa was far and away the leader, followed by Ghana, Mali, and Tanzania.

Africa is a leading producer of other minerals as well. These glitter less than gold and diamonds but are critical to today's high-tech industries:

- ***Chromite*** is used to produce steel, copper, glass, and cement. People use chromium, mined from chromite, in pigments (paints), photography, and plating (a process used to coat something in a thin metal layer). South Africa is the world's leading producer.

Workers do hot strip molding at a steel works in South Africa.
Photo by Neal J. Menschel / © 1990 The Christian Science Monitor
The African continent is rich with natural resources, including manganese used in steelmaking.

- ***Cobalt*** is used to make industrial alloys (a mixture of metals) and high-performance cutting tools. People also use it to color porcelain and other substances. It has medical uses as well. Africa—mostly the DRC and Zambia—accounted for nearly 60 percent of the world's cobalt production in 2006.
- ***Manganese*** is used in steelmaking. South Africa and Gabon are Africa's leading producers of this metal. The world gets about a third of its manganese from Africa.
- ***Uranium*** is fissionable. That is, its atoms *can be split to make nuclear explosions*. People around the world use controlled nuclear explosions to create electricity. They also use uranium to build nuclear bombs. Africa accounts for about one-fifth of the world's uranium production. Almost all of that is from Nigeria and Niger.

Three big African countries also have significant oil resources: Nigeria, Angola, and Sudan.

A Kenyan woman tends to her farm daily, despite dangers due to tribal tensions.

Photo by Melanie Stetson Freeman / © 2008 The Christian Science Monitor

Most African farmers are subsistence farmers—that is, they farm to feed themselves.

Agricultural Resources

Africa's farmers have a tough row to hoe. They're unable to feed their own people. Since 1973 Africa has been a net importer of food. That is, what Africans must buy from others is more than what they can grow and sell on the market. The number of chronically hungry Africans (in other words, people who are hungry most of the time) approaches 200 million—about 20 to 25 percent of the total population.

The good news here, though, is that the World Bank, the United Nations, and other organizations are identifying ways to improve African agriculture. From 1981 to 2001, aid to Africa, adjusted for inflation, declined by about half. Since then, though, aid has bounced back. Many people, in Africa and outside it, are making a renewed effort to pull Africans out of poverty. Observers believe that improving agriculture, including farmers' incomes, is the best way to do this. The New Partnership for Africa's Development (NEPAD) is the main plan behind this effort. NEPAD stresses that "agriculture will provide the engine for growth in Africa."

Most African farmers are *subsistence* farmers—that is, they farm to feed themselves. Most own small plots of one to five acres of land. Women provide about half the labor, and they grow most of the food crops that their families eat.

Africans must work with poor soil, widely varying amounts of rain, and frequent droughts. They have a hard time getting their crops to market. They don't have access to railroads and trucking companies like the ones American farmers rely on to haul their output to the cities. Many African farmers are unable to irrigate—*water*—their fields. They don't have access to credit. That is, they can't borrow money to even out their cash flow over the growing cycle, as American farmers commonly do.

African farmers cope with all these challenges by diversifying. Even on their small plots, they grow many different crops, typically 10 or more. They also grow trees and keep livestock. And they rely heavily on hardy crops—grains such as sorghum and millet, and root crops such as cassava.

Note that these are different from the cereals (rice and wheat) that have been so important to Asia's Green Revolution. Experts say that if African farm output has grown, it's because Africans have planted more land. When Asians' farm output has grown, it's been because their crop yields have been better.

Conflicts Over Resources

As you may have noticed in reading about the Middle East, natural resources are sometimes a mixed blessing to a country. This is true in Africa, too. Controversy rages over who "owns" natural resources, and who should benefit from their development.

Those questions can be hard enough to answer. It all becomes more complicated when resource wealth fuels conflict. This has happened in many African countries in recent years: Angola, the DRC, Sierra Leone, and Liberia.

In cases of civil war, one faction, or *group*, gains illegal control over a resource and uses the money it earns to supply its troops so it can keep fighting. Factional leaders also tap resources illegally to make themselves rich and to gain wealth they can use to "buy" political support.

In Sierra Leone in the 1990s, for instance, a rebel group called the Revolutionary United Front (RUF) forced prisoners of war and others, including children as young as age 8, to dig for diamonds at gunpoint. The diamonds were sold to buyers in nearby Liberia and Guinea, and then resold in the world diamond centers in London and Antwerp, Belgium. The RUF financed its rebellion with the money it got from diamond sales. The group had no real political goals—there was nothing it was fighting for. Its leaders were eventually convicted of crimes against humanity.

Diamonds may be the best-known resource exploited in this way. But illegal sales of oil and timber have also fueled conflict in Africa. The United Nations and other organizations have begun to focus on the links between natural resources and conflict. They are moving to address the problem.

The Distinctive Characteristics of African Culture

Africa's greatest resource is its people and their cultures. Three aspects of African culture are worth examining here: the extended family, the widespread tradition of multiple marriages, and Africa's great storytelling tradition.

The Influence of Extended Families

A strong system of extended families is an essential part of traditional African cultures. Within this tradition, the group is what counts, not the individual. And it's often a very large group. In an African extended family, many people will have a say in how a couple's children should be raised, or where they should go to school, or what careers they should pursue. Not just parents but grandparents and aunts and uncles will have a voice in these decisions. This attitude is summed up in the African saying, "It takes a village to raise a child."

If a father has more than one wife, his children may need to obey not only their mother but their stepmothers—their father's other wives. If a young man has a young woman in mind for his bride, his aunts are likely to "check her out" before the marriage goes forward. By contrast, within the "modern" way of doing things, imported from the West, the individual makes his or her own decisions.

The movement of people to cities is challenging the influence of extended families in Africa. When young people leave their home villages for the cities, they naturally make new friends. They may form these new ties without regard to the social structures they knew at home. They often find their lives revolve around their identities on the job. They make friends at work. And those relationships are likely to cut across family and other traditional ties. They are likely to meet and marry someone whom their relatives don't get a chance to check out, as they would do in the countryside.

On the other hand, many young Africans go to the city and discover their clan is already there. When they first arrive, they are identified according to their family tree and "placed." They typically join a clan-based welfare organization complete with an emergency fund. They know someone is there to help with medical bills in case of serious illness, for instance.

Extended families remain important, whatever stress the system is under. In the absence of Western-style old-age and health insurance, the extended family is an important social safety net. The traditions of the extended family help absorb the shocks of war, disease, and other upheavals.

Africa's system of extended families has helped soften the devastating blow of the AIDS epidemic. This epidemic has affected Africa perhaps more than any other continent. AIDS tends to affect people in their prime earning and child-rearing years, and so it generally creates a lot of orphans. In traditional African culture, however, they don't stay orphans for long. Grandparents, aunts, and uncles step in to raise children. That said, though, so many families have been ravaged by AIDS that there sometimes are no other branches left. And many older grandparents who might otherwise step in to help are themselves already facing dire poverty because of the extended family's breakdown.

Polygamy's Impact

Polygamy means *having more than one spouse at a time*. It is still a fairly common practice in Africa. Having more than one wife at a time is common in largely Muslim parts of Africa. A 2005 survey in Senegal, for instance, found that half of all marriages there were polygamous. Many Muslim men feel that their religion allows them to take up to four wives. But more and more, African women in Muslim countries are deciding they don't want to be wife No. 2 or 3 or 4. Besides, readers of the Koran point out that although this text does allow a man to take more than one wife, to do so he must be able to afford and to treat all equally—a very tall order.

Although polygamy is widespread in Africa—and not just among Muslims—it's been controversial for a long time. European colonial rulers discouraged it. Some modern African leaders, on the other hand—notably President Umar Hassan al-Bashir of Sudan—have encouraged polygamy as a way to increase population.

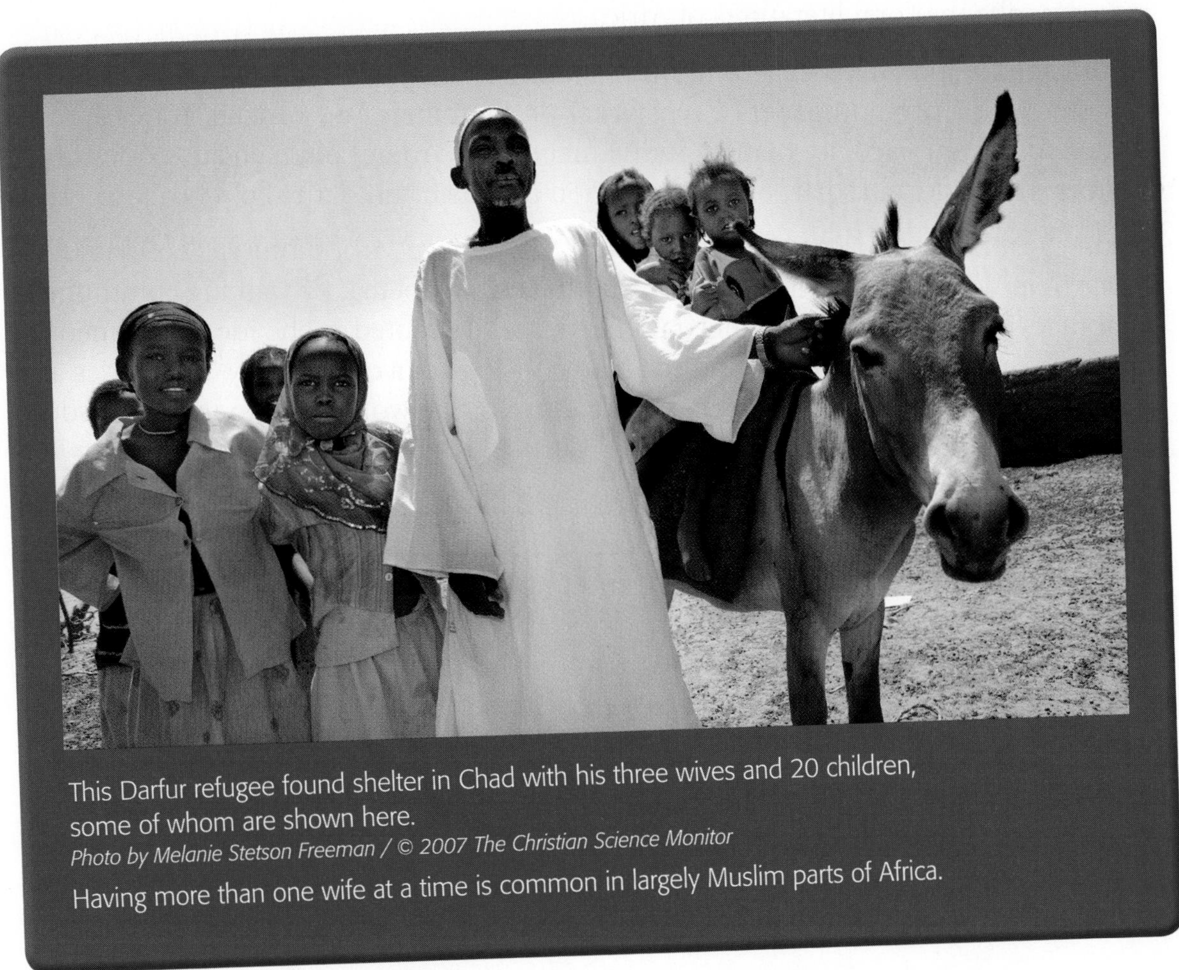

This Darfur refugee found shelter in Chad with his three wives and 20 children, some of whom are shown here.
Photo by Melanie Stetson Freeman / © 2007 The Christian Science Monitor
Having more than one wife at a time is common in largely Muslim parts of Africa.

Christianity, South Africa's leading religion, forbids polygamy. But Jacob Zuma, the country's third president since the end of white rule in South Africa, openly favors multiple marriages and has several wives. Anglican Archbishop Desmond Tutu, the country's most prominent religious leader, has denounced Zuma as a "Zulu peasant" who was "unfit to be president."

A 2009 phone survey of 2,000 South Africans found that 74 percent of respondents objected to polygamy. Attitudes varied widely by race and sex, however.

Even some African men who have practiced polygamy have had second thoughts. In 2005 the BBC interviewed a 56-year-old Ethiopian whose 11 wives had borne him 100 children, 23 of whom had died. As for the rest, he had trouble remembering their names. He had wanted many wives in the first place as a way to share his wealth. But things didn't turn out the way he had hoped. "I want my children to be farmers, but I have no land. I want them to go to school, but I have no money."

The Significance of Oral Tradition

But polygamy is only one characteristic of African culture. Africa is a continent of storytellers. It's a place where oral tradition—language that is spoken rather than written—counts for much. Africans today are still primarily oral people. In fact, the Kenyan novelist Ngugi wa Thiong'o came up with the term "orature" to describe the "oral literature" of Africa.

Africans compose and share orature without writing anything down. There's no writer with a pen and paper or typewriter or computer. And African stories are more of a group activity than an individual one. "Writers" often create stories for groups to perform as part of a presentation of music and dancing.

The griot is an important figure in Africa. A griot is *an African storyteller, especially one from West Africa*. He is a kind of walking encyclopedia, or walking community library. The griot (it's pronounced GREE-o, and it's rooted in the idea of "someone who creates") carries in his head the whole history of a community. His stories are meant to entertain, to help people make sense of the world, and to impart wisdom and traditional morals to his listeners.

Rather like jazz musicians, griots improvise. They don't tell the same story the same way each time. There's no single "correct" version of a story. Rather, griots go back and forth between a memorized text and improvisation. They adapt their story to their audience and to what's going on in the community or the world. If a story becomes irrelevant because of changes in the larger culture, the griots will modify it. Or they may just drop it and replace it with something else. That's how new stories are born.

African languages are less standardized than major Western languages like English or French. A village may share a language with another village just up the road—but may speak it just a bit differently. These language differences mean stories are told slightly differently.

These hairdressers take one to two days to braid a person's hair at their informal outdoor shop in Burundi, in Eastern Africa.
Photo by Melanie Stetson Freeman / © 2006 The Christian Science Monitor
Black Africans are by far the majority of the population of Africa.

The Main Ethno-Linguistic Groups in Africa

A group of people who all grow up with the same body of stories from the same village griot would tend to look at things in a similar way. That body of stories is an expression of ethno-linguistic identity. An ethno-linguistic group is *a group of people who share a common language and culture*. This means they also share a common view of the world and life in general.

Africans

Black Africans are the original inhabitants of sub-Saharan Africa. (Sub-Saharan Africa is *that part of Africa south of the Sahara Desert.*) In fact, scientists believe that modern human beings came from the Rift Valley in Eastern Africa. Black Africans are by far the majority of the population of Africa. They are divided into four main language groups: Niger-Congo, Afro-Asiatic, Nilo-Saharan, and Khoisan. You will read about them later in this lesson.

Arabs and Berbers

The Arabs and Berbers live mostly in North Africa. Some Arabic influence is also noticeable on the east coast, however. Much lighter-skinned than the people of sub-Saharan Africa, they have often been referred to by Europeans as "black." Maybe that's how they looked to the fair-skinned peoples of Europe, especially northern Europe. Another term for the Arabs and Berbers of North Africa is "Moors." The Moors conquered Spain in the eighth century. Shakespeare's tragedy *Othello* is about a Moor in Venice, Italy.

As you read in Chapter 1, Lesson 1, the Arabs originated on the Arabian Peninsula and eventually spread out to North Africa and other places. The Berbers, on the other hand, are the original inhabitants of North Africa west of Egypt. They came under the influence of the Arabs when the Arabs arrived.

> **fastFACT**
>
> St. Augustine has proven to be one of the most important and influential Christians since Bible times. Roman Catholic, Protestant, and Eastern Orthodox Christians still read his books, *The Confessions*—one of the first autobiographies—and *City of God*.

Arabs speak Arabic. Berbers have their own Berber language, spoken by 14 million to 25 million people. Both groups are predominantly Muslim. Two of the most famous Berbers were not, however: the Roman Emperor Severus Septimus and St. Augustine, Christian Bishop of Hippo (354–430).

North Africans in their traditional attire mix with tourists in Tunis, Tunisia.
Photo by R. Norman Matheny / © 1992 The Christian Science Monitor

The Arabs and Berbers of North Africa are much lighter-skinned than the people of sub-Saharan Africa.

White South Africans picnic at a concert at Cape Town's Kirstenbosch National Botanical Gardens.

Photo by Melanie Stetson Freeman / © 2002 The Christian Science Monitor

Whites make up about 10 percent of South Africa's 48 million people.

Afrikaners and Other Europeans

In the seventeenth and eighteenth centuries, Dutch, German, and French Protestant farmers settled in what is now South Africa. Their descendants are known as Afrikaners. They number about 3 million. Together with people of British descent, they make up about 10 percent of South Africa's 48 million people. This group, which speaks Afrikaans and English, is the largest white population in sub-Saharan Africa. All these Europeans, if they are religious, tend to follow the Protestant or Roman Catholic faiths of their ancestral homelands. South Africa has a significant Jewish community as well.

fastFACT

Afrikaans is an Indo-European language that evolved from Dutch among the people who became Afrikaners and coloured (mixed race) in South Africa. More than 6 million people speak it.

People of Mixed Race and Asians

Colored is a term that went out of favor in the United States decades ago as a way to refer to blacks. But in South Africa, *coloured* (with a "u") is the proper way to refer to people of mixed race. They make up about 9 percent of the population. They are generally of mixed African and European background. Some have Asian ancestry as well. Most speak Afrikaans.

In Africa, *Asians* usually refers to people from the Indian subcontinent brought to Africa to work on British-owned plantations. They make up 2.5 percent of South Africa's population. Small groups of Asians live in former British colonies elsewhere in East Africa, such as Kenya. They generally follow the traditional religions their ancestors practiced in South Asia. South and Eastern Africa also have small Chinese communities.

The Main Language Groups in Africa

With its variety of ethno-linguistic groups, it's no surprise that Africa has more languages spoken than any other continent—about 2,000. Most of these have very small numbers of speakers. Only about 50 have half a million speakers or more.

Niger-Congo, Afro-Asiatic, Nilo-Saharan, and Khoisan

The American linguist Joseph H. Greenberg (1915–2001) was the first to classify the languages of Africa. (A linguist is *someone who studies languages*.) He grouped them into four major families.

The Niger-Congo Family

This group consists of more than 1,400 languages. Together they have between 300 million and 400 million speakers. The Atlantic-Congo branch is the biggest of three branches in this family. Its territory stretches across almost all of sub-Saharan Africa. It includes the Bantu group of languages. Swahili, one of the most widely spoken in a geographic sense, is part of this group. So is Shona, the majority language of Zimbabwe.

By contrast, people speak the Kordofanian-branch languages in only a small area of southern Sudan. And they speak the languages of the Mande branch in West Africa.

The Afro-Asiatic Family

Between 200 million and 300 million people in northern Africa, Somalia, Ethiopia, and Eritrea speak these languages. The area around Lake Chad in central Africa is also home to speakers of a group of these languages. The vocabulary of all these tongues—about 350 in all—reflects the life and livelihoods of the people who speak them. That is, they raise and herd livestock and grow food crops. These languages, including the Berber languages touched on earlier in this lesson, have all grown from a language called "ancestral Semitic." This is a sort of "grandfather" language of Arabic and Hebrew as well. This makes today's Afro-Asiatic languages "cousins" of those tongues spoken in the Middle East.

The Nilo-Saharan Family

This is a smaller group, in terms of numbers of speakers—18 million to 30 million. Its languages are so diverse that not everyone agrees that they really belong together as one family. People speak in these languages in the eastern Sahara and the upper Nile Valley. (That is the southern part of the valley because the Nile flows north.) The DRC and the areas around Lake Victoria in east Central Africa are also home to speakers of Nilo-Saharan tongues.

The Khoisan Family

The smallest family of African languages is the Khoisan. There are only about 30 languages in this group, with only about 200,000 speakers altogether. The Khoikhoi and San peoples of Southern Africa account for most of these. The Khoisan language with the most speakers is Nama. People speak it in Namibia and South Africa. Sandawe and Hadza, two other languages in this family, are spoken well to the north, in Tanzania.

The Khoisan languages include "click" consonants, made by clicking or clucking the tongue. Almost every word begins with a click in some of these languages, and there are several different kinds of clicks. One special click is made by pressing the lips together and releasing them by sucking in air. The sound that's made may remind you of the sound of a kiss!

The Roles of European and Asian Languages

Many Africans speak more than one African language. They also often speak one or more European languages, especially if they have a college degree. These include English, French, Afrikaans, Portuguese, and German.

In countries with many different indigenous—*native*—languages, no one tongue is dominant. None has enough speakers to unify the country. And so this role often falls to the "neutral" language of the former colonial power instead.

Most of Africa's South Asians speak English. But some retain their ancestral languages. As evidence of this, the South African Constitution mentions several South Asian languages: Gujarati, Hindi, Tami, Telegu, and Urdu.

How Islam, Christianity, and Indigenous Religions Influence Africa

Africa is a lively spiritual marketplace. During the twentieth century, both Christianity and Islam grew rapidly on the continent. But traditional religions remain as well. Many Africans practice more than one religion.

Africa's Major Religions: Christianity, Islam, and Indigenous

In 1900 Africa had just 10 million Christians, according to the religious scholar Philip Jenkins. This was about 9 percent of a total population of 107 million. Today about 46 percent of Africans are Christian. (Estimates of Africa's total population range from 700 million to 1 billion.)

Jenkins expects to see the numbers rise because Africa's Christian countries have high rates of population growth. He expects that by the year 2050, of the seven countries in the world with the largest numbers of Christians, three will be in Africa: Nigeria, the Democratic Republic of the Congo, and Ethiopia.

A mosque sits on a hill above busy Kampala, Uganda.
Photo by Mary Knox Merrill / © 2009 The Christian Science Monitor

Today the number of those practicing Islam across Africa is only slightly smaller than the number of Christians.

American and European missionaries were behind this growth. Their work also helped standardize native languages, by the way. Translators preferred to create one Bible for as large a group as they could, rather than a different one for every village. These missionaries also brought the Roman alphabet. This is the one used in English and other European languages. Originally, many significant African languages used Arabic script. But it wasn't always a good fit with the sounds of African languages. For instance, Arabic has only three vowels, and Swahili has five: *a*, *e*, *i*, *o*, and *u*. The Roman alphabet worked better to convey the sounds of Swahili.

Islam also grew during the twentieth century. By some reckonings, it attracted even more converts than Christianity. Today the numbers of those practicing Islam are only slightly smaller than for Christians. Muslims are concentrated in North Africa and northern West Africa and along the East African coast.

Oddly enough, European colonialism may have aided Islam's spread in Africa. First, during the colonial era European powers divided their territories artificially rather than paying attention to the natural boundaries between communities. Second, these rulers sometimes adopted Muslim law for these oddly shaped colonies. It provided a single standard that could be applied uniformly. This meant that they didn't have to sort through competing tribal customs.

Also, Christianity came to Africa largely through European colonizers. That made it unattractive to many Africans. Islam, on the other hand, did not have that history and so was more appealing to many.

Not all Christianity in Africa was "imported," however. Africa has two ancient native churches that go back to the very early days of Christianity. They are the Coptic Christian Church in Egypt and the Ethiopian Orthodox Church. And the Copts, by the way, speak a language related to the ancient Egyptian of the Pharaohs.

Despite the rise of Christianity and Islam in Africa, traditional religions are still important. Traditional religions still claim a majority of the population in several countries: Benin, Botswana, Burkina Faso, the Central African Republic, Cote d'Ivoire, Guinea-Bissau, Madagascar, Mozambique, Sierra Leone, Togo, and Zambia.

And of the three African countries that Philip Jenkins predicts will have some of the largest numbers of Christians in the world by the middle of the twenty-first century, all are currently, at least, "mixed," with no one belief system claiming more than 50 percent of the population.

Unfortunately, the large numbers of Christians and Muslims living near each other in many African countries sometimes leads to conflicts. These are often as much ethnic conflicts as they are religious. In the Sudan, for example, the Muslim Arabs of the north and the Christian and traditional black Africans of the south have waged civil war off and on for many years. The black Africans accused the Muslim government of trying to impose Islam on them. The presence of oil reserves in traditionally African areas has complicated the situation.

In Nigeria, conflicts between Christians and Muslims in the country's northern states have grown as Islamic fundamentalists and Wahhabists have pushed to implement Islamic law. They have tried to apply it to Christians and other non-Muslims as well as to Muslims. Nigeria's many ethnic divisions often make the conflict worse.

Worshippers light candles at a Coptic Christian Church in Cairo, Egypt's, Old City.
Photo by Melanie Stetson Freeman / © 1995 The Christian Science Monitor

Africa has two ancient native churches that go back to the very early days of Christianity: the Coptic Christian Church in Egypt and the Ethiopian Orthodox Church.

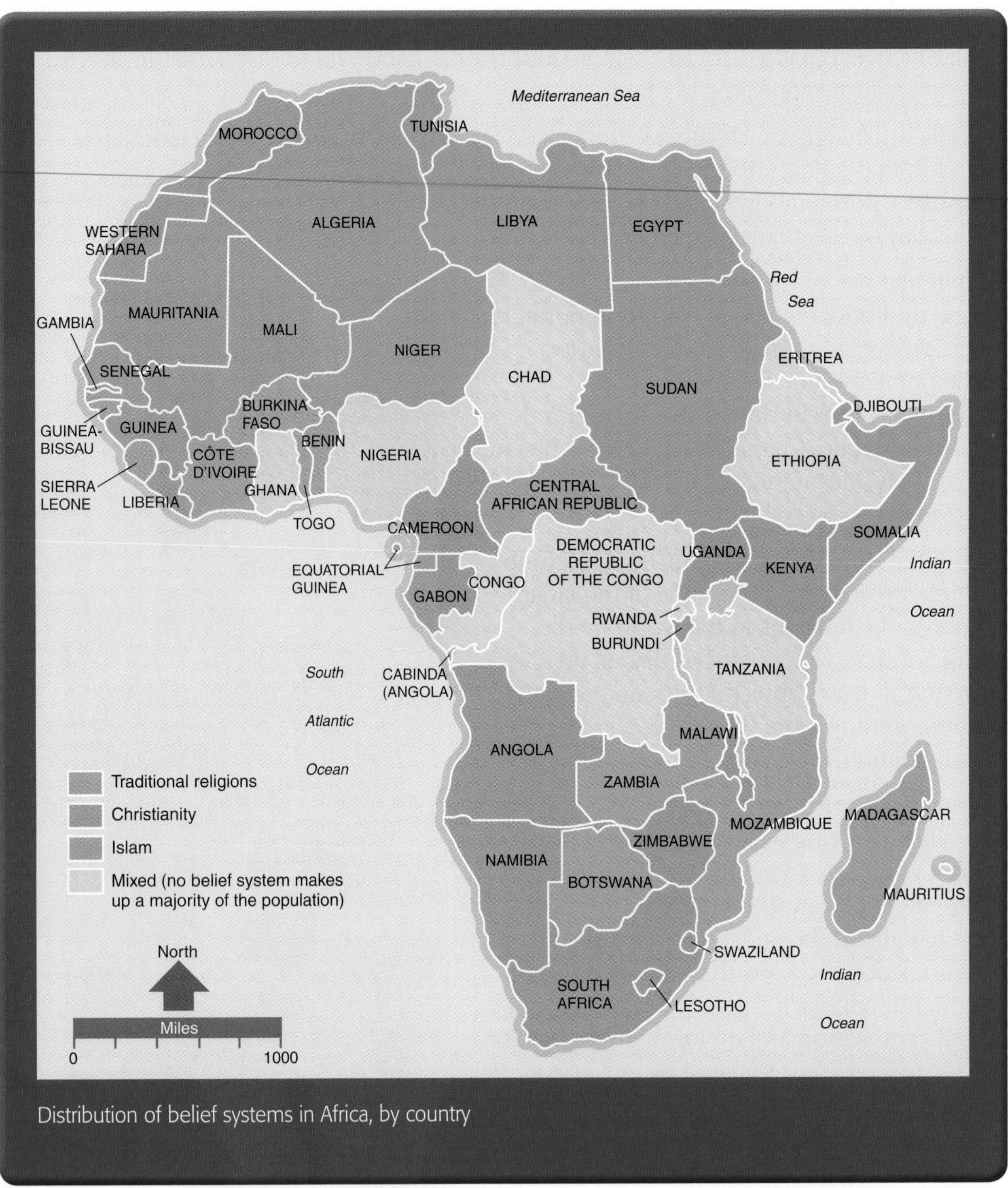

Distribution of belief systems in Africa, by country

Many African dictators, such as Isaias Afwerki in Eritrea, have persecuted Muslims as well as Christians, especially when they refused to do what the government demanded. Much of Africa's religious and ethnic conflict is the aftereffect of the colonial period, when European powers seized control of most of the continent and its resources. You'll read about that in the next lesson.

Lesson 1 Review

Using complete sentences, answer the following questions on a sheet of paper.

1. What is the world's largest hot desert?
2. Where is Africa's Great Lakes region?
3. Why do development officials see agriculture as the "engine for growth" in Africa in the coming years?
4. How did Sierra Leone's RUF guerrillas get diamonds, and what did they do with them?
5. What specific role do a young man's aunts play in a traditional extended family in Africa?
6. How does the Koran limit the number of wives a man may take?
7. What ethno-linguistic group makes up the vast majority of Africa's population?
8. Who are the coloured people of South Africa?
9. What are Swahili and Shona?
10. What group of languages includes distinctive click noises?
11. Why has Christianity grown in Africa since 1900?
12. Where are Africa's Muslims concentrated?

Applying Your Learning

13. If you lived in Africa, what language or languages would you want to know? Why?

LESSON 2 The Shadow of Western Colonialism

Quick Write

Imagine that you are a member of the British Parliament reading about Henry Morton Stanley's explorations of Africa. Should your country do anything in response to his discoveries? Why or why not?

Learn About

- the precolonial period of African history
- the colonial period of African history
- the history and impacts of African independence

In the nineteenth century, a Scotsman named David Livingstone spent more than 30 years exploring Africa. He brought the Congo to the Western world's attention. At one point he completely lost contact with Europe. An American newspaper, the *New York Herald*, sent Henry Morton Stanley to look for him. He found him in 1871 on the shore of Lake Tanganyika. Three years later, the *Herald* and Britain's *Daily Telegraph* commissioned Stanley to continue Livingstone's work (Livingstone had died in 1873). He completed his explorations in 1877 and saw great potential for commerce. He then tried to interest the British government in further exploration and development of this part of Africa. He met with no success, however.

The Precolonial Period of African History

Vocabulary

- social stratification
- polities
- transatlantic
- apartheid
- universal franchise
- repatriate
- hereditary rule

Westerners sometimes think of African history as beginning with the arrival of Europeans. But as you will read in the following sections, many different peoples were moving across the continent before the colonial powers arrived.

The Early Expansion of Islam in Africa

If you had to name the most populous Arab states today, Egypt would surely top the list. But it has not always been the case. Nor has Egypt always been predominantly Muslim. For several centuries after the beginning of the Christian era, Egypt was a largely Christian country. Historians put an exact date on when that began to change—rapidly.

On 12 December 639 a Muslim named Amr ibn al As crossed from the Sinai Peninsula into Egypt. The prophet Muhammad himself had made him a military commander. And now Amr led an army of 4,000 men on horseback. They carried lances, swords, and bows. Their objective was the fortress of Babylon at the top of the Nile Delta.

An Arab chief from Chad.
Photo by Mathew Clark / © 2007 The Christian Science Monitor
Arabs arrived in Africa on 12 December 639 when a Muslim named Amr ibn al As crossed the Sinai Peninsula into Egypt with an army of 4,000 men on horseback.

Six months later, reinforcements arrived. In July, Amr's army, by then numbering as many as 12,000 soldiers, faced off on the plains of Heliopolis against the army of the Byzantines, who then ruled Egypt. The Arabs scattered the Byzantines but won no decisive victory. Their enemy regrouped at the fortress. Finally, after a six-month siege, the fortress fell to the Arabs on 9 April 641.

Amr's men then marched on to Alexandria. It was a fortified city but couldn't hold out against the Arabs. The governor of the city agreed to surrender. The two sides signed a treaty in November 641.

The next year, the Byzantines tried to retake their city. But history was not on their side. In the end, the Muslim conquerors gave them their usual three choices:

1. Convert to Islam
2. Agree to pay a tax to keep their own religion
3. Face the Muslim armies on the battlefield.

The Byzantines chose No. 2. This conquest was an important turning point in Egyptian history. Over the centuries, it changed Egypt from a mostly Christian to a mostly Muslim country. What's more, even those who remained Christian or Jewish adopted the Arabic language and culture.

This conquest of Egypt was part of the Arab/Islamic expansion that began after the death of Muhammad. Arab tribes began to move out of the Arabian Peninsula and into other lands, such as Iraq and Syria.

Once established in Egypt, the Arabs spread out across the rest of North Africa. Invaders from other religions and cultures had passed through this part of the world before the Arabs. But none of them had the same deep, long-lasting effect on the region as Islam. The new faith would make its way into all parts of society. It brought new military leaders, scholars, and fervent religious thinkers. These newcomers would largely replace the tribal practices and loyalties.

The cultural changes happened more slowly than the military conquest, however. The nomadic Berbers converted quickly and helped the Arab invaders. But the Christian and Jewish communities remained significant until the twelfth century.

The Dispersion of Bantu Peoples

As the Arab peoples spread—along with their Muslim religion—across northern Africa, the Bantu peoples were expanding in regions farther south. *Bantu*, as you read in Lesson 1, is the name of a group of languages spoken in much of sub-Saharan Africa. The word *Bantu* means "people" in many of those languages.

The Bantu peoples started out in what is today Nigeria and Cameroon, in the "notch" of West Africa. They first began to expand significantly about 3,500 years ago, about 1500 BC. This was after they learned to grow bananas and yams.

Another wave of expansion came after they learned how to grow cereal crops and to work iron. The timeline of the events is not clear, but many scholars believe the Bantu peoples learned how to work iron around AD 500. Iron tools made it possible for them to cut down trees to clear land for crops. Their ironworking skills let them make other items that were valuable for trade. Perhaps most important, they could make weapons with iron. This gave the Bantu a military edge as they expanded into new territories.

A mother waters her cornfield in Malawi.

Photo by Andy Nelson / © 2002 The Christian Science Monitor

The Bantu peoples began expanding in sub-Saharan Africa starting around 1500 BC—in large part thanks to their agricultural practices and ironworking.

Scientists suggest that the whole development process of the Bantu went something like this: Growing more food (yams and bananas) led to population increases, and more people living closer together. (Scientists call this "social complexity." Sometimes it leads to war.) Feeling the pressure of more people, the Bantu would have been eager to find out about new crops they could grow, including cereals. They may have learned about these crops from other peoples, or figured them out on their own. They also learned to raise livestock. This meant they had even more food.

And more food meant more people. That, in turn, would mean more demand both for food and for land to grow it on—and more social complexity. As they mastered cultivation of cereals, the Bantu could adapt to different kinds of terrain.

Meanwhile, as the Bantu peoples continued their work with iron, they had an advantage compared with ironworkers in other places: their trees. Metalworking requires hot fires. Metalworkers use coal today, but in early times they used wood for their fires. African hardwoods burned very hot.

With these advantages, the Bantus expanded naturally into thinly populated non-Bantu areas. Finally they expanded into just about all the ecological niches where they could fit.

Two separate population streams flowed out of the Nigerian/Cameroonian "notch" on the side of Africa. One went down the west side of the continent. The other crossed the Sahel, the edge of the Sahara Desert, and then moved down the east coast. The two met again in the southern part of the Congo, probably about the start of the Christian era. By AD 300 Bantu speakers occupied most of sub-Saharan Africa.

How the Bantu Dispersion Developed Trade and Exchange

The Bantu peoples had two sets of advantages: their agricultural skills, including raising livestock, and their metalworking skills. And because their iron was so good, it was of interest to people as far away as Eurasia. Since they knew how to cultivate a wide range of crops, they were comfortable in a wide range of terrain. They also had common interests with both peoples who were either cereal-crop farmers or pastoralists, who herded livestock.

All this laid the groundwork for the development of long-distance trading networks running between Africa and Eurasia. Copper and salt were two other goods in the Bantu trade mix. Routes running across the Sahara, up the Red Sea, and across the Indian Ocean tied Africa to the peoples of the Mediterranean, the Near East, and even the Indian subcontinent.

Another aspect of trade and exchange in Africa at this point was its connection to the spread of Islam. Islam expanded its reach by the sword up the Nile Valley. But in most of sub-Saharan Africa, this took place mainly through trade. Muslim merchants, rather than soldiers, spread the new faith. Throughout the Sahel and along the East African coast, Muslims traded with those who practiced traditional African religions. The exchanges benefited both sides. The Muslim communities were often found in dispersed communities along trade routes.

Trade also played a role in still another aspect of the Bantu peoples' development. It increased their wealth. Merchants brought exotic goods from far away into these communities. These goods were common enough that people knew about them, but not so common that everyone had them. People who could afford to buy these special goods had more prestige than those who did not own them. It was probably very much like what you see at your school, in fact. There's likely some brand of shoes, jeans, or accessory that you've told your parents you "had" to have because you wanted to be like the "cool" kids.

How Monsoon Winds Helped Foster Trade

In the days before jet aircraft or steamships, people could travel around the Indian Ocean because they relied on monsoon winds. These are winds that change direction with the season. The word *monsoon* comes from an Arabic word meaning "season." They blow from the northeast from November to March and then from the southwest from April to August. This helped merchants get from the Persian Gulf and the Indian subcontinent to Africa, and then return during the spring and summer.

Scientists use the term social stratification to refer to this *division of a society into layers*. This stratification led to the emergence of "big men," or chiefs, and of polities—*organized political units*, led by chiefs or kings.

The Colonial Period of African History

Colonialism was about money and power. The larger a nation's empire, the more money and power a nation likely controlled. European empires built up their influence by exploiting the natural resources of foreign lands and the labor of native people. They also gathered great wealth through the slave trade. Let's focus here on slavery as it relates to Africa.

As European powers competed for position in Africa, slavery was an accepted institution around the world. The slave trade overshadowed other kinds of trade on the West African coast. Moreover, slavery wasn't just an evil that Europeans imposed on Africans. Many African societies held and traded slaves. Prisoners of war, both men and women, often became slaves. Just as often, however, African slave owners killed the males, but kept the women and children as workers and to bear them more children. This is one reason Africans so readily sold males to the West once the two regions of the world established a slave trade.

However, slavery in Africa was different from the slavery of the New World's plantations. For one thing, it didn't involve a dangerous journey across an ocean. What's more, slaves in Africa often had at least some rights in African communities. Many eventually became part of their masters' families, with full rights.

The Slave Trade of Colonial Africa

The transatlantic—*crossing the Atlantic Ocean*—slave trade began with the Portuguese in the late fifteenth century. Portuguese navigators first came to the West African coast in an effort to bypass Muslim Morocco. From the West African coast the Portuguese gained access to the gold trade of Africa, and the spice trade, too, via the Indian Ocean. For Africa, though, the real legacy of Portugal's adventures there was the slave trade.

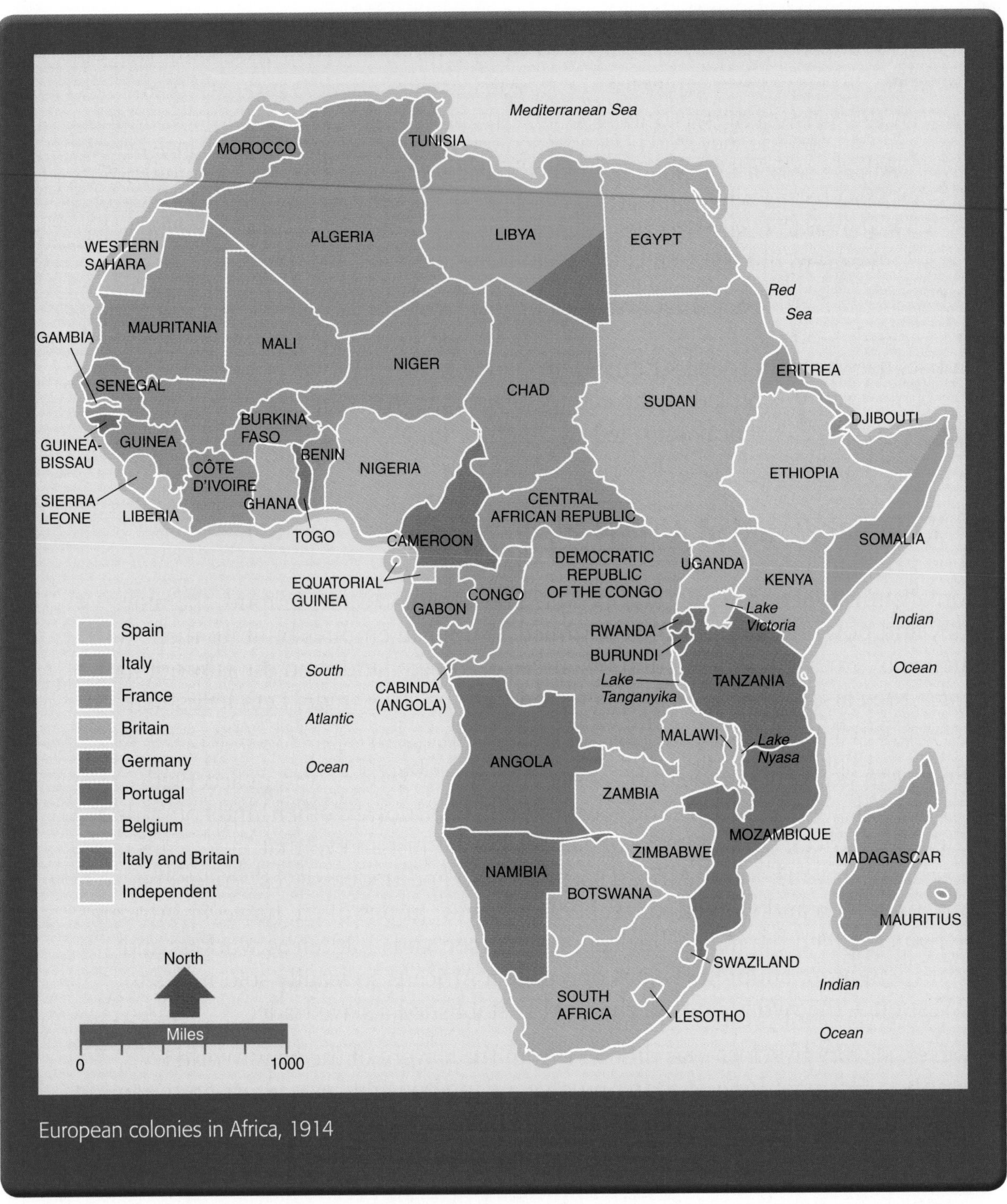

European colonies in Africa, 1914

By 1471 Portuguese ships had reached the Niger Delta. In 1481 emissaries from the king of Portugal visited the court of the oba, or king, of Benin. (This Benin is in modern Nigeria. Don't confuse it with today's Republic of Benin. It's nearby but is a different country.) The two countries had fairly close relations for a time.

The oba's courtiers even started to speak Portuguese. Gwatto, a port in what today is Nigeria, handled peppers, ivory, and, more and more, slaves. These were what the Africans offered in exchange for coral beads, Indian textiles, and European-made items, such as weapons and tools.

At the end of the sixteenth century, the rising naval power of the Dutch challenged the Portuguese monopoly on West African trade. The French and the English later challenged the Dutch in their turn. Ships of other flags got into the trade, too—Denmark, Sweden, the German state of Brandenburg, and even the North American colonies. But Britain was the dominant slaving power in the eighteenth century.

And so when the British Parliament outlawed the slave trade in 1807, the action had wide repercussions. Technically, what the new legislation did was to forbid ships under British registry to engage in the slave trade. But it was meant to shut down traffic in slaves out of West African ports. Other countries followed Britain's lead. Attitudes changed slowly, however.

The American Founding Fathers considered banning slavery in the US Constitution. But to keep the support of Southerners, they agreed to let the slave trade continue until 1 January 1808. On that date, the "importation" of slaves from outside the United States became illegal. Slavery itself continued, however.

Meanwhile, Britain went from being the leading slave-trading nation to being the international enforcer of its new ban. To this end, the Royal Navy maintained a major presence off the coast of West Africa. For years, up to a sixth of its fleet was dedicated to fighting the slave trade. The effort to replace the slave trade with other forms of commerce led to Britain's getting involved in the internal politics of what is today Nigeria. The British government decided to take legal control of the coastal area. This, in turn, led to Britain expanding its colonial presence even further throughout the nineteenth century.

The Development of Partitions and Borders in Colonial Africa

During this period European powers carved up most of Africa into separate spheres of influence. Much of this took place at the Conference of Berlin, from 1884 to 1885. You will notice some patterns coming up again and again:

1. Europeans found coastal areas much easier to reach than Africa's interior
2. Some colonial ventures started out as private businesses, and only later did they come under direct control of a European government
3. As in the Middle East, Europeans did a lot of redrawing of other peoples' maps
4. Many colonies changed hands over time. After Germany's defeat in World War I, its colonies ended up as mandates of the League of Nations.

French Colonies

French West Africa was a federation of eight territories. Many of these have changed their names in the years since:

- Mauritania
- Senegal
- French Sudan (now Mali)
- French Guinea (now Guinea)
- Côte d'Ivoire
- Upper Volta (now Burkina Faso)
- Dahomey (now Benin)
- Niger.

This federation began as a series of coastal trading posts. The French took these over in the seventeenth and eighteenth centuries. Only later during a sort of land rush known as the "Scramble for Africa" in the final decades of the nineteenth century did they move inland in a big way.

The French established *French Equatorial Africa* in 1910. It consisted of these territories:

- Chad
- Congo (then known as "Middle Congo" or the French Congo)
- Gabon
- The Central African Republic (then known as Ubangi-Shari).

Brazzaville, in Congo, served as this federation's capital.

France had large colonies in the Arab north, as well. The countries of *French North Africa* were Algeria, Morocco, and Tunisia.

Women seek shelter from the rain in modern-day Kinshasa, capital of the Democratic Republic of the Congo.

Photo by Robert Harbison / © 1990 The Christian Science Monitor

In the late 1800s Belgian King Leopold II hired Henry Morton Stanley to explore the Congo Basin. Stanley traveled up the Congo River and founded a trading station called Leopoldville, which today is Kinshasa.

King Leopold's African Adventure

King Leopold II was the driving force behind Belgium's move into Africa. The country had become independent only in 1831 when it broke away from the Netherlands. Soon after succeeding his father, Leopold I, to the throne in 1865, he latched onto colonial expansion as a path to glory. He also wanted to get very rich. He hired Henry Morton Stanley to explore the Congo when no one else was interested. This led to the establishment of the Congo Free State. It was a territory 74 times the size of tiny Belgium. And Leopold was utterly in charge of it. It was literally his own personal kingdom. He got the United States and other Western countries to recognize his personal sovereignty over the Congo Free State.

Millions of Congolese died under his brutal rule. By 1895, though, the British press started to expose his atrocities. A Swedish missionary reported that Leopold rewarded his soldiers according to the number of Congolese hands they cut off to punish native workers for not producing enough. Others confirmed these reports. In 1908 Leopold was forced to give up his personal fiefdom to the Belgian state.

The Belgian Congo

When Henry Morton Stanley reported on his explorations of Africa, the "Scramble for Africa" was well under way. But Europeans didn't generally know much about the Congo River basin and weren't much interested. For the ambitious Belgian king, Leopold II, this was a great opportunity.

fastFACT

People have long kept the two countries named "Congo" straight by identifying them by their capitals. Congo (Kinshasa) is the former Belgian Congo. Congo (Brazzaville) is the former French Congo. From 1971 until 1997, Congo (Kinshasa) was known as Zaire.

He hired Stanley to help him. He also set up an international group of bankers to finance Stanley's activities on his behalf. Starting at the mouth of the Congo River in 1879, Stanley worked his way upriver. He founded a settlement called Vivi as a capital. Farther upriver, on the south bank of the Congo, he founded a trading station called Leopoldville. Today it's Kinshasa, capital of the Democratic Republic of the Congo. (The French had already claimed the north bank of the river.) On a later journey, he got local chieftains to sign more than 450 treaties surrendering sovereignty over much of the Congo Basin to Leopold II.

British Colonies

The British were the leading colonizers of Africa. Their holdings in West Africa were:

- Nigeria
- The Gold Coast (later Ghana)
- Sierra Leone
- The Gambia.

On the continent's eastern side, the British controlled a swath running from the Mediterranean to the Cape of Good Hope. It ran through:

- Egypt
- Sudan
- Uganda
- Tanganyika and Zanzibar (today's Tanzania)
- Nyasaland (today's Malawi)
- Northern and Southern Rhodesia (Zambia and Zimbabwe nowadays)
- Swaziland
- Botswana
- Lesotho
- South Africa.

The British also claimed a territory known as British Somaliland on the Horn of Africa—a peninsula in East Africa that juts into the Arabian Sea. They had numerous island possessions, including the Seychelles, the Maldives, and Mauritius.

Paradoxically, the British got more involved as a colonial power in Africa once they decided to combat slavery. Their diplomats made treaties with kings and chieftains who they hoped would help them stop the trafficking. British missionaries active in the area called for government help as they fought what they saw as "barbarous practices" among native Africans.

On the other hand, up until the middle of the nineteenth century, the British were in no great haste to annex colonies. They tended to see them as a drag on finances. If we can trade with these places, isn't that all we need? they wondered. Why bother to annex them? That attitude changed, though, once other European powers began to show more interest in Africa.

South Africa

In 1652 the Dutch established a colony at the Cape of Good Hope, the southernmost tip of Africa. It was originally meant to be just a supply station for the Dutch East India Company's ships. But soon the "Boers" (farmers) spread inland. Their large farms displaced the native San and Khoikhoi peoples.

The British took control of the Cape Colony in 1815. Much of South African history is triangular. The rural Dutch (Afrikaners) and the more urban British were often at odds. So were the Boers and the native peoples. And so were the native peoples and the British. Britain and the Boers fought the Boer Wars in 1880–81 and 1899–1902.

The Union of South Africa was created in 1910. It joined the two British-dominated provinces, the Cape and Natal, and the two "Boer republics." This move gave a big boost to South Africa's prestige. Its new status as a self-governing "dominion" put it on par with Australia, Canada, and New Zealand within the British Empire.

German Colonies

Vasco da Gama of Portugal reached Tanganyika (today known as Tanzania) in 1498. On his way to India, he explored the East African coast. He claimed it all for Portugal, but the Portuguese never really developed it as a colony.

In the middle of the nineteenth century, though, Europeans did begin to explore the interior of Tanganyika. The German explorer Karl Peters persuaded a group of tribal chiefs to accept German "protection." Thus Tanganyika became a German colony. The government in Berlin supported the establishment of the German East Africa Company. This was modeled after the British East India Company and other similar entities. (Germany was a little behind other European powers. For centuries it was a collection of little kingdoms and principalities. It had only just become a unified country in 1870.)

In 1891 the German government instituted direct colonial rule—again, in much the way Britain did in India. After German defeat in World War I, the League of Nations mandated Tanganyika to the British.

Namibia was another challenge to European explorers. The Namib Desert kept them away until late in the eighteenth century. In 1878, however, Britain annexed part of this territory to South Africa. German explorers were active there, too, and in 1890 an Anglo-German treaty acknowledged South West Africa, as Namibia was then known, as a German colony. South Africa, then a British colony, occupied it during World War I. After the war, this rule continued under a League of Nations mandate.

The Portuguese reached the coast of Cameroon in the sixteenth century. But there wasn't much European settlement there until quinine, used to treat malaria, became widely available in the late 1870s. By then, the slave trade was on its way out. In 1884 Germany established a colony it called Kamerun. But after German defeat in World War I, the League of Nations took Kamerun over. Under the League's mandate, Britain and France ruled different regions.

The History and Impacts of African Independence

African nationalism began to stir almost as soon as the ink was dry on Europeans' agreements to carve the continent up among themselves. In Tanganyika, for example, German rule brought the native peoples cash crops, roads, and railroads. But the Africans were unhappy under colonial rule. They rebelled in what's known as the Mahi-Mahi Rebellion of 1905–07. Historians today regard this as one of the first stirrings of Tanzanian nationalism.

The Pursuit of Independence After World War I

Nigeria's quest for independence makes a good case study. Remember that there was no such place as Nigeria before the British created it. So when Nigerians began to talk about "nationalism," they generally meant either a regional ethnic identity—Yoruba or Igbo, for instance—or all Africans.

At first, Nigerians cared more about self-government than American-style independence from Britain. Nationalists in the Islamic north tended to be anti-Western. Nationalists in the south, more influenced by European ideas, opposed indirect (colonial) rule. These new Nigerian activists took some of their cues from American-based black leaders such as Marcus Garvey and W. E. B. Du Bois. The nationalists criticized Europeans for failing to appreciate the richness of indigenous cultures. Nigerian clergy often spoke out in favor of political change, too. Their pulpits gave them a forum to criticize colonial rule that few others had.

As the 1920s wore on, several kinds of groups that weren't obviously political played important roles in the movement for independence. Business and professional associations—such as groups of lawyers or teachers—were one such type. Ethnic and kinship organizations set up to help rural people in the cities were another. A third type was student and youth groups. These attracted people most interested in political change. By 1938 a group called the National Youth Movement was calling for dominion status within the British Empire or Commonwealth of Nations. This would make Nigeria like Canada and Australia.

Nigerians supported the British effort in World War II. They fought against the Italians in Ethiopia as well as in Asia and Europe. For many of them it was a new and broadening experience to have comrades across ethnic and racial lines. But ethnicity and regionalism remained strong forces in Nigerian politics.

After the war, the British saw the need to give up their empire. Two world wars had exhausted Britain and made it more difficult to maintain troops in the colonies. In addition, local peoples, led by leaders like Gandhi in India, were demanding freedom. So the British began to prepare their colonies for independence. And when finally Nigeria had its first "nationwide" political party, it renewed the call for self-government under a democratic constitution. The British finally answered this call. By an act of the British Parliament, Nigeria became an independent country within the Commonwealth on 1 October 1960.

Moves Toward Independence in Other Places

Nigeria's story shows a pattern seen in other British colonies that gained independence, especially after World War II. At first, the Africans' goal was not independence, but fuller participation in the existing system. They gained valuable political experience through some sort of legislative council.

South Africans line up in big numbers to vote in parliamentary elections in 2009.

Photo by Scott Baldauf / © 2009 The Christian Science Monitor

Back in 1994 Nelson Mandela became South Africa's first president elected by people of all races and ethnicities.

And the transitions were generally relatively peaceful. The exceptions were in places with many European settlers—Algeria, a French colony that gained independence in 1962; the Portuguese colonies, which got their independence in the mid-1970s; and Zimbabwe, where a white minority government hung on until 1980.

South Africa is another special case. It gained dominion status in 1910. But its Afrikaner white-minority government and elaborate system of apartheid (a PART height)—*racial segregation*—made the country a pariah state, an outcast.

Eventually even those white rulers themselves saw that something had to give. "We must adapt or die," State President P. W. Botha told his people. His successor, F. W. de Klerk, worked with Nelson Mandela, the long-imprisoned hero of the African National Congress, to end apartheid. In 1994 Mandela became South Africa's first president elected by universal franchise—*when everyone gets to vote, particularly when all races and ethnicities get to vote.*

Zimbabwe, then known as Rhodesia, likewise had a period of white minority rule, from 1964 to 1980. Britain demanded the white settlers give the black majority a bigger political role. But the settlers refused. Prime Minister Ian Smith's government issued a "Unilateral Declaration of Independence" from Britain in 1965. Resulting strife led to guerrilla warfare. Eventually the British negotiated a deal for majority rule.

France was the second great colonial power in Africa, after Britain. Like the British at the end of World War II, the French were starting to think about independence for their colonies. Morocco and Tunisia gained their independence in 1956, shortly after their British-ruled neighbors to the east.

More than a dozen other French colonies in Africa became independent as an indirect result of a major French political crisis in the mid-1950s. France's postwar constitution, the "Fourth Republic," had led to weak and stalemated government. In addition, France had lost its colonies in Indochina after bitter fighting and was engaged in a costly new war in Algeria. The crisis led to the creation in 1958 of France's Fifth Republic, complete with a new constitution. This change made the colonies rethink their status, though. The new constitution provided for a French Community, which the African colonies could join as "autonomous republics." But complete independence was more appealing than mere autonomy, under which France would still be the official ruler. By the end of 1960 more than a dozen French possessions in Africa had become independent.

Workers gather tobacco leaves for drying on a farm in Mozambique run by a white Zimbabwean farmer who has fled there across the border.
Photo by Melanie Stetson Freeman /© 2002 The Christian Science Monitor

After a 1974 revolution in Portugal established democracy, Portugal's three African colonies—Angola, Guinea-Bissau, and Mozambique—became independent states.

Ships carry freight to and from the Port of Luanda in Angola.
Photo by Robert Harbison / © 1990 The Christian Science Monitor

About a million Portuguese citizens were peacefully repatriated to Europe after Portugal's colonies gained independence.

Portugal, the first European colonial power in Africa, was also the last to leave. And as with Britain and France, independence for colonies came after big changes in the mother country.

In the 1970s guerrillas fought for independence for Angola, Guinea-Bissau, and Mozambique. Their struggle inspired democratic activists, including military officers, in Portugal. On 25 April 1974, in a nearly bloodless coup back in the mother country, the Carnation Revolution changed Portugal from an authoritarian dictatorship to a democracy. The new leadership was committed to ending the colonial wars. Fairly soon, all three of Portugal's African colonies became independent states. Afterward, about a million Portuguese citizens were peacefully repatriated—*returned to their homeland*—to Europe.

Nelson Mandela attends a 1992 press conference in Johannesburg, South Africa.

Photo by Robert Harbison / © 1992 The Christian Science Monitor

African history is full of leaders who have overstayed their welcome, which is why Mandela's willingness to step down as South Africa's president in 1999 was so remarkable.

The Struggle for Power Within African Nations During and After Independence

As you've read, there was a pattern for Africans' achieving independence. Sadly, there has also been a pattern for what happens afterward. African history is full of leaders who have overstayed their welcome. Others have found themselves ousted in coups. Robert Mugabe has been president of Zimbabwe for nearly 30 years at this writing, for instance. This is why Nelson Mandela's willingness to step down as South Africa's president in 1999 was so remarkable—like George Washington's refusing to become the king of the new United States.

In a part of the world used to the hereditary rule—*passing down titles, like chief or king, and genes from family member to family member*—of tribal chiefs, Western-style rotation in office hasn't fully caught on. But Africans have had another problem as well: Many of their countries, such as Nigeria, were artificial entities created by the European rulers. They didn't follow the natural borders or respect the traditional homelands of different ethnic groups.

In some cases, colonial masters played one ethnic group against the other. Their reasons for this often seem absurd today. When the Belgians governed Rwanda, for instance, they favored the Tutsi people. The Tutsis were relatively taller and lighter-skinned than the Hutus, another group. When Africans moved toward independence, though, these artificial countries were what they had to work with.

Ghana

In Ghana, for example, Kwame Nkrumah came to power in 1957 as the first prime minister of the first independent African country south of the Sahara. It was an orderly transition. Britain supported it.

Nine years later, though, a group of military officers ousted him in a coup. The plotters called his regime corrupt and abusive. Once he was gone, though, the new leaders still faced many problems. Ethnic and regional divisions remained. So did the challenge of forging a real Ghanaian identity. Under Nkrumah, Ghana seemed to enjoy a spirit of national unity. Once he was gone, people saw that unity as the result of his forceful ways as well as his charisma.

Uganda

Uganda is another, even more extreme, example of these same patterns. After an orderly transition, Uganda achieved independence on 9 October 1962. Less than four years later, though, Prime Minister Milton Obote suspended the constitution. He took over all government powers. In September 1967 he introduced a new constitution that gave him even more powers and abolished Uganda's traditional kingdoms.

Then in 1971 Idi Amin Dada ousted the Obote government in a military coup. Amin was an absolute ruler. His eight-year reign of terror killed at least 100,000 people. It ended in April 1979 when Tanzanian forces backed by Ugandan exiles captured the Ugandan capital. Amin and his remaining forces fled.

Libya

Libya has been such a problem for the United States over the years that a few words about it are in order. Libya's colonial masters early in the twentieth century were the Italians. Like the Germans, they came late to imperialism because they had come late to national unification. Tunisia was the country they really wanted as a colony, but the French got there first.

During World War II, Libyans saw an opportunity for independence. It was likely to come, they thought, if the Allies defeated Italy. And so Libya cooperated with the British war effort in exchange for independence afterward. So it happened. In 1949 Libya became a constitutional monarchy. Ten years later, geologists discovered oil there. Then in 1969 a group of young military officers led by a 27-year-old colonel named Muammar Qaddafi deposed the king in a bloodless coup.

For many years the United States government regarded Libya as a state sponsor of terrorism. US aircraft bombed targets in Libya in 1986 after Libyan agents bombed a nightclub in Berlin, Germany, killing two American service members. The most notable attack blamed on Libya was the 1988 bombing of Pan American Airways Flight 103 over Lockerbie, Scotland. It killed all 259 people aboard and 11 on the ground.

More recently, though, Libya has begun to cooperate with the United States and its allies in fighting terrorism. It renounced its programs to develop missiles and weapons of mass destruction, and paid the United States damages for the Pan-Am bombing. The two countries restored diplomatic relations in 2006 and exchanged ambassadors in January 2009.

The political situation that exists in any region is always a result of its history. For Africans, as for Iraqis, Indians, and Pakistanis, that history is complicated by the aftermath of European colonialism. As artificially created countries sprang up where none had been before, that aftermath has often been round after round of dictators, leadership challenges, and ethnic clashes. You'll read about that in the next lesson.

Lesson 2 Review

Using complete sentences, answer the following questions on a sheet of paper.

1. What major change in North Africa began in 639?
2. What two major advantages did the Bantu peoples have over others in sub-Saharan Africa?
3. How was slavery different in Africa from what it was like in the New World?
4. How did the British role in the slave trade change after 1807?
5. What were the exceptions to a peaceful transition from colonial rule and why?
6. What remarkable thing did Nelson Mandela do in 1999?

Applying Your Learning

7. If you had been an African living under European colonial rule, would you have favored independence? Why or why not?

LESSON  Dictators, Leadership Challenges, and Ethnic Clashes

Quick Write

Why do you think Nelson Mandela's example of leadership was important to South Africa? To Africa as a whole?

Learn About

- how ethnic and sectarian politics undermine democracy in Africa
- the tensions between Arabs and Africans in Sudan
- the tensions between Hutus and Tutsis in Rwanda
- the tensions between Afrikaners, English, and Africans in Zimbabwe and South Africa
- the civil wars of Liberia, Sierra Leone, and the Congo

On 20 April 1964 Nelson Mandela of South Africa's African National Congress (ANC) was on trial for his life. He and other ANC members stood in Pretoria Supreme Court accused of sabotage and other capital crimes. These charges were equivalent to treason. They could all be hanged. They were also accused of plotting a foreign invasion of their country. Mandela denied that charge but admitted the sabotage. The ANC had tried to win political rights for black Africans through peaceful means. But one action after another by the white minority government forced the ANC to rethink its strategy, Mandela said. In the statement he made from the dock, he set forth the reasoning behind the ANC decision to change its tactics. He concluded with these words:

"During my lifetime I have dedicated myself to this struggle of the African people. I have fought against white domination, and I have fought against black domination. I have cherished the ideal of a democratic and free society in which all persons live together in harmony and with equal opportunities. It is an ideal which I hope to live for and to achieve. But if needs be, it is an ideal for which I am prepared to die."

Mandela was sentenced to life imprisonment. He spent the next 26 years in jail, from which he continued to lead his people and party. Released in 1990, he went on to become the first president of South Africa elected by all the people. He served until June 1999, when he retired from public office.

How Ethnic and Sectarian Politics Undermine Democracy in Africa

An essential idea of democracy—the ideal Nelson Mandela was willing to die for—is that all votes are equal. It doesn't matter that some people have more money than others, or more education, or that they have lived in a place longer than some others. It doesn't matter whether they are of European, African, or Asian descent. It doesn't even matter who has studied up more on the issues! When the votes are counted up, everyone's choice has equal weight.

Vocabulary

- disenfranchise
- sectarian
- condominium
- reconciliation
- genocide
- subjugate
- muster out
- demobilize
- amnesty

Young men play soccer under their capital's skyline in Gaborone, Botswana, one of the most stable and democratic countries in Africa.
Photo by Andy Nelson / © 2003 The Christian Science Monitor

An essential idea of democracy is that all votes are equal—no matter that some people have more money and education than others or that they come from a minority group.

That's the way it's supposed to be. But some cultures put great stress on differences—among ethnic, tribal, and other identities. In those places, it's harder to treat everyone equally. It may be hard in such places even to see everyone as fully human. During the genocide in Rwanda, for instance, which you will read about later in this lesson, Hutu militias urged ordinary people to kill the minority Tutsi people by referring to them as "cockroaches." But the two groups are actually closely related. They'd intermarried for centuries. Their conflict is an example of ethnic politics.

This kind of ethnic politics has worked against democracy in Africa. For decades, South Africa's elaborate schemes of racial classification disenfranchised most of its people—*deprived them of their vote*. It also made the whole country an outcast in the family of nations.

As you have read, Africa is a land of immense diversity. Africans speak many languages, practice many religions, and live many different lifestyles. Often these differences result in sectarian strife. Sectarian describes anything *relating to religious or other strongly held beliefs*. As you read in Lesson 2, when the Muslim warrior Amr ibn al As conquered Egypt in AD 639, the Muslims laid down new rules for the vanquished: convert to Islam, pay a special religious tax, or face the Muslims on the battlefield. This was a case of sectarian politics, where different religious and cultural viewpoints went head to head.

You've also read that many African countries were artificial constructs. Their borders were often drawn not to outline natural homelands but to reflect colonial logic. This has only exacerbated Africa's ethnic and sectarian differences and therefore has made it harder to build national unity.

How Sectarian Dictators Make It Difficult to Hold Free Elections

The German writer Max Weber introduced a concept known in English as "the state monopoly on violence." It has many different aspects, including the idea that private citizens don't have their own armies or personal militias. Those who control the US armed forces, for instance, do so as duly elected or appointed public officials. This is part of the rule of law. All service members swear an oath to protect the US Constitution—not to any one personal leader.

But in this lesson, you will read about many political leaders—and military men who took over political leadership by force—who did have their own armies. They used force or the threat of force against:

- Political opponents during election campaigns (as in Brazzaville in 1997)
- Elected leaders (as in Sierra Leone in 1997)
- Their fellow citizens (as in Sudan, Liberia, Rwanda, and other places).

Democracy requires more than just free elections. Even so, you can't have it without them. A country's ability to hold free elections is an index of its health as a democracy. Dictators, or strongmen as they are sometimes called, leading their own personal armies, are a threat to free elections, democracy, and public order.

Zulu women participate in a mass-action rally, marching through Johannesburg, South Africa, in 1992.
Photo by Robert Harbison / © 1992 The Christian Science Monitor

How Sectarian Politics Hinders Justice and Equal Treatment Under the Law

Do people trust the police in their community? Do they trust the courts to treat people fairly? Those two questions are additional important tests of a democracy's health. "Yes" answers to both are a good sign. Good policing and fair administration of justice support the quality of life in a community, at a basic level.

But when sectarian politics intrudes on the life of a country, it often strikes at justice and law. On 21 March 1960, in the South African township of Sharpeville, white police opened fire on an unarmed crowd of black protesters after some of the demonstrators began throwing stones. Protestors then began to flee, but police continued to shoot. They killed 69 and wounded more than 180. This "Sharpeville Massacre" galvanized black South Africa.

The crowd had gathered to protest the hated *pass laws*. The pass law system had been in place for a century and a half. But it had recently been tightened under what *Time* magazine called "the Boer [Afrikaner] regime of stubborn, stiff-necked Prime Minister Hendrik Verwoerd."

Here's how *Time* explained the 1960s pass system—and its larger effects on South African justice: "If an African travels from the countryside to the city, or just across the street for cigarettes, South Africa's ubiquitous, hard-fisted police check his pass. If he stands outside his front door without his pass, the police will not let him walk five feet to get it. He is hauled off to jail, without notice to his employer or family, and fined or imprisoned. Murders go unsolved while the courts are jammed with pass offenders."

How Ethnic Clashes Severely Deter Economic Development for Many People in Africa

Ethnic and sectarian politics affect not only justice, law, and elections, but a country's economy as well. Businesses pursue opportunities wherever these opportunities may be. Much of Africa's wealth is in mineral resources, which are what you might call site-specific. Investors must drill where the oil is.

But the companies of the "new economy," such as clothing manufacturers, can locate anywhere. If ethnic strife makes one location too dangerous or too difficult to do business, they will place their factory elsewhere.

At an even more basic level, much of Africa lacks infrastructure such as paved roads and water systems. Sudan, for instance, is about the size of the eastern half of the continental United States. But it has fewer than 7,500 miles of paved roads, compared with 2.3 million in the United States. Decades of civil war have clearly hindered Sudan's economic development. At times ethnic clashes and related misgovernment have deterred not only investors seeking to make money, but even aid organizations working to fend off starvation in Africa.

The other side of this coin is that peace leads to prosperity. Countries that have suffered through wars and other strife find that once the fighting stops, economic growth resumes. Now that civil war has ended in Liberia, for instance, it is once again able to exploit its mineral and timber resources. Rwanda is still very much a "developing" country. But once genocide and war there ended, its economy picked up markedly. Even Sudan, which is still recovering from decades of strife, has had a similar experience. And countries that avoid war and ethnic strife in the first place find that a peaceful, just environment is itself an economic asset. That's one of the lessons from Botswana, which you will read about later in this lesson.

People ride their bikes along a stretch of road in the Rulindo district of Rwanda.
Photo by Mary Knox Merrill / © 2009 The Christian Science Monitor

Once genocide and war ended in Rwanda, its economy picked up markedly.

The Tensions Between Arabs and Africans in Sudan

Sudan offers a striking example of the effects of ethnic and sectarian strife. As you read earlier, the peoples of Africa fall into two broad groups: the lighter-skinned peoples of the north and the black Africans of the south. Those in the north are of Arab and Berber descent and are largely Muslim. Black Africans in many areas are largely Christian or followers of traditional African religions. The dividing line between these two groups runs through Sudan. The country has been at war with itself for most of its existence as an independent state.

But these two big groups are only the beginning. Sudan has one of the most diverse populations in Africa. Within each of the two distinct major cultures are hundreds of ethnic and religious subdivisions and language groups. This diversity has made it hard for Sudanese to work together politically.

Sudan's northern states cover the greater part of the country and include most of the cities and people. The majority of this region's people are Arabic-speaking Muslims. Most, however, have another non-Arabic mother tongue.

Southern Sudan's population has a mainly rural subsistence economy. For the most part, its people practice indigenous traditional religion. A minority are Christians. The south has many different ethnic groups. It also has many more languages than the north. The Arabic language binds the northern Sudanese together—even though it's not the mother tongue of most. But the southern region is a hotbed of linguistic diversity.

The Arab and Islamic Perspectives of Leaders in Northern Sudan

Sudan's modern history begins in the north. Northerners have traditionally controlled the country. And they have tried to unify it over the years along the lines of Arabism and Islam. They have done this despite opposition: from non-Muslims, from southerners, and from marginalized groups in the east and west.

Sudan's modern history begins around 1820–21. That's when Egypt conquered and unified the northern part of the country. Until that point Sudan was just a collection of independent little kingdoms. And so it remained in the southern part of the country, even after the Egyptians arrived in the north. The Egyptians established a few garrisons in the south, but that was about the extent of their presence. The south remained an area of fragmented tribes. Slave raiders attacked there frequently.

In 1881 a Muslim religious leader named Muhammad ibn Abdalla proclaimed himself "the Mahdi," or "rightly guided one." He began a campaign to unify the tribes in western and central Sudan. Then he and his followers took on the Ottoman-Egyptian government in Khartoum, the Sudanese capital. Since the Ottoman-Egyptian administration was not popular or effective, the Mahdists overthrew it in 1885. The Mahdi then installed what historians call Sudan's first real nationalist government. He was also the first to establish northern and southern Sudan as a single entity.

Despite strict Islamic laws and a lack of political freedom, students such as these at Sudan University's fine arts school in Khartoum find a growing amount of artistic freedom.
Photo by Danna Harman / © 2002 The Christian Science Monitor

The British and Egyptians governed Sudan jointly from 1898 through 1955.

He died soon after, but his state survived. Then in 1898 Lord Kitchener of Britain led an Anglo-Egyptian force into Sudan. It overwhelmed the Mahdists. That led to the establishment of the Anglo-Egyptian condominium in Sudan. A condominium is *a territory subject to joint rule by two or more powers*. In this case, Britain was definitely the senior partner. This arrangement lasted from 1898 through 1955.

In 1953 the two partners reached a deal to give Sudan self-government and self-determination. On 1 January 1956 Sudan gained independence under a provisional constitution. That constitution was silent on some important issues, though, and that led to real trouble.

Southern Sudan's Pursuit of Self-Determination

Sudan fell into civil war almost immediately. Its first civil war grew from a question never settled and a promise never kept. The question never settled was the character, or nature, of the state. Would the new Sudan, governed from the Islamic capital city of Khartoum, be a secular state? Or would it be Islamist?

The promise not kept was to create a federal system for Sudan. A federal system often works well to hold a diverse country together. It can accommodate cultural differences. States or provinces can act independently on local matters, but the country holds together as a whole on matters of defense and foreign policy. Sudan would have faced problems in any case. But a federal system might have helped ease the pressures.

It didn't happen, though. The Arab-led government broke its promise to create a federal system. That sparked a mutiny by southern army officers, and that, in turn, led to civil war. The war lasted 17 years.

Fourteen years into the conflict—in May 1969—Colonel Gaafar Muhammad Nimeiri and a group of leftist officers seized power. You may think that doesn't sound like a path to peace. But Nimeiri's coup would eventually lead to Sudan's 10-year window of peace.

Nimeiri's government marked a break from Sudan's ineffectual leadership. He proclaimed socialism rather than political Islam as the guiding national policy. He also outlined a plan for granting autonomy to the south. This was a move earlier governments had resisted.

But soon Nimeiri became target of an attempted communist coup. After that, he ordered a purge of Communists from the government. In response, the Soviet Union withdrew its support for Nimeiri's regime.

The Islamists had never supported Nimeiri. And now he had lost communist support, too. So to expand his narrow power base, Nimeiri turned south. He pursued peace accords with neighboring Ethiopia and Uganda. He made agreements with each to stop supporting the other's rebel groups.

He then opened talks with the southern rebels in his own country. The deal he signed with them in Addis Ababa, Ethiopia, in 1972 gave the south some autonomy. In return, southerners supported him in putting down two coup attempts.

However warmly southerners felt about the agreement, though, it had no support in the north—not from secularists or from Islamists. Eventually Nimeiri saw this lack of support for the accord as a potential threat to his rule. So he began to pursue national reconciliation—*an end to disagreement*—with the religious opposition.

Then in 1979 Chevron, the oil company, hit black gold in the south. That changed everything. The autonomy Nimeiri's deal granted the south extended to finances. Suddenly southern Sudan controlled a valuable resource no one had even known about when the deal was made. Northerners pushed Nimeiri to cancel the financial parts of the deal.

In 1983 he did more than that. He abolished the southern region. He made Arabic, instead of English, the south's official language. (Among other things, this move cut southerners out of careers in public service.) And he transferred control of southern armed forces to the central government. In effect, he canceled the whole treaty with the south. By doing so, he set off a second civil war. Southern soldiers mutinied rather than accept transfers to the north.

Nimeiri had earlier opposed Islamists, but now he embraced them. He declared that the penal code would include traditional Islamic punishments—amputations of hands to punish theft, and public lashings for alcohol possession. The grievances began to pile up: a collapsing economy, war in the south, and general political repression. A popular uprising in 1985 overthrew Nimeiri while he was out of the country.

In 1989 Sudan got a new Islamic government after General Umar al-Bashir mounted a coup. This intensified the north-south conflict. It also turned Sudan into a haven for Osama bin Laden and other terrorists.

During the 1990s the Sudanese civil war continued through a series of regional efforts to broker peace. Finally in July 2002 the Government of Sudan (al-Bashir's administration) and the Sudan People's Liberation Movement/Army (representing the non-Muslim south) came to terms on the role of state and religion. The agreement also granted southern Sudan a right of self-determination.

On 9 January 2005 the two sides signed a comprehensive peace agreement. It called for wealth-sharing, power-sharing, and security arrangements. It provided for a cease-fire, northern troop withdrawals from southern Sudan, and the resettlement of refugees. After a six-year transition, Sudan will hold new elections at all levels of government. The international community has hailed the peace agreement as a decisive step forward. However, the ongoing strife in the Sudanese region of Darfur has complicated efforts to end the main north-south conflict. (See "The Darfur Crisis.")

The Economic Effects of Constant Strife Within the Country

The war between the Sudanese government and the Sudan People's Liberation Movement lasted 20 years. During that time, violence, famine, and disease killed more than 2 million people. Another 600,000 fled to neighboring countries. The violence also pushed about 4 million other people from their homes. This meant that at one time, Sudan had the world's largest population of internally displaced people. (Sudan has about 40 million people, so that was about 10 percent of the population.) Since the two sides signed the peace agreement in 2005, nearly 2 million of these displaced people have returned to the south, experts say.

In 2004 the end of most of the fighting and the expansion of crude oil exports gave Sudan's economy a real boost. It grew at 6.4 percent—a very respectable rate. And gross domestic product per capita—each person's share of the country's output, in other words—nearly doubled.

fastFACT

The *Sudan People's Liberation Army/Movement* operates in southern Sudan. The *Sudan Liberation Army/Movement,* a separate organization, operates in Darfur, in western Sudan.

The Sudanese are still feeling the effects of their civil war, however. They have very little infrastructure, besides: few paved roads, water systems, and the like. The government is moving toward a market economy, or free enterprise system. But the state and supporters of the governing party remain heavily involved in the economy.

Sudan's civil strife has affected its neighbors as well. They alternately sheltered Sudanese refugees or served as staging grounds for rebel groups.

The Darfur Crisis

Just as Sudan's longstanding north-south conflict was finally ending, reports began to surface, in 2003, of attacks on civilians in Sudan's Darfur region. A rebellion broke out in Darfur, led by the Sudan Liberation Movement/Army and the Justice and Equality Movement. These groups represented farmers, mostly black African Muslims.

To defeat them, the Sudanese government gave arms and money to local militias known as *Janjaweed*. These groups, too, were mostly black Muslims. The differences between the two groups were cultural. The *Janjaweed* were largely "Arabized." That means, in practical terms, that they spoke Arabic. The rebels were largely "non-Arabized." They did not speak Arabic.

The conflict between the two groups was also between two ways of life. The *Janjaweed* were linked to people who herded livestock. Drought pushed them and their herds farther south, into conflict with the farmers. The farmers, meanwhile, were already having trouble trying to coax crops out of the dry ground.

Conflict between farmers and herders surfaces in many parts of the world, including the United States. But the Darfur conflict is remarkable for its scale, and for the role of the national government in supporting attacks on its own people. It has led to the deaths of hundreds of thousands, as well as mass rape. Those internally displaced number 2 million. The US State Department and others have called the killing genocide. Genocide is *the mass killing of one kind of people*, as happened to the Jews during World War II.

But the Darfur crisis has not, at this writing, yielded to intense international efforts to resolve it. On 4 March 2009 the UN's International Criminal Court (ICC) announced that it was issuing an arrest warrant for Sudan's president, Umar al-Bashir. The court charged him with crimes against humanity and war crimes.

This Sudanese woman lives in a camp for internally displaced people in West Darfur, Sudan.

Photo by Danna Harman / © 2004 The Christian Science Monitor

The violence from Sudan's 20-year civil war pushed about 4 million people from their homes, which meant that, at one time, Sudan had the world's largest population of internally displaced people.

The Tensions Between Hutus and Tutsis in Rwanda

Sudan is an example of a country facing strife between groups with genuine ethnic and cultural differences. Rwanda, on the other hand, is a tragedy of strife between two groups whose differences weren't, and aren't, all that great. Bad policies worsened tensions among the people the Belgian colonial power was trying to "elevate."

Background of the Hutu and Tutsi Populations in Rwanda

Of Rwanda's 10 million people, 85 percent are Hutus. They were the country's original inhabitants. Relatively short, they spoke a language in the Bantu group. During the fifteenth century, though, another group began moving into Rwanda. Their descendants are the Tutsi people, who tend to be quite tall and make up 14 percent of today's population. They were cattle breeders from the Horn of Africa. They gradually subjugated—*conquered or subdued*—the Hutus. These newcomers set up a monarchy with a *mwami*, or king, as well as a system of nobles and gentry. This was like what existed in Europe at that time.

The Tutsis didn't control all of Rwanda, however. Some independent Hutu areas remained. And the lines between the ethnic groups weren't always clear. Many Hutus lived as serfs—bound to the land. But many rural Tutsis weren't much better off.

Europeans didn't get to Rwanda until late in the nineteenth century. In 1899 the Rwandan *mwami* submitted to a German protectorate. After World War I, Rwanda and neighboring Burundi became Belgian mandates under the League of Nations. After World War II, Belgian control continued through the United Nations.

Policies during this period sowed the seeds of trouble in the 1990s. The Belgians issued identity cards that classified people by ethnicity. They favored the Tutsis, whom they considered superior to the Hutus, with better jobs and schooling. The two groups responded as you would expect. The Tutsis welcomed their privileged treatment. The Hutus resented being treated as second-class citizens.

In reality, the differences between the two groups weren't great. In any case, whatever differences originally existed had blurred somewhat after centuries of intermarriage. But tensions persisted, and the Belgians made them worse.

Belgium did encourage the Rwandans to develop democratic institutions. But many Tutsis resisted these moves because they threatened their special status. In 1959 the Hutus' resentment boiled over. They rose up and overthrew the Tutsi monarchy. In elections held two years later, the Party of the Hutu Emancipation Movement (PARMEHUTU) won an overwhelming victory. Meanwhile, more than 160,000 Tutsis fled to neighboring countries.

Rwanda (and neighboring Burundi) became independent on 1 July 1962. The PARMEHUTU leader, Gregoire Kayibanda, was Rwanda's first elected president. He talked up ideals of peaceful negotiation and progress for the people. But in reality, his government promoted Hutu supremacy. Inefficiency and corruption soon set in.

On 5 July 1973 the military took over. Major General Juvenal Habyarimana, another Hutu, dissolved the National Assembly and PARMEHUTU. He also abolished all political activity.

Then in 1975 he formed the National Revolutionary Movement for Development (MRND). Its goals were peace, unity, and national development, within a one-party state. The movement was organized at all levels. It included elected and appointed officials.

Rwandans went to the polls in December 1978. They overwhelmingly endorsed a new constitution and confirmed Habyarimana as president. He was reelected in 1983 and 1988. Responding to public pressure for reform, though, in July 1990 he announced a plan to change Rwanda's one-party state into a multiparty democracy.

A formerly displaced Tutsi has been welcomed back to her Hutu neighborhood in Burundi.
Photo by Melanie Stetson Freeman / © 2006 The Christian Science Monitor

While Hutus are Rwanda's original inhabitants, Belgian policies in the post-World War II period favored the Tutsis and sowed the seeds of trouble that would explode in the 1990s.

How the Tutsi Minority Formed the Rwanda Patriotic Front

Rwandan exiles, meanwhile, had banded together as the Rwandan Patriotic Front (RPF). Its members were mostly Tutsis. They blamed the Rwandan government for failing to democratize. They were also unhappy that it had failed to help the Tutsi refugees, now numbering half a million outside Rwanda, in Africa and elsewhere.

On 1 October 1990 the RPF invaded Rwanda from its base in neighboring Uganda. This started a civil war that dragged on for nearly two years. Finally on 12 July 1992 both sides signed a cease-fire accord in Arusha, Tanzania. The accord set a timetable for an end to fighting and a start of political talks. The cease-fire took effect 31 July. Political talks began 10 August 1992.

These three men are all Hutu suspects from the Rwandan genocide in 1994.
Photo by Melanie Stetson Freeman / © 2006 The Christian Science Monitor

During the genocide, which left up to 800,000 Tutsis and moderate Hutus dead, the government-sponsored radio urged ordinary Hutu citizens to go out and kill the "cockroaches," as they called the Tutsis.

The Rwandan Genocide in 1994

On 6 April 1994 the aircraft carrying President Habyarimana and the president of Burundi was shot down on its approach to Kigali, the Rwandan capital. Both presidents died in the crash. No one knows for sure who shot down the aircraft, but the attack seemed to be a signal to those on the ground. Military and militia groups started at once to round up and kill any Tutsis or moderate Hutus they could find. Prime Minister Agathe Uwilingiyimana and her 10 Belgian bodyguards were among the first to die. Her attackers raped her before killing her.

The chaos that ensued was genocide. And it was unprecedented in its swiftness. It began within hours of the attack on the presidential plane. The wave of killings spread quickly from the capital to all corners of the country. It left up to 800,000 Tutsis and moderate Hutus dead.

Key actors in all this were organized bands of militia known as the *Interahamwe*. Their name means "those who stand together." It sometimes gets a darker translation: "those who attack together." Another group, organized somewhat later, was the *Impuzamugambi*, "those who have a single goal." These groups had the backing of the Hutu-led government. These killers had clearly planned their genocide well in advance. The ruling MRND Party was apparently in on the plan, too. Government-sponsored radio urged even ordinary citizens to go out and kill the "cockroaches," as they called the Tutsis.

The Battles for Political Power Between the Hutus and the RPF

Immediately after the presidential plane was shot down, the majority-Tutsi RPF battalion in Kigali came under attack. The RPF forces fought their way out of Kigali and joined other RPF units in the north and resumed their invasion. For two months, civil war and genocide raged at the same time.

Then in June, French forces landed in Goma, Zaire (now the Democratic Republic of the Congo). The French had been major arms suppliers to the Hutu government. But now their mission was meant to be humanitarian. They sought to stop the fighting and the genocide. They set up what was supposed to be a safe zone in southwestern Rwanda. They insisted afterward that this saved many lives. But many members of what was left of the genocidal Hutu regime in Kigali were also able to escape the country through this zone.

Then the RPF defeated the Rwandan Army. This set off another wave of refugees as Rwandan Army soldiers fled across the border to Zaire. More refugees soon followed into Zaire, Tanzania, and Burundi.

The RPF took Kigali on 4 July 1994. The war ended on 16 July. Rwanda was in shambles. As many as 1 million people had been murdered. Another 2 million had fled, and another million were displaced within Rwanda.

People tend to errands in downtown Butare, home to many of Rwanda's educational institutions such as the National University of Rwanda.

Photo by Melanie Stetson Freeman / © 2006 The Christian Science Monitor

In 2003 Rwandans elected a new president and legislature, but the country must remain vigilant to ensure against any recurrence of its 1994 nightmare.

Bringing Rwandans Home

Since the massacre, President Paul Kagame's government has sought to bring Hutus back from abroad and make them a part of Rwandan society again. The British magazine *The Economist* said this about the effort: "Courage and even generosity of spirit in dealing with an awful situation has earned Mr. Kagame's government high marks in the West and in Africa as a whole. After all, Rwanda is the only genocide case where the victims, the Tutsi, have chosen to reintegrate their killers into the country and to live as neighbours again—a uniquely hard task, especially in Africa's most densely populated country. . . . To encourage reconciliation, Rwanda has embarked on an experiment to change completely the way a new generation thinks about itself. Now, officially, no one is a Hutu or Tutsi; there are only Rwandans. Ethnicity, the genocide's alleged cause, is being outlawed."

After the Genocide

Rwanda's new constitution, adopted in May 2003, eliminated reference to ethnicity. No more are people officially labeled as part of one group or another. Later that year, Rwandans elected a new president and legislature.

The country still has work to do. It needs economic growth. It needs democratization and judicial reform. A backlog remains of hundreds of thousands of legal cases against those accused of taking part in the genocide. The country must remain vigilant to ensure against any recurrence of the nightmare of 1994.

The Tensions Between Afrikaners, English, and Africans in Zimbabwe and South Africa

Racial and ethnic differences much deeper than those in Rwanda dominate South Africa's story. As you read in Lesson 2, today's South Africa is the result of joining two Afrikaner provinces, the Transvaal and the Orange Free State, with the British-dominated Cape and Natal provinces. South Africa's white minority long held sway there. Only in recent decades has black majority rule prevailed.

The black-white tensions haven't been the only ones in South Africa, though. Over the years tensions between the two white communities—Afrikaners and British—have affected black-white relations as well.

Neighboring Zimbabwe's story is a little different because it had no Dutch presence. Its European colonial history began in 1888. Cecil Rhodes, an English-born mining magnate, won a concession for mineral rights from local chiefs. The area later known as Southern and Northern Rhodesia became a British sphere of influence. The British South Africa Company ran the territory from Salisbury—now Harare, Zimbabwe's capital.

The company had a royal charter. Its mission was to extend British rule in central Africa without entangling the British government. When the charter ran out, South Africa was eager to incorporate the territory. But the Rhodesians said no. The next year, Britain formally annexed Southern Rhodesia as a colony.

The Dominance of the Minority Afrikaners and English in South Africa

When the Union of South Africa was formed in 1910, all political power remained in white hands. It wasn't just that Africans couldn't vote, either. Several laws marked South Africa as a state that permitted—in fact, called for—racial discrimination. For instance:

- It was illegal for Africans to break a labor contract, but not for whites
- Africans could not become full members of the Dutch Reformed Church
- Mining was an important part of the South African economy. But the Mines and Works Act of 1911 in effect restricted Africans to semiskilled and unskilled jobs in the mines.

The white business class needed Africans' labor but didn't want to give them any more opportunity than they had to. Such restrictions weren't new in practice. What was new was that they were enshrined in law.

The Indian Ocean meets the Atlantic Ocean at the Cape of Good Hope off of Cape Town, South Africa.
Photo by Melanie Stetson Freeman / © 2002 The Christian Science Monitor

When the Union of South Africa was formed in 1910, all political power remained in white hands.

The most important of these was the Natives Land Act of 1913. It divided South Africa into areas in which either blacks or whites could own land. Blacks were two-thirds of the population, but the lands designated for them were only 7.5 percent of the total. Whites, one-fifth of the population, had access to the remaining 92.5 percent. Africans could live outside their 7.5 percent territory only if whites employed them. All this was a source of tension between blacks and whites.

But there was plenty of tension between the Afrikaners and the British in South Africa, too. It began when the British gained control of the Cape of Good Hope at the end of the eighteenth century. The tension worsened after gold and diamonds were discovered in South Africa. (This shows, once again, how mineral riches can be a mixed blessing.)

The Afrikaners' desire to steer clear of the English led them to move north, on what's known as the "Great Trek" up into areas dominated by Zulu tribes. This led to tension and conflict as the Afrikaners and Zulus competed for the same land.

The Afrikaners and English went to war twice in the Anglo-Boer Wars of 1880–81 and 1899–1902. In more recent times, the two groups were divided over what to do about their system of racial division. The Afrikaners were much more conservative than the more-urban English speakers.

The Significance of Apartheid in South Africa

The word *apartheid* first came into use as the name of a public policy in South Africa's 1948 election. It was a "general election" only in a certain sense because most South Africans couldn't vote. Instead, two white parties, Jan Smuts's ruling United Party and D. F. Malan's *Herstigte Nasionale Party* (Reconstituted National Party or HNP), debated what to do about black Africans, who were the majority of the population. The United Party doesn't look "progressive" in the light of today's standards. But it believed that total segregation was impossible.

The HNP, on the other hand, believed that total separation of the races was needed. Otherwise the country might begin to move toward racial equality. HNP supporters believed this was a bad thing. The HNP called for restrictions on Africans in the cities. It believed blacks should return to the countryside regularly to help meet the needs of farmers—white Afrikaners. Blacks should develop political bodies only in the African reserves, the HNP said, referring to lands owned by blacks. They should have no representation in Parliament.

Malan called further for a ban on racially mixed marriages and on black trade unions. He also wanted stricter enforcement of the rules limiting job opportunities for blacks.

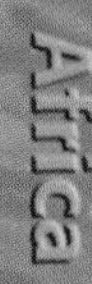

During apartheid in South Africa, facilities such as these public toilets in Johannesburg were divided and labeled by race.
Photo by R. Norman Matheny / © 1984 The Christian Science Monitor

The word *apartheid* first came into use as the name of a public policy in South Africa's 1948 election.

All this added up to a platform called "apartheid." The HNP ran on it. The party won only a minority of the votes cast. But the electoral system gave more weight to rural voters. And so the HNP won a majority of the seats up for election. Renamed the National Party (NP), it would rule South Africa until 1994.

The Nonviolent Revolt Against Apartheid

Black South Africans' efforts to end restrictions based on skin color and to win their political rights began in 1912. That's when they founded the South African Native National Congress. They later changed the name to the African National Congress (ANC).

This, you will note, is well before apartheid became government policy. For most of the ANC's early years, its goals seemed to be receding rather than coming closer to fulfillment. After the National Party (NP) won the 1948 election, it passed laws installing white domination even more strictly. In the early 1960s, after the Sharpeville protest, the government banned the ANC and another organization, the Pan-African Congress (PAC). Nelson Mandela and many other black leaders went to prison, convicted of treason.

The ANC and PAC went underground. They continued their struggle through guerrilla warfare and sabotage. Black protests in 1976 and 1985 convinced some NP members the time had come for change. They began secret discussions with Mandela, still in prison, in 1986. In February 1990, soon after coming into office as state president, F. W. de Klerk lifted the ban on the ANC, the PAC, and other groups. Two weeks after that, the government released Nelson Mandela from prison.

fastFACT

The Group Areas Act assigned different racial and ethnic groups specific areas where they could live and work. The Land Acts reserved most of South Africa's land for whites. The Population Registration Act required that each South African be classified and registered as a member of the black, white, or coloured group. Indian (South Asian) was added later.

The following year, the last three "pillars of apartheid" fell. These were laws that restricted black people's movements and opportunities: the Group Areas Act, Land Acts, and the Population Registration Act.

A long series of negotiations led to a new constitution. It went into effect in December 1993. In their first-ever nonracial elections, South Africans elected Nelson Mandela as their president. He took office on 10 May 1994.

South Africa's Peacemakers

Mohandas Gandhi's ideal of nonviolent resistance was a great influence on Nelson Mandela. But during the struggle to end apartheid, he and other members of the ANC reluctantly concluded that some resort to guerrilla tactics was necessary. This drew criticism from, among others, Archbishop Desmond Tutu, himself black and a critic of apartheid. But the ANC effort to end apartheid was mostly peaceful. And a key element was Mandela's ability to find a negotiating partner on the other side—F. W. de Klerk, the National Party leader who knew the time for change had come. In 1993 the two men shared the Nobel Peace Prize.

The Civil Wars of Liberia, Sierra Leone, and the Congo

While South Africa emerged from apartheid through mostly nonviolent struggle, not all of Africa ended the last century so peacefully. In fact, a number of bloody civil wars marked the final decades of the continent's twentieth-century history. These stories never got much attention from Americans. They had complicated plotlines. It was hard to tell the heroes from the villains. It wasn't always clear there were heroes.

The Liberian Civil War, 1989–1996

Free African-Americans and newly freed slaves founded Liberia, "the land of the free," in 1820. It became an independent republic in 1847. Its model was the United States. Americo-Liberians—immigrants from America and their descendants—ruled. Until 1904 indigenous Africans could not become citizens. It was a one-party state. And the True Whig Party dominated all sectors from independence until 12 April 1980.

That's when things changed. Master Sergeant Samuel K. Doe, an indigenous Liberian, seized power. He and his forces executed President William R. Tolbert and several officials of his government, most of them Americo-Liberians.

Before long, Doe's own Krahn ethnic group dominated Liberia. Human rights abuses, corruption, and ethnic tension soon followed. So did another coup attempt, on 12 November 1985. It failed.

Kinshasa, Democratic Republic of the Congo, on a hazy day.
Photo by R. Norman Matheny / © 1984 The Christian Science Monitor

A number of bloody civil wars marked the twentieth century's final decades in numerous African countries, such as the DRC, Liberia, Sierra Leone, and the Republic of the Congo.

Doe faced yet another challenge not many years later. On Christmas Eve in 1989, a band of rebels invaded from Côte d'Ivoire. Charles Taylor, a former Doe aide, was their leader. His National Patriotic Front quickly gained popular support. They reached the edge of the capital within six months.

The ensuing civil war was one of Africa's bloodiest. It took more than 200,000 lives. Another million Liberians sought refuge in other countries.

In 1990 the Economic Community of West African States (ECOWAS) intervened. Its forces kept Taylor from taking Monrovia, the capital of Liberia. But then two more breakaway factions formed. A former Taylor aide led one. The other consisted of former Armed Forces of Liberia soldiers who had fled the country but then returned.

It took more than a dozen peace accords before Taylor finally accepted one. The factions put down their guns and mustered out—*discharged*—their soldiers. In a special election on 19 July 1997, Taylor won by a large margin. Liberians voted for him mostly because they feared more war if he lost.

The next several years are a story of misrule and foreign misadventure. Instead of working to help his people, Taylor got entangled in Sierra Leone. Back in Liberia, civil war resumed.

Ultimately Taylor went into exile in Nigeria. Then in October 2005 Liberians voted again. The elections were the freest, fairest, and most peaceful in their history. And they voted decisively for their first female president, Ellen Johnson Sirleaf. (Sirleaf is also Africa's first female leader.) The country's problems are immense. But at least its political situation is finally stable.

Strife in Sierra Leone

Meanwhile, fighting was raging next door. In March 1991 a small band calling themselves the Revolutionary United Front (RUF) began to attack villages near Sierra Leone's Liberian border. They wanted control of diamond mines, and they soon got it. They pushed the national army back to the capital, too.

This did not make the government, headed by Major General Joseph Saidu Momoh, look very good. And so on 29 April 1992 Captain Valentine Strasser led some other officers in a coup against Momoh. They exiled him to Guinea and took power as the National Provisional Ruling Council (NPRC).

They didn't do much better than Momoh at controlling the RUF, though. By 1995 the rebels held much of the country. They were on the doorsteps of Freetown, the capital. At one point, the NPRC hired private security contractors to chase the RUF fighters away back to their border hideouts.

But the NPRC soon came under international pressure to restore civilian rule. The country held new elections in April 1996, and the people elected veteran diplomat Ahmad Tejan Kabbah president. But just a year later, the Armed Forces Revolutionary Council (AFRC), under Major Johnny Paul Koroma, ousted him. What's more, he invited the RUF to join the government.

This also didn't last long. A Nigerian-led ECOWAS peacekeeping force known as the ECOWAS Monitoring Group (ECOMOG) reinstated Kabbah. But the RUF tried again to hold the government in its grip, a move that sparked fighting in Freetown that left thousands dead or wounded. Then ECOMOG pushed back again against the RUF.

The international community stepped in again. The Lomé Peace Agreement of 7 July 1999 gave the RUF a role in the government. It also called for international peacekeepers in Sierra Leone. The RUF began to violate it almost at once, though. And so it was swiftly booted out of government, and its leaders arrested.

Episodes of fighting and peacemaking alternated over the next couple of years. Then a program known as DDR—Demobilization, Disarmament, and Reintegration—finally got some traction. Fighting lessened, and the government regained control of rebel areas.

By early 2002 some 72,000 fighters had laid down arms and been demobilized—*taken out of military service*. On 18 January of that year, President Kabbah declared an end to the civil war. He won a second term in a landslide victory in May 2002. The RUF's political wing failed to win a single seat in legislative elections.

At this point the peacekeepers began to leave, and the wheels of justice began to turn. Sierra Leone's Truth and Reconciliation Commission (TRC) started work. The commission's purpose was to let both victims and their attackers tell their stories. This, in turn, was to foster real reconciliation.

The Special Court for Sierra Leone handed up indictments against people from all factions in the conflict. Another figure in the Sierra Leone conflict is former Liberian President Charles Taylor. As of this writing, the Special Court in The Hague is trying him on 11 indictments of war crimes and crimes against humanity.

fastFACT

The Hague, in the Netherlands, is home to the United Nations' International Criminal Court, where the UN tries cases such as crimes against humanity by nations' leaders.

The 1997 Civil War in Congo (Brazzaville)

Elsewhere in Africa, the Congo, or the Republic of the Congo (Brazzaville), had gained from the end of the Cold War. It had long been a one-party Marxist state. But in 1992 it made a transition to multiparty democracy.

Progress soon went off the rails, though. As the July 1997 presidential election approached, tensions between the two leading candidates were high. They started to act more like opposing sides in a civil war than candidates in a civilian election.

On 5 June President Pascal Lissouba's government forces surrounded the Brazzaville compound of his opponent, Denis Sassou-Nguesso. Sassou-Nguesso had troops of his own, though. He ordered them to resist. This touched off four months of fighting. The conflict destroyed or damaged much of Brazzaville.

In early October Angolan troops invaded in support of Sassou-Nguesso. By mid-October, the Lissouba government had fallen. Sassou-Nguesso declared himself president and named a 33-member government.

His government held a National Forum for Reconciliation the following January. Those taking part were to make some decisions about a political transition. The group, under Sassou-Nguesso's tight control, set an election timetable. It chose a transition advisory legislature. It also announced a convention to finalize a draft constitution.

But in late 1998 fighting erupted between forces of the Sassou-Nguesso government and Lissouba. Another group, led by former Prime Minister Bernard Kolelas, entered the fray, too.

This new violence caused great destruction in southern Brazzaville, as well as in other regions outside the capital. Many people died. Hundreds of thousands were displaced. The fighting also led to closure of the key railroad between Brazzaville and Pointe Noire, the country's main port.

In December 1999 the government signed agreements with many but not all of the rebel groups. Then a long national dialogue began. Government and opposition parties agreed to pursue peace.

Lissouba and Kolelas refused to take part, however. Those seeking peace exiled them. They also tried the two men in their absence and convicted them of treason and misuse of government funds, among other charges.

Former fighters received amnesty—*a pardon for crimes*—and in some cases small loans to let them start businesses and therefore more useful lives. Not all opposition groups took part in this process, however. A group called the "Ninjas" continued guerrilla war in the Pool, or southeastern, region of Congo.

The people of Congo approved a new constitution in January 2002. Sassou-Nguesso won the presidential election that followed. The country has been calm and stable since the government signed a peace accord with the Ninjas. Some, but not all, former opposition leaders have received amnesty and returned to the country.

Next Door in Kinshasa

As Congo (Brazzaville) was going through civil war in the 1990s, the Democratic Republic of the Congo next door was also caught in turmoil. Mobutu Sese Seko had taken power there in a coup in 1965. He had renamed the country Zaire and remained in power ever since. By the early 1990s, though, he was losing his grip. And by 1996 war and genocide in Rwanda had spilled over into Zaire. This set in motion the chain of events that led to his ouster.

As noted previously, Hutu militias fled Rwanda after the Tutsi-led Rwanda Patriotic Front took power in July 1994. These fighters used Hutu refugee camps in eastern Zaire as staging grounds for attacks on Rwanda.

In October 1996 Rwandan troops (RPA) entered Zaire. At the same time, Laurent-Désiré Kabila formed an armed group known as the Alliance des Forces Démocratiques pour la Libération du Congo-Zaire (the Alliance of Democratic Forces for the Liberation of Congo-Zaire, or AFDL). Its goal was to oust Mobutu.

Supported by forces from Rwanda and Uganda, the AFDL began a campaign toward Kinshasa. Peace talks with Mobutu failed. In May 1997 Mobutu fled the country. Kabila marched into Kinshasa on 17 May 1997 and declared himself president. He consolidated power and renamed the country. Once again it was the Democratic Republic of the Congo.

Botswana Gets It Right

For a change of pace, you might want to read a little bit about an African country *not* torn by ethnic strife or civil war: Botswana. It came under British protection in 1885. But in 1909 its people resisted inclusion in the new Union of South Africa. They chose to make their own way to democracy. In September 1966 they achieved independence from Britain.

Here's what the US State Department says: "Botswana has a flourishing multiparty constitutional democracy. Each of the elections since independence has been freely and fairly contested and has been held on schedule. The country's minority groups participate freely in the political process. . . . The openness of the country's political system has been a significant factor in Botswana's stability and economic growth."

The roots of Botswana's democracy lie in its native traditions. In its village councils, custom and law limit the powers of traditional leaders. Botswana has a good human rights record, too.

Botswana is not a rich country. It has fewer than 2 million people. It's not without problems. It has a high rate of AIDS infection, for one. But it is a shining example of stability and sturdy democracy in Africa.

Kabila's relations with his foreign backers quickly soured. By 1999 his country was effectively divided into thirds. Kabila's forces controlled part of it. But troops backed by Uganda and Rwanda controlled other sections. A military deadlock led to the Lusaka Accord, which all signed in August 1999. It called for a cease-fire, for United Nations peacekeepers, for withdrawal of foreign troops, and for political dialogue.

Kabila drew criticism for failing to honor his commitments in all this. Then on 16 January 2001 he was assassinated, allegedly by one of his own bodyguards. Joseph Kabila succeeded his father. He reversed many of his father's policies, and the provisions of the Lusaka Accord took effect. The last foreign troops officially departed in 2003.

Some themes here bear mention. Note how often international peacekeepers appear in these stories. Note the role of peace talks—even when they break down. African countries are working together to ensure or restore the rule of law. They have created means for nation-building and reconciliation—even when these work imperfectly. There are still dictators and strife in many areas of Africa. But Africans have come a long way from the days when a European king could control a vast territory in the heart of their continent as his own personal property.

Lesson 3 Review

Using complete sentences, answer the following questions on a sheet of paper.

1. What were the victims of the Sharpeville Massacre in South Africa in 1960 protesting?
2. Which African countries have seen their economies improve after the end of ethnic strife? Name at least two.
3. What are the two broad population groups in Sudan?
4. Who installed what historians call Sudan's first real nationalist government?
5. Which Belgian colonial policy in Rwanda sowed the seeds of trouble in the 1990s?
6. Which policy of Rwandan President Paul Kagame's government has won praise from the West and elsewhere in Africa?
7. After the Union of South Africa was formed in 1910, its legislature passed several laws restricting black Africans' rights. Which was most important and what did it do?
8. Which Indian leader was a great influence on Nelson Mandela?
9. How did fighting between forces loyal to different candidates prevent elections in the Congo (Brazzaville) in 1997?
10. How did war and genocide in Rwanda affect neighboring Zaire?

Applying Your Learning

11. The United States did not intervene to end the genocide in Rwanda. Should it have done so? Explain why or why not.

LESSON 4 AIDS, Health, Poverty, and Human Rights

Quick Write

Were Rwanda's Gacaca courts a good way to pursue justice and reconciliation after the genocide there? Why or why not?

Learn About

- the main health challenges in Africa
- the extent and impact of AIDS in Africa
- the recurring problems with famine in Africa
- the main environmental issues facing Africa
- human rights issues in Africa

Rwanda's 1994 genocide killed nearly a million people. But the killers were almost as numerous: an estimated 800,000 took part. This left the new government that took over after the genocide in a bind: Did they really want to put 800,000 people on trial, even if they could? No. But they had to bring killers to justice somehow.

The United Nations set up the International Criminal Tribunal for Rwanda to try the genocide's leaders. But for those hundreds of thousands accused of being the "ordinary" killers, Rwanda revived the Gacaca courts. These courts are a traditional form of justice. The country aims to conclude these trials sometime in 2009.

"Gacaca" means "on the grass," and that's where judges hold these courts—on the grass, under the trees, in the hometowns of the accused. Confession is key. The process typically starts with a confession from a prisoner, who is then released to his or her hometown to appear before a panel of judges. These judges, ordinary citizens elected by popular vote, hear witness testimony, decide the case, and pass sentence. The courts often limit sentences to time already served plus some community service.

Problems have crept up, however. Guilty parties intimidate and sometimes even kill witnesses to protect themselves. Some Rwandans object that justice and reconciliation can't be combined.

Domitilla Mukantaganzwa is the government official in charge of these courts. Here's how she explained them to the Public Radio International program *The World*: "We don't need only justice. We need also reconciliation. We need also to educate our population to show them that they are really the same population, they are really the same community."

The Main Health Challenges in Africa

Africa has perhaps the most challenging health problems in the world. These problems may strike you, as you read this next section, as hopelessly entangled with one another and self-reinforcing. They are. The good news, though, is that there are ways to solve some of these problems. International bodies like the World Health Organization as well as African national governments are paying attention to them. And they are making some progress.

Vocabulary

- parasite
- vicious circle
- pandemic
- epidemic
- stigma
- famine
- parastatal
- biodiversity
- deforestation
- desertification
- habitat

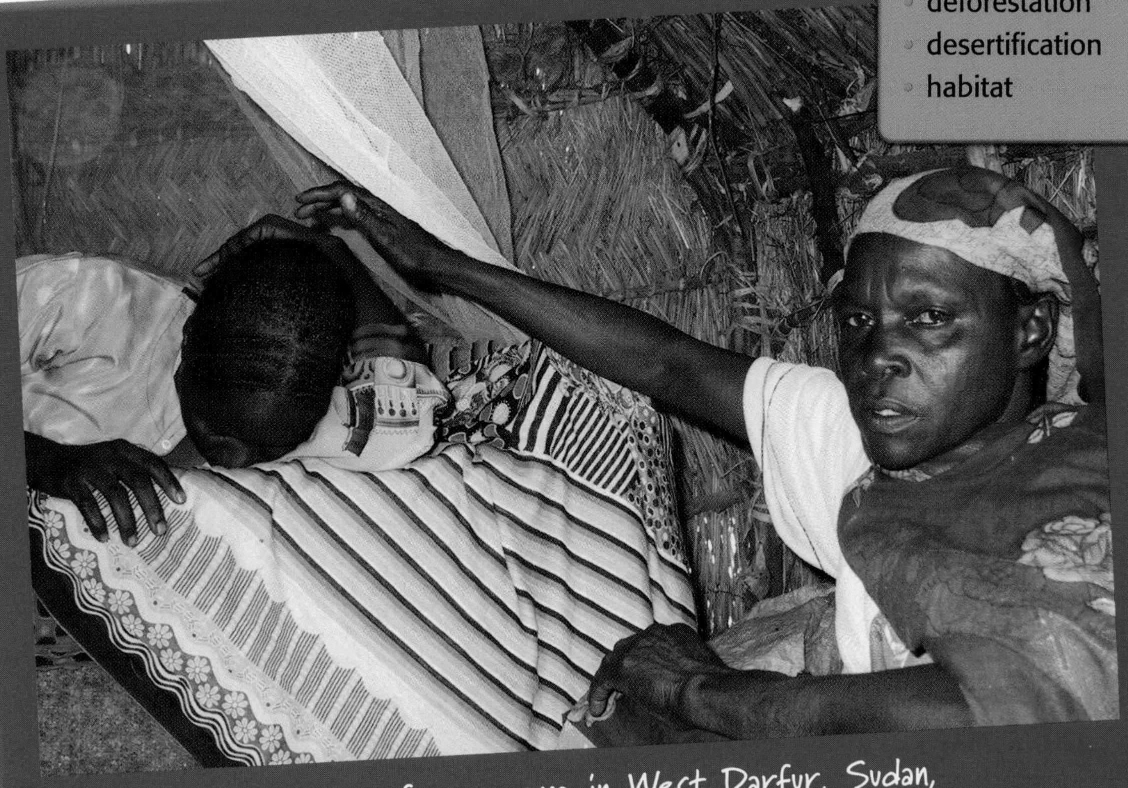

A young woman in a refugee camp in West Darfur, Sudan, rests beneath a mosquito net.

Photo by Danna Harman / © 2004 The Christian Science Monitor

Africa has perhaps the most challenging health problems in the world..

Malaria

Malaria is a mosquito-borne disease caused by a parasite, *a creature that grows and feeds off another organism without contributing to the well-being of the host*. According to the US Agency for International Development (USAID), "every 30 seconds an African child dies of malaria. At least 1 million infants and children under age 5 in sub-Saharan Africa die each year from the mosquito-borne disease."

Ninety percent of the world's malaria-related deaths occur in Africa. The biggest challenge facing those fighting the disease is simply to get their services to people who need them most.

Fortunately many are trying to help. In 2005, US President George W. Bush launched the President's Malaria Initiative (PMI). Its goal has been to cut malaria deaths in half in 15 target countries in Africa by 2010. The PMI has tried to reach 85 percent of each of the two most vulnerable groups, children under 5 and pregnant women, with these effective measures:

- mosquito nets treated with insecticide ("bed nets")
- indoor spraying
- antimalarial drugs
- preventive treatment to keep pregnant women from getting the disease.

USAID is also taking part in the international Roll Back Malaria Partnership. Its 90 partners are striving to "halve the burden" of malaria overall by 2010, meaning cutting in half not only its health effects but the way the disease holds countries back from greater economic development. By World Malaria Day on 25 April 2009, the effort was seeing some success. Malaria deaths had already fallen 66 percent in Zambia, for example.

River Blindness

Mosquitoes aren't the only insects spreading disease. A type of black fly that lives beside streams and rivers in sub-Saharan Africa gets the blame for a disease called *river blindness*. When the fly bites people, it sometimes passes along little worms into their bodies. These worms are another type of parasite. Over time, the worms attack a person's eyes and may eventually cause blindness.

This disease is also known as *onchocerciasis*. It's led to 18 million cases of blindness worldwide. But almost all have been in sub-Saharan Africa.

Fortunately, health authorities have made good progress against the disease. A 30-year campaign to root it out of West Africa concluded successfully in 2002. The numbers of people suffering from river blindness are declining in East Africa, as well. In fact, public health authorities have hailed the campaign against river blindness as a model for other efforts to fight disease.

People went after the black fly breeding grounds with larvicides—substances that kill the black fly larvae. They had to work on a vast regional scale. If they worked merely on a village scale, flies would avoid the sprays by flying to the next village.

Getting river blindness under control is more than a public health issue, though. In West Africa, getting control of the black flies freed up lots of fertile riverfront land for farming. Before, farmers wouldn't work waterfront plots. They feared the black fly and the worms it carried. But now they're farming the land, earning money, and feeding about 17 million people.

Malnutrition

The ravages of disease in Africa are often made worse by malnutrition. All too many Africans are unable to buy or grow enough food for themselves. This leads to chronic hunger, malnutrition, and poor health. When people are hungry or ill, they don't feel well enough to work hard and earn money. And that, in turn, means that they are unable to buy or grow enough food for themselves. And so they are back where they started. People sometimes use the term vicious circle to refer to *a situation where one trouble leads to another that aggravates the original problem.*

Estimates are that 1 in 3 Africans is undernourished. The way out of this vicious circle, African leaders agree, is by expanding the farm sector. One of the United Nations' Millennium Development Goals calls for Africa to cut the number of its hungry people in half by 2015. To meet this goal, officials are looking for ways to expand the agriculture sector and to focus on small-scale farmers.

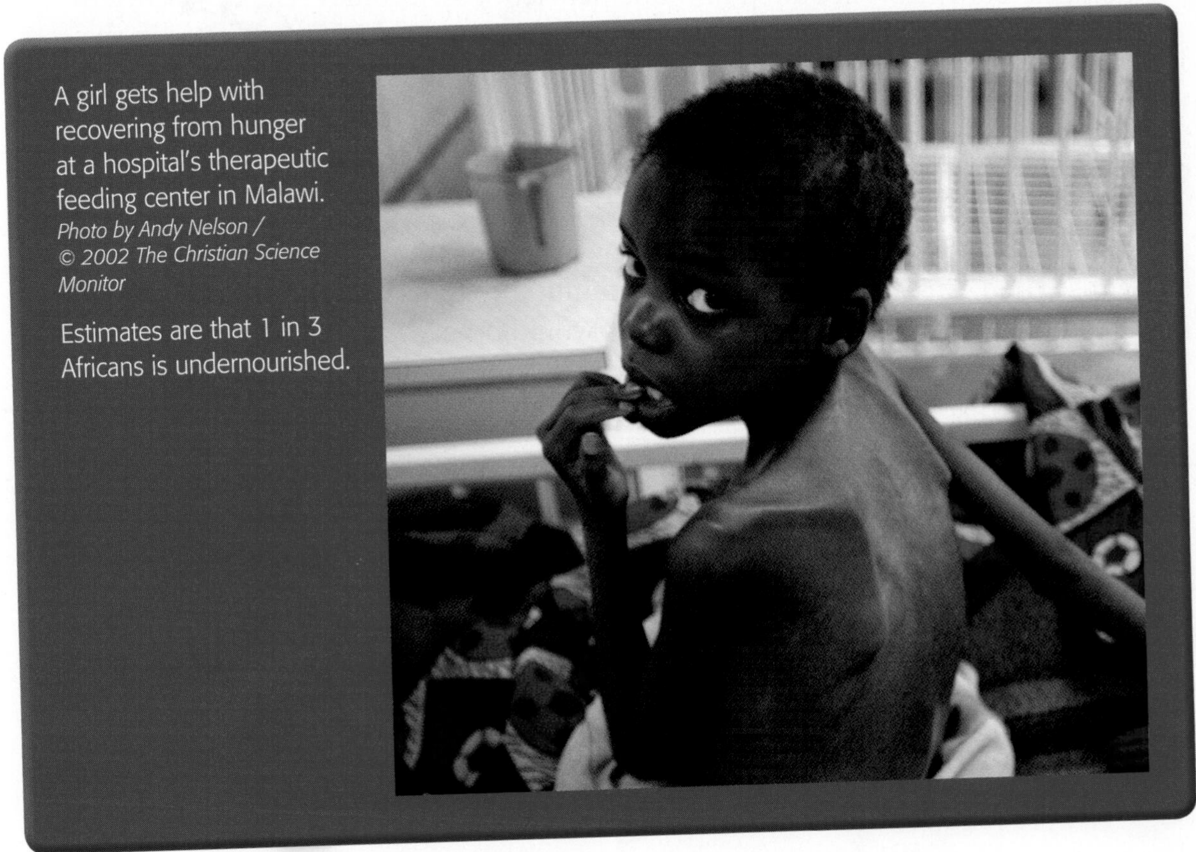

A girl gets help with recovering from hunger at a hospital's therapeutic feeding center in Malawi. *Photo by Andy Nelson / © 2002 The Christian Science Monitor*

Estimates are that 1 in 3 Africans is undernourished.

One problem is that African farmers have little political influence. In developed countries, farmers make up only a very small slice of the labor force. But they tend to have a lot of political clout. Japan's rice farmers, for instance, are a powerful group. In Africa, however, even with far more farmers, political pressure comes from the big cities instead. And so African farmers don't have much political power, nor do they get much attention in parliaments or elsewhere.

Drought is another problem for African farmers. But even worse are the challenges from manmade disasters, such as civil strife and the refugee movements that follow. In 2006, the UN Food and Agriculture Organization reported that 27 African countries urgently needed food assistance. The number of malnourished people totaled 200 million. Of the 27 countries, drought was a factor in only 12. For the other 15, the following factors caused most of the trouble:

- lack of investment in rural areas
- war and other conflicts
- lack of labor because AIDS claims so many people in midlife
- unchecked population growth—despite the many deaths due to AIDS.

The Extent and Impact of AIDS in Africa

People have been trying to treat diseases like malaria and river blindness for decades. But AIDS—acquired immune deficiency syndrome—is a newer health risk. AIDS first came to widespread public attention in the United States in the early 1980s. Doctors and public health officials in New York, Los Angeles, and San Francisco began to find in relatively young gay men diseases generally present in only much older people. Kaposi's sarcoma, a form of cancer, was one. A rare form of pneumonia was another.

Doctors eventually concluded that a new virus, the human immunodeficiency virus (HIV), was attacking its victims' immune systems. This opened them to infections and diseases that their bodies would otherwise have resisted. The virus spreads through bodily fluids, typically through sexual contact or intravenous drug use (that is, drugs injected by needle into a vein).

This history meant that for years, many people around the world saw AIDS as a "gay disease." They viewed it as a plague of the decadent, affluent West. Many people, including African leaders, have refused to accept the disease's medical facts. These attitudes have hindered efforts to contain it. But researchers are sure that the AIDS virus first developed in sub-Saharan Africa. The disease is now a full-blown **pandemic**—*a widespread or even global disease, affecting high numbers of people worldwide.*

The AIDS Epidemic in the African Population

AIDS has hit Africa harder than any other continent. Roughly two-thirds of the world's cases of people living with AIDS are in Africa. Nearly 9 percent of the African population is infected with HIV/AIDS. The disease affects some individual countries much more than others. But especially where the problem is most severe, it affects almost every aspect of life—from the national economy to the question of who will care for the children it orphans.

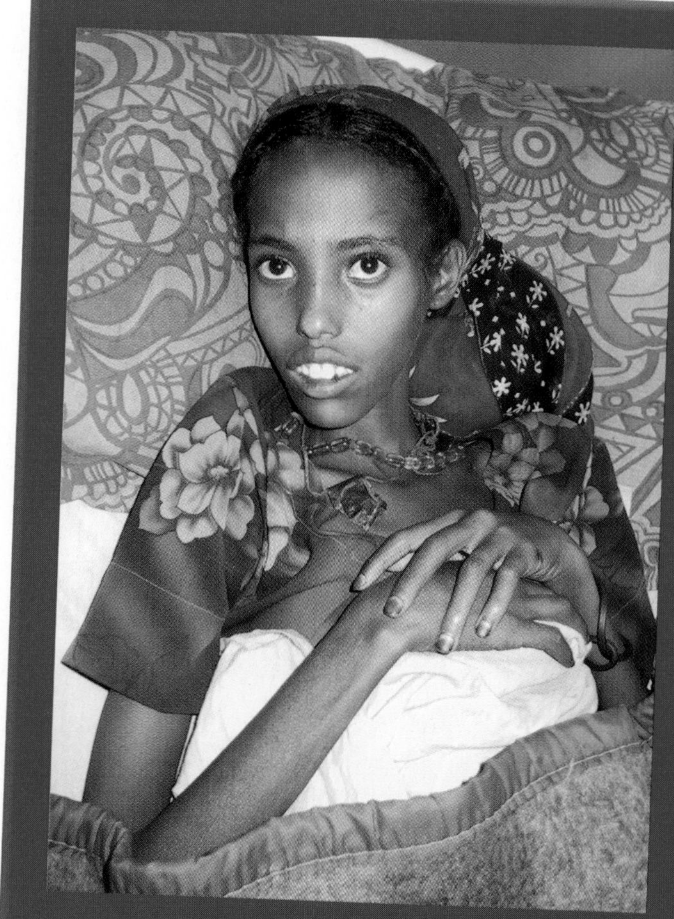

The AIDS disease orphans many of Africa's children, as it did this young girl who is in the last stages of AIDS at a primitive health clinic in Ethiopia.
Photo by Danna Harman / © 2002 The Christian Science Monitor

AIDS has hit Africa harder than any other continent.

The Epidemic's Social and Economic Impacts

AIDS is a health crisis, obviously. But it's much more than that. Peter Piot, head of the Joint United Nations Program on AIDS, has called the disease "a major threat to development and to human society." It's not only causing chaos in society, but it jeopardizes Africa's future, too. In South Africa or Botswana, any given 15-year-old has a 1-in-2 chance of dying of AIDS.

Because of AIDS, Africa stands to lose its hard-won gains in life expectancy, literacy, and education. Some African countries are likely to lose population before they can contain the epidemic—*the sudden and rapid spread of a disease*.

Africans are feeling the impact of AIDS at the household level first. One measure of the direct cost of HIV/AIDS is the loss of income by those who die or lose their jobs because of illness. Households find themselves spending most of their money on health care and funerals.

AIDS is pushing some households that might have stayed above the poverty line back down below it. Two things that individual Africans are likely to do in response to poverty make the epidemic worse: They migrate in search of work, or they go to work in the sex trade—as prostitutes. Both activities throw people into contact with new people to whom they are likely to spread the virus. This is another example of a vicious circle at work. Although you would think that people would do everything they can to avoid AIDS, for many Africans AIDS prevention may seem less critical than simple day-to-day survival.

Over time, the damage AIDS does to household incomes and opportunities weakens the whole society. Extended family networks must strain to care for orphaned kin. Breadwinners who are sick themselves can't take in little nieces and nephews as they would otherwise. Young people growing up in such stressed circumstances have fewer chances to learn from their parents and other elders. Experts call such learning "the transfer of knowledge across generations." It covers everything from family recipes to money management to knowing how to negotiate with in-laws. And it's being lost to an epidemic.

Although this South African couple already has two children of their own, they have taken in six more orphaned by AIDS—the children of the wife's sister and aunt.
Photo by Melanie Stetson Freeman / © 2007 The Christian Science Monitor

Extended family networks must strain to care for orphaned kin.

AIDS has strained Africa's health care systems, too, especially public facilities. In some countries, AIDS patients occupy up to 80 percent of hospital beds. Governments have to make difficult choices: Should they spend their limited resources trying to prevent infections, or treat those already infected? And what about dealing with tuberculosis, malaria, and cholera, which are also serious problems?

AIDS empties schools, too. In some households, children may be the only ones able to tend the sick or to work to support the family. In other cases, children are the only ones left of a family. In Zambia, children 14 or younger head more than 7 percent of the country's households.

Africa

How AIDS affects the labor force in southern Africa

Country	Labor Force Losses Due to HIV/AIDS by 2005	by 2020
Botswana	−17.2 percent	−30.8 percent
Lesotho	− 4.8 percent	−10.6 percent
Malawi	−10.7 percent	−16.0 percent
Mozambique	− 9.0 percent	−24.9 percent
Namibia	−12.8 percent	−35.1 percent
South Africa	−10.8 percent	−24.9 percent
Tanzania	− 9.1 percent	−14.6 percent
Zimbabwe	−19.7 percent	−29.4 percent

Both students and teachers in Africa have high rates of AIDS infection and death. In the first 10 months of 2000, for example, Zambia lost 1,300 teachers to AIDS. That's two-thirds of the number of new teachers the country graduates in a year. Perhaps this explains why early on, many people believed education itself was a cause of AIDS.

The fallout from AIDS on individuals and families ultimately affects the larger economy. AIDS saps production in key sectors, such as farming. Thus AIDS is hitting Africa's food security. Many farms are reverting to subsistence agriculture—done to feed just one's family—rather than cash crops grown to make a living. To give an example from another sector: because of AIDS, Zambia reportedly doesn't have enough engineers to maintain its electrical plants, so power failures repeatedly occur.

AIDS also erodes morale, weakens people's confidence in the future, and undercuts willingness to save and invest. In Botswana, for instance, gross domestic product (GDP, a country's total output) will be 40 percent lower over 25 years than it would be without AIDS.

The High Levels of AIDS Infection in Namibia, Botswana, and South Africa

While AIDS has hit Africa harder than any other continent—in terms of health, economics, and social costs—within Africa AIDS has spread through three countries particularly aggressively: Namibia, Botswana, and South Africa. Cases multiply for various reasons, including the type of work people do, government responses to the disease, and people's beliefs about AIDS.

Namibia

AIDS is the No. 1 cause of death in Namibia. Because Namibia exports so much of what it produces, its economy has a large transport sector. That means many truck drivers spend a great deal of time on the road for long hauls. Away from their wives and children, many of them visit the prostitutes they find at truck stops. The prostitutes become infected, then spread AIDS to their other "customers." Construction workers are another group likely to be away from their families for extended periods. Such men often seek sex from younger girls. The girls are even less likely to seek to protect themselves against disease than are prostitutes.

Public health posters in the truck stops and other places where these mobile workers gather promote condom use as a way to prevent AIDS. But traditional attitudes prevent people from using them as much as they should. Many Namibians are reluctant to discuss sexual matters openly. And many traditional Christians feel that it's not right to sell condoms to those engaging in sex outside of marriage.

Workers clear hills alongside a highway in Rwanda, where there's been a construction and development boom since the 1990s.

Photo by Mary Knox Merrill / © 2009 The Christian Science Monitor

Laborers such as road crews tend to be away from their families for extended periods, and they often seek sex from outside marriage as a result.

The AIDS crisis may be more severe in Namibia than in some other countries. But many of the same factors are at work:

- family life disrupted by men's need to work away from home
- traditional attitudes that make it hard for people to talk frankly about dangerous behavior
- people having multiple sexual partners at the same time
- young women or girls in relationships dominated by older men.

Namibia illustrates the toll AIDS has taken on life expectancy in Africa. You may be used to thinking that people today naturally live longer than their grandparents and great-grandparents did. But AIDS has changed that in Africa.

Two of Namibia's main groups of black Africans have a life expectancy of 43 years, for instance, while the average Namibian lives about 49 years. Both ages are lower than they should be. Health experts worry that it may take until the middle of this century before life expectancy for all Namibians returns to where it was toward the end of the twentieth century—an overall average of 61 years. South Africa, Lesotho, Zambia, and Swaziland are seeing the same pattern.

Botswana

Botswana has the highest rate of AIDS infection in the world. Up to 40 percent of the adult population may be affected. One infant out of every 8 born in Botswana has AIDS at birth.

The disease spread mostly silently through the population once it got a foothold. Like Namibia, Botswana has many migrant workers. People saw AIDS infection as a severe stigma—*symbol of disgrace*. That didn't make it easier for people to seek help. Even once most people had an idea of how the disease was spread, they were reluctant to change their behavior.

But unlike in some other places, AIDS got the attention of Botswana's leaders. "We are threatened with extinction," President Festus Mogae told the UN General Assembly in 2001. "People are dying in chillingly high numbers. It is a crisis of the first magnitude."

> ***fast*FACT**
>
> AIDS drugs can be hard for patients to take. Not that they're hard to swallow, but AIDS patients tend to have a lot of pills and a complicated schedule to follow. This can be challenge enough for well-off Westerners who live with clocks and calendars and are used to following written instructions. It's much harder in places like Botswana.
>
> If people take their pills in the right way at the right time, they can defeat the virus, or at least hold it off for quite some time. But if they don't hit the virus with the full power of the drugs, the virus can develop a resistance to them. "The human immunodeficiency virus is a clever one," says Botswana's Dr. Banu Khan.

In January 2002 Botswana became the first country in Africa to offer the expensive drugs used to treat AIDS to all who need them. It distributes them through the public health system. Observers say that if any country in sub-Saharan Africa can fulfill such a commitment, it's Botswana. But the idea of treating those already infected with AIDS is controversial. Many people argue that it's too late for those who have the virus; resources should go to prevention instead, they say.

With their mother in the hospital with AIDS for the past six months, these South African children ranging in age from 9 months to 18 years are left to fend for themselves. *Photo by Melanie Stetson Freeman / © 2006 The Christian Science Monitor*

South Africa has the largest HIV caseload in the world.

Often drugmakers are reluctant to cut prices for these expensive pills. In Botswana, however, several pharmaceutical companies have agreed to provide medications at significant discounts.

South Africa

South Africa has the largest HIV caseload in the world. Yet for years, its president followed policies that hindered the country's fight against the disease. Thabo Mbeki, who succeeded Nelson Mandela as South Africa's president, rejected scientists' claim that HIV is the sole cause of AIDS. Instead, he suggested that poverty could be the problem. His government rejected offers of free drugs and grants and delayed implementing a treatment program.

In 2008, after he left office, a Harvard University study concluded that policies growing from Mbeki's "denialism"—including the slow introduction of drugs to treat AIDS between 2000 and 2005—led to the needlessly early deaths of 330,000 HIV-positive people. It also led to about 35,000 babies being born with HIV during the same period, the study found.

PEPFAR

But there is hope. Recognizing the toll AIDS was taking on Africans, US President George W. Bush in 2003 launched the President's Emergency Plan for AIDS Relief (PEPFAR). During the next five years, the program spent almost $20 billion to get more AIDS drugs to people with HIV and AIDS in poor countries. It is one of the most expensive foreign aid programs ever.

In January 2009 Stanford University researcher Eran Bendavid announced the findings of a study into PEPFAR's effectiveness. Bendavid found that the number of deaths in the countries where PEPFAR operated was 10 percent below forecasts. That means the program saved 1.1 million lives, although the rates of infection in the countries studied stayed about the same. Congress renewed the program in 2008 with a $48 billion budget.

The Recurring Problems With Famine in Africa

As you read earlier, hunger is another grave danger to Africans. "One in three people are malnourished, and food security today is worse than it was in 1970. Conflict, poor governance, and HIV/AIDS have all reduced basic access to food. Now drought, aggravated by climate change, makes the situation even more desperate," US Senator John Kerry of Massachusetts said in March 2009. Hunger affects 850 million people around the world.

Famine is *a drastic, wide-ranging food shortage*. It's often associated with crop failure due to drought or pest. But many of Africa's famines are manmade. They result from the factors Senator Kerry mentioned: conflict, poor governance (corruption), and HIV/AIDS. Famine leads to hunger, malnutrition, and starvation.

Villagers head home after a World Food Programme distribution in Malawi.

Photo by Andy Nelson / © 2002 The Christian Science Monitor

Hunger affects 850 million people around the world.

You can more easily understand some of Africa's food woes if you think of them as food-distribution problems. For example, Kenya has long been a relatively stable, prosperous country. Its agricultural sector is relatively strong. But ethnic violence after its December 2007 election displaced about a quarter-million people. Many of them lost all they owned. Food was available—but they couldn't afford it. The best way to help them was to give them money to let them buy their own food.

The Extent of Famine in Africa

The 21 African countries with the most severe food crises fall into three broad categories. In the first category, lack of access to food is widespread. The countries in this group are:

- Sierra Leone and Liberia, which are still recovering from years of civil conflict
- Eritrea, on the Horn of Africa, because of the poor state of its economy and its large numbers of displaced persons
- Mauritania, which has endured several years of drought.

Countries in the second category can't grow enough food. These include Lesotho and Swaziland, recovering from years of drought, as well as Somalia, seen as a "failed state," and Zimbabwe. Zimbabwe is one of the most tragic cases because it was once Africa's breadbasket. But its president, Robert Mugabe, has fallen into the all-too-common pattern of a liberation hero who overstays his welcome and becomes a dictator.

The third category consists of countries with food shortages in isolated regions as opposed to a lack of food across the entire nation. This group includes a band of countries along the West African coast, next to Sierra Leone and Liberia: Guinea, Guinea-Bissau, Ghana, and Côte d'Ivoire. It also includes a huge group in East and Central Africa:

- Burundi
- Chad
- Congo
- Democratic Republic of the Congo
- Ethiopia
- Kenya
- Sudan
- Uganda.

The problems in these places are civil strife, refugees, and displaced persons. Crop failures in some places have added to the problem.

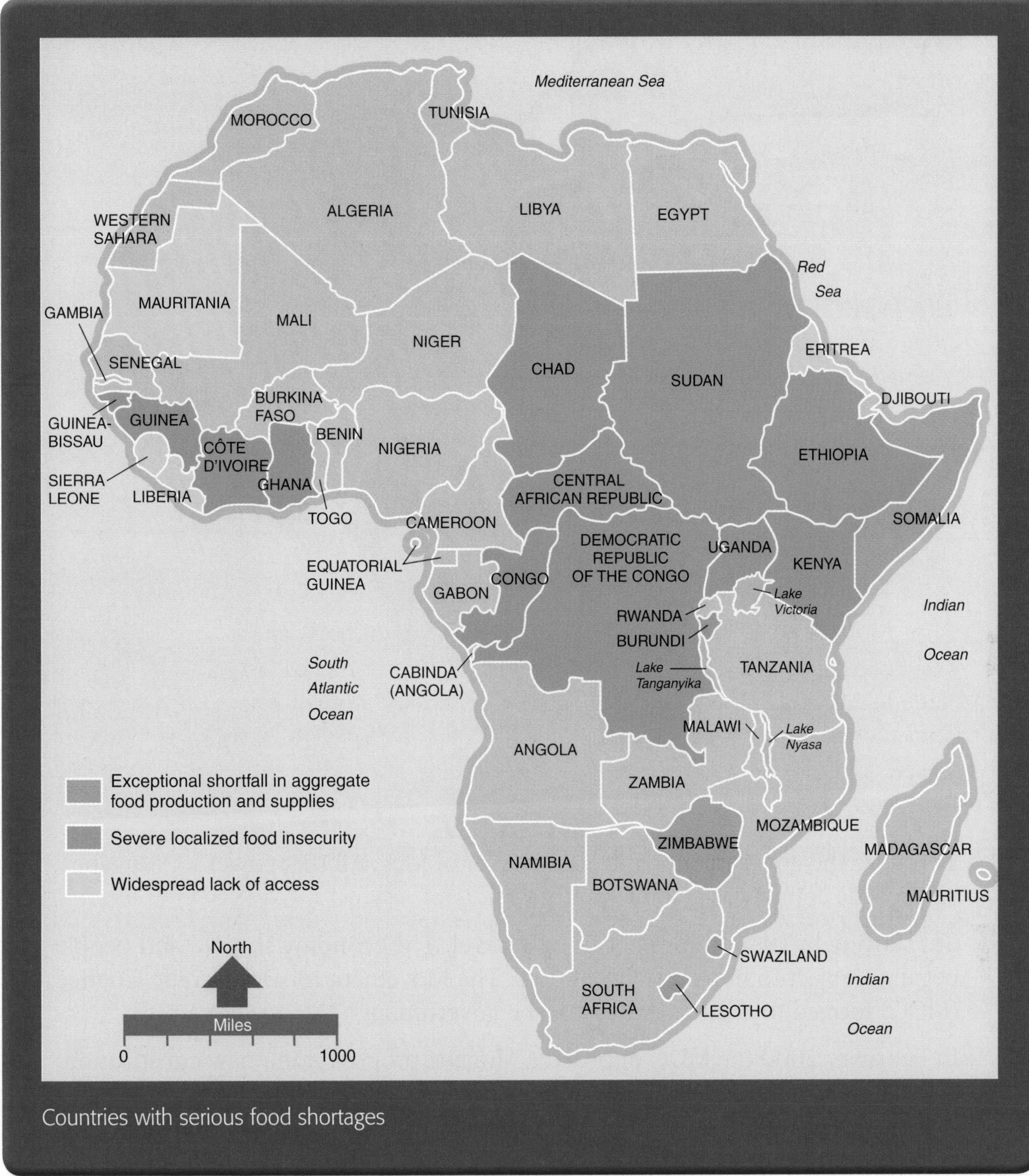

Countries with serious food shortages

How Political and Economic Conflicts Create More Famine

Zimbabwe is a good example of how people can go hungry in a country that should be feeding itself and its neighbors, too. Robert Mugabe was the leader of the new government that took over after white minority rule ended in 1980. For most of its first two decades, Mugabe had a pretty secure grip on things. He controlled the news media and the security forces. Zimbabwe's economy has a huge parastatal sector made up of companies *owned partly or wholly by the government*.

This relocated white Zimbabwean farming family leases nearly 3,000 acres for their dairy in neighboring Mozambique.
Photo by Melanie Stetson Freeman / © 2002 The Christian Science Monitor

Since 2000 Zimbabwe President Robert Mugabe's government has enacted a program to throw white farmers off their land and turn it over to blacks.

This gave the government control over a lot of jobs. All this power let Mugabe control the country as a whole pretty well.

But starting in 1999, things began to unravel. The economy shrank, and people began to object to human rights abuses. The Movement for Democratic Change (MDC) formed to challenge the Mugabe government.

In February 2000 the MDC opposed a Mugabe proposal for a new constitution. The new document, among other things, would have allowed the government to seize white-owned land and give it to black Africans. The proposal went down in defeat. But soon after, the government, working through a loosely organized group of black war veterans, went ahead anyway with a program to throw white farmers off their land and turn it over to blacks. It was an aggressive, even violent, program.

The independent news agency *Zim Online* said at the time: "Zimbabwe's chaotic and often violent land reforms have seen food production in the country drop by about 60 percent because black villagers resettled on former white farms lack the skills and resources to maintain output."

The Challenges Associated With Sending Aid and Relief to Famine Victims

Relief agencies often step in where hunger exists, including in areas of high tension, like Zimbabwe. Even so, people still go hungry. Some of the same issues that make it hard for local farmers to grow food and get it to market in the first place also make it hard for relief agencies to bring food in and distribute it: poor roads, inadequate storage facilities, and corruption. Sometimes corrupt officials or rebel warlords demand bribes from aid agencies or they may hijack a truck full of food aid to feed their own troops.

Development experts are also rethinking the idea of food aid. In the United States in particular, food aid programs have been a way not only to do good but also to take crop surpluses off American farmers' hands. This makes American farmers happy by keeping crop prices up. Food aid has killed two birds with one stone, in other words.

But experts are seeing that flooding a region with food brought in from outside disrupts local economies by taking away local farmers' customers. There are times, however, when airlifting or trucking in sacks of grain and cans of oil is the best way to feed masses of hungry people. This is especially true when they are away from their homes in refugee camps or other locations. In some cases there's no farm sector left to disrupt. But in many situations it's better to provide people cash aid so that they support their local farmers.

A World Food Programme worker in Malawi makes her way across bags of corn.

Photo by Andy Nelson / © 2002 The Christian Science Monitor

Relief agencies often step in where hunger exists, including in areas of high tension.

So it proved in Kenya in 2008. An Irish aid group called Concern partnered with a local African telecommunications company to distribute aid vouchers via cell phone to Kenyans displaced and hungry after ethnic violence. Money can be moved across the country this way in a matter of minutes. Trucking foodstuffs, on the other hand, can take days or weeks. The United Nations World Food Programme has begun to give cash aid as well.

The Kenyan episode illustrates something else: As China and India grow economically, their people have more money and are eating better. This is what economists call "increased demand." It tends to drive up prices for everyone. And it has put poor Africans in competition with newly well-off Asians.

The Main Environmental Issues Facing Africa

Not only hunger and health issues confront the African people. Africa faces significant problems with deforestation, soil degradation, and air and water pollution. Much of its land is at risk of turning into desert.

The tomatoes in a girl's vegetable garden in Zimbabwe never ripened and instead dried out while still on the vine.
Photo by Robert Harbison / © 1992 The Christian Science Monitor

Soil degradation leads to lower crop yields.

Africa's biodiversity, one of its great resources, is also under threat. Biodiversity is *the number and variety of plant and animal species of a place, or of the world as a whole*. As you read about these challenges, one of the things you will note is that everything is related to everything else. It's that old "vicious circle" rearing its head again. Cutting down trees makes soil more likely to blow away. Soil degradation leads to lower crop yields. This may lead farmers to migrate in search of better soil. And more people in an area lead to more stress on the land as people cut down trees to farm. And so the cycle continues.

Deforestation

In Kenya's Rift Valley, for example, farmers can no longer count on the rain that used to come regularly every year. The normal cycles of rising and falling water levels have been disrupted. To explain why, scientists look up to the Aberdare mountain range. It forms the eastern wall of the Rift Valley. Thick forests once covered its mountains. They trapped moisture, kept temperatures cool, and attracted cloud cover. This, in turn, helped produce the plentiful rainfall in the area.

But deforestation—*the removal of trees*—has occurred throughout Kenya over the past few decades. People have cleared land for farms. Timber merchants have cut down more trees than the forests can naturally replace. And government officials have sold or sometimes simply given away large tracts of forest to their friends and relatives. The loss of trees has led to lower water levels in lakes and rivers, and to less rainfall.

The United Nations Environment Program (UNEP) reported in 2008 that Africa was suffering deforestation at twice the rate of the world as a whole. Every year, Africa loses nearly 10 million acres of forest. That's a territory about the size of Switzerland, or a little bigger than the state of Maryland. UNEP called forest loss a major concern in 35 African countries.

Central Africa, especially the Congo Basin, is at the cutting edge of the trend. UN officials want to see Africans conserve their woodlands. But these officials understand that timber production is important to local economies.

Tree Planting as a Path to the Nobel Peace Prize

How important are trees to Africa? Is tree-planting just some "tree hugger" thing, or does it really matter to Africans' peace and prosperity? Consider that Wangari Maathai of Kenya won the Nobel Peace Prize for 2004 because of her efforts to plant trees. The Nobel is one of the most prestigious awards in the world. Typically it goes to people who end wars. But when Dr. Maathai, a biologist by training, served in the National Council of Women of Kenya, she introduced the idea of people planting trees on farms and on school and church property. Her work has led to the planting of tens of millions of trees and to the establishment of the Pan African Greenbelt Network.

A related issue is the loss of glaciers. Africa has only a few of them, and they're shrinking fast. UNEP based its report—covering glaciers and deforestation—on satellite pictures showing how expanding cities, pollution, deforestation, and climate change were damaging Africa's environment.

The Loss of Soil Fertility and Biodiversity

Desertification is *the process whereby land becomes desert*. It's related to deforestation. Trees, like grasses and shrubbery, help retain moisture and soil. Overfarming, on the other hand, depletes soil. As Africa's population has grown, farmers have worked the land harder and harder. They often plant crops on land that isn't very good in the first place. They generally can't afford fertilizers to put nutrients back into the soil. The drought that has plagued Africa in recent years makes all this worse.

And so after a while, the soil yields a smaller and weaker crop. This means less money for the farmers, and starts the cycle of poverty and hunger. Eventually these farmers may give up and move—to some other land they will clear to farm, or maybe to the city, or even to another country.

The tensions in Sudan's Darfur region, which you read about in Lesson 3, stem in part from these kinds of environmental changes. Herders have moved south in search of well-watered pasture for their livestock, and this has put them in conflict with farmers. Development experts see climate change as a leading cause of migration.

Researchers say that to keep pace with population growth, African agriculture needs to expand by 3 percent to 5 percent annually. It hasn't done that. Moreover, the African practice of farming without putting anything back into the earth means that the soil of much African farmland is dead. To restore these soils could be prohibitively expensive.

Conservation farming provides a glimmer of hope here. It is a system of low-cost techniques that farmers can learn and practice, even if they can't afford fertilizers. These include crop rotation, using crop residue to enrich the soil, careful timing of planting, and building and using basins to retain rainwater.

An issue related to deforestation and desertification is biodiversity. Biodiversity is about having a rich mix of different forms of life. It's a good thing. It's something everyone wants more of. Africa has traditionally hosted a lot of it.

Africa's species-rich areas include, for instance, the Succulent Karoo of South Africa and Namibia. That is the world's richest desert. Forty percent of the 4,800 plant species that grow there are found nowhere else on the globe.

But biodiversity is at risk in much of Africa. That's because deforestation and desertification are creating habitat loss. A creature's habitat is the environment to which it is adapted. Habitat is *a creature's natural home*, in other words. When forests disappear and farm fields turn into dusty, dry strips of desert, homes are lost. That means not just human homes, but homes for birds, insects, mammals, even grasses and weeds. Habitat loss is the most important cause of the decline in biodiversity. A species won't stay in a place if it doesn't feel "at home" or can't survive there.

Cracked earth spreads like a carpet across this field in the Sahel Desert in Chad.

Photo by Melanie Stetson Freeman / © 2007 The Christian Science Monitor

Environmental changes have sparked tensions in places like neighboring Sudan and resulted in too many refugees seeking food, water, and shelter in Chad.

Biodiversity is important to Africa because it provides options. Options mean that if one kind of banana is hard to grow, farmers can try out another kind. If cattle growers need to breed animals to withstand certain tough conditions—chronic drought, for instance—it's important that they have many different kinds of cattle to work with. It helps to have a large gene pool to draw on.

Here's another example where biodiversity helps people eat better: In South Africa, people in two villages once again have access to a traditional leafy green vegetable called phara. People eat both its leaves and its fruit. Because of a combination of human and natural factors, phara had disappeared from the two villages. But researchers helped the inhabitants get seeds from other villages. Now there's an organized seed-collection program. The villagers are glad to have their phara back.

Air and Water Pollution

You may be surprised to find out that Africa has air pollution problems. After all, you may think, isn't air pollution a problem of big cities? And isn't Africa a continent of villages? That, it turns out, is an outdated stereotype: The United Nations says Africa has the highest rate of urbanization in the world.

Projected Average Urban Growth Rate, 2005–2010

Region	Urban Growth Rate
Africa	3.31 percent
Asia	2.46 percent
Europe	0.17 percent
Latin America and the Caribbean	1.71 percent
North America	1.31 percent

Source: United Nations Population Division

Air Pollution

In its African Environment Outlook, issued in 2002, the United Nations identified several causes of air pollution in Africa:

- African tax codes tend to encourage the use of "dirty" fuels to run factories and make electricity.
- Africa's factories tend to be outdated and inefficient.
- Africans rely heavily on older cars. These are often "clunkers" brought in from Europe or elsewhere. An older car may emit as much as 20 times the pollution of a newer model. There's a price to pay for dirty air—in human and economic terms. A study of transportation in Senegal found costs tied to vehicle emissions amounted to 5 percent of gross domestic product (GDP).
- Cities in northern Africa have many oil refineries and coal-fired power plants. Their air may have twice as much sulfur dioxide as the World Health Organization thinks is tolerable.

Water Pollution

Africa has a water pollution problem stemming from the same issue you read about in Chapter 2, Lesson 4: lack of sanitation. In Africa, 62 percent of the people lack access to toilets and safe ways to dispose of human waste. Even where facilities exist, many people haven't learned the basics of how and why to use toilet paper, wash their hands, and keep facilities clean. People don't understand that they shouldn't try to flush newspapers down toilets, for instance. Lack of decent toilet facilities often keeps teenage girls out of school. As a result, toilet facilities can cause as many problems as they solve.

Fortunately, African social entrepreneurs see an opportunity here. They are training people to better maintain public facilities. They are opening for-profit "toilet malls," which also include showers. And some are even using the gases from waste to produce electricity.

Africans who want a drink of water can't necessarily just go to the kitchen sink and turn on a tap. Many rely on hand-dug wells, sometimes known as boreholes. This simply isn't the same as getting water piped into your house from a city waterworks that purifies the water beforehand. Wastes of various types often get into the water from these hand-dug wells: not only human waste, but also filth from slaughterhouses, factories, even produce farms. As a result, drinking water contains particles that are unhealthy to drink and carries diseases as well.

Again, social entrepreneurs are moving to clean things up. Efforts are under way in many parts of Africa to divert waste to fuel electricity plants.

A boy takes a shower in a rainstorm in Kinshasa, Democratic Republic of the Congo.
Photo by Robert Harbison / © 1990 The Christian Science Monitor
The lack of sanitation is a major water pollution problem for Africa.

Rather than wait in line, Darfur refugees line up their containers to collect water at this refugee camp in Chad.

Photo by Melanie Stetson Freeman / © 2007 The Christian Science Monitor

Like so many of Africa's health, nutrition, and environmental problems, human rights issues often grow from troubles associated with war, corruption, and large populations in need of basic goods.

Human Rights Issues in Africa

Like so many of Africa's health, nutrition, and environmental problems, human rights issues often grow from troubles associated with war, corruption, and large populations in need of basic goods. In Lesson 3, you read how human rights are violated in parts of Africa. Ethnic strife, no rule of law, and horrific violence are all ultimately human rights issues.

Rape as a weapon of war is another human rights issue in Africa. Rebel groups from Rwanda and Uganda still make trouble in the eastern part of the Democratic Republic of the Congo, for instance. This is despite the provisions of the 1999 Lusaka Accord, meant to bring peace.

The violence in the Democratic Republic of the Congo has displaced a million people. Women have borne the brunt of it. At times a thousand rapes have occurred there every day. When armed groups raid towns and villages, they rape women in front of their families as a way to lay claim to the territory.

Zimbabwe is another country rife with human rights abuses. Government negotiations for a power-sharing deal with the opposition have lumbered along. But what the US State Department calls the "pervasive and systematic abuse of human rights" by Robert Mugabe's authoritarian government has only increased. The ruling party has power so firmly in its grip that it has "effectively negated the right of citizens to change their government," the State Department says. Among the Mugabe government's tactics:

- unlawful killings
- political abductions
- state-sanctioned use of excessive force
- torture by security forces of members of the opposition, student leaders, and civil society activists.

Sudan's human rights practices fall woefully short as well. The government's record "remained poor," according to the State Department. As of 2008 abuses there included:

- curbing citizens' rights to change their government
- killings by government forces and their allies
- "disappearances" of hundreds of civilians
- torture, beatings, rape, and other cruel, inhumane treatment by security forces
- arbitrary arrest and detention
- violence against women and children, including sexual violence and recruitment of child soldiers.

The human rights situation in Eritrea has become particularly dire.

Eritrea won independence from Ethiopia in 1993. This was after three decades of war. By the spring of 2009, though, the advocacy group Human Rights Watch was calling Eritrea one of the most closed and repressive states on earth. The group accused President Isaias Afwerki of keeping the country on a permanent war footing. His pretext for this is an unresolved border dispute with Ethiopia.

The country has no independent civil society. There are no independent news media, either. What's more, the government has also been rounding up and torturing Christians and some Muslims.

Most of Eritrea's adult population is part of an all-draftee army. And there's no getting out. Some who have fled the country have been brought back by force and then have "disappeared."

The Human Rights Issues Associated With War Crimes in Africa

After the ethnic strife and civil wars of the 1990s, national authorities worked with the United Nations to convene two special courts. The Special Court for Sierra Leone was set up in the capital, Freetown. (The government of Sierra Leone asked that the trial of former Liberian President Charles Taylor, however, be moved to The Hague.) The International Criminal Tribunal for Rwanda was established in Arusha, Tanzania. Its mandate is to try defendants on charges of genocide and other serious violations of international law in Rwanda and neighboring countries.

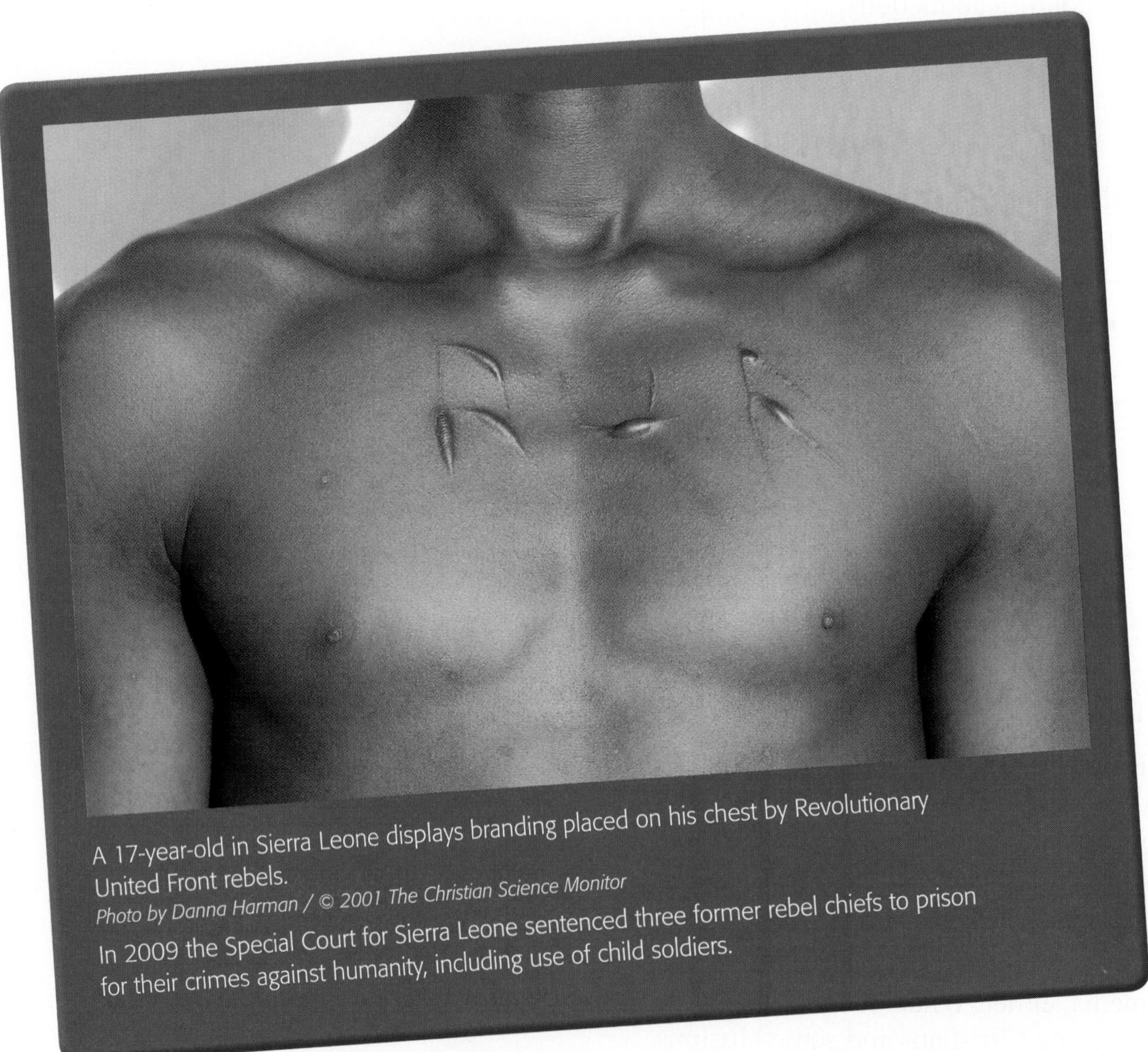

A 17-year-old in Sierra Leone displays branding placed on his chest by Revolutionary United Front rebels.

Photo by Danna Harman / © 2001 The Christian Science Monitor

In 2009 the Special Court for Sierra Leone sentenced three former rebel chiefs to prison for their crimes against humanity, including use of child soldiers.

Both courts are meant to provide justice and accountability. They are also intended to signal an end to war criminals getting away with their crimes, and a warning that Africans will not tolerate such behavior in the future. The Rwanda court's first successful conviction was that of Jean-Paul Akayesu, the mayor of Tabu, Rwanda, in 1998. Court officials hope to have all trials and appeals concluded by the end of 2010. To reach their goal, they are focusing on prosecuting top officials while leaving lower officials' cases to national courts.

In April 2009 the Special Court for Sierra Leone sentenced three former rebel chiefs to prison for their crimes against humanity. Issa Sesay of the Revolutionary United Front (RUF) will serve 52 years. Morris Kallon and Augustine Gbao will serve a maximum of 39 years and 25 years, respectively. The courts found these three senior surviving members of the RUF guilty of murder, rape, sexual enslavement, attacks against UN troops, and the use of child soldiers. The three men led the violence that left tens of thousands of people maimed. The RUF regularly cut off victims' arms, legs, ears, and even noses.

These three men were also found guilty of "forced marriage." This is a euphemism for sexual assault. This was the first time an international tribunal has handed down such a verdict.

Problems Stemming From the Expulsion of Aid Agencies in Africa

Many strife-torn parts of Africa rely on international aid groups to meet their people's basic needs for food, shelter, and health care. But sometimes a national government throws aid groups out, and chaos ensues.

It happened in Zimbabwe in 2008. It happened again in Sudan in March 2009. Sudanese President Umar al-Bashir expelled 13 aid groups working in the troubled Darfur region. Among them were Oxfam, Care, and Save the Children. The government seized the assets of several other aid agencies as well.

The expulsion order came half an hour after the International Criminal Court in The Hague announced it had issued an arrest warrant for al-Bashir. The court wants to try him for war crimes and crimes against humanity in connection with the Darfur crisis.

The expulsion put 2 million Darfuris at risk of starvation, according to Amnesty International. "Millions of lives are at stake and this is no time to play political games," said Tawanda Hondora, an Amnesty official. Sudan is bound by treaty to work with aid groups. But, Hondora said, "the population of Darfur, which has suffered the brunt of this conflict for the past six years, is now being punished by its own government in response to the arrest warrant."

Issues Associated With Genocide in Africa

One of the lessons of the Nazi Holocaust of World War II was "never again." Never again would the civilized world look the other way as a racist ideology was used in an attempt to exterminate a whole people. But in Rwanda it did happen again. And now years later, one of the regrets of many people was that so little was done to stop the killers.

The desire to prevent another Rwandan massacre has been behind some of the multilateral efforts in Darfur. Al-Bashir's move to oust aid organizations is a reminder of just how fragile the mechanisms of international justice really are. So was the fact that al-Bashir was able to travel freely around Africa despite the arrest warrant.

Still, people see the Rwanda genocide as a kind of turning point. Many experts in the human rights field say this tragedy has galvanized international efforts against genocide. The process of bringing perpetrators to justice, both in local courts in Rwanda and at the International Criminal Court in The Hague, has helped the cause of the rule of law.

The problems of disease, malnutrition, environmental damage, and human rights abuses in Africa can seem daunting. Certainly they often threaten to overwhelm the continent's ability to deal with them. Africa's hope, however, stems from two sources. The first is the resilience and resources of the African people themselves. The second is the desire of the world's wealthy nations and the rest of the international community to help. Experience demonstrates that when these two are effectively connected, they can bring about solutions.

Lesson 4 Review

Using complete sentences, answer the following questions on a sheet of paper.

1. What measures are being taken to halve the burden of malaria in Africa? Name at least two.
2. How successful (or not) has the West African campaign against river blindness been? What has been a side effect of this campaign?
3. What proportion of the African population is infected with the AIDS virus?
4. What is the challenge for Africans taking AIDS medications? What is the risk if they don't take them as they should?
5. What proportion of Africans is malnourished?
6. Why are some relief agencies choosing to distribute cash rather than food aid?
7. Why is biodiversity so important in Africa? Give two reasons.
8. Why are old cars a problem in Africa?
9. What are the human rights challenges in Eritrea?
10. Why is the Rwandan genocide seen as a kind of turning point in history?

Applying Your Learning

11. Should the Nobel Peace Prize have gone to someone whose work has focused on planting trees? Why or why not?

LESSON 5 US Interests and Regional Issues in Africa

Quick Write

What do you think the authorities should do about the oil-field violence in the Niger Delta?

Learn About

- the challenges of resources and commerce in the regions of Africa
- immigration trends associated with Africa
- challenges associated with pirating and lawlessness in Somalia
- US and European development efforts in Africa

In March 2009 a series of explosions destroyed a Royal Dutch Shell pipeline that sends crude to the Escravos oil export terminal in southern Nigeria.

The explosions were thought to be sabotage—*acts of deliberate destruction to hinder an operation or cause*. Such sabotage is very common in Nigeria's oil-producing regions. Local youths often destroy pipelines as a way to steal crude oil. Oil theft, also called "bunkering," is a multi-million-dollar business.

The military forces in Nigeria have taken a harder line against oil thieves recently. They have seized several ships full of stolen crude. But this has only prompted the oil gangs to strike back—by attacking the pipeline. A local journalist says the gangs have become very powerful, despite the military crackdowns.

Attacks on oil facilities in the Niger Delta have cut Nigerian output by about one-fifth since early 2006. But the angry local people who are behind the attacks say they have no choice but to strike out at the oil industry. The oil wealth never reaches them, they say. And their own government neglects them.

The Challenges of Resources and Commerce in the Regions of Africa

Vocabulary

- sabotage
- foreign direct investment
- collusion
- brain drain
- maritime
- onus
- sustainable development

The United States has serious economic interests in Africa. These interests are challenged by the continent's political, social, and environmental problems. This lesson will examine some of those more closely.

One example is Nigeria, which shows how oil deposits can be a source of trouble as well as wealth. On the other hand, Uganda's escape from crushing debt may be a model for other African countries facing massive bills. One US response to the many challenges is the African Growth and Opportunity Act (AGOA), a trade law that has opened US markets to African goods.

Children wait for their breakfast outside a village home in Zaire.

Photo by Robert Harbison / © 1990 The Christian Science Monitor

Light-colored hair indicates malnutrition due to a starch-based diet. African nations grapple with a variety of political, social, and environmental problems. The United States has opened its markets to African goods in an attempt to encourage economic growth.

The Challenges Related to Nigerian Oil

The United States trades more with Nigeria than with any other country in sub-Saharan Africa. Nearly half of Nigeria's daily oil production goes to the United States. And the United States gets about a tenth of its oil from Nigeria. Nigeria trades more with the United States than with any other country except Britain. But the American thirst for oil means that Nigeria sells far more to the United States than it buys.

The United States is also Nigeria's largest foreign investor. Foreign direct investment is *what occurs when a company establishes a physical presence in a foreign country*—by buying a mine or building a factory, for instance. In Nigeria, US firms generally buy into and set up oil or mining operations. Exxon-Mobil and Chevron are America's two major players in the region. Foreign companies find Nigeria a hard place to do business because of sabotage, however. For firms in sectors other than oil, it's usually not worth the extra effort because most products don't earn as much money as oil does.

A boy scouts for corn kernels that fell out of bags to be distributed to local villagers in Malawi.
Photo by Andy Nelson / © 2002 The Christian Science Monitor

Hunger often results from government policies. For instance, Nigeria fell into an unhealthy dependence on oil for earnings starting in the 1970s, neglecting its strong farming sector.

During the 1970s oil boom, Nigeria neglected its strong farming and light manufacturing sectors (light manufacturing usually means making goods like clothes and toasters rather than large, heavy products like steel and airplanes). Instead, the country fell into an unhealthy dependence on oil. By 2002, for instance, oil and gas exports accounted for more than 98 percent of the country's export earnings. They also accounted for 83 percent of Nigerian federal government revenue.

As the oil sector boomed, other parts of the economy fell apart. Masses of people poured into the cities. The countryside grew much poorer. Infrastructure and social services collapsed. By around 2000–01 the oil boom was history. The typical Nigerian's income was only about a quarter of what it had been at its peak in the 1970s. Nigerians were poorer, on average, than at independence in 1960.

Meanwhile, the presence of the foreign oil companies in Nigeria is a source of ongoing trouble. They don't get on well with the local peoples, who are poor and desperate for work. Ordinary Nigerians see their corrupt national government in collusion, or *secret agreement*, with the oil firms. The Nigerian government and foreign companies pump the nation's wealth out of the ground and sell it for good money, but the people see none of the profit.

Gangs of young militants vandalize pipelines to steal oil. They also kidnap foreign workers for ransom money. This then goes to fund more criminal operations. On top of all this, the oil industry causes severe environmental damage to the Delta.

The Challenge of African Debt

Despite Africa's rich natural resources, such as oil or diamonds, African nations have large debts. They racked up these colossal debts in the past half-century because of:

- corruption and general mismanagement by political leaders poorly prepared for independence
- oil shocks—which you read about in Chapter 1, Lesson 5—when prices go way up or fall way down
- falling prices for goods that Africa exports
- increased government spending on infrastructure, health care, education, and other services.

African countries owe some of their debt to the United States, but they owe most of it to organizations such as the World Bank, in which the United States plays a dominant role. Debtor nations are like ordinary people who pile up big bills. They charge more and more to their credit cards, but they can only pay the minimum due every month. This means that their total amount due never shrinks. In fact, it continues to grow. And this burden keeps them from moving forward with other things in their lives.

Many people say that finding a way to lift this weight from Africa's shoulders would help lead the continent out of poverty. One program that's had some success in doing this is the World Bank's Heavily Indebted Poor Countries (HIPC) Initiative. Launched in 1996, HIPC reduces loan payments. In return, countries with debts must agree to put the money they save into health care, free schooling, and farming.

In Uganda, for instance, school classrooms used to be half empty. Tuition was only about $50 a year, but many parents couldn't afford it. Under HIPC, Uganda is using the money it would have sent to the World Bank to offer free schooling. The number of children in primary schools rose from 5.3 million in 1997 to 7.6 million in 2003. Immunization rates for common diseases jumped, too. The HIV infection rate fell by half from 1998 to 2004.

Aid donors started to give more, too, once Uganda got debt relief. In fact, the increase in aid was several times the amount of the debt relief.

Children line up in front of a new school in their village center in Uganda.

Photo by Mary Knox Merrill / © 2009 The Christian Science Monitor

The number of children in primary schools in Uganda rose from 5.3 million in 1997 to 7.6 million in 2003, thanks in part to the international community forgiving some of Uganda's debts.

The HIPC Initiative, along with another program known as the Multilateral Debt Relief Initiative, serves 33 African countries. Not every country is stable enough to benefit from debt relief, however. Places with ongoing civil strife are not good candidates for plans like HIPC.

Trade Issues Between Africa and the United States

One of the four pillars of US policy in Africa is to encourage economic growth. This goal includes pushing for open markets, expanded trade, and a bigger role for Africa in the global economy. The African Growth and Opportunity Act (AGOA) is at the center of efforts to meet these goals.

A young Ugandan woman splits her time between cutting sugar cane on her family's farm and getting an education in agriculture through a program meant to lift people out of poverty.
Photo by Mary Knox Merrill / © 2009 The Christian Science Monitor

The export of fruits and nuts, scented oils, and spices are some of the sectors that have grown under the African Growth and Opportunity Act.

AGOA has opened US markets to African goods. It's also helped increase trade between the United States and Africa—both in volume and in the mix of goods traded. In AGOA's first eight years, two-way trade has nearly tripled. By providing markets for African firms, AGOA has helped African companies become more competitive. In fact, AGOA gets a lot of credit for helping African countries develop their garment industries. Hundreds of thousands of Africans now hold newly created jobs in the needle trades. But AGOA has boosted other sectors as well. Prepared vegetables, fruits and nuts, cut flowers, beverages, cocoa products, scented oils for goods like perfume, and spices are some of the sectors that have grown under AGOA. Virtually all of these items enter the United States duty-free—that is, without an import tax.

Immigration Trends Associated With Africa

Jobs and economic growth may be springing up in some African countries, but people still leave the continent in search of new lives elsewhere. Since 1990 more African immigrants have entered the United States than came to American shores before the Atlantic slave trade ended in 1808.

A Rwandan refugee who attends college in New England helps local immigrants such as these schoolchildren adjust to American life.
Photo by Mary Knox Merrill / © 2008 The Christian Science Monitor

African immigrants are like their predecessors from other parts of the world: They want a better life for themselves and their children.

These new African immigrants are still only a trickle. The streams of Latin Americans and Asians are much larger. But all three groups have benefited from legal changes made in 1965. Before then, the law had favored European immigrants.

The new Africans are like their predecessors from other parts of the world: They want a better life for themselves and their children. "Senegal became too small" is how one woman described her journey to America to *The New York Times* in 2005. Marie Lopy arrived as a student in 1996 and later worked as a bookkeeper. Eventually she earned a biology degree from the City University of New York.

Every African immigrant to the United States starts out as an African emigrant. The stream of people out of Africa has been fairly steady in recent years and affects both the African and American economies in a number of ways, as you will read next.

The Increased Levels of Emigration From Africa to the United States

Africans have been arriving in the United States at an annual rate of about 50,000 over the past several years. They come from countries such as Ghana, Nigeria, Senegal, and Mali. But the flow really began in the 1970s. Refugees from Ethiopia and Somalia were in the first wave. During the 1990s the number of black residents of the United States who were born in sub-Saharan Africa nearly tripled. And the proportion of blacks born abroad rose from 4.9 percent to 7.3 percent during this period.

Over time, the immigrant stream from Africa has changed. Now fewer are refugees. More people arrive on family reunification visas instead. That is, the United States lets people into the country who are related to people already living here.

Many speak English. Often, they have grown up in large cities. They have lived in capitalist societies. They live in households headed by married couples. They also are generally more highly educated and have better-paying jobs than many American-born blacks. Like many immigrants, however, these newcomers often work at jobs below their qualifications. They may drive a taxi instead of managing a bank, for instance.

Note that all this applies only to legal immigrants. The numbers of Africans who enter the United States illegally or overstay their visas may be at least four times those of the legal immigrants.

The Impact of Immigration on the US Economy

African immigrants tend to gather in the very biggest cities, notably New York. But they live in many other cities too. For example, Atlanta has drawn large numbers of Africans, perhaps because of its well-established middle-class African-American community. Minneapolis has a notable Somali community. Ethiopians and Eritreans drive most of the taxis in Columbus, Ohio. They run ethnic restaurants in the city center as well.

Immigrants in the United States tend to be entrepreneurial, and these Africans are no exception. They have revived many small communities and depressed neighborhoods in big cities. But tensions sometimes arise when they compete with native-born people for jobs.

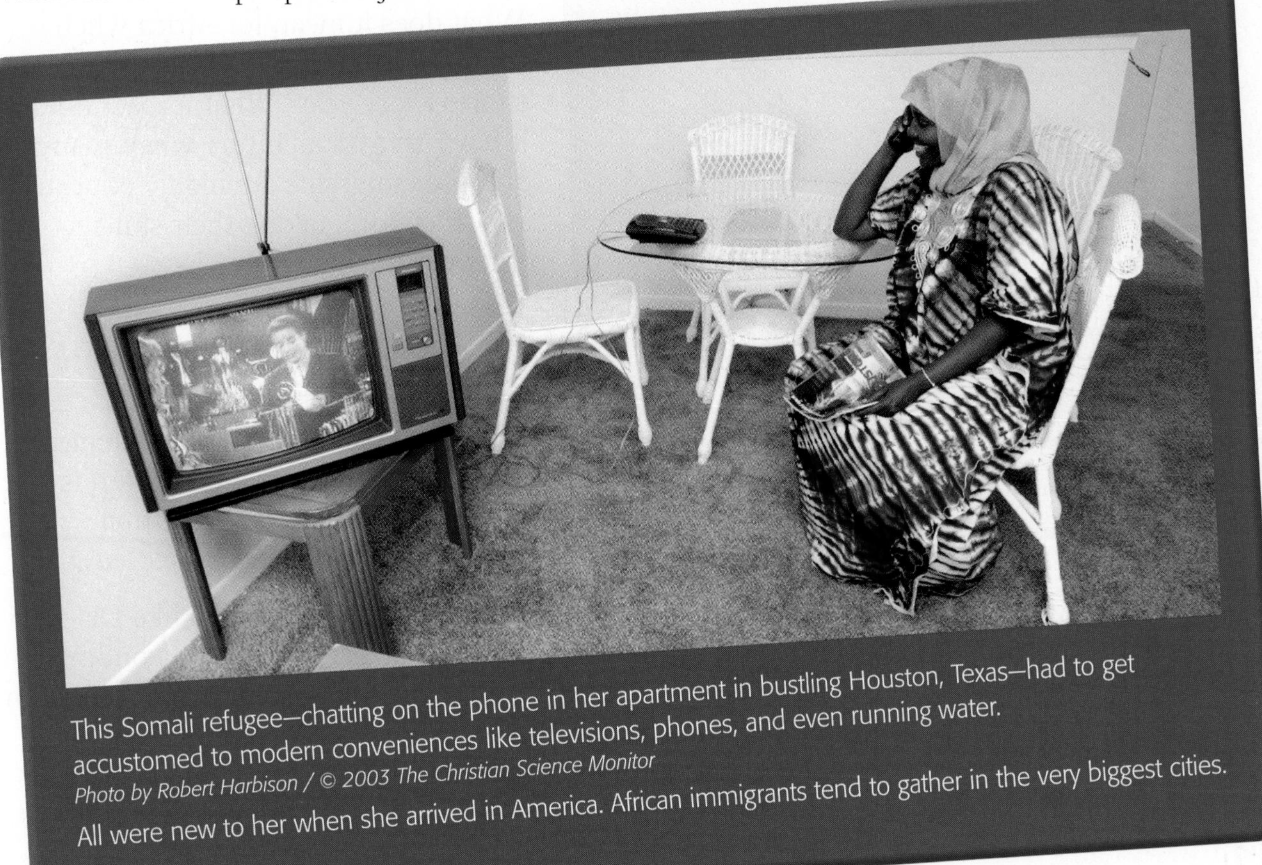

This Somali refugee—chatting on the phone in her apartment in bustling Houston, Texas—had to get accustomed to modern conveniences like televisions, phones, and even running water.
Photo by Robert Harbison / © 2003 The Christian Science Monitor

All were new to her when she arrived in America. African immigrants tend to gather in the very biggest cities.

Students wait for class to start after recess in their UN-built school in Burundi, where many refugees are returning after fleeing conflicts.
Photo by Melanie Stetson Freeman / © 2006 The Christian Science Monitor
Some worry about Africa's future when many of its most highly educated citizens take their skills to other continents.

African immigrants are also likely to change the racial dynamics of the United States. This will affect the society and culture of the country, as well as its economy. The newcomers are redefining the term "African-American." American blacks are a diverse group. But most are just a few generations away from slavery. What happens when skin color no longer sends such a clear signal about someone's family history and culture?

"Historically, every immigrant group has jumped over American-born blacks," Columbia University historian Eric Foner told *The New York Times* in 2005. "The final irony would be if African immigrants did, too."

The Impact of Emigration on African Economies

What does it mean for Africa when tens of thousands of people leave her shores every year? What impact does it have on Africa's future when many of those emigrants are highly educated and, therefore, taking their skills to other continents?

"In 25 years, Africa will be empty of brains," Dr. Lalla Ben Barka of the United Nations grimly predicted a few years ago. Her "brain drain" statement got people's attention. Brain drain is *the loss of skills and knowledge from a place when its educated people leave.*

Each emigrant leaves a hole behind in Africa. The situation has people like Dr. Ben Barka in a state of alarm. Data are sketchy. But her UN agency, the Economic Commission for Africa, estimates that between 1960 and 1989, some 127,000 African professionals left the continent. Since 1990 that rate has risen markedly. It's now up to 20,000 a year. Africa is losing the people it needs most. The United Nations now considers brain drain "one of the great obstacles to Africa's development."

The loss of medical doctors has been the most critical aspect. The United Nations estimates that at least 60 percent of doctors trained in Ghana during the 1980s, for instance, have left the country.

Brain drain means that African countries get little return on their investment in higher education. It also means that they have to hire foreign workers—as many as 150,000 of them—to close the skills gap. All this costs up to $4 billion a year. In Africa, that is very serious money. UN officials are calling urgently for programs and policies "to reverse the devastating effects of the brain drain."

Challenges Associated With Piracy and Lawlessness in Somalia

Another African challenge to US interests is the piracy that has broken out along the coast of Somalia. If someone mentions "pirates," your first thought may be of some popular movie or of Peter Pan's foe, Captain Hook. Or maybe you'd think of music that someone has downloaded illegally over the Internet.

But piracy is a modern problem, not just a fantasy from movies and novels. Merchant ships ply the vast seas alone and mostly unarmed. These modern ships have ways of staying in touch with their home ports beyond anything Christopher Columbus ever dreamed of. But if criminal gangs—pirates—want to attack, there isn't much the merchant crews can do to stop them.

It's bad enough when pirates take over a ship and demand ransom. But security experts see another, far graver danger. They worry that pirates may cooperate with terrorist networks like al-Qaeda to take over a ship and plant a bomb inside one of its freight containers. Agents could set off this bomb once the ship was in harbor at one of America's big cities. The result could be a 9/11-type terror attack.

The April 2009 attack on the Maersk ship *Alabama* off the Somali coast was the first pirate takeover of an American-flagged vessel in more than 200 years. The episode ended with the crew regaining control of the ship and the US Navy's successful rescue of the captain. But that did not end piracy off Africa's shores.

Recent Pirate Attacks on Ships Off the Somali Coast

Somalia is a failed state on the Horn of Africa, with a coastline nearly as long as that of the eastern United States. Piracy became a problem there during the Somali civil war in the 1990s. The situation has been worsening since.

Worldwide, about 250 to 300 pirate attacks occur every year; 2003 was a recent peak year, with 450 attacks. In the year before the attack on the *Alabama*, about 100 attacks had taken place in Somali waters.

A mother tries to get her daughter to drink a nutritional supplement at a hospital center in Malawi that focuses on those recovering from hunger.
Photo by Andy Nelson / © 2002 The Christian Science Monitor

Piracy off Somalia complicates delivery of food aid.

Piracy off Somalia's coast raises two major concerns. First, as mentioned earlier, Islamist terrorists might work with Somali pirates to plant bombs or raise funds through ransoms. Second, more people go hungry because of piracy. Somalia is a poor country that depends on food aid from other countries, but piracy in Somalia complicates delivery of food.

The Impact of Piracy on Imports and Exports for the US

Piracy has been a sensitive issue for Americans since colonial times, when pirates ranged through the Caribbean and up the American coast. After independence, one of the first actions US forces took on foreign soil was on the "shores of Tripoli" in North Africa. That's when the US Marines took action against the Barbary (Berber) pirates.

It seems almost incredible that piracy should resurface in modern times, but in fact it has never completely disappeared. For example, pirates have attacked shipping near Indonesia for years. But the Somali piracy is a concern because it interferes with US trade with other African countries. It endangers the lives of American and other sailors. And it takes place so close to the Persian Gulf's critical oil-shipping lanes that it threatens to drive up the price of oil. Thus, US authorities cannot ignore the situation.

The US Response to Piracy and Lawlessness

The US government is working with the international community, including its NATO allies, to fight piracy. In October 2008 the United Nations Security Council passed Resolution 1838, calling on "all parties" to thwart the pirates, particularly "by deploying naval vessels and military aircraft."

As a result, US Navy ships, along with those of other nations, patrol off Africa's coast. The US government took the lead in setting up an International Contact Group to fight piracy. The United States has also worked with other maritime states to get their court systems to work together better to bring pirates to justice. Maritime means *of or relating to the sea*.

After the attack on the *Alabama*, Secretary of State Hillary Rodham Clinton announced four immediate antipiracy measures. The United States can take such steps on its own as it pursues a broader program with other countries to counter terrorism:

- Work through channels to get Somalis to police their own waters better and to ensure that young Somalis have other career options than crime on the high seas
- Get more ships into the waters around the Horn of Africa and improve communications among them
- Push the Somali government to act more forcefully against pirates operating from bases on its territory
- Work with shippers and their insurers to improve the ships' own capacity for self-defense.

Captain Phillips's Rescue

Richard Phillips, captain of the *Alabama*, had been stuck for five days in a lifeboat off the Somali coast. Pirates had taken over his ship. While his crew eventually seized back control of the ship and took one of the pirates hostage, the other pirates had grabbed Captain Phillips and now held him captive on the lifeboat. At one point, Phillips tried to escape but was recaptured. "It was very, very hot," he said later in an interview. "I really just wanted to jump in that water to get cool."

The USS *Bainbridge*, a Navy ship, was not far away. In fact, it was at the other end of a 100-foot line connecting the two vessels. Aboard the *Bainbridge*, the military tried to negotiate for Phillips's release. But the talks weren't going anywhere.

The Navy's orders were to attack if Phillips's life was in danger. When officers on the *Bainbridge* saw one of the pirates point an AK-47 at Phillips's back, they thought the time had come to act.

It was dusk, and the sea was rolling. But the US Navy SEAL snipers were sure shots. It was all over in a few seconds. Once they were sure Phillips was out of the line of fire, the snipers picked off the three pirates with simultaneous shots.

Phillips, hailed as a hero for giving himself up as a hostage to help his crew, was free and unharmed. He had his own ideas about who deserved the credit. "The real heroes are the Navy, the SEALs, those who have brought me home," he told reporters.

US and European Development Efforts in Africa

Even before piracy grabbed America's notice in recent years, the West had already begun to pay more attention to Africa. President George W. Bush's administration moved to increase aid to Africa significantly. So did European governments.

Former Bush aide Michael J. Gerson once described this focus on Africa as "the upside of foreign policy moralism." Many in the West felt that fighting AIDS, malaria, and other woes in Africa was a moral imperative—something they had to do.

The other reason for the focus on Africa, Gerson went on to say, was "the growing strategic significance of Africa." Africa is where the conflict with radical Islam is playing out. It is home to terrorism and failed states, such as Somalia. And Africa's oil is more important than ever to keeping the supplies flowing around the world.

To Aid or Not to Aid

An even longer-running storyline is that of Western efforts to lift Africa out of poverty. While bright spots exist, many people would argue that half a century after independence, much of Africa is as poor as ever, maybe poorer. Corruption, mismanagement, and poor governance plague the continent. Some say that the West has poured trillions of dollars in aid to Africa with nothing to show for it because of corruption.

A student at Africa Rural University in Kagadi, Uganda, greets residents of the village of Nyamiyaga. As part of her education, the student lived in Nyamiyaga for three months and helped the villagers build a school, improve water sanitation, and expand their farms' profitability.
Photo by Mary Knox Merrill / © The Christian Science Monitor

While bright spots exist, many people would argue that half a century after independence, Africa is as poor as ever, maybe poorer.

Women sweep up corn, which will be cleaned and bagged for distribution, in a World Food Programme warehouse in Malawi.

Photo by Andy Nelson / © 2002 The Christian Science Monitor

While bright spots exist in Africa, many argue that half a century after independence, much of Africa is as poor as ever, maybe poorer. Some say that the West has poured trillions of dollars in aid to Africa with nothing to show for it because of corruption.

It's not just Westerners who hold this view. The respected Tanzanian journalist Ayub Rioba told *The Christian Science Monitor* in 2007, "We have been made permanent recipients of aid, funds, scholarships, food, medicine, from developed countries. . . . And what exactly do we do with all that aid and assistance and help? Almost nothing. Since we gained independence, almost 50 years ago, we have been receiving aid permanently, and statistics today indicate that we are becoming poorer!"

Not so fast! say people like Jeffrey Sachs, an economist at Columbia University. Africa can defeat poverty, and it won't cost that much to do it, he insists. He calculates that Western aid to developing countries works out to about $16 per person per year. To say it has failed, he says, "is a cruel joke." Too much aid really has gone to political purposes (fighting the Cold War in earlier decades, for instance) and to the pockets of high-priced Western consultants.

Sachs is the leader of a group that believes Africa should fight "poverty first." Rioba represents the "governance first" camp that says that the onus—*the burden, or the responsibility*—is on Africans, not on outsiders, to improve the way they govern themselves. A third camp believes in aid, but insists that accountability is key.

In a commentary for the *British Broadcasting Corporation* in 2005, Swedish economist Fredrik Erixon declared that international aid doesn't work. Africans need sound economic policies to escape poverty, he said. He contrasted Africa's experience with Asia's. Where Africa made little economic progress, Asia's economies grew by leaps and bounds. Asians were open to trade and foreign investment, while many Africans closed their borders. Africans also imposed too many rules on businesses. "It is hardly surprising that this strategy of development has failed bitterly," Erixon wrote.

The Millennium Development Goals of the United Nations

Despite Erixon and Rioba's arguments to tackle economic policy and better government before all else, groups like the United Nations are backing the "poverty first" approach to helping Africa. The UN calls its approach the Millennium Development Goals (MDG). The MDG's aims are a sort of global "to do list." They are a group of eight goals that 189 UN member countries adopted at the millennium's start. The target date for achieving them is 2015.

The goals are meant to respond to the world's major development challenges. They combine in a single package some of the most important commitments made at international summits of recent years. They show the connections between growth, reducing poverty, and sustainable development. (Sustainable development is "green" growth—*economic progress that doesn't harm the environment.*) The goals build on democratic governance, the rule of law, respect for human rights, and peace and security as the foundations of human progress.

The goals are also "time-bound and measurable." This means that the UN intends to meet the eight goals by 2015. It also means that the UN has a way of judging whether it has met these goals. The final goal calls for a new way for developing and developed countries to work together for progress.

Efforts to Eradicate Extreme Poverty and Hunger in Africa

The Millennium Development Goals call for cutting poverty in half. Specifically, they call for the share of people who live on less than $1 a day to come down by half by 2015 from what it was in 1990.

The goals also call for "full and productive employment and decent work for all, including women and young people." "Full employment" doesn't mean everybody has to work all the time, by the way. It means that essentially all those who want to work can find jobs. Even so, it's an ambitious target.

The Millennium Development Goals

The following are the eight Millennium Development Goals. As you will notice, they are big, broad ideas:

1. Eradicate extreme poverty and hunger
2. Achieve universal primary education
3. Promote gender equality and empower women
4. Reduce child mortality
5. Improve mothers' health
6. Combat HIV/AIDS, malaria, and other diseases
7. Ensure environmental sustainability
8. Develop a Global Partnership for Development

A woman weaves baskets for a living at a women's cooperative in a UN Millennium Village in Rwanda.

Photo by Mary Knox Merrill / © 2009 The Christian Science Monitor

The UN's Millennium Development Goals call for "full and productive employment and decent work for all, including women and young people."

A child holds a fat ear of corn that her father raised on their land in low-lying wetlands in Malawi.

Photo by Andy Nelson / © 2002 The Christian Science Monitor

The father has been able to raise corn under an irrigation project started by an Irish aid organization, Concern Worldwide. A US program aims to help the UN cut in half the proportion of Africans who suffer from hunger between1990 and 2015.

So is the next one: to cut in half, between 1990 and 2015, the proportion of people who suffer from hunger. The Presidential Initiative to End Hunger in Africa (IEHA) is a leading American effort to help meet this target. This plan seeks to bolster Africa's agricultural sector, especially its small farmers. To this end, IEHA works with governments, development organizations, universities, and the business sector, as well as think tanks and aid groups.

The Effort to Enhance Education Levels in Africa

Goal No. 2 of the Millennium Goals has only one specific target, but it's quite ambitious: "Ensure that, by 2015, children everywhere, boys and girls alike, will be able to complete a full course of primary schooling." In the United States, people usually refer to primary school as elementary school. The African Educational Initiative (AEI) of the US Agency for International Development is an effort to help meet this goal in Africa.

Africa has some of the lowest rates of primary school enrollment in the world. Throughout Africa, teachers, classrooms, and even books are in short supply. The AEI seeks to improve the situation in 39 sub-Saharan countries. It provides scholarships, textbooks, and teacher training. The AEI's goal is to help 80 million African children by 2010.

Schooling for girls is a particular problem. Africa has 33 million primary school-aged children who are not in school, and most of them are girls. The AEI's goal is to provide 550,000 scholarships by 2010. Girls will receive most of these awards, to be used for primary and secondary (or high school) schooling.

These students can then grow up to be educated role models for others in their communities. To this end, the AEI will provide support for tuition fees, books, uniforms, and other needs to make sure the students stay in school. The scholarship program also includes mentoring and other activities.

Other items in the AEI agenda are:

- Providing more and better books and other learning materials
- More and better teacher training
- Outreach to orphans and children out of school for whatever reason (this includes such ideas as teaching classes over the radio)
- HIV/AIDS awareness
- Encouraging parents to get involved in their children's schools.

Two girls team up for a class assignment at their school in Malawi.
Photo by Andy Nelson / © 2001 The Christian Science Monitor

Throughout Africa, teachers, classrooms, and even books are in short supply.

Western governments and organizations continue to work with their African counterparts to find ways out of the various problems the continent faces. For many Westerners, this is a moral demand. For Africans, it is often a matter of sheer survival. Whether these efforts eventually succeed will depend much on how effectively Africans use the aid the United States and other countries offer. Africa's future hangs in the balance.

South African high school girls take part in a basketball camp sponsored by the US National Basketball Association.
Photo by Scott Baldauf / © 2008 The Christian Science Monitor

Schooling for girls is a particular problem in Africa. The US African Education Initiative hopes to provide 550,000 scholarships to African children by 2010. Most will go to girls.

Lesson 5 Review

Using complete sentences, answer the following questions on a sheet of paper.

1. What happened to the rest of Nigeria's economy during the 1970s oil boom?
2. How does the World Bank's Heavily Indebted Poor Countries (HIPC) Initiative work?
3. How is African immigration into the United States different today from what it was before 1808?
4. What is brain drain and how does it affect Africa?
5. What is the *Alabama*?
6. Why does piracy off Somalia's coast concern the US government? Give at least two reasons.
7. Michael Gerson lists two reasons Africa has begun to get more attention from the West. What are they?
8. What are the United Nations' Millennium Development Goals?

Applying Your Learning

9. In this lesson you read about two views of African development—"poverty first" and "governance first." Which do you subscribe to? Why?

CHAPTER 4

St. Basil's Cathedral, located on Red Square in the heart of Moscow, illustrates the profound historical influence of Eastern Orthodox Christianity in Russia and many neighboring countries.
© Stanislav Bokach/Dreamstime.com

Russia and the Former Soviet Republics

Chapter Outline

LESSON 1 Russia and the Former Soviet Republics: An Introduction

Quick Write

What does the August 1991 coup against Gorbachev suggest to you about the way people cope with change?

Learn About

- the geographic locations of Russia and the former Soviet republics
- the major religious groups of Russia and the former Soviet republics
- the historical context of Russia from the Kievan Rus through the time of Peter the Great
- how events of the nineteenth century and World War I contributed to the October Revolution
- the economic and political impacts of World War II and the Cold War on Russia
- the effects of the fall of communism

August can be a good time to make trouble. People tend to let their guard down late in the summer. Many are away on vacation. Those left behind may be too busy holding the fort to pay attention to everything they should.

In August 1991 hard-liners in the Soviet Communist Party decided it was time to take action against their reformist leader, Mikhail Gorbachev. He had called for big changes—in the economy and in foreign relations.

The Soviet Union was a vast country with a huge population. It had abundant resources and a rich culture. But despite these qualities, it was lagging behind Europe and the United States in many ways, including its economy. This downward trend seemed likely to continue. Gorbachev preached "openness," and that sometimes forced the Soviet people to confront painful truths about the consequences of their communist rule. The economic mess they were in was one of these truths.

Gorbachev thought his new ideas would turn the situation around. But the Communist Party hard-liners weren't so sure. A group of these party faithful traveled to Gorbachev's summer vacation home to confront him and put him under house arrest. They went on television to say they were saving the country from a "national catastrophe." Tanks started patrolling the streets of Moscow.

Thousands of people came out to demonstrate against the coup, however. Among them was Boris Yeltsin, president of the Russian Federation—one of the 15 republics that made up the Soviet Union. He climbed onto a tank outside the Russian parliament building to confront the troops. He appealed to them not to turn against the people. He called the coup a "new reign of terror" and called for the people to resist it.

The people responded by turning out in support of Gorbachev, and the troops held their fire. The coup collapsed. In a few days Gorbachev was back at his desk in Moscow. Things were never the same again after that, though. Within just a few months, Gorbachev was out of office and the Soviet Union ceased to exist.

The Geographic Locations of Russia and the Former Soviet Republics

You might consider this lesson an introduction to a country that no longer exists: the Soviet Union. This immense, and immensely diverse, country—made up of Russia and 14 other republics—was for decades a primary focus of US foreign policy. For more than 40 years the Soviet Union was America's Cold War adversary. All of its republics are now independent countries. But for historical reasons, it's still useful to think of them together.

Russia

Even without its former republics, Russia still has the largest landmass of any country on earth. It sprawls across northern Europe and Asia. Its westernmost point is the Baltic city of Kaliningrad. From there it stretches east across 11 time zones to Kamchatka in the Far East.

Vocabulary 

- tundra
- taiga
- steppes
- atheistic
- metropolitan
- anti-Semitism
- principality
- tribute
- primogeniture
- regent
- abdicate
- soviet
- socialism
- Marxism
- collective farm
- cult of personality
- glasnost
- perestroika

A woman hikes a path near a Russian fishing village on the Volga River.
Photo by Robert Harbison / © 1997 The Christian Science Monitor

The Volga is the longest river in Europe, and Russians see it as their "national river."

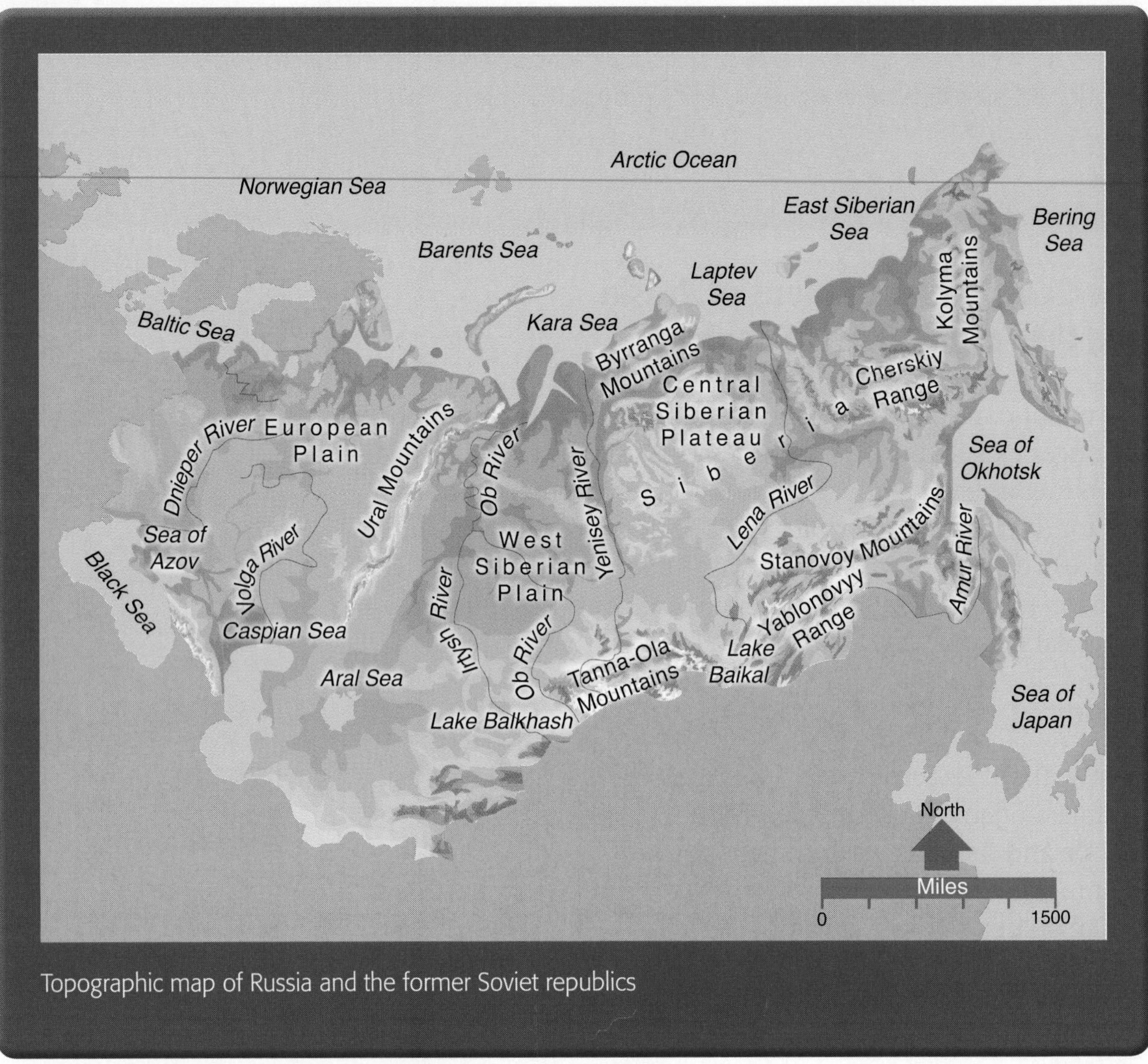

Topographic map of Russia and the former Soviet republics

Its landscape includes tundra, *a vast treeless area between the tree line and the Arctic icecap, with permanently frozen subsoil.*

Farther south are the spruces and firs of the taiga, the *coniferous (cone-bearing) forest.* Still farther south are the mixed and broad-leaf forests, and the steppes, the *vast treeless grass-covered plains*. Near the Caspian Sea, the land changes to semi-desert.

The best-known Russian river is surely the Volga. It's the longest river in Europe, and Russians see it as their "national river." Eleven of Russia's biggest cities are in the Volga basin. The Amur River forms the border with China. It flows into the Sea of Okhotsk. The Lena River flows north through Eastern Siberia to the sea.

Russia's water resources also include Lake Baikal, the deepest freshwater lake in the world and the largest by volume. The Caspian Sea, sometimes classified as the world's largest lake, has three times as much water but is salty.

Russia's mountain ranges include the Urals. These peaks traditionally mark the border between European Russia and Asian Russia. The Caucasian Mountains are in southern Russia. Another important mountain chain, including the Altai range, is in southern Siberia. The Kamchatka Mountains, which have some active volcanoes, stretch along the Pacific coast.

You may think of Russia as far away, especially if you live in the Eastern United States. But remember that Russia is a near neighbor to part of the United States—Alaska, just across the Bering Strait. You may remember from your American history studies that the United States bought Alaska from Russia in 1867.

Russia's Languages and Ethnic Groups

The 140 million people of Russia represent more than 100 ethnic groups. But ethnic Russians make up a little more than 80 percent of Russia's population. The other significant groups are Tatars (3.8 percent) and Ukrainians (3 percent). Other still smaller groups generally account for less than 1 percent each of Russia's population.

Russian, one of the world's great literary languages, is the official language of Russia. Russian is the language of such writers as Pushkin, Tolstoy, Dostoevsky, Chekhov, Pasternak, and Solzhenitsyn. It is also one of the United Nations' six official languages. Another 100 or so languages are spoken in Russia today, too.

Belarus, Ukraine, Moldova, Estonia, Latvia, and Lithuania

Belarus is about the size of Kansas. It's a flat, landlocked country, without any natural borders, tucked in between Russia to the east and northeast, Latvia to the north, Lithuania to the northwest, Poland to the west, and Ukraine to the south. The Belarusian language is a member of the Slavic subgroup of the Indo-European language family, related to Russian.

Ukraine is much bigger—the biggest country in Europe, if you discount Russia on the grounds that it's mostly in Asia. Ukraine has even more neighbors than Belarus. In fact, Ukraine means "at the edge," and its strategic position has become even more obvious with the fall of the Soviet Union. Poland, Slovakia, and Hungary lie to the west, Belarus to the north, Moldova and Romania to the southwest, and Russia to the east.

The Carpathian Mountains' northern peaks are an important feature of Ukraine. Most of the country is a steppe north of the Black Sea, divided by the Dnieper River. It divides the country east and west before it flows into the Black Sea. Ukraine's rich dark soil and long agricultural traditions have earned it the nickname "breadbasket." At some points it was "breadbasket of the Soviet Union," and at other times, "breadbasket of Europe." The Ukrainian language is a Slavic tongue.

Political map of Russia and the former Soviet republics

Moldova lies between the southern Ukraine and Romania. This is significant because before World War II, it was part of Romania. Before that, it was part of the Russian Empire. The Soviet Union seized it back at the beginning of World War II. It obtained its independence when the Soviet Union collapsed. Most Moldovans are ethnic Romanians, and the "Moldovan" language is really Romanian, an Indo-European Romance language related to French, Spanish, Italian, and Portuguese.

Estonia, Latvia, and Lithuania are often thought of together as "the Baltic states." That is, they're on the Baltic Sea. They look across the sea to Sweden and Finland. They are largely wooded, with extensive meadowlands and pasturelands. The highest elevation in any of these three states is only about 1,000 feet. The Lithuanian and Latvian languages are related; Lithuanian may be the most like the original Indo-European language of all Indo-European languages. The Estonian language is related to Finnish.

Armenia, Azerbaijan, and Georgia

These three small and quite different countries lie in the mountainous Caucasus region between the Black and Caspian Seas. Armenia is surrounded by Turkey to the west, Georgia to the north, Azerbaijan to the east, and Iran to the south. The Armenian culture is an ancient one; the Kingdom of Armenia adopted Christianity in the fourth century (the 300s). Armenians speak an Indo-European language.

Oil-rich Azerbaijan borders the Caspian Sea to the east, Georgia and Russia to the north, Armenia to the west, and Iran to the south. The Azerbaijani language is from the Turkic family. Shiite Muslims are the largest religious group. Relations with neighboring Armenia are tense: since independence, the two have fought over Azerbaijan's Nagorno-Karabakh region—largely populated by Armenians. A 1994 cease-fire is still in effect.

The Republic of Georgia sits between Russia to the north; the Black Sea to the west; and Turkey, Armenia, and Azerbaijan to the south. The Georgian people were also early adopters of Christianity, converting in the fourth century. The Georgian language comes from the South Caucasian language family, which scholars believe to be unrelated to other language groups.

Kazakhstan, Kyrgyzstan, Tajikistan, Turkmenistan, and Uzbekistan

These five countries are the Central Asian republics of the former Soviet Union. Kazakhstan is very dry, largely desert or semi-desert, with hot summers and cold winters. Its mountain ranges reach elevations of more than 20,000 feet and get heavy snowfall, despite the country's otherwise dry climate. It borders Russia to the north, the Caspian Sea to the west, Turkmenistan, Uzbekistan, and Kyrgyzstan to the south, and China to the east.

A Kazakh sheepherder watches over his flock on Russian steppes near Russia's border with Mongolia.
Photo by R. Norman Matheny / © 1996 The Christian Science Monitor
Steppes are vast treeless grass-covered plains.

The Tian Shan, Pamir, and Alay mountain ranges dominate Kyrgyzstan. Flat expanses are only in its northern and eastern valleys. Many lakes and fast-flowing rivers drain from the mountains. The country borders China to the east, Kazakhstan to the north, Uzbekistan to the west, and Tajikistan to the south.

Tajikistan is also mainly mountainous. The lower elevations are in the northwest, southwest, and Fergana Valley in the country's far northern zone. The highest elevations are in the southeast in the Pamir-Alay system. Glaciers are thick in the mountains. A dense river network has created valleys through the mountains. The country lies between Kyrgyzstan and Uzbekistan to the north, Uzbekistan to the west, Afghanistan to the south, and China to the east.

Turkmenistan is mostly flat. It is surrounded by Uzbekistan and Kazakhstan to the north, the Caspian Sea to the west, Iran and Afghanistan to the south, and Uzbekistan to the east. The Turan Depression and the Garagum Desert cover nearly 80 percent of the country. Turkmenistan has some mountains in the west and southwest and the Kugitang Range in the far east.

Uzbekistan is largely flat desert, with few lakes and rivers. Mountain ranges dominate the southeast and northeast; they cut east-west across the middle of the eastern provinces. Uzbekistan shares the Aral Sea with Kazakhstan. Once the fourth-largest salt lake in the world, this sea has been shrinking since the 1960s. That's when the Soviet government diverted the rivers that fed it to irrigate desert instead. Efforts are under way to repair the damage resulting from this decision. The country stretches between Kazakhstan to the north and west, Turkmenistan and Afghanistan to the south, and Tajikistan and Kyrgyzstan to the east.

The people in all these Central Asian countries are mostly Muslim. The exception is in Kazakhstan, where a large Russian Christian minority resides. The Kazakh, Turkmen, Kyrgyz, and Uzbek languages all belong to the Turkic language group. Tajik, on the other hand, is an Indo-European language.

The Major Religious Groups of Russia and the Former Soviet Republics

The main faiths in Russia are Orthodox Christianity and Islam. For most of the twentieth century, the Soviet Union was officially atheistic—*believing God doesn't exist*. But even so, more than a third of the people claimed faith in some religion during that period. And since the fall of communism in 1991, the Russian Orthodox Church has rebounded notably.

The Major Christian Traditions in Russia and the Former Soviet Republics

The Russian Orthodox Church goes back to Kievan Rus, the first forerunner of the modern Russian state. In AD 988 Prince Vladimir made Byzantine Christianity Russia's state religion.

While self-governing, the Russian church answered spiritually to the patriarch—or the head bishop—of Constantinople. Today this city is called Istanbul, which is in Turkey. The Russian church had its seat, or base, in Kiev, however. Today Kiev is the capital of Ukraine. But as power moved to Moscow in the fourteenth century, the church moved as well. This started a tradition in the Russian church: The metropolitan of Moscow—*a church leader, like an archbishop in the West*—would head the Russian church.

Students gather in Moscow's Red Square with world-famous Saint Basil's Cathedral—built by Russian Czar Ivan IV in the sixteenth century—towering behind them.
Photo by Robert Harbison / © 1997 The Christian Science Monitor

In AD 988 Prince Vladimir made Byzantine Christianity Russia's state religion.

Other Orthodox churches exist in the former Soviet republics as well:

- The Georgian Orthodox Church
- The Ukrainian Orthodox Church
- The Belarusian Orthodox Church.

Like the Russian Orthodox Church, all these Orthodox churches are part of the worldwide Eastern Orthodox Church. It's one of the three major forms of Christianity, together with Roman Catholicism and Protestantism.

The Armenians are another former Soviet people with a distinctive religious tradition. They were the first people in the world to adopt Christianity as a state religion. Their Armenian Apostolic Church endured harassment during the Soviet era. Today, though, it operates freely in the newly independent Republic of Armenia.

Russia and the former Soviet republics have millions of Roman Catholics, too. They live mostly in Belarus, Latvia, and especially Lithuania, which has a Catholic majority. Baptists and Lutherans are the two leading Protestant denominations in the former Soviet Union; Lutherans are the largest religious group in Estonia and Latvia.

The Influence of Judaism in Russia and the Former Soviet Republics

In 1492 Queen Isabella expelled the Jews from Spain. Many of them moved eastward—through Germany to Poland, Lithuania, Ukraine, and Belarus. In the years after, many continued on to Russia. Jews first arrived there in the sixteenth century.

But opportunities for the Jews under czarist rule were few. The best jobs available to them were as tax collectors or managers of large estates. Their work in these roles only angered the Slavic peasants working on those estates. This in turn intensified the anti-Semitism—*prejudice against Jewish people*—that had followed the Jews from Western Europe.

Still, after absorbing much of Poland at the end of the eighteenth century, Russia had the largest Jewish population (about 1.5 million) in the world. Jewish culture and the Yiddish language flourished, and their numbers grew. But Russia has historically not been a happy home for Jews.

As you read in Chapter 1, Lesson 2, the czars restricted the Jews' movements and subjected them to pogroms. Later, during the Soviet Union's early years, things got better for the Jews. But then their situation tightened up again under Joseph Stalin's harsh dictatorship. And during World War II, some 2.5 million Soviet Jews died at the hands of the Nazi Germans and their local sympathizers.

After the war, the Jewish community dwindled. Many emigrated to Israel and the United States. This movement slowed somewhat after the Soviet Union's fall. Much official anti-Semitism ended at that point. Some people felt free for the first time to claim their Jewish identity. And so the official number of Jews in Russia rose from 500,000 to 700,000. The 1990s also saw a modest renewal of Jewish cultural and religious life in Russia. However, Jews remain mindful of their history in Russia. They worry that these more open conditions may not last.

This fairly new Turkish-built mosque in Russia's southwest is evidence of a recent mosque-building binge taken on by the Turks in Central Asia.
Photo by Robert Harbison / © 1997 The Christian Science Monitor
Arab conquerors first brought Islam in the eighth century to what became the Russian empire.

The Influence of Islam in Russia and the Former Soviet Republics

Arab conquerors first brought Islam to what became the Russian empire in the eighth century. By the 1980s Islam was the second most widespread religion in the Soviet Union. Between 45 million and 50 million citizens called themselves Muslims. But most lived in Central Asia, in former Soviet republics that are now independent countries.

In 1996 Muslims made up an estimated 19 percent of all Russians who practice a religion. Muslim communities are concentrated among the minority peoples between the Black Sea and the Caspian Sea. Researchers today aren't always sure how many actually practice Islam as a religion, however. Many people may simply claim a Muslim identity. Almost all Russian Muslims are Sunni.

Muslims and the Russian government have an uneasy relationship. Muslims fear that the government still clings to the idea of the Russian church as a privileged state religion. And the government, for its part, fears the possible rise of political Islam. Officials remember how things went for the Soviet Union in Afghanistan, which you read about in Chapter 2, Lesson 3. And they also saw how the Islamic revolution played out in Iran.

The Historical Context of Russia From the Kievan Rus Through the Time of Peter the Great

As the previous section mentioned, what people think of as "Russia" actually began in Kiev, which today is in Ukraine. But as you will read, when the Mongols invaded Kiev, the center of what would become Russia shifted to Moscow.

The Dominance of the State of Kievan Rus in Early Russian History

The East Slavs and the Varangians, a group of Scandinavian warriors and merchants, settled around Kiev in the middle of the ninth century. They established Kievan Rus, the state that would lead to modern Russia, in Kiev in 962. It lasted until the twelfth century, when various invaders began to attack. Finally the Mongols under Batu Khan destroyed most of the main cities in the thirteenth century.

Snow blankets this small, rural town that sits about 85 miles from Moscow.

Photo by Melanie Stetson Freeman / © 2008 The Christian Science Monitor

When the Mongols invaded Kiev back in the thirteenth century, the center of what would become Russia shifted to Moscow, then a minor trading post.

The two most important figures of the Golden Age of Kiev were Prince Vladimir, who ruled from 978 to 1015, and his son Prince Yaroslav the Wise, who ruled from 1019 to 1054. Vladimir, as you read earlier, brought Byzantine Christianity to Kievan Rus. Yaroslav created the first East Slavic law code. Both men increased their power by marrying off their female relatives to European kings. Vladimir married the sister of the Byzantine emperor.

Prince Vladimir's adoption of the Eastern Orthodox form of Christianity opened Russia to the influence of Byzantine culture. Russians studied Greek texts and philosophy at a time when educated Western and Central Europeans learned Latin. But Vladimir and the rest of Kiev were reading Orthodox literature in translation. They didn't have to learn Greek, in other words, which meant they didn't really connect with the Greek cultural tradition. This is the beginning of an important theme in Russian civilization: cultural isolation.

The Rise of Muscovy and the Evolution of the Russian Aristocracy

The Mongol invasion of Kiev was an opportunity for Moscow, almost 500 miles away to the northeast, to gain importance. Moscow in those days was just a minor trading post. Its remote wooded location gave it some protection against the Mongols. It had access by river to the Baltic and Black Seas, and to the Caucasus as well. Even more important, Moscow was home to a series of princes who were ambitious, determined, and lucky. Moscow was the center of a principality—*a territory ruled by a prince*—known as Muscovy. So this period is known as the rise of Muscovy.

Ivan I, otherwise known as "Ivan Money Bags," was an early Muscovite prince. He cooperated with the Mongol overlords and collected tribute money—*a tax*—for them from other principalities. This boosted his power and gave him an edge over his rivals. It was during Ivan's reign that the Orthodox metropolitan, the church leader, moved to Moscow. This change increased Moscow's standing as well.

fastFACT

The title "czar," or "tsar," is a Russian form of "Caesar," a Roman imperial title. The title also survived in "Kaiser," the term German emperors used. By calling themselves "czars," Ivan III and his descendants put themselves on a par with the Byzantine emperors or the Mongol khan.

Also at about this time, the grand princes of Muscovy brought more and more Russian lands—and wealth and people—under their rule. The prince who was most successful at this was Ivan III. He reigned from 1462 until 1505 and was the first to use the titles of "czar" and "ruler of all Rus." In 1480 Mongol rule officially ended and all the ethnically Russian lands came under Muscovite control. Ivan III continued to expand his territory, by conquest and persuasion. By the end of his reign, Muscovy had tripled in size.

Ivan III married Sophia Paleologue, the niece of the last Byzantine emperor. At their marriage, the Muscovite court adopted many Byzantine terms, rituals, titles, and emblems. In this way, the Muscovite dynasty claimed itself to be the successor to Rome and Constantinople (Byzantium). In later centuries this concept would be important to Russians' self-image.

The czars owned everything in Russia. Each nobleman swore an oath once a year as the czar's "slave." Unlike most of Europe, Russia had no primogeniture—*the right of first-born sons to inherit all their fathers' property*. This was a good thing for second and third sons, but not necessarily a good thing for the noble families overall. With the passing of each generation, the heirs split their estates into smaller and smaller shares (rather than the whole of it going to the eldest son). This carving up of estates kept individual noblemen from accumulating, or keeping, enough property to let them challenge the czar. As a result, the czar held more and more power and the people less and less.

The Influence of Peter the Great in Developing the Russian Empire

One of Russia's greatest czars was Peter I, or Peter the Great. He played a big role in shaping modern Russia. He is also known for his efforts to turn Russia westward. He even built a new capital, St. Petersburg, on the Gulf of Finland, close to the rest of Europe.

Peter was born in 1672, at a time of great turmoil in Russia. At first it was by no means clear that he would ever rule. He was a child of Czar Aleksey's second marriage, so others were ahead of him in line for the throne. Various groups at court, meanwhile, struggled for control. But when his sickly half-brother died, Peter became co-czar at age 10 with yet another half-brother. His half-sister Sofia held real power, however. She ruled as regent—*one who rules for a lawful monarch who is too young for the throne*—and he went off to play with soldiers.

Many little boys play with toy soldiers. Peter, as a boy, played soldiers with real men, and when he staged battles, they used live ammunition. He developed a keen lifelong interest in Western military practice and technology. Military engineering, artillery, shipbuilding, and navigation all fascinated him.

His war games later paid off when the soldiers he had drilled foiled a plot to crown Sofia. He eventually became the sole czar of Muscovy in 1696 after the deaths of his mother and half-brother.

Peter spent much of his time making war. He sought to secure his southern borders against the Tatars and the Ottoman Turks. To that end, he created Russia's first navy, and with it took the port of Azov. He traveled to Europe to seek allies against the Ottomans. The first czar to make such a trip, he visited Germany, the Netherlands, and England. He learned a great deal and hired hundreds of technical specialists from Western Europe.

Peter failed to forge a European coalition against the Ottoman Empire. But he did see an opportunity to make war on Sweden. He wanted a Russian port on the Baltic, and taking land from Sweden was a way to get one. He built his new capital, St. Petersburg, on former Swedish lands. It sits on the Gulf of Finland, an arm of the Baltic.

Peter's military victories gave him a direct link to Western Europe. In celebration, Peter assumed the title of emperor as well as czar, and Muscovy officially became the Russian Empire in 1721.

Among his reforms that modernized Russia, he reorganized the army on a European model, streamlined government, and put money and people to work. His army drafted soldiers for lifetime service from among the taxpayers. It drew officers from the nobility and again required lifelong service in either the military or civilian administration. He defined ranks in terms of service to the czar rather than birth or seniority. He tripled state revenues through a variety of taxes—on salt, alcohol, and even beards! He required Western-style education for all male nobles.

But some historians say that his Westernization was less than successful, because Peter did things by force. He seemed not to grasp the importance of the individualistic spirit in the West. He could order his subjects to shave their beards to look more Western. He couldn't order them to think for themselves or adopt Western ideas.

How Events of the Nineteenth Century and World War I Contributed to the October Revolution

Had Peter the Great been able to return to Russia a century and a half after his death, he probably would have been disappointed. Russia had progressed in many ways—but other countries were moving faster. Germany, finally united into a single country under Bismarck, was an economic competitor. So was Japan in the Far East. The United States had emerged from its Civil War and become a force to be reckoned with.

Russia's population was much larger than most other major countries, and it was growing faster than that of any other country except the United States. Most Russians lived in rural communities and practiced only primitive agriculture, however.

The czarist regime faced two choices:

- It could try to develop faster economically and technologically, and risk domestic upheaval
- Or it could move more slowly and risk full economic dependency on its nimbler neighbors.

How World War I Exposed the Weakness of the Czarist Government

World War I—sparked by the June 1914 Serbian assassination of Archduke Franz Ferdinand, heir to the Austro-Hungarian throne—exposed the Russian system's deep flaws. The major powers of Europe and beyond fell in line on one side or another. Russia marched into the war in August 1914 with a show of national unity and solidarity with the Serbs, their fellow Slavs.

But military reversals and government incompetence soon soured many Russians. In short order, Russia suffered several defeats, leaving Germany controlling the Baltic Sea and, with its Turkish allies, the Black Sea. This cut Russia off from most of its foreign suppliers and markets. Russian military leaders seemed inept and ill prepared for battle. Meanwhile, prices went up and up. Inflation became a real problem.

Troops lacked the supplies they needed for battle. A War Industries Committee tried to ensure that needed goods made it to the front. But army officers quarreled with civilian leaders, took control of front line zones, and refused to cooperate with the committee.

In 1915 Czar Nicholas II went to the front to take charge of the army, at least in theory. He left his wife, Princess Alexandra, behind at home. Although she and Nicholas were cousins—both descended from Britain's Queen Victoria—she was German born, and thus considered by many Russians to be one of the "enemy." She had also fallen under the influence of a controversial monk named Grigori Rasputin. Alexandra had initially turned to Rasputin for help with her young son, Alexei, who suffered from hemophilia—uncontrolled bleeding. But Rasputin gained sway over government policy and appointments because of his supposed holy powers. Scholars still debate Alexandra and Rasputin's role and influence in the court. But it's clear that popular concern about a foreign princess and a "mad monk" did not help the czarist regime's image.

Meanwhile, the Russian legislature quarreled with the government's war bureaucracy. And some deputies (legislators) formed the Progressive Bloc to create a genuinely constitutional government rather than one wholly subject to a czar.

The 1917 Riots and Strikes in Response to Food and Fuel Shortages

The strain of war led to popular unrest. High food prices and fuel shortages caused strikes in some cities in 1916. Workers who had won the right to representation on the War Industries Committee used it as a forum for political opposition. The countryside was stirring, too. Soldiers grew ever more unwilling to follow orders. They balked at becoming cannon fodder on the orders of inept leaders.

In December 1916 a group of nobles took matters into their own hands and murdered Rasputin. But his death brought little change. Continuing conflict between Nicholas and the Duma—Russia's version of Congress—didn't help either.

Then in early 1917 deteriorating rail transport led once again to acute shortages of food and fuels. Riots and strikes followed. The government called in troops to quiet the unrest in the city then known as Petrograd (a more "Russian" version of St. Petersburg).

The government had summoned troops some years before, in 1905. At that time, 200,000 Russian workers had marched on the czar's Winter Palace in St. Petersburg. Troops fired on the workers. They killed several hundred. But they saved the monarchy.

Twelve years later, though, the poorly trained troops in the capital were less willing to do the dirty work of an authoritarian monarch. In 1917 troops turned their guns over to the angry crowds. Public support for the czar just melted away. The Romanov dynasty had ruled Russia for three centuries. In March 1917 its reign ended.

Someone had to lead Russia in the czar's absence. So the Duma created a body called the Provisional Government. The new government's delegates met Nicholas the evening of 15 March at Pskov. Rebellious railway workers had stopped the czar's train at Pskov as he was trying to return to Moscow. When his generals told him he lacked the country's support, he announced he would abdicate—*give up the throne*—in favor of his brother, Grand Duke Michael. But Michael refused the throne, and so imperial rule came to an end.

How Lenin and the Bolsheviks Overthrew the Russian Provisional Government and Established the Soviet Union

With the czar gone, the Provisional Government's leaders intended to bring democracy to Russia. They also wanted to continue Russian participation in World War I, alongside its Allies (including the United States, France, and Britain). They were moderate in their policies and appealed to the wealthy classes. But the Provisional Government wasn't the only body claiming to rule Russia at that point. A political contest among these competing bodies was about to result in the October Revolution.

A group of workers' councils called "soviets" had sprung up to protect workers' rights. (Soviet is *a Russian word that means council.*) One of these, the Petrograd Soviet, thought it ought to govern Russia. It drew its members from deputies elected in factories and regiments, and it coordinated the activities of other soviets across Russia. While the Provisional Government was working toward democracy in Russia, the Petrograd Soviet was working toward a moderate form of socialism.

Socialism is *a form of rule in which the government controls everything from businesses to how much land people may own.* Communism, as you read in the Introduction, is *an economic system in which property belongs to everyone and work is organized for the benefit of everyone.* Most socialists want to bring about change by democratic means. Communists, on the other hand, usually support change through force, suppress freedom, and install authoritarian governments.

In the third corner were the Bolsheviks, a radical group led by Vladimir I. Lenin. The Bolsheviks pushed for socialist revolution in the streets and in the workers' councils. Lenin called for taking land from the rich and dividing it equally among all Russians. He also backed the idea that the state should control all means of production, such as factories. Unlike the Petrograd Soviet, his ideas weren't moderate.

By November the Bolsheviks had overcome the moderates within the Petrograd Soviet and had seized power from the Provisional Government. But the new Bolshevik regime, which didn't call itself "communist" until March 1918, wasn't really secure until after a long and bloody civil war, fought from 1918 to 1921, during which the Bolsheviks murdered the former czar and his entire family.

Children walk across Red Square in front of a huge poster of former Soviet leader Vladimir Lenin.
Photo by Melanie Stetson Freeman / © 1989 The Christian Science Monitor

Lenin led a radical group called the Bolsheviks, who pushed for socialist revolution and in 1917 seized power in Russia.

Why the October Revolution Really Happened in November

The year 1917 was a busy one for Russians. They went through two revolutions. The first occurred when the czar abdicated. It's known as the February Revolution. Later that year came the October Revolution. That's when the Bolsheviks took over. But wait, you may say. The text I've just read says that the czar abdicated in March and the Bolsheviks took over in November. Here's the explanation: Russia was still following the Julian calendar in 1917. Not until 1919 did the Soviet Union (as it was by then) switch to the Gregorian calendar, which was widely in use in the West. To "catch up" with the Gregorian calendar, the Russians had to add extra days. This pushed the February Revolution into March, and the October Revolution into November.

The Economic and Political Impacts of World War II and the Cold War on Russia

The Communists came to power with some big ideas about how to run a country. But their execution was often faulty. Trial and error is one of the themes of this period from the Bolshevik Revolution into World War II. During the 1918–21 civil war, the Soviet government tried to centralize the national economy, in accord with Marxism—*the political and economic theories of Karl Marx, a founder of socialism and communism*. This theory didn't work well for the Soviets, however. And so during the 1920s the government allowed some private businesses to coexist alongside state-owned industry. After Lenin's death in 1924, potential successors jockeyed for power among themselves. The economy was one of the issues Soviet leaders used to make a name for themselves.

The Rise of Stalin

The most successful of these successors to Lenin was Joseph V. Stalin. He gradually consolidated his influence and isolated his rivals within the party. By the end of the 1920s, he was the sole leader of the Soviet Union.

In 1928 he introduced the First Five-Year Plan for building a socialist economy. The state took control of all factories. The state also took over all farms, by force if necessary, to establish collective farms. A collective farm is *a farm or a group of farms organized as a unit and managed and worked cooperatively by a group of laborers under state supervision*. Stalin's plan produced endless misery, however. Tens of millions of peasants starved to death. The government killed many who resisted forced collectivization.

The Effects of Stalin's Repression and World War II on the Russian People

Later on in the 1930s, after the collectivization disaster, Stalin began a purge of the Communist Party. This set in motion a campaign of terror. He ordered the execution or imprisonment of untold millions from all walks of life.

Then as World War II loomed, Stalin tried to avoid conflict with other countries. He signed a nonaggression pact with Germany in 1939. That didn't keep Hitler from invading the Soviet Union, however, in 1941. Stalin and his forces fought back. They stopped the Nazi offensive at Stalingrad in 1943 and pushed back through Eastern Europe, all the way to Berlin before Germany surrendered in 1945. World War II ravaged the Soviet Union. Its death toll is still uncertain more than half a century later, but the estimate is that more than 26 million perished. Even so, the Soviet Union emerged from the conflict an undisputed world power.

By the time Stalin died in 1953, he had been the Soviet dictator for a quarter century. On his watch, the country had gone from a backward agricultural society to a powerful industrial state. But he had been responsible for the deaths of tens of millions of people. Repression was part of the system he created. Indeed, when he died he was thought to be planning a new wave of terror. Even his inner circle secretly rejoiced to learn he was dead.

For years after his death, a vital question for Soviet leaders would be, How many changes can we, or should we, make? Nikita S. Khrushchev took a while to emerge as Stalin's successor. But he signaled a sharp break with the past.

Khrushchev and Other Leaders After Stalin

Stalin had named no political heir, and none of his associates dared claim to be his successor. So in the first years after his death, his associates tried to rule collectively. Eventually Khrushchev emerged as the most powerful figure in the Soviet Union. His tenure (1953–1964) brought about a relative liberalization, or opening up, in Soviet life.

In February 1956, in a dramatic speech at the Twentieth Party Congress, he denounced Stalin's crimes. He revealed that Stalin had killed thousands of party members and military leaders. This had hurt the Soviet Union militarily during World War II, he said. Stalin had also encouraged a cult of personality, he said—*an unhealthy intense personal focus on a leader.*

Khrushchev also proved more tolerant of arts and culture, in contrast with the repression of the arts under Stalin. And he did not use the secret police as an instrument of repression, as Stalin had done.

Khrushchev tried reforms in both domestic and foreign policy, with mixed results. During his tenure, world politics became much more complex. The insecurities of the Cold War persisted; he almost got into a nuclear war with the United States over Soviet missiles in Cuba. The Khrushchev era came to an end after a combination of failed policy innovations in agriculture, party politics, and industry undid him.

A vendor sells traditional nesting dolls at a market in Moscow.

Photo by Melanie Stetson Freeman / © 1999 The Christian Science Monitor

Soviet leader Nikita Khrushchev was more tolerant of arts and culture, in contrast with the repression of the arts under Stalin.

The Politburo, or chief executive committee of the Communist Party, removed him in 1964. This opened the way for another period of collective rule.

Brezhnev Takes Power

In place of Khrushchev, Leonid I. Brezhnev ruled at first with Alexei Kosygin and Nikolai Podgorny, but eventually emerged as the only leader. The Brezhnev era was more conservative; that is, more authoritarian and less liberal. Stalinism did not reappear, but de-Stalinization largely ended. Brezhnev didn't allow much room for individual expression the way Khrushchev had tried to do. Relations with the West were subject to wild swings. The Soviet invasion of Afghanistan in 1979 was a major setback in relations with the West.

But the Soviet leadership was basically stable—maybe too stable, analysts began to say. The age of the average Politburo member rose from 55 in 1966 to 68 in 1982. By the late 1970s Brezhnev's health was in decline. He refused to leave office, though, even after suffering two strokes. He died in November 1982. The two leaders who followed him ruled for only a year or two each. For real change, and real leadership, the Soviet Union would have to await Mikhail S. Gorbachev.

The Gorbachev Era

When Gorbachev's turn came, it came quickly. At the death of Konstantin U. Chernenko, a former Brezhnev aide, the Politburo acted within hours to name Gorbachev his successor. Gorbachev was a unanimous choice. He moved swiftly to put his allies in key positions. But he gave little hint at first of how radical his leadership would become.

Soon, though, he was promoting "new thinking." By this he meant foreign policy based on shared moral and ethical principles rather than Marxist-Leninist concepts of unending conflict with capitalism. Rather than flaunt Soviet military power, he sought to exercise political influence instead. He was a dealmaker. He pulled Soviet troops out of Afghanistan. He and US President Ronald Reagan agreed that they would remove their short- and mid-range nuclear missiles from Europe. And in a July 1989 speech, Gorbachev insisted on "the sovereign right of each people to choose their own social system."

For years, the Soviet Union had held to the Brezhnev Doctrine—that "socialist" (communist) states needed to stay socialist. With his speech, Gorbachev came within a whisker of rejecting that doctrine.

The General Pattern of Economic Growth Following World War II

Once Gorbachev came to power, he became such an international celebrity that everyone learned at least a few words of Russian. One of them was glasnost. It's hard to find an English equivalent, but it means something like *open public discussion of problems.*

This was a wholly new concept in the Soviet Union. Had the Russians had it in the years following World War II, they might have understood their own economy better. The Soviet Union had developed a powerful industrial economy, despite the turmoil of the early Stalin years. After World War II, the country first rebuilt and then expanded its economy. The economic growth rates of the Soviet Union between the early 1950s and 1975 were impressive. They averaged 5 percent per year. This outpaced the United States and kept pace with growth in many Western European economies.

But those numbers were misleading—they hid a lot of inefficiency. The Soviet Union hit impressive growth rates by making "extensive investments." That is, the Soviets put lots of labor, capital, and resources into their system. But prices set by the state did not reflect actual costs of these investments. This led to misallocation of resources—putting money in the wrong place. Government interference with business decisions kept industries from adapting to new opportunities. It also hindered productivity growth.

The quality of Soviet goods and services wasn't very good, either. That was another unhappy truth the growth figures hid.

The Soviet Union's Slow Economic Decline

The Soviet Union paid a high price for the stability it had under Brezhnev. He and his team avoided tough political and economic change. And that doomed the country to the decline it experienced during the 1980s. This deterioration was a sharp contrast to the energy that marked the early days of the Soviet experiment.

The Soviets stuck with the central planning that Stalin introduced, even though this model didn't fit with the modern world that was taking shape all around them. Eventually the tricks they used to make their growth rates look better than they actually were stopped working. The Soviets didn't have unlimited resources. Soviet birthrates were declining, especially in the European parts of the country. That meant fewer workers were available, especially in the areas where factories were located. Capital, resources, and technology were also in decline. By the mid-1970s, official average growth rates in the Soviet Union were down to 2 percent per year.

That might have been acceptable in a mature, fully modern economy. But the Soviet Union wasn't that. It was still playing catch-up with the United States, with Europe, and with Japan. By the 1980s Asian economies were giving the Soviets some tough competition.

Soviet standards of living, never very high in the first place, were getting worse. And thanks to the global communications revolution—tools like phones, computers, satellites, radios, and televisions—ordinary Soviet citizens began to see and understand their relative position in the world. Gorbachev came to power under these conditions.

Gorbachev understood that the Soviet Union could not keep up with the United States in developing new military technology. This made it all the more necessary to do whatever was needed to take the chains off the Soviet economy and let people use their own initiative and creativity to create economic growth.

The Effects of the Fall of Communism

As it turned out, Gorbachev was the last general secretary of the Soviet Communist Party. He preached glasnost and also perestroika, or *restructuring of the economy*. But his attempts at reform from within didn't work. The people of the Soviet Union weren't content with half-measures. They demanded more and the system collapsed.

In June 1991 Boris Yeltsin, a popular reformer, became the Russian Federation's first democratically elected president. This federation was the successor state to the Soviet Union. The former Soviet republics of Russia, Ukraine, and Belarus formed the Commonwealth of Independent States in December 1991. On 25 December, Gorbachev resigned as Soviet president. Eleven days later, the Soviet Union ceased to exist.

The Transition From Central Planning to a Market-Based Economy

Russia went through immense stress during the 1990s as it moved from a centrally planned economy to a free-market system. Two factors came together in 1998 to cause a serious crisis:

- The government had trouble raising money to fund public services
- The government borrowed too much money to pay for its budget deficit.

Moscow Mayor Boris Yeltsin strolls through Red Square with his wife on May Day in 1989 following festivities.
Photo by Melanie Stetson Freeman / © 1989 The Christian Science Monitor
In June 1991 the popular reformer became the Russian Federation's first democratically elected president.

It only made matters worse that this was playing out at a time when prices for Russia's main export earners (oil and minerals) were down. At the same time, investors worldwide were nervous generally because of a financial crisis in Asia.

The value of the ruble—Russia's currency—abruptly fell 60 percent. Foreign investors took their money and went home. Payments and commercial transactions seemed to get lost going through the banking system. Inflation hit 85 percent annually—a dangerously high rate.

It was all over fairly quickly, however. A string of nine boom years followed, with growth at a healthy average annual rate of 7 percent, until the global economic crisis hit in 2008.

The Policies of Boris Yeltsin and Vladimir Putin

The crisis back in 1998 came toward the end of Boris Yeltsin's eight-year term as president. Yeltsin had long been seen as a reformer. He had promoted the kinds of policies that free-market Westerners endorsed. But by the time of the 1998 economic crisis, he appeared increasingly erratic, both personally and in policy terms. He named and then dismissed several prime ministers. Many worried that free-market reforms had lost legitimacy and that Russia itself might be lost to some post-communist chaos.

Then on 31 December 1999 Yeltsin resigned and turned power over to his prime minister, Vladimir Putin. Putin became acting president and in March 2000, Russians elected him president, as Yeltsin had asked. Putin served two terms as president and after that took on a new role as prime minister. Putin's background in Russia's secret police has given some people pause. He has reined in freedom of the press, carried out a brutal war in the breakaway region of Chechnya, sent troops into neighboring Georgia, supported criminal prosecution of some opponents, and interfered in private business decisions. But he gets high marks for his overall economic policies.

Soon after Putin took over, the worst of the crisis ended. Several factors figured in the rebound. The underpriced ruble helped, as did higher prices for materials like oil and minerals. But so did some important government policies: tight controls on spending and reforms of tax, banking, labor, and land laws.

Furthermore, the amount of goods people bought for themselves, as well as the money people put into businesses, grew 10 percent a year during this period. The ruble recovered its value. Inflation dropped sharply, though it was still high. Russia had a budget surplus from 2001 to 2008.

Members of the pro-Putin youth group, Nashi, march in Moscow to protest visas denied to some of their associates by the European Union.

Photo by Melanie Stetson Freeman / © 2008 The Christian Science Monitor

Vladimir Putin, who served two terms as Russian president before becoming prime minister, has reined in freedom of the press and interfered in private business decisions, among other controversial and sometimes brutal steps.

Russia's holdings in other countries' currencies grew to nearly $600 billion by mid-2008. That's the third-largest such reserve in the world. If oil prices drop sharply, for instance, the fund can help cushion the blow. In 2006 the ruble, long a controlled currency, was made "convertible"—meaning it could be exchanged for US dollars, European Union euros, or any other "real" money.

The global economic downturn that began in 2008 posed severe challenges for Russia, however—as it did for many other countries. These difficulties threatened to reduce the popularity of both Prime Minister Putin and Russia's governing party.

The Opening of the Soviet Market to Foreign Trade and Investment

Before 1987, Western companies had few opportunities to do business with the Soviet Union. The main exceptions were companies such as Occidental Petroleum or several Finnish firms, which were willing to trade on a barter basis—taking Soviet raw materials or goods as payment instead of cash. But Gorbachev meant to change all that with his perestroika campaign. Soon his government was allowing foreign companies—from both free-market and communist countries—to set up business. It was a first in 60 years.

By the end of 1988, more than 70 Soviet ministries and enterprises had the right to deal directly with foreign firms. In fact, experts pointed out, Gorbachev felt so strongly about increasing economic ties with the West that he had that goal written into the Five-Year Plan.

Nowadays, the flow of foreign investment into Russia equals that flowing into Brazil, India, and China. Per capita, though, foreign investment in Russia lags behind that in Hungary, Poland, and the Czech Republic. Most foreign investment is in the manufacturing, real estate, oil and mining, and trade sectors.

Russia is still a politically risky place to invest, though. Its business climate is challenging. The rule of law remains weak. Corruption remains a problem. Investors also worry about a lack of openness, explicitness in rules, and clarity of relationships.

The people of the former Soviet Union have been through a lot of history since the beginning of the twentieth century. The 15 successor republics are very much works in progress. A few enjoy full democracy, others have almost returned to Stalinism. The relations between many of them are strained, and some accuse Putin and Russia of purposely stirring up trouble. Some are friendly to the West and are members of NATO, while others continue to be hostile to the United States and its friends. Some are enjoying economic growth, while others remain stuck in the old Soviet-style rut. Together, they pose difficult policy challenges for the United States. You'll learn more about these issues in the following lessons.

Lesson 1 Review

Using complete sentences, answer the following questions on a sheet of paper.

1. What is the Volga?
2. What does the name Ukraine mean?
3. Which action by Prince Vladimir in AD 988 affected Russia's religious life?
4. Which action by a Spanish queen led to the arrival of large numbers of Jews in Russia?
5. Who was Ivan "Money Bags"?
6. Who was Peter the Great?
7. Which weaknesses in the Russian system did World War I expose?
8. What was the difference between the Provisional Government and the Petrograd Soviet?
9. What was Stalin's farm collectivization, and how successful was it?
10. What price did the Soviet Union pay for stability under Brezhnev?
11. Which two factors caused a serious crisis in 1998?
12. What about Vladimir Putin gives some people pause, and why does he get high marks?

Applying Your Learning

13. Was Gorbachev a successful leader? Why or why not?

LESSON 2 Economic Restructuring: Communism and Capitalism

Quick Write

How would you advise Joseph Stalin?

Learn About

- the characteristics of communism as an economic system
- the economic and political influence of Marx, Lenin, and Stalin on communism in Russia
- how the Soviet economic system worked and eventually failed
- the importance of the export of resources for the restructured Russian economic system

Picture this scene: The year is 1927; the place is Moscow. You're a senior official at Gosplan, the State Planning Commission established six years earlier under Vladimir Lenin. He's been dead for three years now. After some jockeying for power, it's become clear that Joseph Stalin, the Georgian with the bushy mustache, is the new leader of the Soviet Union.

One day he summons you to his office because he has a big idea he wants to tell you about. "A Five-Year Plan!" he blurts out. "This country has been trailing behind the Germans and the British and the Americans for decades now. Even the Japanese are ahead of us! We need to do something to—what was the expression that fellow from the embassy used?—'to pull ourselves up by the bootstraps.'"

He's pacing the room by now. "I know there's really nothing in Marx's writings to support this. But Lenin did say we could follow different paths, as long as we ended up in the right place. I'm thinking of a plan that would *command* the economy, all our industrial sectors, and even the peasants, to *produce*. Everyone needs goals. But we can't count on them to figure out what the goals should be. What does some plant manager know, anyway? Or some grubby peasant? We have to tell them!"

Suddenly he stops short. He turns to you and asks, "What do you think of my idea?"

The Characteristics of Communism as an Economic System

Vocabulary

- egalitarian
- collectivization
- free enterprise
- totalitarian
- class struggle
- dialectical materialism
- proletariat
- dictatorship of the proletariat
- authoritarian
- autocratic

In the previous lesson you read an overview of Russia's experience with communism within the broader context of Russian history. In this lesson you will read in more detail about communism as an economic system.

The Ideal of an Egalitarian Society Based on Common Ownership and Control of the Means of Production

The Communists who came to power in the Soviet Union after the Bolshevik Revolution of 1917 promoted the ideal of an egalitarian society. They wanted, in other words, a society *without class divisions*. There would be no upper class, no middle class, no working class, or peasant class. This egalitarianism rested on the concept of common ownership and control of the means of production.

Means of production is a term that refers to productive assets such as farms and factories. In theory, under communism, "the people"—that is, the citizens—owned these assets. Farmers no longer worked land their families had owned for generations, for instance.

Moscow's subway system carries millions of people every day.
Photo by Melanie Stetson Freeman / © 2008 The Christian Science Monitor

The Communists who came to power after the Bolshevik Revolution of 1917 wanted a society without class divisions.

"The people" owned and farmed the land for the good of all. Companies could no longer list and trade shares on a stock exchange because "the people" owned the companies. Bright young people finishing their education and starting out couldn't launch their own companies. Rather, they looked to a career in a government ministry (department) or at a state-owned enterprise.

Time and again, Russia has followed a path unlike that of other major countries. This is true of its economic development, too. These differences affected Russia socially and politically.

In many ways, Russia was ripe for a communist experiment in ways that other countries were not. Heavy industry—steel mills and the like—dominated Russia's late nineteenth-century economy more than it did other countries' economies. All this heavy industry meant that Russia had a relatively larger urban working class than the rest of the world. These workers cut a higher profile in Russia than in the West. And they tended to be politically active.

Because so much of Russia's industry was owned either by the state or by foreign investors, industrialists (capitalists) didn't have much of a profile. What's more, the nobles and the upper-middle classes, groups that normally play a big role in a country's politics, avoided the political stage.

In your own local community, you may be aware of business owners and professionals who get involved in civic and political affairs in different ways. Think of the Rotary Club or Chamber of Commerce inviting congressional candidates to speak to their members, for instance; or the businessman who runs for governor; or the dentist who serves on the school board. Business and middle-class people like this were largely absent from czarist Russia.

All this meant that socialist working-class parties developed in Russia before parties closer to the center of the political spectrum did. The working-class parties focused on equality. The parties of the center—which in most countries tend to represent the middle and business classes—concentrated more on opportunity. This order in the rise of political parties—socialists first, center second—is the reverse of the pattern in Europe and North America.

The Concepts of Nationalization and Collectivization

As you read earlier, communism assumes that the people control all means of production. In reality, this meant the state owns them. Back in Chapter 1, Lesson 2, you learned that nationalization is the process of putting something—a bank or a steel mill, for instance—under state control and ownership.

A related concept is **collectivization**—*the process of putting something under the ownership or control of the "collective"—a group of people*. Though this term is sometimes used to refer to factories and other industrial facilities, people use it especially in talking about farms. Nationalization and collectivization are two concepts particularly linked to Joseph Stalin's rule and the way the Soviet economy developed.

The Soviet Army drills in Moscow's Red Square for the 1989 May Day parade.

Photo by Melanie Stetson Freeman / © 1989 The Christian Science Monitor

During the Soviet Union's 1918-1921 civil war, the government ran the economy as if it were a military operation with a series of measures known as "war communism."

How Central Planning, Bureaucracy, and State Control Are Associated With Communism

Stalin's fingerprints are also all over central planning, bureaucracy, and state control. The founder of communism, Karl Marx (more on him later), set forth a number of big ideas. But he didn't call for a centrally planned economy.

In its early years, in fact, the Soviet Union experimented with a number of different economic policies. It even allowed free enterprise—*private companies owned by individuals*—to coexist with state-owned enterprises. (Private businesses often outdid the state-owned ones.) But those experiments also included, during the 1918–21 civil war, a group of drastic measures known as "war communism."

These measures included nationalizing industry and running it from a central office in Moscow. The government also took over day-to-day control of factories from workers. They installed expert managers instead. To feed people living in the cities, the government seized grain from farmers. Government officials would simply show up and order peasants to turn over their supplies.

War communism meant the government ran the economy as if it were a military operation. In many ways it was. This governing style took place during a civil war, after Russia had already been through the traumas of World War I and two revolutions. War communism wasn't popular, and it didn't last forever. But that it happened under the leadership of much-admired Vladimir Lenin gave Stalin a precedent he could draw on years later when he wanted to take the country in a very different direction.

The Economic and Political Influence of Marx, Lenin, and Stalin on Communism in Russia

Karl Marx was dead long before the revolutions of 1917. But he provided the ideas that Russian communism built on. Vladimir Lenin provided revolutionary leadership as the czarist regime crumbled. Things could have gone differently. Russia could have become a social democracy after it toppled the Romanovs. But Lenin pushed Russia into radical Bolshevism. And Stalin reinforced and strengthened this communist system. Under Stalin, Soviet communism became a totalitarian system—*featuring absolute government control of every aspect of life*—characterized by the use of terrorism, even against the country's own citizens. But the Soviet Union also became one of the world's two undisputed superpowers—along with the United States.

A defaced statue of Joseph Stalin stands in Tbilisi, Georgia, one of the former Soviet republics.
Photo by Melanie Stetson Freeman / © 1990 The Christian Science Monitor

Under Stalin, Soviet communism became a totalitarian system characterized by the use of terrorism, even against the country's own citizens.

The Influence of Karl Marx on the Rise of Communism in Russia

Karl Marx (1818–83) was a nineteenth-century German philosopher and political theorist. He is known as the founder of communism. He was an idea man and a phrasemaker. He contributed a number of terms to the international political vocabulary. His ideas, set forth in his book, *Das Kapital (Capital)*, may be hard to take seriously today. But they were hugely influential for decades. You need some understanding of them to make sense of the twentieth century, and even the world you live in.

Marx had a progressive view of history. He predicted that, just as feudalism had led to capitalism, capitalism would eventually progress to socialism, which would then progress to communism. He preached a vision of **class struggle** (one of his key phrases) that sees *the working classes locked in conflict with the "oppressive" property-owning classes.* **Dialectical materialism** was his phrase for *the process by which the class struggle leads to the dictatorship of the proletariat, socialism, and then communism.*

Proletariat is Marx's term for *the working classes.* He borrowed it from ancient Rome, where the proletarians were the lowest class of citizens. The **dictatorship of the proletariat** is *an early stage of socialism, marked by the workers' dominance in putting down the resistance of the property-owning classes.* Marx may not have been the best judge of human nature. And he completely disregarded the role of agriculture. But he correctly foresaw that the privileged classes would not give up their advantages without a fight.

Socialism, in Marx's view, was a transitional stage. Its guiding principle was "from each according to his abilities, to each according to his work." In this stage, the state would own the means of production.

The final stage, Marx said, would be communism. Once communism was achieved, the state would wither away. Goods and services would be distributed fairly to everyone. As you may realize by now, it hasn't worked out that way in any country with a communist system.

Lenin adapted Marx's ideas to conditions in Russia. He added the idea of a communist party leading the workers' revolution and establishing communism. This system was known as Marxism-Leninism. It became the official ideology of the Soviet Union. It called for an **authoritarian** government—one *requiring absolute obedience*—run by the Communist Party. The party would have sole control of the state-owned means of production.

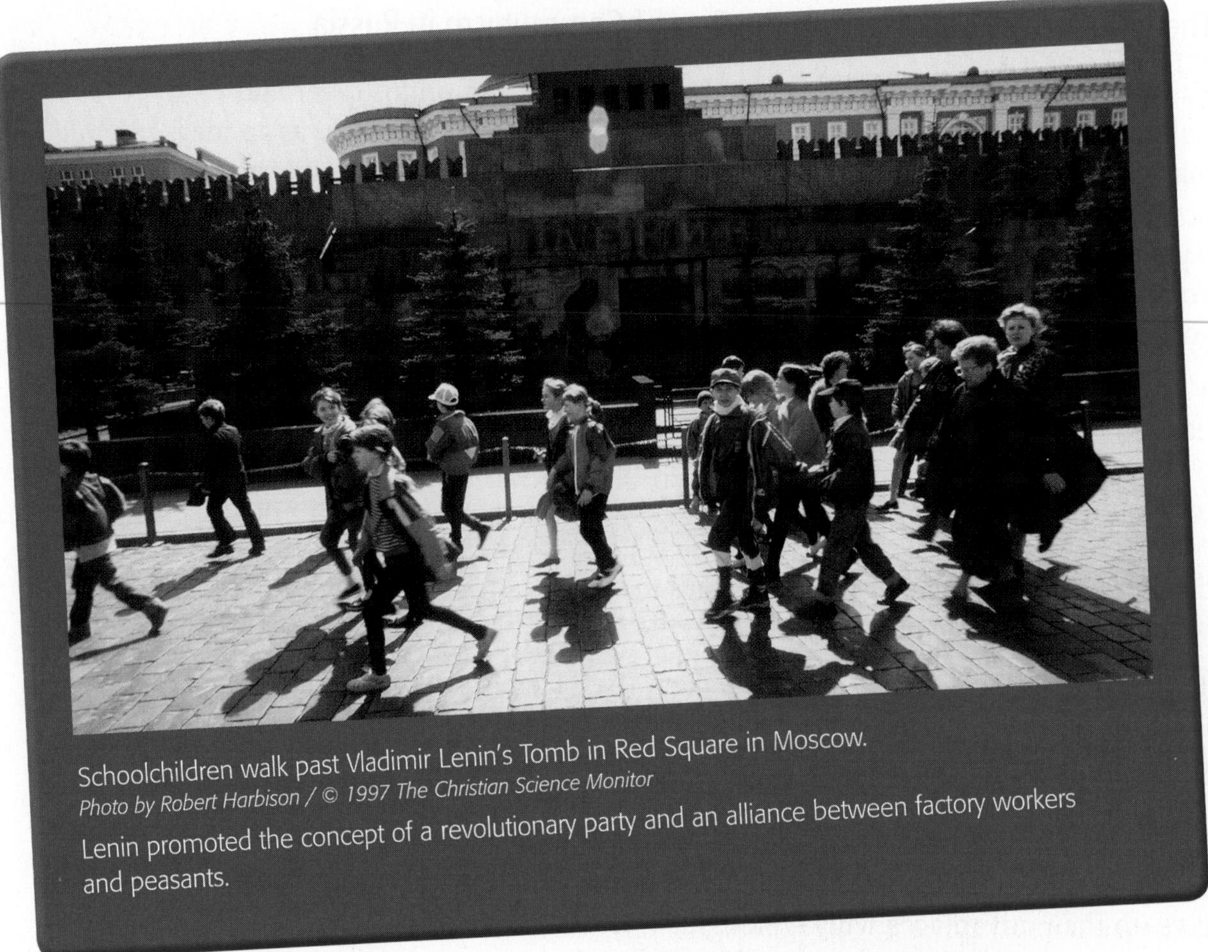

Schoolchildren walk past Vladimir Lenin's Tomb in Red Square in Moscow.
Photo by Robert Harbison / © 1997 The Christian Science Monitor

Lenin promoted the concept of a revolutionary party and an alliance between factory workers and peasants.

Vladimir Lenin's Role in Establishing the Soviet Union

If Marx was the theorist, Lenin was the pragmatic tactician. He was the most politically talented of Russia's revolutionary socialists. During the early 1890s, Lenin wooed Russia's other radicals over to Marxism. In 1900 he founded a newspaper, to be published in Germany, called *Iskra*—"the spark." Two years later, he published a book promoting the idea that a newspaper published abroad could help a revolutionary political party direct the overthrow of an autocratic government. (An autocratic government is one in which *total power rests in one person.*)

Lenin then set about establishing a well-disciplined party that would do just that. After all, he already had his newspaper. He joined the Russian Social Democratic Labor Party. This was the forerunner of the Communist Party of the Soviet Union. There he stirred up internal divisions. This led to his followers—the Bolsheviks—gaining the upper hand. Lenin promoted the concept of a revolutionary party and an alliance between factory workers and peasants. These ideas drew on those of other Russian thinkers as well as of Marx. Stalin and other young Bolsheviks looked to Lenin as their leader.

Leaders of the Soviet Union and Russia, 1922–2008

Leader	Period	Accomplishments
Vladimir Lenin	1922–1924	Led Bolshevik Revolution, won Russian civil war, established Soviet Union
Joseph Stalin	1927–1953	Implemented centralized economy, five-year plans, totalitarian state; murdered millions of people who opposed or were thought to oppose his policies; allied with United States and Britain in World War II
Nikita Khrushchev	1953–1964	Denounced Stalin, fought economic ministries, tried agricultural reforms, legalized small garden plots; Cuban Missile Crisis
Leonid Brezhnev	1964–1982	Held firm against economic and political reforms; liberalized some foreign trade; negotiated arms-limitation treaties with United States as part of détente policy; invaded Afghanistan
Yuri Andropov	1982–1984	Longtime head of KGB, Soviet secret police and spy agency; died before he could implement any major policies
Konstantin Chernenko	1984–1985	Close to Brezhnev, governed as a caretaker for a year before his death
Mikhail Gorbachev	1985–1991	Tried to save Soviet economy with economic reforms, but did not go far enough; ushered in period of significant political liberalization; presided over final collapse of Soviet Union
Boris Yeltsin	1991–1999	First president of noncommunist Russia; implemented wide-ranging democratic and free-market reforms; increasingly erratic policy shifts led to brink of chaos
Vladimir Putin	1999–2008	Former KGB officer; Yeltsin's last prime minister and successor as president; reined in democratic reforms and some human rights; interfered in business decisions; invaded breakaway Chechnya; became prime minister again at end of term—many believe he holds the real power in Russia
Dmitry Medvedev	2008–	Close to Putin; many believe he is a figurehead president with Putin as the real authority

Once in power, the Bolsheviks let peasants seize land and workers take over factories. They also abolished the nobles' privileges. They nationalized banks. Their "revolutionary tribunals" replaced courts of law.

Like Marx before him, Lenin called for "dictatorship of the proletariat." He saw no need for parliamentary democracy. Nor did he think Russia needed more than one political party. Under his leadership the Soviet government created a secret police to attack "enemies of the state"—anyone who opposed his ideas, including liberals and moderates.

Lenin set the tone of the new Soviet Union. The strict party discipline, the lack of tolerance for organized opposition, and the focus on "enemies" would all endure throughout Soviet history. But Lenin had a pragmatic streak, too. He had his own version of Marxism that suggested that the party should follow any course if it led to communism.

Joseph Stalin's Era of Leadership in Russia

At Vladimir Lenin's death in 1924, the Soviet Union was not yet a totalitarian state. By the time Joseph Stalin had settled in as Lenin's successor, however, it absolutely was one.

Stalin set the Soviet Union onto a new course, a program of intensive socialist construction. Between 1927 and 1929 the State Planning Commission—Gosplan—worked out the First Five-Year Plan. It was a "revolution from above."

Stalin sought to centralize the economy. The plan pushed for the economy's rapid industrialization. It emphasized heavy industry. But the regime nationalized small-scale industry and services, too. Managers strove to fulfill their output targets. Trade unions, once the foot soldiers of the struggle for labor rights, got the job of increasing worker productivity.

But Stalin's plan ran into trouble in short order. He had insisted on unrealistic production goals, for one thing. And his emphasis on heavy industry meant that consumer goods were in short supply. It wasn't the first time this had happened in Russia, nor would it be the last. Inflation grew.

To provide more food for the state, the First Five-Year Plan called for collectivizing the peasants and their lands and livestock. That is, the private farms were combined into collective farms, so the state could better control them. This meant taking away the peasants' land and animals. Peasants worked on these collective farms under the direction of party leaders, from plans the party had approved. Laborers' wages rose or fell partly based on a harvest's success or failure. The government also set up state farms. The government owned and managed these directly, like factories. Workers there earned salaries.

Stalin's regime largely restricted peasants' movements from these farms. In effect he reintroduced serfdom, a type of bondage that Alexander II had abolished in 1861.

In his agriculture "reforms," Stalin was also keen to go after the wealthiest peasants, known as kulaks. These landowning kulaks were "wealthy" only by comparison with other peasants. But the party claimed that the kulaks trapped poorer peasants in "capitalistic relationships."

Both kulaks and the poorer peasants fought back against the Stalinist campaign. They slaughtered their animals rather than turn them over to the collectives. The resulting livestock shortage lasted for years. The government pushed ahead with its collectivization, however. It deported kulaks and other rebels to Siberia, a vast, freezing cold region in eastern Russia, where many died.

Farmers know that a farm is not a factory. Communists found it hard enough to run factories. But they found farming even harder. Coaxing crops out of the earth and tending livestock are not mechanical or ideological processes. They require sensitive attention to conditions on the ground day by day. But the Stalin regime's general mismanagement of agriculture led to widespread starvation. In some cases, the state deliberately withheld food shipments. In the Ukrainian Republic, for instance, millions died this way. And Ukraine has some of the richest soil in the world!

By 1932 Stalin realized he had serious problems on his hands. Industry was failing to meet its production goals and agriculture had actually lost ground. His solution was to declare that the First Five-Year Plan had met its goals early, and then to order another plan, with more realistic goals.

The Second Five-Year Plan (1933–37) was in fact more successful. It devoted more attention to consumer goods, and production from factories built during the first plan actually helped increase total output during the period of the second plan.

The Third Five-Year Plan was less successful. This was largely due to a sudden shift in emphasis. With war clouds gathering on the horizon, the government stepped up weapons production.

By the end of the 1930s, Stalin's plans had led to an increase in industrialization. But agriculture continued to show poor returns.

How the Soviet Economic System Worked and Eventually Failed

People often think of the Soviet economy as being focused on big heavy industry—steel mills and the like. It was. But this focus predated communism; it went back to the late nineteenth century. In those days, foreign investors took the lead, seeking to exploit Russia's natural resources, such as coal and iron. Under communism, the state took over the leadership role from foreign investors. Russia's own merchant class, meanwhile, was reactionary—opposed to change of any sort. Russia largely lacked a truly entrepreneurial class. It lacked, in other words, people who would start not only new businesses but whole new industries. This put Russia, from the beginning of the twentieth century, at a disadvantage. To this day, it has not made up the lost ground.

Women sell food at the Danilovsky market in Moscow.

Photo by Melanie Stetson Freeman / © 1999 The Christian Science Monitor

Then-Soviet leader Nikita Khrushchev introduced plans in the 1950s for growing more corn and for stepping up meat and dairy production, but they turned out to be disastrous.

The Subordination of Industry and Agriculture to the State

In a totalitarian system, the government controls just about everything. In a communist country, the state—the government—owns and controls most means of production. The Soviet Union was both communist and totalitarian. Both industry and agriculture were subordinate to the state. This meant, obviously, that the government had a lot of power. But it also meant it had a lot of responsibility when things went wrong. It was up to the Soviet leaders to fix problems, whether those troubles were a food shortage or a lack of efficiency at factories. In the United States, on the other hand, the president isn't responsible for the corn harvest; corn farmers are.

Soviet leader Nikita Khrushchev, who came to power after Stalin's death, introduced plans for growing more corn and for stepping up meat and dairy production. They were disasters. Likewise, his efforts to merge collective farms into ever-larger units also backfired, leading to mass confusion in the countryside.

In the mid-1950s Khrushchev opened to farmers vast areas of land in the northern part of the Kazakh Republic and in nearby sections of Russia. These "new lands" produced excellent harvests in some years, but they were also subject to drought. This campaign also failed in the end.

This failure was an example of the kind of thing that happened when the state controlled the farm sector. The land in question was grassland that had never been farmed before. People had lived there for centuries, but no one had ever thought the land looked promising as a place to grow crops. Under the Soviet system, however, top-down orders from politicians and bureaucrats in Moscow carried more weight than the views of people literally "on the ground."

One of Khrushchev's innovations in the farm sector was successful, though. He encouraged peasants to grow more on the tiny private farm plots they were allowed to keep. By the end of the Soviet era, these little private farms were a major source of food in the country. They were much more productive than the state-owned collective farms. And they showed how the profit motive spurs output on the farm as well as in the factory.

The Impact of Central Planning on the Quality and Quantity of Production

Everything about the Soviet Union was big. Its manufacturing capacity was immense. It eventually became one of the world's largest producers of all manner of goods, from nuclear warheads to canned fish. What the Soviets made, however, wasn't always top quality. The canned fish, for instance, would languish on shop shelves because the taste was so foul no one would eat it.

One reason the system failed was that it's just not possible to plan for every possibility in an economy. Take an automobile, for example. It has many parts. In the United States, hundreds of small companies make these parts for the big auto companies. If spare parts are needed, they can fairly easily step up production and supply them. But the Soviets often didn't even plan for spare parts. Or they didn't plan for enough of them. Or the parts were poorly made and didn't fit. It was not unusual in the Soviet Union for factory and farm equipment to stand idle for long periods because no parts were available to repair them. Food stores might have refrigeration units, but they often didn't work.

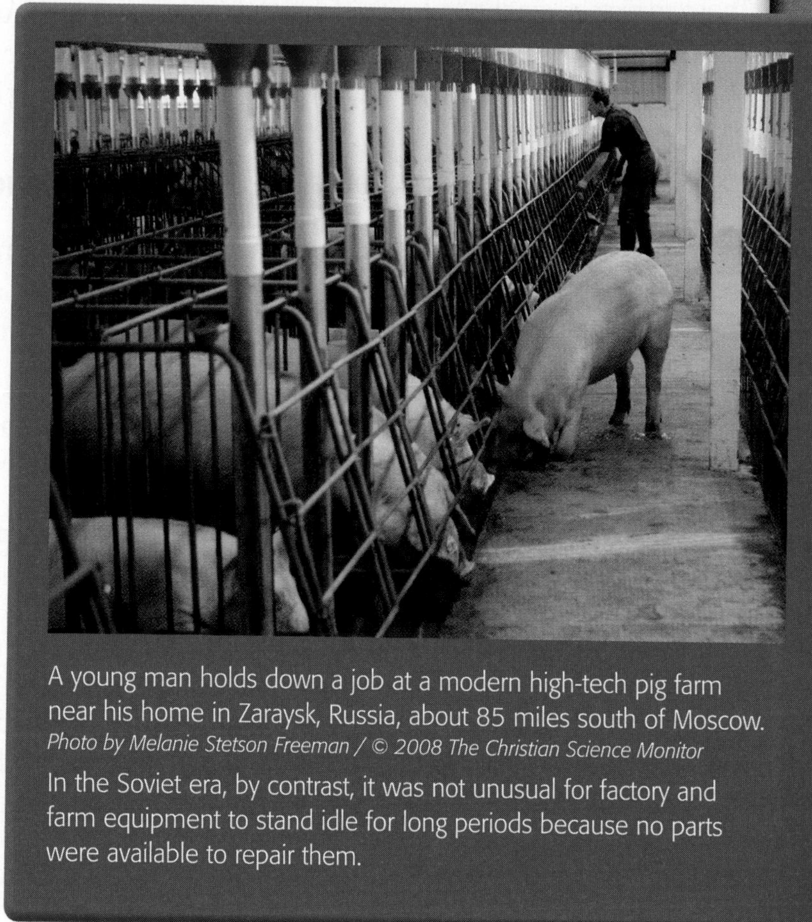

A young man holds down a job at a modern high-tech pig farm near his home in Zaraysk, Russia, about 85 miles south of Moscow.
Photo by Melanie Stetson Freeman / © 2008 The Christian Science Monitor

In the Soviet era, by contrast, it was not unusual for factory and farm equipment to stand idle for long periods because no parts were available to repair them.

The problem was that the Soviet system never strove for efficiency. It never tried to get the most output from its inputs—getting the most bang for the buck, you might say. Soviet plant managers never had to worry about the costs of production. Soviet wages were low, and workers had no incentive to work harder or more efficiently. No one received any financial reward for doing a better job or making a better mousetrap. This led to an old Soviet joke: "As long as the state pretends it is paying us," the workers would say, "we'll pretend we are working."

But the central planning system, however cumbersome it was, proved hard for the Communists to give up. In one attempt at reform, Khrushchev in 1957 abolished the so-called industrial ministries in Moscow and replaced them with regional economic councils. It was a political move, meant to undercut the centralized Moscow bureaucracy.

But the decentralization merely caused disruption and more inefficiency. A few years later he tried a political restructuring. This time he tried reorganizing the Communist Party. This move, too, backfired badly. It got everybody angry with Khrushchev. By the following year, 1963, the economy was in such a mess that the government abandoned a special seven-year plan it had been pursuing. And by the end of 1964, the other Soviet leaders pushed Khrushchev out of power. The industrial ministries returned.

fastFACT

For most of Soviet history, each economic sector had its own government ministry—equivalent to US Cabinet-level departments. There were ministries for the automobile industry, for the wood-processing industry, and for the chemical industry, for example. These ministries ran the factories in their industry sectors.

The Decline of Soviet Creativity and Productivity

Some situations call for decisive, action-oriented, military-style leadership. Imagine, for instance, a river about to flood, and a county sheriff directing volunteer sandbaggers. Someone needs to give clear orders, set a tempo for the work, and get everyone to move.

But a national economy is different from a natural disaster. Think of your own experiences as a shopper. When you're in the market for new electronics, you notice new features that last year's models didn't have. When you shop for clothes, you want that color that's really hot this season, or the style that the people you admire are wearing.

This is exactly the kind of thing that the Soviet economic system could not deliver. Analysts say it was more effective in its early years. It did a relatively good job of mobilizing resources, including labor, and directing them to certain industrial goals. When the Soviet Union had few tractors, and basic tractors were needed to increase agricultural production, this system could work up to a point.

Commuters rush through a Moscow metro station, complete with artistic mosaics on the walls.
Photo by Melanie Stetson Freeman / © 2008 The Christian Science Monitor

The Soviet system relied on commands, rather than incentives. It did little or nothing to foster innovation or improvements in quality.

But the system relied on commands, rather than incentives. It focused on meeting production quotas, on "making the numbers." It did little or nothing to foster innovation or improvements in quality. Factory officials saw progress in terms of "more of the same" rather than creative improvements. A director who tried to innovate risked not making his targets—the mark of failure. It became impossible to make any kind of change.

The Soviet system had a particular weakness in technological innovation. In the early days, Soviet enterprises could borrow technology from foreigners. As the Cold War continued, such channels froze up, since the government closed access to the world outside of the Soviet Union, and foreign countries became less willing to share technology. In the early 1970s the Soviets bought licenses to produce some Western products—Pepsi Cola and out-of-date Fiat cars, for example. But little of the technology such licenses brought was shared with other sectors of the economy.

Intellectual freedom is also an important part of the creative process, even in science and technology. But many of the Soviet Union's most important and creative intellectuals spent years in prison camps or under house arrest. Stalin simply had thousands, if not millions, of intellectuals arrested, jailed, and even murdered. Khrushchev largely put an end to the killing of dissidents. But even under Leonid Brezhnev two of the Soviet Union's premier intellectuals—physicist Andrei Sakharov and novelist Alexander Solzhenitsyn—found themselves under house arrest or in foreign exile. You cannot stifle creative people and hope for creativity in society.

By the end of the Brezhnev era, the Soviet economy had largely run out of steam. Grocery stores that three decades before were full of goods had little to sell. Corruption in the retail "industry" meant that what goods were available were often sold to friends and relatives on the black market. People waited for up to 10 years on waiting lists to buy an automobile. There wasn't enough housing: Millions of people still lived in "communal apartments"—two, three, or four families each living in one room of an apartment and sharing the kitchen and bathroom. And as computerization and technology gains led to economic growth and rising living standards in Western countries, the Soviet Union was simply unable to keep pace.

Throughout this period, however, one Soviet product remained readily available: vodka. Alcoholism affected creativity and productivity not just in the economy but in the whole society. By the end of the Brezhnev years, life expectancy in the Soviet Union was on the decline, and infant mortality on the rise. Runaway alcoholism was a factor in both.

The Shift to the Open Market Forces of Capitalism

Mikhail Gorbachev took office in 1985 and inherited a Soviet system that cried out for change. The first reforms he introduced didn't go much beyond what some of his predecessors had tried. They amounted to mere tinkering, such as his anti-alcoholism campaign. They weren't enough. So he tried again.

In his next move, Gorbachev brought in the more fundamental changes known as perestroika—restructuring. New legislation in 1987 set state enterprises free to decide their own levels of production in response to customers' orders. No longer did they have to fill targets set by a central planning agency. That was a truly radical idea in the Soviet Union.

Perestroika also required enterprises to be self-financing—to figure out how to operate at a profit. Most significantly, the law allowed joint ventures with foreign companies. Workers' collectives took over control of enterprises from government ministries. The central planners shifted from making detailed plans to offering broad guidelines. And for the first time since Lenin, Soviet law even allowed private ownership of small businesses—although not the land or the buildings they occupied. Private taxis and restaurants began to appear in Soviet cities.

Gorbachev also eased up on repressing dissent. He released Dr. Sakharov and allowed him to return to Moscow.

These looked like bold changes. But in the end, they weren't much more effective than Khrushchev's private farms. Gorbachev's new system was neither fish nor fowl. It wasn't enough of a market system to jump-start the sluggish economy. And it wasn't quite central planning, either. It did, however, retain some of the key elements of Stalin's system: price controls, a currency that couldn't be freely exchanged, a ban on private property ownership, and the government monopoly over most means of production. These elements blocked significant progress.

By the end of 1991, when the Soviet Union dissolved, its economy was in a tailspin. Although far from what he intended, Gorbachev had pushed his country onto a path of real reform. As he disappeared from public life, Russia embarked on a difficult transition.

Shoppers brave the chill to run errands at this open-air market in a town south of Moscow.

Photo by Melanie Stetson Freeman / © 2008 The Christian Science Monitor

After Gorbachev took office in the 1980s, Soviet law allowed private ownership of small businesses for the first time since Lenin.

The Importance of the Export of Resources for the Restructured Russian Economic System

In the previous sections, you've read about the shortcomings of the Soviet system. However, Stalinist central planning couldn't ruin Russia's natural resources. These extensive resources have helped Russia through a challenging transition back to a market economy.

A mill worker processes flax fibers at a textile factory in modern-day Russia.

Photo by Fred Weir / © 2006 The Christian Science Monitor

Right up through the Gorbachev era, however, the Soviet Union lagged behind other countries in churning out high-quality factory-made goods.

Russia as an Exporter of Raw Materials, Not Manufactured Goods

Russia has greater wealth in raw materials than almost any other country. Many of these materials are the building blocks of an industrial economy.

Russia is also self-sufficient in almost every major industrial raw material. And this is true even now that it no longer controls the productive mines of Ukraine, Kazakhstan, and Uzbekistan, which are now independent countries.

Even in a high-tech electronic age, wood is still an important material, and Russia has a lot of it. You might think of Russia as the Saudi Arabia of timber. The forests of Siberia hold about one-fifth of the world's timber. Most of this is conifers—the evergreens of the taiga you read about in Lesson 1. Much of it is exported to Europe, Russia's immediate neighbors, and China and Japan.

Natural resources are place-dependent. An oil deposit, or a seam of coal, for instance, is where it is. Such resources stay put until they can be pumped or mined. On the other hand, human resources—people—are mobile. Even in a society where the government controls people's movements as tightly as the Soviet Union did under Stalin, people still have ways of gravitating toward opportunity.

Because Soviet leaders clung to central planning, right up through the Gorbachev era, their country lagged behind others in churning out high-quality factory-made goods. This is especially true of consumer goods. There was no Soviet equivalent of Italian sports cars, microwave ovens, or personal computers.

The only exception to this mediocrity was in the arms industry and space exploration. The Soviets made excellent automatic rifles, fighter planes, and tanks. And Soviet space technology allowed the country to almost keep pace with the United States—to the point where today's Russia remains an essential player in space exploration and the International Space Station. But these were not consumer goods available both in the country and for export.

As a result, Russia is known mainly as an exporter of raw materials, not manufactured goods. The Soviet Union could export timber, oil, and minerals, but it failed to develop a system to add value to things that came out of the ground. And that failure lives on in today's Russia. The country exports raw lumber, but not goods made of wood.

Military Arms, Minerals, and Crude Oil as Three Major Russian Exports

The economy's tilt in favor of heavy industry fostered the Soviets' ability to manufacture military hardware for export. During the Cold War, the Soviet Union gained power and influence by supplying military hardware and other aid to developing countries.

Sometimes the Soviets supported governments, such as that of Gamal Abdul Nasser in Egypt during the 1950s and '60s. Other times they supported guerrilla movements, such as the armed wing of the African National Congress.

Russia inherited most of the Soviet Union's defense industrial base. The government has made some efforts to convert some of this to civilian production. But these efforts have met with mixed results. Russia remains a major arms exporter.

Indeed, as former President and current Prime Minister Vladimir Putin has reasserted Russia's role as a global power, Russia has pushed arms sales abroad, in the Middle East, Asia, and Latin America. Both economic and political interests are behind this policy. In early 2009 the head of the Russian arms export monopoly said it had $27 billion in orders on its books. This backlog would keep domestic defense firms busy for four to five years, he added. The Russian defense sector employs more than 2.5 million people, about a fifth of the country's industrial labor force.

Russia has significant deposits of both oil and natural gas. Its production accounts for about one-fifth of the world's total. Russia is self-sufficient in energy and is a major exporter of both oil and gas. These fuels are primary hard-currency earners for Russia, as they were for the Soviet Union.

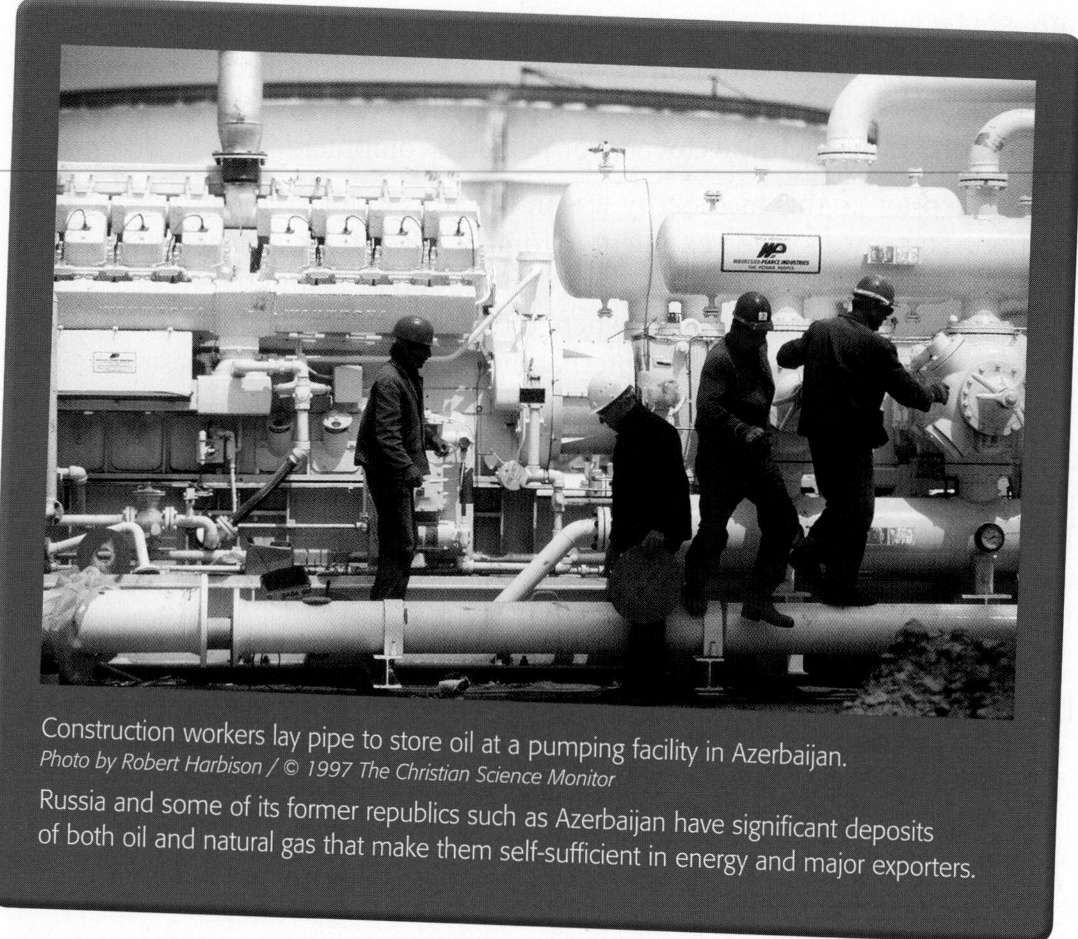

Construction workers lay pipe to store oil at a pumping facility in Azerbaijan.
Photo by Robert Harbison / © 1997 The Christian Science Monitor

Russia and some of its former republics such as Azerbaijan have significant deposits of both oil and natural gas that make them self-sufficient in energy and major exporters.

Russia's nonfuel mineral reserves include:

- iron ore
- manganese
- chromium
- nickel
- platinum
- titanium
- copper
- tin
- lead
- tungsten
- diamonds
- phosphates
- gold.

Russia manages to be a leading exporter of these minerals even though they are deposited largely in remote areas that are frozen solid much of the time. Minerals and other raw materials account for 90 percent of Russia's exports to the United States. Energy is the dominant element in this mix.

The Importance of Russian Exports in a Free Market Economy

Economists may lament the fact that Russia's economy remains underdeveloped. Some may wish that Russians would do more with their resources. That would enable them to export at a higher level. Still others worry that energy prices have been too unstable of late to provide a solid base for Russia's economy.

But these regrets notwithstanding, Russia's exports have been a lifeline since the Soviet Union dissolved. In a period of economic weakness and painful transition, Russia nonetheless had things the world needed, and could sell them: especially oil and gas.

Likewise, Russia's renewed emphasis on arms exports may worry outside observers. But arms sales are good for Russia's economy. The arms plants keep people working, for one thing. And that means they're good for domestic political stability.

Trade with other countries is also drawing Russia into the family of nations. This in turn helps ease its longstanding cultural isolation. In his day, Stalin tried to have Russia pull itself up by its own bootstraps. But it didn't work. Only by trading with other countries can Russia develop its own economy.

And there are signs development *is* taking place. Freed of central planning and control, the economy is diversifying. Since the rebound from the 1998 crisis that you read about in Lesson 1, consumer spending and fixed capital investment have both grown briskly. They have overtaken exports as the main driver of economic growth.

Russian President Vladimir Putin (left) and US President George W. Bush hold a press conference at the White House in 2001.
Photo by Andy Nelson / © 2001 The Christian Science Monitor

Trade with other countries is drawing Russia into the family of nations. This in turn helps ease its longstanding cultural isolation.

Russia is now developing a capitalist economy, although it still faces many challenges. Land ownership remains a difficult issue: While limits on owning land were thrown out in 1995, there is still no constitutional protection for land ownership. Business and contract laws remain inadequate. The tax system keeps changing, and tax evasion is widespread. The government continues to interfere in business decisions when it wants to, sometimes unfairly punishing both Russian and foreign businesspeople and investors.

But in abandoning communism, Russia has set the stage for harnessing its one great underused resource: the creativity and labor of the Russian people themselves. It will take a long time for Russians to free themselves from the mistrust of foreigners and the old economic and political habits that have prevented economic growth and development in the past. But without the heavy hand of czars or Communists preventing them from doing so, Russians face a brighter future than seemed possible just a couple of decades ago.

A young couple strides past a Russian Orthodox church in Moscow.

Photo by Melanie Stetson Freeman / © 2008 The Christian Science Monitor

In abandoning communism, Russia has set the stage for harnessing its one great underused resource: the creativity and labor of the Russian people themselves.

Lesson 2 Review

Using complete sentences, answer the following questions on a sheet of paper.

1. Why did Russia have such a relatively large urban working class in the late nineteenth century?
2. Which leader developed the Soviet Union's central planning?
3. What did Karl Marx mean by dialectical materialism?
4. How did Lenin set the tone for the new Soviet Union?
5. Why did Khrushchev's "new lands" campaign fail?
6. Why was it hard for the Soviet economic system to deliver technological innovation?
7. Why has Russia, like the Soviet Union before it, been known as an exporter mainly of raw materials rather than manufactured goods?
8. Why are exports and trade so important to post-communist Russia?

Applying Your Learning

9. If you were Gorbachev, what steps would you have taken in 1985 to reform the Soviet system?

LESSON 3 Russia and the Republics

Quick Write

In general, is it a good idea to stick with the map you've got? Or under special circumstances, such as the Soviet Union's collapse, is some reassignment of territory in order?

Learn About

- the political and economic influence of Russia on the Ukraine, Belarus, and Moldova
- the political and economic influence of Russia on the Baltic States
- the political and economic influence of Russia on Armenia, Georgia, and Azerbaijan
- the political and economic influence of Russia on Kazakhstan, Kyrgyzstan, Uzbekistan, Tajikistan, and Turkmenistan

Imagine this: You've landed a job with your congressman. Mostly you just answer the phones. But the conversations you overhear—or even get to take part in!—make you feel as if you're at the center of the world.

Your boss is young; he's only in his second term. But he's been named to the House Foreign Affairs Committee, and he's thrilled. He's looking for an issue where he can make a name for himself. And you think you know what he's going to settle on.

It's something a lot of constituents have been calling about. One part of your district has a lot of older people from Eastern Europe and places that used to be part of the Soviet Union. They want your boss to push to get the United States to recognize a new country over there. It's a little strip of land on the other side of one of the big rivers—someplace way on the other side of Romania. You've never quite gotten the name.

Members of the congressman's staff keep kicking the idea around. Would this be a good thing for the congressman to support? Would it be good for the United States? Would it be good for the people who live along that river in Eastern Europe?

A nice guy from the State Department dropped by to talk the other day. He was all business in his blue suit. He tried to seem nonchalant. But he obviously didn't think US recognition of this new little country was a good idea. "Stability," he kept saying, "we diplomats like stability. To recognize that territory's independence will only make our allies mad and increase ethnic tensions there. It might even lead to war. We like to stick with the map we've got."

But that nice older man from the district, who's been so helpful to your boss, happened to be in Washington that week, in your office in fact. When he heard the man from State talk about "stability," you thought he was going to blow a gasket. You saw him take a deep breath, walk over, and say, "The map of the Soviet Union is the map that Stalin drew. He's gone now. The Communists are all gone. We can draw a better map."

The Political and Economic Influence of Russia on the Ukraine, Belarus, and Moldova

Vocabulary 

- bilateral
- subsidy
- separatist
- émigré
- secretariat

Ukraine, Belarus, and Moldova sit between Russia to the east and the expanding European Union to the west. These neighbors are often grouped together, but each has a very different story.

Ukraine and Belarus were founding members of the United Nations in 1945. Yet, like Moldova, they were part of the Soviet Union. That is, they were all part of one country. Russian leader Joseph Stalin, who otherwise kept a tight grip on things, wanted each of the Soviet Union's 15 republics to count as an "independent" member state within the United Nations so the Soviet Union would get more votes. The Western allies rejected this idea.

A warm day draws people out of doors in Lvov, Ukraine.

Photo by Melanie Stetson Freeman / © 1990 The Christian Science Monitor

As a Soviet republic, Ukraine was one of the United Nations' founding members in 1945.

But as a compromise, Ukraine and Belarus were given their own seats at the UN. Moldova, one of the smallest and poorest of the former Soviet republics, did not get a seat.

As of this writing, Ukraine is trying to join the European Union (EU), a Western economic alliance, and NATO, a Western military alliance. Belarus, on the other hand, has been backsliding in its progress toward democracy. In fact, the EU has reduced its relations with Belarus. Moldova, meanwhile, has been reaching out to the West as it seeks new connections outside the former Soviet Union.

The Diplomatic and Trade Relationship Between Russia and the Ukraine

Ukraine's top foreign-policy goal is Euro-Atlantic integration. That means eventual membership in the EU and in NATO. Ukraine was negotiating an "association agreement"—a forerunner to full membership—with the EU as of this writing.

Despite the European focus, Ukraine still seeks good relations with Russia and, on balance, has them. Significant issues remain between the two countries, however. Membership in NATO is one of them. Moscow still sees NATO as an alliance targeted at Russia, and so opposes Ukraine's joining it.

NATO, for its part, has affirmed that Ukraine will eventually join the alliance. But it has put off, for review "at a later date," Ukraine's request for a concrete plan for admission. Even while sending encouraging signs to Ukraine, NATO leaders are sensitive to Russian concerns. NATO must ask itself, if Russia ever felt threatened, would it attack Ukraine? One of NATO's core tenets is that an attack on one is an attack on all—generally referred to as "mutual assistance." So would NATO really come to Ukraine's aid? How? Those questions remain unanswered for the moment. The Western military alliance must think through all possible outcomes when adding new members.

Natural gas is another issue that stands between Russia and Ukraine. Under Vladimir Putin's leadership, Russia has not hesitated to use its energy resources to exert power and influence over other nations. Some see Putin as particularly interested in working out bilateral deals—*deals between two individual parties*—with individual countries rather than working with the EU as a whole.

Russia's natural gas flows by pipeline across Ukraine and on to the rest of Europe. In the first few weeks of 2009, the Russian national gas distributor, Gazprom, cut supplies to Ukraine. This led to a crisis for both Ukraine and the rest of Europe. Ukraine had domestic reserves of its own, but other Europeans were cut off. The situation was grim. Slovakia alarmed its neighbors by considering restarting an obsolete nuclear reactor to provide energy. Putin and his Ukrainian counterpart, Prime Minister Yulia V. Tymoshenko, signed an agreement resolving the dispute on 19 January 2009. But tensions remain between the two countries.

A bird's-eye view shows the Dnieper River running through Kiev, Ukraine.
Photo by Robert Harbison / © 1991 The Christian Science Monitor

Although Ukraine's top foreign-policy goal is Euro-Atlantic integration, it still seeks good relations with Russia.

Yet another source of strain lies in the stationing of the Russian Black Sea Fleet at the Crimean city of Sevastopol. In 1997 Ukraine agreed to allow this until 2017. More recently, however, Ukrainian officials have hinted they will not renew the lease when it expires. In the same area, the two countries dispute the boundaries in the Sea of Azov and the Kerch Strait.

One of the most dramatic recent examples of Russian interference in one of its former Republics took place during the 2004 Ukrainian presidential campaign. Russia favored pro-Russia contender Viktor Yanukovych. But Ukrainians supported Viktor Yushchenko, a pro-West candidate.

Shortly before the election, Yushchenko fell ill. His face swelled, developed pockmarks, and showed alarming signs of aging. Doctors from Austria, Britain, the United States, and France conducted tests. Their diagnosis was massive dioxin poisoning.

Britain's *Daily Mail* reported in 2009, "The president's pro-Western allies have accused Russia of being behind the plot to kill him, but Moscow maintains its innocence. Ukrainian prosecutor general Oleksandr Medvedko has said only three countries—one of them Russia—in the world produce dioxin TCDD." Yushchenko recovered; Russia's involvement has never been proved.

The Diplomatic and Trade Relationship Between Russia and Belarus

Relations between Russia and Belarus are smoother than they are between Russia and the Ukraine. Russia is Belarus's No. 1 partner, both economically and politically. A third of Belarusian exports go to Russia. Belarus relies heavily on Russia, along with other former Soviet republics, both for export markets and for raw materials, cheap energy, and parts to build things.

Market prices are a factor in these relationships. A spike in natural gas prices in 2007, as well as higher prices for Russian oil and oil-based products, led to a crisis. The Belarusian government had to cut subsidies and borrow money from Russia. A **subsidy** is *government money used to keep prices artificially low for goods such as food and oil.*

The two countries are supposedly on track to form a "union." The founding treaties for this union call for single citizenship, a common currency, and a common foreign and defense policy. It would be like the EU, with some institutions following the EU model, although it would be a union of two, rather than two dozen, members.

Belarus has postponed carrying out the currency union. The 2007 energy crisis slowed the two countries down. Although some other entities have expressed interest in joining the "union state," the whole project remains vague.

The Diplomatic and Trade Relationship Between Russia and Moldova

Poor, landlocked, and densely populated, Moldova is a textbook example of a former Soviet republic trying to find its way in a new world. Moldova got most of its energy and raw materials from other parts of the former Soviet Union. The breakdown in trade after the Soviet Union dissolved hit Moldova hard. Drought and civil conflict made the situation worse.

Tucked between Ukraine and Romania, Moldova has an economy in which industry accounts for only 15 percent. Agriculture makes up 35 percent. With its mild, sunny climate, the country grows wheat, corn, barley, tobacco, sugar beets, and soybeans. Its farmers also raise beef and dairy cattle and keep bees.

Moldova's best-known product, though, is its world-class wines. In March 2006, however, Moldova lost one of its main markets when Russia banned imports of its wine and meat—supposedly because of health concerns but really due to political tensions between the countries.

Then in November of that same year, Russia reversed the ban after Moldova threatened to block its effort to join the World Trade Organization (WTO). Russia remains the largest economy outside the WTO, which it wants to join. It took nearly a year after Russia lifted the ban for Moldova's wine trade to return to its earlier levels. Nowadays Moldovan wineries are pursuing new markets in Western Europe.

Like Ukraine, Moldova has also been subject to Russia's gas politics. In January 2006 Gazprom shut off Moldova's gas supplies. By the time the gas began to flow again, the price had doubled. It's been on the rise ever since.

The Moldovan region of Transnistria, a sliver of land on the east bank of the Dniestr River, is controlled by ethnic-Russian separatists. A separatist is *a member of a movement to break away from a larger body*. The region's population is 40 percent Romanian, 28 percent Ukrainian, 23 percent Russian, and 9 percent other groups. This dispute has also strained Moldovan relations with Russia, which still has forces stationed in the region.

The Political and Economic Influence of Russia on the Baltic States

Like their southern neighbors, the Baltic states share a long but varied history under Russian rule. Estonia, Latvia, and most of Lithuania belonged to the Russian Empire by the end of the eighteenth century. After World War I, all three enjoyed periods of independence and cultural flowering. But in 1939 the Molotov-Ribbentrop Pact between Germany and the Soviet Union allowed the Soviets to seize them while the two aggressors divided up Poland.

All three Baltic states regained independence after the Soviet Union collapsed. Always the most Westernized in terms of culture and religion, they are among the most successful "new democracies" to emerge from the end of the Cold War. All three belong to both NATO and the EU. All three are strong friends of the United States. And all three still have some issues with their large neighbor to the east.

A woman and child walk through a field on Saaremaa, an Estonian island in the Baltic Sea.
Photo by Melanie Stetson Freeman / © 1990 The Christian Science Monitor

The Baltic states—Estonia, Latvia, and Lithuania—are among the most successful "new democracies" to emerge from the end of the Cold War.

The Diplomatic and Trade Relationship Between Russia and Estonia

Alone among the three Baltic states, Estonia regained its independence completely without bloodshed. It began to call itself "the Republic of Estonia" in 1990. It declared full independence in August 1991, during the coup against Gorbachev. The Supreme Soviet of the USSR (the legislature) officially recognized Estonia as an independent country on 6 September 1991.

But the transition was not all smooth as silk. Estonia wanted Soviet troops off its soil as soon as possible. Moscow objected. Kremlin officials said they had no place else to house the troops.

Meanwhile, the Russian civilians who made up a significant minority of Estonia's population had a rude awakening. They found that a new law would require them to speak Estonian fluently if they wanted to qualify automatically for citizenship. Most of them wouldn't meet the new standard. The Soviet government cried foul. This was a human rights violation, Moscow insisted. The Kremlin signaled that Soviet troops would stay put in Estonia until the issue was resolved.

One of the sticking points was the pace of Russian withdrawal from Paldiski, some 20 miles from the Estonian capital. The Soviet navy had a base there with two nuclear submarine training reactors.

The Russians under Peter the Great first occupied Estonia's capital, Tallinn, in the eighteenth century. This view shows part of the old city.

Photo by Melanie Stetson Freeman / © 1989 The Christian Science Monitor

The country's modern transport and communications links mean it has great potential as a safe bridge for trade between the Nordic countries and northwest Russia.

Moscow kept control of the reactors until 1995, although its last warship sailed out of port in 1994. As for the Soviet troops in Estonia, the few remaining also left in 1994. And by then they were once again Russian soldiers, rather than Soviet troops.

There was also a dispute over some 750 square miles of territory. The Soviet Union had granted this to Estonia in 1920. But Stalin had annexed it directly to the Soviet Union in 1945. In the 1990s Estonia pushed to have the land returned. The Russians resisted, and in the end Estonia gave in. But it was a measure of how far the mighty Soviet Union had fallen that plucky little Estonia, with not even 1.5 million people, felt it could press the issue.

Through all this Estonia did not want to go undefended. The likelihood that Estonia would ever be able to defend itself against the only country likely ever to attack it—Russia—was remote. But that didn't stop the Estonians. During the 1990s they worked to build up their armed forces. They appointed an Estonian émigré named Aleksander Einseln as their commander. An émigré is *someone who leaves his country, especially during war*. Einseln left Estonia in 1944 when the Russians marched on the small country. He eventually came to America and became a citizen.

Because Einseln was a US citizen and a retired US Army colonel at the time Estonia contacted him, the US State Department objected forcefully to his appointment. It feared Russia would be upset if former US military personnel served in high posts in the former Soviet republics. Several US senators intervened in the matter, however, and that calmed the waters.

More recently, Russia has complained that Estonia does not do enough to maintain Soviet-era war memorials or to investigate when they are vandalized. In northern Estonia, unknown vandals have twice attacked a monument to soldiers who died fighting Hitler's force in 1944. In April 2007 mass protests greeted Estonian efforts to remove a Soviet-era monument and the graves of some World War II-era Soviet soldiers from the center of Tallinn, the capital. Riots ensued, in which more than 1,000 people were arrested.

Estonia's new relationships with the West mean that it trades much less with Russia than it did with the old Soviet Union. But Estonia sits at a crossroads between East and West. Its modern transport and communications links mean it has great potential as a safe bridge for trade between the Nordic countries and northwest Russia. Looking further into the future, many observers foresee a role for Estonia as a link in the supply chain between the rest of the EU and the Far East.

The Diplomatic and Trade Relationship Between Russia and Latvia

Like Estonia, Latvia looks west to new allies and trade partners. But it looks over its shoulder to the east often enough to keep an eye on the Russian bear. The issues that arose as Latvia tried to slip free of the bear's hug track the Estonian experience very closely.

Once again, the Soviet Union pressed for citizenship rights for ethnic Russians who had settled in the Baltic states only as part of Stalin's occupation. Once again, the Soviets insisted on keeping troops in place as a bargaining chip on the citizenship issue. Once again, the Soviets argued that they couldn't withdraw their troops because they had no housing for them back home. (Latvia helped answer that argument by getting some of its Western friends, including the United States, to fund construction of new housing for Russian troops in Russia.)

And as in Estonia, the Soviets claimed that a sensitive military installation in Latvia prevented their pulling out. In this case it was a radar base at Skrunda, part of its antimissile early warning system.

Latvian citizens go about their daily activities in downtown Riga about the time of independence.

Photo by Melanie Stetson Freeman / © 1990 The Christian Science Monitor

Latvia exports more than six times as much to the EU as to the former Soviet republics.

Latvia's Embassies in Waiting

One of the challenges of becoming an independent nation is setting up a foreign policy apparatus from scratch. That means setting up a foreign ministry, and finding diplomats to represent the new country in foreign capitals. After all, every independent country needs an agency to manage its relations with other countries. That's what the US State Department does for the United States.

Latvia wasn't really starting from scratch, however. It had been independent between the world wars. And as the Soviet Union neared its end, Latvia had a group of people thinking about foreign policy. They were a kind of government in exile, preparing to lead.

What's more, throughout the years of Soviet domination, Latvians maintained embassies in Washington and elsewhere. Their officials had no real power, since their government had ceased to exist. But the Latvian embassies maintained outposts of what had once been a free country. The United States never recognized the Soviet takeover of the three Baltic states.

Before World War II, the Latvian government brought gold and cash to the United States for safekeeping. Money from these funds continued to finance these embassies during the Soviet era. And through them, Latvians made useful contacts and got advice from host governments. So when Latvia regained independence in 1991, it had people ready to lead.

The Latvia that regained independence in 1991 is slightly smaller than the Latvia Stalin took over during World War II. Unlike the Estonians, though, the Latvians never demanded their little strip of territory back. But they were reluctant to sign a new border treaty that would formalize the Russian land grab. In the end they did, and the new treaty went into effect at the end of 2007.

Russia remains Latvia's largest non-EU trade partner. But EU imports into Latvia, by value, outweigh those of all former Soviet republics more than 4 to 1. And Latvia exports more than six times as much to the EU as to the former Soviet republics.

The Diplomatic and Trade Relationship Between Russia and Lithuania

Lithuania had the most difficult transition back to independence of all the Baltic states. It declared itself an independent state on 11 March 1990. Gorbachev, as leader of the Soviet Union, informally agreed not to use force against the Lithuanians. In return, the West agreed not to push the Soviets to accept Lithuanian independence.

Things changed, however, on the night of 13 January 1991. Soviet troops attacked a TV tower in Vilnius, the Lithuanian capital. They killed 14 civilians and injured 700. Gorbachev, it turned out, had authorized the use of force after all. After that, Western nations no longer felt bound by their earlier promise. They started recognizing independent Lithuania one by one. On 6 September 1991 the Soviet Union, then in its last months, recognized Lithuania along with the other Baltic states

As with the other Baltic states, the question of Soviet troop withdrawals arose in Lithuania. So did the claim from Moscow that it lacked housing for its officers in Russia. Ultimately, though, Soviet troops did pull out, ahead of schedule and a year earlier than from Estonia and Latvia.

Lithuania and Russia began a new chapter in their relationship after that, including working together on economic matters. The two countries took a while to exchange ambassadors, though. And Lithuania continued to complain about Russian violations of its airspace.

In the years since, Vilnius has found escaping from Soviet economic policies harder than ousting Soviet troops. As part of the Soviet Union, Lithuania acquired an economic base in line with what you've read about so far: heavily industrial. Its farm sector was heavily mechanized, dependent on chemicals, and not very productive. Output improved, but only at a cost to the environment.

The availability of cheap Soviet energy had gotten Lithuanians into some bad habits. Their economy used too much energy. It didn't use resources wisely. Ninety percent of its products went to the Soviet Union. That was perhaps just as well because Lithuanian goods wouldn't have held their own in world markets.

All that had to change. The Lithuanians had to privatize most state-owned business. This they did successfully. And they had to cut their trading links to the East and retool, literally, to deal with the West.

A few figures show how dramatically Lithuania shifted in just a few years. In 1997 Lithuania was sending 45 percent of its exports to the former Soviet Union. By 2006 that number had fallen to 21 percent. And by that year, 63 percent of Lithuanian exports went to members of the European Union. Some of those members were once part of the Soviet bloc. The shift shows how Lithuania is trading not only with new partners, but also with familiar partners who have changed their own systems.

The Political and Economic Influence of Russia on Armenia, Georgia, and Azerbaijan

The Baltic states' greatest challenger over the centuries has been Russia. But three small countries at the Russian Federation's southern border have been squeezed repeatedly not only by Russia, but by the Turks and the Persians (Iranians) as well. Armenia, Georgia, and Azerbaijan are the three countries that make up this southern region known as the Caucasus—the region between the Black and Caspian Seas. Territorial disputes and violence have marred their transitions to independence.

The Diplomatic and Trade Relationship Between Russia and Armenia

Armenia is a much-invaded country at the hinge of Europe and Asia. The Ottoman Turks ruled it until 1918. It was briefly independent. Then it became part of the Soviet Union in 1920. But on 21 September 1991 it once again declared its independence.

Signs written in Roman letters show how Azerbaijan has changed since the Soviet days when everything was written in the Cyrillic alphabet.
Photo by Robert Harbison / © 1997 The Christian Science Monitor

Azerbaijan, Armenia, and Georgia have been squeezed over the centuries not only by Russia, but by the Turks and the Persians as well.

The top item on Armenia's foreign policy agenda is the territory of Nagorno-Karabakh. Its dispute is with Azerbaijan. But Russia likes to stay involved in what its politicians call the "near abroad." So the issue has a Russian side to it, too.

Armenia deals with Russia in other contexts, as well. Like many other former Soviet republics, it depends on Russian fuel imports. These cost more nowadays. Soon Armenia will be paying world-market prices for Russian oil and gas. Armenia gets almost all of its electricity, though, from other sources. Nuclear power provides 40 percent, hydropower 30 percent, and thermal energy 30 percent.

Since independence, Armenia has restructured its economy. It has carried out wide-ranging reforms. These have led to lower inflation and steady growth. Armenia exports more of its goods to Russia than to any other country. Germany and the Netherlands aren't far behind, though. Russia is also Armenia's No. 1 source of imports. Ukraine and Kazakhstan are in second and third place.

The Diplomatic and Trade Relationship Between Russia and Georgia

While Armenia was under Ottoman rule, Georgia was under Russian rule. Georgia, too, had a brief period of independence after the October Revolution before it fell under Soviet rule. Indeed, some of the most notorious Soviet leaders were Georgians, such as Stalin and his murderous secret police chief, Lavrenti Beria.

A man greets visitors to the house where Stalin was born in Gori, Georgia.
Photo by Melanie Stetson Freeman / © 1990 The Christian Science Monitor

Some of the most notorious Soviet leaders were Georgians, such as Stalin and his murderous secret police chief, Lavrenti Beria.

This house with many balconies is typical of the architecture in old Tbilisi, Georgia.
Photo by Melanie Stetson Freeman / © 1990 The Christian Science Monitor

Despite a war that Georgia and Russia fought most recently in 2008 over a breakaway province, the two countries maintain trade ties. Georgia imports more than twice as much as it exports.

Georgia declared its independence anew in March 1991. After a few rough years, it began to stabilize in 1995. But marred elections and massive corruption marked this period, too. Since 2004, however, President Mikheil Saakashvili's government has helped turn the country into a maturing market democracy. Sweeping reforms have decentralized power. Local governments now have more authority. And Georgian elections have been largely free and fair.

Two separatist conflicts affect Georgia's relations with Russia. One is in Abkhazia in western Georgia, where the Commonwealth of Independent States (CIS) maintains a peacekeeping force. The troops making up this force are all Russian, however. A UN force also maintains a presence there. Abkhazia declared its independence from Georgia in the early 1990s, and the territory often sides with Russia when there is tension in the region.

fastFACT

After the Soviet Union collapsed, 12 of the 15 republics (minus the Baltic countries) decided to band together in the Commonwealth of Independent States. The CIS loosely coordinates economic, trade, and security policies. Ukraine and Turkmenistan are not full members, and as this is written, Georgia is withdrawing.

South Ossetia in north-central Georgia is the other region attempting to break away. It has asserted its independence since the early 1990s. But Saakashvili campaigned for president on a promise to regain control over the region. This led to a brief war with Russia in August 2008.

Russia intervened on the side of the South Ossetians. Russian President Dmitry Medvedev said Russia had to defend South Ossetia's civilians. Russia has offered them Russian citizenship, and most of them have accepted it.

A French-brokered cease-fire took effect on 12 August 2008. On 26 August Russia recognized the independence of both Abkhazia and South Ossetia. Human rights observers have faulted both Georgia and Russia, as well as the separatists, for their actions in South Ossetia. And while Russia's actions drew wide condemnation, some argued that Saakashvili should have held his fire, too.

Despite the war, Georgia and Russia maintain trade ties. Georgia imports more than twice as much as it exports. Russia is more important to Georgia as a source of imports than as a market for exports. In 2006 the Russians banned the import of Georgian wine, mineral water, and agricultural products and severed transportation links.

Georgia's economy is built on heavy industry—steel, aircraft, machine tools, and the like. It exports to Turkey, the United States, Azerbaijan, Britain, Bulgaria, and Ukraine, as well as Russia.

The Diplomatic and Trade Relationship Between Russia and Azerbaijan

Azerbaijan is an oil state whose people are mostly Shia Muslim. Russians, Persians, and Ottoman Turks have fought over its territory through the centuries. Its current borders go back to 1828. That's when the Russians split the territory with the Persians.

Four young women enjoy a view of the Caspian Sea from a promenade in Azerbaijan's capital, Baku.
Photo by Robert Harbison / © 1997 The Christian Science Monitor

Azerbaijan is an oil state whose people are mostly Shia Muslim.

Nagorno-Karabakh and Other "Frozen Conflicts"

Nagorno-Karabakh is the main foreign-policy issue for both Armenia and Azerbaijan. This territory is within Azerbaijan. But its people are mostly ethnic Armenians. During Soviet rule, Moscow considered the territory "autonomous"—meaning it had a limited degree of self-rule.

In 1988 the ethnic Armenians began to protest because they were unhappy with Azerbaijan. They voted to link their territory to Armenia. In July 1988 the Supreme Soviet (council or legislature) of Nagorno-Karabakh voted to secede from Azerbaijan. The Supreme Soviet of Armenia voted to make the territory part of Armenia. It did this even though Armenia had no common border with the territory. The Supreme Soviet of Azerbaijan immediately voted to declare the Armenian vote null and void.

In 1990 violence broke out, with Azeris, the main ethnic group in Azerbaijan, attacking ethnic Armenians. Moscow declared a state of emergency in Nagorno-Karabakh. It sent in troops. It also forcibly occupied the Azerbaijani capital, Baku, as well as the seaside town of Sumgait.

The Soviet Union was collapsing as all this played out. In April 1991 Azerbaijani militia and Soviet troops targeted Armenian paramilitaries in Nagorno-Karabakh. Moscow also sent troops into the Armenian capital, Yerevan.

But on 30 August 1991 Azerbaijan declared independence from the Soviet Union. Things changed after that. Soon Moscow said it would no longer support Azerbaijani military action in the disputed territory. Armenian militants then stepped up the violence. In October 1991 the voters of Nagorno-Karabakh chose independence.

Eventually all-out war broke out. More than 30,000 people died between 1992 and 1994. A cease-fire has held since 1994. But negotiations have not yet led to real peace. Russia co-chairs the Minsk Group, which is leading these talks. The Minsk Group is part of the Organization for Security and Cooperation in Europe.

Nagorno-Karabakh is one of four so-called "frozen conflicts" within the former Soviet Union. The two breakaway regions of Georgia are also part of this group. So is Transnistria in Moldova. These places have seen actual war at times, followed by long peace talks. The talks haven't led to peace but have mostly kept a lid on violence. Many accuse Russia of supporting the separatists to stir up trouble in the former Soviet republics.

All four separatist regions seek independence from states that don't want to let them go. And all four are finding it hard to win international recognition.

Azerbaijan's history is like that of its neighbors. After czarist rule, the country had a brief window of independence. Then came a time as a republic within the Soviet Union.

But Azerbaijan was one of the few places to suffer bloodshed as the Soviet Union broke up. During the 1980s Azeri nationalism began to stir again. In January 1990 Soviet troops killed 190 Azeri demonstrators. (This was related to the conflict over Nagorno-Karabakh.) Soon after that Azerbaijan declared its sovereignty. On 30 August 1991 it became independent once again.

Like Armenia, Azerbaijan's trade links extend both east and west. Italy, in fact, edges out Russia as its leading trade partner. Azeri trade with the EU and other Western countries, as well as with Iran, is on the rise. Trade with the former Soviet Union is on the decline. The main Azeri exports are oil and gas, chemicals, oil field equipment, textiles, and cotton. Durable consumer goods, food, and textiles account for most Azeri imports.

The Political and Economic Influence of Russia on Kazakhstan, Kyrgyzstan, Uzbekistan, Tajikistan, and Turkmenistan

As with other former Soviet republics, Kazakhstan, Kyrgyzstan, Uzbekistan, Tajikistan, and Turkmenistan's relations with Russia are constantly evolving. For the first time in modern history, these five Central Asian republics are independent countries. All remain closely tied to Russia and to one another. But some manage their relations with Russia from a position of strength, and others from a position of weakness.

The Diplomatic and Trade Relationship Between Russia and Kazakhstan

Parts of Kazakhstan came under Russian control voluntarily. Other parts the Russians simply took over. Kazakhstan was an important Central Asian base for Russia during the days of "the Great Game," Russia's competition with Britain in Central Asia. But the Kazakhs pushed back against Russian domination. They wanted to keep their nomadic lifestyle. They rebelled repeatedly, first against czarist rule and later against the Communists. And many fled to China.

The Soviets turned the grasslands of Kazakhstan into a grain belt. During World War II they exploited Kazakhstan's mineral resources, and conscripted its people into the armed forces. Five national divisions of draftees served in the Soviet war effort.

Kazakhs enjoy tea in their log hut in southern Russia.

Photo by R. Norman Matheny / © 1996 The Christian Science Monitor

Over the centuries, the nomadic Kazakhs have rebelled repeatedly, first against czarist rule and later against the Communists.

By the 1980s Kazakhstan was experiencing the same tensions and calls for reform as were other parts of the Soviet Union. On 16 December 1991 Kazakhstan declared independence.

Under President Nursultan Nazarbayev, Kazakhstan largely transformed its command economy into a free-market system. Its energy resources made its transition easier.

From the start, Nazarbayev tried to find a place for Kazakhstan as a bridge between East and West, Europe and Asia. As a newly independent country, Kazakhstan found out that nuclear weapons get people's attention. At the Soviet Union's dissolution, Kazakhstan found itself a nuclear power because many Soviet weapons happened to be based on its soil.

Kazakhstan quickly won diplomatic recognition and membership in international organizations. President Nazarbayev signed the Strategic Arms Reduction Treaty (START) and its so-called Lisbon Protocol. This committed Kazakhstan, along with Belarus and Ukraine, to give up nuclear weapons. In May 1995 the Kazakhs destroyed the last nuclear warhead on their soil. They met their goal of being "nuclear free."

Kazakhstan has stable relations with all its neighbors. It has led efforts to get former Soviet republics, including Russia, to work together as a regional community. These have met with only mixed success, however. In 1992 Kazakhstan also tried to broker peace in Nagorno-Karabakh. The idea was not only to resolve this specific conflict, but to set a precedent for settling similar conflicts within the former Soviet republics.

Kazakhstan is a large country, as big as all of Western Europe, and an ethnically diverse one. More than one-quarter of its people are ethnic Russians. Emigration means there are fewer of them than before, though. Many Kazakhs speak Russian, however. Russian is the "official" language: Kazakh is the "state" language.

One of the most important symbols of Russia-Kazakhstan cooperation is the Baykonur space complex. This was the main launching center for the Soviet space program; Russia now leases it from Kazakhstan.

The Diplomatic and Trade Relationship Between Russia and Kyrgyzstan

The land the Kyrgyz Republic occupies became part of the Russian Empire in 1876. Under communism, the country became the Kyrgyz Soviet Socialist Republic.

The early years of Gorbachev's glasnost had little effect there. Nationalism stirred within the population, but economics worked against this movement. Indeed, in March 1991, 88.7 percent of the voters approved a proposal to maintain the Soviet Union as a "renewed federation."

But within months the winds had changed. On 19 August 1991 the coup against Gorbachev began. At the same time, Askar Akayev, the Kyrgyz Republic's reform-minded president, became a target of plotters as well.

After the coup against Gorbachev collapsed, Akayev and his vice president quit the Soviet Communist Party. The whole Politburo and secretariat—*the offices that manage a country's or an organization's affairs*—resigned their posts. On 31 August 1991 the legislature voted to declare independence. On 21 December 1991 the Kyrgyz Republic formally joined the new Commonwealth of Independent States.

Kyrgyzstan has close ties to other former Soviet republics, particularly Kazakhstan and Russia. And it has been alert to Russian concerns about Russian-speaking minorities in former Soviet republics. Russian is an "official language" under the Kyrgyz constitution.

Kyrgyz economic relations have been less smooth at times. Kyrgyzstan resented Russian restrictions in the so-called ruble zone, of which it was part. This was a trading organization that used the ruble as a common currency. And so Kyrgyzstan introduced its own currency, the *som*.

Kyrgyzstan failed, though, to warn its neighbors Kazakhstan and Uzbekistan about the currency change. These two countries feared an influx of rubles and a spike in inflation. Both neighbors halted trade for a time. The crisis soon calmed, though. In January 1994 the three countries formed an economic union. Since then, the Kyrgyz Republic has pushed regional cooperation. It has held joint military exercises with troops from Uzbekistan and Kazakhstan, for instance.

These same two countries, along with Russia, are among Kyrgyzstan's leading trade partners. So are Switzerland and China. Kyrgyz exports include cotton, wool, meat, tobacco, gold, mercury, uranium, hydropower, machinery, and shoes. Kyrgyz imports come from Russia, China, Kazakhstan, and Uzbekistan. They include oil and gas, machinery and equipment, and foodstuffs.

The Diplomatic and Trade Relationship Between Russia and Uzbekistan

Russia is Uzbekistan's leading trade partner. A little more than a quarter of Uzbekistan's exports go to Russia; the same share of its imports comes from there. Ukraine and Kazakhstan are two other important trade partners. And trade with non-CIS partners has grown, too. The European Union, Turkey, South Korea, and Japan figure prominently.

Uzbekistan maintains close ties to Russia. In November 2005 it signed a mutual defense treaty with Moscow. Uzbekistan also seeks stronger ties to China to balance its relationship with Russia.

A mother brings her baby to be blessed at the Pakhlavan Makhmud Mausoleum in Khiva, Uzbekistan.
Photo by Robert Harbison / © 1996 The Christian Science Monitor

Uzbekistan seeks stronger ties to China to balance its relationship with Russia.

Like many of its neighbors, Uzbekistan is something of a "joiner." Since independence it has joined groups as varied as the Organization of the Islamic Conference and NATO's Partnership for Peace. It's also joined some of the groups that have developed within the former Soviet Union. Some of these groups include Russia; others do not. Uzbekistan also supports US efforts against worldwide terrorism. It has taken part in a number of peacekeeping forces in Central Asia.

The Diplomatic and Trade Relationship Between Russia and Tajikistan

Tajikistan is an example of a poor country falling back under Russian sway even though it's still independent. It first came under the Russian Empire's control during the late nineteenth and early twentieth centuries. Russian rule lapsed for a few years after 1917. But the Bolsheviks soon reasserted Russian control. Tajikistan became a Soviet socialist republic in 1929.

As the Soviet Union broke up in 1991, Tajikistan became independent again. But it soon fell into civil war. By 1997 the two main factions had reached a power-sharing peace agreement. This took effect in 2000.

Tajikistan shares an 800-mile border with Afghanistan. The last Russian border guards protecting this frontier pulled out only in 2005. But an army division, the 201st Motorized Rifles, has never left.

Tajikistan is one of the poorest countries in the world. During the Soviet era, Moscow gave aid amounting to up to 23 percent of the Tajik GDP. Today Tajikistan depends on exports of cotton and aluminum for its foreign revenue. It also counts on money sent back home by Tajiks working abroad. Most of these are in Russia.

Tajikistan exports more to the West than before. Most of its imports, though, are from within the CIS. Electricity, natural gas, and oil come from Uzbekistan and Russia. Grain comes from Kazakhstan.

Like many former Soviet republics, Tajikistan looked westward in the first years of its independence. But more recently it has turned back toward Moscow. Russia has taken a harder foreign-policy line in recent years. Moscow has shown itself willing to fight for, or at least over, former Soviet territory. In August 2008 it fought the brief war with Georgia over the breakaway region of South Ossetia, for instance. And the Tajiks have taken note. Just weeks after Russia's involvement in South Ossetia, Tajik President Emomali Rakhmon agreed with his Russian counterpart that Russia would increase its military presence in Tajikistan.

The Diplomatic and Trade Relationship Between Russia and Turkmenistan

From the sixteenth century on, raiders on horseback went after the caravans that passed through Turkmenistan. The raiders pillaged and took prisoners for the slave trade. When the czar's armies thundered into Central Asia to consolidate his empire, their excuse was that they were looking to free Russian citizens.

By 1894 Turkmenistan was part of the Russian empire. Thirty years later, the Turkmen Republic was part of the Soviet Union. On 27 October 1991 Turkmenistan regained independence.

This didn't mean a flowering of democracy, though. Rather, the Turkmens traded authoritarian rule from Moscow for a despot closer to home. Saparmyrat Niyazov was the new republic's first president. He remained the supreme decision maker and "president for life" until his death in 2006.

His successor took office after a popular vote. But Turkmenistan otherwise retains much of the worst of the old Soviet Union. It has a centrally planned economy. The government restricts personal liberties by requiring internal passports, for instance. And no political opposition is allowed.

Some 85 percent of the citizens are ethnic Turkmens. Another 4 percent are ethnic Russians. Turkmen is the official language. But the 1992 constitution refers to Russian as a "language of interethnic communication."

Turkmenistan is an important producer of oil and gas. Its natural gas reserves are significant, though probably not so great as it would like the world to believe. It is the No. 2 gas producer within the former Soviet Union, behind Russia. This gives it an energy independence that other countries might envy. To bring its gas to market, however, Turkmenistan must rely on Russia because most of the pipelines run across Russia.

Russia is one of Turkmenistan's leading trade partners. The two countries are also involved in some water resource issues. Among them are marine boundaries in the Caspian Sea.

Russia's Continuing Influence

By now you see that it's difficult to make general statements about the former Soviet republics. They all have very different relationships with Russia and with each other. In many cases, these relationships depend on geography and history. The Baltic states, for example, lie close to the West and have direct land and sea connections. For centuries they traded with the West. They have cultures influenced by the Roman Catholic or Lutheran churches and use the Roman alphabet. So it's only logical that they would have quickly reasserted these ties after independence.

But geography isn't everything. Ukraine and Belarus are Slavic neighbors, yet one is a democracy and the other a dictatorship. In the Central Asian republics, respect for democracy and human rights varies widely, as you have read. These republics are still working out their relations with Russia, each other, and the rest of the Islamic world.

One common fact remains, however: Russia is still the dominant figure in the territory of the former Soviet Union. With a large population, huge territory, vast resources, and a still-powerful military, Russia will remain a major player in the neighborhood for a long time to come. For the leaders of the other republics, this is a fact of life they will always have to take into account.

Lesson 3 Review

Using complete sentences, answer the following questions on a sheet of paper.

1. How have Ukraine and Belarus behaved differently since the breakup of the Soviet Union?
2. Why is wine so important to Moldova, and why did Russia lift its ban on Moldovan wines?
3. What caused the three independent Baltic states to become part of the Soviet Union?
4. How was Lithuania's transition to independence more difficult than that of the other Baltic States?
5. What did Georgian President Mikheil Saakashvili promise to do in his election campaign?
6. What are four "frozen conflicts" of the former Soviet Union?
7. As the Soviet Union dissolved, Kazakhstan found itself in possession of which major item that got people's attention? What did it do with these?
8. How has Turkmenistan retained much of the worst of the old Soviet Union?

Applying Your Learning

9. Do you think the brief war between Russia and Georgia in August 2008 was a reason for NATO to act swiftly on Ukraine and Georgia's membership requests—or to slow down? Explain.

LESSON 4 Russia and World Relationships

Quick Write

What does the tradition of doctored maps tell you about Russia?

Learn About

- the historic relationship between Russia and the United Nations
- the historic relationships between Russia and neighboring European nations
- the historic relationships between Russia and China, Japan, and Korea
- the historic relationship between Russia and the United States

Bruce Morrow is an American oil engineer who spent three frustrating years in Siberia. He worked for a joint venture of BP, the British energy giant, and some Russian investors at the Samotlor oil field. Morrow told a reporter with *The New York Times* in 2005 that he could never tell from the maps the Russians gave him just where he was. The maps showed no latitude or longitude, and their grid diverged from true north.

Morrow said he knew that these maps were the work of a special group of map doctors at his company. They were following a practice well known during the Cold War, but deeply rooted in Russian history. It's called *maskirovka*: a Soviet military term for "deception, disinformation, and deceit," the *Times* wrote.

During the Cold War, maps were doctored for security reasons—in this case, to protect the Siberian oil fields from missile strikes, according to the *Times*. The practice has continued in recent times, partly to keep some control over foreigners like Morrow, and partly to keep a special class of Russian cartographers employed. People know about mapping programs like Google Earth. But foreign workers like Morrow hear rumors of jail time for those who turn to it. Map doctoring also serves as a subtle trade barrier: It makes it harder for foreign firms to do business in Russia.

According to rules enforced by the Russian Federal Security Service (known by the Russian acronym FSB), or secret police, accurate large-scale maps are available only to those with a Russian security clearance, the *Times* reported. As the Kremlin tightens its control on strategic industries such as oil, it is not letting up on the map rule.

The Historic Relationship Between Russia and the United Nations

Vocabulary

- rehabilitation
- warm-water port
- détente

In Lesson 3 you read about Joseph Stalin's efforts to get a separate seat at the United Nations for each of the Soviet Union's republics. President Franklin D. Roosevelt countered that he should then get a separate seat for each of the then-48 United States. That apparently pushed Stalin to compromise on just three seats: one each for Russia, Ukraine, and Belarus. Since the Western Allies wanted the Soviets in the UN, they went along.

The churches inside the Kremlin, the government seat, are bathed in sunlight on a winter's day.
Photo by Melanie Stetson Freeman / © 2008 The Christian Science Monitor

Since the Western Allies wanted the Soviet Union in the UN after World War II, they gave Stalin three seats.

The Soviet Union's Role in Establishing the United Nations

The Soviet Union had, in fact, a founding role in the UN. President Roosevelt wanted it that way.

The United States had never joined the League of Nations, a forerunner of the UN established after World War I. Roosevelt saw the League's weaknesses. But even in the early days of World War II, he also saw value in planning for an organization to pick up where the League had left off. Even before the United States had entered the war, it joined Britain in issuing a declaration that became known as the Atlantic Charter.

The charter outlined a vision for a new world order. It would be one built in part on a more effective world body than the League. This new group's mission would be "to maintain international peace and security." Roosevelt suggested "the United Nations" as its name.

In January 1942 the governments of the United States, the Soviet Union, Britain, and China formalized the Atlantic Charter ideas. These four major Allies, plus 22 other states, agreed to work together to defeat Germany, Japan, and Italy. They committed in principle to set up the United Nations after the war.

The effort to launch the UN began in earnest at an organizing conference in San Francisco in April 1945. On 24 October 1945 the United Nations officially came into existence. The Soviet Union was one of its charter members.

Russian Influence on the UN Security Council's Veto Rights

One of the problems with the old League of Nations was that it didn't have ways to enforce its rules. Roosevelt wanted to be sure that the new United Nations had the power to make its decisions stick.

As the new world body took shape, the five major Allied powers—the United States, the Soviet Union, Britain, China, and France—accepted important roles. These countries were the major winners of World War II. (Within a few years, they would be the five countries in the world with nuclear weapons.) They became the "permanent five" members of the 15-member UN Security Council. The council is the part of the United Nations that has the most power. The other slots rotate among all the member nations.

The UN founders were practical. They knew that to be effective, the power relationships within the UN had to match those of the real world. The special status of the "permanent five" was one way to ensure this.

The word "veto" doesn't appear in the UN Charter. But the charter specifies that to pass, a Security Council resolution needs "the concurring votes of the permanent members." In Washington, when the president vetoes legislation, Congress can try to pass it again. At the UN Security Council, a single veto sinks a resolution, with no second chances.

The Soviet Union insisted on this veto right in the Security Council. It also insisted that any changes to the UN Charter have unanimous approval of all five permanent members. British Prime Minister Winston Churchill and Roosevelt understood that veto rights were the price of Soviet participation in the new system. Along with membership for Ukraine and Belarus, it was a price they were willing to pay.

fastFACT

In the Soviet period, Ukraine was called the *Ukrainian Soviet Socialist Republic.* Belarus was the *Byelorussian Soviet Socialist Republic.*

How the Soviet Union Used Its Veto Power

A turning point in Soviet policy at the United Nations came in January 1950. China had just gone through a revolution. Communists had taken over, and the Nationalist government had fled to Taiwan. As far as the UN was concerned, though, the government on Taiwan was the "real" China and entitled to a seat on the Security Council. The Soviet Union, unsurprisingly, felt differently. In a show of solidarity with the Chinese Communists, its envoys boycotted UN functions. (The Communist government was finally awarded the seat in 1971.)

Russians walk across Red Square—next to the Kremlin—in front of a mall that used to be the state department store, GUM.
Photo by Melanie Stetson Freeman / © 2008 The Christian Science Monitor

The Soviet Union insisted that any changes to the UN Charter have unanimous approval of all five permanent members of the Security Council.

In June of that year, North Korea attacked South Korea. With no Soviet representative at the table, the Security Council passed a resolution that the Soviets would otherwise have vetoed. It called for the intervention of UN military forces in Korea. The Soviets would not make this mistake again. Their return in August 1950 marked the beginning of a new period of active participation at the UN.

In the UN's first 10 years, the Soviet Union issued 79 vetoes. During that period China used its veto once and France, twice. Britain and the United States issued no vetoes at all. Soviet vetoes became so routine that Andrei Gromyko, the longtime Soviet foreign minister, was nicknamed "Mr. Nyet"—"Mr. No."

Over time, the Soviets used their veto less. And post-communist Russia, as successor state to the Soviet Union, has used the veto scarcely at all. The Soviets understood the veto as a way to prevent UN action in areas they saw as properly within their sphere of influence. That's why the Korean vote mattered to the Soviets. In hindsight, they realized they should have been there to block it. The veto was also a way to maintain their influence and to protect friends and allies. Since the end of the Cold War, the permanent members have tried to work out their differences before bringing resolutions to a vote.

The Historic Relationships Between Russia and Neighboring European Nations

To understand Russian behavior in more recent times, it helps to reach back a little further into the past. Russia's history with its European neighbors is one of invasions and counterinvasions. Poland and Lithuania, both Soviet satellites in the twentieth century, were relentless invaders of czarist Russia. So was Sweden, even though it's known today as militarily neutral.

Russia played major roles as a US, British, and French ally during both world wars. During World War II, its participation was decisive in turning the tide against Nazi Germany.

Russia's experiment with Soviet communism had repercussions across Europe. *Ten Days That Shook the World* was the name of one well-known book about the revolution that created the Soviet Union. It was an apt title. And the undoing of that revolution 70 years later would reverberate equally widely.

The Centuries of European Invasions of Russia

Students of twentieth-century history may not think of the Soviet Union as a victim. But for centuries, Russia was on the receiving end of invasions.

Consider the early years of the seventeenth century, for instance. In Moscow, this was a chaotic period known as "the Time of Troubles." Rivalry among the nobility complicated a struggle over the throne. Then Poland and Sweden—serious regional powers—stepped in. A Polish garrison backed one claimant to the throne.

Tourists cross the famed plaza in front of the Hermitage—the czars' former Winter Palace, now an art museum—in St. Petersburg, Russia.
Photo by R. Norman Matheny / © 1993 The Christian Science Monitor

Peter the Great built St. Petersburg on land he took from the Swedes in the early eighteenth century.

Another contender turned to the Swedes for support. Then a third claimant, allied with the Poles, appeared. He was proclaimed czar, and the Poles occupied Moscow. This whole period is also known as the Polish-Muscovite War (1605–18).

In 1707 King Charles XII of Sweden invaded Russia. He and Peter the Great attacked and counterattacked each other repeatedly. Peter eventually built his new westward-looking capital, St. Petersburg, on land he took over from the Swedes. He would have said it was land he took back from the Swedes.

In 1812 French Emperor Napoleon I invaded Russia. This episode ends rather better for the Russians. Czar Alexander I was at one point an ally of the French leader. But the alliance became strained. Alexander worried about the intentions of the Poles, whom France controlled. Napoleon worried about Alexander's plans for two vital straits between the Black and Mediterranean Seas, the Dardanelles and the Bosporus.

Napoleon decided to invade Russia with 600,000 troops—twice as many soldiers as the Russian army had. But the Russian winter turned out to be Alexander's most important ally. Although Napoleon took Moscow, fewer than 30,000 of Napoleon's men made the trip back home. And as Napoleon retreated in defeat, Alexander pursued him—to the gates of Paris. When Russia and its allies, such as Britain and Spain, finally defeated Napoleon, Alexander was hailed as Europe's savior and was given considerable say in redrawing the map of Europe at the subsequent peace conference.

The invasions did not stop with the dawn of the twentieth century. Germany invaded Russia during both world wars.

The Russian Roles in World Wars I and II

World War I

World War I was czarist Russia's last war and formed the background for the two revolutions of 1917. Russia had allied with Britain, France, and Belgium against Austro-Hungary and Germany. Its large population meant it could field a large army. Its soldiers held up well against the Austrians, who were as poorly armed as the Russians were. The Russians had far less success against the Germans, however.

Through the war's early years, the advantage seesawed between the Germans and the Allies. At first, Russia's moves into the German state of East Prussia drew enough German troops from the western front to let the French, Belgians, and British stop the German advance. Then one of Russia's armies was almost wiped out in the disastrous Battle of Tannenberg. And so it went.

A monument in St. Petersburg commemorates the reign of Czar Nicholas I, who fought the Crimean War against Britain, France, and the Ottoman Empire. *Photo by Robert Harbison / © 1991 The Christian Science Monitor*

That war helped set the stage for World War I, czarist Russia's last war.

By 1917 the new Soviet government was eager to get Russia out of the war. It agreed to a cease-fire. Peace talks began but then broke down. Fighting resumed, though the Russian forces were crumbling. Some in the Bolshevik government sought to prolong the war—all the better to stir up class warfare and provoke revolution in Germany, they argued. But Lenin insisted that Russia had to make peace at any price. On 3 March 1918 Soviet government officials signed the Treaty of Brest-Litovsk.

St. Petersburg

St. Petersburg went through a succession of names in the twentieth century. This led to an old Soviet joke:

"What city were you born in?"
"St. Petersburg."
"What city did you grow up in?"
"Petrograd."
"What city do you live in now?"
"Leningrad."
"What city would you like to live in?"
"St. Petersburg!"

This joke came true.

With this treaty, the Soviet government gave away an enormous part of what had been the Russian Empire. It handed Poland, the Baltic lands, Finland, and Ukraine over to German control. It also gave Turkey part of the Caucasus. Moreover, the new borders came dangerously close to Petrograd—the new name for St. Petersburg. The government moved the capital back to Moscow for safety. All in all, it was a package of desperate measures. But Lenin saw no other way to ensure the new Soviet state's survival.

After the Bolsheviks won the Russian civil war, they began a campaign to retake lands that had been lost through the treaty. By 1940 they had regained everything except Finland. Soviet troops attacked Finland, but the Finns' heroic resistance kept their country independent—although they did surrender some land in the east.

World War II

Meanwhile, World War II had begun with Germany's invasion of Poland on 1 September 1939. The Soviets thought their nonaggression pact with Germany—the Molotov-Ribbentrop Pact you read about in Lesson 3—would keep the same fate from befalling them. They were wrong, however. All it would really do was buy them some time.

By the summer of 1940 Hitler's forces had overrun much of Europe. As Hitler was advancing, the Soviet Union sought to protect itself by seizing territory within its sphere of interest—such as eastern Poland and the Baltics—and attacking Finland.

Stalin kept trying to calm Hitler in the hope of avoiding war. But early in the morning of 22 June 1941, 180 German divisions swept across the border into the Soviet Union. The invasion, code-named Operation Barbarossa, nearly broke the Russians. By November the Germans had taken Ukraine. They had besieged Leningrad, as Peter the Great's city was then called. And they threatened Moscow itself.

By the end of 1941, however, the German forces had lost their momentum. Like Napoleon, the Germans struggled against the bitter Russian winter. And the Red Army had regained its footing. It was beginning to strike back.

There was a lull in the fighting over the winter of 1941–42. Then the Germans renewed their offensive. To gain control over the lower Volga River region, they decided to try to take Stalingrad, on its west bank. The Soviet forces put up fierce resistance even after the Germans had turned the city to rubble. Soviet troops finally surrounded their attackers and forced them to surrender in February 1943. It was a decisive victory. Afterward, the Soviet Union had the upper hand for the rest of the war. By January 1944 the Red Army had broken through the siege of Leningrad. By May 1945 the Soviets made it all the way to Berlin, and the war in Europe was over.

fastFACT

An estimated 650,000 to 800,000 people died in the 900-day siege of Leningrad. About 500,000 are buried in mass graves in the city's Piskaryovskoye Cemetery.

It was a great victory for the Soviet Union—one generally unappreciated in the West. World War II was also important, from a Russian perspective, in that it brought about a temporary alliance with two great powers, one new and one old—the United States and Britain. Mutual mistrust ran deep between them. But they had to cooperate to defeat Hitler. The Soviets benefited from weapons and equipment from the Western allies. By tying the Germans down and eliminating hundreds of thousands of German troops, the Soviets gave the British and Americans time to prepare to invade German-held Western Europe.

The Effect of the Cold War and the Warsaw Pact

This temporary alliance began to sour even before the Allies had won the war, however. In February 1945 Stalin met with Roosevelt and Churchill in the Ukrainian city of Yalta, on the Black Sea. They clashed over Stalin's plan to extend Soviet influence to Poland. By August of that year, Japan had surrendered. There was nothing left to hold the alliance between the Soviet Union and the Western democracies together.

The war had been devastating to victors and vanquished alike. Many survivors were just grateful to be alive. And many in the West were grateful for Soviet contributions to the war effort. But quite quickly, things began to change. More and more territory was falling under Soviet control. Cease-fire lines began to harden into de facto new international frontiers, as in Korea and Germany. Communist governments seized power. Churchill was one of the first to notice. Measures that had seemed merely defensive when the Soviets had taken them to hold Hitler at bay suddenly seemed aggressive instead.

As Churchill memorably put it in a speech he gave on 5 March 1946, at a small college in Fulton, Missouri, "From Stettin in the Baltic to Trieste in the Adriatic, an iron curtain has descended across the Continent." He ticked off the great European cities that lay behind that curtain "in what I must call the Soviet sphere." He noted that they were subject to an "increasing measure of control from Moscow."

The Cold War was a period of tension and hostility between the United States and its allies and the Soviet Union and its allies. Fortunately it never led to direct all-out conflict between the two sides. But there were many nervous moments along the way. The two did fight one another indirectly in a number of smaller, costly, and bloody wars in faraway places like Korea and Vietnam, however.

Because of Russia's long history of invasion from the West, Stalin tried to create a buffer zone of compliant "allies" around the Soviet Union. The Red Army had occupied many of these countries during the war. Afterward, taking advantage of its position as an occupying power, the Soviet Union actively helped local communist parties take power. By 1948 seven East European countries had Communist governments.

In 1949 the Western allies established the North American Treaty Organization, or NATO, a defensive alliance to protect against Soviet attack. In 1955 West Germany became a NATO member. This was an early step in the rehabilitation—*restoring one's good reputation*—of Germany back into the family of nations. The Soviet Union responded to this step by establishing the Warsaw Pact that same year.

Members of the Warsaw Pact

- The Soviet Union
- Albania (withdrew in 1968)
- Bulgaria
- Czechoslovakia
- East Germany (German Democratic Republic)
- Hungary
- Poland
- Romania

Up until that point, the Soviet Union had bilateral relationships with each of its "satellites." This word was much used to describe Eastern European nations in the Soviet "orbit." The Warsaw Pact essentially took all those one-to-one relationships and merged them into one big alliance. It was supposed to be a defensive alliance. But actually it was a way for the Soviets to keep the other members under their control. The pact used the terms "collective action" and "mutual support" as cover for Soviet domination and sometimes even military intervention into its allies' internal affairs.

Warsaw Pact forces were even used against its member nations. Soviet troops put down the Hungarian uprising of 1956. And when the Kremlin decided that Czech leader Alexander Dubcek had gone too far in a wave of liberalization known as "the Prague spring" of 1968, Warsaw Pact tanks rolled in to bring things to a stop.

The White House in Moscow was the seat of the Russian republic's parliament during the Soviet era. After the Cold War ended, it was until 1993 the home of Russia's parliament. It now houses the Russian government.
Photo by R. Norman Matheny / © 1996 The Christian Science Monitor

The Effect of Perestroika and Glasnost on Russia's Neighboring European Nations

As you read in earlier lessons in this chapter, everything changed when Mikhail Gorbachev came to power in 1985. He dropped Marxist-Leninist talk about irreconcilable conflict with the West. Instead, he stressed common moral and ethical principles.

In December 1987 he and US President Ronald Reagan signed a treaty—the Intermediate-Range Nuclear Forces Treaty (or INF)—eliminating mid-range nuclear missiles from Europe. This was an immense relief to Europeans, east and west. It led to better relations between the Soviet Union and Europe generally. But Gorbachev's new approach offered more than just relief. His policies of perestroika and glasnost—"restructuring" and "openness," respectively—set in motion big changes in the satellite nations. In fact, change came to the Eastern European countries before it came to the Soviet Union.

In June 1989 Poland's Communist government held relatively free parliamentary elections. The Communists lost every seat they contested. Hungary, meanwhile, pursued reforms, too. It also restored the reputation of Imre Nagy, the reformist leader whom the Soviets had executed after they crushed the 1956 uprising. In the summer of 1989 Hungary took down the barriers along the border with officially neutral Austria.

By the end of the summer, vacationing East Germans were pouring through this tear in the Iron Curtain. Others sought escape at the West German embassy in Prague, Czechoslovakia, now the Czech Republic. (An embassy is considered sovereign soil of the country it represents. During the years of division, West Germany offered citizenship to all Germans who reached its soil by whatever means. Once within the embassy gates in Prague, East Germans were literally home free.) Thousands temporarily camped on the embassy grounds.

It was big enough news that East Germans were voting with their feet for another life. Their country had long been held up as the big success of the Soviet bloc. But change didn't stop there. One night in November 1989 East German authorities almost absent-mindedly opened the Berlin Wall—a concrete barrier the Communists had built through the middle of Berlin in the early 1960s. That same night the Bulgarians deposed their longtime Communist leader, Todor Zhivkov. Two weeks later Czechoslovakia deposed its Communist leaders in what's known as the Velvet Revolution. At an impromptu summit in Malta in December 1989, Gorbachev and President George H. W. Bush declared an end to the Cold War.

The Historic Relationships Between Russia and China, Japan, and Korea

While much of Europe was gladly shedding its communist ties—and had tried to for decades—some forces in Russia and China were more wedded to their "red" ways. In fact, the Sino-Soviet relationship during most of the twentieth century turned on the question of whether the worldwide communist movement was big enough for both of them. The answer often appeared to be no.

In another corner of Asia, Russia's relationship with Japan got off on the wrong foot at the beginning of the twentieth century. That association is still hobbled by territorial disputes, despite the strong and growing trade ties between the two. For much of the past century, Russia's partner in Korea was the Communist North. But with the collapse of communism, Moscow has changed its mind about South Korea. It no longer dismisses Seoul as a US puppet.

Russia's Early Support for Communist China

The Communists under Mao Zedong took control of China in 1949. They had defeated the Nationalists (Kuomintang or Guomindang) with help from the Soviet Union. In 1950 China and the Soviet Union made a mutual defense treaty to protect themselves against the United States and Japan. The two communist giants were partners. But Mao drove a hard bargain in his dealings with the Russians. He signaled that, with its own Communist Party and its immense population, China would be no mere "satellite" following Moscow's dictates.

A rare sunny winter day in Moscow bathes the Kremlin wall and behind it the yellow Duma (legislature) building (right)—in warm light.

Photo by Melanie Stetson Freeman / © 2008 The Christian Science Monitor

Kremlin leaders remained neutral when tensions flared along the Sino-Indian border, displeasing China and contributing to the split between Soviet leaders and Mao Zedong.

For a time, though, the two countries were quite close. As the People's Republic of China was getting established, its leaders had a pressing domestic agenda. And with so much to do, they felt that their best approach to foreign policy was to stand with other communist countries against the United States and Japan. China had no choice, Mao declared, but to "lean to one side" in international relations. By that he meant the Soviet side.

The Break Between Soviet Leaders and Mao Zedong

During the late 1950s, though, strains emerged in the Sino-Soviet alliance. The Soviets didn't do enough, in Beijing's view, to help China regain what it considered the breakaway province of Taiwan. When tensions flared along the Sino-Indian border, the Soviet Union remained neutral. That displeased China.

What's more, Nikita Khrushchev's moves toward de-Stalinization alarmed the Chinese. So did his efforts on behalf of peaceful coexistence with the West. The Chinese under Mao considered that this violated communist doctrine.

In 1957 Moscow's successful launch of the *Sputnik* satellite was an immense boost to the prestige of the Soviet Union, and of communism generally. It strengthened Mao's view that the winds of history were blowing in the Communists' favor. "The east wind prevails over the west wind," he said. So why, then, the Chinese wondered, was the Kremlin so interested in coexistence with the West?

Finally, in 1960, after Mao introduced the radical economic policies of the "Great Leap Forward," Moscow withdrew its advisers from China. And China did not object. Mao and his colleagues had reached the point where the benefits of its Soviet alliance no longer outweighed the limits it placed on Chinese independence. In 1966, as China moved into its Cultural Revolution, the two countries' Communist Parties broke off relations. A deep freeze remained until well into the 1980s.

Current Economic Relations Between Russia and China

In more recent years, Russia and China have strengthened their ties. China takes part in the Shanghai Cooperation Organization, along with Russia and four of the Central Asian republics. A November 1997 agreement resolved almost all outstanding border issues between Russia and China. China is a major market for Russian exports, notably oil. China has overtaken Japan in recent years as the No. 2 consumer of primary energy, after the United States. Construction began in the spring of 2009 on a pipeline to carry Russian oil to China. It is expected to be up and running in 2010.

This Russian missile factory is located in Samara, along the southern Volga River.
Photo by R. Norman Matheny / © 1993 The Christian Science Monitor

China is a major market for Russian exports, notably oil. Arms sales have also been an important element of Russia's economic relations with China.

Arms sales have been an important element of Russia's economic relations with China. Between 2001 and 2009, Russian arms sales have brought in $16 billion from China. But by the end of that period, Russia was selling only about $1 billion worth of weapons to China annually.

As the network of international relations continues to expand, Russia and China work together in many different forums. By some accounts, though, their economic relations are less effective than their political ties.

Military Encounters Between Russia and Japan, 1900–45

In the Russo-Japanese War of 1904–05, Czar Nicholas II's forces faced off against those of imperial Japan. Not long before, European powers had forced Asia open to foreign trade. Many major powers were seeking to carve out a sphere of influence for themselves in Asia as they had done in Africa.

The issue between Russia and Japan was control of Korea and Manchuria (part of China today). The Russians wanted a warm-water port—*a port that does not ice up during the winter*. They had their eye on Port Arthur, in Manchuria. Unfortunately for them, so did the Japanese.

Diplomatic messages went back and forth between the two camps. The czar's more progressive-minded envoys tried to get him to accept a compromise. But his reactionary cabinet ministers kept squabbling among themselves. As a result, he had trouble putting together a coherent policy for the Far East. As the Russians dithered, the Japanese prepared to attack. And when they did, they astonished the world with their military success.

Financially, though, the war was a strain for Japan. Eventually both sides accepted President Theodore Roosevelt's offer to mediate. This led to the Treaty of Portsmouth, named for the US Navy facility in New Hampshire where it was negotiated. Among other things, the treaty awarded the use of Port Arthur to the Japanese and recognized Korea as a Japanese sphere of influence.

People remember the Russo-Japanese War as the first major military defeat of a European power at Asian hands. It was a humiliation for the Russian government. And it helped push the Russian people toward revolution.

This defeat of Russia marked the beginning of a period of poor relations with Japan. After World War I, Japan took over the key Russian port of Vladivostok for four years. The Soviet Union had a neutrality pact with Japan during much of World War II. But as the war was winding down, Stalin declared war on Japan at the Allies' request and moved to occupy vast tracts of East Asia that Japan had occupied. This led to the incorporation of the Kuril Islands and the southern half of Sakhalin Island into the Soviet Union. These moves created an issue that kept Japan and the Soviet Union from signing a peace treaty to bring the war to an official end. The issue froze Russo-Japanese relations for decades.

Soviet navy ships out of Baku, Azerbaijan, practice maneuvers in 1990.
Photo by Melanie Stetson Freeman / © 1990 The Christian Science Monitor

Japan's defeat of the Russian navy in the Russo-Japanese War of 1904–05 was a humiliation for the Russian government and helped push the Russian people toward revolution.

Russo-Japanese Economic Relations Since the Cold War

Gorbachev's ascent to power changed much in the Soviet Union. It didn't, however, change the stalemate in his country's relations with Japan. Nor did the Soviet Union's collapse erase strains between the nations. So the two countries are still technically at war, although they don't behave that way.

Russia continues to hang onto the Southern Kurils, seized by the Soviet Union as World War II was winding down. The United States considers the islands Japanese. Russian Coast Guard boats still harass or even seize Japanese fishing vessels in waters surrounding the disputed territory. In August 2006 a Russian patrol even fired on a Japanese vessel, killing a crew member. Even so, Japan and Russia find ways to work together. They are building two large energy projects on Sakhalin Island, for instance.

In addition, the volume of trade between the two has risen sharply in the first decade of the twenty-first century. According to figures from the Russian Federal Customs Service, the total value of Russo-Japanese trade increased between 2003 and 2008 from less than $5 billion to more than $50 billion. Russia buys cars (new and used) and other vehicles, as well as various types of electrical-engineering products, from Japan. Japan buys oil, timber, metal, and metal products from Russia.

Russian Support of North Korea During the Korean War and the Cold War

The division of Korea at the 38th parallel began as an administrative matter at the end of World War II. Japan had occupied Korea. When Japan went down in defeat, someone had to be there to accept the surrender of its forces in Korea. US and Soviet forces took on this duty. When the United States asked Stalin to limit his occupation to the 38th parallel, he agreed. At that point he did not have time to devote his attention to Korea. And neither side was interested in another war.

Within a few years things had changed. The US-Soviet alliance had fallen apart. Each country was arming the military forces of "its" part of Korea—Kim Il-sung in the North, and Syngman Rhee in the South. Stalin was beginning to see an opportunity to build up communism in Asia.

According to historian Mark O'Neill, in April 1950 Kim Il-sung begged Stalin for the chance to invade the South and unify Korea. It would all be over in three days, he said. Stalin agreed, as long as the Chinese promised to provide troops. Mao was desperate for Soviet aid at that point and readily agreed. He turned 60,000 ethnic Koreans in the (Chinese) People's Liberation Army over to the Korean People's Army, the North's fighting force. The invasion began 25 June 1950.

The Korean War took much longer than three days. The United States and other nations rallied to South Korea's defense. As you read earlier in this lesson, when the Korean issue came up before the United Nations Security Council, no Soviet representative was there to block a resolution. So the council authorized a "police action" to defend South Korea.

After three years of fighting, and Stalin's death, all parties agreed to an armistice, signed on 27 July 1953. No peace treaty has ever been signed. In fact, on 27 May 2009 North Korea, under the leadership of Kim Jong-il, unilaterally withdrew from the armistice.

As the split between the Soviet Union and China widened during the Cold War, North Korea leaned closer to China. Currently both Russia and China are participants in the Six-Party Talks meant to denuclearize the Korean Peninsula.

Economic Relations Between Russia and South Korea Since the Cold War

For decades, South Korea was an object of scorn for the Soviet Union, which considered it a creature of "US imperialism." The Soviet Union didn't even have diplomatic relations with Seoul until Gorbachev established them.

But since then Russia has worked to improve its ties with South Korea in many different forums, including the Six-Party Talks. With links to Japan hampered by a territorial dispute, and with China as a potential rival, Russia can look to South Korea as a new partner with which it has a less unhappy history.

Trade between Russia and South Korea was worth about $20 billion in 2008. The two countries cooperate in such sectors as energy, transport, and construction. Russia needs South Korean support in its bid to join the World Trade Organization. South Korea wants Russian energy. The two countries are also trying to link the Trans-Korean and Trans-Siberian railways.

The Historic Relationship Between Russia and the United States

In 2007 the US Embassy in Moscow celebrated 200 years of diplomatic relations between the United States and Russia. The first US minister to Russia was John Quincy Adams. In 1823, as secretary of State, he wrote the Monroe Doctrine. This historic foreign policy statement dictated that Europe keep "hands off" the Americas.

People associate the Monroe Doctrine with Latin America. They see it as a warning to any European power that would seek to take over former Spanish colonies there. But the specific issue that prompted the Monroe Doctrine had to do with imperial Russia. Czar Alexander I wanted to pursue commercial fishing in the coastal waters off the US Pacific Northwest. In 1821 he had declared the waters above the 51st parallel north under the Russian American Company's control alone. He was interested in ports as far south as San Francisco. President James Monroe would not stand for that. So he directed Secretary of State Adams to formulate the famous statement.

Another significant event in US-Russian relations took place in 1867, when Secretary of State William Seward bought Alaska from Russia for $7.2 million.

The story of US-Russian relations, though, begins in earnest in the twentieth century. Both the United States and Soviet Union fought on the Allied side during World War I, but the Soviets pulled out of the war not long after the US entry. The US-Soviet relationship during World War II was much more of a partnership.

Young Russian Army recruits chat in Moscow's Gorky Park.

Photo by Melanie Stetson Freeman / © 1999 The Christian Science Monitor

The US-Soviet relationship during World War II was a partnership.

The Relationship During World War II

Americans greeted the first Russian Revolution of 1917 with great enthusiasm. But that cooled when the Bolsheviks took power later that year. After all, the new Communist regime had not been democratically elected. Nor did it show much respect for human rights and private property. The United States, like many other governments, withheld diplomatic recognition. US policy finally changed when President Franklin Roosevelt established full relations with the Soviets in November 1933. The United States was the last major power to do so.

Within a few years, though, American opinion again turned away from the Soviets. Stalin was at that point invading Finland and seizing territory in the Baltics and elsewhere. Hitler's invasion in June 1941, though, changed American minds once more. The Soviet Union began to look less like a conqueror and more like a victim of fascism.

Under the Lend-Lease Act, the United States sent vast amounts of aid and war materiel to the Soviet Union. This was critical in helping the Russians withstand the Nazi onslaughts. Eventually, as you read earlier, the Soviet forces were able to regain the initiative against the Germans. The continuing Soviet battles with German forces in the east bought the Western Allies time to prepare for the invasion of German-held France. That Western front would eventually relieve pressure on Soviet forces.

Coordinating all this took long, intense diplomatic negotiations among "the Big Three"—Roosevelt, Churchill, and Stalin. In these talks, Roosevelt and Churchill granted Stalin some things he asked for. Others would later complain about their giving too much to the Soviet leader. But Roosevelt and Churchill thought it was necessary at the time. The Big Three also started laying the groundwork for a postwar world—one with a United Nations as a place where countries could discuss their concerns.

After a fierce battle, Berlin fell to the Soviets on 8 May 1945. The Soviets and their Western allies had met on the Elbe River in Germany beforehand to shake hands and congratulate each other on their anticipated victory. Months of fighting lay ahead against another Axis Power—Japan—however. Not until August 1945 did Japan surrender—and then only after the United States had dropped two nuclear bombs.

The US-Soviet alliance was born out of necessity. Each country knew it needed the other to defeat one of the most destructive forces of modern times. The Allies put ideology aside in the interest of winning the war against fascism.

The Soviet effort in World War II, still largely underappreciated in the West, cost more than 20 million lives. It destroyed towns and cities and laid waste to the country's economic infrastructure.

US-Soviet cooperation was a brief moment in history. It would soon be replaced by the beginnings of the Cold War. But the significance of the US-Soviet wartime effort in winning World War II cannot be overestimated.

The Cold War's Effect on Soviet-US Relations

The way the Soviets moved after World War II to assert control in the Eastern European lands they occupied angered the West—the United States in particular. But there didn't seem to be much the West could do to stop it short of going to war.

One early crisis, the Berlin Airlift, demonstrated how the West could push back against the Soviets without getting into all-out war. In 1948 the Soviets tried to cut off outside supply lines to West Berlin. Under the Western Allies' control, West Berlin nonetheless lay deep within the heart of the Soviet occupation zone in Germany. When the Soviets closed off road and rail links, the Western Allies responded by supplying the city wholly by air for nearly a year. On 12 May 1949 the Soviets lifted the blockade. The airlift became a symbol of Western resolve to stand up to the Soviets without having to engage in direct conflict.

The Cuban Missile Crisis of October 1962 was another critical point in the Cold War. US military intelligence discovered that the Soviets had installed nuclear missiles in Cuba. After several days of great tension, President John F. Kennedy's administration ultimately negotiated their removal from Cuba. But the period is widely regarded as the closest the United States ever came to nuclear war with the Soviet Union. Here, too, diplomacy, creative thinking, and a willingness to give the other side ways to "save face" helped avoid a disastrous confrontation.

Before the arrival of Gorbachev, the high point of US-Soviet relations came in May 1972. That's when leaders from the two countries signed two important arms control agreements: the Anti-Ballistic Missile Treaty and the Interim Agreement on the Limitation of Strategic Offensive Arms. This marked a period of détente, or *relaxation of international tension*, between the two countries.

The Effect of Perestroika and Glasnost on Russian-US Relations

Americans were less hopeful about Gorbachev's new ideas than were Europeans. After all, the Americans' Cold War experience was different from the Europeans'. For Americans, the Cold War was largely a drawn-out nuclear standoff with an enemy who was distant—geographically, but also culturally and ideologically.

For Europeans, the Cold War divided countries that were at least neighbors, if not always exactly friends. Eastern Europeans had only limited travel opportunities. But Western Europeans could and did visit cities like Prague, Czechoslovakia, and Budapest, Hungary. West German Chancellor Willy Brandt had already introduced his *Neue Ostpolitik*. This was a "new Eastern policy" of dialogue with the East bloc. It was hugely controversial in some quarters. But it won him the Nobel Peace Price of 1971.

Relations between the Soviets and the United States began to thaw, however, when it seemed that Ronald Reagan was hitting it off with Gorbachev. It helped that President Reagan's friend Margaret Thatcher, Britain's "Iron Lady" prime minister, had approved of Gorbachev. Her anticommunist credentials were never in doubt, and she had said, "I like Mr. Gorbachev. We can do business together."

And so, it turned out, could President Reagan. The Reagan-Gorbachev dialogue led to the INF Treaty. This accord, signed in 1987, was the ban on mid-range nuclear weapons you read about earlier in this lesson. It was the first arms-control treaty that actually called for destruction of existing weapons. Other treaties had merely set future limits on the deployment of weapons.

After Reagan left office, George H. W. Bush continued the dialogue with Gorbachev. It led, among other things, to the Strategic Arms Reduction Treaty (START) and the astonishingly swift merging of East Germany and West Germany into, once again, a single, united Germany.

With the fall of communism and the election of Boris Yeltsin as president of the new Russian state, relations between the United States and Russia grew perhaps as close as they have ever been. President George W. Bush took office hoping for a close relationship with Yeltsin's successor, Vladimir Putin. But Putin's policies led instead to a cooling of relations between the two countries. These included a brutal invasion of the breakaway Chechnya region and moves to rein in Russian business, political opposition, and the free press. Russia has also undermined American interests in the former Soviet republics as it has tried to regain its influence in what it considers its backyard.

But the two countries continue to work together in many ways that were unthinkable during the Cold War. You'll read about some of them in the next lesson.

Muscovites and tourists take advantage of a warm day at a new park just outside Red Square.
Photo by Melanie Stetson Freeman / © 1999 The Christian Science Monitor

Relations between the Soviets and the United States began to thaw when President Ronald Reagan hit it off with Mikhail Gorbachev.

Lesson 4 Review

Using complete sentences, answer the following questions on a sheet of paper.

1. When did planning for the United Nations begin?
2. Which countries make up the UN Security Council's "permanent five" and how did they get this status?
3. Which countries have invaded Russia over the centuries? Name at least three.
4. What was the Warsaw Pact?
5. How did Russia get off to a bad start in its relations with Japan?
6. How has Russia changed its view of South Korea since Gorbachev?
7. What was the Lend-Lease Act and whom did it help?
8. What did British Prime Minister Margaret Thatcher say about Mikhail Gorbachev?

Applying Your Learning

9. Was it a good idea to grant a veto to the UN Security Council's permanent five members? Should more countries have permanent status and a veto?

LESSON 5 US Interests and Regional Issues in Russia and the Former Soviet Republics

Quick Write

Do you think Ambassador Ushakov was right in what he said about competition in space between the United States and Russia? Does that space rivalry have anything to do with other issues between the two countries? How so?

Learn About

- the impact of the restructured Russian economic system on worldwide democracy
- the Russia-US challenges of nuclear threats, nonproliferation, and missile defense
- the effects on the United States caused by Russian oil production and distribution
- the importance of the cooperation in space between Russia and the United States

On 20 February 2007 the US State Department marked 200 years of diplomatic relations between the United States and Russia. Officials chose to highlight an aspect of that relationship that John Quincy Adams could never have imagined as the first US minister to Russia: cooperation in outer space.

At the celebration, Yuri Ushakov, the Russian ambassador to the United States, said, "In exploring outer space, we are not only partners but rivals as well. That rivalry, that competition, however, produced brilliant results. . . . A half a century ago, in 1957, the Soviet Union launched the first man-made satellite, and America [responded] by establishing NASA and the launch of their own space vessels."

Now the United States and Russia cooperate in space on a daily basis in support of the International Space Station.

The Impact of the Restructured Russian Economic System on Worldwide Democracy

Vocabulary

- normalization
- geopolitical

Even in the twenty-first century, Russia has an authoritarian streak. Russians still play hardball on the international political stage. But they are no longer promoting communism or Marxism in Europe or the Third World. Nor are they pushing the idea of a global "class struggle."

That is a big change. These activities were a constant of the Cold War years, even during the golden age of US-Soviet détente in the mid-1970s. At that point, Soviet leader Leonid Brezhnev insisted that better relations with the United States did not mean that the Soviets would stop supporting Cuban troops in Africa.

Proxy wars—involving Soviet allies fighting allies of the West—are now a thing of the past. More states have given up socialism in favor of capitalism. Even China, once a leader of the Communist bloc, has turned to free-market economics.

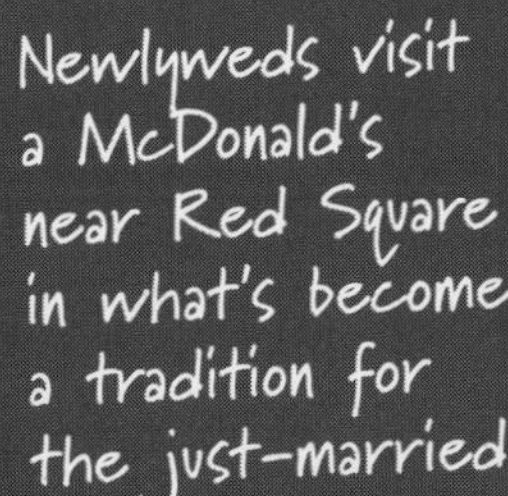

Newlyweds visit a McDonald's near Red Square in what's become a tradition for the just-married in Moscow.

Photo by Melanie Stetson Freeman / © 1992 The Christian Science Monitor

In the post-Cold War world, more states have given up socialism in favor of capitalism.

Russia's Shift Away From Pushing the Socialist Model

The move away from proxy wars was a long time in coming, though. The Soviet Union and the West had many differences to overcome to get where they are today. For instance, the Soviet Union installed Communist governments in the many Eastern European countries it occupied at the end of World War II. People in the West often called these Eastern European states "puppet regimes." That is, they knew the Soviets were still pulling the strings. Likewise, in Asia, the Soviets set up a communist government in the part of Korea they controlled. By 1950 they were willing to support North Korea's invasion of the South.

The Soviet Union backed Fidel Castro's socialist revolution in Cuba in 1959. That put a communist country within 100 miles of Florida's coast. It also gave the Soviets a useful ally to do its revolutionary dirty work in Latin America, Africa, and elsewhere.

In long civil wars in Angola and Mozambique, for instance, Cubans helped factions fighting US-aided forces. In the decade-and-a-half after the Portuguese withdrew from Angola in 1975, some 300,000 Cubans fought there. Their opponents included guerrilla armies backed by the United States and, in some cases, by South Africa's white-minority regime.

It's true that during the Cold War, the United States and the Soviet Union rarely exchanged fire. There was never a "hot war" between the two big powers. The Cuban Missile Crisis and the 1973 Arab-Israeli War were as close as they ever came to one. But there were many hot wars carried out by the two superpowers' proxies. That era has now ended, and its significance for world peace is immense.

The Worldwide Shift Away From Socialism

Just as the Soviet Union and the United States fought a tug-of-war in the last century over communism and capitalism, so other countries around the globe were working out their relationships with these economic systems. In the late 1970s some 60 percent of the world's population, by one estimate, lived under some form of communism or socialism.

But that didn't last long. Many countries soon made changes that can be broadly described as shifts away from socialism. In China, for instance, the reformer Deng Xiaoping introduced new economic ideas that harnessed the power of each individual's drive to succeed. Change came to India, too. It is and always has been a democracy. But its economic system had long included socialist elements. Then in 1991 it introduced significant free-market reforms.

These changes amounted to new answers to the question, how much of the economy should remain in the hands of the state? As the Indian example shows, this swing in thought wasn't happening just in Communist-bloc countries. Britain is another example. It is unquestionably a Western democracy. Its economic system is broadly capitalist. But after World War II, under Labour Party governments, Britain had nationalized some important sectors of the economy. After Prime Minister Margaret Thatcher's Conservatives came to power in 1979, they privatized much state-owned enterprise. For instance, public housing residents in Britain got to buy their homes from local authorities. And the privatization of British Telecom, the national phone company, gave millions of ordinary Britons the chance to become stockholders by buying shares. It was one of the largest share offerings in history.

At the same time that many states were moving away from socialism, many states were also moving toward greater democracy. Throughout the former Communist bloc, newly independent countries voted in free elections for the first time since the early twentieth century. In some cases, it was for the first time ever. But this trend didn't affect just the Communist bloc. In 1998 in Indonesia, for instance, the people overthrew authoritarian President Suharto after he had ruled for more than 30 years. And in 1994 South Africa held the first election in which all adults, including black people, were eligible to vote.

A young man and his fiancée place an order at a coffee house in Moscow.
Photo by Melanie Stetson Freeman / © 2008 The Christian Science Monitor

The last few decades have seen a historic shift away from socialism.

Young Russians visit an underground mall just outside Red Square in Moscow.

Photo by Melanie Stetson Freeman / © 2008 The Christian Science Monitor

The breakup of the Soviet Union took place against a backdrop of broader changes in the world and the global economy, including a rise in free trade.

These many swings represented a historic shift toward greater liberties in the world. They prompted Freedom House, a human rights organization, to report in 2002, "The highest-ever proportion of the world's population is living in freedom today."

In 1972 Freedom House started tracking the numbers of "free," "partly free," and "not free" countries around the world. In 2002 it found that "free" countries had risen to 89, up from 43 in 1972. The number of "partly free" countries had risen from 38 to 55. The number of "not free" countries had fallen from 69 to 48.

However, in 2009, Freedom House reported what it saw as a troubling shift in the wrong direction. Five "influential authoritarian states," it said, are "actively undermining democracy within their borders and abroad." It identified them as China, Russia, Iran, Venezuela, and Pakistan.

The Rise in Free Trade Around the World

The breakup of the Soviet Union took place against a backdrop of broader changes in the world and the global economy. These transformations included a rise in free trade around the world.

Theorists and writers have been thinking about free trade since the beginning of the modern science of economics. As you read in the Introduction, David Ricardo argued that all countries benefit when each focuses on what it does best and all countries trade freely. Since the mid-1930s US government policy has broadly favored free trade. And since World War II, most countries have signed on to the effort to lower trade barriers, such as taxes, globally. They have done this by joining the General Agreement on Tariffs and Trade and later, its successor, the World Trade Organization.

Meanwhile, many countries have also joined regional economic and trade blocs. The European Union (EU), for instance, began as a "common market" for a small group of countries to trade freely in coal and steel across national borders. Today's EU has 27 members. It governs trade in much more than just coal and steel. North America has its North American Free Trade Agreement, and South America has its Mercosur. This trading bloc goes back to 1991. It's known as the "Common Market of the South."

The Soviet Union had its trade bloc, too: the Comecon, also known as the Council for Mutual Economic Assistance. Just as the Warsaw Pact gave the Soviet Union military partners, the Comecon provided the Russians with economic alliances. Comecon, set up in 1949, was meant to be a counterweight to Western European efforts at aid and cooperation.

These Soviet-era apartment buildings house many Muscovites at the edge of the bustling city.
Photo by Melanie Stetson Freeman / © 2008 The Christian Science Monitor
In front of them stands a post-Soviet "Planet Sushi" Japanese restaurant.

The Soviet Union provided its Comecon partners with cheap oil and a market for their generally poor-quality manufactured goods. This led Gorbachev to complain that his government was subsidizing a system that let partners trade their better goods to the West and dump the rest in Moscow.

Once Comecon fell apart in 1991, many of its former member countries found themselves facing enormous increases in energy costs, as you read in Lesson 3. On the other hand, those who were energy producers, such as Russia, were suddenly able to sell their oil and gas at much higher world-market prices.

The Russia-US Challenges of Nuclear Threats, Nonproliferation, and Missile Defense

Like economic issues, defense issues changed when the Soviet Union dissolved and the Cold War ended. Today's nuclear threat is far different from what it used to be. No longer is it a standoff between two superpowers. Russia is now working with the United States on several different aspects of the nuclear threat. These include proliferation—the spread of nuclear weapons, nuclear terrorism, and the threats falling under the heading of "loose nukes."

But the two nations disagree strongly on missile defense. This dates back to the 1980s, when President Ronald Reagan introduced what he called the Strategic Defense Initiative. Most people remember it as "Star Wars." The idea was to develop weapons that could block incoming nuclear missiles on their way to the United States.

Reagan and his team presented this as peaceful technology, not aimed at anyone. They promised to share it with others, in fact. The technology itself was still very much in development. It drew criticism, and even ridicule, from some quarters.

But aside from that, many critics saw missile defense as destabilizing. Here's why: US relations with the Soviet Union were based on a concept of "mutual assured destruction." That theory held that each side had enough weapons to wipe the other out so completely that neither would ever use them. The Star Wars idea shifted the balance, however. Some people believed that if the United States could protect against incoming Soviet missiles, it might be tempted to launch its own missiles against the Soviets. If you have a shield to protect yourself, you may be tempted to use your sword, in other words. If you have no shield, you're more likely to keep your sword in its sheath.

Despite the criticism, Reagan's successors continued to develop missile defense. These efforts were aimed, not at Russia, but at possible nuclear threats from countries like Iran and North Korea. The new leaders in Moscow continued to oppose missile defense, however. They saw it and still see it as anti-Russian. They have warned that sustained US pursuit of missile defense could lead to a new cold war. Fortunately, though, other aspects of the US-Russian dialogue on nuclear matters have been more positive.

This square in Moscow houses some typical Russian architecture, including apartments, a church, and some fast-food kiosks.
Photo by Melanie Stetson Freeman / © 2008 The Christian Science Monitor

The Cooperative Threat Reduction (CTR) Program

One of these areas concerns the security of nuclear materials. As the Soviet Union was breaking up, nuclear scientists and arms control experts began to worry: "Are Russian nukes secure?" It was bad enough that during the decades-long Cold War, Americans and Russians had to lose sleep over the prospect of nuclear war. Once the Soviet Union began to break up, though, the concern shifted. You can think of the new concerns broadly as the problem of "loose nukes."

This situation has several aspects. For one, experts began to worry about the threat of an accidental nuclear launch at a time when it wasn't always clear who was in charge of the Russian government. They were also bothered by the thought that gangsters or terrorists might be able to steal warheads. Experts also feared that poorly paid Soviet nuclear scientists would give in to the temptation to steal nuclear materials to sell them on the black market—along with the scientists' nuclear expertise.

Fortunately, the transition from the Soviet Union to the Russian Federation was relatively smooth. It did not lead to civil war. And as you read in Lesson 3, Belarus, Kazakhstan, and Ukraine all decided to give up the nuclear weapons they had in their possession when the Soviet Union dissolved.

But there was still work to do. Two US senators, Sam Nunn, a Georgia Democrat, and Richard Lugar, an Indiana Republican, recognized this. They worked to establish the Cooperative Threat Reduction (CTR) program to address the "loose nukes" problem. Some people refer to it simply as the Nunn-Lugar program.

The plan was launched in 1992; it was renewed in 2006 to run until 2013. The CTR program helps Russia and the former Soviet republics control and protect their nuclear weapons, materials that could be made into weapons, and weapons-delivery systems, such as missiles. CTR also has helped dismantle and destroy weapons and delivery systems, as in Kazakhstan.

Several departments of the US government have a role in the CTR program: Defense, Energy, Commerce, and State. The program's budget is about $1 billion annually. The Nunn-Lugar program focuses primarily on the nuclear threat. But it has also addressed the threats posed by chemical and biological weapons.

US and Russian Efforts Toward the Global Initiative to Combat Nuclear Terrorism

Russia and the United States announced the Global Initiative to Combat Nuclear Terrorism in St. Petersburg in July 2006. Its goal is to keep terrorists from getting nuclear materials. Within two years, 75 nations had signed on, including all EU members.

The initiative addresses some of the same problems as the Nunn-Lugar program. But it is a global effort, with Russian partnership. Countries taking part commit voluntarily to support its principles.

They agree to do such things as improve their systems for keeping track of how much nuclear material they have, and where it is. They commit to better guard their nuclear power plants. They promise not to let terrorists use their countries as bases. And they promise not to provide financial support to those trying to obtain nuclear materials for terrorist purposes.

Joint Efforts to Restrain Nuclear Weapons in Iran and North Korea

As you have read in earlier chapters, Iran and North Korea have a special place on the global worry list. Both are pressing ahead with development of nuclear technology. Russia is part of efforts to contain both.

Russia is cooperating with the United States and the rest of the UN Security Council to bring Iran's nuclear programs into compliance with the rules of the International Atomic Energy Agency (IAEA). The council has passed a number of resolutions demanding Iran follow those guidelines.

Russia also has a role in the Six-Party Talks seeking to keep the Korean Peninsula free of nuclear weapons. In 1994 the United States and North Korea reached an "Agreed Framework." It called, in effect, for North Korea to give up nuclear ambitions in exchange for aid from the United States and normalization—*a return to normal relations without tensions* between the two. The accord was troubled from the start. It effectively broke down in 2003. As diplomatic efforts continued, North Korea demanded bilateral talks with the United States. It wanted to bargain one on one. The United States, on the other hand, has insisted on involving others in the negotiations. Russia has stepped forward to take part.

The Soviet Union had a role in North Korea from the beginning. It was present as an occupying power when Korea was first divided after World War II. The Soviets backed the North Korean invasion of the South in 1950. But now Russia is working with the United States, plus China, Japan, and South Korea, to bring Pyongyang into the family of nations.

Tractors ride on a railcar in Samara headed toward the Urals.
Photo by R. Norman Matheny / © 1993 The Christian Science Monitor

Under the Global Initiative to Combat Nuclear Terrorism, Russia and the United States agree to do such things as improve their system for keeping track of how much nuclear material they have, and where it is.

The Effects on the United States Caused by Russian Oil Production and Distribution

Russia may be skilled when it comes to dealing with big issues like nukes, national defense, and politics. But it's had less success over the years when managing its natural resources. As you read in Lesson 2, Russia has immense wealth in natural materials, such as oil. Over time, however, its manufacturing economy and service economy have simply limped along. Russia hasn't done well at adding value to what's simply there in the ground, in other words.

An oil rig, intended for use in the Caspian Sea, is under construction in Astrakhan, Russia.
Photo by Robert Harbison / © 1997 The Christian Science Monitor

Russia is the world's second largest crude oil producer and exporter.

Russian resource industries, especially energy, helped keep the country afloat during its transition from communism. But to really flower in the long term, Russia needs to use income from natural resources to develop a manufacturing or services economy.

The World's No. 2 Producer and Exporter of Crude Oil

When people think about oil supplies, they tend to think of the Middle East—specifically Saudi Arabia. The Saudis' reserves are immense. They often have played the role of guiding oil prices by increasing or decreasing their own oil production. But Russia is the world's second largest crude oil producer and exporter. Russia exports almost as much oil as the next three top exporters—Norway, Iran, and the United Arab Emirates—combined.

So when a Russian newspaper reported in early 2009 that Russian oil production fell for the first time in 10 years, oil analysts took note. The production decrease was slight—less than 1 percent. But it could be a major turning point in the world's crude oil production. It might mean that only a few countries can still increase production: Saudi Arabia, Kuwait, and Iraq.

Russia's Geopolitical Advantages and Disadvantages as a Major Oil Producer

Russia's immense energy resources have the potential to earn it billions and billions of dollars. This could help fund government operations. It could also help further develop the Russian economy.

Russia's oil and gas reserves give it a certain amount of geopolitical leverage. Anything that's geopolitical revolves around *how a country's geography—in this case its natural resources, too—affects its relations with other nations*. Russia has already shown a willingness to take advantage of its pricing power. It has withheld supplies to get vastly higher prices from former Soviet republics and countries in Europe. Down the line, Russia could manipulate energy supplies or prices to force its partners into actions they would not otherwise take.

Mid-day traffic jams Moscow's Ring Road, a major highway encircling the city.

Photo by Robert Harbison / © 1997 The Christian Science Monitor

Russia's immense energy resources could help further develop the Russian economy.

Gas Versus Oil

Gas usually travels by pipeline. Pipelines run across Russian territory, giving Russia control over gas prices it charges regional markets. Oil, on the other hand, is easier to transport by ship to markets all around the world. That offers world markets greater control in setting prices (although producers can decrease or increase the amount of oil they pump to manipulate prices).

Think of it this way: You can buy a major-brand soft drink from any of a hundred different places in your town. But if you want a drink of municipal water, your only choice is to turn on the tap in your kitchen. And that means you don't get a whole lot of say in how much you're going to pay for water coming out of your kitchen tap. But you can shop around town for the best deal on major brand soft drinks.

But these energy resources also represent a vulnerability for Russia. Yes, the world needs energy, and the earth's oil resources are finite. Ultimately, the price of oil and gas will rise. But in the near term, energy prices rise and fall in fairly wide swings. At this writing in 2009, relatively high prices are helping Russia weather the world economic downturn. But when prices are low, Russia, like other resource economies, risks running short on revenue. It could end up without enough money to fund its government and to expand its economy.

The US Consumption of Oil and the Threat of a Loss of Oil Supplies

The United States is another leading energy producer. It was the world's leading producer of crude oil until 1973, in fact. Even in recent years, the United States has been as high as the No. 3 producer of crude.

But the US economy is so thirsty for oil that even though it produces a great deal, it must import even more. Over the years, the US government has identified keeping oil supplies flowing as a vital national interest. This has led to trade and diplomatic relationships with Saudi Arabia and other oil powers.

But other relationships make the United States potentially vulnerable to a loss of oil supplies. So do the unresolved conflicts in the Middle East. In 1973 US support for Israel during the Yom Kippur War led to an Arab oil embargo against the United States. Something similar could happen again.

Iran could also move to tighten the oil spigot as it did during the 1970s. And many observers worry that Israel might mount a military attack to try to halt Iran's nuclear program. If this happened, it would likely disrupt world oil supplies, including those of the United States.

Oil can be loaded onto tankers and shipped around the world. If one supplier withdraws, the United States can turn to other sources. But the options aren't unlimited. Disruption of supply leads to higher prices.

Ships crowd into the port at Vladivostok, Russia.
Photo by R. Norman Matheny / © 1996 The Christian Science Monitor
Oil can be loaded onto tankers and shipped around the world. The United States could at some point need to turn to Russia for oil.

Russia is already known as a "price hawk" among oil producing countries. In other words, it works to raise prices. It's ready to use its pricing power to geopolitical advantage. And it needs the money it gets from higher prices.

The bottom line: The United States could at some point need to turn to Russia for oil. At the very least, it will have to cope with an oil market in which Russia has considerable say.

The Importance of the Cooperation in Space Between Russia and the United States

The Soviet-US rivalry didn't end with oil drawn from the earth's depths or with their vast economies. It long ago reached into space. From the beginning, human efforts to explore space were seen as a race between the United States and the Soviet Union. And it was a contest between two ideologies, Western capitalism and Soviet communism. The Soviets made it into space first, with their launch of the *Sputnik* satellite in October 1957. That was a tremendous blow to American prestige. It prompted China's Communist ruler Mao Zedong to comment, "The east wind prevails over the west wind."

Soviet cosmonaut Aleksei Leonov describes his experiences to Boston museumgoers in 1990.
Photo by R. Norman Matheny / © 1990 The Christian Science Monitor

When the US *Apollo* and Russian *Soyuz* spacecraft docked in 1975, Leonov and astronaut Thomas Stafford greeted each other with the first international handshake in space.

Cooperation and Competition in Space

And yet if competition was present from the start, cooperation came along soon after. Already in 1962 President John F. Kennedy opened talks with Soviet Premier Nikita Khrushchev about teaming up in space. The Apollo-Soyuz Test Project in 1975 was the two countries' first major effort at working together in this way.

Apollo-Soyuz was the first international manned spaceflight. Its mission was to test how well American and Soviet spacecraft would be able to meet and dock—to "hook up" in space. The flight opened the way for international space rescue and future joint manned flights. When the two spacecraft docked on 19 July 1975, astronaut Thomas Stafford and cosmonaut Aleksei Leonov greeted each other and shook hands. It was the first international handshake in space.

Experiments by NASA and Russian Scientists in the Shuttle-Mir Program

The US-Soviet détente that made that handshake in space possible ended when the Soviets invaded Afghanistan in 1979. But cooperation in space between Russians and Americans resumed after the Soviet Union broke up. The United States, now in partnership with the Russian Federation, renewed an earlier space agreement from 1987. The two countries also issued a "Joint Statement on Cooperation in Space." These agreements led to the NASA-Mir program.

In February 1994 cosmonaut Sergei Krikalev became the first Russian to fly aboard an American space shuttle. The following year, astronaut Norman Thagard became the first American to fly aboard the *Mir* Space Station. He spent 115 days from March to July 1995. Later in 1995 shuttle *Atlantis*, on mission STS-71, became the first US space shuttle to dock with *Mir*.

NASA scientists conducted a number of important experiments with their Russian colleagues during this time. They addressed such vital questions as:

- How plants and animals, including humans, function in space
- How the solar system originated and developed
- How to build better technology in space
- How to build future space stations.

The Joint Efforts of the US and Russia in Developing the International Space Station

Even before Krikalev made history as the first Russian aboard an American space shuttle, plans for US-Russian cooperation in space had moved well beyond the Shuttle-Mir program. Space scientists were already thinking about the International Space Station (ISS).

The ISS is the largest international science project in space. It involves not only the United States and Russia, but also Canada, Japan, and Brazil, as well as 11 other countries represented by the European Space Agency.

The purpose of the space station is primarily research. It serves as a lab for zero-gravity experiments of all kinds. The station has had a continuous human presence aboard since the first crew arrived on 2 November 2000. That crew, by the way, included Sergei Krikalev, the space shuttle pioneer.

The International Space Station

The International Space Station is the largest space station ever. It's also the largest artificial satellite orbiting the earth. Its only competition is the moon. It's being assembled in space in stages, like an out-of-town vacation home. And as often happens with such a project, it's taking awhile. Construction began in 1998. It is expected to be complete by about 2011.

The space station makes nearly 16 orbits around the earth every 24 hours. It's only about 220 miles up, and if you know where to look, you can see it with the naked eye.

The ISS may be the flagship of international scientific cooperation at this point. But the tone of the US-Russian relationship has darkened over the past few years. Some experts worry that Moscow could try to use the ISS as a bargaining chip. It might seek to limit US access to the ISS, for instance. During the Cold War, US-Soviet cooperation in space tightened or slacked off in response to changes in the larger relationship between the two countries.

The Communist Party has fallen away. But the natural rivalry between two great nations with different ways of looking at the world has not. That's true about space exploration. And it's true in other realms as well. It's fair to conclude that managing the ups and downs of US-Russian relations will test both governments long into the future.

Lesson 5 Review

Using complete sentences, answer the following questions on a sheet of paper.

1. Did the number of countries classified as "free" rise or fall between 1972 and 2002?
2. What was Gorbachev's complaint about Comecon?
3. What problems does the Global Initiative to Combat Nuclear Terrorism address?
4. Russia is working with the United States and other countries to contain the nuclear ambitions of which two countries on the global worry list?
5. What risks does Russia run when oil prices are low?
6. The United States was the world's leading producer of oil until what year?
7. When Thomas Stafford and Aleksei Leonov greeted each other on 19 July 1975, what did they do? What was the significance of this action?
8. What is the purpose of the International Space Station?

Applying Your Learning

9. Do you think Russia and the United States will continue to cooperate on issues of common interest or not? What have you read that makes you feel that way?

CHAPTER 5

The statue of Christ the Redeemer, 130 feet tall and built in the 1920s, has become a symbol of Rio de Janeiro, Brazil. Portuguese-speaking Brazil is the largest country in Latin America and the fifth largest in the world.

Latin America

Chapter Outline

LESSON 1 Latin America: An Introduction

Quick Write

What advantages did Pizarro and Atahuallpa each have? Was any other outcome of their encounter possible?

Learn About

- the geographic locations of the major regions of Latin America
- the major religious groups and languages of Latin America
- the region's history before and after the European conquest
- some key historical events associated with Latin America since independence

On 16 November 1532 the Spanish explorer Francisco Pizarro had his first encounter with Atahuallpa, the emperor of the Incas. The scholar Jared Diamond has called it one of the most dramatic moments in relations between Europeans and the native peoples of the New World. In his book, *Guns, Germs, and Steel*, he calls it "the collision at Cajamarca," referring to the Peruvian highland town where the two men met.

Pizarro led a ragtag band of 168 soldiers, 62 on horseback and the rest on foot. They had steel armor, but only a dozen or so guns called *harquebuses*, plus swords, daggers, and other such weapons. He represented King Charles I of Spain, monarch of the most powerful state in Europe.

Atahuallpa, on the other hand, was himself a monarch. He was the head of the New World's largest and most advanced state. He had the home-court advantage. Millions of obedient subjects and—more to the point—an army of 80,000 surrounded him.

Yet, as Diamond relates, within minutes of their first setting eyes on each other, Pizarro had captured Atahuallpa. He held him for ransom for eight months. It was quite a ransom: enough gold to fill a room 22 feet long by 17 feet wide to a height of eight feet. And once the gold was delivered, Pizarro broke his promise to release the emperor. Instead he executed him.

The Geographic Locations of the Major Regions of Latin America

Latin America spreads over more than one continent. Its five major regions fill not only all of South America; they include Central America and extend into the ocean as well.

Mexico and Central America

Mexico is a large country with massive mountain ranges: the Sierra Madre Occidental in the west, the Sierra Madre Oriental in the east, the Cordillera Neovolcánica in the country's center, and Sierra Madre del Sur in the south. The areas along the coasts

Vocabulary

- navigable
- isthmus
- commonwealth
- secularization
- infidels
- evangelizing
- proselytizing
- syncretism
- conquistadores
- polytheistic
- creoles

Pollution and smoke from forest fires blanket Mexico City.
Photo by Robert Harbison / © 1998 The Christian Science Monitor

A topographic map of Latin America and the Caribbean

and in the Yucatan Peninsula are lowlands. The interior is high plateau. Mexico has few navigable rivers—rivers *that can carry ships or boats*. Most Mexican rivers are short and run from the mountains to the coast.

Because Mexico stretches so far from north to south, and varies so much in altitude, its climate varies widely, too—from desert to jungle. Rainfall is sparse in the north and in the interior. It is abundant, though, along the east coast, in the south, and in the Yucatan Peninsula. Mexico also has frequent earthquakes.

Central America is a string of seven small countries between the southern tip of Mexico and the northern tip of South America. The countries are Guatemala, Belize, El Salvador, Honduras, Nicaragua, Costa Rica, and Panama. They are sometimes described as an isthmus—*a narrow strip of land, with water on either side, that connects two larger bodies of land*. In this case, the two bodies are North and South America. People also use the term *isthmus* to refer to Panama, the narrowest part of Central America. It's the site of the Panama Canal, a shortcut for ships traveling between the Atlantic and Pacific Oceans.

Like Mexico, Central America is prone to earthquakes and volcanoes. A "bridge" between the two continents, Central America is also important for its biodiversity. Its small territory is home to many different kinds of plants and animals, including birds, reptiles, and butterflies. People come from all over to see and enjoy all this wildlife. Such tourism is an important industry for Central America.

The Caribbean Islands

The southern tip of Florida points like a thumb to the Caribbean region. The Caribbean Sea is a roughly rectangular body of water. Cuba, the biggest Caribbean island, lies in the sea's northwest corner. Jamaica is due south of Cuba's eastern end. Hispaniola sits east of Cuba. Two countries share Hispaniola: Haiti, in the west, and the Dominican Republic, in the east. Still farther east is Puerto Rico, a US territory.

These four islands make up the Greater Antilles. They account for about 90 percent of the Caribbean's landmass. To Puerto Rico's east lies an arc of smaller islands. It curves south. Then it turns west, running roughly parallel to the coast of Venezuela, on the northeastern "shoulder" of South America. The islands of this arc are the Lesser Antilles. They include the Virgin Islands (some of which are also a US territory), the Leeward Islands, and the Windward Islands, plus Trinidad and Tobago.

The Caribbean has a rich mix of political "flavors" to match its spicy food. Cuba is the only communist country in the Western Hemisphere, while Puerto Rico is a US commonwealth. A commonwealth in this case is *a self-governing territory voluntarily associated with the United States*. Puerto Ricans have been US citizens since 1917.

The Caribbean includes sovereign states but also territories under American, British, Dutch, or French control. These are reminders of the time when Europe ruled much of the New World.

South America

The South American continent is home to 12 countries plus French Guiana, which is part of the French Republic. Brazil is the largest country in South America and the fifth largest in the world. Suriname is the smallest South American nation. Although South America experiences a wide range of climates, most of it is tropical. Its northernmost portion sticks north of the equator and its southernmost tip dips into the sub-Antarctic regions.

Venezuela, Colombia, and Ecuador

Venezuela has four major regions—the Maracaibo lowlands of the northwest, the northern mountains from the border with Colombia along the Caribbean Sea, the plains of the Orinoco River, and the highlands of the southeast. The climate ranges from tropical humid to alpine.

Colombia also has four major regions: the Andean highlands; Caribbean lowlands; Pacific lowlands; and the *llanos* (plains) and tropical rainforest in the east. Colombia has coasts on both the Caribbean Sea and the Pacific Ocean, and it has islands in both bodies of water. As in Mexico, differences in elevation make for big differences in climate across the country. There is little seasonal variation, however.

Ecuador is on the Pacific Ocean, and the equator slices right through it, just north of the capital, Quito. Ecuador is much smaller than Venezuela and Colombia. But like them, it, too, has four regions. There's the coast, for one. Second is the mountain region. It has two major mountain chains that are part of the Andes Mountains running north and south down the middle of the country, with a basin between them. The third region is the eastern (inland) side of the country, with piedmont and lowlands. The fourth region is the Galápagos Islands. They lie about 600 miles to the west off the mainland's coast.

The Andean States and Uruguay

The Andean States are Peru, Paraguay, Bolivia, Chile, and Argentina. This group takes its name from the mountains these countries share. The Andes are the longest mountain range in the world. They run 4,500 miles down South America's western side.

In addition to the mountains, these states share a common history as part of the ancient Inca empire (more on that later). They are also home to the Quechua group of languages.

A political map of Latin America and the Caribbean

This famous view from the Inca ruins' mountaintop perch in Machu Picchu, Peru, includes the Urubamba River and the Andes Mountains.
Photo by Alfredo Sosa / © 2002 The Christian Science Monitor

Uruguay sits on South America's east coast just north of Argentina. This tiny country's western border also touches big Argentina and its northern border butts up against even bigger Brazil. Its capital, Montevideo, stands at the mouth of the Rio de la Plata—a river that flows into the Atlantic Ocean.

Brazil and the Guyanas

Brazil takes up nearly half of South America's landmass—47 percent. It sprawls across four time zones and shares a border with all but two of the other countries in South America: Chile and Ecuador.

The Amazon Basin—home of the world's largest rainforest—and the Central Highlands dominate Brazil's landmass. The country's main mountain ranges follow the Atlantic coast. Northern Brazil has a mostly tropical climate, where it is seldom cold. The south is more temperate and gets some snowfall. But Brazil is better known for rain. Some parts get more than 10 feet of rain a year. The Amazon River, one of the world's longest, and the world's largest in terms of water volume, flows for more than half its length through Brazil.

"The Guyanas" refers to three territories that sit atop Brazil. Once they were known as British Guiana, Dutch Guiana, and French Guiana. Today the first two are known as Guyana and Suriname, respectively. Both are independent states. French Guiana is an "overseas department" of France. All three lie on the so-called "Guiana Shield," a geologically stable part of the continental crust.

Guyana is about the size of England. It has about 1 million inhabitants, largely of African, South Asian, or Native American origin. Ninety percent of them live along the coast. Suriname is about the size of the US state of Georgia. Its terrain is rainforest, savanna, coastal swamps, and hills. Its climate is tropical.

Suriname has only about half a million people. But they make up one of the most diverse populations in Latin America, in terms of religion and ethnicity.

French Guiana, the smallest of the three, is about the size of Portugal, but with only about 200,000 inhabitants. It is mostly rainforest, with a coastal strip where most of its people live. French Guiana is home to the European Space Agency's Guiana Space Center, at Kourou. The territory's location near the equator makes it a good place for launching rockets into space. According to the National Aeronautics and Space Administration, this is because rockets get a "big boost from Earth's rotational motion" at the equator where the planet is spinning an extra fast 1,041 miles per hour. The center has helped bring a desperately poor area into the modern world.

Lush tropical growth makes up the Atlantic rainforest such as this patch in Brazil.
Photo by Howard LaFranchi / © 1998 The Christian Science Monitor

The Amazon Basin—home of the world's largest rainforest—and the Central Highlands dominate Brazil's landmass.

The Major Religious Groups and Languages of Latin America

Despite all the countries it includes and the landmasses it covers, Latin America exhibits a common trend in both religion and language: European imports predominate. But indigenous religions, or at least religious practices, remain. So do the languages spoken there before European settlement.

The Influence of Catholicism

Roman Catholicism is the main religion of Latin America. But its role differs from place to place. And that role is changing. The Roman Catholic Church is responding, for one thing, to Protestant missionary efforts. It's also responding to a larger trend toward secularization—*a movement away from religion in general.*

In some places, Catholic clergy have supported authoritarian governments. This has hurt the church's prestige and moral authority. In Chile, for instance, many of the clergy supported the military government of General Augusto Pinochet after he overthrew a leftist government in 1973. But Catholic priests and bishops have also engaged on the left, working for the poor.

Brazil is one of the largest Catholic countries in the world. Its Catholic tradition goes back to the missionary zeal of the Spanish and Portuguese. They came to the New World in the fifteenth century eager to win converts among those it considered infidels, or *nonbelievers*. Catholic missionaries in Brazil sought to convert both the native peoples and the slaves brought in from Africa.

Men and women mostly stand on separate sides of this Catholic church during Sunday mass in Pisac, Peru.
Photo by Alfredo Sosa / © 2002 The Christian Science Monitor

Roman Catholicism is the main religion of Latin America.

In later centuries, Brazil attracted immigrants from traditionally Catholic countries—notably Italy, but also Poland and Germany. Brazil has no official state religion. Its separation of church and state is weak, however. In 1996, some 76 percent of the population—122 million people—called themselves Catholic. This was a strong majority. But the figure was down from 89 percent in 1980.

The situation in Mexico is similar. In 1970, 96.2 percent of those five years old or more identified themselves as Roman Catholic. By 1990 the census showed Catholics accounting for 89.7 percent of the population. That's still an overwhelming majority. But it's eroding somewhat. The 1990 census also showed strong regional variation. Various forms of Protestantism appeared much stronger in the southeastern part of the country.

The Remanso de Paz Christian church in Sincelejo, Colombia, is a meeting place for displaced persons in the community.
Photo by Sara Miller Llana / © 2007 The Christian Science Monitor

The number of Protestants in Latin America has been growing in recent decades.

The Influence of Protestantism

Catholicism's loss has been Protestantism's gain. Or rather, much of the shift has been due to Protestant missionary efforts.

Look again at Mexico. Many different Protestant groups have been evangelizing—or *recruiting*, to use the more secular term—since the 1970s. (Proselytizing is another term for *efforts to win converts to a religion*.) The overall Protestant share of Mexico's population has risen from 1.8 percent in 1970 to 3.3 percent in 1980 to 4.9 percent in 1990.

So-called "mainline" Protestant groups have been in Mexico since the late nineteenth century. But much of the growth in Protestantism since the 1970s has been on the part of churches such as the Assemblies of God, the Seventh-day Adventists, the Church of Jesus Christ of Latter-day Saints (the Mormons), and the Jehovah's Witnesses. By the early 1990s, for instance, more than half a million Mormons lived in Mexico.

All this has spurred the Roman Catholic Church to seek more visibility itself. Catholic clergy have spoken out more on sensitive public issues. For many years they ignored constitutional limits meant to keep them out of politics. Then in 1992 Mexico made dramatic changes in its constitution, which had strictly separated church and state. Mexico also resumed diplomatic relations with the Vatican.

The Influence of Native American and African Religions

Native American and African religious traditions also play a strong role in Latin America. People often fold these into more conventional Christian practice. In Mexico, for instance, being Catholic doesn't keep people from supporting traditional folk religious practices, especially in the countryside.

In Brazil, to give another instance, many people combine Catholic teaching with Afro-Brazilian cults. Syncretism is the term for this *combination of different forms of religious belief or practice*. People may turn to these combinations because they simply see no conflict between different religious beliefs. Other forms of syncretism have roots in traditional religious persecution. People "go underground" with practices they don't want to give up.

An extreme form of syncretism is a kind of black magic called *macumba*. People use this for either good or evil purposes. Those who practice it leave offerings to their deities, or gods. These offerings may include chicken, rum, flowers, and candles at crossroads, beaches, or other similar public places.

Haitian voodoo may be one of the best-known but most poorly understood examples of African religion in Latin America. The belief system of voodoo revolves around family spirits, known as *loua* or *mistè*. Individuals believe they inherit these spirits, almost like a family property. They are "handed down" through their mother's or father's side of the family.

The spirits protect from misfortune. But the families have to "feed" the *loua* with food, drink, and other gifts. This generally happens annually. Families hold a second, more elaborate service once in a generation. Some poorer families, though, wait until they really feel a need to restore their relationship with the spirits before they hold a service.

Haitians tend to distinguish between the practice of voodoo, on one hand, and black magic, on the other. Roman Catholics who practice voodoo don't see themselves as practicing a separate religion, or as outside the bounds of Catholicism. Protestants, however, tend to have another view. They have been present since Haiti's founding, and they see *loua* as demons. And many Haitians see Protestantism as opposing voodoo.

Santeria is another example of syncretism. The name means literally "the way of the saints." Santeria is a religion based on the beliefs of the Yoruba people of Nigeria, with some elements of Roman Catholicism. It grew out of the slave trade in Cuba. Its center is in Cuba, but it has also spread to the United States.

The Major Languages of Latin America

You probably already know that Spanish is the dominant language of Latin America. It is the language spoken in Mexico and Central America, as well as in most of South America. But Portuguese, with about 200 million speakers in Brazil, is a strong second.

Each of the three Guyanas has a different official language, and each is the only territory in South America to have its particular language as its official tongue. English is the official language of Guyana. Dutch is the official language of Suriname. And French is the official language of French Guiana.

The main languages of the Caribbean are English, Dutch, French, and Spanish. Haitian Creole, derived from French, is another important European-related language in Latin America. And German-speakers, too, are a significant minority in almost every Latin American country. Brazil's German community may be the best known. But German speakers abound in Argentina, Chile, Colombia, Paraguay, Uruguay, and Venezuela, too.

Latin America's Many Indigenous Languages

The languages listed above may seem like a large group. But they're nothing compared with the indigenous languages—those the native peoples spoke before Europeans arrived.

These tongues may have numbered as many as 1,750. Many have disappeared. But somewhere between 550 and 700 remain, according to one estimate. Scholars have grouped these languages into 56 different language families. They have also identified 73 *isolates*—languages with no known relatives.

By contrast, the European languages fall into just two families: Indo-European and Finno-Ugric. Finno-Ugric includes Finnish and Hungarian. The Indo-European family includes just about everything else. Europe has only one isolate: Basque, spoken in parts of Spain and France.

No indigenous language of Latin America has anywhere near as many speakers as Spanish or Portuguese. But some do have large numbers. And two of them coexist with Spanish as official languages: Quechua in Peru, and Guaraní in Paraguay.

The Region's History Before and After the European Conquest

Europe hasn't been the only outside influence on Latin American culture. In fact, the first people came to Latin America from Asia. It wasn't until thousands of years later that they were followed by conquistadores—*conquerors*—from Spain and Portugal. Further down the road, the American and French revolutions inspired revolution in Latin America, too.

The pyramids of the ancient Teotihuacán civilization still stand near Mexico City.
Photo by Melanie Stetson Freeman / © 1991 The Christian Science Monitor

While the Teotihuacán culture developed during Mexico's Classic Period (0 to AD 700), archaeologists have found evidence showing that people reached Mexico as far back as 10,000 to 8000 BC.

The Origins of the Indigenous People of Latin America

The first humans in the Americas wandered across from Asia tens of thousands of years ago—perhaps as early as 30,000 BC. They crossed at the Bering Strait, walking across the ice bridge between Asia and Alaska. Then over many long years, they worked their way slowly down and across North America. Archaeologists have found evidence showing that people reached Mexico around 10,000 to 8000 BC. They learned to grow corn, squash, and beans. These native plants have been food staples of the Americas for thousands of years since.

With their food supply assured, people began to settle down. They established villages and developed tools and cultural skills. By 1500 BC, early Mexicans were making figurines and other sophisticated wares out of clay.

The march of humanity didn't stop at Mexico, either. Rather, people proceeded on to and through Central and South America.

The Importance of the Mayan, Aztec, and Incan Civilizations

When the European explorers arrived at the end of the fifteenth century, they encountered three great native civilizations: the Maya, the Aztec, and the Inca. The first two of these flourished in what is today Mexico. The third flowered in the Andean States of South America.

The Mayans

The time between 200 BC and AD 900 is known as the Classic Period in the Mayan region. Archaeologists have called it the Golden Age of Mexico. The arts and sciences flourished. People developed systems for writing and elaborate calendars for recording time. Their language is known as Mayan or Quiché.

The religion of these early Mexicans was polytheistic—*worshipping many gods*. These gods represented forces of nature: rain, water, the sun, and the moon. Quetzalcóatl, a feathered serpent, was the most important of these. This god was understood as the essence of life and the source of all knowledge.

The early Mexicans lagged behind other comparable civilizations in their metalwork. This came into use only by the Classic Period's end. Still, these people were great builders. Many of the impressive structures they constructed survive today. These include pyramids near Mexico City and in the state of Veracruz, as well as the Temple of the Sun at Palenque in present-day Chiapas.

The feathered serpent Quetzalcóatl was the most important deity during Mexico's Golden Age.

A reclining figure carved from stone watches over Mayan ruins in Mexico.

Photo by Melanie Stetson Freeman / © 1991 The Christian Science Monitor

The Mayans produced pottery, statues, and ornate buildings.

A very simple farm economy, based on the cultivation of a few staple foods, underlay these civilizations. But they also produced pottery, statues, and ornate buildings. Their society was stratified—divided into layers or classes, including a ruling class of priests and intellectuals who managed the work of the peasant majority.

Teotihuacán, the largest non-Mayan city, fell around AD 650. At this point the center of power shifted from central Mexico to the Mayan city-states of the Yucatan Peninsula. The lowland Mayan culture flourished from AD 600 to AD 900 and then abruptly declined. Scholars aren't sure why this happened. But they suggest a number of possible causes: crop failure, plague, drought, strain from overpopulation, or pressure from more warlike neighbors.

Whatever its cause, this decline of the Mayans brought the Classic Period to an end. The Post-Classic period followed. Its hallmark was a sudden surge of militarism. This was a chaotic period of turmoil and mass migration. People went wherever they could to find allies against common enemies. Architecture became defensive as builders shifted from palaces and temples to creating fortifications. War, though, was less a means of expansion and more a source of revenue: One group conquered another to collect tribute money and, more frighteningly, to capture prisoners for sacrifice to the gods.

The Aztecs

The Valley of Mexico—roughly the site of today's Mexico City—has been prime real estate for as long as humans have lived in Mexico. The valley has an abundance of water. It has an abundance of game and vegetation. It's easy to get to. It was a main route for migrating groups passing through as well as those seeking to settle down.

The last nomads to arrive in the valley are the ones you are most likely to have heard of: the Mexica, also known as the Aztecs. The origins of this group are obscure. They appear, however, to have come to the Valley of Mexico during the turmoil of the Post-Classic period.

Legend has it that they arrived there around AD 1100. The story goes that the chirps of their sun and war god Huitzilopichtli guided them. (The impressive-sounding name of their war god translates as "hummingbird on the left.")

The people already living in the crowded valley looked on the newcomers with suspicion and tried to keep them from settling. After some more wandering and fighting, the Aztec reached the marshy island in Lago (lake) of Texcoco, the site of present-day Mexico City. There they saw an eagle perching on a cactus tree and holding a snake in its beak. This, legend says, they took as a sign that they should build their new capital on that spot. The Mexican flag today bears an image of an eagle holding a snake.

That capital was Tenochtitlán (tay-noch-teet-LAHN). It became an important center in the area and the seat of the monarchy the Aztec established in 1376. By the early sixteenth century, they controlled most of central and southern Mexico, except for the Mayan areas in the southeast.

After the Aztecs built Tenochtitlán, their society became more complex. They chose their emperor by merit from among the ruling dynasty. The nobility consisted of high priests as well as military and political leaders. The merchants lived in a separate part of the city. They had their own courts, guilds, and even gods. The biggest class was commoners: farmers, artisans, and low-level civil servants. At the bottom were conquered peoples brought to the capital as slaves.

Mexico's flag bears the image of an eagle holding a snake.
© Dusipuffi / Dreamstime.com

The Aztecs, who saw just such a sight, took this as a sign to build their capital on the site of present-day Mexico City.

The Aztec Empire was rather like the feudal system that Europe had developed not long before: a loose coalition of city-states, with a lot of alliances and obligations to provide soldiers and laborers. The Mexican city-states paid taxes to Tenochtitlán. The Aztecs sought to expand to collect tribute, or tax, from conquered peoples. Tributes came "in kind"—in goods of some sort, rather than in cash. Precious metals and stones; crops such as cocoa, cotton, and corn; or even feathers, shells, or jaguar skins were among the forms of tribute the Aztecs accepted.

But the Aztecs never really consolidated their dominance over their territory. That eventually led to their empire's fall. Even so, their language, Nahuatl, is still spoken in many parts of Mexico today.

The Incas

The Incas of Cusco, or Cuzco, started out as a small, relatively minor ethnic group, the Quechuas. Their language, Quechua, is the ancestor of the modern Quechua language spoken today. They began to expand their territory as early as the thirteenth century. Then around the middle of the fifteenth century, the pace of conquest picked up.

The ruins of Machu Picchu, Peru, are the remains of either an ancient Incan city or a home to Incan rulers.
Photo by Alfredo Sosa / © 2002 The Christian Science Monitor
At their peak, the Incas controlled a large portion of South America.

The Inca emperor of that time, Pachacuti Inca Yupanqui, has been likened to Alexander the Great or Napoleon. At their peak, the Incas controlled a large portion of South America, and a population of 9 million to 16 million people. The empire extended more than a thousand miles along the spine of the Andes: north to southern Colombia and south to northern Chile. It stretched from the Pacific Ocean in the west to the Amazonian rainforest in the east.

The Incan Empire

The Incas were remarkable for the scale on which they did things. At the beginning, they had the same basic skills as most of their neighbors: weaving, pottery, metallurgy, architecture and engineering, and irrigated agriculture.

And it's worth pointing out what they did not have. The Incas had neither the wheel nor a formal writing system. Instead, they used an intricate system of knot-tying to keep records.

The Incas also lacked markets in the usual sense—places where free buyers and sellers could meet to exchange goods for an agreed price. Instead, their system was an elaborate cooperative or mutual aid system. Grazing land was held in common. People received allotments of farmland according to the size of their families. All people had both the right to ask relatives and others for help farming their own land, and the responsibility to respond to others' requests for help in working their lands.

The Spanish and Portuguese Conquest and Colonization of Latin America

This story starts with Christopher Columbus. In 1492 he really did sail the "ocean blue," as the familiar rhyme has it. On 12 October of that year he (or one of his crew) spotted land. They came ashore somewhere in the Bahamas or the Turks and Caicos. On subsequent voyages he explored other parts of the Caribbean, looking for a way to Asia. And on his fourth and final voyage, he made the first European contact with the civilizations of Central America.

His voyages were the beginning of more than three centuries of Spanish conquest and colonization of the New World. These lasted until the nineteenth-century independence movements.

In 1513 Vasco Núñez de Balboa crossed the Isthmus of Panama. He and his expeditionary crew were the first Europeans to see the Pacific Ocean from the New World's west coast.

On 22 April 1519 Hernán Cortés landed in Mexico and founded the city of Veracruz. He led his forces on to the Aztec capital, Tenochtitlán, which they conquered by 1521 with the aid of their native allies.

Farther south, and a few years later, Francisco Pizarro of Spain toppled the Inca empire, also with the aid of some native allies. Some five years before Pizarro arrived in 1532, the Inca empire had been rocked by a civil war. The reigning emperor, Huayna Cápac (1493–1524), died prematurely. Some attribute his death to measles; others to smallpox or some other disease brought from Spain. The death touched off a struggle for power between his two sons. This conflict, along with European diseases, left the Incas poorly positioned to defend themselves.

A Spanish conquistador built Aliaga House in Lima, Peru, in 1535. His descendants still live there.
Photo by Alfredo Sosa / © 2002 The Christian Science Monitor

Christopher Columbus's voyages in the late fifteenth century were the beginning of more than three centuries of Spanish conquest and colonization of the New World.

Spain, Portugal, and the Treaty of Tordesillas

Just months after Christopher Columbus returned from his first voyage to the Americas, Pope Alexander VI issued a decree, called a *papal bull*, that gave Spain a big boost in its efforts to conquer the New World. The pope in effect drew a line on the globe, a meridian (a north-south line) about 300 miles west of the Cape Verde Islands, off the west coast of Africa. He decreed that any land discovered west of this line should belong to Spain. New land to the east should belong to Portugal.

These two countries were the great sea powers of their time. But the New World of the Americas was a Spanish discovery. The Portuguese were more interested in clear sailing around Africa and on to India and China. They did have some interest in the New World, too, however. And they weren't happy with the line the pope had drawn.

So Portugal's King John II, nephew of the famous Prince Henry the Navigator, took the matter directly to Spain's King Ferdinand and Queen Isabella. They met at the Spanish city of Tordesillas, and they agreed to move the line about 800 miles to the west. This gave Portugal a claim on South America—the land that today is Brazil.

In 1542 the Spanish established the Viceroyalty of Peru where the Incan empire had been.

Meanwhile, the Portuguese were taking advantage of opportunities granted by the Treaty of Tordesillas. They started out interested in trade rather than settlements. Portugal didn't have enough people to establish colonies the way the English were about to do in North America.

The Portuguese pattern in Africa was to set up trading posts on the coasts, with just enough land around them to support them. At first the Portuguese followed this pattern in South America, too. But then competition from the French forced them to shift from a commercial to a colonial empire. They needed more Portuguese people on the ground. At this time the Portuguese shifted from trading tropical hardwood (known, aptly, as brazilwood) to cultivating sugarcane. This required control over large stretches of territory and over large numbers of slaves. Slave hunters were the first to jump over the Tordesillas Line.

The Quest for Independence in Latin America

At the beginning of the nineteenth century, the colonies of Latin America were beginning to get restless under their European masters. They looked north to the 13 former British colonies' experiment in democracy and self-government, and they wanted to try it themselves. (British colonies in Canada remained loyal to the king.) They also were aware of the French Revolution of 1789, which sparked revolutionary idealism in many parts of the world.

In 1808 French Emperor Napoleon I invaded Spain and installed his brother Joseph on the Spanish throne. The ensuing turmoil distracted Spain enough that it gave the colonies an opening to start their own independence movements throughout the Spanish Empire.

As the Spanish colonies' political leaders began to think about unity and independence, one of the issues was whether to have a federalist system, like that of the United States, or a more centralized one. Another issue was finding the right relationship between church and state. Latin America had experienced much less tolerance and religious pluralism than North America.

By the 1830s Spain had lost all its colonies on the mainland. By the nineteenth century's end, its last two Caribbean colonies, Cuba and Puerto Rico, were under US occupation. Spain was no longer a colonial power in Latin America. Led by a series of "liberators," the Spanish colonies had set themselves an independent course.

La Paz, Bolivia, is the world's highest city.
Photo by Melanie Stetson Freeman / © 2007 The Christian Science Monitor
Bolivia is named for Simón Bolívar, who is credited with helping Colombia, Venezuela, Panama, Ecuador, and Bolivia achieve independence in the early nineteenth century.

Simón Bolívar

Simón Bolívar (1783–1830) was the Latin American leader who, more than any other, is known as "the liberator." He helped overthrow the Spanish, and served as the president of "Gran Colombia" ("Greater Colombia") from 1821 until his death. This area consisted of modern-day Colombia, Venezuela, Panama, and Ecuador. Bolivia, named for him, is another country whose independence he is credited with helping achieve. Bolívar is a revered national leader in all these countries.

José de San Martín

José de San Martín (1778–1850) was born in what is today Argentina. But he lived most of his early life in Spain. He returned to South America in 1812 to help train an army to defeat Spain and win independence. He led a rebel force across the Andes in 1817. They defeated the Spanish at Chacabuco, Chile, and occupied Santiago, the Chilean capital. The following year he won a decisive victory at Maipu. Then he established a nationalist government in Chile.

In 1820 he moved on to Peru, defeating the Spanish there, too, occupying the capital, and proclaiming Peruvian independence on 28 July 1821. The following year, continued resistance from Spain forced him to call on Bolívar for help. The two men disagreed on policy, though. In September 1822 San Martín resigned in favor of Bolívar. In 1824 he moved back to Europe and stayed there until his death.

Bernardo O'Higgins

Bernardo O'Higgins (1778–1842) was the illegitimate son of Isabel Riquelme and Irish-born Ambrosio O'Higgins, later the viceroy of Peru. That is, his father was the governor of the Spanish colony that Bernardo would eventually help overthrow. Bernardo was brought up by foster parents in Chile, educated in Lima, and finally sent to England. There he was exposed to liberal ideas, including the ideals of independence for Spain's colonies. After living in poverty in Spain for a couple of years, he returned to Chile in 1802 to join the cause of independence.

At that point he took his father's name. And eventually he took control of patriot forces. He fought alongside José de San Martín at Chacabuco. And he became the first president of an independent Chile in 1818 after San Martín refused the position.

O'Higgins spent several years trying to clear the Spaniards out of Chile and to prepare to move into Peru. A liberal at heart, he found himself having to rule more and more like a dictator. In 1823 he resigned and left for exile in Peru.

Miguel Hidalgo y Costilla

Miguel Hidalgo y Costilla (1753–1811) was a Mexican priest and revolutionary. Influenced by the ideals of the French Revolution (liberty, equality, and brotherhood), he tried to improve the lot of the native people in his parish. He helped them plant olive groves and vineyards and build a porcelain factory. Under his direction they also engaged in the silk industry. All these projects were forbidden and got him into trouble with the Spanish government. He was even brought before the Spanish Inquisition to be tried for heresy. But fortunately for him, his case was suspended.

When the French invasion of Spain gave the independence movement a boost, Hidalgo was one of a group of creoles—*people born in Latin America of European parentage*—who met to plot a revolution. When authorities discovered the plot, he openly adopted the cause of independence. He gathered an immense army of local Indians. Though poorly organized, they achieved some military victories. Eventually he was betrayed, captured, and shot to death by the Inquisition. Leadership of the liberation movement passed to others, but he is remembered as a hero.

Toussaint Louverture

Louverture (approximately 1743–1803) was a leader of the Haitian Revolution (1791–1804). This uprising led to the establishment of Haiti as the first republic ruled by blacks. It went from being a French colony to an independent country.

Louverture was a black slave born in Saint-Domingue (today's Haiti) to a father who had been a free man in Africa. He had the further advantage of being the personal servant to a humane master who provided him with an education. He was thus one of the few literate black revolutionary leaders.

The French Revolution of 1789 reverberated particularly strongly in Saint-Domingue, which was a French colony, after all. It had long been troubled with racial conflict as escaped slaves returned to plantations to attack whites. This led to a full-scale slave rebellion in 1791. It brought down the colony and led to the Haitian Revolution. Louverture was one of the leaders who were fighting for the end of slavery.

By May 1800 Louverture held sway over the entire island of Hispaniola. He ruled as something of a dictator. He could see Haiti needed to continue exporting sugar to survive economically.

Haiti's first round of independence didn't last long. It was never official. By 1802 Napoleon, then governing France, decided to send some 20,000 troops to the island to recapture it. Louverture was promised he would be allowed to retire quietly, but instead he was arrested and brought to France. He died there of neglect in a frigid dungeon.

The Monroe Doctrine and Latin American Independence

You read about the Monroe Doctrine in Chapter 4, Lesson 4, as it relates to Russia. But the doctrine applies particularly to Latin America.

President James Monroe first stated this policy in an address to Congress on 2 December 1823. The doctrine spoke to the new political order developing in the Americas and Europe's role in the Western Hemisphere. His speech drew little attention at the time from Europe's great powers. But the Monroe Doctrine has settled in over time as a foundation stone of US foreign policy.

In formulating this doctrine, Monroe and Secretary of State John Quincy Adams drew on two important diplomatic ideals that had already taken shape in the few decades of the young nation's history:

- Disentanglement from European affairs
- Defense of neutral rights.

The doctrine has three main concepts:

- Separate spheres of influence for the Americas and Europe
- An end to colonization of the New World
- No European intervention in the Americas.

Monroe was issuing a clear warning to European powers: They must not interfere in the affairs of the newly independent Latin American states or potential US territories. The doctrine was also intended to support expanding US influence and trading ties to the south. Americans worried that Spain and France might reassert control over newly independent states, or impose trade restrictions on them that would be almost as bad. And as you read in Chapter 4, the prospect of a Russian presence on the west coast of North America was troubling, too.

By the middle of the nineteenth century, the Monroe Doctrine and the belief that the United States had a "Manifest Destiny" to spread across the continent provided the justification for US expansion across North America. By century's end, the United States had the economic and military power to enforce these ideas.

Later administrations, especially that of President Theodore Roosevelt, used the Monroe Doctrine to justify unilaterally intervening in Latin America. You'll read about one of those interventions in the following section.

Some Key Historical Events Associated With Latin America Since Independence

Latin America's history since independence shares some of the same themes that ran through its colonial history. These include questions of legitimacy and spheres of influence. As the United States found after 1776, independence is only the beginning of a large set of challenges.

US War With Mexico in 1846

From the early colonial period, Texas was part of New Spain, as the Spanish domains of North and Central America were known. But the territory needed more people. So in the 1820s the Spanish authorities invited "Catholic" immigrants from the United States into Texas. They could buy land for 10 cents an acre. Americans—most not Catholic—poured in. And soon they outnumbered Mexicans in Texas 4 to 1.

Worried about losing Texas to the United States, Mexican authorities tightened up on American immigration. They even abolished slavery in Texas in 1829 to make Texas less appealing to those from the southern United States.

These moves backfired. In March 1836 Texas declared its independence from Mexico. But Mexican General Santa Anna wasn't going to let Texas go without a fight. He marched 3,000 men north to San Antonio. His forces laid siege to the Alamo. This was an old Franciscan mission where 150 armed Texans had taken refuge. All but five died in the assault. The Mexicans executed the survivors. A couple of weeks later, Mexican forces surrounded the Texan town of Goliad and forced the commander to surrender. On orders from Santa Anna, they executed 365 prisoners there.

This brutality fueled an anti-Mexican reaction in the United States. American volunteers poured into Texas to fight Santa Anna. They ambushed and roundly defeated his forces at the San Jacinto River near what is now Houston on 21 April 1836. Two days later, they also captured Santa Anna, who had fled the scene. In custody, he signed two treaties. One ended the fighting. The other, a secret treaty, recognized Texan independence.

A quiet scene from the Amazon River shows villages lining the banks in Peru.
Photo by Mark Sappenfield / © 1999 The Christian Science Monitor

The idea of bringing Texas into the United States gained support in both Texas and Washington. But Mexico severed diplomatic relations as soon as Congress voted to annex Texas in 1845. Mexico's legislature had never ratified Santa Anna's secret treaty. A further complication was that Texas had expanded its territorial claim. Suddenly "Texas" included parts of New Mexico, Colorado, Oklahoma, and Kansas, as well as all of present-day western Texas.

Texas soon became the Union's 28th state, despite Mexican objections. President James K. Polk sent a special envoy to Mexico to settle the boundary issue and also to buy California. However, Mexican President José Joaquín Herrera was in no mood to bargain. He could have accepted an independent Texas. But a Texas doubled in size and annexed to the United States was too much. He refused to meet Polk's envoy. Instead, he started reinforcing Mexican army units along the Rio Grande. Fighting broke out 25 April 1846. The two sides declared war soon after.

The United States pursued a three-front strategy. One column of troops occupied California and New Mexico. These territories fell with little bloodshed. A second column, under General (later President) Zachary Taylor, entered northern Mexico. Fierce fighting took place there against Santa Anna's forces. General Winfield Scott commanded the third column. He landed at Veracruz and took the city. Then he marched on to Mexico City. The battle for the capital lasted more than three weeks. US victory there (in the "halls of Montezuma") led to a cease-fire and peace talks.

French Rule of Mexico Under Maximilian

Just a decade later, Mexico was once again engulfed in war. This time it was a civil war, lasting from 1858 to 1861. It came to a clear end, with the liberals victorious. But it left the national treasury empty. And so the new president, Benito Juárez, called a time-out on repayment of foreign debts.

This made Mexico's debtors unhappy. In fact, Spain, Britain, and France were so unhappy that in October 1861 they decided to launch a joint invasion to get their money. They were unable to agree on how to enforce the debt collection, though. So the Spanish and the British soon returned to Europe. That left the French, who decided to occupy Mexico.

Soon a group of Mexican conservatives who had supported the French occupation invited Ferdinand Maximilian Joseph von Habsburg of Austria to accept the Mexican crown. The Habsburgs were a leading royal family of Europe. But Maximilian was actually more liberal than the conservatives knew. He continued some of the Juárez government's policies, even as Juárez himself retreated into exile from the capital.

The whole situation was a test of the Monroe Doctrine. A European power seeking to impose a monarch on an American state was exactly what Monroe and Adams had tried to prevent. But at first, the United States was too caught up in its own Civil War to respond to Mexican liberals' calls for help.

fastFACT

The Cinco de Mayo (May 5) holiday celebrates the Mexicans' victory in an 1862 battle against the French.

That changed after the American Civil War ended in 1865. The following year, Napoleon III began pulling out of Mexico. He needed troops back home to defend France. In Mexico, the campaign to oust the French resumed on 19 February 1867. Within three months, Maximilian surrendered and went on trial. Then, on Juárez's orders, a firing squad executed him on 19 June 1867.

Regional Disputes Between Bolivia and Chile and Between Panama and Colombia

The situation in South America during the nineteenth century was just as turbulent as that in Mexico. Disputes within countries and between countries led to bad feelings across the continent.

Chile and Bolivia, for example, have been arguing for more than 100 years. Chile is the one country in the Western Hemisphere with which Bolivia does not have normal diplomatic relations. Bolivia's defeat during the War of the Pacific (1879–83) strained ties. In that war, Bolivia lost the coastal province of Atacama, which left the country landlocked.

The two countries' relations were severed from 1962 to 1975 in a dispute over the Lauca River. Relations resumed but then were broken again in 1978. This latest break happened when the two countries failed to agree on a way to grant Bolivia access to the sea. Bolivia and Chile have only partial diplomatic relations. The two countries do not exchange ambassadors.

Panama's issue with Colombia ended more definitively. Even before the construction of the Panama Canal, Panama was a crossroads of trade in Spain's New World empire. In 1821 Central America revolted against Spanish rule, and Panama joined Colombia, which had already declared its independence.

Panama then spent the next 82 years trying to become independent of Colombia. Panamanian efforts to break free between 1850 and 1900 included five attempted secessions and 13 interventions by the United States. The last straw, though, came in 1903. That's when Colombia failed to ratify a US proposal for canal rights over the narrow isthmus.

At that point, Panama proclaimed its independence. Seeing an opportunity, the United States backed the Panamanians and worked with them to realize the plan for a canal.

How the Spanish-American War Led to the Building of the Panama Canal

In a larger sense, however, the Panama Canal was a direct result of the Spanish-American War in 1898. That conflict ended Spain's colonial empire in the Western Hemisphere. It also secured the US position as a power in the Pacific. No wonder future Secretary of State John Hay called it a "splendid little war."

By 1898 when the war began, Cuban revolutionaries had been fighting for independence from Spanish rule for three years. The conflict was too close for Americans to ignore. They were eager to see Spain out of the New World, in keeping with the Monroe Doctrine's principles. Spain's brutal tactics also won American sympathies for the Cubans.

Tensions mounted. Then on 15 February 1898 the US battleship *Maine* exploded and sank under mysterious circumstances in Havana harbor. US military action began to look likely.

The US goal was a stable government in Cuba. Washington wanted to ensure peace for both Cubans and American citizens there. On 20 April the US Congress acknowledged Cuban independence. It demanded that Spain give up control of the island. But it also promised the United States would not annex Cuba. Congress authorized President William McKinley to take military action to ensure Cuban independence.

Spain rejected this ultimatum and severed diplomatic relations. McKinley responded with a naval blockade of Cuba and a call for 125,000 military volunteers. By the end of April, Spain and the United States were at war. The first battle, though, was fought on 1 May 1898 in Manila Bay in the Pacific. The US Navy defeated the Spanish naval forces defending the Philippines.

Ships pass through the Panama Canal's Gaillard Cut on their way to the Atlantic Ocean.

Photo by Andy Nelson / © 1998 The Christian Science Monitor

Even before the construction of the Panama Canal, Panama was a trade crossroads in Spain's New World empire.

The next month US forces landed in Cuba, defeating Spanish land and naval forces. By late July the French ambassador to Washington put out peace feelers on Spain's behalf.

The resulting Treaty of Paris, signed 10 December 1898, guaranteed Cuban independence. It forced Spain to give the Pacific island territory of Guam, along with Puerto Rico, to the United States. Spain agreed to sell the Philippines to the United States for $20 million. And McKinley used the war as a pretext to acquire Hawaii.

The Spanish-American War had involved naval operations in both the Pacific Ocean and the Caribbean Sea. And that convinced President Theodore Roosevelt, McKinley's successor, that the United States needed a better way to get from one ocean to another. The United States, he decided, needed to control a canal in the Western Hemisphere.

The Hay-Herrán Treaty with Colombia, signed 22 January 1903, would have made that possible. It would have given the United States a 100-year lease on a strip six miles wide on which to build a canal. But then the Colombians failed to ratify the treaty.

The Isthmus of Panama, then part of Colombia, seemed clearly the right place for the canal, however. Roosevelt and other Americans figured that if Colombia balked, perhaps the United States would do better if the site it wanted were under the control of a different political entity. At that point the United States started supporting the Panamanian separatist movement.

In late 1903 some Panamanian revolutionaries, with US naval support, rose up against the Colombian government. US forces blocked Colombians from going to Panama City to put down the rebellion.

President Roosevelt recognized the new Panamanian government in November 1903. For the Panamanian patriots, the uprising was about more than just a canal. They might have felt elbowed aside. But there was no real alternative to the deal worked out with Secretary of State John Hay. By February 1904 the Isthmian Canal Convention, as the treaty was known, had been ratified by both the Panamanians and the US Senate. Roosevelt would get his canal.

The Cuban Missile Crisis

The Cuban missile crisis was an important moment in US relations with the Soviet Union. But it is also an important chapter of Latin American history.

As a new president in 1961, John F. Kennedy decided that Cuban President Fidel Castro was working for the Soviet Union to undermine Latin America. Kennedy wanted Castro out. This concern led him to authorize a secret invasion of exiled Cubans to topple Castro. The operation, known as the Bay of Pigs invasion, failed spectacularly within a couple of days. Kennedy shouldered the blame. But he remained keen to rid Cuba of Castro.

It was against this background that Soviet Premier Nikita Khrushchev brought mid-range nuclear missiles into Cuba. US intelligence saw signs of a general buildup of Soviet arms through routine surveillance. On 4 September 1962 Kennedy warned against introducing offensive weapons into Cuba. Then on 14 October an American U-2 surveillance plane brought back pictures of the Soviet nuclear missiles. Kennedy couldn't ignore the evidence.

He gathered 18 top advisers to decide what to do. It was one of the most dangerous moments in human history because it could have triggered nuclear war. Some advisers wanted an airstrike against the missiles, followed by a US invasion of Cuba. Others favored stern warnings instead.

The president chose a middle course. On 22 October he ordered a naval quarantine of Cuba—a blockade by a less warlike name. He also sent a letter to Khrushchev, calling on him to remove the missiles. This opened a channel of communication between the two men that stayed open throughout the crisis.

There were nervous moments along the way. But on 27 October Kennedy accepted the Soviet offer to withdraw the missiles in return for an end of the quarantine and a pledge not to invade Cuba.

That same day, Robert Kennedy, who was the attorney general and the president's brother, met with Soviet Ambassador Anatoly Dobrynin. He delivered two messages: The stern one was that if the Soviets did not remove the missiles, the United States would. The gentler one was that if they removed the missiles from Cuba, the United States would remove some obsolete American missiles from Turkey that worried Moscow. This message helped the Soviets save face.

Based on this, the Soviets agreed on 28 October to remove their missiles from Cuba. The Cuban missile crisis remains one of the most keenly discussed episodes of the Cold War.

The Organization of American States

Given their common history as former European colonies and their shared environment, the countries of the Americas have worked for more than 100 years to try to solve common problems. In 1890 they launched the International Union of American Republics. It became the Pan American Union in 1910. Its current name, the Organization of American States (OAS), dates from 1948.

The OAS membership includes 35 independent countries in the Americas. Most controversial among these is Cuba. While Cuba is technically a member, the OAS has for several years excluded Cuba's Communist government from participating on grounds of its "incompatibility with the principles of the inter-American system."

Pedestrians cross a street in the heart of the theater district in downtown Buenos Aires, Argentina.

Photo by Andy Nelson / © 2002 The Christian Science Monitor

The country is one of 35 members of the Organization of American States.

The OAS aims to:

- strengthen peace and security in the Western Hemisphere
- promote democracy
- ensure peaceful settlement of disputes
- provide for common action in the event of aggression
- promote economic, social, and cultural development.

The OAS also has 63 permanent observers. These include the European Union plus dozens of countries in Europe, Asia, and Africa. The OAS has four official languages: English, French, Portuguese, and Spanish. It works on a regional scale on many of the same issues the United Nations tackles globally.

Many of these issues grow out of Latin America's serious economic challenges. You'll read about those in the next lesson.

Lesson 1 Review

Using complete sentences, answer the following questions on a sheet of paper.

1. Identify two things that the Andean States share, in addition to the mountains.
2. Why is the European Space Center in French Guiana?
3. What is syncretism? Give an example.
4. How many indigenous languages survive in Latin America? How many families of indigenous languages are there?
5. How did the first humans come to the Americas?
6. What line drawn by Pope Alexander VI did the rulers of Spain and Portugal agree to move?
7. Why was installation of Maximilian as the ruler of Mexico a test of the Monroe Doctrine? Why was the United States slow to respond?
8. What two messages did Robert Kennedy have for Anatoly Dobrynin on 27 October 1962?

Applying Your Learning

9. In what way did the Spanish-American War of 1898 provide a boost for building the Panama Canal?

LESSON 2 Economic Reform, Leadership, and the Political Pendulum

Quick Write

How do you think these twentieth-century experiences have affected Mexicans' attitudes toward land ownership and new technology?

Learn About

- the challenges of the region's economic systems
- the challenges related to the political struggle for power
- how weak governments, corruption, and crime affect economic development
- the struggle for power between church and state
- how free trade agreements have affected the region

The turn of the twentieth century was a time of great modernization. Around the world, new technologies and new means of transportation changed the nature of work. They increased people's wealth.

Mexico took part in this modernization. But its peasants bore most of the costs. For instance, during this time, machines became available to do work that peasants had done by hand. The new machines helped the country realize immense gains in productivity. But they tended to put manual laborers out of work faster than the workers could find their way into new factories.

During the same period, the government seized much private and collectively owned land. The idea was to create fewer but bigger and more-productive farms. By 1910 most villages had lost their communally owned lands. Much of the country's most productive lands were in the hands of just a few hundred wealthy families. More than half of all rural Mexicans worked on these families' estates. By 1911 the average Mexican's income, adjusted for inflation, had only just recovered to the level of 1821, the year Mexico won independence from Spain.

The Challenges of the Region's Economic Systems

A common thread runs through Latin American history. As countries developed and more or less prospered, most of their people did not. Most citizens simply never had much of a stake in society. During the immense economic expansion of the nineteenth century, they had never been "dealt into the game" as their North American counterparts were. A number of factors contributed to this.

Vocabulary

- hacienda
- co-opt
- junta
- anticlericalism
- liberation theology

A man pushes a wooden rake through raw coffee beans at this farm in Chiapas, Mexico.
Photo by Howard LaFranchi / © 2000 The Christian Science Monitor
As Latin American countries developed and more or less prospered, most of their people did not.

Why Feudalism and Mercantilism Continue in Latin America

A major factor was that European nations established their colonies in the New World primarily to make money. Mercantilism, which you read about in the Introduction, was the economic philosophy behind these ventures. Europeans at the time saw trade as a "zero-sum game." That is, they believed there was a limit to how much trade could take place. If one country gained, another had to lose. Modern ideas about economic growth, on the other hand, are more expansive. They hold that trade can benefit everyone who takes part. But those ideas lay far in the future as the first Europeans put down roots in the Americas.

Trade Rules

The colonial powers had strict rules about who could sell what to whom. The colonies were to produce raw materials for export back to Europe and to buy pricey finished goods from Europe. (As you may recall, the British made these demands of their colonies, too. The North American colonists didn't like them at all.) And the government always took a cut. The king of Spain, for instance, charged a 20 percent levy—a tax known as "*la quinta real*," or "the royal fifth"—on all production in the colonies.

Local Peruvians shop at an open-air barter market in Pisac, where Incas once bartered with one another.

Photo by Alfredo Sosa / © 2002 The Christian Science Monitor

The plantations of New Spain operated largely as self-sufficient communities, also relying mostly on barter.

In Latin America, land was abundant and so were people. A relatively small number of Europeans received grants of land from their rulers and set up vast *haciendas*. The term **hacienda** is another way to say *an estate*. But it can refer to a mine or even a factory as well as, more commonly, a plantation. Europeans forced native peoples into laboring on these haciendas—as farm laborers, as miners, and sometimes eventually as skilled tradespeople.

The plantations of New Spain operated largely as self-sufficient communities. They relied mostly on barter and exported very little. Mines, on the other hand, were soon turning out large quantities of gold and, even more important, silver. By the late sixteenth century, silver accounted for 80 percent of New Spain's exports. Today we get produce and even fresh meat from around the world. But in those days agricultural produce was consumed near where it was grown or raised. Silver, however, was not perishable, and it was well worth the cost of shipping back to Europe.

The same was true of sugar. It was a high-value, portable exception to the rule about farm produce staying local.

Social Classes

As these haciendas developed, natives and Europeans naturally came into contact with each other. Soon they began to intermarry. An elaborate racial classification developed, as in India, or in South Africa during apartheid. It was a very stratified, or layered, society.

At the top were the white Europeans. *Peninsulares* was the term for those born on the Iberian Peninsula, that is, in Spain or Portugal. Down just a notch were the *criollos*, or creoles, whites born in Latin America. They sometimes "married up" to *peninsulares* to get ahead in society. The next group was those of mixed European and Native American parentage, known as *mestizos*. Then came the full-blooded indigenous people. And then there were African slaves. They were brought to the New World early on to work the sugar cane and other plantations.

A hacienda owner was called *hacendado* or *patrón*. The economic system was similar to feudalism—the owner was very much like a feudal lord in Europe, with serfs and peasants below him, along with cowboys on horseback.

Southern Colonies vs. Northern Colonies

The same mercantilist philosophy lay behind the colonization of territories farther north. But in the future United States and Canada, conditions were different. There were fewer indigenous people and relatively fewer colonists. Land was harder to farm. Laborers were fewer, so they were in a better position to bargain with landowners and employers. They could demand, and get, more money. North American laborers were not as replaceable as their South American counterparts. What's more, North American colonists often arrived as complete families, or with extended families or communities. They often brought their pastors with them.

All this meant that North America's European colonies tended to become home to smaller populations. People were more likely to come from the same racial and ethnic backgrounds. There was far less intermarrying with native peoples. And so the north didn't form the same racial classes as did Latin America. There were fewer "layers" to society. More people took part in the economy at a higher skill level, too. There were more blacksmiths and carpenters, for instance, rather than unskilled farm laborers.

North American colonists also had greater rights. More people there had the vote. More had citizenship rights and legal protections than in South America. They had local assemblies early on, such as the House of Burgesses in Virginia. They had rights that an African slave on a Brazilian sugar plantation, for instance, did not.

North Americans had slaves, too, of course. But there were fewer of them. And they became important to the economy much later—especially in the nineteenth century, after the invention of the cotton gin. Many important institutions of society were already set up by the time slavery became economically significant in North America. The European colonies of Latin America, on the other hand, developed with less equality in wealth, human capital, and ultimately political influence.

Historical Patterns

In 2003 the World Bank published a major report—*Inequality in Latin America and the Caribbean: Breaking with history?* Its authors said that these developments at the colonial period's beginning set the tone for this region. The World Bank authors discussed how these patterns took hold in Latin America. They also considered how the patterns continued after independence in the nineteenth century. Their study focused on the importance of institutions such as schools and universities.

The authors found that extreme inequality persisted in Latin America because, even after independence, institutions continued to favor the wealthy. The system shut most people off from opportunity. The elites developed impressive universities, for instance, because they wanted to send their own children there. But they did little to develop primary schooling, which would have benefited everyone.

Independence brought new leadership to Latin America. But in practice, it didn't always amount to much change. Local creole elites simply took over from European-born elites. Sometimes the new locally born leaders were even more conservative than the old colonial ones. In fact, in some cases, notably Mexico, creoles wanted independence because they thought Spain was getting too "liberal" for them. The World Bank authors concluded: "[I]ndependence did not fundamentally alter the structures of political power in Latin America." And nearly two centuries after independence, many of the same forces remain at work.

The GINI Index

Economists use a number called the GINI index to measure income inequality in a country. (GINI is pronounced "genie," like the one you let out of the bottle.) The higher the number, the more unequal the incomes. If everyone in a country had the same income, the GINI index would be zero.

Researchers have found that from the 1970s through the 1990s, Latin America's and the Caribbean's GINI inequality index reading was nearly 10 points higher than Asia's. It was 17.5 points higher than for the 30 countries of the developed world. And Latin America and the island nations scored 20.4 points higher than Eastern Europe.

The Inequalities of Income and Wealth

The gaps between rich and poor are wider in Latin America and the Caribbean than in almost any other region on earth. It's not just that rich Latin Americans have bigger incomes. There are big gaps between rich and poor in terms of all kinds of access, also: to education, to health care, and even to water and electricity.

The region also exhibits what a World Bank official called "huge disparities" between the rich and poor in assets. The Latin American poor have much less voice in their societies. And they have fewer opportunities to improve their lot.

Women pack avocadoes for export from Mexico.
Photo by Melanie Stetson Freeman / © 1991 The Christian Science Monitor

The model for land ownership in Latin America was set early on—vast *haciendas* controlled by rich *peninsulares* and creoles, but worked by vast armies of landless peasants or *campesinos*.

The Imbalance of Land Ownership

These inequalities help explain why one of the themes of Latin American history is land reform. The model for land ownership was set early on: vast *haciendas* controlled by rich *peninsulares* and creoles, but worked by vast armies of landless peasants or *campesinos*. That model continues, in some form, even today.

The nineteenth century was a time of expanding political rights. The liberal ideas imported from Europe should have helped improve the peasants' lot. But the nineteenth century was also a time of falling transportation costs. New railroads and faster steamships made remote places less remote. It helped increase land values, and this led to a small group of people owning more and more land. The new waves of development also helped hold down wages.

A World Bank study of rural land ownership around 1900 showed some striking gaps between Latin America, on one hand, and the United States and Canada, on the other. These numbers showed how many farmers owned their own land compared with how many merely worked other people's land. In 1910, on the eve of the Mexican revolution, only 2.4 percent of heads of households in rural Mexico owned land. The Bank called this number "astoundingly low."

Roughly comparable numbers for Argentina in 1895 were higher—around 20 percent. But the numbers for the United States in 1900 and Canada in 1901 were 74.5 percent and 87.1 percent.

The Wide Gaps Between the Very Rich and Very Poor

What do these gaps matter for a society? Economists say that great inequality doesn't just make it hard for poor people to escape poverty. It tends to hold back the whole society. Countries with higher inequality have to grow faster to lift their people out of poverty. If wealth were spread around as evenly in Latin America as it is in Europe, Latin America would have a poverty rate of only 12 percent instead of 25 percent.

A Small Middle Class

A related point is that a society where the gaps between rich and poor are wide tends to have a small middle class. That's not good for growth and development. Middle-class consumption is an important economic engine. A society's middle classes tend to be the people moving "up"—wherever "up" happens to be at any given time. For example, Chinese people these days are buying new refrigerators and television sets. Indians are buying their first family car. This is part of the demand fueling economic growth in these two countries.

Another key point about Latin America: The racial divisions that developed in early colonial times continue to have economic effect. The World Bank study found that race and ethnicity still limit people's opportunities and welfare. Indigenous people and those of African descent are "at a considerable disadvantage with respect to whites," according to the Bank. Whites continue to earn the highest wages in the region.

The World Bank, focusing on seven different Latin American countries, found that indigenous men earn 35 percent to 65 percent less than white men. White women earn more than indigenous ones by a similar margin. In Brazil, men and women of African descent earn only about 45 percent of what their white counterparts do.

The Challenges Related to the Political Struggle for Power

History has also set political patterns in motion in Latin America: Turmoil prevalent in the past still crops up in many of the continent's nations today. The region has fought its share of civil wars. Three of its major countries have swung back and forth between military and civilian rule. And two of its important modern leaders have developed poor relations with the United States.

The Traditions of Political Authoritarianism

When George Washington stepped down after two terms as president of the United States, he set an important precedent. He showed self-restraint despite all the power his position gave him. The Constitution didn't require him to serve only two terms. But he thought it was a good idea.

A Nicaraguan woman shows off her inked thumb, which proves she has voted in an election.

Photo by Melanie Stetson Freeman / © 1990 The Christian Science Monitor

Three of Latin America's major countries have swung back and forth between military and civilian rule.

Early decisions matter. They establish traditions. In August 1828 Simón Bolívar, several years into independence from Spain, took steps that helped establish a less fortunate political tradition in Latin America.

Bolívar assumed dictatorial powers as the leader of Greater Colombia. He tried to put in place a constitution that he had developed for Bolivia and Peru. His constitution increased the central government's power. It also called for a president-for-life who would name his own successor.

A large share of the people didn't like it, though, and it failed to gain acceptance. In 1830 Greater Colombia fell apart. Venezuela and Ecuador broke off as separate countries. Bolívar resigned, and by year's end he was dead.

The Results of Civil Wars in Mexico, Colombia, Argentina, El Salvador, and Nicaragua

The countries named above have each waged more than one civil war. Many of these conflicts have lasted for years—in some cases, decades. Some have seen many revolutions.

In Mexico and El Salvador, land ownership has come up as an issue again and again. In other countries, tension between different political parties has ignited into open warfare.

Mexico

You read in Lesson 1 about a Mexican civil war known as the War of the Reform (1858–61). But early in the twentieth century, Mexicans lived through more years of civil war as part of their revolution.

The liberals' overthrow of Maximilian I in 1867 led to a peaceful, tolerant period known as the Restoration. But in 1876 a political mastermind named José de la Cruz Porfirio Díaz Mori took power. He would lead the country, directly or indirectly, for a remarkable 34 years. Historians call these years "the Porfiriato."

It was a time of modernization and progress. Mexico began to play a bigger role in the global economy. The Díaz formula combined natural resources, cheap labor, and foreign capital and technology. This made export production possible. Railroads—the high technology of the day—helped expand agriculture, manufacturing, and mining.

fastFACT

In many Hispanic countries, children receive two surnames—one from the father and one from the mother. The "middle" or next-to-last name comes from the father's surname, while the last name is the mother's surname. On first reference, the entire name is given, with both surnames. On second and following references, just the father's surname is given. Thus José Alvarez García would be more commonly referred to as José Alvarez or Mr. Alvarez. Fidel Castro's full name is Fidel Alejandro Castro Ruz.

But times were not so good for ordinary Mexicans and their civil liberties. Díaz courted foreign interests. He let the clergy get involved in politics. He let the army violate people's guaranteed rights. He either co-opted his opponents—*exploited them for his own purposes*—or jailed them.

By 1908 Mexicans thought they saw change coming. That's when Díaz told an American reporter he wouldn't run for reelection. Seizing the apparent opportunity, liberals put up Francisco Madero González as their candidate.

Then Díaz changed his mind. He ran and won in June 1908. He had to take some harsh measures to do so, though. These included arresting thousands of his opponents.

Within a few months, Madero, then in exile, was calling for the people to rise up in protest. They welcomed his call. By January 1911 a large-scale revolt had broken out. Madero returned to lead the revolution. By the end of May the 80-year-old Díaz had quietly set sail for exile in France.

The story doesn't end there, though. Madero soon saw that the revolution had raised hopes it wouldn't be able to fulfill—at least not under his leadership. He saw a split between moderates and radicals. Moderates wanted political change. Radicals wanted land reform.

Madero soon fell victim to a coup. Next came a period of dictatorship that ended on 8 July 1914. A period of civil war and anarchy followed. At that point, Mexico had four different governments. Each claimed to represent the will of the people.

The leader of one of these, Venustiano Carranza Garza, won out. Carranza took office as president on 1 May 1917.

By then Mexico had a new charter: the Constitution of 1917. It was the product of the revolution. It guaranteed civil liberties. It limited the president to a single term. And it promised to protect all Mexicans from foreign or domestic exploitation.

Colombia

A clear division between liberals and conservatives has marked Colombia's politics from the beginning. Simón Bolívar was the Republic of Greater Colombia's first president. His supporters became the core of the Conservative Party. They favored strong centralized government and an alliance with the Roman Catholic Church. They also wanted to limit the right to vote.

Followers of Bolívar's vice president, Francisco de Paula Santander y Omaña, became the core of the Liberal Party. They wanted decentralized government. They wanted the state, not the church, to control education and other civil matters. And they wanted more people to be able to vote.

By 1850 the two groups had formed organized political parties. Elections over the years gave each a roughly equal period in control of the government. In fact, Colombia has a solid tradition of civilian government and regular free elections.

But conflict between the two parties has more than once led to civil war. The War of a Thousand Days (1899–1903) claimed 100,000 lives. It was as part of this conflict that Panama, with US help, declared its independence from Colombia in 1903. Decades later, a civil war known simply as "*La Violencia*" (the violence) took about 300,000 lives from 1946 to 1957.

Argentina

Early in the twentieth century, Argentina was one of the world's wealthiest countries. But by mid-century, a string of military governments was struggling to keep the economy going. They also tried to contain terrorism and other political violence.

Tango dancers entertain local people and tourists in downtown Buenos Aires, Argentina.

Photo by Andy Nelson / © 2002 The Christian Science Monitor

Early in the twentieth century, Argentina was one of the world's wealthiest countries, but by mid-century it fell into violent political struggles.

By the early 1970s a charismatic but long-exiled leader, Juan Domingo Perón, sensed the time was right to return to his homeland. By October 1973 he was once again the country's elected president. His third wife, Maria Estela Isabel Martinez de Perón, became vice president.

It was a triumph for the Peróns. But it was a turbulent time for the country. Political violence was rife. The government responded with emergency measures, including holding people in prison without charge and without a clear release date.

Then on 1 July 1974 Perón died. His widow succeeded him in office. The armed forces removed her on 24 March 1976, however. A junta—*a group of military officers ruling a country after seizing power*—took control of the government.

The junta took harsh measures against those it deemed political extremists or their sympathizers. Gradually basic public order returned. But the human costs of this so-called "Dirty War" were immense. Tens of thousands of people "disappeared." The authorities simply rounded them up and killed them.

Understandably, this meant the public had little trust in the junta. Meanwhile, the economy was weak. And charges of public corruption kept piling up.

Trying to stir up public support, the junta in 1982 tried to seize from Britain a group of islands in the South Atlantic. The Argentines called these islands the Malvinas, and they had long claimed them as part of Argentina. To the British, who had controlled them for centuries, they are "the Falklands."

The Argentines hadn't reckoned with British Prime Minister Margaret Thatcher, however. Nicknamed "the Iron Lady," she insisted the Falklands were British—and would remain so. When Argentina attacked and conquered the islands, Britain's air, land, and naval forces counterattacked and threw them out. The conflict lasted just a few months and ended with the Argentine surrender on 14 June 1982.

Argentina's crushing defeat in the Falklands/Malvinas and the souring economy cost the junta its hold on power. Democracy returned. Raúl Alfonsín of the Radical Civil Union won the presidency and took office on 10 December 1983.

El Salvador

Like much of Central America, El Salvador has a long history of revolutions. By the beginning of the twentieth century, the country had reached some degree of calm. But by the 1970s its democratic institutions were on the decline again. Arturo Armando Molina Barraza won the 1977 presidential election. Yet people believed the vote was rigged—and clumsily so. In 1979 a reformist coup took place. Soon the situation deteriorated into civil war.

One especially shocking event of this period was the murder of the Roman Catholic archbishop of El Salvador, Oscar Arnulfo Romero y Galdámez. Police intelligence agents shot Romero as he was saying Mass on 24 March 1980. The war took an estimated 75,000 lives, with the US government actively backing the moderate-conservative government against leftist rebels.

In January 1992, after lengthy peace talks, the two sides came to terms. The military came under civilian control. The peace accord allowed former guerrillas to become a normal political party and take part in elections.

Nicaragua

The Monroe Doctrine warned Europe to keep its hands off the New World. There's another side to that coin, however. The United States has seen Latin America as its own sphere of influence and often intervened there.

Nicaragua is a clear example of this. The United States kept troops there almost without a break between 1909 and 1933. From 1927 to 1933 the US Marines in Nicaragua fought a long-running battle with a rebel force led by General Augusto Calderón Sandino. He was a Liberal who had rejected a US-sponsored peace agreement between his party and the Conservatives.

But by 1933 the American public wanted to bring the Marines home. After they left, a general named Anastasio Somoza García outfoxed his opponents, assassinated Sandino, and took over the presidency.

Despite the way he came to power, Somoza kept close ties to the United States. So did his sons, who succeeded him. Their dynasty lasted until 1979. Then the Sandinista National Liberation Front, which had been fighting Somoza's sons since the early 1960s, toppled them.

The Sandinistas were authoritarian rulers. Voicing Marxist slogans, they seized property. They nationalized industry. And they supported guerrilla and terrorist groups in the region. The United States halted aid to, and trade with, Nicaragua. Eventually Washington even began to support the resistance.

Eventually the Sandinistas yielded to pressure from both home and abroad. They began peace talks with their opponents. These led to national elections in February 1990. Violeta Barrios de Chamorro won the presidency. She was well known as the widow of an influential slain journalist, Pedro Joaquín Chamorro Cardenal. Her nearly seven years in office were a time of great progress for Nicaragua. Its democracy strengthened, its economy stabilized, and its human rights practices improved.

At the end of her term she handed power over to her successor, José Arnoldo Alemán Lacayo, a former mayor of Managua. It was the first such peaceful transfer of power in recent Nicaraguan history.

A young girl runs her family's food stall at a market in Managua, Nicaragua.
Photo by Melanie Stetson Freeman / © 1990 The Christian Science Monitor

After much turmoil, Nicaragua's first modern-day peaceful transfer of power took place in 1997.

The Up-and-Down Patterns of Democracy in Argentina, Chile, and Brazil

Like Argentina, Chile and Brazil have swung over the years between civilian and military rule. In all three, rising middle classes pushed for change and more democracy. Then conservatives pushed back. And all three spent many years under military rule.

In Chile, Salvador Allende Gossens, a Marxist, headed a group that took power in 1970. He nationalized industry, including US interests in Chilean copper mines. The economy did not run well under his leadership. On 11 September 1973 General Augusto Pinochet Ugarte threw out Allende in a military coup in which Allende was killed.

Human rights abuses marked Pinochet's rule. It ended after a popular vote on 5 October 1988 denied him a second eight-year term as president. Soon after, Chile began its return to democratic rule.

Brazil's constitutional republic ended with a military coup in 1930. In the 1970s, though, two of its more enlightened military rulers, Ernesto Geisel (1974–79) and João Baptista de Oliveira Figueiredo (1979–85), began a democratic opening. Brazil completed its transition to a popularly elected government in 1989.

The Influence of Perón and Peronism in Argentina

Around the world, political parties tend to have similar names: "Liberal" or "Conservative," for instance. What's much rarer is a political movement named for a person. But that's what Juan Perón, the Argentine leader whom you read about earlier, founded: Peronism.

Perón first burst onto the political scene as an army colonel in 1943. He was part of a military coup that ousted Argentina's constitutional government. He's hard to place on the usual left-to-right political spectrum. His first role in the new government was as labor minister. He worked to give the working class more power. He also moved to nationalize industry. He produced five-year plans, not unlike Joseph Stalin. All that may make him sound like a socialist.

Some call Perón a fascist, however. Himself of Italian descent, he openly admired Italian fascist Benito Mussolini. In 1955 a military coup ousted Perón as Argentina's elected civilian president. So he went into exile in Spain, where the fascist dictator Francisco Franco Bahamonde still ruled.

Even without Perón, Peronism lives on in Argentina. Since the restoration of civilian rule in 1983, Argentina has elected several Peronist presidents. Along with Perón's, their record hasn't been good: They have often mismanaged the economy, bankrupted the government, allowed labor unions too much influence at the expense of business, and propped up unprofitable industries.

The Influence of Castro and Communism in Cuba

Fidel Castro first came to wide public notice in 1953. He was a revolutionary activist in Cuba. The country may have won its independence back in 1902, but by the 1950s it was languishing under a corrupt dictator, Fulgencio Batista y Zaldívar. People wanted a return to constitutional rule. Many resistance groups, urban and rural, wanted to topple Batista. But on New Year's Day 1959, after rebel forces led by Castro had won a series of victories, Batista simply fled.

As Castro took power, he promised a return to constitutional rule and democratic elections. He promised social reforms, too. But it didn't work out that way. He used his control of the military to increase his power. He repressed dissent. He pushed other resistance fighters aside. And he jailed or executed thousands of opponents. As Castro turned more radical, hundreds of thousands of Cubans fled, most to Florida. He declared Cuba a socialist state on 16 April 1961.

All this—plus Cuba's takeover of US property—quickly soured relations with the United States. Washington had already imposed an economic embargo on Cuba in October 1960.

For years, Castro worked closely with the Soviet Union. He provided the foot soldiers for Soviet military adventures, notably in Africa. The period of greatest tension between the two countries was the 1962 Cuban missile crisis.

A half-century later, an ailing Castro has turned over some powers to his brother Raúl. But the real "post Castro" era lies still in the future.

The Influence of Hugo Chávez in Venezuela

As Fidel Castro has begun giving up power in Cuba, Hugo Chávez Frías of Venezuela has moved into the role of Latin America's leading leftist troublemaker. Venezuela long had a reputation as one of the most stable democracies in Latin America. But that began to change in 1989. That's when people rioted in response to such things as inflation and government program cutbacks—referred to by historians as an "austerity program"—intended to deal with the nation's huge debts. Some 200 people died in the riots. In 1998 Chávez ran for president on a reform platform and won.

Chávez, a career military officer, argued that the system had lost touch with ordinary people. He called for, and got, a new constitution. Voters reelected him in 2000. In 2002 a military coup briefly deposed him. But he regained office. In 2004 he faced a recall election and won with 59 percent of the vote. In 2006 he won the presidency again, with 63 percent of the vote.

But the following year, voters narrowly defeated a package of reforms he proposed. These would have, among other things, scrapped presidential term limits and redefined private property. It was his first electoral defeat. Many saw it as a rebuke to his efforts to increase his power. He has signaled his intent to make many of the changes by presidential decree—that is, without input from anyone but himself.

Under Chávez, US-Venezuelan relations have been tense. The United States is a major trading partner with Venezuela. But Chávez has used particularly fiery rhetoric to refer to Washington and US policies. He has also called for a "multipolar world" devoid of US influence. And he has made overtures to—or deals with—several countries the United States finds problematic: Iran, North Korea, Belarus, and Syria. His purchase of Russian shoulder-fired missiles in the summer of 2009 sparked alarm in Washington, where officials feared Chávez would give the missiles to the Colombian rebels.

How Weak Governments, Corruption, and Crime Affect Economic Development

One way to understand Latin America's political instability throughout history is to look at the different forces shaping the economy. These forces include weak governments, corruption, crime, and, more specifically in Colombia's case, the drug trade.

Farmers used to harvest coca crops for cocaine on this land in Peru, but a group of farmers now grows a healthy alternative: bananas and plantains.
Photo by Howard LaFranchi / © 2000 The Christian Science Monitor

Forces shaping Latin America's economy include weak governments, corruption, crime, and the drug trade.

Colombia's economic report card through the 1980s was not bad. Its solidly middle-tier economy was growing at a respectable rate. The country had good trade relations, a skilled workforce, and good levels of investment and savings.

But there were some blots on its record as well. Careful observers had to admit that Colombia's relative prosperity was built at least in part on the illegal drug trade. And drugs created problems.

For a start, the drug lords' political and economic power rivaled the government's. The parts of Colombia where the drug trade was concentrated were notably better off than other parts of the country. Another problem was inflation. A steady stream of dollar bills from the United States meant prices kept rising higher than they would have otherwise. People put more money than necessary into the financial, real estate, and construction sectors because they were such good places to introduce illegal drug money into everyday use.

Finally, the drug trade drew more and more people into a life of crime. As a result, violence and corruption spread throughout the country. Colombia is by no means the only country running into drug-related issues. Mexico, for instance, is facing such serious drug violence that some observers are beginning to compare the country to a "failed state."

How Bribery Affects Government Officials

George Friedman, an analyst writing for Stratfor Global Intelligence, has described how drug money and bribery affect governments and their employees. Drug cartels have the power both to bribe government officials at all levels and to kill them, he noted. "Government officials are human; and faced with the carrot of bribes and the stick of death, even the most incorruptible is going to be cautious in executing operations against the cartels."

Government officials who take bribes either look the other way and allow crime to occur, or they actively participate in criminal activity. Perhaps they issue permits that criminals do not qualify for or hand out phony identification papers that allow criminals to operate. In any event, they violate their responsibilities to the people they are supposed to serve. Instead of working for the government, they work for the drug lords.

How Violence and Assassination Affect Economic Development

In these ways, outlaws can gain enough power against a government that the two sides trade places. The cartel governs the government. Public officials become the drug cartels' tools.

It's similar to what happened in Chicago during the 1920s. Alcohol smuggling created a huge pool of money, which criminals used for bribes. The city government was effectively "absorbed," to use Friedman's word. Only with major reinforcements brought in from Washington—the FBI—did the forces of law and order get a grip on the situation. Such high levels of lawlessness—actual violence, or the threat of it, combined with bribes—make it hard for a state to function at all. Normal economic forces can no longer operate, as businesses are forced to cooperate with the criminals and do their will. The criminals often "tax" legitimate businesses—skimming part or all of the profits—thus increasing the costs of doing business. Some businesses give up and close, and their owners leave.

The Economic Results of the Flight of Prominent Citizens From a Society

When rich people leave a place, they tend to take their money with them. That's the principle analysts have in mind when they think about how general lawlessness affects a local economy. It leads to less investment.

A business owner worried about his son or daughter being kidnapped on the way to school is likely to move to where he feels safer. So is a merchant concerned about his shop being looted and his goods stolen. And when affluent Latin Americans move to Miami or Houston or Los Angeles, their new investments are likely to go into their new city. This has been Latin America's recurrent theme for decades.

Prominent citizens often exercise a degree of informal leadership in their communities as well. They help "get things done," not only with their money but also with their contacts and connections. The ability and push to improve conditions go away when such people no longer live in a place, even if they retain property there.

The Struggle for Power Between Church and State

Another power historically exerting influence in Latin America is religion. The United States largely settled its question about the relationship between church and state long ago through the First Amendment to the Constitution. Yet many Latin American countries still struggle with the issue.

As you read in Lesson 1, Protestantism has made significant inroads in Latin America in recent decades. But the region is still overwhelmingly Catholic. In fact, the Roman Catholic Church has tried to exert influence in Latin America for centuries. But from country to country, the role of the church in politics has varied. A look at four countries in particular tells the story.

Ecuadoran rebels signed the 1809 Act of Independence at San Agustin (shown here), a seventeenth-century Roman Catholic church in Quito, Ecuador.
Photo by Alfredo Sosa / © 2006 The Christian Science Monitor

From country to country, the role of the church in Latin American politics has varied.

The Conflicts Between the Mexican Government and the Roman Catholic Church

Mexico has been Catholic since soon after the Spaniards arrived. Priests traveled with Spanish conqueror Hernán Cortés when he first came to Mexico in 1519. Spain claimed new territories in the name of the cross as well as the crown. But since Mexican independence, church-state relations have been complex, as governments have tried to limit church power and influence.

The nineteenth-century liberals who fought for Mexican independence embraced the French revolutionary ideal of anticlericalism. This means *opposition to the involvement of the clergy in secular affairs*. Liberals favored decentralization and free competition. They couldn't help noticing that in Mexico the church was practically a state within a state. After all, the church was a major landowner. And it controlled most schools, hospitals, and charitable institutions. The liberals saw the church as resisting needed reforms.

The constitutions of 1857 and 1917 restricted the church in many ways. Those went well beyond forbidding the "establishment" of the church as a state religion. Rather, they amounted to what Americans would consider limits on the "free exercise" of religion. One provision, for example, gave the state ownership of all church buildings.

By the 1980s, though, the church was demanding an end to these restrictions. Widespread political corruption was becoming more and more blatant. The clergy demanded the right to speak out on national affairs. And so in 1992 Mexico abolished constitutional limits on the church. Church-state tensions have not disappeared. But they have eased considerably.

The Influence of Catholic Social Reform Initiatives on Government in Paraguay

Paraguay is another country where the Catholic Church challenged a corrupt government. From 1954 until 1989 Alfredo Stroessner Matiauda was the government strongman in charge. Stroessner kept the country under one successive 90-day state of emergency after another. Only during election campaigns did he lift it.

By the late 1960s the church, traditionally neutral on politics, decided it could no longer play along. It spoke out against human rights abuses and the lack of social reform. The church was one of very few independent voices in the country.

The Stroessner regime soon cracked down on the church's social activism. But the church bounced back. By the early 1980s it had become the regime's most important opponent. The Stroessner era ended with a military coup in 1989. Civilian rule soon followed. Church activists can fairly claim credit for preparing the way for the transition.

The Relationship Between Church and State in Brazil

Brazil is yet another Latin American country where clergy have heeded the call to social action. Liberation theology is the term for *an activist movement of Roman Catholic priests who make direct efforts to improve the lot of the poor*. Brazil has been a center of this movement. Brazilian theologian Leonardo Boff played a leading role in it.

The movement drew its inspiration from the Second Vatican Council of 1965 (Vatican II). This council liberalized and modernized some church procedures. The "liberationists," as they're sometimes called, also got a push from the Latin American Bishops' Conference in Medellín, Colombia, in 1968. This conference endorsed direct action on behalf of the poor.

During Brazil's years under military rule, progressive priests defended human rights. They made the church a focus of resistance to an undemocratic regime.

The liberation theology movement has faded somewhat in recent years. The end of military rule has given Brazilians new channels of political expression. And as conservative Pope John Paul II's appointees have risen within the church, Brazil's bishops have become more conservative, too.

The Church's Mediating Role in El Salvador

Liberation theology was an important movement in El Salvador as well. Luis Chávez y González served for nearly 40 years as the archbishop of San Salvador. He was a strong advocate for the poor. He did things such as trying to help peasants who had lost their farms to large businesses.

As in Brazil, so also in El Salvador—the Second Vatican Council and the Medellín bishops' conference of 1968 moved the clergy to act on behalf of the poor. Activist clergy and church members set up so-called Christian Base Communities to work for social change.

But as civil unrest grew during the late 1970s, right-wing groups started attacking priests who worked to help the poor. The church became divided. Most bishops supported the church's traditional role and the government's authority. But a small group of parish priests favored developing the Christian Base Communities. They continued to call for more aid to the poor.

In 1977 Bishop Chávez resigned. His successor was Monsignor Oscar Arnulfo Romero y Galdámez. Bishop Romero was seen as a moderate, not a radical. But like Chávez, he spoke out publicly for social justice. He became the leading advocate for the poor. Every Sunday morning, he gave radio addresses. As tensions rose, his outspokenness was too much for the right wing. That led to his assassination.

Truckers haul goods from *maquiladoras*—factories owned by US companies but stationed outside US borders—in Mexico.
Photo by Robert Harbison / © 1995 The Christian Science Monitor

The United States has free-trade agreements with several Latin American countries.

How Free Trade Agreements Have Affected the Region

One of the difficulties developing countries around the world have experienced is finding markets for their goods. Without such markets, it's difficult for their economies to grow and a middle class to develop.

Since World War II, US policy has been that the best way to expand trade in all directions is to have freer trade. The US government has found that free trade agreements are one of the best ways to open foreign markets to American goods. By allowing other countries to sell goods in the United States without trade barriers, these countries are then able to buy more US goods. The United States has such agreements with 17 different countries in place. Of these, half are with Latin American countries.

Free Trade With Latin American Countries

Latin American countries having free trade agreements with the United States:

- Chile
- The Dominican Republic
- El Salvador
- Guatemala
- Honduras
- Mexico
- Nicaragua
- Peru

Of the three other free trade agreements pending at this writing—that have been worked out but not put into effect—two are with Latin American countries: Panama and Colombia.

One measure of the success of these accords is that they account for far more US exports than the size of the trading partners' economies would suggest. In 2007 US free-trade partners, in Latin America and elsewhere, made up 7.5 percent of global production. But they bought more than 42 percent of US export goods.

The Purpose of Free Trade Agreements

The basic idea of free trade goes back to the early days of classical economics. If each country produces the things it does best and trades freely with other countries doing what they do best, everyone is better off. Among economists this view has wide support.

Among politicians, however, it's a different story. Free trade means opening a nation's doors to foreign competitors. And letting foreign firms compete means letting them win when they're better—or cheaper—than their domestic counterparts. That benefits consumers, who get lower prices, more innovative products, or both. But for the producers—including the local firms that fail and their employees—it can be a tough process.

The Scope and Benefits of the North American Free Trade Agreement

The North American Free Trade Agreement (NAFTA) created a free trade zone among the United States, Canada, and Mexico. It's the largest free trade zone in the world. It connects 444 million people whose annual production of goods and services comes to $17 trillion.

The agreement entered into force on 1 January 1994. NAFTA called for some duties and other trade restrictions to be phased out over time. That process was completed on 1 January 2008.

Two-way trade by the US with Canada and Mexico now exceeds US trade with the European Union and Japan combined. And US exports to the NAFTA partners have risen from $142 billion to $418 billion.

The Mexican economy grew by 30 percent between 1993 and 2003. Mexican exports to the US reached more than $138 billion, while its exports to Canada grew from $2.7 billion to $8.7 billion during the same time. But Mexico's small farmers, whose plots are tiny and not very productive, complain that they cannot compete with more efficient US farms. While US farms receive US government subsidies, in the past few years the Mexican government has cut its farm subsidies. This has increased problems for Mexican farmers.

Workers manufacture Otis elevators at this *maquiladora* factory in Nogales, Mexico.
Photo by Robert Harbison / © 1995 The Christian Science Monitor

The North American Free Trade Agreement connects 444 million people whose annual production of goods and services comes to $17 trillion.

The Scope and Goals of the Central American Free Trade Agreement

The Central American-Dominican Republic Free Trade Agreement (CAFTA-DR) is the first trade accord the United States has signed with a group of developing countries. The United States approved the agreement on 5 August 2004. The other parties include:

- Costa Rica
- El Salvador
- Guatemala
- Honduras
- Nicaragua
- The Dominican Republic.

CAFTA-DR has been put into practice on a rolling basis as individual parties have fulfilled its requirements. Like other trade pacts, it's meant to create new opportunities by doing away with tariffs, opening markets, and reducing barriers to services. It also aims to establish state-of-the-art rules for twenty-first-century commerce. Advocates of CAFTA-DR say it will make trade and investment in the region easier and will promote closer relationships between the countries. Like all such agreements, however, it has many opponents in the United States and the partner countries, especially among labor unions, who fear that free trade endangers jobs.

The CAFTA-DR countries are the third-largest market for US exports in Latin America, after Mexico and Brazil. US policymakers hope that such agreements will lead to more economic development in the region, ending the cycles of poverty, political turmoil, violence, and drug smuggling that have troubled it for so long. They also hope more opportunity in Latin Americans' home countries will lessen the pressure many feel to illegally emigrate to the United States.

US military intervention in the region over 200 years has not greatly altered the patterns that have hindered Latin America. Free trade advocates are betting that their policies can be effective where armed force has not.

Lesson 2 Review

Using complete sentences, answer the following questions on a sheet of paper.

1. What was the importance of silver and sugar in the New World?
2. What does the GINI index measure, and how does Latin America compare with other regions?
3. What did Simón Bolívar do in 1828 that helped establish a tradition in Latin America?
4. What patterns have Argentina, Chile, and Brazil followed?
5. What country has drug violence so serious that some are comparing it to a "failed state"?
6. Which American city in the 1920s had conditions similar to those in Colombia?
7. What ideal was behind Mexican liberals' efforts to limit the Roman Catholic Church?
8. What is "liberation theology"?
9. What is the basic purpose of free-trade agreements?
10. What is the largest free trade zone in the world? How many people does the zone connect, and how much do its members produce?

Applying Your Learning

11. How does drug money affect an economy like Colombia's?

LESSON 3 Cartels and the Growing Drug Trade

Quick Write

What effect do you suppose the rescue of the 15 FARC hostages had on Colombians? On FARC members? On the Colombian government?

Learn About

- the key factors that drive and sustain the drug trade
- how the drug trade undermines local governments and damages economies
- how the US and local governments have tried to cut off the drug trade

The drug trade is dangerous not just because it produces problems such as addiction and gang violence—serious though those are. The drug trade also generates immense amounts of money, enough to fund a whole army.

In Colombia, the drug trade supports a Marxist guerrilla group called the Revolutionary Armed Forces of Colombia, or FARC. FARC began its campaign to topple the Colombian government in 1964. It has funded its efforts with hundreds of millions of dollars in drug profits.

The government has fought back. In recent years, it has met with some great successes, including killing top FARC leaders. In addition, the ranks of FARC's foot soldiers have shrunk by about half over 10 years. But the rebels still have some things going for them: the drug trade and hostages. FARC has nabbed hundreds of civilian and military hostages over the years.

None was higher profile than one particular group of 15 hostages that included three American contractors and Ingrid Betancourt Pulaceo. Betancourt, a former Colombian presidential candidate, was held captive for six years. With family in France, she had become a cause célèbre—her circumstances aroused a lot of sympathy and interest—especially in the European press.

In a daring operation in July 2008, the Colombian military rescued all 15 hostages "safe and sound." Not a single shot was fired, Betancourt said afterward. It was a more forceful blow against FARC, analysts said, than the government could ever have delivered with a missile.

How did they do it? A "mole"—a secret government agent—had infiltrated FARC. He had persuaded his FARC superiors to transfer the 15 hostages to the camp of the group's new top leader, Alfonso Cano.

The hostages thought they were going to be part of a prisoner exchange. The rebels tied the hostages' hands and feet. They took the hostages to a camp supposedly belonging to a "friendly" nongovernmental organization (NGO). When the hostages saw what looked like more guerrillas at the NGO camp, their hearts sank.

But the "guerrillas" turned out to be Colombian Army commandos in disguise. As the commandos tied up the rebel leaders, one of the pilots called out to the hostages: "We are with the army. You are free."

Vocabulary

- graft
- narcotic
- extradition
- forfeiture

The Shadow Wolves, the last Native American US Customs unit, load bales of confiscated marijuana onto a pickup truck in Arizona to haul it away and burn it.
Photo by Robert Harbison / © 2002 The Christian Science Monitor

The drug trade generates immense amounts of money, enough to fund a whole army.

The Key Factors That Drive and Sustain the Drug Trade

The drug trade is a dangerous, criminal business. But it is a business. Looking at it that way will help you understand better how the illegal trade works.

The Importance of a Good Climate for Growing Coca and Marijuana

Classical economics teaches that every country should do what it does best. Unfortunately, much of Latin America is well suited for growing coca—from which cocaine is made—or marijuana, or both. Marijuana plants thrive under the intense sun of places like Mexico. Coca flourishes in the Andes Mountains.

fastFACT

People of the Andes region have chewed coca leaves for thousands of years. But pure cocaine was extracted from coca leaves only in the mid-nineteenth century.

How Widespread Poverty Contributes to the Drug Trade

Widespread poverty makes coca and marijuana irresistibly attractive to farmers as cash crops. Not unlike sugar in the colonial period, they are relatively lightweight, high-value commodities. They are well worth the cost of shipping to markets in North America and elsewhere. Farmers can feed their families much more easily on the earnings from a small plot if it's planted in marijuana or coca than if they raised wheat or corn. In strictly business terms, such farmers are seeking the best return on their investment.

Lack of opportunity feeds the drug trade in another way. In crowded Latin American cities with few job choices, many people take work as a lookout or messenger for a drug merchant. In these communities the richest and most "successful" businessmen are often drug lords. People who are poor and looking for work have a hard time resisting the wages drug lords are willing to pay.

Why Being Close to the United States Matters

Classical economics also teaches that if demand is great, suppliers will enter the market to meet that demand. There is, unfortunately, great demand for illegal drugs in the United States. In an economic sense, demand for drugs means not just the desire for them, but desire backed with money to pay for them. Latin American countries have their own problems with drug use among their citizens. But being so close to such a large market of potential US customers is an important factor in the Latin American drug trade.

Traffic, backed up into Mexico, waits to pass through customs to get into the United States.

Photo by Robert Harbison / © 2001 The Christian Science Monitor

Drug smugglers sometimes stuff their illegal payloads into car fenders and other ingenious hiding places to try to get past US Immigration and Customs Enforcement officers.

During President Ronald Reagan's administration, his wife, Nancy, promoted an antidrug campaign with the slogan "Just say no!" It drew widespread criticism as too simplistic. But its underlying logic was sound: The market for drugs would vanish if Americans ceased to demand them.

How Sea, Land, and Air Access Makes Smuggling Drugs Easier

The US-Mexican border runs for nearly 2,000 miles and is one of the most frequently crossed frontiers in the world. NAFTA, the North American Free Trade Agreement, has only tightened the connections between the two countries since it took effect. And that in turn has only increased the opportunities for smuggling.

Some drugs come into the United States by water—in small craft making their way through the Caribbean Sea or the Gulf of Mexico and making landfall on the Florida coast. Others get into America by land—stuffed into car fenders and other ingenious hiding places as smugglers try to get their payloads past US Immigration and Customs Enforcement officers. Some people, called drug mules, simply carry their illegal loads across the Southwestern deserts into the United States. Other smugglers bring drugs in by air. They often use small planes that evade detection by radars at the edge of US territorial waters.

How Weak Local Governments and Widespread Corruption Impact the Drug Trade

As you read in Lesson 2, the drug trade can bring so much money into an area that it overwhelms the local economy and corrupts local governments. Pablo Escobar Gaviria, who controlled the Colombian drug trade in the 1980s, used the phrase "*plata o plomo*" to describe the choice he offered those who got in his way: "silver or lead." They could accept a bribe or face his bullets. It's believed that Escobar ordered the killings of hundreds if not thousands of politicians, judges, and policemen. You might say the way weak local governments and widespread corruption impact the drug trade is by enabling it to continue.

A woman studies a bullet-riddled wall where a drug cartel killed two men in the border town of Palomas, Mexico.

Photo by Tony Avelar / © 2009 The Christian Science Monitor

The drug trade can bring so much money into an area that it overwhelms the local economy and corrupts local governments.

How the Drug Trade Undermines Local Governments and Damages Economies

In a speech a few years ago, Dante Caputo, secretary for political affairs for the Organization of American States (OAS), described drug trafficking as a form of organized crime that ultimately amounts to an attack on democratic power. He reminded his listeners of Latin America's special vulnerabilities when it comes to the drug trade. "Our American hemisphere is the first region in the world—there have been no others—to bring together such democracy, poverty, and inequality," he said.

This triangle of factors requires special attention, Caputo suggested. Poverty makes a society fragile, he said. This fragility opens doors for the drug trade. And once the doors are open then the weaknesses of Latin American democracies—still relatively young—make it hard to defend against the drug lords' power.

Mexican agents talk to a group of would-be migrants about the dangers they face when crossing the border–which can include drug smugglers, gangs, and dehydration.
Photo by Howard LaFranchi / © 2000 The Christian Science Monitor

An OAS official has described drug trafficking as a form of organized crime that ultimately amounts to an attack on democratic power.

How Violence, Bribery, and Graft Lead to Corruption in Government and Business

In his speech, Caputo told of his experience as an election monitor in an unnamed Latin American country. He saw drug traffickers buying votes to install their own mayors in certain towns. If traffickers control a city's mayor and town council, he said, they need not fear the law holding them to account. In fact, with their own politicians in place, the drug kings can then also engage in graft—*the illegal use of power to get more power, money, and property*.

Drug lords are no longer interested in just selling drugs, Caputo warned. They want power, too—at a local level first, but ultimately at a national level. "In some of our countries," he added, "they are knocking on the doors of the central government."

Carlos Lehder Rivas, a Medellín Cartel leader in Colombia, is an example of a drug lord who tried to become a political power. US authorities eventually prosecuted him and got him convicted. But before that, Lehder bought interests in local Colombian radio stations and newspapers. He even created something he called the Latino Nationalist Party. He promoted his political ideology, a combination of nationalism and fascism, through his newspaper, *Quindio Libre*.

Pablo Escobar is another drug lord who tried—with success—to buy his way into the people's hearts. He could certainly afford to do so. At the peak of his power, Forbes magazine identified him as the seventh-richest man in the world. He handed out cash to the poor. He built housing for poor people. He bought sports teams and built stadiums for them.

Like Lehder, he, too, made his way into politics. In 1982 Escobar won election as an alternate congressman—a sort of deputy representative to fill in during the absence of the main representative—in the national legislature.

A campaign mural for former Mexican President Vicente Fox covers the US-Mexico border fence on the Mexican side.
Photo by Robert Harbison / © 2001 The Christian Science Monitor

Now drug lords want in on the political scene, too—at a local level first, but ultimately at a national level.

Colombian Marines patrol a river for signs of cocaine labs in their country's southern jungle.

Photo by Howard LaFranchi / © 2001 The Christian Science Monitor

In the early 1980s many young Colombians became addicted to *basuco*, a highly addictive and damaging form of cocaine.

The Influence of Increased Levels of Drug Addiction on the Workforce

The drug trade doesn't just corrupt governments and tarnish legitimate economies. It leads to health problems as well. As the drug trade developed during the 1960s and 1970s, Latin Americans tended to think serious drug use was a problem just for North Americans. But over time, they learned they were wrong.

In Colombia during the early 1980s, for instance, many young people became addicted to *basuco*. *Basuco* is a highly addictive and damaging form of cocaine, normally smoked with marijuana or tobacco. Smugglers dumped it on the domestic market at low prices because it wasn't of "export" quality.

Basuco caused the same kinds of problems that crack cocaine was causing in the United States around the same time. It was cheap. And it soon became more popular than marijuana. Hundreds of thousands of Colombians grew addicted. Many suffered permanent nervous disorders.

In Mexico, which has become a major drug smuggling center, more than 460,000 people are addicted to drugs, according to a study reported by the *Los Angeles Times*. That's an increase of 51 percent between 2002 and 2008, the newspaper said.

This has obvious implications for society as a whole. But it also has special significance for the workforce. As you have read, income inequality in Latin America is extreme. And so it is crucial for individual men and women to better their lot by finding ways to take part in the economy at a higher skill level. Latin America needs fewer farm laborers and more technicians. Its people need to find ways to work smarter, not harder. But it's hard to do that while addicted to drugs.

In addition, drug addiction among the population tends to drive away outside investors. A company looking to build a state-of-the-art factory in a particular town, for instance, will study its working-age population. Company officials will ask, "Will we be able to find enough people who can operate our expensive high-tech equipment safely and effectively? Will they be able to use our sensitive instruments correctly?" If company officials see evidence of widespread drug addiction in the community, they will answer those questions "no." And they will put the factory somewhere else.

How Illegal Monies From Drug Trades Creates Economic Inflation

The drug trade has other damaging economic effects. Among them is inflation, or an increase in prices. To put it the other way around, inflation is a decline in purchasing power. Inflation is the reason you get less for your money. Too much money chasing the same amount of goods causes a jump in prices.

Not all price rises are because of inflation. Sometimes prices rise because values rise. If house prices rise in a neighborhood because the streets and sewers have been improved and the neighborhood becomes a more attractive place to live, that's not necessarily inflation. That's increased value. Nor is it inflation if wages rise because workers become more productive.

> **fastFACT**
>
> Cocaine is not a new problem. The United States first banned its importation in 1914.

But drug money coming into an area tends to force up prices generally, without any real value added. Consider a farmer needing help with his banana crop. If he has to compete with marijuana or coca growers for the same pool of workers, he's likely to have to pay more—even though bananas are still bananas and still sell for the same price.

Similarly, drug barons drive up land prices. Every time a drug lord can outbid a banana farmer on a piece of property, for instance, that higher sale price affects the whole land market. The higher price becomes "the new normal"—even though the land hasn't really become more valuable in any legal way. It's just that someone with more money to spend has come along.

How the US and Local Governments Have Tried to Cut Off the Drug Trade

The US government has spent most of the twentieth century and all of the twenty-first so far fighting the importation and use of illegal drugs. Under heavy pressure and with help from the US government, Colombia was finally able to rein in the two biggest drug cartels, in Medellín and its rival in Cali.

But Americans' continuing demand for illegal drugs has led new suppliers to enter the marketplace. The focus of US concern has now shifted to Mexico, where at least 6,500 people—mostly criminals—died in drug-related violence in 2008 and the first quarter of 2009.

The US Department of Justice has called Mexican drug cartels the greatest organized crime threat facing the United States. People usually think of "organized crime" as the Mafia, or "the Mob." But now US officials see the Mexican drug cartels as posing a similar threat.

The picture is not entirely bleak, however. The federal government has scored some important victories against the Mafia. Now it's using the same approach to choke off the Mexican drug trade and its violence.

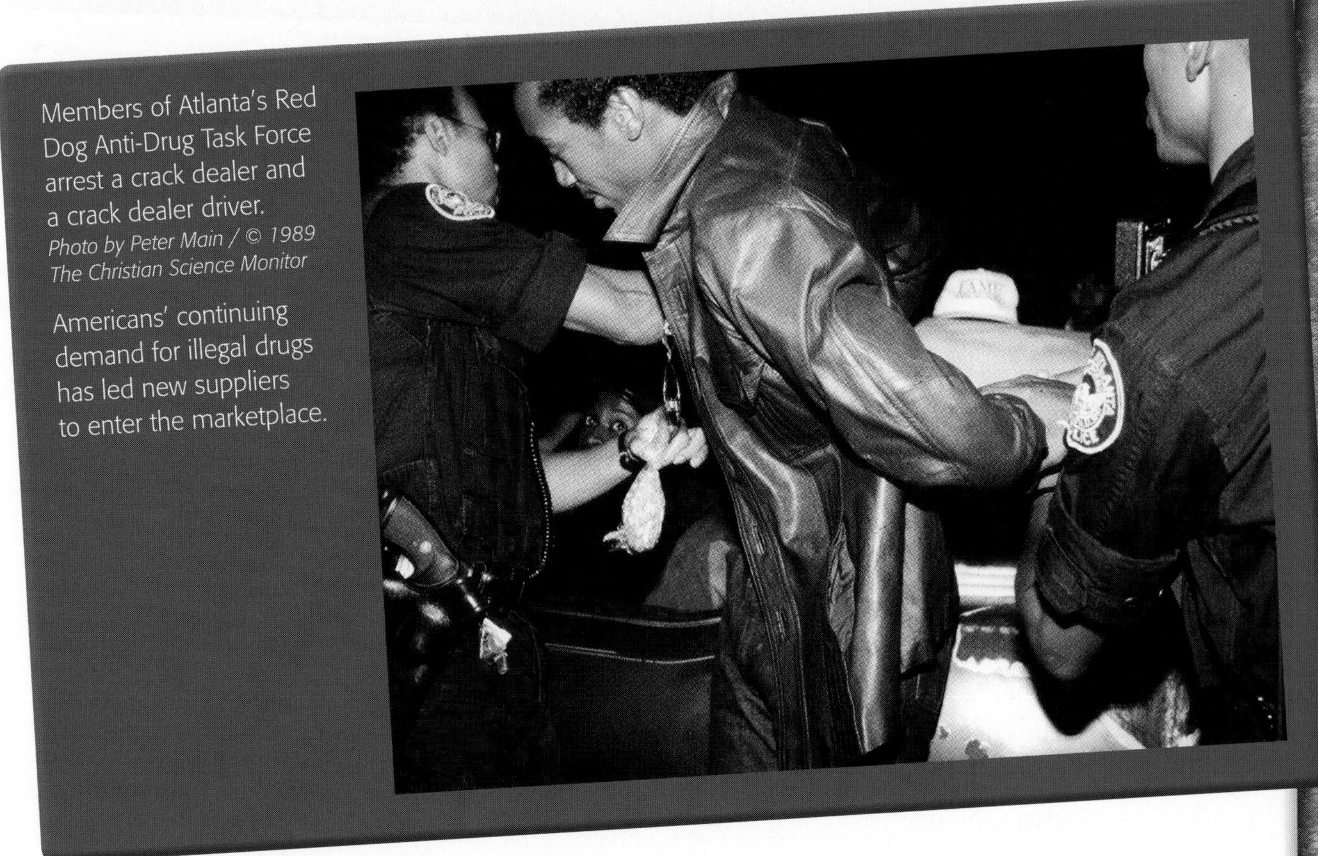

Members of Atlanta's Red Dog Anti-Drug Task Force arrest a crack dealer and a crack dealer driver.
Photo by Peter Main / © 1989 The Christian Science Monitor

Americans' continuing demand for illegal drugs has led new suppliers to enter the marketplace.

Law enforcement officials in the Bahamas look over their latest drug seizure, 2,900 pounds of marijuana found buried in the sand on the island of Mayaguana.
Photo by Kris Axtman / © 1999 The Christian Science Monitor

All anti-drug efforts start with intelligence.

Two Justice Department officials testified before Congress in March 2009. They said that task forces are the best way to fight these drug cartels. Prosecutors must lead the task forces. And they must be backed by solid intelligence. This approach also brings local, state, federal, and even international resources to bear on the problem.

This worked well in the late 1980s and 1990s during groundbreaking Mafia prosecutions in the United States and Italy. In their testimony, the Justice officials said this approach "broke the back" of the Mafia. And today federal authorities are fighting the drug cartels in the same way.

This approach has five key elements:

- The extensive use of coordinated intelligence
- A strong focus on key cartel leaders—on investigating them, arresting them, and bringing them to the United States for trial
- Investigation and prosecution of gun-, cash-, and drug-smuggling cases
- Police action against the "spillover" effects in the United States of cartel violence in Mexico
- Prosecutions in federal court of those responsible for smuggling, kidnapping, and violence.

The Justice testimony described Operation Xcellerator. This two-year operation led to the arrest of more than 750 people on narcotics charges. (A narcotic is *an addictive drug that alters mood or behavior and usually induces sleep.*) It was a multiagency, multinational effort that began in May 2007. Its target was Mexico's Sinaloa Cartel. This cartel has brought tons of cocaine into the United States and distributed it through an extensive network.

Mexico is fighting hard against the cartels. In some locations, the federal government and the drug lords are waging open warfare. Along with the criminals, many Mexican officials, police, and soldiers have died in the violence.

The United States and its neighbors and partners aren't the only ones in Latin America fighting the spread of drugs. The seven countries of Central America plus the Dominican Republic have united with Mexico to fight drugs, crime, and terrorism. These countries have found themselves caught in the middle. The world's biggest cocaine consumer—North America—lies to the north. And the world's biggest supplier, South America, lies to the south.

In high-level meetings in the first half of 2009, representatives of those countries stressed the need for greater border security, more and better drug-abuse prevention and treatment programs, and stronger efforts against organized crime. Trafficking in drugs and arms is of special concern to these countries.

Efforts to Identify, Arrest, and Prosecute Drug Cartel Leaders

It all starts with intelligence. Since 2003 the US Justice Department has worked with other agencies to develop a target list of the world's "most wanted" drug kingpins. This list helps the Justice Department and its partner agencies focus their resources.

Extradition is another part of the effort. Extradition is *the legal process by which one country surrenders a criminal or criminal suspect to another for punishment or trial*. It's often quite a sensitive issue. This is especially true when a country extradites one of its own citizens. "Will our citizen get a fair trial in this foreign country?" officials have to ask themselves.

For this reason, it's important that in recent years both Colombia and Mexico have returned fugitives to the United States in unprecedented numbers. Extradition is key to prosecution. Some of those extradited have been major drug lords, including leaders of Mexico's Tijuana and Gulf cartels.

Efforts to Seize Drug Cartels' Assets

Another part of the US strategy against the cartels is *asset forfeiture*. Forfeiture is *the government's seizure of property involved in criminal activity*. The US government wants to take the cartels' arms and cash away from them. Asset forfeiture is a powerful tool to strip criminals of illicit wealth, including homes and cars. It's part of every US government operation thought to involve drugs. Between 2007 and 2008, for example, the Justice Department seized $2.9 billion in forfeited assets.

In the case of the Sinaloa Cartel, for instance, agents not only made hundreds of arrests but also seized around $59 million in currency, more than 12,000 kilos of cocaine, 1.3 million Ecstasy pills, and thousands of pounds of other drugs. They also seized 169 guns, 149 motor vehicles, three aircraft, and three boats.

Mexican soldiers chopper in for a drug raid on a marijuana plantation on an isolated mountainside.
Photo by Sara Miller Llana / © 2006 The Christian Science Monitor

The National Drug Intelligence Center estimates that Mexican cartels gross between $17 billion and $38 billion annually from drug sales.

Efforts to Disrupt the Flow of Cash and Arms

The US government focuses not just on eliminating the drug cartels' leadership. Attacking and dismantling their financial systems is also a top priority. The National Drug Intelligence Center estimates that Mexican cartels gross between $17 billion and $38 billion annually from drug sales. Much of that ends up as "bulk currency"—suitcases or even truckloads of cash.

A policeman keeps his eyes open for trouble in São Paulo, Brazil.
Photo by Robert Harbison / © 1989 The Christian Science Monitor

When drug cartel members fall into authorities' hands, it's often state troopers or local police who make the arrests. But state and local law agencies may lack resources for drug investigations. So federal agents often step in to take over that work.

When drug cartel members fall into authorities' hands, it's often state troopers or local police who make the arrests. They seize cash at the scene. The actual banknotes often can provide valuable clues. These notes help lead the police to the cartel leaders. But state and local law agencies may lack resources for such investigations. So federal agents often step in to take over that work.

Although the drug cartels are Mexican, US officials know that money from the United States fuels the drug trade. They also know that guns from the United States play a role in much of the drug violence. Stopping the gun trade is primarily the charge of the Bureau of Alcohol, Tobacco, Firearms, and Explosives. It's a part of the Justice Department and is widely known simply as ATF.

ATF agents seize individual weapons when they can. But the real work of stopping the flow of arms involves identifying the sources of trafficked guns. Project Gunrunner is the ATF's plan for combating firearms violence by cartels along the Southwest border. It involves spotting the relatively small number of dealers who don't follow the rules for gun sales. Then agents go after them to investigate. Ultimately they seek to eliminate them as sources of illegal arms.

The drug trade is one of the most important issues in inter-American relations. It affects countries from the mountains of South America to the shores of Hudson Bay. North Americans like to blame South American governments for not doing enough to stop it. South Americans reply that without demand from wealthy North Americans, there would be no supply in the first place. But it's not so simple—plenty of North Americans are involved in the supply network, and many Latin Americans have become consumers.

The fact is that both supply and demand are responsible for the situation. They can only be controlled if North America and Latin America cooperate. Working out the details of that cooperation will keep diplomats busy for years to come.

Lesson 3 Review

Using complete sentences, answer the following questions on a sheet of paper.

1. Why would a farmer with only a small plot of land be tempted to grow coca or marijuana instead of wheat or corn?
2. What, in economic terms, does the phrase "demand for drugs" mean?
3. What is *basuco* and what problems does it cause?
4. What's an example of how drug money creates inflation?
5. What is extradition and why is it important?
6. What is asset forfeiture?

Applying Your Learning

7. Do you think the United States can win the war on drugs? Why or why not?

LESSON 4 Poverty, Educational Limitations, and Environmental Challenges

Quick Write

What advantages do you think the banana trade brought to Honduran people? Do you think it brought any disadvantages?

Learn About

- how reliance on commodities versus manufactured goods impacts poverty
- the impact of racial and socioeconomic divisions in Latin America
- how poor education, urban overcrowding, and high population growth contribute to poverty
- the challenges of environmental pollution and deforestation

The year 1899 was important for Honduras. For one thing, for the first time in decades, the Central American country had transitioned peacefully from one president to another. General Terencio Sierra Romero had succeeded Policarpo Bonilla Vásquez as president.

But something else happened that year that probably mattered more for Honduras in the long run. The Vaccaro brothers of New Orleans shipped their first boatload of bananas from Honduras to New Orleans.

Bananas are probably as familiar to you as apples. But Americans weren't really used to eating bananas at the turn of the last century. The Vaccaros were bringing in something new. This yellow tropical fruit was a big hit with the public. The banana trade boomed. Within a few years railroad lines were under construction along the Caribbean coast to help haul the fruit to the banana boats.

Soon bananas were Honduras's main export. They were just about its only export, in fact, since its mines had largely played out. The Honduran government was eager to do what it could to support the new industry. It gave the banana companies—the Vaccaros and their competitors, also based in the United States—tax breaks. The businesses got permission to build wharves and roads. The government let them go ahead with improvements to interior waterways and gave them charters to build new railroads.

How Reliance on Commodities Versus Manufactured Goods Impacts Poverty

Vocabulary

- maquiladora
- subsistence farming
- social mobility

"How can we bring more value to the marketplace?" That's a fundamental question that businesses ask themselves as they think about what goods and services to offer their customers.

It's also a question that governments have to consider. As you have read in other chapters, their countries can do better, and their people can climb out of poverty, as they find ways to produce higher-value goods. That means not just raw materials but finished goods. Even a simple product like a bar of soap embodies the labor of those who made it. More-sophisticated products may reflect highly skilled labor, leading-edge technology, good design, and even a good sense of which colors are really "hot" just now.

In this section you'll read about Honduras as an example of a country that's had trouble finding ways to add value. It's a pattern found in other parts of Latin America and the developing world as a whole.

Visitors browse at a high-end merchandise shopping mall in downtown Buenos Aires, Argentina.
Photo by Andy Nelson / © 2002 The Christian Science Monitor

Countries can do better, and their people climb out of poverty, as they find ways to produce higher-value goods.

A factory owner walks through his plant that employs 10 people to assemble bags in Buenos Aires, Argentina.

Photo by Andy Nelson / © 2002 The Christian Science Monitor

Many Latin American countries have made efforts to develop a manufacturing base, but some, such as Honduras, have been only moderately successful.

Honduras as a Nation Historically Dependent on One Commodity

Honduras is one of the Western Hemisphere's poorest countries. After independence, its economy languished for years. Hondurans couldn't figure out how to produce things that the world needed.

The country's limited success has rested in exporting commodities, such as agricultural products and minerals. For a century and a half, Honduras has been largely dependent on exports of one commodity or another.

Minerals came first: principally silver but some gold, too. Miners dug ores containing gold, silver, lead, zinc, and cadmium out of the earth and shipped them to the United States and Europe for refining. But the ore didn't last forever—

the New York and Honduras Rosario Mining Company, the main operator there, shut down its works in the 1950s. By the early 1990s minerals accounted for only 2 percent of Honduras's gross domestic product.

Around 1900 another commodity became important: bananas. The country's fortunes rise or fall with the world price for bananas. It's not a good position to be in. The government has tried to get its farmers to diversify—to grow other crops. But this hasn't worked well. There have also been efforts to develop manufacturing in Honduras. But they have been only moderately successful. The country lacks a dependable source of economic growth.

fastFACT

Copper is a good example of a commodity. It gets processed into such things as wire, piping, and roofing. Wheat is an agricultural commodity. It is ground into flour that ends up in the bread at your supermarket. People sometimes speak of "a rare commodity" or "a useful commodity." But for the most part, an economy based on commodities is relatively low on the scale of development.

Why Bananas and Coffee From Honduras Have Been Unreliable Sources of Income

Like all farmers, banana growers have to contend with drought, disease, and disaster. In 1974, for instance, Hurricane Fifi destroyed about 95 percent of the banana crop, as well as killing thousands of people. Like any agricultural commodity, bananas are subject to price variations. Even more important for Honduras, international corporations grow and market most of its bananas. They keep most of the wealth this generates, too. That's another reason bananas aren't the best foundation for Honduras's economy.

Coffee is the other main commodity that Hondurans grow. In the mid-1970s coffee moved past bananas as the country's leading export earner. But its prices vary more wildly than those of bananas. A steep price decline around 2000 underlined the risks of building a national economy on coffee beans.

Part of the problem was that many countries saw coffee as an extremely popular product and therefore a crop they would like to grow. But coffee was a mature industry. People around the world, including Europeans and North Americans, have been drinking it for centuries. Yes, demand was strong—coffee is the second most valuable commodity in the world after oil. But plenty of growers were already supplying this demand.

Many of those who wanted to get into the business didn't see this, however. Or else they failed to see how prices could fluctuate. Many small farmers in Vietnam, for instance, started growing coffee when prices were strong in the mid-1990s. They briefly made Vietnam the world's No. 2 coffee producer. But when prices collapsed a few years later, these farmers were left in a difficult position.

Why Honduras Has Never Developed a Manufacturing or Industrial Sector

It's not that Honduran governments haven't understood the basic problem. After 1950 they pushed modernization of the country's farm sector. They also tried to encourage the development of a richer mix of national exports. They urged Honduras to deliver more than just bananas to the world marketplace. To this end, they spent heavily on better roads, telephone lines, and other infrastructure. They increased credit to farmers, and they provided technical assistance of various kinds. With help from strong prices on world markets, these efforts began to pay off.

Then during the 1960s the Central American countries banded together to form the Central American Common Market, or CACM. They lowered tariffs between member countries but erected a high external tariff. The CACM was meant to encourage trade among its members. It also stimulated Honduras's industrial sector. Some Honduran manufactured goods, such as soaps, sold well in other Central American countries.

But the industrial sectors of El Salvador and Guatemala were bigger, stronger, and more efficient. So Honduras bought more goods from these trade partners than it sold to them. Nobody would call El Salvador or Guatemala industrialized countries. Yet both were more industrialized than Honduras, which just couldn't compete with them. After fighting a war with El Salvador in 1969, Honduras effectively withdrew from the CACM.

In more recent years, Honduras has experienced some strong economic growth—more than 6 percent annually for 2004 through 2007. A bright spot has been its maquiladoras, or *export-reprocessing centers*. These factories take raw materials from elsewhere and turn them into finished goods such as textiles for export. The centers employ about 130,000 Hondurans, out of a workforce of 2.8 million.

But the maquiladoras have another effect. The manufacturing sector in Honduras is tiny. And the small companies that make up the country's manufacturing sector have been under stress the past few decades. The foreign-owned maquiladoras

From Grinding Stones to Wiring Harnesses

In times past, a maquiladora was a gristmill. Farmers could bring their corn or other grain to be ground there. Once it was turned into flour they'd collect and sell it. Nowadays, maquiladora has come to mean primarily assembly plants in Mexico or elsewhere in Latin America. The idea is that like the workers at the gristmill, those at the assembly plant do one phase of the work, and then return the goods to those who brought them. For example, maquiladora workers assemble garments—sewing together pieces of fabrics made elsewhere. Or they may make wiring harnesses, as another example. Wiring harnesses are tedious to produce but are a necessary part of automobiles and other vehicles.

An indigenous woman prepares food for tourists in Ecuador as part of an ecotourism program her tribe has started to earn money.
Photo by Melanie Stetson Freeman / © 1993 The Christian Science Monitor

One way to look at a country's economy is to consider what opportunities it provides to its people to add value.

contribute to this stress. They can afford to pay relatively high wages. The small Honduran firms have to match them or risk losing workers. Unable to pay the costs, many of these firms have folded.

The Effect of National Economic Weakness on the Honduran People

One way to look at a country's economy is to consider what opportunities it provides to its people to add value. An economy with a large manufacturing sector needs a lot of people to do a lot of high-value work. If these high-value sectors are big enough, they lift up even people who hold jobs outside the manufacturing sector.

The engineers and other high-skilled—and highly paid—employees of an aircraft-manufacturing plant, for instance, can afford comfortable homes, expensive cars, well-made clothing, and good food. The money they spend "turns over" in their communities. It creates opportunity for homebuilders, auto dealers, clothing salespeople, and supermarkets and restaurants—even the dishwashers and the parking valets.

But Honduras doesn't have that kind of base, despite efforts to diversify its economy. What it does have is too many unskilled and uneducated laborers. The farm sector accounts for more than half the labor force. In the United States, the comparable figure is less than 3 percent.

Honduras has a large population of subsistence farmers. Subsistence farming is *a type of farming in which the farmers and their families eat most of what they produce and sell very little*. More than half of the rural population gets by on farms of only about five acres. Such people have few economic opportunities.

In addition, skilled laborers are generally scarce in Honduras. About a third of the workforce is in the service sector or the "urban informal sector." This informal sector consists of street vendors, poorly paid household servants, and other "off the books" jobs.

Because there is so little economic opportunity in Honduras, many Hondurans are drawn to the United States. The money they send back to their families accounts for almost one-quarter of the country's gross domestic product—the total of goods and services a country produces.

Like other countries in its situation, until Honduras finds a way to move its economy away from commodities and into manufactured goods, such challenges will continue.

The Impact of Racial and Socioeconomic Divisions in Latin America

Race plays a part in the Latin American economy as well. It means generally lower incomes for blacks and indigenous people. Race and ethnicity lead to gaps in opportunity, including education and other benefits. A look at Brazil and Colombia illustrates the issues.

The Social Stratifications Between the Wealthy and Poor

A *stratified* society is one with "layers." Colombia and Brazil are two good examples of such societies.

Colombia

Traditions brought over from Spain four centuries ago remain a strong influence in Colombia. The social "layers" are clearly separate from one another. Individuals' occupation, income, family background, education, and power determine people's social class. These align with race to a large degree. The more European or white one is, the more likely that person is to belong to the upper class.

Colombians know it can be hard to move up into a higher social class. Social mobility is the expert term for this *ability of individuals or groups to move up or down within a class structure according to changes in income, education, or occupation*. As elsewhere, social mobility is somewhat greater in the cities.

A study done during the 1980s found that the upper class made up 5 percent of Colombia's population. The middle class made up 20 percent. The lower class accounted for 50 percent. The bottom 25 percent were called simply "the masses."

These groups included a couple of important subgroups. The "new rich" were those who had made enough money to get a toehold in the upper class. Blue-collar workers who had the protection of membership in a trade union belonged to the oddly named "upper lower class." And so did poorer white-collar workers. You might say these two groups were the "top of the bottom."

Indigenous women in traditional garb wait to congratulate a young Bolivian couple on their wedding day.

Photo by Melanie Stetson Freeman / © 2007 The Christian Science Monitor

Race and ethnicity lead to gaps in opportunity for blacks and indigenous people in Latin America.

The Paradox of Colombian Blacks

As Colombian society developed, it was so tightly based on Spanish culture that any other influence was seen as "un-Colombian." This attitude made it hard for indigenous people to find a place in Colombian society.

You might think, then, that the African slaves would have had an even harder time. But in fact, blacks in Colombia were actually more fully part of national society, and left a greater mark on it, than the indigenous people. This was true even though the native peoples had been in Colombia for thousands of years. But Africans had worked as household servants in Spain since the Middle Ages. Unlike the indigenous people, they didn't seem "alien" to the Spanish. And black slaves had no "homeland" in the New World to retreat to. That made it harder for them to preserve African culture, and easier for them to adopt Spanish culture. And their relationship as servants or slaves put them into close contact with their masters.

This black woman in Bolivia says that Afro-Bolivians are starting to assert their rights in society.

Photo by Sara Miller Llana / © 2009 The Christian Science Monitor

In other Latin American countries, such as Colombia, blacks have been more fully part of national society, and left a greater mark on it, than the indigenous people.

The Teatro Amazonas is a 100-year-old opera house in Manaus, Brazil, with a sparkling white bas-relief over the entrance.
Photo by Robert Harbison / © 1997 The Christian Science Monitor

Brazil is a highly stratified society with extreme gaps between rich and poor.

Brazil

Brazil is another highly stratified society. Among its particular features—slavery in Brazil lasted for nearly three generations after independence in 1822. The country's income distribution—one of the worst in the world—is also highly skewed. In other words, its gap between rich and poor is extreme, even by regional standards.

Brazil's relatively high per capita income masks this deep inequality. An estimated one-fifth of the people suffer extreme poverty. And, especially if they live in rural areas, these poor people are almost invisible to their better-off fellow citizens.

However, another feature of Brazilian society is "vertical" relationships—close ties between people of property and prestige and those who may both work for them and depend on them. In the countryside, this was known as *coronelismo*, or "colonelism." The idea was that a wealthy landowner (often a former military officer, hence the term) would "take care" of the poor. This was seen as necessary in the absence of effective education and other public services. The relationship was rather like that of a European feudal lord and the servants he protected. And the tradition lives on today.

Town leaders in Florida, Bolivia, are looking for money to repair this schoolhouse's leaky roof.
Photo by Sara Miller Llana / © 2008 The Christian Science Monitor

Public primary and secondary schools in Latin America tend to be underfunded and of poor quality.

The Lack of Adequate Educational Opportunities for the Working Poor

Such arrangements highlight the fact that public primary and secondary schools in Latin America tend to be underfunded and of poor quality. They fail to teach basic skills in mathematics, language, and science. Poor school funding leads to poorly trained and motivated teachers. Fewer than 30 percent of students in the region finish high school. And many who do finish lack skills to compete in the workplace.

In Brazil, for instance, public education is free, in theory at least. It's also required for children ages 7 to 14. But coverage is incomplete and uneven. The lower classes attend public schools, while the middle and upper classes turn to private education. This changed somewhat during the economic squeeze of the 1990s, which led many middle-class parents to move their children from private to public schools.

One of Brazil's biggest problems is children who don't go to school at all. Enrollment varies from richer to poorer states, and between black and white children. But the dropout rate after the second year is about 25 percent.

In 1994 UNICEF, the United Nations' children's fund, ranked countries by per capita income compared with the rates of school absence in the first five grades. Given its position as a vibrant emerging country, Brazil should have been a winner in that competition. Instead it came in dead last.

Colombia has done better at getting children to school, but it, too, has high dropout rates. The average Colombian adult has received only 5.3 years of schooling. The average Brazilian has only 4.9 years.

In Mexico, by contrast, the number is 7.2 years. In recent decades, Mexico has made some impressive gains in enrollment. Between 1950 and 1995, for instance, the number of students enrolled increased eightfold. Still, many of Mexico's education problems are typical of the region. Instruction is of poor quality. Dropout rates are high. Laws that require children to attend school are largely ignored. And the system fails to prepare students for the global economy.

The Patterns of Discrimination Against Indigenous Populations in Latin America

About 10 percent of those who live in Latin America are indigenous, or native, people—about 40 million to 50 million. They lag behind other Latin Americans in both income levels and other measures:

- education
- health
- access to water
- access to sanitation.

Experts see this gap as evidence of discrimination against Latin America's indigenous people. A United Nations official has called this discrimination a "structural problem"—something that's built into the way a society works. Governments do not devote enough resources to indigenous peoples' problems.

In Panama, for instance, 95 percent of the indigenous population is poor. Among the nonindigenous, only 37 percent are poor. In Mexico, the corresponding numbers are 80 percent and 18 percent. The same pattern prevails elsewhere in the region. In 2000 three of the world's highest rates of child mortality were in Latin American countries with relatively large indigenous populations: Bolivia, Guatemala, and Peru. Experts see this pattern as likely to hold Latin America back from meeting its development goals and from overcoming poverty.

A Cuna Indian woman displays a mola, her people's traditional clothing.

Photo by Melanie Stetson Freeman / © 1991 The Christian Science Monitor

She makes molas and sells them to tourists in Panama City, Panama. About 10 percent of those who live in Latin America are indigenous, or native, people, and they lag behind other Latin Americans in income levels and other measures.

In a poverty-stricken area southwest of Buenos Aires, Argentina, two girls—out of a family with six children—tend to their young brother.
Photo by Andy Nelson / © 2002 The Christian Science Monitor

Experts say that in Latin America, richer, better-educated, city-dwelling women are far likelier to have smaller families than poorer, poorly educated women in the countryside.

How Poor Education, Urban Overcrowding, and High Population Growth Contribute to Poverty

Besides class and racial divides, other factors contribute to high poverty levels in Latin America. These include the state of education, overcrowding in the cities, and the size of the population.

Not only are Latin American schools poor, as the last section illustrates—the region lags behind much of the world in education. A study by the Inter-American Development Bank in 1999, for instance, found that in Southeast Asia, 80 percent of young people got a high school education. In Latin America, the figure was only about 33 percent.

Lack of opportunity in rural areas pushes many of these poorly educated people into Latin America's cities. At times, more newcomers arrive than the cities can employ. The newcomers often overwhelm the cities' ability to provide housing, schools, hospitals, police protection, and other services.

The brightest news in this poverty mix is that high population growth is now less of a problem than it was. Latin America used to be known for its high rates of population growth. But these have fallen significantly. On the US Central Intelligence Agency's 2009 list of estimated population growth rates for 234 states and territories around the world, most of Latin America was somewhere in the middle.

Latin America's giant, Brazil, had an annual growth rate of 1.20 percent. This put it ahead of the world average rate, 1.17 percent, by just a whisker. Mexico, with a rate of 1.13 percent, was just a few places behind.

However, those figures are for countries as a whole. As with the income statistics mentioned above, a single figure that represents a national average can mask a wide disparity. Experts say that in Latin America, richer, better-educated, city-dwelling women are far likelier to have smaller families than poorer, poorly educated women in the countryside.

The Lack of Skilled Job Opportunities for Those Who Have Little or No Education

It's as true in Latin America as it is anywhere on the globe—the future belongs to those with an education. But even if the region's young people manage to finish school, many are still unprepared for the demands of the modern workplace.

A consultant gave this grim assessment as the twentieth century drew to a close: "We are creating two urban classes: those who are prepared to lead, with broad technological and scientific knowledge, and their subordinates, who have a deficient education and are ill-prepared for the challenges of the next century."

Schoolchildren play a game at a park in Chile.

Photo by Robert Harbison / © 1989 The Christian Science Monitor

It's as true in Latin America as it is anywhere on the globe—the future belongs to those with an education.

Attitudes are changing, however. Brazil, for instance, is home to some fine universities. Literacy rates in its big cities match those of the developed world. Brazilian parents have noticed the economic and social changes going on around them. This has led them to more highly value education for their children. As in the United States, school availability has become an important factor for Brazilians in deciding where to live and how to make a living. It's even helping people decide how many children to have.

The Effects of Mass Migration From Rural to Urban Areas

Urbanization has been one of the great trends across Latin America over the past few decades. Two-thirds of the region's people once lived in rural areas, with the rest in cities. Now those proportions have been reversed. In some countries the cities account for an even larger share of the population.

Peruvians gather after Sunday Mass in rural Pisac, Peru, to consult with their local Catholic priest about community issues.
Photo by Alfredo Sosa / © 2002 The Christian Science Monitor

Two-thirds of Latin America's people once lived in rural areas, with the rest in cities. Over the past few decades those proportions have been reversed.

"Self-Help Housing"

Affordable housing for low-income people has been a problem in Mexico since World War II. The government had some success in financing new apartment complexes, but the units tended to end up occupied by government employees. For most of the urban lower class, "self-help housing" has become the only real option.

Such a community starts when investors buy a tract of land on the outskirts of a city. The tract is typically acreage too poor to farm and not well suited for more upscale development. The investors slice up the property into many small lots. They sell them to poor families who jump at the chance to become landowners. They put up simple brick structures—sometimes just a single large room. On paper, the investors are required to put in water and sewer lines and streets. In fact, though, they often do little more than mark the lots for sale.

Brazil, for instance, saw some 20 million people move from rural to urban areas during the 1950s, 1960s, and 1970s. This migration was one of the largest of its kind in history. By 1991 city-dwellers were 75 percent of the population.

What are the effects of such mass migrations? For individuals, a move to the city is likely to mean more opportunity for education and work. People can acquire the skills that make them more valuable to employers. But the city is a demanding environment. The cost of living is higher. And to survive in an urban economy you must have cash to survive. In the country, people can live off the land, growing their own food.

Urban growth requires governments to do a lot of building. They're not always up to the task. Roads, power lines, telephone cables, and water and sewer lines have to be installed. People also need schools, hospitals, and police stations. The result of uncontrolled growth is the overcrowding mentioned earlier.

Mexico, for instance, became much more urban over the course of the twentieth century. The share of the population living in towns or cities with at least 15,000 inhabitants increased more than fivefold. It went from 10.5 percent around 1900 to 57.4 percent in 1990. This dramatic growth, much of it concentrated in three of the country's biggest cities—Mexico City, Guadalajara, and Monterrey—strained the federal government's ability to build urban infrastructure. Housing was in especially short supply.

The growth of cities tends to bring with it the development of an urban middle class. These people make their way in the world on the strength of what they know, or know how to do, rather than what they own. They tend to be white-collar workers, technicians, civil servants, unionized workers. They also tend to be politically active. The rising middle classes have helped bring in, or bring back, more democratic rule in many parts of Latin America over the years.

Unemployment Patterns in Large Urban Areas

It's an ancient tale, told throughout history around the world—a young person from the country arrives in the big city, full of hope. And then he discovers its streets are *not* paved with gold.

Moving to the city doesn't always lead people to success. Many arrive and find no jobs. Or they may discover that they lack the right skills for the jobs available.

In either case, they will be unemployed, a situation much more common in the city than in the country. That's because in Latin America unemployment is largely an urban phenomenon. Joblessness in the cities generally averages 15 percent—about five times the rural unemployment rate.

That's a dramatic difference. But to understand why that should be, remember that to be "unemployed," someone must be actively looking for work. Rural people who may work a few months at a time but then don't actively look for other jobs—perhaps because they know there aren't any—aren't "unemployed." They're considered out of the labor force altogether.

But in the city people have no choice but to be in the labor force. They have to pay rent and buy food at a grocery store. There's no garden out back as there is in the country. Therefore, city dwellers who lose their jobs must find new ones quickly,

For Latin Americans, leaving the countryside for the city is a matter of leaving a relatively low-risk, low-reward situation for a high-risk, high-reward one. As the numbers you've seen throughout this lesson indicate, it's a move that millions have made.

The Challenges of Environmental Pollution and Deforestation

As you might imagine, this kind of urban growth greatly affects the environment. With all its social and economic challenges, Latin America boasts some of the greatest environmental treasures on the planet. Its biodiversity is one of its strengths. But the region has some of the worst environmental problems on the planet, too. Fortunately, it's made remarkable progress cleaning up certain trouble spots, especially recently.

Girls wash the family laundry in a river near their home in Ecuador.
Photo by Melanie Stetson Freeman / © 2009 The Christian Science Monitor

Plaintiffs charge in a lawsuit that the oil industry has polluted many rivers in this area. Local people usually swim, bathe, wash clothes, and cook with water from these rivers. Latin America has some of the worst environmental problems on the planet.

Efforts to Fight Air Pollution in Places Such as Mexico City

It used to be that when the children of Mexico City drew pictures with their crayons, they reached for their brown crayons when they colored in the sky. Cyclists routinely wore surgical masks to keep from breathing in too much soot on the road. Birds fell dead from the sky. Ozone in Mexico City reached unsafe levels 97 percent of the year.

That's how serious the air pollution was. In 1992 a United Nations report called Mexico City the most polluted metropolis on earth.

Mexico City's air-quality challenges are unique. It's a megacity of 20 million people. Its high altitude means the air is thin. Fuels burn less efficiently and cleanly there. And volcanoes ring the city, spewing gases into the air.

But in recent years the city has made a dramatic turnaround. Though ozone remains a problem, some of the worst contaminants have been cut back by three-fourths.

Mexico has cleaned up its act with new technology and new laws. It has phased out leaded gasoline. It has required new cars to have catalytic converters, as they do in the United States. Environmental police have started ticketing drivers of smoke-belching old cars. The government leaned on power plants to switch from burning oil to natural gas.

Other Latin American cities are fighting smog, too. For instance, São Paulo, Brazil, the largest city in South America, cut the number of the largest soot particles in the air by 21 percent between 2000 and 2004. São Paulo, Mexico City, and the region's other major cities are part of the Clean Air Initiative for Latin American Cities, formed by the World Bank. The Clean Air Initiative seeks to improve air quality in Latin American cities by developing or improving city clean-air action plans in which everyone with an interest participates. This includes governments, the private sector, and the public in general.

Sewage—including that flowing from this Mexicali, Mexico, neighborhood—and garbage pollute the New River, which eventually empties into California's Salton Sea.
Photo by Robert Harbison / © 2001 The Christian Science Monitor

Some 127 million people in Latin America lack access to sanitation services.

The Region's Attempts to Provide Clean Drinking Water and Sanitation

Water extraction—the pumping of water out of the ground—increased tenfold in Latin America over the twentieth century. A major share of this water—71 percent—goes to irrigate crops. But a lot goes to quench people's thirst, too. And there are some hopeful statistics. In 1990, 82.5 percent of Latin Americans had access to improved drinking water. By 2004, 91 percent did. Access to safe water in urban areas rose from 93 percent to 96 percent during this time. In rural areas, the number rose from 60 percent to 73 percent. Even so, some 50 million people in Latin America still lack access to safe drinking water. Of these, 34 million are in rural areas.

Sanitation services—the safe removal of sewage, including human waste—reached 77.4 percent of Latin Americans in 2004. This was up from 67.9 percent in 1990. But only 14 percent of the sewage was adequately treated. As a result, both surface and groundwater are subject to serious pollution. And some 127 million people still lack access to sanitation services.

Social scientists use the term "improved drinking water" to refer to water coming from any of several different safe sources. These can include ordinary household taps, communal wells, protected springs, and even rainwater.

Effects of Deforestation and Desertification on the Region's Biodiversity

Latin America is one of the world's most important regions for biodiversity. The Amazon River basin alone is home to about 50 percent of the planet's biodiversity. Brazil, Colombia, Ecuador, Mexico, Peru, and Venezuela are in a league of their own, even within Latin America. Each one has more plant and animal species than most of the rest of the world.

Tree trunks and stumps litter the floor of a clearcut rainforest in Brazil.

Photo by Robert Harbison / © 1997 The Christian Science Monitor

Latin America is one of the world's most important regions for biodiversity.

But this biodiversity is under threat. Deforestation leads to habitat loss. When land is cleared for farming or building new roads and housing and shopping centers, plants and animals end up with fewer places to live. This can endanger species.

A study by the Worldwide Fund for Nature (WWF) identified 170 eco-regions within Latin America, including the Caribbean. Of these, only eight are relatively intact, and another 27 relatively stable. Another 82 are endangered, 31 of those critically so. Still another 55 are vulnerable.

Latin America contains about a quarter of the world's forest cover, but these forests are disappearing rapidly. About two-thirds of the loss of forest cover that occurred in the world between 2000 and 2005 took place in Latin America. The largest net loss happened in the Brazilian rainforest. There people have cleared forests to grow crops for biofuels, such as ethanol.

When an area loses its forests, it loses at least some of its ability to keep its rainwater. Soil washes away and clogs rivers and other bodies of water. Emissions of carbon dioxide, one of the major greenhouse gases, increase.

Unchecked deforestation can lead to desertification, which affects some 25 percent of this region. Just as Mexico has made a rapid reduction in its air pollution, so, too, the region is beginning to address deforestation. Paraguay stands out as a positive example—a 2004 law has helped reduce deforestation by 85 percent.

Latin America faces some difficult and unique economic, social, and environmental issues. While many of these are left over from the colonial period, others result from current government policies. Whatever their cause, the conditions that result affect not only the people of the region—they often deeply affect the United States and its relations with its Latin American neighbors. You'll read about this in the next lesson.

Lesson 4 Review

Using complete sentences, answer the following questions on a sheet of paper.

1. Since 1900 Honduras has been economically dependent on what?
2. Why was Honduras unable to compete against El Salvador and Guatemala within the Central American Common Market?
3. What are the "vertical" relationships typical in Brazilian society?
4. Indigenous people lag behind other Latin Americans in terms of income and what other measures?
5. How are attitudes toward education changing in Brazil?
6. How is unemployment in the cities different from joblessness in rural areas?
7. Cyclists in Mexico City used to wear surgical masks on the road. Explain why.
8. What is Paraguay's recent standout achievement in environmental protection?

Applying Your Learning

9. Maquiladoras have been good for Honduras' economy as a whole but a problem for the country's small manufacturing firms. Explain why.

LESSON 5 US Interests and Regional Issues in Latin America

Quick Write

What would you think of someone who tried to organize a group similar to the Rough Riders today to fight in Afghanistan?

Learn About

- the history of US relations with Cuba
- the history of US relations with Haiti
- the challenges of migration from Latin America to the United States
- the effects on the United States of the political and economic challenges in Latin America

One of the most colorful episodes of the Spanish-American War is the story of the Rough Riders. The story also illustrates how much has changed in US relations with Latin America—and how much has changed in the way people fight wars.

When the war broke out, 39-year-old Theodore Roosevelt was assistant secretary of the Navy under President McKinley. He was also a leading advocate for the liberation of Cuba. He got permission from the War Department to raise a regiment of soldiers to aid the Cuban cause.

He enlisted his friend Dr. Leonard Wood to help with this quest. Wood was an army doctor who had won the Medal of Honor fighting Apaches in the 1880s. In 1898 he was also President McKinley's own doctor.

Roosevelt lacked military experience himself, so Dr. Wood became the commander of this volunteer regiment, as a colonel. Roosevelt became a lieutenant colonel.

The regiment consisted of 1,250 men from all over the United States. It drew cowboys, Indians, and other men from the Wild West. (And the West was still pretty wild in those days.) It also drew Ivy League athletes and sons of privilege from back East. They were a very diverse group. But what they had in common was that they could all ride and shoot. They were in good shape and could be ready for war with little training.

They gathered in San Antonio, Texas, in May 1898. On 14 June 1898 they shipped out to Cuba from Tampa, Florida. On 1 July, now-Colonel Roosevelt led the Rough Riders and several regular Army units up Kettle Hill and the San Juan heights overlooking Santiago, Cuba. Their capture of these positions led to the city's surrender, virtually ending the war in Cuba.

The History of US Relations With Cuba

Vocabulary

- covert
- visa
- remittance
- amnesty
- guest worker
- resource nationalism
- expropriation

As you read earlier, the United States entered the Spanish-American War in large part to get Spain out of the New World. Cuba was the last major Spanish colony to gain independence. Cubans began their struggle to throw off Spanish rule in 1868. In 1895 Cuba's national hero, José Martí Pérez, started a final push for independence.

Cuban farmers plant sugar cane by hand.

Photo by Melanie Stetson Freeman / © 1991 The Christian Science Monitor

Cuba was the last major Spanish colony to gain independence. Cubans began their struggle to throw off Spanish rule in 1868.

The US Relationship With Cuba From the Spanish-American War Through the Batista Regime

In order to protect American citizens during the fighting between the Spanish and Cuban rebels, President McKinley sent the battleship USS *Maine* to Havana Harbor. The Spanish government permitted this deployment. On 15 February 1898, however, the *Maine* blew up and sank, leading to more than 250 fatalities. More than five tons of powder charges for the *Maine*'s guns ignited. Why it happened remains a mystery.

But its effect was clear. Americans assumed the Spanish had torpedoed the ship. The incident brought the United States into Cuba's war with Spain. "Remember the *Maine*!" was a rallying cry around the United States. For advocates of an assertive American foreign policy, joining the conflict was a smart move. "A splendid little war," Ambassador John Hay called it in a letter to Theodore Roosevelt.

The war didn't last long. In December 1898 Spain signed a peace treaty handing control of Cuba over to the United States. On 20 May 1902 the United States gave Cuba conditional independence, under the terms of the Platt Amendment.

fastFACT

The Platt Amendment was a set of eight conditions that Cuba had to fulfill before the US government would withdraw its military forces from the island. The amendment led to the treaty that gave the US government a perpetual lease—one lasting for as long as the United States wishes to keep it—on the Guantánamo Bay naval base.

The US government wanted a stable, independent Cuba. But it also wanted the right to intervene militarily to defend US interests on the island. These were considerable. In 1934 the US government decided Cuba had met the Platt Amendment's conditions, and granted Cuba full independence.

The leaders of independent Cuba were generally authoritarians who won or held onto power by force. Fulgencio Batista y Zaldívar was an army sergeant who wielded power behind the scenes and then won the presidential election in 1940. Defeated for reelection in 1944, Batista didn't run in 1948. Four years later he changed his mind and ran again. But three months before the date of the scheduled election, he took power in a bloodless coup. He suspended the election and began ruling by decree. After a decade of misrule, forces led by Fidel Castro and others ousted Batista on 1 January 1959.

US Attempts to Undermine Fidel Castro's Regime

Soon it became clear that Castro was a communist allied with the Soviet Union. Presidents Dwight D. Eisenhower and then John F. Kennedy didn't want Castro spreading communism through the Americas.

Old Havana's streets are fairly empty of cars even in the twenty-first century.
Photo by Alfredo Sosa / © 2008 The Christian Science Monitor

Besides going after the Castro regime through economic embargoes, the Kennedy administration implemented Operation Mongoose in 1961 to undermine and overthrow Castro.

In November 1961 the Kennedy administration decided to implement something called Operation Mongoose. This code name referred to a covert—*hidden or secret*—program to undermine and overthrow Castro. This was after the Bay of Pigs invasion, but before the Cuban missile crisis, which you read about in Lesson 1. The idea was to stir up a rebellion in Cuba that the United States would then support. It would be an excuse for ousting Castro.

The Central Intelligence Agency and the State and Defense departments were involved. So was Robert Kennedy, the attorney general. Operation Mongoose included military attacks, sabotage, and political propaganda.

Throughout 1961 and 1962, though, the United States kept after Cuba with some more mundane means, too: trying to isolate the island economically. The US government also supported military raids by anti-Castro guerrillas. Castro and his government knew these raids had US support. Both sides understood that these raids were likely to kill Castro and other Cuban officials, even if that wasn't their main goal.

Bracing for a US attack, Castro asked for and got more military aid from the Soviet Union. As US agents worked on Operation Mongoose, Soviet Premier Nikita Khrushchev secretly sent mid-range nuclear missiles into Cuba. Operation Mongoose, in other words, was part of the context for the Cuban missile crisis.

After the missile crisis, Kennedy agreed to stop the raids on Cuba. This decision sorely disappointed the Cuban exiles in the United States. They wanted Castro out. Some even began to turn against Kennedy. They wanted to see him out, too.

Some evidence suggests that by the fall of 1963, a year after the missile crisis, Kennedy had approved some efforts to improve relations with Cuba. But other evidence suggests that the raids against Castro continued. They were just under a thicker blanket of secrecy.

In an interview with an American news agency in the fall of 1963, Castro warned against the United States "aiding terrorist plans to eliminate Cuban leaders." He added that US leaders would be in danger if they tried to oust or kill Cuba's leaders. When Kennedy was assassinated in November 1963, some suspected that Castro was involved. (No link has ever been proved.)

In the mid-1970s a US Senate committee revealed that the US government had sponsored efforts to kill Castro at various times during the 1960s.

It found the CIA involved in two kinds of operations. One was a plan to organize a coup to overthrow Castro. It included a relationship with an important Cuban who, though trusted by Castro, had told the CIA he would be willing to organize such a coup.

The other kind of operation was a joint effort between the CIA and organized crime to kill Castro. Sam Giancana, leader of the Mafia in Chicago, was seen as part of this effort. After several years in Mexico, he was deported back to Chicago. He was murdered there in 1975, probably by Mafia rivals, shortly before he was scheduled to testify before the Senate committee.

The Effects of Cuban Immigration to the United States in the Castro Era

Many Cubans fled their country after Castro's revolution. More than 200,000 came to the United States from 1959 to the 1962 missile crisis. Flights were suspended after that. But refugees kept coming—they just came by boat instead of air.

In 1966 Congress passed the Cuban Adjustment Act. It assumed that any Cuban reaching American soil was by definition a refugee from communism and was welcome in the United States.

This was significant. "Refugee" is a term that has some political status and rights acknowledged in international law. A refugee is different from an economic migrant. "Refugee" was not a status the United States would bestow casually.

But American policymakers in the mid-1960s believed that by accepting Cubans as refugees, they could show up communism's failings in the Caribbean and make a humanitarian gesture at the same time. Thousands of Cubans took advantage of the opportunity. But as Cuban authorities tightened their grip on the island, the flow of refugees slowed to a trickle.

Suddenly, however, the trickle became a flood again. Dissent was growing in Cuba. The economy was not. People lacked housing and jobs.

Castro responded to these rumbles of protest with a gesture so subtle the United States overlooked it at first. On 4 April 1980 he withdrew the Cuban guards at the Peruvian embassy in Havana. That opened the embassy to ordinary Cubans. They could go there and request asylum. More than 10,000 did so.

Then Castro announced that the port of Mariel was also "open." Anyone who wanted to climb into a boat to leave Cuba could. For six months people streamed out of Cuba in whatever vessels made their way into Mariel to pick them up. The Cubans of Florida pressed all manner of small craft into service for this Mariel boatlift, as it's called.

Cuban men people watch on a stoop in Old Havana. *Photo by Alfredo Sosa / © 2008 The Christian Science Monitor*

While Cubans continue to try to reach American soil, the US has received two especially large waves of Cuban immigrants: first in the 1960s and next with the Mariel boatlift in the 1980s.

By the time it was over, more than 125,000 Cubans had left. Most of them ended up in Florida. Under US law, they were welcomed as refugees. But the often dangerously overloaded boats that carried them were in violation of US maritime law. The US Coast Guard's response to the boatlift was the largest peacetime operation it had ever undertaken. It combined rescue and law enforcement.

The boatlift was controversial in the United States. The 1950s to '60s wave had included many highly educated citizens—mostly whites. The *Marielitos*, as they were known, were poorer and generally darker-skinned than the earlier waves of Cubans. Additionally, a small percentage of the latest wave was criminals and people who were mentally ill. Castro had simply released them from prisons or hospitals. This made many Americans think Castro was flooding Florida with "undesirables." That was a misimpression. But the boatlift also made people think the United States had lost control of its borders.

Eventually most of the *Marielitos* found homes in their new land. The United States absorbed them, as it has absorbed newcomers for centuries.

Today Cuba's government once again restricts freedom of movement. It prevents some people from leaving the country because of their political views. It denies exit permission even to those who have permission to enter other countries.

At this writing, Cuba has begun a transition from Fidel Castro's rule. The Cuban dictator is elderly and in poor health. No one knows for sure what the island will be like when he's gone. But whatever changes occur are likely to affect people's movements between Cuba and the United States.

The History of US Relations With Haiti

As two large island-nations in the Caribbean, Cuba and Haiti make for some interesting contrasts and comparisons. Since 1959 the United States has—officially—stayed out of Cuba. But it's returned to Haiti again and again.

Haiti is the world's oldest black republic. After the United States, it's the second-oldest republic in the Western Hemisphere. In fact, its success against Napoleon I helped persuade the French emperor to sell Louisiana to the United States.

US Interventions in Haiti Through the Duvalier Regimes

As a former French colony, Haiti has lived a different history from Latin America's mostly Spanish-speaking countries. But it has at least a couple of things in common with them. Haiti saw political unrest throughout much of the nineteenth century, and a lengthy period of US military occupation in the twentieth century's early years. After 19 years, US forces withdrew in 1934.

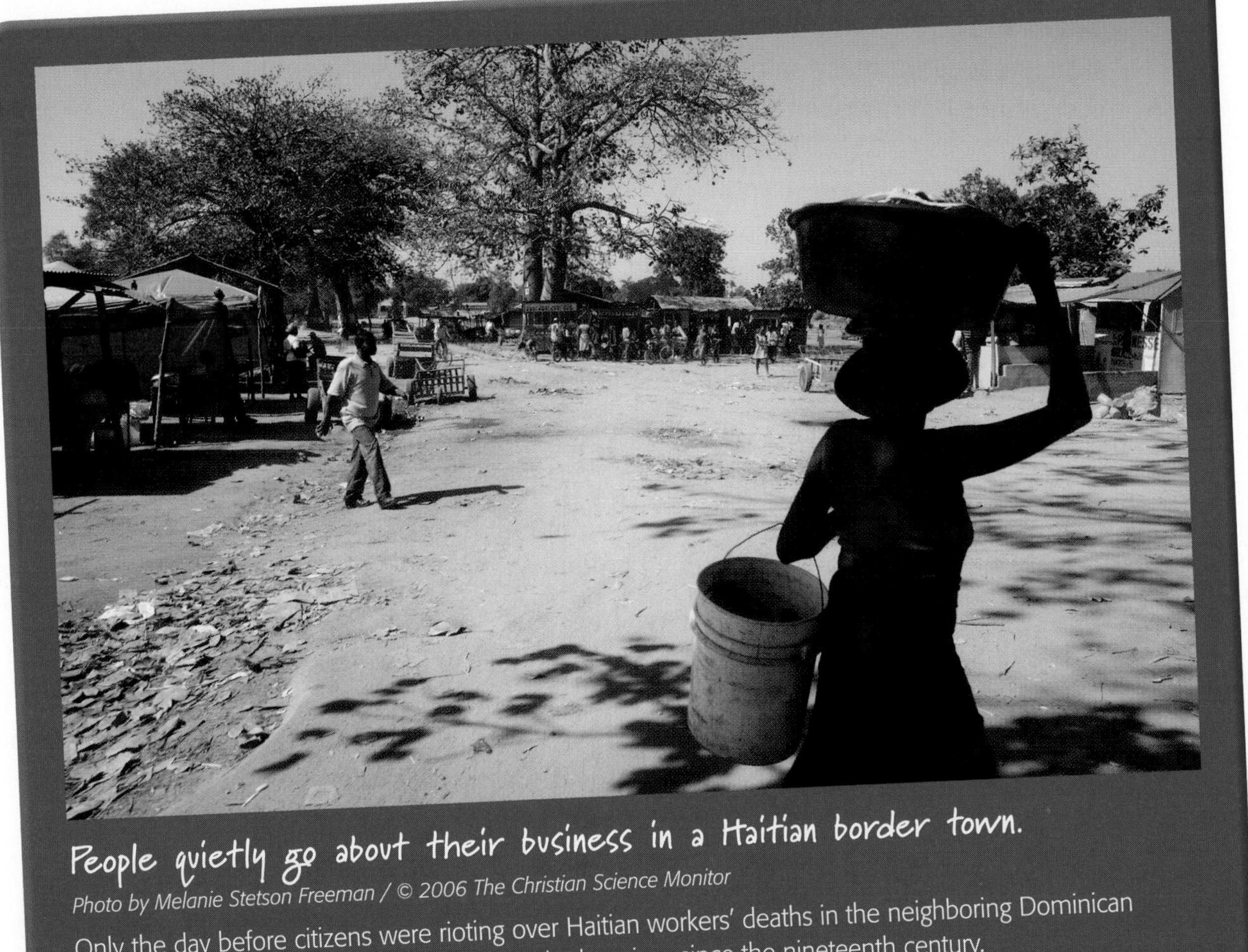

People quietly go about their business in a Haitian border town.

Photo by Melanie Stetson Freeman / © 2006 The Christian Science Monitor

Only the day before citizens were rioting over Haitian workers' deaths in the neighboring Dominican Republic. Haiti has seen unrest—political and otherwise—since the nineteenth century.

'Papa Doc'

In 1957 François Duvalier won election as Haiti's president. The Haitian physician enjoyed being called by his nickname, "Papa Doc." Duvalier had made a name for himself running a US-funded public health campaign. He entered public life without any particular ideology. But he began to see himself as "the personification of the Haitian fatherland."

His harsh, corrupt rule disturbed President Kennedy. Especially troubling was the charge that Duvalier had used American military aid not to train Haiti's regular army but to strengthen the *tonton macoutes*. These were a paramilitary force loyal to Duvalier personally.

This misrule made the United States suspend its aid to Haiti. US aid was actually a good share of Haiti's national budget. But the cutoff didn't matter much to the Haitian people because officials had been siphoning off aid money to their own pockets. In fact, the aid cutoff gave Duvalier an excuse to look as if he were standing up to an outside power.

After Kennedy's death in 1963, US pressure on Duvalier eased. Because of Haiti's strategic location near communist Cuba, Washington settled into grudging acceptance of "Papa Doc."

'Baby Doc'

"Baby Doc," though, was something else. Jean-Claude Duvalier was a clueless 19-year-old when he succeeded his father as Haiti's president-for-life. Haiti's elite were content to see a second generation of Duvalier rule. But Baby Doc had even less political competence than his father. He stumbled into one crisis after another, including a bizarre episode involving the country's pig population. Haiti's widespread poverty made this all worse.

Things began to change after 1983. On a visit to Haiti in March of that year, Pope John Paul II declared, "Something must change here." He called for fairer distribution of income, more social equality, and more concern for the masses.

Two years later, a revolt began. Duvalier responded with a cut in food prices but also a police and army crackdown and the closure of independent radio stations. A military plot to remove him was under way, however. By early 1986 President Ronald Reagan was pressuring Duvalier to leave Haiti. Finally on 7 February 1986 he and his wife did. Duvalierism was over. But it wasn't clear what would follow.

These Little Piggies Did Not Go to Market

When people speak of a "US intervention" in a foreign country, they generally mean military action. At one point in Haiti, however, US intervention involved pigs rather than guns.

In mid-1978 African swine fever plagued pigs in the Dominican Republic, next door to Haiti on the island of Hispaniola they share. Washington feared that the disease would spread to North America. So the US government pressured Jean-Claude Duvalier to slaughter the entire Haitian pig population. American officials promised that US and international aid agencies would replace the pigs with animals certified as disease free.

Duvalier went along. But his regime failed to see how the cull angered his people. For many of them, black Haitian pigs were like savings banks. The Haitians could sell their pigs whenever they needed cash. And the animals were low maintenance. They took neither special food nor special care. The replacement, non-native pigs needed both. Haitians deeply resented this US intervention. Their anger would help bring Duvalier down.

US Policy Toward Haiti From the Cédras Regime to the Present

As the Duvaliers headed off to exile in France, most Haitians said they wanted democracy. But they didn't really know what it was or how to bring it about.

Haiti had a series of provisional governments as it created a new constitution. In December 1990 Jean-Bertrand Aristide won two-thirds of the vote in a free and fair presidential election. He took office in February 1991. But after just a few months, a group of military officers overthrew him. They were very much like the people who had supported the Duvaliers.

From October 1991 on Haiti had military rule. The regime may have been responsible for thousands of deaths. The UN and the OAS tried repeatedly to restore the Aristide government. They failed.

Then the UN Security Council adopted Resolution 940. It authorized members to do whatever it took to oust the military rulers and reinstate the legally elected government. The United States took the lead in forming a multinational force to go to Haiti and show General Raoul Cédras and his team to the exits.

fastFACT

Haiti has two official languages—French and Creole (Kreyol). While the elite can read and write French, almost the entire population speaks Creole. Most of the Creole vocabulary comes from French words. But the grammar and pronunciation are so different from French that a French-speaker cannot understand it and must study it as a foreign language.

On 19 September 1994 the first of 21,000 troops arrived in Haiti. On 15 October President Aristide and his government returned from exile.

Then on 7 February 1996 Haiti enjoyed its first-ever democratic transition of power. Aristide handed off power to his ally, René Préval.

Things began to go downhill from there, though. Aristide broke with his party to form a new one. It did well in the next round of parliamentary elections. But international monitors called the voting flawed. It was the first of a string of problems with voting. Soon Préval and his government were ruling by decree.

Aristide won another presidential election, taking office again on 7 February 2001. But monitors called this election flawed, too. It led to a political stalemate. Violence followed, including attacks by police on civilian marchers. On 29 February 2004 Aristide resigned his office. He flew off on a chartered plane into exile in Africa. At this writing, René Préval is once again president of Haiti.

Since April 2004 the UN Stability Mission in Haiti has helped to ensure public order. It's made up of several thousand military troops from 18 countries and civilian police from 39 countries. The Security Council votes to renew it every six months.

A vendor walks through muddy, filthy streets in Haiti's capital, Port-au-Prince, where there's no trash pickup.
Photo by Melanie Stetson Freeman / © 2006 The Christian Science Monitor

From 1957 to 1982 about 1 million people left Haiti, which today has 8.5 million people.

How the US Has Dealt With Haitian Immigration

Over the years, so many people have left Haiti that there are some special terms for them. These emigrants are known as "the Diaspora" or "the Eleventh Department." (A "department" in Haiti is roughly comparable to a state.) These emigrants' No. 1 destination has been the United States.

From 1957 to 1982 about 1 million people left Haiti, which today has about 8.5 million people. The coup against Aristide prompted another wave of émigrés. Like the *Marielitos* from Cuba in 1980, these Haitians were largely "boat people." They risked their lives on the Caribbean in vessels better suited for staying close to shore.

The former US Immigration and Naturalization Service reported the arrival of some 55,000 Haitian "boat people" in Florida between 1972 and 1981. The actual number was probably closer to 100,000. No one knows how many perished at sea.

Unlike Cubans, though, Haitians did not count as refugees. They were fleeing a corrupt, authoritarian government. But they weren't leaving a totalitarian communist regime. The United States considered them economic migrants rather than refugees.

Some critics have seen other factors at work here. They point out that Florida's Cubans are well connected politically, while the Haitians are not. Some critics also see racism. After all, Haitians tend to be darker-skinned than even the *Marielitos*.

Haitian emigrants aren't fleeing just political unrest, either. They're fleeing chaos brought on in large part by natural and ecological disasters. In 2008 four hurricanes hit the country. They killed nearly 800 people. They destroyed most of the harvest. Entire cities were left uninhabitable.

The Haitian government wants the US government to grant "temporary protected status" for Haitians in the United States illegally. The hope is to avoid mass deportations back to Haiti. These would flood Haiti with more jobless returnees than it could absorb. Haitians abroad send money back to their families, and the Haitian government doesn't want to cut off this funding.

The Challenges of Migration From Latin America to the United States

Haiti and Cuba are only part of the immigration picture. Immigration to the United States has tended to come in waves. The United States is currently in the midst of a flood of people from Latin America, most from Mexico. Some experts see it as likely to match the immigrant influx of the early twentieth century.

Latin Americans are a much larger part of immigration to the United States today than a century ago. Most of those immigrants were from Europe. In 2007, on the other hand, Mexico was the top country of origin for foreign-born residents of the United States. Latin Americans made up 54 percent of the United States' foreign-born residents.

Two men peer over a fence into the United States from Tijuana, Mexico, in hopes of crossing the border.

Photo by Melanie Stetson Freeman / © 1997 The Christian Science Monitor

The United States is currently in the midst of a flood of people from Latin America, most from Mexico.

Another difference between today's immigration situation and that of a century ago is that so many people are here illegally: 12 million is one often-cited estimate, although it's hard to know the exact tally.

The Difference Between Legal and Illegal Immigration

Americans often talk about immigration as though all immigrants shared the same legal status. But this isn't the case. *Legal immigration* refers to those who work within US law to come to the United States to settle permanently. They may take out citizenship. Before they come, they apply to a US embassy abroad for an immigrant visa. A visa is *a document that gives the bearer permission to travel to a particular country*.

Illegal immigrants, by contrast, arrive in a country without permission. Many come as tourists or students but stay on after their visas expire. Others sneak across the border in the middle of the night. They may even pay smugglers to help them across. Still others are brought in as small children by their parents. Such children may grow up not even knowing their own illegal status.

It is quite common to find more than one immigration status within a single family. Because the United States Constitution's 14th Amendment grants citizenship to anyone born on US soil, parents who have entered the country illegally may have children who are native-born citizens. Some members of Congress have introduced legislation to change this, but so far they have not succeeded.

The Debate Over the Benefits and Damages From Illegal Immigration

There's no doubt that illegal immigrants significantly affect the US economy. But people disagree mightily on whether these effects are positive or negative. The vast majority of illegal immigrants work in low-skill, low-wage jobs. More than half are in construction, manufacturing, hotels, and restaurants. All these sectors depend heavily on these workers.

Damages From Illegals

Some people who believe the negative effects outweigh the positive want to see a crackdown on illegal immigration. They charge that foreign workers take jobs from Americans.

Critics of illegal immigration want the government to punish companies that hire illegal immigrants. With fewer foreign-born workers, these critics say, employers would be forced to hire American citizens. They would have to pay more, however, to win and keep them. They would have to cover health-care benefits and their fair share of taxes. That would be good for those American workers. It might also mean more money rolling through the US economy.

A case in point is a Georgia-based chicken-processing plant, Crider Inc., which lost most of its Hispanic workforce, here illegally, to an immigration raid back in 2006. *The Wall Street Journal* reports that soon the plant owners were hiring local African-Americans for an average of one dollar more per hour than they had paid their illegal employees. The report added, "For the first time since significant numbers of Latinos began arriving in Stillmore[, Georgia,] in the late 1990s, the plant's processing lines were made up predominantly of African-Americans."

Benefits

On the other side of the illegal immigration debate are those who say that the economy would stall without immigrants' "elbow grease." Illegal immigrants do jobs Americans don't want to do, these people argue. If an employer can't find low-wage workers for a factory in the United States, for instance, the firm is likely to ship the whole operation abroad. That would eliminate not only low-wage assembly jobs but better-paying managerial jobs as well.

Jorge Borgas of Harvard University has estimated the effects of immigration, legal and illegal, on American earnings. Between 1980 and 2000, he figured, immigrants increased the labor supply enough to hold down the average annual earnings of American-born men by $1,700, or 4 percent.

Most illegal immigrants who enter the country compete for jobs with Americans who have less than a high school education. These workers represent roughly the bottom tenth of the labor force. Immigrant labor held their wages down by 7.4 percent, Borgas found.

Illegal Immigration to the Rescue of Social Security?

Illegal immigration, one observer has suggested, could be the fastest way to shore up the troubled finances of Social Security.

The suggestion was mostly a joke—but not completely. The idea is that employers withhold money from all employee paychecks. They pay this money, on behalf of their employees, into Social Security, the national retirement system. This includes those who won't ever collect Social Security benefits, as most illegal immigrants won't.

This inclusion of everybody goes back to 1986. Congress passed a law that year making it harder for employers to pay workers "off the books"—that is, in cash, with no tax withheld. Nowadays, however, everyone has a Social Security number, even if it's only a fake number bought from a street-corner vendor. The extra money has been a real windfall for the Social Security Administration.

A cruise ship anchors off Haiti's coast while passengers enjoy a local beach.

Photo by Melanie Stetson Freeman / © 2006 The Christian Science Monitor

The tourists create jobs and bring money to the impoverished island country. Latin American countries also depend heavily on remittances sent back home by relatives living and working in the United States.

The Economic Effect on Latin American Countries of Money Sent Home by Immigrants in the United States

The other side of immigration in the United States is remittances to the immigrants' home countries. *Remit* means "to send back." A remittance is *a sum of money a worker abroad sends back home to his or her family*.

These remittances are important in Latin America. They have increased an average of 19 percent per year since 2000. And they are often significant chunks of each country's gross domestic product.

The value of remittances to Honduras, for example, grew from $440 million in 2000 to $2.6 billion in 2007. As you read in the last lesson, this amounts to nearly 25 percent of Honduras's gross domestic product (GDP). Guatemala and El Salvador have seen similar rate increases. El Salvador, Haiti, and Jamaica are three countries where remittances count for about a fifth of GDP.

Studies find that remittances don't do much to level out Latin America's income inequality. But they do help the very poorest stay afloat.

However, remittances to Latin America fell drastically due to the global recession that began in 2007, according to *The New York Times*. The Inter-American Development Bank told the *Times* in mid-2008 that more than three million Latin American immigrants had stopped sending money to families in their home countries during the previous two years.

Federal, State, and Local Government Efforts to Contain Illegal Immigration

To many Americans, the presence of illegal immigrants in their country represents a failure. To some it's a failure of government to enforce laws and secure national borders. To others, it's a failure to pass laws that acknowledge the place of these newcomers within the economy.

In 1986 Congress passed legislation meant to pardon employers who hired illegal immigrants. It also granted amnesty—*forgiveness or pardon*—to millions of people in America without authorization. The law required that employers obtain documentation that an employee is legally in the United States. One principle effect of the law was to create a market for fake Social Security cards. Some people argue that it also increased the flow north of illegal immigrants across the US-Mexico border.

In May 2006 the US Senate passed legislation that offered a "path to citizenship" for illegal immigrants. It also provided for a "guest worker" program. Guest workers are *migrant workers who work abroad temporarily and then return home.*

Latin Americans look across the Mexican-US border to suburbs in El Paso, Texas, while a US Border Patrol agent stands watch.
Photo by Robert Harbison / © 1995 The Christian Science Monitor

Some people argue that the 1986 US immigration law increased the flow north of illegal immigrants.

Latin America

The Senate bill had support from both parties in that chamber. But its backers couldn't bridge the gaps with what the US House had passed. The House did not favor a path to citizenship for illegal immigrants. So the legislation died. A few months later, Congress passed a bill ordering construction of some 700 miles of border fences between the United States and Mexico.

Border security has generally been a federal matter. But some communities have given up waiting for Congress to act. They are taking matters into their own hands. They are enforcing laws already on the books as a way to stop illegal immigrants.

For example, in Santa Rosa County on the Florida Panhandle, the Sheriff's Department investigated local businesses, seeking evidence that some workers were using stolen Social Security numbers. Many were arrested and charged with violations of state identity-theft laws.

Around the country, police have rounded up thousands of immigrants. The charges are often minor: fishing without a license, for instance. But such arrests have led to deportation in some cases. In others, groups of people simply disappear—like many of the Hispanics of Santa Rosa County.

In 2008 *The New York Times* reported that nearly 150 local police forces were part of, or applying to join, a federal program that trains local law enforcement to investigate and detain suspected illegal immigrants. In other jurisdictions, police are simply acting on their own, with backing from local officials.

The Effects on the United States of the Political and Economic Challenges in Latin America

Even as the United States grapples with immigration issues, Latin America itself has been transformed over the past few decades. Authoritarian rule has given way to democracy in almost every country. That is good news even if those democracies are sometimes a bit shaky. Latin America is also important as a free-market region of the world. Its role as a global provider of energy, minerals, and food is crucial.

A study by the Council on Foreign Relations found that since the end of the Cold War, Washington has shifted its focus in Latin America. The old priorities were containing communism and fighting insurgency. The new priorities are:

- opening markets
- strengthening democracy
- stemming the flow of illegal drugs.

The council study found that both political parties in Washington have consistently supported these goals over the years. The council's report also came up with four other "urgent priorities." These, it suggests, should guide US policy toward Latin America:

- poverty and inequality
- citizen security
- migration
- energy.

The United States still plays a strong role in Latin America. James Monroe would be pleased. But there are fewer situations now in which the US government simply steps in and takes over. The four urgent priorities, the council study said, are opportunities for new direction in US policy and dialogue.

Meanwhile, Latin Americans have pursued interests outside the Western Hemisphere of late. For instance, they have new ties with Africa and Asia, especially China. But even so, ties within the Americas—both trade and the movement of people—have tightened.

Haitian schoolchildren chat with a US soldier in 1994 when the United States led a multinational force to restore the island nation's rightfully elected president to power.
Photo by Robert Harbison / © 1994 The Christian Science Monitor

A Council on Foreign Relations study suggests that ensuring citizen security is among priorities that should guide US policy toward Latin America.

How Poverty and Inequality in Latin America Affect the United States

At this point it should come as no surprise to see "poverty and inequality" at the top of the agenda. It's an issue that spills over into the United States. It spurs much of the immigration to the United States. And it's not just economic inequality between the United States and Latin America—inequality within individual countries causes Latinos to hit the road and head for "El Norte."

In some cases that means north to the United States from Mexico. In others it means north to Mexico from Central America. But as economic and other ties continue to deepen, and given the facts of geography, US well-being is not separate from Latin America's.

Old Havana, the old quarter of Cuba's capital, sits on the island's north coast.

Photo by Alfredo Sosa / © 2008 The Christian Science Monitor

Poverty and inequality in Latin America spur much of the immigration to the United States.

How Challenges to Law and Order in Latin America Affect the United States

As you read in Lesson 3, years of effort to control the drug trade in Latin America have been largely ineffective. Victories are won in one location, only to have new drug lords pop up in another. The battle has led to a sharp increase in public insecurity. Crime and violence are two of the region's top threats.

Drug-related violence, particularly from the Mexican drug cartels, continues to spill over the US border. This danger reaches more than Arizona, New Mexico, Texas, and southern California along their border with Mexico. *The New York Times* reported in March 2009 that US law enforcement has identified 230 cities where the Mexican cartels and their allies maintain drug-distribution networks or supply drugs.

How Latin America Can Help Supply US Energy Needs

Although Latin America has its drug-cartel challenges, it also produces a rich flow of oil. When Americans think of "foreign oil," they tend to think of the Middle East. But as a region, Latin America is the largest foreign supplier of oil to the United States. Latin America accounts for nearly 30 percent of imports, compared with 20 percent from the Middle East. Latin America is also a strong partner for the United States in the development of alternative fuels.

However, Latin America is not a zero-risk energy source. One of the issues is resource nationalism. This refers to *policies or efforts to nationalize a country's natural resources*. People use this term especially with reference to oil. It's sometimes used to refer to nationalization by expropriation—*seizure of a foreign firm's assets, with no compensation paid*.

In an echo of earlier times, Venezuela and Bolivia have recently sought to renationalize the investment of foreign oil producers. (So has Russia, to give an outside example.)

Mexico's constitution, meanwhile, restricts foreign investment in the country's oil sector. Those restrictions affect how long, and how well, Mexico will be able to carry on as an energy producer.

From a free-market perspective, these moves aren't good for energy production. They don't help the cause of diplomacy, either. They risk making Latin America an unreliable energy partner.

The Western Hemisphere's energy ministers used to meet regularly. From 1999 to 2004 they gathered annually under US leadership to discuss issues of mutual interest. Those meetings have fallen away during this resurgence of resource nationalism. Some observers would like to see them return.

Energy in Latin America isn't just about oil, by the way. The region is big in hydroelectric power. In fact, hydropower supplies 23 percent of energy needs there. (The figure for the United States is 3 percent.) Argentina, Brazil, and Chile are big on solar and wind technologies, too.

Some observers suggest that the United States should work with Latin Americans on alternative energy as well as oil and gas. Such cooperation could pay off not only in strengthened diplomatic ties but also in progress in the areas of economic development, climate change, and sustainability.

For much of US history, Americans have acted as though they could ignore what was going on south of the border. When they did turn their attention to Latin America, the result was often military intervention. But the days are long gone when the United States could close its eyes to the continuing political, economic, and social difficulties Latin Americans face. These problems have spilled onto the streets of American cities and into American neighborhoods. Solving them will take a good deal more patience, effort, and understanding on both sides. The consequences for the US and its neighbors of failing to do so would be immense.

Lesson 5 Review

Using complete sentences, answer the following questions on a sheet of paper.

1. What was the Platt Amendment?
2. What did the Cuban Adjustment Act assume about any Cuban reaching US soil?
3. Why did the cutoff, under President Kennedy, of US aid to Haiti not make much difference to the Haitian people?
4. How did Haitian "boat people" differ from those coming from Cuba?
5. What are remittances and how are they important in Latin America?
6. How is the presence of illegal immigrants in the United States seen as a failure?
7. In how many US cities do Mexican drug cartels maintain drug-distribution networks?
8. What is resource nationalism?

Applying Your Learning

9. How should the United States address illegal immigration?

CHAPTER 6

People around the world recognize the Eiffel Tower in Paris. France is one of many countries that demonstrate the enduring influence of the Roman Empire in culture, public works, architecture, and language.

Europe

Chapter Outline

- LESSON 1 Europe: An Introduction
- LESSON 2 The European Union
- LESSON 3 Immigration, Terrorist Cells, and Ethnic Strife
- LESSON 4 The Creation and Collapse of Yugoslavia
- LESSON 5 US Interests and Regional Issues in Europe

LESSON 1 Europe: An Introduction

Quick Write

What does this episode suggest to you about the influence of ancient Rome and the rest of Europe on American civilization?

Learn About

- the geographic locations of the major nations of Europe
- how Ancient Greece and the Roman Empire influenced Europe's development
- how Christianity, Islam, and Judaism affected the development of Europe
- how nationalism destroyed the continental European empires
- how Marxism, socialism, and fascism affected the development of Europe

On 22 September 1776 a 21-year-old schoolteacher named Nathan Hale was hanged as a spy in New York City during the American Revolution. How had this happened?

In early September General George Washington desperately needed to know the site of the upcoming British invasion of Manhattan Island. The best way to find out would be to send a spy behind enemy lines. Hale, a gifted and patriotic young man, volunteered for the mission.

Arriving by boat from Connecticut, he moved around the city in civilian clothes pretending to be a schoolmaster looking for work. But before he could gather much information, the British attacked. They soon had captured most of Manhattan and torched the city. In the ensuing chaos, Hale was captured.

The British found intelligence information on his person. He had been found out. He was a soldier out of uniform behind enemy lines. The rules of war were clear. Hale was sentenced to hang the next day.

No one can be certain what his last words were. But there is strong evidence for the tradition that his final utterance was this: "I only regret that I have but one life to lose for my country."

Educated people of the day—Washington as well as the British officers who witnessed the execution—would have recognized it as a paraphrase of a line from a 1713 play, "Cato," by the English writer Joseph Addison. In it the hero, Cato, makes ready to defend the last vestige of the Roman Republic against the imperial ambitions of Julius Caesar.

The Geographic Locations of the Major Nations of Europe

Europe stretches from Spain in the west to Russia's Ural Mountains in the east. The European mainland's northernmost point is the Norwegian town of Knivskjellodden. The southernmost point is in Gavdos, Greece. Europe looks east to Asia, south across the Mediterranean to Africa, and west to the Atlantic Ocean.

Vocabulary

- Crusades
- schism
- simony
- sacraments
- vernacular
- ethnic cleansing
- nation-state
- scapegoat
- quisling

A bagpiper plays traditional Scottish tunes in a square in Inverness, Scotland.

Photo by Robert Harbison / © 1997 The Christian Science Monitor

Scotland is part of Britain, which in turn is one of several nations making up Northern Europe.

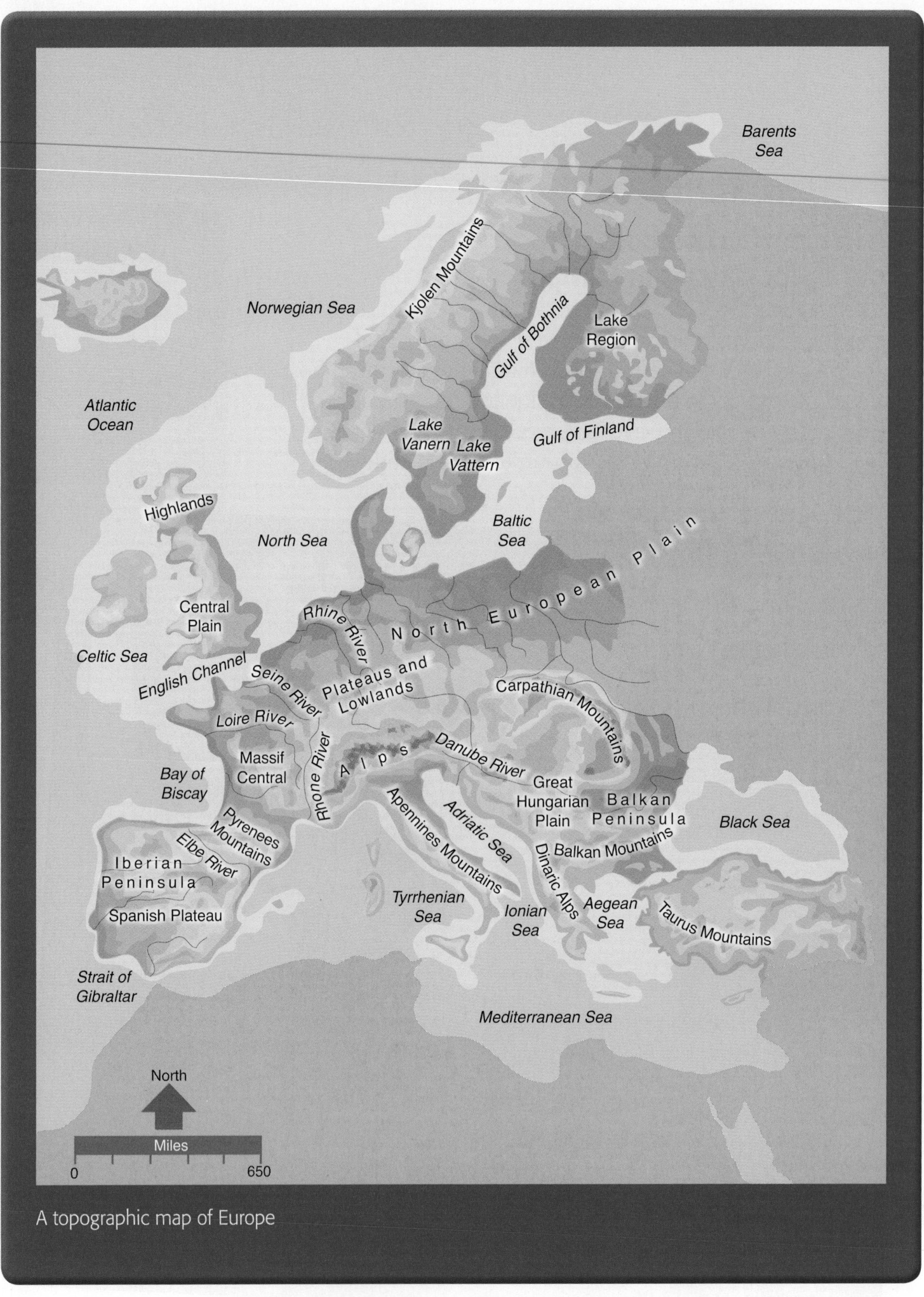

A topographic map of Europe

Western Europe

Western Europe includes Germany and France. Twice during the twentieth century these two countries and their allies faced off to fight wars so terrible that people call them "the world wars." Germany and France's postwar reconciliation has been one of the engines of European unification. Other important countries here are Belgium, the Netherlands, Austria, and Switzerland.

Northern Europe

Northern Europe includes the nations of the British Isles—Britain and Ireland—off the European mainland's coast. It also includes the three Scandinavian countries—Denmark, Norway, and Sweden. Iceland and Finland are also part of Northern Europe. Some people group these latter two with Scandinavia. But the Danes, Norwegians, and Swedes share ethnic roots. They can also understand each other's languages. Finns are outside this common heritage, while Icelanders speak an older language the Scandinavians can't understand. All five, though, fit under the umbrella term, "the Nordic Countries."

Eastern Europe

Eastern Europe has undergone a transformation over the past generation. As the 1980s began, the Czech Republic, Hungary, Poland, and Slovakia were part of the Warsaw Pact. They were "satellites" in the former Soviet Union's orbit. Now they are part of the European Union and NATO. So, too, are Bulgaria and Romania.

Southern Europe

Italy, with the Holy See (Vatican City), and Spain and Portugal are some of the more powerful Southern European countries. Southern Europe also contains the small states or territories of Andorra, Malta, San Marino, and the divided island of Cyprus.

The south also includes the countries of the former Yugoslavia: Bosnia and Herzegovina, Croatia, Kosovo, Macedonia, Montenegro, Serbia, and Slovenia. As one country during the Cold War, they were communist but not part of the Soviet bloc. Greece lies to the south. Albania, another communist outlier, lies along the Adriatic coast between Greece and the former Yugoslavian states. This region is often known as the Balkans, or Southeastern Europe. It also includes Turkey, partly in Europe but mostly in Asia. Turkey, long a member of NATO, aspires to join the European Union as well.

A political map of Europe

Visitors take in the Austrian Alps, which are enveloped in an early morning fog.
Photo by David Clark Scott / © 2003 The Christian Science Monitor

The Alps, which stretch from Austria to France, are Europe's highest mountains.

Major Mountain Ranges

The Alps are Europe's highest mountains. They stretch from Austria and Slovenia in the east; through Italy, Switzerland, Liechtenstein, and Germany; to France in the west. The Pyrenees separate the Iberian Peninsula (Spain and Portugal) from the rest of continental Europe. The Carpathians, stretching a thousand miles from the Czech Republic to Romania, are Europe's largest mountain range. Turkey shares the Taurus Mountains with Syria. The Apennines are a chain of mostly green and wooded mountains that run down Italy's spine.

Major Seas and Rivers

The Rhine is one of Western Europe's "main streets." It starts in Switzerland, flows north past France and through Germany and the Netherlands into the North Sea. The Danube is the longest river within the European Union. It flows through or along the edge of 10 countries. The Loire, the Rhone, and the Seine are great rivers of France. The Elbe is a great river of Central Europe, flowing from the mountains of the Czech Republic through Germany until it flows into the North Sea at Hamburg.

Important among Europe's seas are two seas north of the continental mainland, on either side of Denmark, the North Sea and the Baltic Sea. Farther to the east, east of Bulgaria and north of Turkey, is the Black Sea. And the Mediterranean lies south of the European mainland, with the boot of Italy stretching out into it.

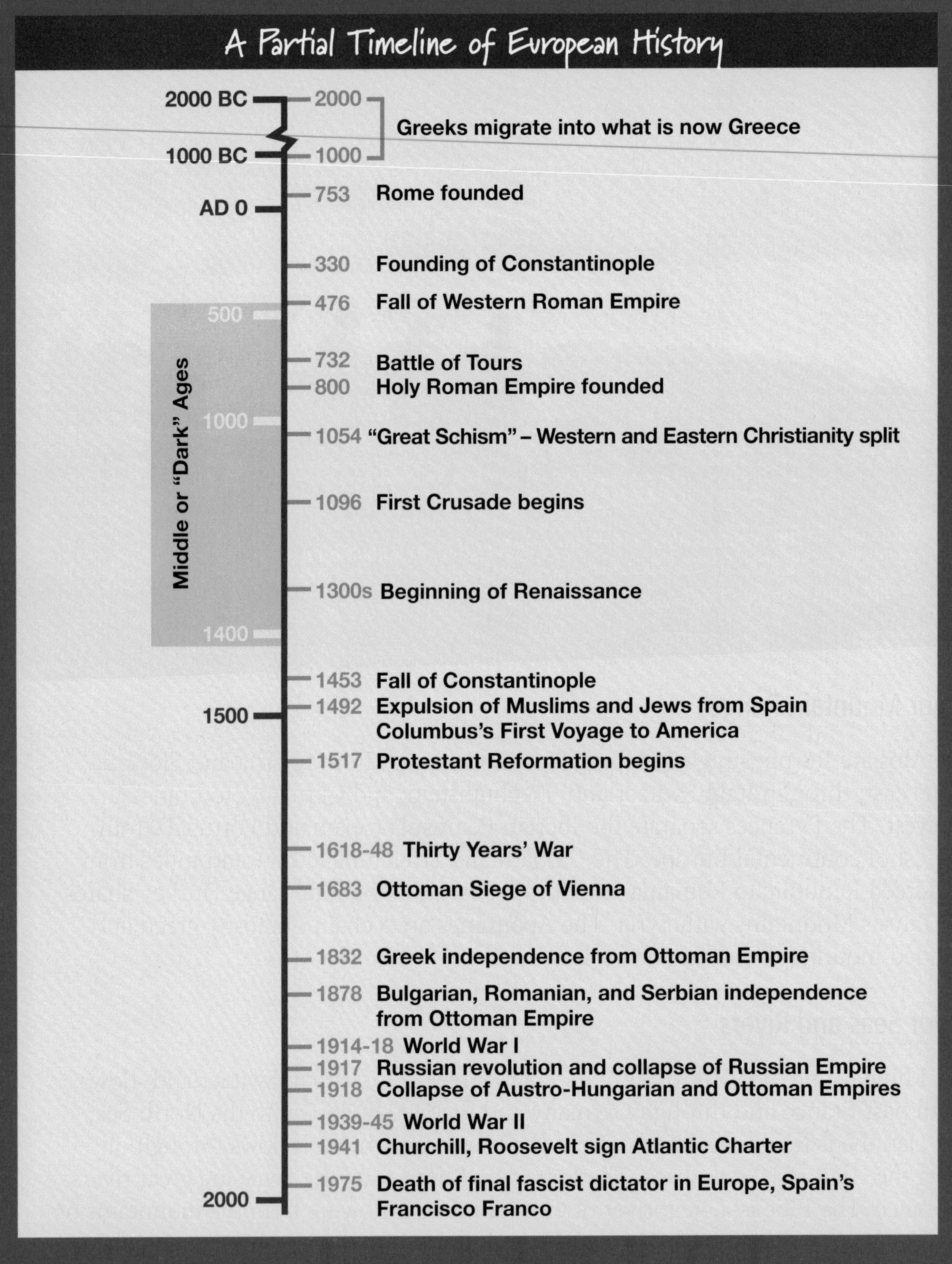
A Partial Timeline of European History
2000 BC
1000 BC
AD 0
1500
2000
Middle or "Dark" Ages
500
1000
1400
2000
1000
Greeks migrate into what is now Greece
753 Rome founded
330 Founding of Constantinople
476 Fall of Western Roman Empire
732 Battle of Tours
800 Holy Roman Empire founded
1054 "Great Schism" – Western and Eastern Christianity split
1096 First Crusade begins
1300s Beginning of Renaissance
1453 Fall of Constantinople
1492 Expulsion of Muslims and Jews from Spain
Columbus's First Voyage to America
1517 Protestant Reformation begins
1618-48 Thirty Years' War
1683 Ottoman Siege of Vienna
1832 Greek independence from Ottoman Empire
1878 Bulgarian, Romanian, and Serbian independence from Ottoman Empire
1914-18 World War I
1917 Russian revolution and collapse of Russian Empire
1918 Collapse of Austro-Hungarian and Ottoman Empires
1939-45 World War II
1941 Churchill, Roosevelt sign Atlantic Charter
1975 Death of final fascist dictator in Europe, Spain's Francisco Franco

How Ancient Greece and the Roman Empire Influenced Europe's Development

No matter Europe's massive landmass and its wide access to oceans, two empires were also massive enough to shape the continent. Greece and Rome were the ancient world's two giants. Study of their literature and history formed the backbone of the Founding Fathers' education. Even today, a university's classics department is the one offering courses on Classical Greek and Latin literature and history.

You might say that that Greeks provided the big ideas, and the Romans put them into practice, first in a Republic and later in a wide-ranging empire. As the Roman Empire broke down, Europe sank into what is known as the Dark Ages. It was a time of political disorder. It was also a time of far less cultural achievement than had taken place in earlier centuries. Centuries later, European culture had a great rebirth known as the Renaissance. It began in Italy in the fourteenth century. From there it spread across Europe. During this period of artistic flowering, scholars also began to rediscover the writings of the classical period.

The Renaissance led to the Enlightenment, an eighteenth-century cultural and political movement. Thinkers within this movement believed that reason and natural rights should be the basis for governments. They believed that "governments . . . deriv[e] their just power from the consent of the governed," to borrow from the Declaration of Independence.

Americans study Europe in particular because Europeans settled America. The Founding Fathers were European-Americans steeped in the classics. It would be hard to overstate the influence of this literature on them.

Since its founding, the United States has become vastly more diverse. It has drawn people from all around the world. To many people, that is one of the measures of its success. But the country is still based on ideas that, however universal their appeal, came to the United States from Europe.

The Influence of Ancient Greece on the Democracy, Philosophy, Architecture, Mythology, Language, and Religion in Europe

Democracy—rule by the people—developed in Greece around 500 BC. The Greek city-state of Athens was the model that thinkers of the Enlightenment studied and held out as the ideal.

Socrates, Plato, and Aristotle were tremendously influential philosophers—students of philosophy. Philosophy is a Greek word meaning "love of wisdom." The term also refers to the investigation of reality, on the basis of logical reasoning rather than experiments and field research. Aristotle (384 BC–322 BC) in particular represented the "cutting edge" of Western science for centuries and remained influential until the Renaissance.

The Parthenon, a well-known example of ancient Greek architecture, sits on the Acropolis, a hill in Athens, Greece.
Photo by R. Norman Matheny / © 1992 The Christian Science Monitor

The ancient Greeks produced architecture that remains influential in Europe and beyond for its expressions of harmony, symmetry, and balance.

The ancient Greeks produced architecture that remains influential in Europe and beyond. Their structures expressed ideals of harmony, symmetry, and balance. Greek architects used mathematical formulas to produce ideal proportions in their buildings.

fastFACT

The ancient Greeks knew that the eye plays tricks and makes stately marble columns appear thinner in the middle. And so they designed their columns with a slight bulge in the middle so that they would appear straight.

Before humans had science to explain the world around them, they developed stories to make sense of things they observed. Every day, for instance, the sun travels from east to west across the sky. The Greeks developed the story of Helios, the sun god, who drove a four-horse chariot across the sky every day. This story is an example of a myth. Mythology is a group of such stories. Greek mythology is the body of stories about the Greek gods of Mount Olympus, as well as human heroes and monsters.

The US Supreme Court building in Washington, D.C.
Photo by Andy Nelson / © 2005 The Christian Science Monitor

The Parthenon in Athens has architectural "descendants" in the United States as well, such as the US Supreme Court.

These gods are not like the God of Abraham, whom you read about in Chapter 1. These gods, with their multiple marriages and love affairs, are more like characters in a soap opera. But these myths live on in painting, sculpture, and other forms of art. And even when their science is unsound, these myths represent keen insights into human nature. The story of Helios and Phaeton, for instance, sounds like a very contemporary tale of a young man who's been given the keys to the family car before he's ready for them. When Phaeton's father, Helios, lets him drive the "sun" across the sky, the chariot goes out of control and burns the earth. Zeus has to stop the disastrous ride with a thunderbolt.

Unlike its myths, the Greek language didn't spread the way Latin did. Modern Greek has about 15 million native speakers, mostly in Greece and Cyprus. But Greek has strongly influenced the vocabulary of English and other Western languages. People tend to use Greek words for Greek ideas.

Democracy, *philosophy*, and *mythology*, for example, are English words with Greek roots. Many important fields of study have names with Greek origins—*politics*, *economics*, *physics*, *theology*, *astronomy*, and *biology*.

Many other words you use—such as at school or work—also come from Greek. When you *analyze* a piece of writing, or *synthesize* available materials to create a coherent *thesis*, you're drawing on Greek vocabulary.

Furthermore, the original language of the New Testament was Greek. The Apostle Paul and other biblical writers used *koine*, a form of Greek that was later than classical Greek, though not as modern as today's Greek.

The Influence of Ancient Rome on Law, Engineering, Architecture, Government, Religion, and Language in Europe

In Chapter 5, Lesson 5, you read that the United States grants automatic citizenship to anyone born on US soil. This is known as *jus soli*—the law of the soil. That's a Latin phrase. Does that give you a hint at the influence of Roman law? Emperor Justinian codified Roman law around AD 530. His code influenced European legal systems until the eighteenth century. The English-speaking countries based their legal systems on English common law. But even in those countries Roman law was influential. Countless legal concepts are referred to with Latin terms.

An Italian family takes a break in front of Rome's famed Colosseum, an ancient sports arena.

Photo by Robert Harbison / © 1999 The Christian Science Monitor

The ancient Romans were peerless engineers and builders of roads, bridges, aqueducts, and other structures, as the Colosseum shows.

The ancient Romans were also peerless engineers and builders of roads, bridges, aqueducts, and other structures. The Roman road system was the Interstate Highway System of its day. You might even say it was the Internet of its day. These roads held the sprawling Roman Empire together. Look at any road map of Europe today, and it will show many roads used back in the days of the ancient Romans.

fastFACT

During his Fascist rule during the early twentieth century, Italian dictator Benito Mussolini ordered the initials SPQR stamped on manhole covers throughout Rome. The letters stood for "the Senate and the People of Rome." The ancient Romans had used them. In doing this, Mussolini was trying to claim a connection between his government and ancient Rome. That he chose to make this point on manhole covers tells you something about the ancient Romans' reputation for public works.

In architecture, the Romans followed Greek models, which they spread throughout the Roman Empire. In fact, the Romans are considered the founders of many modern European cities, notably London and Paris. The ruins, at least, of many Roman structures are found all over Europe. Europe is also full of newer structures modeled on ancient ones. The Arch of Triumph, which Napoleon had built in Paris in the early nineteenth century, mimics the Arch of Titus in Rome, for instance, from around AD 81.

The government of the Roman Republic, like the Greek Athenian city-state, was an important political model during the Age of Enlightenment. From the republic comes the term *senate*, used today for the upper chamber of the US Congress.

Regarding religion, within Western Christianity, Rome has been influential as the seat of what is known as the Roman Catholic Church.

Latin as the International Language of Europe

Latin was the language of ancient Rome. It spread with the Roman Empire throughout the Mediterranean region and across much of Europe. It was long the language of government, even in places where most people spoke some other tongue. Around the ninth century, Vulgar Latin—the form of Latin that most people spoke—began to break down. The so-called Romance languages, such as French, Spanish, and Italian, began to develop at that time. But Latin remained the international language of science and scholarship into the seventeenth century. The main scientific writings of the Renaissance—those of Copernicus and Galileo, for instance—were in Latin. Today, Latin is still the Vatican's official language. And if you consider the Romance languages to be modern forms of Latin, you could say that hundreds of millions of people worldwide still speak it.

The Languages of Europe*

Family	Branch	Language
Afro-Asiatic	Semitic	Maltese
Basque		Basque
Indo-European	Albanian	Albanian
	Baltic	Latvian, Lithuanian
	Celtic	Breton, Irish Gaelic, Scots Gaelic, Welsh
	Greek	Greek
	Germanic	Danish, Dutch, English, Frisian, German, Icelandic, Norwegian, Swedish, Yiddish
	Indo-Aryan	Romany (Gypsy)
	Romance (descended from Latin)	Catalan, Corsican, French, Italian, Ladino, Portuguese, Romanian, Romansch, Spanish
	Slavic	Belorussian, Bulgarian, Czech, Macedonian, Polish, Russian, Serbo-Croatian, Slovak, Slovenian, Sorbian, Ukrainian
Turkic	Turkic	Turkish
Uralic	Finno-Ugric	Estonian, Finnish, Hungarian, Sami (Lapp)

*(*excluding Russia and the former Soviet republics in Europe)*

The Influence of the Eastern Roman Empire

Around the fifth century AD the western half of the Roman Empire crumbled. But the eastern part survived another thousand years. One sign of this looming change was that around AD 330 the Roman Emperor Constantine shifted the seat of his realm from Rome to Byzantium, on the Bosporus—the gateway to Asia and so a good strategic location. He renamed the capital city for himself, Constantinople. (Today it's the Turkish city of Istanbul.) The empire was still known at the time as the Roman Empire, although later scholars called this Eastern Roman Empire the Byzantine Empire. It lasted until 1453.

The Byzantine Empire was the continuation of the Roman Empire, but over the centuries it became more and more Greek. In the seventh century, under Emperor Heraclius, Greek replaced Latin as the official language. Neighboring peoples referred to the empire as the Empire of the Greeks.

Meanwhile, back in Rome, a succession of emperors there had to contend with invading barbarian tribes. The date of the Western Empire's collapse is usually given as AD 476.

During this period, the Eastern Empire was the only civilized European power. It helped preserve learning and literature that were lost to the West. (Western Europe would rediscover this during the Renaissance.) The Eastern Empire was an important cultural influence in Eastern Europe and Russia. It helped spread Christianity and established a written language among the Slavic and other peoples.

How Christianity, Islam, and Judaism Affected the Development of Europe

In addition to the Greek and Roman empires' major influences, three religions with Middle East origins also molded Europe's character. To understand Europe, you need to understand these Abraham faiths: Christianity, Islam, and Judaism.

The Unifying Influence of Christianity in Europe

Christianity was Europe's great unifier, especially after the Western Roman Empire's decline. You might say that the Roman Catholic Church was the successor institution to the empire. The church ran schools and universities. It sponsored scientific research. It commissioned important buildings, notably churches, and works of art such as paintings and sculpture. European music was largely church music, from the Gregorian chant of the Middle Ages on through the cantatas of Bach and the sacred compositions of Mozart.

What's more, Europe's traditions of caring for the poor, the aged, and the sick all go back to church activities. This continued well into the nineteenth century. By that time, however, there were many different churches, not just the Roman Catholic Church.

The Impact of the Crusades, the Schism of 1054, the Protestant Reformation, and the Church-State Battles on European History

Christianity also played a large role in defending Christian Europe and Christian lands in Egypt, Syria, Palestine, and Anatolia (Turkey) from Islamic invasion. For instance, Muslims had conquered Andalusia—a region in Spain—as far back as the eighth century. For nearly two centuries, from 1095 to 1291, Christians engaged in the Crusades. These were *a series of wars intended to liberate Jerusalem from Muslim rule*.

The Crusades began with a speech by Pope Urban II. No text of it survives, but he supposedly called for the nobles of Western Europe, known as the Franks, to defend their fellow Christians, the Byzantines, to the east. Much of the Eastern Empire had come under Islamic rule. The Byzantines were calling for help.

The pope also apparently called for the overthrow of Jerusalem's Islamic government and its replacement with a Christian kingdom. The city had come under Muslim control in AD 638. Originally these rulers allowed Christians free access to Jerusalem. But by the time of the pope's speech, the rulers of Jerusalem were making it hard for Christian pilgrims to visit their faith's holiest sites.

The Franks responded to the call. Both nobles and commoners streamed east in great waves. They managed to retake Jerusalem on 15 July 1099. They established several Crusader states. These would last nearly two centuries. In 1291 the last of them fell to Islamic forces. That was, in one sense, the end of the Crusades.

But the Crusader ideal lived on. A few words are in order on the men who fought these campaigns. They were in effect armed pilgrims. Each went through a special religious ceremony in which he vowed to carry out his mission of defense of "holy places." He wore a cross on his chest, not unlike a team jersey. A Crusader had to have some demonstrated military skill. And if he failed to fulfill his pledge he could get thrown out of the church.

The Great Schism

When Pope Urban called for the defense of Eastern Christians, he was asking for help for a group with which he had just parted company, theologically speaking. The eastern and western parts of the Roman Empire had been drifting further and further apart since it first broke into two. In 1054 the Latin-speaking Western Church and the Greek-speaking Eastern Church reached a point of irreconcilable differences.

They were at odds on matters of doctrine, theology, and politics. Geographic distance and language were factors in the split as well. At this point the church broke into two, as the empire had done earlier. This split is known as the Great Schism of 1054. (A schism is *a break or split within a group, such as a religious body*.)

This schism led to the development of the modern Roman Catholic and Eastern Orthodox churches. Despite the split, Pope Urban evidently felt close enough to Eastern Christians to call for their defense from the Muslims.

The Protestant Reformation

Another important division in the Western Church was the Protestant Reformation. It was a series of divisions, actually. And it led to the formation of three major strains of Protestantism: Lutheranism, Calvinism, and Anglicanism. These churches followed the theology of Martin Luther, of John Calvin, or of the Church of England, respectively.

The unity of the Roman Catholic Church began eroding during this period when spiritual matters clashed with political interests. In 1378 the College of Cardinals—a body of senior clergymen—elected an Italian, Urban VI, as the new pope.

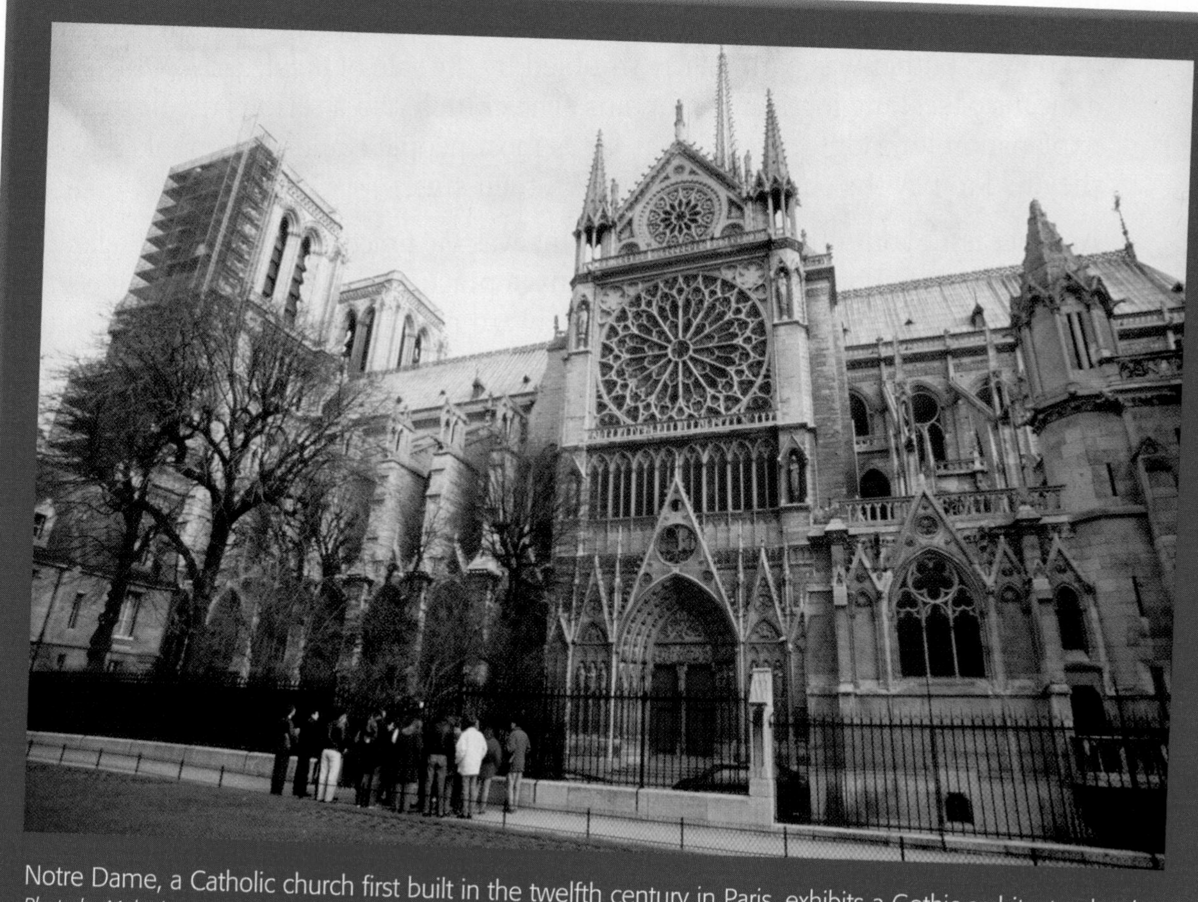

Notre Dame, a Catholic church first built in the twelfth century in Paris, exhibits a Gothic architectural style.
Photo by Melanie Stetson Freeman / © 1993 The Christian Science Monitor

The Great Schism of 1054 led to the development of the modern Roman Catholic and Eastern Orthodox churches. Western Christianity split further during the Protestant Reformation, which began in 1517.

But a faction of cardinals allied with France refused to accept him. They named Clement VII pope instead. He withdrew to Avignon, in the south of France, and ruled from there. Urban VI, meanwhile, stayed in Rome.

Europe was divided over which was the "true" pope. The spectacle of two rival popes competing for the role of successor to St. Peter continued for 40 years, until a new one whom everyone could agree on became the new pope. The episode, the Great Western Schism, damaged the papacy's prestige. It also foreshadowed more trouble to come.

The Protestant Reformation really began in 1517. That's when Martin Luther, a monk and a professor at the University of Wittenberg, in Germany, nailed 95 theses—a kind of essay—to the door of All Saints' Church. He was calling for reforms in the church. And so he was posting these theses for debate in traditional fashion, just as you might post something on an online message board.

Luther and others saw a church that had become corrupt because of its monopoly on power. Luther was particularly troubled by the sale of *indulgences*, which were a means of seeking forgiveness for sins. The church had a serious theological explanation for indulgences. But as far as most people could see, it looked as if they had to pay the church to be forgiven their sins.

Another issue for Luther was **simony**. This was *the practice of buying and selling church offices*. Simony was like the patronage practiced by big-city "machine" politicians of later centuries, who would award plum jobs to friends, contributors, and people whose votes they wanted.

Luther had other ideas as well. He believed that the clergy should be free to marry. He wanted fewer **sacraments**, or *religious rites*. He challenged the pope's authority. He also opposed several Catholic traditions that had arisen over time but had no biblical basis, such as devotion to the Virgin Mary and other saints.

Luther also called for the Scriptures in the **vernacular**—*the language people actually speak*. He wanted people to be able to read the Bible in their own languages, since most people couldn't read Latin.

John Wycliffe of England and Jan Hus of Bohemia (the Czech Republic today) were among Luther's spiritual role models from earlier times. His contemporaries, those who lived at the same time Luther did, included Ulrich Zwingli and John Calvin in Switzerland, and somewhat later, John Knox, the Scottish Calvinist—or Presbyterian—leader.

In England, King Henry VIII broke with the pope over a matter closer to home. Henry needed a son as an heir to his throne. His wife, Catherine of Aragon, failed to bear him one. Henry wanted a divorce so that he could start again with a new wife. But church teaching—and the pope—forbade divorce. So Henry pulled the Church of England out from under papal authority and made himself its head. Even today, the British king or queen is the formal head of the Church of England.

Church-State Battles in European History

You read earlier in this lesson that the Roman Catholic Church was the successor institution to the Roman Empire. That is, the church had both spiritual (religious) and temporal (worldly, or political) power. In fact, after the Western Roman Empire fell, the church was often left as the most powerful political player in many regions. But as the modern European nations began to form, the new secular authorities often found themselves in direct political conflict with the pope. Often these conflicts involved competing claims to the throne; other times they involved land reform or taxing church property.

One of the most keenly remembered episodes took place in January 1077. It concerned an encounter between Pope Gregory VII and the Holy Roman Emperor, a German king named Henry IV.

History remembers Gregory as one of the great reforming popes, but in his own day he was seen as something of a power-grabber. He insisted on new church law providing that the College of Cardinals elect the pope without interference from temporal rulers such as Henry. Henry and other rulers also wanted to be able to appoint bishops. Gregory stood up to Henry—making Gregory the first pope to do so. And Gregory excommunicated the king—threw him out of the church.

Henry wanted to be let back into the church. He traveled, in winter, to make his case before the pope in person. Gregory was at his winter palace in Canossa, in northern Italy. Tradition has it that he made Henry stand barefoot in the snow for days until he would accept his penance and readmit him to the church.

It was a short-lived peace. The pope excommunicated Henry again a few years later, this time for keeps. The move affected more than Henry's soul. It left the king out in the cold as a temporal power as well. Once he was expelled from the church, all his feudal relationships—the service he expected from those beneath him—were void. A Christian knight owed no allegiance to an excommunicated lord. Princes and dukes abandoned Henry and threw their support to other leaders.

The Impact of the Muslim Invasions of Europe

As Europe for centuries was going through political turmoil from within, so it was coming under attack from the outside. From the seventh century onward, Muslim warriors spread out in waves from the Arabian Peninsula. They moved across the Middle East, into North Africa, and across the Strait of Gibraltar into Spain and Portugal. Soon they controlled almost all the Iberian Peninsula except for the northern sections of Spain. The border with the Christian north changed continuously.

The new Islamic territories were known as al-Andalus. Their provincial government had its base in the city of Cordoba. Al-Andalus was part of the Umayyad caliphate, a Muslim empire based in Damascus. Muslim rule rose and fell continuously between 711 until 1492, when King Ferdinand and Queen Isabella finally retook Granada, a Muslim kingdom in southern Spain.

Within al-Andalus itself, Muslims, Christians, and Jews appear to have coexisted in relative peace and prosperity. Along the frontier and the Mediterranean coast, however, war and slave raids marked those centuries.

Al-Andalus was home to great scholars who eventually helped reconnect Western Europe with classical learning. Averroes, or Ibn Rushd, hailed from Cordoba, and helped Europe rediscover Aristotle and Plato. Moses Maimonides, a great Jewish thinker, was another son of Cordoba. He helped codify Jewish law. His classic "Guide for the Perplexed" linked religion, philosophy, and science. It was an important influence on medieval Christian scholarship. Both men were physicians, too.

Other contributions of Al-Andalus included agriculture, textiles, poetry, and even personal hygiene. The ancient Romans had been great bathers, but standards slipped after the empire fell.

Things played out a little differently along the frontier between Islam and Christendom in France, however. By 732, when Muslims were establishing themselves on the Iberian Peninsula, they had also moved up into France.

On 10 October of that year Muslim forces squared off against the Franks. These were a German tribe that had moved into the old Roman province of Gaul (today's France) a few centuries earlier. Charles Martel (his name means "hammer") was the leader of the Franks. The two sides met on a high wooded plain near the northern city of Tours.

Martel had chosen the site to make the Muslim cavalry charge uphill. His side had no horses but had the advantage of surprise. He was also able to infiltrate the Muslim forces, who broke off the battle to try to preserve their plunder. But the Franks continued to press the charge. They drove the Muslims off the field. Charles Martel's victory at Tours marked the end of Muslim expansion into northwestern Europe.

The sun casts a golden hue over Istanbul, Turkey.

Photo by Robert Harbison / © 1994 The Christian Science Monitor

In 1453 the Eastern Roman Empire collapsed when Constantinople (now Istanbul) fell to the Ottoman Turks after a siege of nearly eight weeks.

It wasn't the last Christian-Muslim confrontation in Europe, however. In 1453 the Eastern Roman Empire collapsed when Constantinople fell to the Ottoman Turks after a siege of nearly eight weeks. The empire had already begun to come apart into a series of Greek monarchies. But Sultan Mehmed II's army turned a Greek-speaking Eastern Orthodox Christian city on the eastern edge of Europe into a Muslim city on the western edge of Asia Minor. It became the new capital of the Ottoman Empire, and in a sense, the successor institution to the Eastern Roman Empire.

Over the next two centuries the Turks advanced deep into Europe and North Africa. Their control of the overland trade routes between Europe and Asia gave Christopher Columbus an important reason to seek a westward sailing route to Asia. In 1527 the Ottomans laid siege to Vienna, Austria, seat of the Holy Roman Empire. The Austrians pushed back. But in 1547 the Habsburg ruler, Ferdinand, ceded control of Hungary and other Southeastern European territories to the Ottomans. Centuries later some of these countries—Albania and Bosnia-Herzegovina—are still predominantly Muslim. Others have significant Muslim minorities, such as Bulgaria with around 12 percent of its population. And still others show lingering signs that they were once under Ottoman rule, such as Romania with a Muslim population just under 1 percent.

In 1683 the Ottomans made another assault on Vienna. Once again, the Habsburg forces pushed back, with help from the Germans and from Polish forces under the heroic leadership of King Jan Sobieski. They swept the Ottomans away at the Battle of Vienna. It might be premature to call this the beginning of the end of the Ottoman Empire. But it was the high-water mark for Turkish efforts to expand into what is today Western Europe.

The History of the Jews in Europe From 1492 to the Twentieth Century

Americans grow up with the date 1492 etched in their minds. No wonder—it's the date when Christopher Columbus sailed for the New World. But it was also the year that Spain expelled its Jewish community—200,000 strong.

This wasn't the first, or the last, time that Jews faced expulsion from a place where they had long been established and lived peacefully. But they remembered this one with special bitterness because they had for so long been so happy in Spain.

The Jews had benefited from the relative religious tolerance that marked Muslim rule in Iberia. Indeed, the period from the eighth to the twelfth centuries is known as the golden age of Jewish culture in Spain. And so Spanish Jews saw their expulsion as a terrible betrayal.

It took place as part of the Spanish Inquisition. This was an effort, under King Ferdinand and Queen Isabella, to ensure the Catholic orthodoxy of the Spanish people. They thought they were being faithful to what they saw as "the one true faith." But in modern terms you would describe the Inquisition as, at the very least, a gross assault on civil liberties. It led to a form of ethnic cleansing—*the organized elimination of an ethnic group or groups from a region or society by deportation, forced emigration, or genocide.*

Spain's Jewish community dated back to the Diaspora—the scattering—of the Jewish people in the wake of the Roman occupation of Judea (today's Israel) during the first and second century. In addition, as part of this effort at religious purity, Spanish officials leaned hard on Jews to get them to convert to Catholicism. Many did.

But then Tomas Torquemada, the cleric behind this effort, feared that these converts might return to their original faith if they saw anyone still practicing it. And so, he insisted, any Jews who failed to convert must go.

The fortunate ones made it to Turkey. Sultan Bajazet welcomed them warmly and liked to chide the Spanish king for his actions: "How can you call Ferdinand of Aragon a wise king, the same Ferdinand who impoverished his own land and enriched ours?"

Other Spanish Jews, known as "Sephardim," settled in North Africa, Italy, and elsewhere in Europe. This period from the High Middle Ages on was not a good time for the Jews in Europe. The same Crusader fervor that energized European Christians to go after Muslims in Jerusalem also led to moves against Jews closer to home.

The Spanish expulsion followed the banishing of Jews from England in 1290, from France in 1396, and from Austria in 1421. Many of them fled east to Poland. Jews were blamed for causing the plague epidemics of the period, and hundreds of their communities were destroyed across Europe.

It was not all darkness, however. It was during this period that Yiddish culture arose. Spanish Jews spoke Ladino, a form of Spanish written with Hebrew letters. Ashkenazim, or German Jews, spoke Yiddish, a form of German written with Hebrew letters. The Yiddish language developed in the Rhineland of Germany, in those communities that suffered during the time of the Crusades and afterward.

As the Ashkenazim moved farther east, to Poland, Ukraine, Belarus, Russia, and Romania, they brought Yiddish with them. It became the basis of a rich culture of poetry, storytelling, and other literature, and of music (*klezmer*) and theater.

The Jewish Emigration to the United States and Palestine

By the Age of the Enlightenment, however, progressive voices were calling for granting Jews full political rights. Jews had full protection as citizens of the United States from the very beginning. By the end of the eighteenth century, Britain, France, and the Netherlands had granted Jews equal rights with Gentiles. Eastern Europe would follow only in the next century.

By the late nineteenth century, the Zionist movement had begun to take shape. As you will read in more detail later in this lesson, this period was one of nationalism, and the rise of the nation-state. A nation-state is *an autonomous political entity that is home to a more or less homogeneous group of people*. France, for instance, was the nation-state that was home to the French people. As the nineteenth century began, however, there was no political entity called "Germany." There was instead a German people who lived in a collection of independent German states. Under the leadership of German Chancellor Otto von Bismarck, these states combined to form Germany.

Italy had a comparable experience. Nationalists believed that a people deserved their own state. Early Zionists, influenced by this view, began to feel the Jewish people deserved a Jewish state.

A turning point in Western Europe, particularly France, was the Dreyfus Affair of 1894. It exposed the depths of anti-Semitism in France, most scandalously within French institutions such as the army. The scandal involved a Jewish officer in the French Army named Alfred Dreyfus. He was accused of leaking intelligence to a German military attaché. He was convicted of treason in a secret court-martial and banished for life to Devil's Island, a penal colony off the coast of South America. Doubts about his guilt began to surface. But it became clear that the army had little interest in seeking the truth of the matter.

Eventually the novelist Émile Zola published a denunciation of the French Army coverup in the daily newspaper *L'Aurore*. Reactionary politicians and the leadership of the Catholic Church, both hostile to France's latest effort at republican government, called the case a conspiracy of Jews and Freemasons intended to damage the army and destroy France. Dreyfus eventually won his freedom. But the whole affair had made people think again about just how free and open France—and Europe as a whole—really was.

Theodor Herzl, who set up a political movement for a Jewish state, witnessed mobs shouting "Death to the Jews!" in France. For him and his fellow Jews, there was only one answer: mass immigration to a country of their own.

In little more than half a century later Herzl's vision would result in the founding of the State of Israel. But at the same time, many other European Jews were turning to another land to build a secure future: the United States.

At the World War II concentration camp Auschwitz in Poland, the Nazis killed more than a million people, most of them Jews. The message over the camp's entrance reads *"Arbeit macht frei,"* which means "Work brings freedom."
Photo by Robert Harbison / © 1993 The Christian Science Monitor
The slogan over the gate was a lie—Hitler called for the systematic extermination of Europe's Jews.

The period from 1820 to 1924 was a time of relatively open immigration. Between 1820 and 1880 America's Jewish population increased from about 3,000 to as many as 300,000. The immigrants came largely from Central Europe and established themselves not only in New York and Philadelphia, but in smaller cities as well. After 1880 Jewish immigrants came from farther east. Persecution and lack of opportunity pushed them westward to America.

How World War II Devastated the Jews Living in Europe

The horrors of Nazi Germany are uniquely associated with the twentieth century. But some aspects of German leader Adolf Hitler's treatment of the Jews hark back to the High Middle Ages. The requirements to wear yellow badges and live in closed "ghettoes" would have been familiar to a medieval Jew who had time-traveled to the twentieth century. The role of scapegoat—*one who is forced to take the blame for others' failings*—would have been familiar, too. Medieval Jews were blamed for the plague. In the 1930s Jews were blamed for economic collapse and German defeat in World War I.

When Hitler came to power as chancellor—in effect, prime minister—in 1933, Germany was an advanced society with a weak political culture, specifically a weak culture of democracy. Its economy was in distress as a result of the Great Depression. Hitler preached a racist ideology that promoted the idea of "Aryan supremacy."

The battlefield deaths of World War II were bad enough, to say nothing of those of civilians who died during air raids and other military action. But Hitler called for the systematic extermination of Europe's Jews. The Nazis and their allies murdered six million Jewish people. Many of the Jews who survived emigrated to the United States or Israel.

How Nationalism Destroyed the Continental European Empires

As the previous sections have discussed, ancient cultures, religion, and geography all had a hand in fashioning Europe's history and character. Nationalism is another force that shapes countries. Nationalism is loyalty to country. It affected four important empires in European history: the Holy Roman Empire, as well as the Ottoman, Austro-Hungarian, and Russian empires.

The Impact of Nationalism on the Holy Roman Empire

The French philosopher Voltaire (1694–1778) joked that the Holy Roman Empire (HRE) was neither holy, nor Roman, nor an empire. What was it, then? It was an attempt to bring much of Europe under one authority, to fill the void created by Rome's fall in AD 476.

Voltaire was arguably right that the HRE wasn't holy. But for centuries its emperors sought coronation from the pope. Voltaire was certainly right that it wasn't Roman. It was largely German. As for whether it was an empire—by the end of its existence, it was more like an alliance instead.

Folk singers in traditional Austrian dress entertain tourists in a plaza in Salzburg's Old City.

Photo by David Clark Scott / © 2003 The Christian Science Monitor

The Austro-Hungarian Empire was one of four affected by nationalism in European history. The other three were the Holy Roman Empire, the Ottoman Empire, and the Russian Empire.

But it did last more than a thousand years. And its (mostly elected) emperors saw themselves as successors to the Romans. Founded in 800 by the Frankish king, Charlemagne, the HRE was at its peak during the twelfth century. It was formally dissolved in 1806, during the Napoleonic wars.

One date to point to as a way of understanding how nationalism ultimately undid the HRE is 1648. That was the year the Peace of Westphalia ended the Thirty Years' War. That series of conflicts was the second of two sets of religious wars touched off by the Protestant Reformation. The map of solidly Catholic Europe had turned into a patchwork of mixed jurisdictions as some rulers embraced the new faith and others stayed true to the old one.

The Holy Roman Empire at its twelfth-century peak

The first round of religious wars ended in 1555 with a treaty known as the Peace of Augsburg. An alliance of Lutheran princes came to terms with the representative of Emperor Charles V, a Catholic. The treaty provided a legal basis for both Catholicism and Lutheranism to coexist within the empire. It established the principle of *Cuius regio, eius religio*—"whose region, his religion." In other words, it allowed the prince or other ruler of a region to choose its religion. The idea behind a ruler deciding the religion of all his people seems alien to modern thought. But at the time it represented an advance for religious pluralism, or the practice of many religions in one country or empire.

By 1648 much of Europe was exhausted by 30 years of fighting. The Peace of Westphalia is the term for the two treaties that brought this second round of wars to an end. These treaties established the principle of state sovereignty. That is, the real power lay with the states that made up the empire. It was a victory for smaller, homogeneous units, rather than a far-flung empire.

The Fall of the Ottoman Empire

In 1853 Czar Nicholas I of Russia called the Ottoman Empire "the sick man of Europe." Nationalism was stirring among the Ottomans' peoples. Europeans generally assumed that the empire was breaking up. Their main concern was that any newly emerging independent states might upset the balance of power in the region.

The Ottoman Empire's disintegration was like a pickup baseball game. Once a game has already begun, any new player to arrive can't join the ongoing game until a second person arrives to once again balance out the teams.

Greece was the first new state to emerge from the Ottoman Empire. It achieved independence in 1832. In 1877, after the Ottomans tried to suppress the uprisings of the Bulgarians, Russia went to war against the Turks. The result was a large independent state of Bulgaria under Russian protection.

Soon, though, other Europeans decided that Russia was becoming too dominant. In 1878 they renegotiated a much smaller Bulgaria. It was autonomous rather than independent. And it was back under Ottoman rule rather than allied with Russia. Serbia and Romania emerged as independent states at the same time. And Bosnia-Herzegovina went from Ottoman to Austro-Hungarian rule. What was left of the Ottoman Empire finally collapsed after World War I.

Tourists flock to the baroque-style Imperial Palace Schönbrunn, completed in the early eighteenth century, in Vienna, Austria.
Photo by Neal Menschel / © 1992 The Christian Science Monitor

By the nineteenth century, the Austro-Hungarians were picking up territory from the Ottoman Empire and undergoing reforms, including setting up a "dual monarchy" in 1867 with two capitals—Vienna and Budapest.

How Nationalism Changed the Austro-Hungarian Empire

But even as they were picking up territory from the Ottoman Empire, the Austro-Hungarians were feeling the same forces of nationalism at work on them, too. Austria controlled Hungary, the German-speaking state of Bohemia, and part of Romania, Italy, Poland, and Ukraine. But German-speaking Austrians made up only about a quarter of the population of the whole empire. Slavs—Czechs, Slovaks, Poles, Ukrainians, Serbs, Croats, and Slovenes—were about half the population. Hungarians and Italians made up the rest.

Each of these groups made its nationalist demands. They wanted countries of their own. The emperors tried to hold nationalism in check and sought to play the various ethnic groups off one another. It was a difficult game. The empire was so diverse that it didn't really have the option of political unification, as Germany had managed.

Austria-Hungary was economically liberal and progressive, with prosperous middle classes. But its government remained monarchist and authoritarian. About all it managed in the way of reform was to set up in 1867 a "dual monarchy" of Austria-Hungary, with two capitals—Vienna and Budapest. This arrangement lasted until the defeat of the Habsburgs in World War I. This, in turn, led to the carving up of the empire into many newly independent republics.

How Poland and Finland Affected the Russian Empire

Nineteenth-century nationalism affected even the Russian Empire. It included, at that point, part of Poland and all of Finland. But the empire would lose both after World War I and the Bolshevik Revolution.

As World War I opened, Poland was divided three ways. Part belonged to the Russian Empire, which was part of the Allied coalition with Britain and France. Germany and Austria-Hungary, two of the Central Powers, controlled the other two parts. All three powers were keen to have Polish support—and soldiers. And so, they were willing to do favors for the Poles, including making gestures toward self-rule.

What the Poles really wanted, though, was independence. As the war settled down into stalemate, the cause of Polish self-rule became more urgent.

At the end of World War I, US President Woodrow Wilson made a famous speech called "the Fourteen Points." In this he called for the establishment of a unified, independent Poland, with access to the Baltic Sea.

Germany and Austria-Hungary had lost the war, so were in no position to object to Wilson's plan for their Polish territories. Neither were the Russians, having withdrawn from the Allied war effort after the Bolshevik Revolution. Poland regained its independence as the Second Polish Republic.

The Finns emerged from more than a century of Russian domination when they broke away at the time of the October Revolution of 1917. They declared their independence, and on 31 December 1917, Lenin's Bolshevik government recognized it. After a brief but intense civil war between their own leftist Reds and rightist Whites, the Finns averted a leftist takeover and settled down into a parliamentary democracy.

After 20 years of Finnish independence, World War II broke out in 1939. The Finns declared themselves neutral. But then the Soviet Union invaded Finland in what was known as the Winter War of 1939–40. Despite fierce resistance, the Finns had to concede. They lost 10 percent of their territory to the Treaty of Moscow, which ended the war.

People shop at an outdoor market in Finland's capital, Helsinki.

Photo by Peter Ford / © 2005 The Christian Science Monitor

Finland declared its independence from Russia in 1917, and by the end of that year Lenin's Bolshevik government recognized it. Finland remains a free country today. It joined the EU in 1995.

After Germany invaded the Soviet Union, however, Finland fought with the Nazis against the Soviets. It withdrew from the war as the tide turned against Germany and signed a new peace treaty with new concessions to the Soviets. For the rest of the Soviet era, Finland maintained a policy of "friendly neutrality." As the Soviet Union dissolved, this led to true neutrality and eventually an openly Western orientation. On 1 January 1995 Finland joined the European Union.

How Marxism, Socialism, and Fascism Affected the Development of Europe

As powerful as nationalism and religion are in sculpting a country's borders and character, so are certain forms of government and economics. Marxism and socialism governed the Soviet Union for decades. But any story about government types wouldn't be complete without mention of a third movement: fascism.

Fascism was in many ways Marxism's mirror image. Fascism was an ideology of the far right, as communism was of the far left. Fascism was nationalistic, in a tribal or racist sense. This went far beyond people simply wanting their own country. Fascists also saw individuals as subservient to the state.

Some use the term fascism to refer only to Italy under the dictatorship of Benito Mussolini during World War II. But others insist that Adolf Hitler's National Socialism, or Nazism, was a form of fascism. Both Roosevelt and Churchill saw Nazism and fascism as a threat so great that they were willing to ally with Joseph Stalin to defeat Hitler and Mussolini.

Politics of the far right are often known as "reactionary" because they react to other political actors—trade unionists organizing for better working conditions, for instance. This goes well beyond principled conservatism. Fascists' nationalism leads them to look for scapegoats. They seek these especially among those they consider "outsiders" or "others"—Jews, as you have read, but also Freemasons, homosexuals, Communists, and Protestants.

Fascists tend to believe conspiracy theories and suggestions of betrayal. Many Germans blamed "Jews and Communists" for their defeat in World War I. According to the "stab in the back" theory, these "outsiders" had sabotaged Germany's war effort.

Victims' suitcases lie piled high at the Auschwitz death camp in Poland. *Photo by Robert Harbison / © 1993 The Christian Science Monitor*

Fascists in Germany blamed "Jews and Communists" for their defeat in World War I. On the foundation of these theories grew the Nazi movement that built the concentration camps where millions of Jews died during World War II.

The Influence of Marxism on the Development of Europe

The ideas of Marx and his colleague, Friedrich Engels, caught on as Europe industrialized. Lenin made those ideas the basis of a party that would run a totalitarian state. He realized this vision with the founding of the Soviet Union.

After World War II, Stalin made the most of his position as one of the victorious Allies to expand Marxist influence by creating the "Soviet bloc" in Eastern Europe. But Europe had long been full of communist, socialist, and other Marxist parties. Even during the Cold War of the twentieth century, leftists of various stripes took part in European politics. In the 1970s so-called "Eurocommunists" ran effective local governments in Western Europe, notably in Northern Italy.

The Effects of Socialism in Europe

Europeans generally accept a larger state role in the economy than Americans are used to. Europeans pay more taxes than Americans. In return they have publicly funded health care ("socialized medicine"). They also have a more generously funded network of social services. Labor unions are generally stronger and more politically active in Europe than in the United States.

All this may be seen as a legacy of democratic socialism in Europe. This movement has taken form in political parties such as Germany's Social Democrats and Britain's Labour Party. These parties have often been well to the left of the American political mainstream. But they are committed to peaceful parliamentary democracy. As such they are quite unlike the Soviet Communists.

The Consequences of Fascism in Twentieth-Century Europe

Besides Hitler's Germany and Mussolini's Italy, the term *fascism* also describes the rule of another dictator of this period, Francisco Franco. Until his death in 1975, he was both chief of state and head of government in Spain. All real power was in his hands. Although Franco came into power in a civil war with the backing of Hitler and Mussolini, during World War II, Spain was officially neutral. Franco and Hitler discussed bringing Spain into the conflict on the Axis side. But the two never came to terms.

Spain was once one of the most powerful countries in the world. But its antidemocratic government for much of the twentieth century held it back and kept it out of the mainstream. Since Franco's death, though, Spain is once more taking its place on the European stage.

fastFACT

One writer has described fascist economics as "socialism with a capitalist veneer." Advocates saw it as a middle way between liberal capitalism and Marxism. In fact, the official name of the German Nazi party was the "National Socialist German Worker's Party." Socialism sought direct state control of the economy. Fascism sought that control indirectly, by dominating supposedly private owners of businesses.

Berliners climb onto the Berlin Wall near the Brandenburg Gate to celebrate just hours after the Wall opened in 1989.

Photo by R. Norman Matheny / © 1989 The Christian Science Monitor

Fascists showed up elsewhere than in the Italian and Spanish governments, however. In France, for instance, many French fascists collaborated with the Germans after France fell in 1940.

In Britain, a group of aristocrats gathered around Sir Oswald Moseley flirted with Nazism to a degree that horrified the British government. After Edward VIII had given up the British throne to marry an American divorcée, he and his wife visited Germany in 1937 as Hitler's guests. This left the lasting impression that they were Nazi sympathizers as well.

In Norway, a fascist group called "the National Gathering" was widely regarded as a local counterpart to Hitler's Nazis. Its leader, former defense minister Vidkun Quisling, headed the Norwegian government under Nazi occupation. Today, quisling means *a traitor who serves as the puppet of the enemy occupying his or her country*.

In the final analysis, fascism wrought death and destruction throughout Europe before and during World War II. Tens of millions of innocent civilians were killed along with soldiers, sailors, and airmen. Tens of millions died under Lenin's and Stalin's communism, too. So it's not hard to conclude that the consequences of fascism and communism in Europe were among the most disastrous in history.

Happily, the defeat of fascism opened a whole new chapter of democracy and prosperity in Western Europe. The collapse of Soviet communism has brought the same to Eastern Europe. With all that could divide it—the aftermath of World War II, politics, religion, nationalism, even geography—the continent is one of the most developed and prosperous in the world. Elections are vigorously free and open, for the most part. Its people are well educated overall and regularly informed by a free press. In order to preserve that peace, prosperity, and liberty—and to prevent any further disasters like the two world wars—the European states have sought common footing through the European Union. You'll read about that in the next lesson.

Lesson 1 Review

Using complete sentences, answer the following questions on a sheet of paper.

1. What is the significance of the postwar reconciliation between France and Germany?
2. What do the three Scandinavian countries have in common?
3. Why did the ancient Greeks make their columns bulge in the middle?
4. What did the initials "SPQR" stand for, and why did Mussolini stamp them on manhole covers?
5. What was the significance of the date 1453?
6. What happened in 1492 that made the Jews of Spain feel betrayed?
7. What was the Holy Roman Empire?
8. In the nineteenth century, what were Europeans concerned about as the Ottoman Empire began to break up?
9. What was the "stab-in-the-back" theory?
10. What effect did Franco's government have on Spain?

Applying Your Learning

11. How do you think historic memory of the Crusades, Charles Martel, the Siege of Vienna, and the fall of Constantinople has affected relations between Europeans and the peoples of the Middle East?

LESSON 2 The European Union

Quick Write

What do you think Kohl and Mitterrand might have been thinking about as they stood before the crowd?

Learn About

- the origins of the European Union
- the countries that are members of the European Union
- the political and economic structure of the European Union
- the importance of the euro as a world currency

Verdun: It was World War I's longest single battle. It lasted nearly 10 months, which is longer than some entire wars. Verdun-sur-Meuse lay about 150 miles northeast of Paris. It had been an important fortress since Roman times. The French had reinforced it since the previous war with Germany, in 1870–71. It would be an important objective psychologically, the Germans reasoned.

The German commander's plan was to subject Verdun to intense bombing. This would pull French troops in from all along the Western Front to the eight-mile-wide front around Verdun to defend the ancient fortress. All those troops would be easy targets for his big artillery guns. He would "bleed France white," he said.

It began with a German artillery barrage at 7:15 a.m. on 21 February 1916. It didn't end until 16 December. Nobody really knows how many soldiers died there, but estimates run into the hundreds of thousands. The Germans lost very nearly as many soldiers as the French did. And when it was all over, neither side had gained any tactical or strategic advantage.

Nearly 70 years later, on 22 September 1984, West German Chancellor Helmut Kohl went to Verdun. There he met French President François Mitterrand for a ceremony to honor the dead—of both world wars. As their national anthems played, the two leaders clasped hands. The two men side by side, hands joined, became a living symbol of reconciliation between France and Germany.

The Origins of the European Union

The European Union, or EU, is a union of 27 democratic countries, ranging from Germany (with 82 million people) to tiny Malta (with 400,000). It is not the United States of Europe. Nor is it an empire. It started small—with only six members. And it has changed names as its missions and functions have changed.

The basic idea of the EU was political union through economic union. The reasoning behind postwar efforts to unite Europe was that democratic, law-abiding countries whose people traded freely with one another would be unlikely to go to war against each other. The first steps toward union began with some of the same industries that had fueled the war machine: coal and steel.

Vocabulary

- customs union
- referendum
- Euroskeptics
- central bank
- reserve currency

People walk and bike along the narrow streets of Amsterdam, the Netherlands, on a rainy day.
Photo by Neal J. Menschel / © 1991 The Christian Science Monitor

The Netherlands was a founding EU member. The reasoning behind postwar efforts to unite Europe was that democratic, law-abiding countries whose people traded freely with one another would be unlikely to go to war against each other.

The Goal of the European Union: to End Wars Among European Nations

World War I was supposed to be "the war to end all wars." That's what US President Woodrow Wilson called it. He also called it "a war to make the world safe for democracy."

But it didn't work out that way. Barely a generation after the conflict killed millions of people, Europe was at war again. Germany, Austria, and Italy—three pillars of modern European civilization—were under fascist rule. In fact, Germany and Italy had *elected* fascist governments. In Austria, parliamentary democracy had literally "switched itself off" when Austrian Chancellor Engelbert Dollfuss seized power after several prominent members of parliament resigned over a vote in chambers. And the Nazi war machine was rumbling across the continent.

When World War II ended, Europeans said, "Never again!" As they dug out of the rubble and began to rebuild in the years after 1945, they sought creative but practical ways to keep the peace that had been so hard won.

The Influence of the European Coal and Steel Treaty in Creating the EU

The European Union began on 9 May 1950 with the publication of the Schuman Plan. In it French Foreign Minister Robert Schuman proposed that France and Germany's coal and steel industries be put under joint control.

These two industries were essential for producing war materiel. A modern state cannot go to war without them. If the two countries' defense industries were merged, they presumably couldn't go to war with each other. As Schuman put it, "The solidarity in production thus established will make it plain that any war between France and Germany becomes not merely unthinkable, but materially impossible."

He reached out to Konrad Adenauer, chancellor of the new Federal Republic of Germany (or West Germany). Adenauer agreed to his idea. Schuman also wanted an organization that would be open to other countries as well.

On 18 April 1951, six countries—France, Germany, and Italy, plus Belgium, the Netherlands, and Luxembourg (the so-called Benelux countries)—signed a treaty based on the Schuman Plan. This written agreement between the countries put the coal and steel sectors in all six under common management. This would keep them from making weapons to turn against each other.

The treaty created the European Coal and Steel Community (ECSC). The ECSC established free trade among its six members in iron ore, coal, coke (a form of coal), and steel. It did this by:

- removing tariffs (import taxes) and other trade barriers
- regulating production and sales
- establishing a common external tariff on imports from other nations
- aiding investments in coal and steel in member states.

Border traffic from France approaches Italy.

Photo by R. Norman Matheny / © 1992 The Christian Science Monitor

In 1957 France, Italy, Germany, Belgium, the Netherlands, and Luxembourg signed the Treaty of Rome, creating the European Economic Community or Common Market. The treaty aimed to promote free trade among the members and integrate their economies.

The Treaty of Rome and the Development of the Common Market in 1957

The coal and steel experiment was a success. It confounded the pessimism of critics who were sure it would fail. Today Europeans mark 9 May, the anniversary of Schuman's presentation of his plan, as "Europe Day," the EU's "birthday."

Soon "the Six" decided to take another step toward a united Europe. On 25 March 1957 they signed the Treaty of Rome. It took effect on 1 January 1958. It established the European Economic Community (EEC) or Common Market.

The Common Market was essentially a **customs union**—*an association of nations to promote free trade within the union and set common tariffs for nations that are not members*. The idea was that increased trade among the members would help integrate their economies. It was an early step in weaving such a tight web of connections among these six countries that war would become more and more unthinkable.

fastFACT

Two "Treaties of Rome" were signed at the same time. The other established the European Atomic Energy Community, or Euratom, to support the development of peaceful nuclear energy in Europe.

The Countries That Are Members of the European Union

The European Union has grown in two main ways, since the signing of its earliest treaties. It has acquired new members. And it has taken on new missions and functions.

A young student reads a book by a fountain's edge in Portsmouth, England.

Photo by Melanie Stetson Freeman / © 2004 The Christian Science Monitor

Britain was not an original member of the EC, but joined in 1973.

The European Union's Six Founding Nations

The Common Market began with the same six members as the coal and steel group. Britain's wartime leader, Winston Churchill, was a great advocate of a united Europe as a way to prevent further wars. But the Common Market sidelined Britain at first. This had partly to do with resistance from French President Charles de Gaulle. It also had to do with Britain seeing itself as not exactly part of "Europe," since Britain is an island nation.

The EU's 27 Current Members

The Common Market first expanded in 1973. France by then had a new president, Georges Pompidou. He came to terms with Edward Heath, the very pro-European British prime minister, to bring Britain into the European Community (EC), as the Common Market was renamed. Two other new members joined at this time—Denmark and Ireland.

The 1980s saw another three new members. Greece, already a NATO member, joined the EC in 1981. Spain and Portugal joined in 1986, after both had thrown off right-wing dictatorships and established democratic rule. That was a requirement for joining the EC.

Kemer, Turkey, used to be a small coastal village. Today it's a tourist destination for Russians, Germans, and other Europeans. *Photo by Melanie Stetson Freeman / © 2007 The Christian Science Monitor*

As of 2009 Turkey is an EU candidate member along with Croatia and the Former Yugoslav Republic of Macedonia.

In 1990 the EC expanded again, not because it took a new member, but because an existing member had itself expanded. West Germany reunified with the former communist East Germany after the fall of the Berlin Wall. In 1993 the Treaty of Maastricht came into effect, changing the EC to the European Union. The next expansion came on New Year's Day 1995, when Austria, Finland, and Sweden joined.

The year 2004 was one of big expansion for the EU. It added 10 new members. These included the four central European states seen as strong candidates for membership as soon as the communist era ended: the Czech Republic, Hungary, Poland, and Slovakia. They also included the three Baltic states (Estonia, Latvia, and Lithuania); two Mediterranean island republics, Malta and Cyprus; and Slovenia, the most progressive and Westernized of the former Yugoslav republics.

Two more countries, Romania and Bulgaria, joined the EU in 2007. At this writing the EU has three candidate members—Turkey, Croatia, and the Former Yugoslav Republic of Macedonia.

fastFACT

The Greeks insist that only they have a right to use the name Macedonia, since a neighboring region also called Macedonia is part of Greece. Do you remember Philip of Macedonia and Alexander the Great? The Greeks therefore insist that the former Yugoslav republic use the awkwardly long name Former Yugoslav Republic of Macedonia (FYROM) rather than call itself simply "Macedonia." Negotiations over the issue continue.

The EU's Member States

- Austria
- Belgium
- Bulgaria
- Cyprus
- Czech Republic
- Denmark
- Estonia
- Finland
- France
- Germany
- Greece
- Hungary
- Ireland
- Italy
- Latvia
- Lithuania
- Luxembourg
- Malta
- Netherlands
- Poland
- Portugal
- Romania
- Slovakia
- Slovenia
- Spain
- Sweden
- United Kingdom

The Political and Economic Structure of the European Union

Have you ever tried to organize a couple of friends to go to the movies, but then found the group had suddenly grown to half a dozen—so you had to take two cars and see a later showing? Then you have some idea what the European Union has experienced since its modest beginnings. The following sections will give you an overview of the rules and institutions that help manage the union, and how they work together.

The "Rule of Law" and the Importance of Treaties for the EU

The EU member states have negotiated and signed many treaties over the years. They are generally named for the city where they were signed.

A Belgian shopkeeper shows off her line of merchandise, which she designed with the European Union's star theme to honor passage of the Treaty of Maastricht in 1992.
Photo by Andy Nelson / © 2000 The Christian Science Monitor

The Treaty of Maastricht created a structure with three "pillars"—the European Community, a Common Foreign and Security Policy, and joint action in Justice and Home Affairs.

There's a particular reason treaties loom so large within the EU. In the United States, the Congress passes laws for the entire country. But the EU is still a collection of sovereign states. So, for the EU, a treaty is often the correct mechanism through which to work.

Beyond that, though, treaties are an expression of the rule of law. Through much of Europe's history, the principle of "Might makes right" had reigned. That's the kind of thinking the EU was created to overcome. Thus if Germany wants Belgium to do something (to cite a not totally random example), there has to be discussion and agreement, rather than just one-sided action—especially military action.

Besides the Treaty of Rome, the EU's founding document, other important EU treaties include:

- ***The Treaty of Maastricht***, which created a structure with three "pillars":
    - the European Community—including the customs union, economic and monetary union, and other forms of European economic cooperation
    - a Common Foreign and Security Policy—covering defense and international relations
    - joint action in Justice and Home Affairs—to foster international cooperation on police and criminal matters.

  This new three-pillared structure is the European Union.
- ***The Treaty of Nice***, signed on 26 February 2001, reformed the EU's institutions to help it function smoothly after growing to 25 states.
- ***The Treaty of Lisbon***, signed on 13 December 2007, aims to further streamline EU institutions and make the EU more democratic. Its other purposes are to improve the Union's accountability, openness, transparency, and participation. At this writing the parliaments of all 27 member states have approved the treaty. While the parliaments have OK'd the treaty, however, the president of the Czech Republic had not given final approval as of mid-2009. Ireland, which voted the treaty down in a referendum—*a vote by the people*—in 2008, passed it during a second referendum in late 2009. To become law, the treaty must be approved by all 27 EU members.

The Treaty of Lisbon followed an attempt to pass an EU constitution a few years earlier. A treaty establishing such a constitution was adopted by heads of state and government in June 2004, and signed later that year. But it was never ratified, as French and Dutch voters defeated the constitution in referendums in 2005.

The European Parliament Committee of the Regions counts votes during a meeting in Brussels, Belgium. The committee members offer advice to the Parliament.
Photo by Andy Nelson / © 2000 The Christian Science Monitor

The Parliament's job is to pass laws based on proposals from the European Commission. Europeans elect representatives to the European Parliament every five years.

The European Parliament's Role

Europeans elect representatives to the European Parliament every five years. The number of representatives that each country votes into office depends on that country's population. Parliament's job is to pass laws based on proposals from the European Commission, which is the executive of the EU (more on that later). Parliament shares this responsibility with the Council of the European Union (more on that later, too). Parliament and the Council also share joint budget authority for the EU.

Parliament also has the power to dismiss the European Commission. This corresponds to the way a national parliament can "bring down" the government of a prime minister, as with a vote of no confidence. The Parliament also elects the European Ombudsman, who investigates citizens' complaints about bad conduct by EU institutions. The European Parliament meets mainly in Strasbourg, France, and occasionally in Brussels, Belgium.

The Parliament is organized by party rather than national delegations. The European People's Party, for instance, is a mainstream conservative party allied with the Christian Democratic parties on the Continent. The European People's Party in the European Parliament includes representatives from across the different member nations. The Parliament as a whole includes the usual spectrum of views from left to right. It has socialists, liberals, greens, and others.

The Parliament also includes a range of views on European integration. Some members are strongly pro-federalist. In European terms, this means stronger integration and closer ties among members. At the other end of the spectrum are the Euroskeptics—or Eurosceptics, as they often spell it—*people who oppose further EU integration*. They are happy with the EU as a customs union. But they feel that closer integration limits their own national sovereignty. Over the years, the British have been the leading Euroskeptics.

Many Euroskeptics worry about too much European-wide regulation from officials at EU headquarters in Brussels—many of them unelected. They note that their countries have their own sturdy traditions of parliamentary democracy and rule of law.

Moreover, the Euroskeptics complain, the EU has become more cumbersome as it has expanded. For example, it continues to have a large number of official languages—currently 23. This requires armies of translators and interpreters.

The Council's Role

The Council is the EU's main decision-making body. It consists of government ministers from member governments—rather like Cabinet secretaries in the United States.

The actual makeup of the Council varies according to the issue or issues on the table at any given time. For example, if the EU is trying to settle an environmental issue, each member state will send its minister responsible for the environment. If there is a financial issue to decide, the Council will consist of finance ministers, and so on.

Every six months, a different member state holds the so-called presidency of the EU. The state with the presidency chairs the meetings and sets the overall agenda. Each state's turn at the presidency is an opportunity to "show its stuff." It's a time to demonstrate leadership and good management. This time in the spotlight has been especially important for newer and smaller members.

Each country's number of votes within the Council reflects its population. But the system gives some weighting in favor of smaller countries. (Does this remind you of something about the way the US Congress is organized?) The council decides most issues by majority vote. But the really sensitive ones require everyone to agree.

Several times a year the presidents and/or prime ministers of the member states meet as the European Council. These so-called summit meetings set overall policy.

The European Commission's Function

The European Commission is the EU's executive organ. It corresponds very roughly to the departments of the US executive branch, just as the European Parliament corresponds very roughly to the US Congress. It drafts proposals for new laws. It also manages the day-to-day business of carrying out policies and spending money. The Commission ensures that everyone follows European treaties and laws. And it can take rule-breakers to the European Court of Justice if necessary.

Twenty-seven men and women, one from each member state, make up the Commission. An army of some 24,000 civil servants, most of them in Brussels, supports them. The Commission also has a president, chosen by the governments of the EU members.

The Role of the EU Courts

As you can imagine, within a community that so emphasizes the rule of law, courts are very important. The Court of Justice of the EU ensures that EU law is interpreted and applied the same way in all countries. That is, the court makes sure that a German court doesn't interpret a given law differently from a Belgian court. The court also ensures that member states and institutions meet their legal commitments. The Court of Justice has its headquarters in Luxembourg. It has one judge from each member country.

The European Central Bank's Role

A central bank is *a government body that issues currency, regulates the supply of credit, and holds the reserves of other banks*. It isn't a commercial bank, or the kind of bank where you or your family—or even very rich people or big corporations—would have an account. Rather, it's a "bankers' bank." It's the bank where commercial banks go to get money. The central bank of the United States is the Federal Reserve Bank. Its counterpart in Europe is the European Central Bank, or ECB.

The ECB has its headquarters in Frankfurt, Germany. Its chief job is managing the euro—the new common European currency. It does that mainly by setting interest rates. Its biggest concern is ensuring stable prices—fighting inflation. During the early twentieth century Germany suffered a terrible bout of hyperinflation. Prices skyrocketed. The banknotes in people's wallets lost value even on the streetcar ride into town to shop. Almost no Germans alive today remember that from personal experience. But the episode stamped itself on collective memory. Germans today remain strong inflation fighters. And they've brought that attitude to the management of the euro.

The European Investment Bank

Another EU bank makes loans for many different kinds of projects within the EU and EU candidate members. It is especially active in poorer areas. It finances rail and road-building projects and other infrastructure projects, as well. It also supports programs to protect or clean up the environment. EU governments own the bank, and so it can raise capital and provide loans at attractive rates. A particular focus of the bank right now is projects that will help the EU become the world's leading knowledge-based economy.

The Importance of the Euro as a World Currency

The idea behind the European Union was, in simplest terms, "trade not war." If Europe's national economies were integrated closely enough with one another, no one would go to war. After all, what business wants to bomb its customers? Or attack its suppliers?

The introduction of a common currency has been one of the crowning achievements of this integration. The euro has succeeded not only as Europe's common coin, but also as an important world currency—to the point that some observers say it may take over the role the US dollar has played in the global economy.

Passengers make their way along a platform at Gare du Nord in Paris, France, to board a high-speed train.
Photo by Andy Nelson / © 2000 The Christian Science Monitor

The introduction of a common currency has been one of the crowning achievements of European integration.

So just what's meant by "common currency," and what are some of the basics of currency exchange? In the United States, people use dollars to buy things. Printed on each bill is the line: "This Note Is Legal Tender for All Debts, Public and Private." No matter where a person travels in the United States, the dollar is accepted all across the country. The accents are different, the scenery is different, and the weather is different. But the dollar is everywhere. That's because the United States is one vast sovereign nation.

The nations of Europe, though, are much smaller. Until the euro came in, each had its own currency, with a few exceptions. This meant tourists were always having to change money—from dollars to francs to marks to florins. They had to pay for this service. For tourists on a bus tour, this was a minor inconvenience. For European companies trying to expand across national frontiers, it was a major problem.

People take in the outdoor air in Poiana Tapului, Romania, which sits in the shadow of the Transylvanian Alps.

Photo by Robert Harbison / © 1990 The Christian Science Monitor

Romania, Poland, and Estonia are not yet members of the euro zone, but all have set national target dates for joining.

But what if they shared a currency? What if there were a European coin as universally accepted in Europe as the dollar is in America? Those were the questions behind the development of Europe's common currency, the euro.

The Countries That Use the Euro as a Currency

At this writing, 16 countries use the euro as their currency. Its symbol looks like this: €. People often refer to this group of countries, with about 330 million citizens, as the "euro zone." (The official term is "euro area.") It started out in 1999 with a group of 11 countries: the original "Six" of the EU, plus Ireland, Finland, Austria, and the Iberian duo, Spain and Portugal. All these countries had to meet certain "convergence criteria" to join the euro zone—more on that later.

Greece joined in 2001, Slovenia in 2007, the island republics of Cyprus and Malta in 2008, and Slovakia in 2009. Additionally, Poland, Estonia, and Romania have national target dates for joining.

The launch of the euro took place in two phases. On 1 January 1999 Europeans began using the euro as "virtual money" or "book money" before there were actual coins and banknotes. Banks and other businesses would enter sums into ledgers in the national currency and also in euros. On 1 January 2002 banknotes and coins began to circulate.

The Euro's Advantages for EU Members

Using the common currency means people and businesses don't have to pay the cost of exchanging money. Currency exchange is a service, and it has to be paid for. It's somewhat like the interest someone pays on a loan.

But there's more to it than that. Currency exchange rates go up and down over time. Let's take the case of a manufacturer who contracts to deliver a container full of finished goods to an international customer. The manufacturer may pay his employee and his suppliers in one currency but be paid by the customer in another. When the manufacturer and the customer first agree to the contract, including prices, they can figure in the price of currency exchange. But over the life of the contract, as the factory produces the goods and then the shippers deliver them, the exchange rate may shift. It may be enough to give the customer an unexpected bargain—and to wipe out all of the manufacturer's profit.

Currency fluctuations occur for reasons beyond the control of people such as this hypothetical manufacturer and customer. A government may "print money," as the expression goes, to cover a budget deficit. When supply increases, the price falls. That is, the value of that currency will fall on international markets. On the other hand, the value of the US dollar often goes up in times of turmoil in the world. People who lose confidence in their own national currency go to the bank to buy dollars. As the demand rises, the price—the value of the dollar—rises.

This "flight to security," by the way, is ultimately a vote of confidence by world markets in the United States, both as an economy and as a free country. But in the near term it can wreak havoc as buyers and sellers try to come to terms. Is it any wonder that much of Europe has been glad to put these problems behind it?

Why Some EU Countries Don't Use the Euro

On the other hand, not all the EU is within the euro zone. Why not?

Some countries remain outside because they haven't yet met the criteria to join. Several EU members outside the euro zone are former communist countries. They are making the transition from centrally planned economies to free markets. This is a big change. But all are keen to make the transition. As small, "open" economies (with lots of imports and exports) already doing a lot of trade with euro countries, they should benefit greatly from adopting the common currency.

But the euro-zone criteria, known as "convergence criteria," are fairly tough. They weren't easy for even longtime EU members to meet at first. To enter the euro zone, a country must show that it has:

- ***Price stability.*** A country's inflation rate must be low.
- ***Sound public finances.*** Government budget deficits and national debt must be under control.
- ***Exchange-rate stability.*** The value of the national currency the prospective new member is about to give up should not swing wildly in the markets.
- ***Low long-term interest rates.*** Long-term rates are the markets' way of predicting the future. Low rates are a sign that a member wanting to join the euro zone will be able to continue to meet the criteria over the long term, and not for a short time only, just to get in.

Any close relationship involves some tradeoffs between freedom and flexibility, on one hand, and support and strength, on the other. If you take a friend along on a trip, you'll have to pay attention to his or her preferences on how early to start out and where to stop for lunch. That may cramp your style somewhat. But if your car breaks down, or you get lost in the woods, you may be glad to have company.

That basic principle comes into play in the euro zone as well. The biggest EU member outside the euro area is Britain. The British, whose pound sterling was once the world's dominant currency, have not wanted to give up their ability to steer their own economy independently. Their economy is big enough that they can do this. They have been allowed to "opt out" of the euro zone. So have the Swedes. Their situation is similar, although their currency was never so dominant, nor is their economy so big.

Denmark is the other country outside the euro zone. The Danes have twice voted down referendums on joining. Their currency is pegged to the euro, however. This means that the Danes have to keep pace with euro standards but don't get the benefit of a common currency—the worst of both worlds.

How the Euro Compares With the Dollar as a World Currency

If you were to visit the mythical Republic of Bananaland, for instance, you might have to exchange some of your dollars for Bananalandish money. But you wouldn't want to exchange any more than you really needed on your visit. When you got ready to leave, you might try to change any unspent Bananalandish money back into dollars. Or you might just give the taxi driver who takes you to the airport a really big tip. After all, what are you going to do with Bananalandish money? There's no place to spend it except Bananaland.

Not all currencies are like this. The dollar, for instance, is a currency people accept widely outside the United States—even where it's not the official legal tender. In the mid-1990s research by officials of the Federal Reserve found that between 55 percent and 70 percent of all dollars circulating were doing so *outside* the United States.

Some of these dollars go into dubious transactions—drug deals, for instance. But in other cases, people just need a safe store of value. Dollars represent people's emergency reserves—stashes of cash under the mattress of someone living in a war zone, or under a repressive government.

There's evidence that euro notes are beginning to fill that role of emergency cash reserve, too. And the euro is available in €500 notes. The biggest dollar note widely available is the $100 bill. That means that the euro has become an even better way to pack a lot of value into a single suitcase.

In sum, both the dollar and the euro are currencies that individuals, banks, and governments are willing to hold on to. In technical terms, the dollar and the euro are both examples of reserve currencies. A reserve currency is *a currency that governments keep on hand to pay international debts*.

The US dollar is the most widely traded currency in the world, and the euro is in second place. The euro is also the No. 2 reserve currency after the dollar. At its launch, the euro accounted for 18.1 percent of global foreign exchange reserves. By the summer of 2009 that had risen to 25.9 percent. At the end of 2006 the combined value of euro notes in circulation surpassed that of US dollars.

Cargo ships dock in Barcelona, Spain, along the Mediterranean Sea.
Photo by R. Norman Matheny / © 1989 The Christian Science Monitor

To date, it appears that the EU has been a smashing success. First, there have been no wars between its members. France and Germany, for example, have been at peace for decades after centuries of conflict. The EU has increased Europe's economic importance on the world scene. Free trade between its members has helped bring economic growth to some of the continent's poorer corners. It has advanced the causes of freedom, democracy, and human rights, since countries wanting to join must agree to protect and promote them.

But the process of adding new members has brought growing pains. The defeat of recent referendums may indicate that Europeans have reached the limit of how much national sovereignty they are willing to give up—for now, at least.

This was a problem for the early United States, as well. In that case, Americans were willing to give up some state authority to the federal government, exchanging the Articles of Confederation for the Constitution. But the 13 original American states shared a common English language and British heritage. For the multilingual European nations, with different cultures, religions, and histories, the process is proving much more difficult. How much further European unity develops will determine much about the continent's future.

CHECK POINTS

Lesson 2 Review

Using complete sentences, answer the following questions on a sheet of paper.

1. What did the Schuman Plan propose?
2. What did the Treaty of Rome establish?
3. What did Spain and Portugal have to do before joining the European Community?
4. Why did the EC expand in 1990?
5. What are the three pillars of the European Union?
6. Which people have been the leading Euroskeptics, and what do they worry about?
7. Why should entering the euro zone be good for the EU's formerly communist new members?
8. Why has Britain remained outside the euro zone?

Applying Your Learning

9. Compare and contrast the governments of the United States and the European Union.

LESSON 3 Immigration, Terrorist Cells, and Ethnic Strife

Quick Write

Was it a good idea for the Danish newspaper to publish the 12 cartoons?

Learn About

- why European countries have permitted immigration
- why immigrants have had difficulty assimilating into European societies
- the difficulties al-Qaeda and its allies have posed for Europe
- the background of ethnic and religious strife in Northern Ireland

On 30 September 2005 the Danish newspaper *Jyllands-Posten* published a dozen editorial cartoons on Islam. Most depicted the prophet Muhammad. The idea, the newspaper said, was to contribute to the debate over criticism of Islam and self-censorship within Western media.

Danish Muslims were not happy. Some 5,000 of them marched in protest against the cartoons. Muslims traditionally regard depictions of Muhammad to be blasphemous, or sacrilegious. They claimed that their religion had been insulted. After that the matter seemed to die down somewhat.

Then in the early weeks of 2006, the controversy blew up again. A group of diplomats from Muslim countries sought to meet with the Danish prime minister to discuss the cartoons. They wanted the Danish government to force *Jyllands-Posten* to apologize. The prime minister refused to meet with the diplomats, saying that there was nothing to discuss. Denmark is built on a tradition of freedom of the press, he explained. He neither had nor wanted the power to limit that freedom.

Over the following weeks, hundreds of thousands of protesters took to the streets throughout the Muslim world. An estimated 100 people died in violence connected with the protests. Protesters burned Danish flags, and many people announced they would boycott Danish goods. The Danish prime minister called it his country's worst international crisis since World War II.

Why European Countries Have Permitted Immigration

Vocabulary

- assimilate
- demographics
- terrorist cell
- established church

Europeans moved to the New World partly because of overcrowding in the Old World. Now Europe has several times as many people as when it settled the New World. But the tide has turned. Since the mid-twentieth century, Europe has no longer been just a source of emigrants. Rather it has been a destination for immigrants.

The Need for Labor

Right after World War II, Europeans had a lot of rebuilding to do. The West German economy, in particular, was expanding so fast there was a labor shortage. To supply needed workers, Germany turned to Turkey. The first Turkish *Gastarbeiter*, or "guest workers," arrived in the early 1960s. The Berlin Wall had by then shut down most emigration from East Germany. The Turkish guest workers thus helped fill a gap in the West German labor force. And by leaving Turkey, they helped relieve overcrowding and unemployment there.

Children play in the narrow streets of Istanbul, Turkey.

Photo by Robert Harbison / © 1994 The Christian Science Monitor

After World War II, West Germany had a labor shortage. So the country invited *Gastarbeiter*, or "guest workers," from Turkey. In turn, by leaving Turkey, the guest workers helped relieve overcrowding and unemployment in their own country.

France and Belgium also brought in large numbers of foreign workers during this period. They came in waves. The first came from Southern and Southeastern Europe: Greece, Italy, Spain, Portugal, and Turkey. Eastern Europeans—notably Poles—made up the second wave. The third wave came from former European colonial possessions—from the South Asian subcontinent, North Africa, and French-speaking West Africa.

As Western Europeans grew more affluent and their birthrates fell, there were fewer young workers to take up the slack. They became choosier about the jobs they would take. Service jobs—cleaning, waiting tables, washing dishes—became the province of non-Europeans. Meanwhile, the Turks, in particular, made a place for themselves as skilled workers in Germany's high-tech manufacturing industries.

The first guest workers had short-term work permits. The plan was for them to return home at the end of their contracts and for others to take their places. The plan didn't work out quite that way, however. Employers were reluctant to let workers go once they had invested time and effort to train them. And guest workers got used to life in a more liberal and affluent society. They didn't want to return home.

A North African worker prepares crêpes at an outdoor stand in Paris, France.
Photo by Neal J. Menschel / © 1991 The Christian Science Monitor

Like West Germany, France brought in large numbers of foreign workers during the post-World War II period, including many from North Africa.

Recruitment of foreign workers came to an abrupt stop in the economic downturn of 1973. Family reunification continued, though. And the guest workers began to have children. By the 1990s some 70 percent of Germany's Turkish community was German-born.

The Turkish community increased roughly fourfold from that "immigration stop" of 1973 to 2005. Likewise, the numbers of North Africans in France grew nearly tenfold between 1957 and 2002, according to another study. Other countries have seen similar increases.

Freedom of Immigration Within the European Union

Meanwhile, the great expansion of the European Union (EU) has created new migration issues. That's because an EU citizen may travel freely to any EU country with only a passport or even just a valid identity card. The latter is a state-issued document rather like an American driver's license. No EU citizen can be required to have an entry or exit visa for any EU state.

If you've lived all your life in the United States, you may not fully appreciate what this means. And it means most in the countries formerly under communist rule. Just a generation ago many rail trips involved hours of waiting time. A train would pull off to a siding at a national border and government customs officials could carefully—very carefully—inspect everyone's passport and maybe luggage as well. Within the EU, that's no longer true.

The EU right of entry includes the right to stay in a place for up to three months. For longer stays, EU citizens must prove they will not burden the social services of the country they are visiting. In the main, though, EU citizens can travel across national frontiers unimpeded to work or study in another EU country. What's more, an EU citizen who moves from one EU country to another acquires the right of permanent residence in the new country after five years of uninterrupted legal residence.

But the 2004 expansion of the EU did bring with it some curbs on the free movement of labor. Much of "old Europe" worried that giving citizens of the new member states unfettered job access would lead to a flood of "Polish plumbers" and other Eastern Europeans. These workers, the reasoning went, would compete for jobs and/or drive down wages. At worst, they would swell the welfare rolls.

And so, acting as individual states, a dozen of the EU countries temporarily closed their job markets to these Eastern Europeans. An important exception was the British, who chose not to restrict their job market. As a result, economists reckon, about 1 million immigrants came to Britain after May 2004, creating something of a miniboom in the economy.

Under the treaty governing the 2004 expansion, all EU states must open their labor markets to the 2004 entrants by 2011. The treaty that brought Bulgaria and Romania into the EU in 2007 provides that all curbs on the free movement of labor from those countries must end on 31 December 2013.

The Humanitarian Aspects of Immigration

So the past few decades have forced a number of European countries to rethink their views on human migration. Countries that for years sent people abroad—Ireland, for example—have in recent years seen many of those natives return. What's more, these nations have drawn immigrants from other countries as well.

fastFACT

A country that offers *asylum* gives persecuted people a safe place to live. To qualify for asylum under international law, an asylum-seeker must have a well-founded fear of persecution by enemies in his or her home country.

But unlike the United States, which actively recruited immigrants to populate a vast land, European countries haven't thought of themselves as destinations for immigrants. Well into the 1990s German officials would scarcely use their word for "immigration." They would insist that Germany is not an "immigration country," like the United States or Canada. They held that Germany has refugees and asylum-seekers, but not immigrants.

Europeans have long looked at the immigration issue through a humanitarian lens. World War II not only killed millions of Europeans—it displaced millions as well. Masses of people were on the march as borders were redrawn and governments fell. The "never again" ideal within European thinking—"never again another terrible war"—called for taking seriously the human rights issues tied to migration.

During the boom years, guest-worker programs sometimes solved more than one problem at once. Europeans got the labor they needed. And the immigrant workers got an escape from poverty and political repression into a new life.

The economic contractions of the 1970s, however, brought a halt to recruitment of guest workers. That didn't mean an end to immigration. But governments began to look harder at people's requests for asylum. They drew a sharper distinction between asylum-seekers and economic migrants—those who were merely seeking better economic opportunity.

A pattern has developed—when things go wrong in a land that used to be a European colony, a good many people of that former colony often turn up on the doorstep of the onetime "mother country." Applications for asylum have risen significantly since the end of the Cold War. Only 104,000 people sought asylum in Western Europe in 1984. But by 1992 the figure was 692,000. More recent numbers are down from that peak but still well above those of the early 1980s. Figures for 2008 showed 20,000 asylum applications per month within the EU. Asylum has become one of the main means of immigration into Europe.

This is in part because the end of the Cold War "lifted the lid" on a number of small conflicts around the world. Many of these wars are fought by regular troops and paramilitaries who target civilians. Multitudes flee "ethnic cleansing" and seek safety in Europe. Many of these try to make their way to Europe illegally. No one knows how many people do this. In 2000 one European expert cited a "reputable estimate" of 400,000 illegal migrants smuggled into the EU each year. The problem mirrors that of the United States and illegal immigrants from Latin America.

Why Immigrants Have Had Difficulty Assimilating Into European Societies

Immigration, whether legal or illegal, raises issues such as *assimilation*. People often use the word assimilate when they talk about immigrants. Referring to the immigrants, it can mean *to become like one's environment; to blend or fit in*. When *assimilate* refers to what a society does to its immigrants, it can mean *to make (something or someone) similar, to absorb, to take in*.

Shoppers run errands at Whitechapel Market in an East London borough called Tower Hamlets. The borough is home to one-third of London's Muslim population.
Photo by Mary Knox Merrill / © 2006 The Christian Science Monitor

Europeans have long looked at the immigration issue through a humanitarian lens.

But assimilation has not always been easy for immigrants in Europe or the societies where they settle. Part of the problem is ordinary racism. Most Europeans are used to living in countries where almost everyone belongs to the same ethnic group, or a dominant ethnic group. But observers suggest a number of other factors at work as well:

- Europeans don't have the same sense of themselves as living in "a nation of immigrants" as Americans do
- European governments often hesitate to engage with culturally conservative immigrant communities (such as Muslim communities that may require women to wear burqas)
- Immigrants to Europe haven't always had a clear path to gain citizenship and otherwise take part in public life.

This lack of a path, along with other factors, can keep newcomers anchored in their immigrant communities. Some would say it keeps them "stuck."

Immigrants once had to let go of one world to embrace another. Nowadays, though, many immigrants have one foot in each of two worlds. They rely on cell phones, the Internet, and cheap airfares to keep in touch with extended family. But these modern conveniences can also bind them to their homelands' political and ethnic grievances. They can tie immigrants to social attitudes—say about women's roles and rights—that are unhelpful in the modern world, as well.

Another factor at work is that Europe began to experience large-scale immigration just as the assimilation or "melting pot" ideal was giving way to the idea of "multiculturalism." This more recent concept has made governments more hesitant to push for assimilation, not wanting to seem disrespectful of other cultures.

Still another overarching factor: Europe's newcomers are largely Muslim. With longer historical memories than most Americans have, many Europeans have not forgotten Europe's many confrontations with the Islamic world over the centuries. In addition, the twenty-first century is a time when Islam is struggling to come to terms with the relationship between religion and the state. Muslims are wrestling with questions of the legitimacy of secular governments. This spotlights issues such as whether a French Muslim girl can wear a headscarf to a public school, or whether sharia, or Muslim religious law, should have jurisdiction over a European divorce case.

The Christian West has been through this before. You read in Lesson 1 about its years of religious conflict. This involved not only Christians and Muslims, but also Christians and Jews, Protestants and Catholics, and spiritual and temporal leaders within Christianity. These questions were settled eventually, mostly in favor of tolerance, pluralism, and freedom of religion. But it took centuries.

The following sections look at some of Europe's immigrant communities.

The Persecution of the Roma in Europe

Most people refer to this ethnic group as Gypsies. That reflects an old misconception that they came from Egypt. Their itinerant lifestyle—the way many of them continually move around—has made "gypsy" a synonym for people with no fixed place to live.

But those who know more about them call them Roma, or Romani. These people came from India and arrived in Europe around 1300. Their language is related to Sanskrit, the Indo-European parent of modern-day Hindi and other languages of South Asia.

The Roma number about 4 million, although some estimates run higher. They're one of the most oppressed minority groups in Europe. They've been persecuted one way or another since they arrived. The Nazis rounded them up and murdered them during the Holocaust, just as they did the Jews. The Germans required the Roma to wear black triangles on their clothing.

The Romas' lifestyle often puts them at odds with governments. France, for example, requires those with "no fixed abode"—no permanent place to live—to have certain travel documents. These sometimes require renewal every three months. These rules affect mostly Romani people, who consider the regulations discriminatory. Similarly, new legislation lets British police order Roma in their jurisdictions to "move along" from highway rest stops. Local officials also seek to evict Roma from what they see as illegal camps.

Much more seriously, however, hard times in Europe have led to treatment much worse than that, especially in Eastern Europe. Far-right politicians play on old stereotypes. They call the Roma petty criminals and drains on social services. Recent Roma experiences include:

- The Italian government announced plans for a national registry of all of the country's estimated 150,000 Roma, including those born in Italy. Some observers found it especially troubling that other European leaders raised few objections to this.
- In the Czech Republic, right-wing groups have clashed with police as they tried to march through neighborhoods where the Roma have established permanent homes.
- A string of attacks on Roma in Hungary—18 in 18 months—was carried out in 2008–09. The attackers used crude firebombs, as well as firearms. The attacks were so precise and stealthy that authorities suspect that rogue police or military officers were behind them.

Harassment of Foreigners and Immigrants in Germany

Meanwhile, in Germany harassment of immigrants, foreigners, and people who "look foreign" remains an issue. The US State Department has called such harassment, including beatings, "a frequent problem throughout the country."

Many of these crimes are connected to right-wing political groups. Ironically, harassment also seems to occur more often in the formerly communist east, which is poorer than the west.

Germany has been trying to attract foreign scholars and students. But Viadrina University, in the poor state of Brandenburg, has received reports of harassment and attacks on foreign students since it reopened in 1991. The state is home to a small but violent subculture based on an ideology of racial purity.

German authorities use the term "politically motivated crime" to identify offenses related to victims' ideology, race, and so forth. In other words, these are hate crimes. With a population of 82 million, Germany has experienced about 1,000 violent politically motivated crimes annually in recent years.

The Challenges of Employment, Education, and Housing Faced by Immigrants in France

More than many of their neighbors, the French tend to see themselves as a nation that welcomes immigrants. France has long seen a relatively high level of immigration. More than 1 million North African Muslims arrived in the 1960s and early 1970s. France has the largest Muslim and Jewish populations in Europe.

This doesn't mean, though, that immigration hasn't been an issue. On the contrary, it's long smoldered. In the fall of 2005 it burst into flames with three weeks of rioting by North African immigrants. The episode turned a spotlight on the challenges of employment, education, and housing that young immigrants, or the children of immigrants, face in France.

The trouble began on 27 October 2005 with a power failure in the Paris suburb of Clichy-sous-Bois. It later turned out that two young men—one from Mali, the other from Tunisia—thought the police were chasing them for an identity check. They climbed into an electric relay station and touched a high-voltage transformer. They were immediately electrocuted. The whole neighborhood was blacked out.

People blamed aggressive policing for the young men's deaths. The immigrants' anger touched off riots. The official report said the police were not actually after the two young men who died. But routine police checks are so much a part of life for young immigrants that not everyone believed the official report.

Public school students in Paris are escorted home at the end of the day's lessons.

Photo by R. Norman Matheny / © 1989 The Christian Science Monitor

The 2005 riots in France turned a spotlight on the challenges of employment, education, and housing that young immigrants, or the children of immigrants, face in France.

In France, poor people tend to live in the "suburbs," not in the inner city. To Americans, "suburb" may suggest tree-lined streets and big houses. But the French term for suburb, *banlieue*, has the same negative connotations that "inner city" carries in English. The *banlieues* that ring Paris are concrete deserts filled with sterile housing projects. Joblessness there reaches 30 percent to 40 percent. It's even higher among young men, such as the two who died in the relay station.

Many see the *banlieues* as symbols of France's failure to integrate more of its Muslims, some of whom have been in France for three generations. The 2005 rioting spread to other Paris suburbs, and then elsewhere in France. The government called a state of emergency. By the time it was over, rioters had torched nearly 3,000 cars. Police had arrested nearly 9,000 people. One man died, in addition to the two whose deaths set off the rioting. Damages were estimated at €200 million (about $286 million in 2009 dollars).

Religious Freedom and Secularism in France

France has a strong tradition of religious freedom. But it's coupled with a strong tradition of secularism. This means, among other things, that students or employees in public schools may not wear "conspicuous" religious symbols. The law applies equally to Muslim headscarves, Jewish skullcaps, and large Christian crosses. But members of those groups see the ban as an infringement on their religious freedom. The ban affects immigrants out of proportion to their numbers, in part because they haven't adopted France's secular ways.

A woman in a headscarf walks past an Islamic bookstore in a Muslim community in Roubaix, France.

Photo by Neal J. Menschel / © 1989 The Christian Science Monitor

According to French law, students or employees in public schools may not wear "conspicuous" religious symbols. The ban affects immigrants out of proportion to their numbers, in part because they haven't adopted France's secular ways.

But even when it was officially "over," car burnings continued. The *banlieues* remained a tinderbox. In March 2006 the French parliament passed an "equal opportunity" law. It meant to improve education, create jobs, and open up the *banlieues*. The government launched programs such as one to encourage young people to start their own businesses. But it's not clear that much has changed since 2005. And people still torch cars in the *banlieues*.

Racial and Ethnic Discrimination Against Immigrants in Britain

British law prohibits racial discrimination. But that doesn't mean it doesn't happen. In 2009 the US State Department, for instance, cited evidence of discrimination against people of African, Afro-Caribbean, South Asian, and Middle Eastern origin. A British group called Victim Support fielded nearly 30,000 calls for help in cases of "racially motivated incidents" between April 2005 and March 2007. This was a big increase over a prior period. The group said, though, that the higher number reflects better referrals from the police rather than more incidents.

However, prosecutions for "racially aggravated crimes" have also risen. Prosecutors in England and Wales, with a combined population of around 55 million, brought cases against 7,430 defendants in connection with such crimes between April 2005 and March 2007.

In October 2008 the British government minister in charge of policing said she would review the way English and Welsh police forces recruit and promote officers. This came shortly after Boris Johnson, the Conservative mayor of London, announced his own investigation of race and London's Metropolitan Police Force, or MET.

Word of Johnson's inquiry followed a statement from the MET's Black Police Association (BPA) that it would boycott efforts to recruit officers from ethnic minority communities. In fact, the BPA said it would actively discourage black and Asian recruits. Such recruits would be "treated unfairly," the BPA said.

The National Association of Muslim Police, however, said it would not take part in the boycott. That group said that the MET was making progress in race relations.

The Difficulties al-Qaeda and Its Allies Have Posed for Europe

Europe is dealing not only with difficulties associated with changing **demographics**—*a population's makeup in race, ethnicity, and culture, among other characteristics*. It is also confronting terrorism within its borders from radical groups, many of them Muslim. The 9/11 terror attacks weren't felt just in the United States. They were felt in Europe, too. Soon after the event, *Le Monde*, an influential French newspaper, ran a headline saying, "*Nous sommes tous Américains*"—"We are all Americans."

This touched Americans deeply. But Europeans weren't just expressing moral support. The 9/11 attacks affected them directly. Dozens of Europeans died when the Twin Towers of the World Trade Center in New York collapsed.

The 9/11 attacks weren't Europe's first encounter with terrorism. Britain has faced the Irish Republican Army (more on them later), as well as Zionists trying to get the British out of Palestine. Spain has long confronted Basque separatists, who want a state of their own. During the 1970s West Germany suffered violence at the hands of radical leftist groups such as the Red Army Faction and the Baader-Meinhof Gang. Italy had its extreme-left Red Brigades.

People wait for the "tube"—subway train—at Oxford Street in London, England.

Photo by Mary Knox Merrill / © 2006 The Christian Science Monitor

Europe has borne its share of terror attacks. On 7 July 2005 four suicide bombers in the London subway killed 52 people and injured 700 others.

But the new challenge from al-Qaeda is different. It's different in its scale of operations, for one thing. During the first few years of the twenty-first century, al-Qaeda struck on nearly every continent.

Al-Qaeda is different in the scale of its ambitions, too. History is full of examples of guerrillas, and even terrorists, who have laid down arms to take a seat at the negotiating table and pursue achievable, concrete goals. By contrast, al-Qaeda's agenda is global. As you read in Chapter 1, Lesson 4, it seeks to unite all Muslims and to reestablish the caliphate, the Muslim empire of centuries past. Al-Qaeda leader Osama bin Laden has said that this can be done only by force. Al-Qaeda seeks to overthrow nearly all Muslim governments. It sees them as hopelessly corrupt. It also aims to drive Western influence out of Muslim lands. Eventually it would abolish state boundaries. This is not a group with which the West can negotiate.

At this writing, Europe has suffered two significant terror attacks since 9/11. On 11 March 2004 bombs in a Madrid commuter rail station killed 191 people and injured some 1,500. On 7 July 2005 four suicide bombers in the London subway killed 52 people, as well as themselves, and injured 700 others. It was the deadliest bombing in London since World War II.

Analysts differ in their interpretation of the Madrid bombings. Immediately afterward the Spanish government blamed the Basque separatists. But evidence soon suggested that Islamic extremists were behind the attacks. Then the question became whether they were connected to al-Qaeda, and if so how. Spanish officials described them as "homegrown." But other analysts weren't so sure. They saw the bombers as "local," but certainly linked to the al-Qaeda network. A British Broadcasting Corporation report in 2005 called the Madrid attacks "the bloody calling card of the new al-Qaeda, a loose network of jihadi groups, locally recruited and acting independently of Osama Bin Laden."

The al-Qaeda connection to the London bombings was apparently even looser. The group that carried out these attacks was made up of homegrown terrorists. While they were not members of al-Qaeda, they modeled themselves after that organization.

The Dangers Associated With Radical Terrorists

Radical terrorists have shown themselves willing to throw away their own lives, and to take those of their neighbors and fellow citizens with them, for the sake of a cause that promises only more death and destruction.

As you have read, Islamic civilization at its height saw a flourishing of science, mathematics, astronomy, medicine, literature, and other forms of learning. Muslim scholars helped reconnect medieval Western Europe with its Greco-Roman heritage. But al-Qaeda and its ideological running mates have distorted Islam. They have pressed it into service of an ideology that leads only to more hatred, anger, fear, ugliness, destruction, and death.

One of the lessons of the London and Madrid bombings was the need to fight al-Qaeda's ideology, and not just its organized killers. Al-Qaeda influences far more people than it controls.

The Tension Between Allowing Freedom and Protecting Citizens' Security

As in the United States, Europe's struggle against terrorism has created tensions between citizens' rights and their security. A national government's two chief tasks are defending its borders and protecting its citizens. Even people who believe less government is better agree that those two tasks are important.

But for most Europeans and Americans, security isn't the only thing that counts. Personal freedoms—civil liberties—are essential, too. To give them up would be to give up something that's at the heart of national identity. To spend too much freedom to buy security would mean the terrorists have won.

In time of war or great emergency, though, citizens sometimes give up some freedoms in the short term in the interest of security in the long term. The balance between freedom and security becomes harder to maintain at these moments. Societies must think through, What's really different now? Is this new threat severe enough to require us to give up some of our freedom?

In some cases, the answer may be yes. The British, for instance, have a robust tradition of free speech and freedom of religion. But they have felt a need to act against radical Islamist preachers. One of these was Abu Hamza al-Masri. An Egyptian-born British citizen, he has called for God to destroy the United States. He was mentor to, among others, Richard Reid. Reid was the "shoe bomber," who tried to blow up an American Airlines flight from Paris to Miami in December 2001.

In 2003 the Charity Commission, which has some control over houses of worship, dismissed Abu Hamza al-Masri for making "inappropriate political statements." A British court subsequently convicted him of inciting murder and racial hate. The United States has sought to bring him to New York for trial on terrorism charges.

The Internal Threat of Radical Terrorists Who Emigrate Into a Country

In this atmosphere, opening up to the world can put a country at risk. That's the challenge Europe has faced as it has sought to open its borders to newcomers. As the European Union has worked toward a "single market" and the free movement of people, officials of different countries have surrendered some control and learned to take one another's word about whom to let in and whom to exclude. It isn't always easy.

Mohamed Atta was any immigration official's nightmare. An Egyptian architectural student, he went to Germany to study at the Technical University of Hamburg. He had studied German at Cairo's Goethe Institute. The institute is one of the many such centers the German government supports around the world to teach and share German language and culture.

For Atta, though, German language study led indirectly to involvement with political Islam. It was a case of the law of unintended consequences. While in Hamburg, he attended the Al Quds Mosque in Hamburg, known for its harsh, militant version of Sunni Islam. It apparently radicalized him.

Atta eventually became the leader of a terrorist cell known as the "Hamburg cell" of al-Qaeda. A terrorist cell is *a small group of usually three to five terrorists who work together, separate from other groups nearby*. For reasons of secrecy, such groups are intentionally kept "in the dark" about one another's existence.

The Hamburg cell helped plan and execute the 9/11 attacks. Atta was at the controls of American Airlines Flight 11 when it crashed into the North Tower of the World Trade Center at 8:46 a.m. on 11 September 2001.

In the case of the Madrid bombings, those who see a closer rather than a looser link to al-Qaeda point to the participation of people from outside Spain. One analyst who studied the record closely found that most of those involved in the attacks were Moroccan immigrants, not native-born Spaniards.

But, on the other hand, for many people the real horror of the London bombings the following year was that the attackers weren't immigrants, but native sons. Moreover, there was little in their backgrounds to suggest they were particularly vulnerable to radicalization, an official report found. Learning to understand how young men and women become radicalized is essential to fighting terrorism.

Suicide bombers may be terrorism's foot soldiers. But its followers who grew up in Europe are considered some of al-Qaeda's most dangerous members. They tend to be better educated than their counterparts who grew up in the Middle East or South Asia. As Europeans, they blend better into Western societies, too. So Europe remains an important front for al-Qaeda.

The Legal Challenges of Arresting and Prosecuting Suspected Terrorists

Many observers have said that the United States has tended to see the fight against terrorism as a war. Europeans, in this view, have tended to see terrorism as a law-enforcement problem. Others say those descriptions oversimplify the issue. In either case, since the Madrid and London bombings, Europeans have ratcheted up their counterterrorism efforts much as their American cousins already had.

European governments have faced many of the same challenges as the United States did with regard to sharing information on terror suspects among agencies and countries. In some cases, analysts see gaps in the law that make it hard to prosecute terror suspects.

In response to terror attacks, Europe has moved to "harmonize" or standardize its national laws. Europeans have also introduced a European arrest warrant. In theory this eliminates problems with extradition.

British and German counterterrorism officials in particular have moved from a reactive to a preventive approach. That is, they have moved forward with preventive measures rather than waiting for something to happen. They are also going after suspected terrorists for any minor violation they can identify. In this way they hope to disrupt large-scale plots before they can be carried out.

Like the United States, both Britain and Germany have changed their policies about cooperation between different kinds of agencies. In all three countries, intelligence agencies (the CIA and its counterparts) can now share information with agencies investigating crimes (the FBI and its counterparts). In all three countries, law enforcement can step in and make arrests earlier in the development of a terror plot.

Some countries don't have the laws they need on their books for successful prosecution of terrorists. Many laws have been changed since the 9/11 attacks. But more changes are needed.

The Background of Ethnic and Religious Strife in Northern Ireland

Britain in recent decades had to deal with native-born terrorists, not just conflicts with outside terrorist groups such as al-Qaeda. The roots of these troubles date back for centuries in England's relationship with Ireland. English kings started crossing the Irish Sea trying to assert control over Ireland during the Middle Ages. But the best place to start this story would be in 1536, nearly a century past the Middle Ages, right after the Protestant Reformation. That's when King Henry VIII became serious about getting Ireland under the English crown's control. He was worried about the loyalty of Catholic lords.

What Henry began, Elizabeth I and James I completed. English authorities in Dublin unified the island under a central government. They were less successful in winning the Catholic Irish over to Henry's new Church of England, though. The brutal methods the English used to put the Irish down created resentment that has endured right up to today.

Into the early seventeenth century, crown governments colonized Ireland. They sent Scottish and English Protestants—often against their will—to settle there and overwhelm the Catholics with their numbers. The British settlers became Ireland's ruling class. They worshipped at the Church of Ireland. This is a Protestant church, the Irish branch of the Church of England. It was the established church. This means that it was *a church officially favored by the state and supported by tax revenues.* A series of Penal Laws discriminated against all other faiths. They hit Roman Catholics especially hard, but affected Scottish Presbyterians, too.

Members of the Royal Ulster Constabulary (RUC) patrol downtown Londonderry, Northern Ireland, in 1994.
Photo by Melanie Stetson Freeman / © 1994 The Christian Science Monitor

The roots of the "troubles" between Catholics and Protestants in Northern Ireland date back at least to 1536, under Henry VIII. The brutal methods the English used to put the Irish down created resentment that has endured right up to today.

By the late eighteenth century the same political ferment that led to the American and French revolutions led also to an Irish uprising against British rule. The Irish Rebellion of 1798 was unsuccessful, though. In response, the British in 1801 merged their Kingdom of Ireland with the Kingdom of Great Britain (England, Scotland, and Wales). This created the United Kingdom.

Perhaps the bitterest period in Irish history followed when a disease struck the island's potato crop between 1845 and 1852. Potatoes were the main food for a large share of the population. As the crops failed, and the British government failed to respond adequately, more than 1 million Irish people starved and another 1 million emigrated—many to the United States.

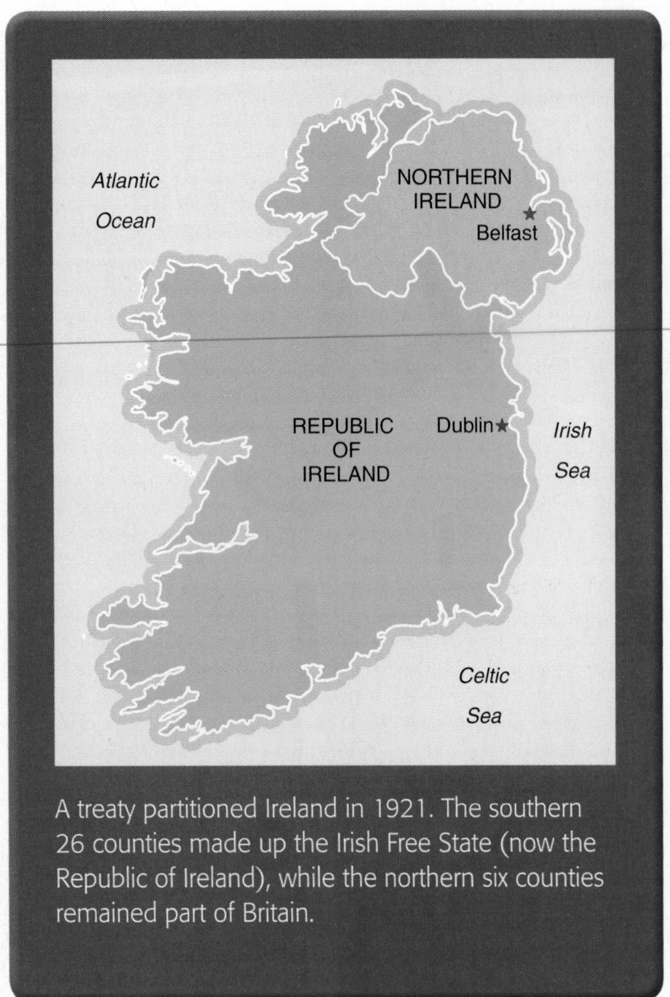

A treaty partitioned Ireland in 1921. The southern 26 counties made up the Irish Free State (now the Republic of Ireland), while the northern six counties remained part of Britain.

As a result of the famine, the cause of Irish independence regained traction in the nineteenth century. The first years of the twentieth century saw an experiment in "home rule" and then an Irish civil war.

In 1921 an Anglo-Irish treaty partitioned, or divided, Ireland. The partition created the Irish Free State, made up of 26 counties to the south, and Northern Ireland, consisting of six counties in the north. The Irish Free State had "dominion" status within the British Empire, like Canada or Australia. Northern Ireland had "home rule." It managed its own domestic affairs. But it was considered an integral part of Britain, or the United Kingdom.

The partition was made along religious lines. The six counties to the north had a Protestant majority. This was Henry VIII's legacy, since he had "planted" the strongly Catholic north with Protestants to keep it under control.

Soon after its launch the Irish Free State went through more civil war. The issue then, as earlier, was whether half a loaf, or three-fourths of a loaf, was better than none. In principle, Irish nationalists wanted to see all of Ireland out from under British rule. But they were divided. Should they accept the Irish Free State as a first step, and hope to regain the six counties eventually? Or should they hold out for all 32 counties?

Those willing to accept the Irish Free State as a first step won out. It became simply "Ireland" in 1937 and officially a republic in 1949. At that point it left the Commonwealth, the successor institution to the British Empire.

An independent Ireland was conceived of as "a Catholic state." The Republic of Ireland's constitution lays (theoretical) claim to the entire island. It embodies the hope, in other words, that partition is only temporary.

The people of Northern Ireland, on the other hand, fear that partition is only temporary. The majority of its people, of Scottish or English descent, are known as loyalists or unionists. They are loyal to the link to Britain. They want the union maintained. Northern Ireland was conceived of as "a Protestant state for a Protestant people." For years, its majority discriminated against its nationalist, or Irish Catholic, minority in jobs and housing. Nationalists faced almost complete exclusion from the political process.

From 1921 to 1973 Northern Ireland had its own parliament and prime minister. The government handled local issues, such as education and law enforcement, leaving matters such as defense and foreign policy to the British national government in London. It was a division rather like that of the American federal system.

But by 1973 conditions in the province had gotten so bad that the British government suspended home rule and imposed direct rule from London. Sectarian violence was getting out of hand. Bombings and shootings were the order of the day. Organized crime raised money for paramilitary forces on both sides. The police force, the Royal Ulster Constabulary, was overwhelmingly Protestant. It did not enjoy the confidence of the Catholic population.

The British government put an official in London, with the title of secretary of State for Northern Ireland, in charge of the province and of resolving the issues behind "the troubles."

The Views of Catholic Nationalists and Protestant Loyalists in Northern Ireland and the Tensions Between Them

The situation in Northern Ireland is often regarded as purely a religious conflict. American news organizations tend to describe the two sides as Catholics and Protestants. Those are familiar categories. They take less explanation. But there's a difference between political views and religious identities.

Many early Irish nationalists were in fact Protestants. It's a point that's often overlooked. The leaders of the Irish Rebellion of 1798, for instance, were largely Protestant.

But broadly speaking today, the overwhelming majority of Protestants want to remain within the United Kingdom. That is, their political views are unionist or loyalist. Catholics tend to be nationalist or republican. That is, they want to be part of an independent Irish Republic.

Another critical difference is over people's willingness to use force to achieve their ends. Constitutional nationalists seek to reunify Ireland by means of political persuasion. Not so the more radical elements on the republican side, who have often resorted to violence. Likewise, on the loyalist side, some work through political channels. Others have taken up arms.

A mural with a bright British flag covers the end of a building in a Protestant neighborhood in Belfast, Northern Ireland.

Photo by Melanie Stetson Freeman / © 1994 The Christian Science Monitor

Each side in Northern Ireland tends to see itself as a minority. Nationalists see themselves as an oppressed minority within the six counties. Unionists see themselves as a minority within the whole of Ireland; they fear being abandoned by Britain and being swallowed up in a "popish"—Catholic-dominated—Republic.

The Protestant population of the Republic of Ireland has fallen since partition, from a little more than 7 percent to about half that today. But the Catholic population of the North has risen since partition. This is a result of higher birthrates among Catholics. In the near term, new electoral procedures make nationalist votes count for more. Politicians have to pay more attention to them. Protestants have to look ahead to a time when they won't have the votes to block a referendum on joining the Republic of Ireland.

The Conflicts Between the Irish Republican Army (IRA) and the British Military

A civil rights movement arose in the 1960s to win fairer treatment for Northern Ireland's Catholics. Its leaders consciously took African-Americans' struggle for racial justice in the United States as their model. When British soldiers arrived in Northern Ireland as "the troubles" began, they came to protect the Catholics' civil rights. It was similar to the way federal troops had protected the rights of young American blacks to attend certain schools and universities just a few years before in the United States.

But by that time, the British had oppressed the Irish for so long that the British Army wasn't credible as defenders of Catholic civil rights. Instead, they soon became a party to the dispute. The Irish Republican Army (IRA) was one of their main adversaries. For decades the IRA ran a terrorist campaign against the British military presence in Northern Ireland.

Bold colors make up a mural with a "Free Ireland" message in a Catholic neighborhood in Belfast, Northern Ireland.
Photo by Melanie Stetson Freeman / © 1994 The Christian Science Monitor

A civil rights movement arose in the 1960s to win fairer treatment for Northern Ireland's Catholics. Its leaders consciously took African-Americans' struggle for racial justice in the United States as their model.

The IRA is the armed wing of Sinn Fein ("We Ourselves"), a leading nationalist party, which has long pushed for Irish reunification. Because of its armed wing, Sinn Fein was kept out of discussions on Northern Ireland's future, even though it draws a considerable share of the vote. The IRA's laying down of arms under the Good Friday agreement of 1998 has allowed Sinn Fein a seat at the table.

The Good Friday Agreement of 1998

The door to restored local government in Northern Ireland began to open in the mid-1990s. Successive British governments and the Clinton administration in the United States encouraged a number of peace gestures in Northern Ireland. In response, the main body of the IRA called a cease-fire. And former US Senator George Mitchell led a series of negotiations that lasted nearly two years. These finally resulted in the Good Friday Agreement.

fastFACT

To put the casualty figures in context, note that Northern Ireland has only about 1.75 million people. If the United States were to suffer a loss on the same scale, it would mean more than half a million fatalities. That's almost as many as died in the American Civil War.

By the time the accord was signed, "the troubles" in Northern Ireland had cost 3,600 lives. Of these, 2,000 were civilians, another 1,000 were members of the security forces, and 600 were members of paramilitary groups. These last were members of the IRA and their loyalist counterparts.

The Good Friday Agreement won support from majorities in both the Republic and the North's six counties. Its key parts include:

- "Devolved government"—home rule by local authorities rather than from London (that is, the British government)
- Commitment to work toward "total disarmament" of paramilitary groups, the IRA and its allies, and their unionist counterparts
- Police reform, so that both communities have confidence in local law enforcement
- New, stronger mechanisms to ensure equal rights and equal opportunity
- Mechanisms for involving the Republic of Ireland's government in the governance of the North, such as the British-Irish Council.

As of December 1999 Northern Ireland once again had its own government. The Good Friday Agreement called for an elected assembly, with 108 seats, plus a cabinet of 12 ministers. Unionists and nationalists share responsibility within the cabinet. Northern Ireland also elects 18 members to the Westminster Parliament in London.

A British soldier in a Catholic neighborhood in Belfast in 1994 lets a local boy peer through his rifle sight. To build trust, British soldiers began wearing their dress berets in the 1990s rather than their combat helmets while on patrol.

Photo by Melanie Stetson Freeman / © 1994 The Christian Science Monitor

The 1999 Good Friday Agreement called for Unionists and nationalists to share responsibility in Northern Ireland's cabinet. The St. Andrews Agreement of 2007 cleared the way for actual home rule.

Real progress has taken place. A new police force has replaced the Royal Ulster Constabulary. The IRA has laid down most of its arms. After a few bumps in the road to peace, the St. Andrews Agreement of 2007 cleared the way for actual home rule.

Elsewhere, however, Europe in the 1990s saw the outbreak of its worst ethnic violence since World War II when the multiethnic federation of Yugoslavia fell apart following the end of the Cold War. The fighting in and among the former Yugoslav republics and the atrocities that took place there became so severe that NATO was forced to intervene. That story is the subject of the next lesson.

The Cyprus Conflict

Ireland isn't the only divided island in Europe. The Mediterranean island of Cyprus has been unofficially partitioned since 1974. It has two communities, Greek and Turkish. Each has a distinct identity based on religion, language, and ties with its "motherland."

In 1960 Cyprus won independence from the British. It became a republic. Its constitution included protections for the Turkish Cypriots. (A *Cypriot* is a citizen of Cyprus.) The Greek Cypriot leadership, though, soon sought to do away with these. The stated reason was more government efficiency. To the Turkish Cypriots, however, the talk about efficiency was cover for something else. The Greek Cypriots wanted *enosis*, or union, with Greece. Violence broke out. The Turkish Cypriots soon after set up a "provisional administration," a kind of alternative government.

In 1974 the military junta then ruling Greece sponsored a coup against the Greek Cypriot government. The plotters thought the Cypriot leadership wasn't pushing hard enough for *enosis*. At this point, the Turkish government intervened militarily to help the Turkish Cypriots. A treaty that was signed when Cyprus gained independence allowed this. Today the Turkish Cypriot administration controls about a third of the island.

The UN has long tried to resolve the division. A UN peacekeeping force maintains a buffer between the two sectors. In recent years, Cyprus has joined the EU. But the Turkish part of Cyprus does not benefit from the EU membership. And the EU has signaled that the Cypriot dispute must be settled before Turkey's own EU membership bid can proceed.

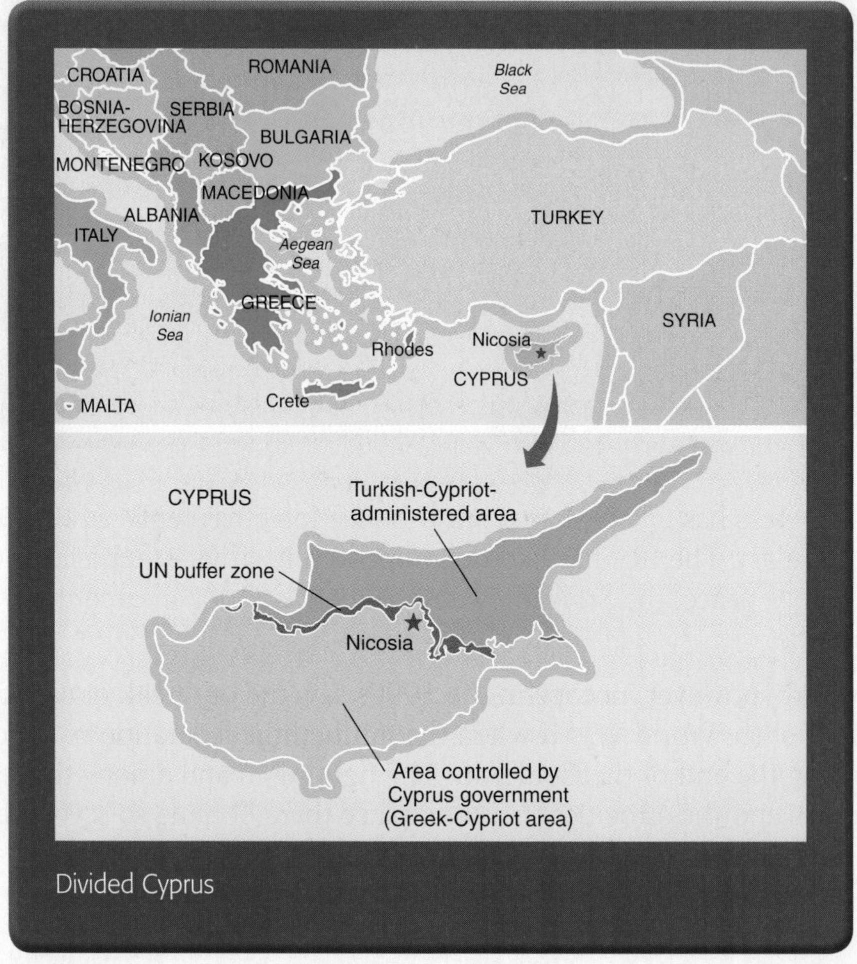

Divided Cyprus

Lesson 3 Review

Using complete sentences, answer the following questions on a sheet of paper.

1. When and why did the first Turkish "guest workers" arrive in Germany?
2. Why did the EU curb the free movement of labor at its 2004 expansion?
3. Members of which ethnic group in Europe were required to wear black triangles at one point during the twentieth century? Under what circumstances?
4. Aggressive policing was blamed for which series of events in France in late 2005?
5. Who was Mohamed Atta and what was the Hamburg cell?
6. Why are European Muslims seen as some of al-Qaeda's most dangerous members?
7. What is the difference between Northern Ireland's nationalists and unionists?
8. What is the Good Friday Agreement?

Applying Your Learning

9. How do you think governments should best balance freedom and security in the face of terrorism?

LESSON 4 The Creation and Collapse of Yugoslavia

Quick Write

What signs of trouble do you see in this incident?

Learn About

- how Yugoslavia was created after World War I
- how World War II affected Yugoslavia
- the role of Josip Broz Tito in uniting Yugoslavia after World War II
- how Yugoslavia dissolved into seven independent countries
- the history of ethnic cleansing in the Balkans

In the spring of 1987 the Serbs of Kosovo were feeling like victims of discrimination. Kosovo was a province of Serbia, within the multiethnic state of Yugoslavia. The province had been Serbia's heartland during its glory days in the Middle Ages.

But by the 1980s ethnic Albanians (mostly Muslims) had long made up a majority of Kosovo's population. The neighborhood had changed. Yugoslavia's postwar constitution had given Kosovo special "autonomous" status. In 1974 ethnic Albanians got fuller control of the province. Serbs began to complain about employment discrimination and unfair treatment by the police.

On 24 April 1987 a Serb politician named Slobodan Milosevic gave a speech from the balcony of the House of Culture in Kosovo Polje, a town a few miles outside the provincial capital. His speech was supposed to encourage the town's significant Serb minority, but also to calm them down:

"You should stay here," he told them. "This is your land. These are your houses, your meadows and gardens. Your memories. You shouldn't abandon your land just because it's difficult to live."

The line people most often quote from Milosevic's speech that day is: "No one should dare beat you."

At first glance, Milosevic's language seems pretty tame. But it was rare for a high-ranking Yugoslav official to talk about ethnic tensions. Many heard this as a call to the Serbs to confront the ethnic Albanians running the province. That line, historians say, helped bring Milosevic to power, first in Serbia, and then in Yugoslavia.

How Yugoslavia Was Created After World War I

Vocabulary

- sedition
- reparation

One of the new states to emerge after World War I was Yugoslavia. It was made up of several distinct peoples who had lived under different empires. They had little in common, really, except being near one another. You could say that Yugoslavia held together more because of pressures on it from outside than by any internal unity.

The country lasted rather longer than many expected, in fact. When it did come apart, in the twentieth century's final years, it raised dark questions for Europeans. Among them: Had they really learned the terrible lessons of two world wars?

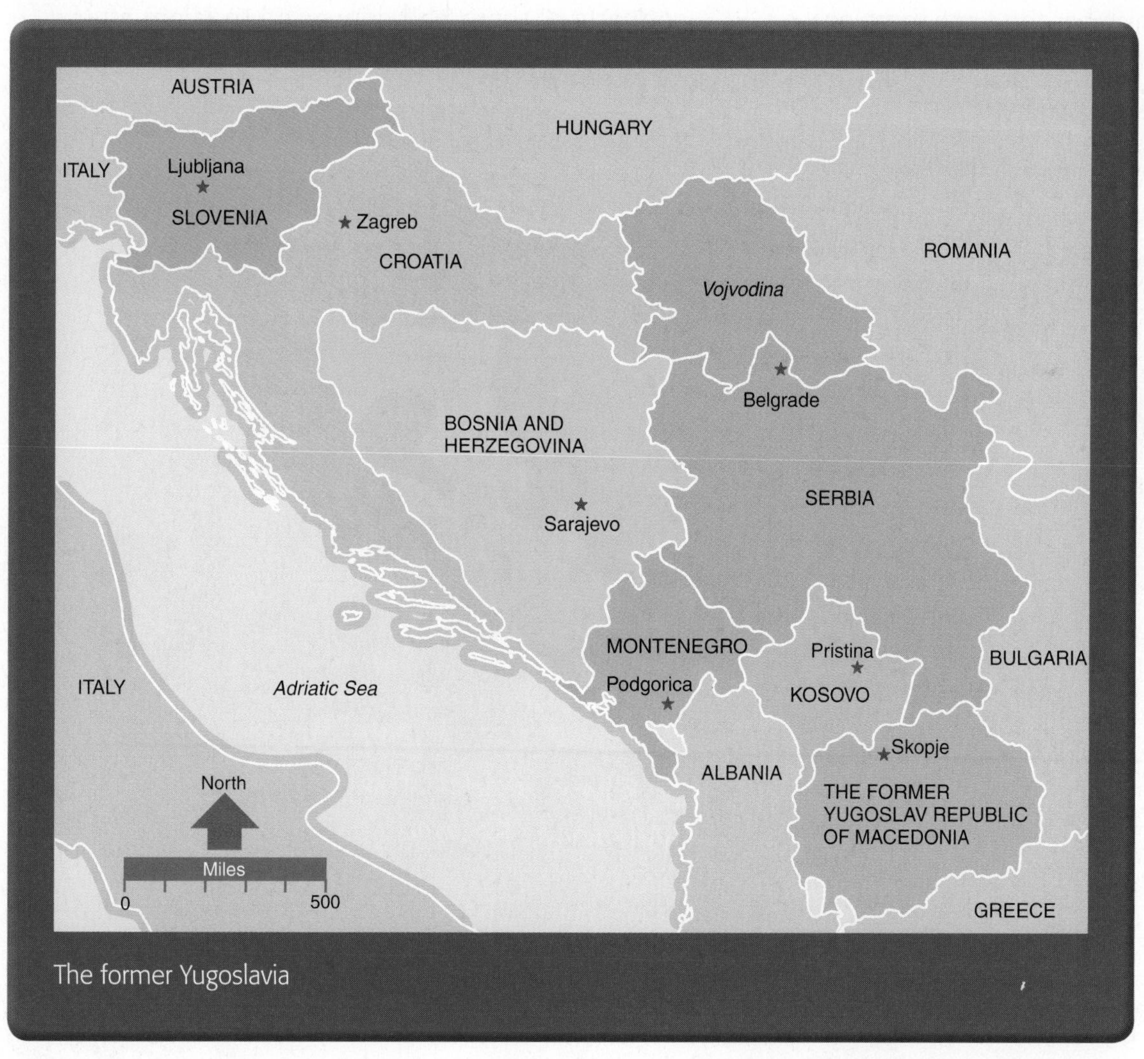

The former Yugoslavia

The Former Yugoslav Republics of Serbia, Croatia, Slovenia, Bosnia and Herzegovina, Kosovo, Macedonia, and Montenegro

The peoples who became part of Yugoslavia all had very independent histories. The Slovenes had been part of the Frankish Kingdom. The Franks fought in the Crusades. Later the Slovenes were part of the Austrian Empire. They kept wrestling with the question of nationhood.

Some of the Croats had briefly been independent before falling under Hungarian and Austrian rule. The Croats in Dalmatia, on the Adriatic coast, were at various times under Byzantine, Venetian, and French rule, as well.

The Serbs briefly rivaled the Byzantine Empire during the Middle Ages. But then they fell under Turkish domination for 500 years. Only in the late nineteenth century did they emerge independent of Ottoman rule after the Russians defeated Turkey in the Russo-Turkish War of 1877–78.

> **fastFACT**
>
> *Montenegro* is Italian for "black mountain." Montenegrins, who speak a Slavic language, call their country *Crna Gora* (CHURna GOHra), which has the same meaning.

The Montenegrins lived for centuries under a dynasty of bishop-priests. They defended their mountain homeland against all foreign aggressors. As for the Bosnians, their distinction was that so many of them had converted to Islam after the Turks invaded.

This bridge over the Ibar River divides the Serbian and Albanian sections of Mitrovica, Kosovo.

Photo by Andy Nelson / © 1999 The Christian Science Monitor

Back in the Middle Ages, Kosovo was the center of the Serbian empire. It was in Kosovo that invading Ottoman Turks defeated the army of Serbian Prince Lazar.

Macedonia was home to many different ethnic groups over the centuries. As the Ottoman Empire weakened, Serbs, Bulgars, Greeks, and Albanians all began to jockey for power there. So did the major European powers.

Finally, a few words about Kosovo: Its people were Albanian. It had been something of an Ottoman backwater until the early twentieth century. But back in the Middle Ages it had been the center of the Serbian empire. Many important Serb religious sites were in Kosovo. These included a number of architecturally significant Serbian Orthodox monasteries. It was in Kosovo that invading Ottoman Turks defeated the army of Serbian Prince Lazar.

These territories ended up as the six republics of Yugoslavia:

- Bosnia and Herzegovina—a single republic with a two-part name
- Croatia
- Macedonia
- Montenegro
- Serbia, including the autonomous provinces of Kosovo and Vojvodina
- Slovenia.

The Threat of Italian Expansionism to Serbia, Croatia, and Slovenia Following World War I

World War I pitted the Croats and the Slovenes against the Serbs. But during the war they began to think of an independent southern Slav state that would bring them all together.

This began to seem like an even better idea once Bolshevik Russia disclosed the supposedly secret 1915 Treaty of London. The treaty was between Italy and the Triple Entente—Britain, France, and Russia. It was basically a deal to bring Italy into the war on the Allied side.

> **fastFACT**
>
> A Serb is a member of the Serb ethnic group. A Serbian is a resident of Serbia, regardless of ethnic group. Likewise, a Croat is a member of the Croat ethnic group, while a Croatian is a resident of Croatia. There are Croatian Serbs, for example, and Serbian Croats.

In return, the Entente would award territory to Italy after the war. Italy had its eye on many attractive pieces of real estate. But Yugoslavia's future founders were especially concerned about certain of their territories going to the Italians under this deal. One of them was Istria, the westernmost part of Croatia. It's a peninsula across the Adriatic from Venice. In addition to Istria, the three Entente allies had also promised to hand over to Italy much of Dalmatia, another part of Croatia along the Adriatic coast. The Slovenian lands, too, were to go to Italy.

The people who lived in those places weren't happy about this. They didn't want to come under Italian rule. Croat nationalist leader Ante Trumbic and others formed the London-based Yugoslav Committee. Its mission was to promote the creation of a south-Slav state.

Croatia's western border runs along the Adriatic Sea.
Photo by Kristen Browman-Worthington / © 2000 The Christian Science Monitor
The Kingdom of the Serbs, Croats, and Slovenes, which became Yugoslavia, was founded in 1918.

Serbian, Croatian, and Slovenian Leaders Form Yugoslavia

In July 1917 Croat leader Trumbic and Nikola Pasic of Serbia signed the Declaration of Corfu. This document called for a union of Serbs, Croats, and Slovenes. The new state would be a constitutional monarchy. The king would be from the Karadjordjevic dynasty, which had been ruling Serbia. But the new state would be democratic, too, with a parliamentary system.

Serbs and Croats speak essentially the same language. But Serbs use the Cyrillic alphabet. Croats use the Latin. The Declaration of Corfu provided equal recognition for both. The three predominant religions—Roman Catholicism, Serbian Orthodoxy, and Islam—would also get recognition in the new state.

A major question remained unsettled: Would the new state be centralized or federal? Trumbic pressed for a federation, one that would grant the regions some power of their own. Pasic wanted a centralized state.

The issue moved forward when Austria-Hungary, defeated in World War I, lost authority over its south-Slav lands in October 1918. A National Council of Slovenes, Croats, and Serbs became, for all practical purposes, the region's government. As the war ended, Italy started grabbing parts of Dalmatia. The Allies gave it the city of Trieste. This was what the south Slavs had feared. Those trying to organize the new state knew they had to act quickly. Additional territories, such as Bosnia and Herzegovina, joined the Slovenes, Croats, and Serbs.

On 1 December 1918 Prince Regent Alexander Karadjordjevic announced the founding of the Kingdom of the Serbs, Croats, and Slovenes. The new kingdom won recognition from the Paris Peace Conference the following May. Alexander's father, Peter I, ruled the kingdom until his death in 1921, when Alexander assumed the throne.

How World War II Affected Yugoslavia

The kingdom faced big problems from the start: ethnic hatred, religious rivalry, language barriers, and cultural conflicts. The question of central versus federal authority bitterly divided the Serbs and Croats. The logic of Yugoslavia (as the country was known from 1931 on) was "economy of scale." A unified Balkan state could make the most of the region's resources. And it would provide collective strength against external threats.

But the new state's political leaders lacked vision and experience in parliamentary government. They weren't good at compromise either. In 1929 King Alexander took over as a dictator. He canceled civil liberties and abolished local self-government. He decreed strict laws against sedition—*words or deeds meant to stir up rebellion against the government*. He also made it illegal to promote communism.

The king changed the country's unwieldy original name to Yugoslavia—"the land of the south Slavs." He unified the six regional legal systems. He restructured government ministries. To ease separatist pressures, he did away with traditional provincial boundaries.

At first, he had wide support. It is not uncommon for a new democracy to lean on a monarch. (King Juan Carlos helped set Spain firmly on a democratic track after Franco, for instance.) Alexander's actions seemed to make government more efficient and less corrupt. He has gone down in history as "the unifier." But some have seen him as a fascist.

The tension between the center and the parts is one of the threads through Yugoslav history. The Serbs wanted a centralized government that they could dominate. The Croats wanted a federal system, to give them (and the many other ethnic groups) more autonomy. This was the balance that Yugoslavia never got right. The lack of it eventually tore the country apart.

From the beginning, Serb dreams of restoring their medieval glory dominated the new state. They wanted to bring back "Greater Serbia." What did it mean when a Serbian prince became king of a new state made up of many disparate peoples? Was that unity in the Balkans—or a Serbian takeover? A takeover, clearly, some would say. And they would see this as part of a pattern that would play out later under the leadership of Josip Broz Tito and beyond that of Slobodan Milosevic.

Many of Yugoslavia's neighbors, notably the Italians, wanted the new state to fail. Rome supported various separatists to hasten Yugoslavia's end. Then in October 1934 a Bulgarian agent of the Croat fascists assassinated King Alexander in Marseille, France. The assassin had received help from Italy and Hungary. Yugoslavs genuinely mourned their king. Even his opponents feared that his death would lead to Yugoslavia falling apart.

Other forces were at work, too. The king's efforts toward unity backfired in the end. They set off more ethnic strife, which continued through the 1930s. Only as another European war threatened in 1939 did Serbs and Croats get serious about reaching a settlement. But by then it was too late.

World War II broke out on 1 September 1939. The Yugoslavs were desperate for allies. They had hoped for help from the French. But the fall of France in 1940 put an end to that. Hitler pressed the Balkan countries to ally with the Axis powers—Germany, Italy, and Japan. Romania did so in November 1940. Bulgaria followed in March 1941. Almost surrounded by enemies, Yugoslavia turned to the Soviet Union. It decided to recognize the Soviet government and sign a nonaggression pact with it.

But Hitler kept pressing Yugoslavia to join the Axis. Convinced the country's military situation was hopeless, the government finally agreed. It did so despite pro-Western public opinion. The government won a promise from Hitler to leave Yugoslavia alone. Germany would not demand military assistance from Yugoslavia, violate Yugoslav sovereignty, or station the German army on Yugoslav territory.

On 27 March 1941 military officers ousted the government that had made a deal with Hitler. General Dusan Simovic was the new prime minister. Anti-German fervor swept Belgrade. Demonstrators flew British, French, and American flags along with their own. Crowds shouted out slogans against the Axis. All this began to make the new Simovic government nervous. It affirmed Yugoslav loyalty to the agreement its predecessor had made.

But Hitler was unimpressed. On 6 April 1941 the Luftwaffe, the German Air Force, bombed Belgrade, killing thousands. Axis forces invaded, the Yugoslav army collapsed, and the king and government fled. On 17 April the remaining resistance forces surrendered unconditionally.

The Danube River flows through Belgrade, Serbia.

Photo by Robert Harbison / © 1990 The Christian Science Monitor

On 6 April 1941 the German Air Force bombed Belgrade—then the capital of Yugoslavia—killing thousands.

The invasion caused panic in Yugoslavia. Foreign occupiers partitioned the country and terrorized its people. The next four years would be very bloody. The Communist-led Partisans came to dominate the country's resistance movement. By the end of the war, they would be in firm control of the entire country.

The Partition of Yugoslavia by Germany, Italy, Hungary, and Bulgaria

After the invasion, Germany, Italy, Hungary, and Bulgaria dismembered Yugoslavia. Germany occupied parts of Serbia, including parts of Vojvodina, an autonomous Serbian province. It created a puppet state, the "Independent State of Croatia," which also included Bosnia and Herzegovina. Germany also annexed northern Slovenia, bordering Austria, which Germany had already taken over.

Italy took southern Slovenia and much of Dalmatia. In addition, Italy joined Kosovo with its Albanian puppet state and occupied Montenegro.

Hungary occupied part of Vojvodina and the Slovenian and Croatian border regions. Bulgaria took Macedonia and part of southern Serbia.

The Violence, Massacres, and Devastation in Yugoslavia During World War II

World War II was a brutal time for all Yugoslavs. Northern Slovenia faced a reign of terror and "Germanization" under German control. The Nazis cleared Slovenes off their own farms and replaced them with German colonists. They resettled the Slovenes in Serbia. Southern Slovenia fared somewhat better. The Catholic hierarchy there collaborated with the Italian occupiers, who were less brutal than the Germans.

In the Croatian puppet state—the Independent State of Croatia known by its initials as the NDH—the Nazis installed a new leader because the previous one wasn't willing to collaborate. The new man, Ante Pavelic, sent out storm troopers from the *Ustase* (oo-STAH-sheh)—a fascist Croatian group—to eliminate 2 million Serbs, Jews, and Gypsies. They accomplished this through forced religious conversion, deportation, and murder. The violence was enough to appall even the Nazis. Berlin feared that the bloodbath would prompt further resistance from the Serbians.

Jews and Serbs were also massacred in areas occupied by the Albanians and Hungarians. Thousands of Serbs who had been living elsewhere in Yugoslavia fled back to Serbia. The German puppet regime there was under General Milan Nedic's leadership. He thought of himself as a custodian rather than a collaborator. He tried to keep violence under control.

In Macedonia, many people welcomed the Bulgarian occupation force. They expected to be granted some autonomy from Sofia, the Bulgarian capital. Instead, they bore the brunt of a harsh campaign to "Bulgarianize" Macedonia.

The Yugoslav Resistance Movement and Tensions Between Serbs and Croats

Serb-Croat tensions had made it hard to run a country. But they made it even harder to try to run a national resistance campaign in a country under military occupation. Even during the ghastly violence of World War II, Yugoslavia's Serbs and Croats seemed more interested in fighting each other than in fighting the Germans. This ethnic strife eventually led the Western Allies to shift their support from the Serb nationalists to the Communists.

Resistance in Yugoslavia developed mostly in scattered units of the Yugoslav army and among Serbs fleeing genocide in the Nazi puppet state of Croatia. Armed groups in Serbia organized under the name *Cetnik* (CHET-nik), meaning "detachment."

The best known were the followers of Colonel Draza Mihajlovic. He was a Serb nationalist, monarchist, and staunch anticommunist. Mihajlovic expected that the Allies would soon invade the Balkans. He advised his troops to avoid small clashes with the Axis forces. Instead, he said, they should prepare to rise up in force to back up the Allied push when it took place.

Europe

In October 1941 the British recognized Mihajlovic as the Yugoslav resistance leader. In 1942 the Yugoslav government-in-exile in London promoted him to commander of its armed forces. The Cetnik forces in effect became Yugoslavia's defense forces.

But Serb-Croat tensions within the government-in-exile were extreme. They were so bad that the British began to look around for someone other than Mihajlovic to back in Yugoslavia. The Yugoslav cabinet made decisions unanimously rather than by majority vote. That sounds "inclusive," as people say today. But the cabinet could grind to a halt over even a minor decision. On major issues—such as genocide against Serbs in the Nazi puppet state of Croatia—it was hopeless.

The British were keen to stabilize the Balkans. They wanted a steady Yugoslavia to anchor the region. But stability was not what they saw in the squabbling ministers-in-exile in London. In 1943 the Allies, led by the British, ended their support of Mihajlovic. They planted their hopes for a secure, multiethnic, postwar Yugoslavia in Josip Broz Tito and his Communist Partisans.

fastFACT

Languages don't often draw their verbs from the name of a part of the world. But *Balkanize* is one verb that does come from maps. To *Balkanize* an area is to divide it into small, often hostile units. At this point you've read enough of the history of Yugoslavia to understand why the verb means what it does.

The Role of Josip Broz Tito in Uniting Yugoslavia After World War II

Josip Broz was born in Croatia in 1892. He was the son of a poor Croat-Slovenian peasant family. He was drafted into the Austro-Hungarian army during World War I. The Russian Army captured him and held him prisoner in Russia. During his time there, he converted to communism. He fought in the Red Army during the Russian Revolution. He returned to the new state of Yugoslavia a member of the Communist Party.

"Tito," a Croatian form of "Titus," was an alias he used during his time underground. It became the name by which he is remembered.

How Tito Led the Communist Resistance Movement During World War II

If you'd seen the Communist Party of Yugoslavia (CPY) in the mid-1930s, you might not have guessed that 10 years later it would be running the country. The government had banned the CPY in 1921. It endured years of police repression and internal conflict. Stalinist purges didn't help, either. Membership was down to only a few hundred.

But under Tito, the party had a real rebirth. He became a member of its Central Committee in 1934. In 1937 he rose to secretary general of the still-outlawed party. In the four years before the war, he built a strong organization of 12,000 full party members, plus 30,000 youth members.

The crowds who gathered to demonstrate against the pact with the Axis in the spring of 1941 included Tito's Communists. "Death to Fascism, Freedom to the People" was the Partisans' slogan. Tito's appeal was "pan-Yugoslav." It spoke to all of Yugoslavia rather than just one ethnic group. He drew recruits from across the country. The Partisans eventually became the largest, most active resistance group.

In July 1941 the Partisans launched uprisings that won control of much of the countryside. But in September the Axis struck back. Germany warned that it would execute 100 Serbs for every German soldier the resistance killed. At Kragujevac, the Germans showed they meant what they said. They killed several thousand civilians in a single reprisal.

Tito believed that such actions would only backfire against the Germans, bringing the Partisans more recruits. He ignored the threat and continued his tactics. His rival Mihajlovic, leader of the Cetniks, feared that German reprisals would turn into a Serb holocaust. He ordered his forces not to engage the Germans. Soon he turned on Tito and the Partisans. They became his main enemy. Cetnik units began cooperating with the Germans and Italians to keep Tito from winning.

At this point Stalin began to worry that the Partisans' activity might make the Allies lose trust in the Soviet Union. So Moscow refused to supply arms to Tito. Instead, the Soviets maintained ties to the government-in-exile in London. This, you may recall, was made up of the ministers the British were losing faith in.

In November 1942 the Partisans held the first meeting of the Anti-Fascist Council for the National Liberation of Yugoslavia. They were eager to gain political legitimacy. The council was known by its Serbo-Croatian initials, AVNOJ, and was a sort of provisional government.

The following year was a turning point in the war. In March the Partisans outmaneuvered the German army and defeated the Cetnik forces decisively in Herzegovina and Montenegro. Then German, Italian, Bulgarian, and Croatian forces launched a major attack on the Partisans. But they escaped. When the Italians surrendered in 1943, the Partisans captured their arms, gained control of much of the coast, and began receiving supplies from the Allies fighting in Italy.

A second session of AVNOJ in November 1943 laid the groundwork for the postwar government of Yugoslavia. The council named Tito marshal of Yugoslavia and prime minister. The session also dealt with King Alexander's son, Peter II, who had been living in exile in London since 1941. It issued a declaration forbidding King Peter to return to the country until a referendum had been held on the status of the monarchy.

People walk through a crowded square in Belgrade, Serbia.

Photo by Robert Harbison / © 1990 The Christian Science Monitor

A joint Partisan-Soviet force liberated Belgrade in October 1944. Unlike in other parts of Europe, there was little Soviet presence in Yugoslavia after the war.

At the Tehran summit meeting in December 1943 Roosevelt, Churchill, and Stalin decided to support the Partisans. The British then worked to reconcile Tito and Peter. In September 1944 the king yielded to British pressure. He called on all Yugoslavs to back the Partisans.

As the Soviet Union's Red Army moved toward Yugoslavia in September 1944, Tito traveled secretly to Moscow to make a deal with Stalin. They agreed that Soviet troops would enter Yugoslavia but leave as soon as the country was secure. Stalin gave his word that his army would keep out of domestic politics.

And so it happened. Soviet troops crossed the border on 1 October. A joint Partisan-Soviet force liberated Belgrade on 20 October. After that, most of the Red Army went on to Hungary. The Partisans and Western Allies were left to crush the remaining German, Ustase, and Cetnik forces.

The Formation of the Federal People's Republic of Yugoslavia in 1945

At the end of the war, the Communists, under Tito, emerged as Yugoslavia's sole rulers. They had received only limited help from the Soviets, so there wasn't much Soviet presence in the country after the war. This was unlike the situation in other parts of Europe, where the Soviets made the most of their position as an occupying power.

Tito did yield to Allied pressure, however, on one point. He agreed to work with Ivan Subasic, a noncommunist Croat, to form a new government. Subasic was a compromise between the royalists and the communists. On 7 March 1945 a provisional Yugoslav government took office. Tito was prime minister and war minister. Subasic was foreign minister. Tito supporters held most of the rest of the cabinet posts.

A Communist-dominated Provisional Assembly—a legislature—convened in August. The government held elections for a Constituent Assembly in November. New laws required all candidates to be nominated by the Communist-controlled People's Front. The police harassed noncommunist politicians—as they had earlier harassed Communists. They also suppressed noncommunist newspapers.

Subasic and other noncommunist ministers resigned in protest. Many parties boycotted the elections. As a result, of the votes cast, the People's Front won 90 percent.

An ethnic Albanian family rumbles under a sign in Prizren, Yugoslavia (now Kosovo), on their journey home from Albania. They had been refugees for three months.
Photo by Andy Nelson / © 1999 The Christian Science Monitor

Yugoslavia's postwar constitution made Kosovo, whose people were mostly ethnic Albanians, an autonomous province within Serbia.

On 29 November 1945 the new Constituent Assembly dissolved the monarchy. In its place, it established the Federal People's Republic of Yugoslavia. Soon after, it adopted a Soviet-style constitution. This provided for a federation. It would have six republics under a strong central government. The new regime took a number of steps to hold the Serbs in check:

- It made Montenegro and Macedonia full-fledged republics
- It created within Serbia an ethnically mixed autonomous province of Vojvodina
- Kosovo, whose people were mostly ethnic Albanians, also became an autonomous province within Serbia.

The constitution set up a rubber-stamp Federal Assembly and a presidential counsel to administer the federal government. But Tito was the one in charge of it all—party, government, and armed forces.

How Tito Led Efforts to Repair Wartime Damage

World War II claimed 11 percent of Yugoslavia's prewar population: 1.7 million lives. Only Poland lost a higher share of its people. Another figure may be even more stunning: About 1 million of Yugoslavia's war dead—a clear majority—were killed by other Yugoslavs.

Yugoslavia's major cities, production centers, and communications systems were in ruins. Starvation was widespread. A quarter of the population was homeless.

Tito's government was in charge of repairing it all, with help from the United Nations. By 1946 Yugoslavia's national income had recovered to its 1938 level.

But that 1938 income level was no great achievement. Yugoslavia was one of Europe's most underdeveloped countries. Its per capita income that year was 30 percent below the world average.

The lands of the south Slavs had begun the twentieth century as a feudal society. Or perhaps it would be better to say, as a collection of different feudal societies. German, Austrian, and Hungarian families owned vast estates in Slovenia, Croatia, and Vojvodina. Turkish feudalism remained in Kosovo and Macedonia. In Bosnia, Christian sharecroppers worked farms owned by Muslim landlords. In Dalmatia, some tenant farmers followed a system going back to ancient Rome. Serbia was a jumble of independent small farms.

After Yugoslavia was established in 1918, it put its farm sector through a radical reform. The new state may have erased reminders of a system that much of the rest of Europe had left behind centuries before, but it failed to relieve rural poverty. Furthermore, land reform gave peasants plots too small to farm efficiently. More than 75 percent of the population lived in poverty, dependent on tiny farms.

This was the picture on the eve of World War II. And these were the problems that Tito had to address immediately after the war's end.

The Institution of Land Reform and the Establishment of a Soviet-Style Economic System

In August 1945 Tito's new government seized large and medium-size land holdings. It also took property belonging to banks, churches, monasteries, absentee landlords, private businesses, and the German minority, which had been expelled. Half the land went to peasants. The other half went to state-owned enterprises.

The authorities held off on forced collectivization for a time. But once they started, they did a thorough job. In January 1949, 94 percent of farmland was in private hands. The next year, 96 percent was in the hands of the social sector. What's more, the government required farmers to sell surpluses from private plots to the state at prices below the market. Peasants got incentives to join state or cooperative farms.

Yugoslav planners thought that all this would boost food production, improve standards of living, and get people off the farm so they could work in industry. But it didn't pan out that way. They abandoned the program after just a few years.

The Communists also followed the Stalinist model for rapid industrialization. By 1948 they had nationalized almost all wealth. The Yugoslavs also practiced central planning, like Stalin. State officials set wages and prices. They created elaborate five-year plans. These stressed use of domestic raw materials and the development of heavy industry. They also tried to foster economic growth in the parts of the country that needed it most.

The Yugoslavs generated capital through a combination of war reparations—*the act of making amends for an injury, often through payments to the injured party*—along with Soviet credits, and exports—foodstuffs, timber, minerals, and metals. They traded mostly with the Soviet Union and Eastern Europe.

How Yugoslavia Dissolved Into Seven Independent Countries

As time went on, Yugoslavia's path split from the Soviet Communists' course. Or rather, it followed Tito's path. During the 1940s Tito made several key foreign policy decisions without checking with Moscow. So Moscow threw Yugoslavia out of the Soviet bloc. This was a major split. It left Tito free to accept support from the Marshall Plan. This was the American aid program that helped rebuild Western Europe after World War II. The Soviets had forbidden the new Communist states in Eastern Europe from accepting such aid.

Yugoslavs also, under Tito, developed their own economic system. They called it "socialist self-management." Its slogan was "Factories to the workers!" Workers' councils, rather than party officials, ran factories and other enterprises.

For a time, Yugoslavia represented a "third way." It followed a path down the middle, you might say. On one side was Western capitalism, with booms and busts, and winners and losers. On the other side was Soviet communism. Rigidity and inefficiency—to say nothing of a lack of freedom—plagued this route.

At first, the "third way" worked. In the early decades, Yugoslav standards of living improved greatly. But by the late 1970s the system, like other socialist economies, was running out of steam. It was clear as well that a system held together by the iron leadership of one man would not survive his death. At least, it wouldn't last without some big changes. After Tito died, shortly before his 88th birthday in 1980, ethnic tension reasserted itself.

The country soon began to fall apart. It blew up rather spectacularly, in fact. As the United States and its European allies saw this happen, the question was, What does all this mean for us? What is the Western interest in preserving Yugoslavia as a unified entity?

Yugoslavia sat on the edge of Europe. But it was clearly part of Europe. On the other hand, it belonged to neither NATO nor the EU. Nor was it part of the Communist Warsaw Pact. It was part of no regional "club" that could influence events.

Western efforts to prevent war from ever happening again in Europe had focused on developing the EU and maintaining the NATO alliance. Western military planners had zeroed in on the Soviet threat. Their scenarios featured Russian tanks rolling across Germany. They were unprepared to confront ethnic strife in the Balkans.

Out of fuel and desperate to get out of Kosovo, an ethnic Albanian pushes his car from the no-man's land between Yugoslavia and Albania in April 1999.
Photo by Andy Nelson / © 1999 The Christian Science Monitor

Western military planners had prepared for the Soviet threat. They were unprepared to confront ethnic strife in the Balkans.

But Americans and Europeans both knew the lessons of history. They wanted to avoid repeats of fascist aggression and Nazi genocide. Was Slobodan Milosevic, the Serbian leader who emerged after Tito, another Hitler, they wondered? And they recalled that a political assassination in Yugoslavia had touched off World War I.

The Rise of Serb Nationalists and Slobodan Milosevic After Tito's Death

Yugoslavia under Tito looked like a federal system. Power appeared to be shared. But for the four decades of the Tito era, Serbian Communists ruled Yugoslavia's political life. This was so even though Tito's own roots were outside Serbia.

Tito had kept a firm lid, though, on Serb and other ethnic nationalism. Communists generally opposed nationalism. As head of such a fractious country, Tito had more reason than most to feel that way.

After Tito's death, however, a new leader arose who was quite willing to break the taboo on nationalism. This was Slobodan Milosevic. His speech at Kosovo Polje in April 1987 was all over the news in Belgrade that evening. It made him a popular hero overnight. It was highly unusual for an official of his high rank to talk about ethnic tensions. He seemed to be calling on the Serbs of Kosovo to take on the ethnic Albanians of their local Communist Party.

He had become the head of the Serbian Communist Party the year before. But his speech transformed his public image. He went from a colorless party hack to a firebrand of Serb nationalism. He seemed to have acquired charisma. He turned out to be a skillful exploiter of mass media, too. In 1989 he became president of Serbia.

The Declarations of Independence From Yugoslavia in the Early 1990s

With Tito gone, Yugoslavia's constituent republics decided, one by one, to pursue their future outside the federation. Each took a different way out. In the end, Serbia was alone.

Slovenia

Slovenia became Yugoslavia's most prosperous republic. It was the model of Yugoslavia's "third way." But political and economic power remained concentrated in Belgrade. This only increased after Tito's death.

Meanwhile, however, Slovenia was going its own way. Its democracy flourished. Its cultural, civic, and economic realms opened up to a degree unheard of in the communist world.

In September 1989 Slovenia amended its constitution to assert a right to secede from Yugoslavia. On 23 December 1990, 88 percent of Slovenian voters chose to do so. On 25 June 1991 the Republic of Slovenia declared independence. A nearly bloodless 10-day war with Yugoslavia ensued. Yugoslav forces withdrew after Slovenia showed stiff resistance.

Slovenia—a Model for Jefferson?

A 16th-century French political philosopher named Jean Bodin described in his writings an unusual Slovenian custom. His account suggests that democracy there grows from deep roots. For almost 1,000 years, until the late fourteenth century, the dukes of Carinthia, in Austria, governed Slovene farmers. Each time a new duke was installed, the farmers gave formal consent to being governed.

The Declaration of Independence refers to governments "deriving their just powers from the consent of the governed." Some scholars think Bodin's account of the Slovene farmers may have influenced Thomas Jefferson in drafting the Declaration.

Croatia

Croatia was the second Yugoslav republic to declare its independence. Things didn't go nearly as smoothly as in Slovenia's case, however. While there were few Serbs in Slovenia, there were many in Croatia.

In 1990 Croatia held its first multiparty elections since World War II. Longtime Croat nationalist Franjo Tudjman won the presidency. A year later, Croatia declared independence from Yugoslavia. Conflict between Serbs and Croats within Croatia escalated. Then, just a month after Croatia had declared its independence, actual war broke out. You'll read more about this later in this lesson.

Bosnia and Herzegovina

Bosnia's story wasn't exactly one of seeking independence from a larger entity. At least, it wasn't at first. Rather, it faced secession from within. Slovenia and Croatia had both declared independence in June 1991. On 1 March 1992 the Bosnian government held an independence vote. It passed. On 5 April 1992 the parliament declared Bosnia's independence.

The Bosnian Serbs had other ideas, however. Back in late September 1991 Radovan Karadzic, the Bosnian Serb leader, had proclaimed four "Serb Autonomous Regions" in Bosnia. By the next month, Karadzic's group announced the formation within Bosnia of a "Serbian Republic of Bosnia-Herzegovina." It would have its own constitution and legislature. Then in January 1992 Karadzic proclaimed an independent "Republic of the Serbian People in Bosnia-Herzegovina."

Bosnian Serbs backed Karadzic. They had already voted in their own referendum to remain within Yugoslavia, so they did not support the Bosnian government's March 1992 independence vote. With support from Serbia, the Bosnian Serbs responded to the 1992 Bosnian move with armed force. The Bosnian Serbs' goal was partition. They wanted to divide the republic along ethnic lines to create a "Greater Serbia."

An ethnic Albanian refugee family, fleeing fighting in Kosovo in 1999, walks to waiting trucks that will drive the group to Kukes in western Albania.
Photo by Andy Nelson / © 1999 The Christian Science Monitor

As Yugoslavia broke up, Montenegro and Serbia were the last republics left. The Montenegrins were a check on the Serbians' nationalist campaign against Kosovo. Montenegro declared its independence in 2006.

Nonetheless, the United States and most of Europe recognized the independence of Bosnia and Herzegovina on 7 April 1992. It joined the United Nations on 22 May 1992.

Macedonia

Macedonia's culture and language had flourished in Tito's Yugoslavia. But as communism was collapsing throughout Eastern Europe, Macedonia decided to leave Yugoslavia in late 1991. Macedonia's exit was the only one not marred by some sort of armed conflict. The only blot was that the country's ethnic Albanians chose not to take part in the independence referendum. The new Macedonian constitution took effect on 20 November 1991.

Montenegro

The breakup of Yugoslavia left Montenegro in a difficult position. Montenegro and Serbia were the last republics left. On 27 April 1992 they passed a new Constitution of the Federal Republic of Yugoslavia. This reaffirmed Montenegro's tie to Serbia. But the Montenegrins kept their own identity. They were a check on Milosevic and his nationalist campaign against Kosovo (more on that later).

Ten years later, the two states redefined their relationship once again. But on 3 June 2006, after a referendum, Montenegro declared independence.

With that, the Republic of Serbia was alone. There was no more Yugoslavia.

After the Breakup, Seven Independent Governments

Tito's Yugoslavia had six republics. But seven different national governments now occupy its territory. Here's how the situation looks today:

As an independent republic, Slovenia has pursued stabilization and further openness. It has joined both NATO and the EU.

Croatia has been through a number of peaceful elections since President Tudjman's death in December 1999. One government after another has worked to carry out peace agreements. They have promoted national reconciliation and democracy. Croatia is a candidate member of the EU. It joined NATO in April 2009.

Bosnia and Herzegovina today consists of two "entities." You might think that they are "Bosnia" and "Herzegovina." But they are the Federation of Bosnia and Herzegovina and the Republika Srpska. The first is largely Bosniak (Bosnian Muslim) and Croat. The second is mostly Serb. In the most recent national elections, wartime nationalists lost ground to more moderate groups. But the latter, too, relied heavily on ethnic messages to win votes. The national government is a six-party coalition.

A strong civilian and military international presence still resides in Bosnia. This stems from the Dayton Peace Agreement. This agreement ended the ethnic wars of the early 1990s. In December 1995 NATO deployed 60,000 troops to Bosnia to oversee the carrying out of the accord. A smaller presence remained until 2004. At that point the EU took over from NATO. Some 2,000 EU troops remain there now.

Macedonia was the only republic to break away without fighting. Kiro Gligorov, its first post-independence president, became the first head of state in a former Yugoslav republic to leave office. He stepped down in November 1999 after serving eight years.

Macedonia's history since independence hasn't been all peaceful, however. Its bouts of ethnic violence didn't come until several years later. In late 2000 many ethnic Albanians there began to wonder where they fit in. Tensions erupted into actual fighting in February 2001.

Mediators brokered a cease-fire. Then all parties, with help from US and EU diplomats, agreed to end the fighting in August 2001. They also worked out agreements to give minority groups improved civil rights.

Like other new democracies in Europe, Macedonia wants to join the EU and NATO. Macedonia is an official candidate member of the EU. And at a NATO summit in April 2008 all members agreed that Macedonia had qualified to join the alliance. They did not reach consensus on inviting Macedonia to join, however. As you read in Lesson 2, Greece still disputes the new country's use of the name Macedonia.

Montenegro adopted its first post-independence constitution in October 2007. Its leaders seek to connect with Europe. They have taken first steps to join the EU. The government continues to promote reforms. It's made considerable progress since independence. But Montenegro still has some ethnic tensions. Rule of law is not yet fully established. And economic development is uneven throughout the country.

Kosovo Albanians loaded into trucks head for the Albanian-Kosovo border as they begin the repatriation process back into Kosovo following the 1999 conflict.
Photo by Andy Nelson / © 1999 The Christian Science Monitor

Kosovo broke away from Serbia several years after the constituent republics had decided to pull out of Yugoslavia.

Serbia and Kosovo

Demonstrating crowds helped bring Slobodan Milosevic to power in the late 1980s. Crowds brought him down a decade later. In October 2000 he was forced to concede defeat. He had—officially—won the presidential election the month before. But it had become clear that his victory was fraudulent. Citizens took to the streets to march for his opponent, Vojislav Kostunica, a democrat.

Serbians were very happy to see Kostunica replace Milosevic. Initial reform efforts went well. But within a couple of years, happiness had slid into apathy. Things were not going well in Serbia. The new president was in open conflict with his prime minister. Elements from organized crime assassinated the prime minister. Elections took place but drew too few voters to be valid.

More recently Serbia has moved onto a better path. It has yet another constitution, adopted in 2006, to reflect its solo status. It's more democratic and more oriented toward Europe. But the Kosovo issue remains a delicate one. Even progressive-minded Serbians see the province as an integral part of their country.

Kosovo is the seventh national government in the former Yugoslavia. It was part of Serbia—the heart of the country, Serbs would say. It was a province, not a republic. It broke away from Serbia several years after the constituent republics had decided to pull out. You will read more about Kosovo's struggle for independence in the next section.

The History of Ethnic Cleansing in the Balkans

In addition to moves toward independence, ethnic cleansing has also marked Balkans' history. Ethnic cleansing is the very dark side of a people wanting "a homeland of their own." President Woodrow Wilson's call for "self-determination" was a strong influence as Europe's map was redrawn after World War I. A nation's borders should align with its people, the logic goes. Poland should be one country where the Poles live, for instance. Poland shouldn't be split among three different empires, as it was before World War I.

But people move around. Minority groups will always exist. A modern, pluralistic country must be able to accommodate them.

Children gather around a US Air Force staff sergeant as she hands out coins and candy during a humanitarian mission in the Novo Brdo region of Kosovo.
Photo by 1st Lt. Maksym Nedria, Ukrainian Army

While Serbia today is more democratic and oriented toward Europe, the Kosovo issue remains a delicate one. Even progressive-minded Serbians see the province as an integral part of their country.

Yugoslavia was from the beginning an artificial country. But as it broke apart, many politicians wanted more than just independence from Belgrade. They wanted a homeland of their own with no ethnic minorities. They wanted to "cleanse" their turf from peoples unlike them. Estimates of the numbers of people affected have run up to 2.5 million people.

The Conflicts Between Serbs and Croats in Croatia

Earlier in this lesson you read about how fighting broke out between Croats and Serbs after Croatia's declaration of independence in 1991. The United Nations mediated a cease-fire in January 1992.

But the following year, fighting broke out again. The Croats were trying to get back land they had lost the year before. A second cease-fire followed in May 1993. A more formal "joint declaration" of peace between Croatia and Yugoslavia came some months later. The Serbs had established something they called the "Republic of Krajina" within Croatia, however. In September 1993 the Croatian Army went on an offensive against this new entity.

March 1994 brought the third Serb-Croat cease-fire in as many years. But it, too, was broken twice the following year, in May and August 1995. At this point, Croatian forces regained parts of the border region known as the Krajina. After that, thousands of Serbs poured out of the area.

In November 1995 Croatia signed the Erdut Agreement, arranged by the UN. It called for the return of Serb-held territories to Croatia. These territories rightfully belonged to Croatia. That is, they were within Croatia's internationally recognized borders, even though Serbs held them.

In December 1995 Croatia signed the Dayton Peace Agreement. This committed it to a permanent cease-fire and the return of all refugees. The agreement also called on Croatia to reintegrate these Serb-held territories peacefully, over three years. In other words, Croatia got its land back, but was asked to be patient about it. This took place as promised, and was completed in November 1998.

The Tensions and Conflicts Between Muslims, Serbs, and Croats in Bosnia

You read earlier about Serb attempts to take a chunk out of Bosnia as well. Croats, meanwhile, had similar ideas about carving up Bosnia. They wanted to combine the Bosnian Croats' territory with Croatia itself.

This move did not go well for the Croats, or for Croatia. When they attacked, the Bosnian army pushed back. The Bosnians drove the Croatian army out of several different towns and brought it to the verge of total defeat. They killed an estimated 7,000 Croats. Some 200,000 others ended up as refugees in small, isolated enclaves.

On the diplomatic front, the attempt at a land grab cost Croatia its international standing. It drew threats of sanctions from some European Community members. It destroyed the domestic popularity of Franjo Tudjman and his ruling party.

Eventually the Croat-Bosnian clash came to an end. In March 1994 Muslims and Croats in Bosnia signed an agreement creating the Federation of Bosnia and Herzegovina. This simplified a three-way conflict. Serbs, Croats, and Bosniaks had all been fighting one another. The accord put Bosniaks and Croats on the same side against the Serbs. The Serbs had cut off food and other supplies to Sarajevo, the Bosnian capital, in 1992. The United States and 20 other countries began an airlift to keep the people of Sarajevo from starving. Meanwhile, NATO created a no-fly zone for Serbian aircraft over Bosnia.

The fighting continued through most of 1995. Soldiers committed many atrocities. One of the worst was by the Army of Republika Srpska in and around Srebrenica in July 1995. They murdered about 8,000 unarmed Bosniak men and boys.

When Bosnian Serb forces shelled Sarajevo again in August 1995, NATO began a bombing campaign against Bosnian Serb positions. Soon after that, Bosniak, Bosnian Croat, and Bosnian Serb officials met in Geneva, Switzerland to hammer out a cease-fire. The presidents of Bosnia, Croatia, and Serbia then met at Wright-Patterson AFB in Dayton, Ohio, and negotiated the Dayton Peace Agreement of 21 November 1995. This agreement ended the conflicts in Bosnia and Croatia.

The International Criminal Tribunal for the Former Yugoslavia in The Hague, Netherlands, indicted Bosnian Serb leaders Radovan Karadzic and Ratko Mladic. It charged them with genocide and crimes against humanity for their roles in the Srebrenica massacre. Serbian authorities—the post-Milosevic authorities—apprehended Karadzic in July 2008. They turned him over to the tribunal. Mladic remains at large at this writing.

The Displacement of Albanian Workers in Serbia Ordered by Slobodan Milosevic

To pick up another strand of the tangled story of the Balkans—the story of Kosovo—you have to return to 1989. In that year Milosevic, as Serbia's new president, eliminated Kosovo's autonomy. From then on, he decreed, the province would be ruled directly from Belgrade. Belgrade ordered the firing of large numbers of ethnic Albanian state employees. Serbs then took their jobs.

In response to this, the Kosovo Albanians began a peaceful resistance movement. They established a parallel government, too. They funded this mainly with money from Albanians outside the country.

KLA rebels peer into a home in Korenica, Yugoslavia, where Serbian police shot a family of five and then set their house on fire during the Kosovo War.
Photo by Andy Nelson / © 1999 The Christian Science Monitor

Starting in late 1998 Serbian soldiers and police forces committed atrocities against civilians. Experts estimate that Serbians drove 800,000 ethnic Albanians out of Kosovo during this time.

The Kosovo Liberation Army's War for Independence From Serbia

After a while, however, the Kosovars—Albanians living in Kosovo—lost patience with peaceful resistance. The international peace efforts in the former Yugoslavia during the 1990s failed to deal with their concerns. And so in 1997 the Kosovo Liberation Army (KLA) began armed resistance. Its main goal was independence for Kosovo.

The Police and Military Force Used Against the KLA and NATO's Intervention

In late 1998 the Milosevic regime unleashed a brutal campaign against the KLA. Serbian soldiers and police forces committed atrocities against civilians. They displaced or even killed large numbers of them. Ethnic Albanians fled in terror to the border with Albania. Experts estimate that Serbians drove 800,000 ethnic Albanians out of Kosovo during this time.

Intense mediation efforts led to the Rambouillet Accords. These called for autonomy for Kosovo. They also provided for a NATO presence to keep the peace. Milosevic rejected the accords, however. He refused to sign them.

This provoked nearly 80 days of bombing by NATO air forces, from March to June 1999. On 10 June 1999 the UN Security Council passed Resolution 1244. This authorized an international presence in Kosovo. This would include civilian officials as well as military forces. The UN would take charge for a time. Resolution 1244 also called for a political process to determine Kosovo's status.

After Milosevic surrendered, two international forces moved in to Kosovo. One was the UN Mission in Kosovo. The other was a NATO-led security force known as KFOR (Kosovo force).

Meanwhile, as ethnic Albanians returned to their homes, some elements of the KLA abducted or killed ethnic Serbs and Roma in Kosovo. Thousands of people from these minority groups fled Kosovo during the latter half of 1999. Many remained displaced 10 years later.

As of this writing, about 14,000 KFOR troops from NATO and its partners remained in Kosovo. Despite Serbia's opposition, Kosovo declared its independence in February 2008. The United States recognized the new state the next day. By June 2009, 60 countries had done so. The World Bank and International Monetary Fund admitted Kosovo as a member that same month.

A Romani woman reacts as her neighbor's home burns in Pec, Kosovo. The home belonged to another Roma who had been helping Serb police. Many Romani feared reprisals for their work for Serbs.
Photo by Andy Nelson / © 1999 The Christian Science Monitor

As ethnic Albanians returned to their homes, some elements of the KLA abducted or killed ethnic Serbs and Roma in Kosovo. Thousands of people from these minority groups fled Kosovo during the latter half of 1999.

After Milosevic fell from power, the new Serbian government arrested him. It turned him over to the International Criminal Tribunal for the Former Yugoslavia in 2001. He died in jail in March 2006 during the fourth year of his trial.

For several decades the Serbs dominated the Yugoslav federation. But in the end, Serb nationalism went too far. It caused the exact opposite of what the Serbs had hoped for. It created seven independent countries instead of a Serb-run central state. With the independence of Kosovo, the defeat of radical Serb nationalism seemed complete—at least for the time being. Given the history of the Balkans, one can never be sure.

Lesson 4 Review

Using complete sentences, answer the following questions on a sheet of paper.

1. Why was Kosovo important to the Serbs?
2. Why were the people of Istria, Dalmatia, and the Slovenian lands not happy about the promises made in the 1915 Treaty of London?
3. What did Hitler promise Yugoslavia when its government signed on to the Axis?
4. Serb-Croat tensions during World War II eventually led the Allies to do what?
5. What deal did Tito make with Stalin in September 1944?
6. What steps did the postwar Yugoslav regime take to hold the Serbs in check?
7. What effect did Milosevic's April 1987 speech at Kosovo Polje have? What topic did it show him willing to talk about?
8. Who was Radovan Karadzic, and what did he do in September 1991?
9. Which agreement ended the fighting in Bosnia and Croatia?
10. What happened after Milosevic refused to sign the Rambouillet Accords?

Applying Your Learning

11. Explain why the Kingdom of the Serbs, Croats, and Slovenes was a flawed idea. Name some other countries in the world that have the same flaws.

LESSON 5 US Interests and Regional Issues in Europe

Quick Write

What do President Truman's reminiscences suggest to you about the connection between the United States and Europe?

Learn About

- why the United States intervened in the two world wars and fought the Cold War
- the historic purpose and current activities of the North Atlantic Treaty Organization (NATO)
- the importance of trade with Europe to the US economy
- the development of human rights and democracy in Eastern Europe following the Soviet Union's collapse

Everyone knows that US presidents have to make a lot of difficult decisions. Harry S. Truman may have faced more than most. One of his most difficult involved Berlin soon after World War II.

Berlin was then the divided capital of a divided country under military occupation. West Berlin was an "island" under control of the Western Allies—the United States, Britain, and France. But it was surrounded by territory under Soviet rule. All its supplies came overland from the western sectors of Germany.

But on 24 June 1948 the Soviets halted all rail, road, and water access from the west. They wanted to starve West Berlin into submission and to force the Western Allies out.

What options did Truman have? There really was only one path left into West Berlin: the sky. Military planners scrambled to prepare for the unimaginably dangerous prospect of supplying a major city entirely by air—indefinitely.

In a 1964 interview President Truman told how he had made the decision to go ahead with the Berlin Airlift.

"Many thoughts went through my mind. How does a city blockaded from the rest of the world survive? Where does food come from? Medicines? Coal for heat and the making of electric power? Raw materials for the factories?

"And what about milk? I was told that 6,000 newborn babies would die [without milk]. The Kremlin was telling the people of Europe that the United States would back away from any military risks.

"People were wondering what I would do. Europe was waiting. The Russians were waiting to see whether or not the Berlin crisis would be met.

"Our position in blockaded Berlin was precarious. If we wished to remain there, we would have to make a show of strength. But there was always the risk that Russian reaction might touch off a catastrophe. There was always a chance that some trigger-happy Russian pilot might light a powder keg and create a situation that would create trouble for all of us.

"I called a Cabinet meeting for June 25. . . . I made it abundantly clear that the blockading of Berlin was a major propaganda move. They were determined to force us out of Berlin. They were bringing us to the brink of war.

"You think about a lot of things when you have to make a decision like that. . . . You think about our young men, the youngsters, who are in the Army, that will be killed.

"But the decision had to be made. I made the decision. We would stay in Berlin, come hell or high water."

Vocabulary

- isolationism

An officer with the 3rd Infantry Regiment pays his respects at the gravesite of a World War II and Korean War veteran in Arlington National Cemetery outside Washington, D.C.
Photo by Andy Nelson / © 2006 The Christian Science Monitor

In both World Wars I and II, the United States fought to stop aggression, especially German aggression, and to preserve people's right to self-determination and self-government.

Why the United States Intervened in the Two World Wars and Fought the Cold War

The spirit of Woodrow Wilson pervades much of the following section of this lesson. The only political scientist ever elected president of the United States, he embodied the idealist strain of American foreign policy. His ideas, however imperfectly carried out, were a major influence on the peace process at the end of World War I. They continued to influence American policy through World War II and the Cold War.

A maritime issue was the United States' immediate reason for entering World War I. Japan's attack on Pearl Harbor in Hawaii prompted US entry into World War II. But in both wars the larger issue that brought the country into the fight was the need to stop aggression, especially German aggression, and to preserve people's right to self-determination and self-government.

By the Cold War, the United States had a new adversary: the Soviet Union. An ally of necessity during World War II, it had become America's enemy in short order at its conclusion. But for the United States, the Cold War issues were similar to what they had been during both world wars: standing up to aggression, in terms both of territory and of individual rights. Woodrow Wilson would have understood.

How German Actions Drew the United States Into World War I

The conflict now known as World War I started as a European war. It was the United States' first military adventure in Europe in more than a century. President Wilson had run for reelection as a peace candidate in 1916. He tried to maintain strict US neutrality. This had the advantage, in theory, of allowing the United States to trade with both the Allies (Britain, France, and Russia) and the Central Powers (Germany and Austria).

But on 2 April 1917 Wilson went before Congress to seek a declaration of war against Germany. The immediate issue at hand was German use of submarines against passenger and merchant ships. These were civilian vessels, not warships, although many of the merchant ships were carrying military supplies to the Allies.

Washington had protested vehemently against the loss of American lives when German submarines torpedoed unarmed ships in the Atlantic. At one point, Wilson threatened to sever diplomatic ties with Germany. Germany responded in 1916 with the "Sussex pledge," named for a French ship that had gone down. Germany said it would cease attacking passenger ships. In the case of merchant vessels, it would give crews time to escape before an attack.

By January 1917, though, German policy had changed. Naval officials had become convinced that Germany could defeat Britain within five months if only the Sussex pledge were abandoned. The officers argued that, after all, the United States was already helping the Allies. It couldn't credibly claim neutrality. Germany's military leaders and Kaiser Wilhelm agreed. In February Germany announced it would resume unrestricted attacks on civilian vessels.

German Chancellor Theobald von Bethmann-Hollweg protested the decision. He predicted it would bring the United States into the war on the Allied side and lead to German defeat.

President Wilson got his declaration of war from Congress in early April. He proved the chancellor right. You know the story by now: the United States entered the war, and Germany and its allies in the Central Powers went down in defeat in 1918.

The Formation of the League of Nations in 1920

The League of Nations was the UN's forerunner. President Wilson was the first to propose the League. He did this in 1918 in his Fourteen Points speech, which sketched out a vision of postwar Europe.

Wilson and his collaborators on both sides of the Atlantic managed to establish the League. Once they had, he gave his all to getting the United States to join it. In fact, he campaigned so fervently for it on a tour around the United States in 1919 that he collapsed, never to fully recover before his death in 1924. Despite these efforts, Congress would not approve joining the League.

Boats pass under Westminster Bridge—with Big Ben and Parliament in the background—in London.

Photo by R. Norman Matheny / © 1989 The Christian Science Monitor

German naval officials argued that Germany could defeat Britain in World War I if German submarines were allowed to attack civilian vessels. The German chancellor correctly argued that doing so would bring the United States into the war on the Allied side and lead to Germany's defeat.

Nonetheless, the League was a new kind of peacekeeping organization. Previously, after a period of war the countries involved would meet for a peace conference and a settling of accounts. The Peace of Westphalia after the Thirty Years' War (1618–48) was such a conference. Another occurred after the Napoleonic wars and France's defeat, when diplomats at the Congress of Vienna redrew the map of Europe in 1815.

But Wilson saw a need for a permanent organization. Many of the individual items on his list of Fourteen Points called for regulation or enforcement. He pushed for an organization that could act on international disputes as soon as they arose. So did other likeminded scholars. (Remember that Wilson had been a professor before he went into politics.)

The League was meant to foster international cooperation, provide security for its members, and ensure a lasting peace. The idea was wildly popular. Creation of the thing itself, however, would prove exceedingly difficult. Wilson got the Covenant of the League, its charter, attached to the Treaty of Versailles. Versailles was the treaty that settled World War I. Wilson went to Paris to negotiate it. It was the first instance in American history of a sitting president traveling outside the United States.

People refresh themselves at a sidewalk café near the University of Paris-Sorbonne.
Photo by R. Norman Matheny / © 1989 The Christian Science Monitor

President Wilson went to Paris to negotiate the Treaty of Versailles, which ended World War I. He was the first president in American history to travel outside the United States.

Several of the League's main organs may remind you of those of the United Nations:

- An assembly of all members
- A council, with five permanent members and four rotating ones
- An International Court of Justice.

The League would guarantee member nations' "territorial integrity"—their borders—and their political independence. In case of trouble the League would be able to take "any action . . . to safeguard the peace." It could set up arbitration, that is, it could try to settle arguments between countries. And it could impose sanctions, or punishments, on any member who misbehaved.

Wilson couldn't get the backing he needed from Congress to join the League of Nations, however. Specifically, Henry Cabot Lodge, the Senate majority leader and chairman of the Foreign Relations Committee, opposed it. Republicans were concerned that the League would limit the United States' ability to defend its own interests. Beyond that, many Americans still remembered George Washington's warning against "foreign entanglements." Let Europe take care of its own affairs, they said. Many historians say today that the League would have been a much more effective organization with American involvement.

Ultimately, the League failed because it had no way to enforce its decisions. It depended on the major powers to lend their own troops to do so—something they were reluctant to do. In the end the League proved unable to prevent aggression against other nations by Italian dictator Benito Mussolini, and Germany's Adolf Hitler, and Japan's militarist government. They simply withdrew from the League.

The US Commitment to Promote Freedom and Democracy Around the World

As you read earlier in this lesson, the immediate issue that brought the United States into World War I was German submarine attacks. But there was more to it than that.

In Wilson's address to Congress he said that the American goal was "to vindicate the principles of peace and justice in the life of the world." In several different speeches he called for an end to the war on terms that would bring "a just and secure peace," not merely "a new balance of power."

He brought together a group of experts referred to as "The Inquiry" to help him think issues through. In December 1917 he asked this task force to draw up specific recommendations. What would be needed for a comprehensive peace settlement? Wilson took the group's recommendations and turned them into the program known as his Fourteen Points. He presented these to Congress on 8 January 1918.

Eight of the points speak to specific territory issues among the combatants. Five others speak to general principles for running a peaceful world. One of these ("open covenants") was meant to put an end to secret treaties, such as the Treaty of London that would have given so much of the Balkans to Italy. The 14th point was the call for the League of Nations.

Wilson's idealism runs through all these points. But he had practical goals in mind, too. He wanted to keep Russia in the war, and he tried to do it by convincing the Bolsheviks that they would get a better peace from the Allies. He wanted to bolster Allied morale. And he wanted to undercut support for Germany. The United States was full of German immigrants and people of German descent. They didn't think of the British as their natural allies in the same way as did Washington's political class, especially those at the White House and the State Department, who were largely of British descent.

Wilson's address to Congress won praise in the United States and among Allies. Even Lenin hailed it as a landmark of enlightened policy. The Fourteen Points became the basis from which Wilson negotiated the Treaty of Versailles. The treaty fell short of Wilson's vision. But the Fourteen Points still stand as the most powerful expression of the idealist strain in American foreign policy.

Wilson's Fourteen Points, Paraphrased

1. Open covenants openly arrived at
2. Freedom of the seas
3. The removal of economic barriers and equality of trade conditions among nations
4. Reduction of national armaments
5. A readjustment of colonial claims, with colonial peoples' interests given weight equal to those of the colonizers
6. A pullout of foreign troops from Russia, and Russia left to determine its own political destiny
7. Pullout of foreign troops from Belgium, with its independence restored
8. Pullout of foreign troops from France and the return of Alsace-Lorraine to France
9. Readjustment of Italy's frontiers along national lines
10. Self-determination for the peoples of the Austro-Hungarian Empire
11. Boundaries of the Balkan states redrawn along historical lines
12. Self-determination of the peoples under Ottoman rule and freedom of navigation through the Dardanelles and the Bosporus
13. National independence for Poland, with free access to the sea
14. Formation of the League of Nations.

To read the Fourteen Points in full, you can visit the Web at: http://web.jjay.cuny.edu/~jobrien/reference/ob34.html

The failure of the Treaty of Versailles to prevent World War II and the aftermath of that war left many Americans more concerned about the future of democracy and human rights around the world. For many, these concerns were enough to justify the Cold War with a communist enemy that respected neither. In 1977 President Jimmy Carter returned to Wilsonian ideals when he made the promotion of human rights an official goal of US foreign policy. He convinced Congress to create a human rights bureau in the Department of State. Today, US embassies around the world monitor human rights conditions in their host countries. The department issues annual reports highlighting the human rights problems in each country, trying to increase the pressure on governments to correct them.

The Influence of Henry Luce and the Internationalists on Twentieth Century US Foreign Policy

The US refusal to participate in the League of Nations was an example of the isolationism that swept the United States after World War I. Isolationism is the special term for *a policy of avoiding alliances and other forms of international relations*. The term came into use in the early 1920s. This was just as Wilson's hopes for US participation in the League foundered.

Isolationism was a powerful force in the United States right up until the attack on Pearl Harbor in December 1941. Even as Hitler's troops overran Poland and France, leaving Britain alone against the Nazis in 1940, many Americans wanted to stay out of another European war. This sentiment kept President Franklin Roosevelt from sending US forces to help until the United States itself was attacked.

There was another American view circulating on international affairs, however: internationalism. Henry R. Luce (1898–1967) was one of its leading advocates. He commanded the forces of *Time*, *Life*, and *Fortune*. Or at least, he published magazines with those names. They gave him a sturdy platform from which to proclaim his views.

On 3 March 1923 Luce and a Yale classmate published the first issue of *Time*. He favored US involvement overseas and democratic reform in China. He opposed Soviet communism and, at home, the ban on alcohol sales known as Prohibition. (It lasted from 1920 to 1933.)

In February 1941 Luce published in *Life* an editorial called "The American Century." In it, he urged the United States to join Britain in its war against Germany. Even more important, he said that the United States must replace Britain as the world's leader. "American principles" must transform international relations.

Luce aligned himself with Wilson and Theodore Roosevelt. He argued that the United States had the moral obligation to use its power to promote freedom and democracy around the world.

Born in China of missionary parents, Luce had a particular interest in Asia. After China's communist revolution, he blamed the Democrats in Washington for having "lost China" and being "soft on communism." He later focused on the fight against communism elsewhere in Asia. His feelings were so strong that they blinded him to the weaknesses of some of the anticommunist leaders he supported.

But whatever his shortcomings, Luce was a powerful voice in American foreign policy. His "American Century" editorial, written just months before the United States entered World War II, marked the rise of internationalism over isolationism in American foreign policy thinking.

The Atlantic Charter and Conference of 1941

The outbreak of World War II revived the question of how different countries could harmoniously work together in the future. President Franklin Roosevelt met with British Prime Minister Winston Churchill in Newfoundland in August 1941 to discuss postwar plans, among other issues. World War II was far from over at this point. For the United States, it hadn't even begun. But the two were already planning for arrangements for after the war, such as a successor to the League of Nations.

Winston Churchill rides in a limousine after giving a speech at the Massachusetts Institute of Technology's Mid-Century Convocation in 1949.
Photo by Gordon N. Converse / © 1949 The Christian Science Monitor

Back in 1941 Prime Minister Churchill and President Franklin D. Roosevelt met in Newfoundland to discuss postwar plans. They signed the Atlantic Charter to bind the two countries together.

The Atlantic Charter that they signed served to bind the two countries together. It committed them both to supporting the restoration of self-government for countries occupied during the war. It also pledged them to allow all peoples to choose their own form of government. This was significant for Britain, which still had an extensive empire.

The war that Churchill and his fellow Britons were fighting was not going well for them as he met with Roosevelt. The Axis powers had just invaded and partitioned Yugoslavia. The Germans threatened, moreover, to take over the Suez Canal. That would have shut Britain off from India. The Germans had also invaded the Soviet Union. The Soviets would eventually prove able to hold on longer than anyone else had expected. But at the time of the meeting in Newfoundland, policymakers in London and Washington were expecting the Soviets to fold within weeks.

Against this background, Churchill had come to Newfoundland hoping to "get the Americans into the war." That was his chief goal. He did not achieve it. Roosevelt refused even to discuss American entry into the war with Churchill. And Roosevelt, for his part, was disappointed that the signed Atlantic Charter didn't do more to move American public opinion toward entering the war.

The Atlantic Charter wasn't a binding treaty. It was simply a document that spelled out postwar goals. But it was significant for a number of reasons:

- It affirmed solidarity between Britain and the United States against Axis aggression
- It laid out Roosevelt's vision for the postwar world—a vision that owed much to President Wilson
- With its commitment to self-determination, it served as an inspiration for colonial subjects around the world as they fought for independence.

The Historic Purpose and Current Activities of the North Atlantic Treaty Organization (NATO)

The Atlantic Charter helped lead to the formation of the North Atlantic Treaty Organization (NATO) after the war. NATO, sometimes called the Atlantic Alliance, is today a military security organization of 28 North American and European member countries. Its 12 founding members signed the North Atlantic Treaty, also known as the Washington Treaty, on 4 April 1949. The group pledged itself to mutual defense in accord with the United Nations Charter.

Western leaders had negotiated the treaty with an eye to the east. In just a short period after 1945 the Soviet Union had gone from an ally in the fight to stop Hitler to the West's principal adversary. NATO's 12 original members focused on the defense of Western Europe against Soviet aggression. They promised to consider an attack on any one of them as an attack on all.

Red rooftops surround the Cathedral of St. Vitus in central Prague, Czech Republic.

Photo by Neal Menschel / © 1996 The Christian Science Monitor

As the Cold War ended, Eastern European nations such as the Czech Republic saw joining NATO as a good way to counter Russian influence and stay free.

NATO's Continuing Purpose

After both the Soviet Union and the Warsaw Pact dissolved in 1991, though, the question arose—does NATO still have a purpose? After all, the reasoning went, isn't the Cold War over, and didn't the West win?

For Eastern Europe, the answer was emphatically, yes, NATO still has a purpose, and we want to join. Membership in the two big Western "clubs," NATO and the EU, would show that these emerging democracies had "made it."

These East European countries wanted the world to know they had broken free of the Soviet bear's powerful hug. NATO membership would let them reconnect with the democratic West. (The original connection, it's worth noting, had been stronger in some of these countries than others.) They also wanted to be sure they stayed free, and joining NATO seemed a good way to counter Russian influence and ensure that.

Meanwhile, policymakers in the West thought that including the "emerging democracies" under NATO's umbrella was a good way to help them cement the gains they had made. NATO looked likely to be able to bring new members in faster than the EU. Some would say that was because military organizations can move more quickly than civilian organizations. Others would explain the difference by noting that the United States is part of NATO but not of the EU.

At any rate, NATO found itself in the midst of a mission change. Once a military alliance focused primarily on security, it became an engine of democratic and economic change. And not just in Europe either, but more broadly.

Russia had other ideas, though. NATO always insisted it was a defensive alliance. But the Soviets nonetheless saw it as "aimed" at them, and not without some reason.

Though Russia may have moved past communism, it hadn't given up on traditional ideas about spheres of influence. It was reluctant to give up territory that had belonged to its empire. The West may have embraced twentieth-century Wilsonian self-determination. But Russia's mindset was still nineteenth-century balance-of-power statecraft.

"Squaring the circle" was the term people used at NATO headquarters during the 1990s. By this they meant the challenge of bringing former Warsaw Pact nations into NATO without angering postcommunist Russia. Western advocates of enlargement stressed that NATO was about democracy and free-market economies.

This was true, if not quite the whole truth. NATO was also about military security. NATO was, in fact, the most powerful military alliance in human history. The wonder was that NATO headquarters in Brussels didn't hear more growls from Moscow.

But somehow Alliance leaders managed to square the circle. The first new members from the former Warsaw Pact joined in 1999. That was five years before the EU brought in any Eastern European members. And it happened peacefully.

NATO's Member Nations

The list in the adjacent box names all 28 NATO members. You might want to compare its membership roster with the European Union's. NATO is very much a European organization, and so its membership largely overlaps with that of the EU. But six EU members do not belong to NATO: four historically neutral countries (Austria, Finland, Ireland, and Sweden), plus the two island republics of Cyprus and Malta.

NATO's Members

- Albania
- Belgium
- Britain
- Bulgaria
- Canada
- Croatia
- the Czech Republic
- Denmark
- Estonia
- France
- Germany
- Greece
- Hungary
- Iceland
- Italy
- Latvia
- Lithuania
- Luxembourg
- the Netherlands
- Norway
- Poland
- Portugal
- Romania
- Slovakia
- Slovenia
- Spain
- Turkey
- United States

And NATO has seven members that are not part of the EU at this writing. These include the two North American partners, the United States and Canada. They were founding members of the Alliance, along with Iceland and Norway. Turkey joined in 1951, part of the first enlargement of NATO. The two newest NATO members, Albania and Croatia, are part of the continuing adjustments to the political landscape in the Balkans. They joined in 2009. As of this writing, both Turkey and Croatia were candidate members of the EU.

NATO's Role in the Cold War

One of NATO's most important actions during the Cold War might be one that it never took. In its first 40 years, NATO never fired a shot. It expanded from its original 12 members in 1952, when Greece and Turkey were brought into the Alliance. The two have long been rivals in Southeastern Europe. With pressure from the United States, NATO brought them in at the same time.

In 1955 NATO leaders thought the time was right to add West Germany to the Alliance. They did so, over Soviet objections. The following year, the Soviet Union formed the Warsaw Pact with Albania, Bulgaria, Czechoslovakia, East Germany, Hungary, Poland, and Romania.

Pedestrians cross a busy street in Syntagma Square in Athens, Greece.

Photo by Melanie Stetson Freeman / © 2007 The Christian Science Monitor

NATO expanded from its original 12 members in 1952, when it brought Greece and Turkey into the Alliance. Since the two have long been rivals, NATO brought them in at the same time.

Russians in NATO?

A couple of years after NATO took in Greece and Turkey, the Soviet Union made a provocative request: It asked to join NATO. After all, the logic went, the Alliance had just shown its willingness to take in new members. The Soviets seemed to be asking what the requirements for membership in NATO were.

They appeared to be completely unclear about NATO's purpose. The whole point of NATO was to defend against the threat of Soviet aggression. The diplomatic reply sent to Moscow was, "It is unnecessary to emphasize the completely unreal character of such a suggestion."

In one of his own memos, Lord Ismay, NATO's first secretary general, was less diplomatic. He wrote, "To put it very bluntly, the Soviet request to join NATO is like an unrepentant burglar requesting to join the police force."

The subject would come up again, though. In 1991 Boris Yeltsin wrote to NATO to ask for Russian membership in the alliance. It was a "long-term political aim," he said. The NATO ministers were too stunned to respond. At this writing, there has been no movement on the issue.

NATO's Intervention in the Balkans

NATO's movement into the Balkans in 1995 was its first large-scale operational peacekeeping mission. Known as IFOR—for "implementation force"—it was meant to ensure that the terms of the Dayton Peace Agreement were met. IFOR's main task was to end the inter-ethnic fighting in Bosnia-Herzegovina and to separate the armed forces of the two "entities" in Bosnia: the Federation of Bosnia and Herzegovina and the Republika Srpska.

IFOR deployed 60,000 troops with a one-year mandate starting in December 1995. Their mandate came from UN Security Council Resolution 1031. Note this reference to the UN. And remember that NATO's founding treaty invokes the United Nations Charter's peacekeeping principles. That important document goes back four years earlier than the North Atlantic Treaty.

The UN had tried to police the situation in Bosnia with one of its own peacekeeping forces. UN peacekeepers have been deployed in crises around the world since the mid-1950s. But the wars in Yugoslavia saw the worst violence in Europe in half a century. The UN troops were in over their heads.

In the case of the Bosnian war's worst single atrocity, a detachment of Dutch "blue helmets," as UN troops are known for their distinctive light blue headgear, proved unable to protect a group of thousands of Muslims who had fled to Srebrenica. They had been promised a "safe haven" there from the Bosnian Serbs. Some 8,000 men and boys were marched off and shot to death by Bosnian Serbs. After that, the call for a "more robust" peacekeeping force was heard.

The new force, IFOR, was notable for several reasons. For one, it was not carried out to defend a NATO member, but rather, to help bring peace to a country without allies of its own. IFOR was also an "out of area" operation. It was a deployment outside the territory of NATO members.

The NATO mission was also an opportunity to try out some new relationships that had developed since the Cold War's end. After the Warsaw Pact broke up, NATO established a program called "Partnership for Peace." It was a series of bilateral agreements with individual Eastern European countries. To a large extent, these partnerships were preparation for NATO membership. But not always. Indeed, Russia took part in the Partnership program. And Russian troops, along with troops from other Partner countries, served alongside NATO troops in IFOR.

IFOR had met its goals by September 1996. But the situation on the ground was still potentially unstable. So NATO agreed to deploy SFOR, a "stabilization force" from December 1996.

SFOR was still deployed in Bosnia when NATO found itself with another mission in the Balkans: the Kosovo crisis. This time NATO acted without UN approval. For 78 days in early 1999 NATO aircraft flew more than 38,000 sorties without a single Allied fatality. Beginning in June 1999 some 46,000 troops from 39 countries were deployed in KFOR, or "Kosovo force," to keep the peace there (see Lesson 4). Some 14,000 remained in Kosovo in mid-2009.

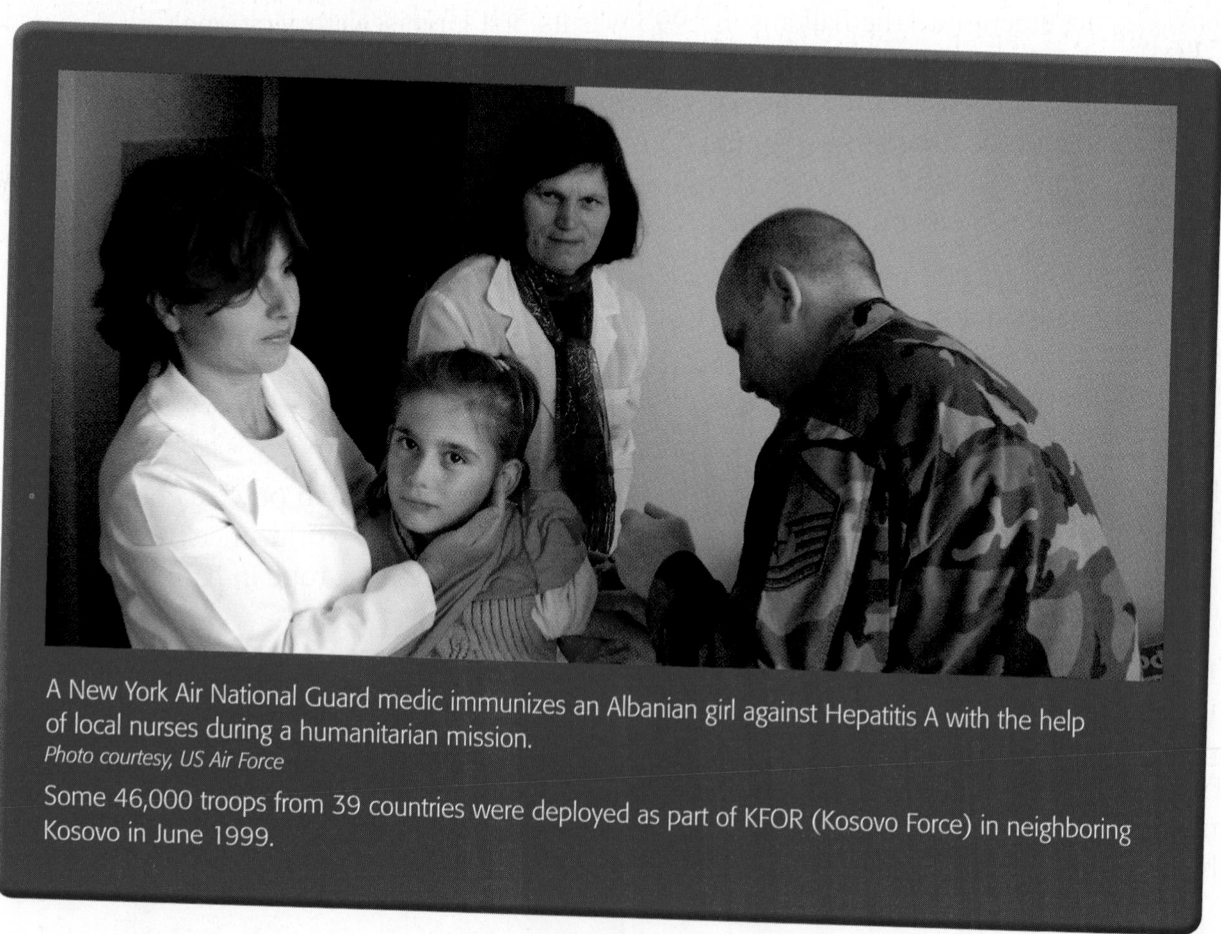

A New York Air National Guard medic immunizes an Albanian girl against Hepatitis A with the help of local nurses during a humanitarian mission.
Photo courtesy, US Air Force

Some 46,000 troops from 39 countries were deployed as part of KFOR (Kosovo Force) in neighboring Kosovo in June 1999.

NATO's Role in Afghanistan

If the Balkans were "out of area," Afghanistan was *really* out of area. How did NATO get so far from Europe? The story starts in the weeks after the terrorist attacks of 11 September 2001.

On 7 October the United States, with British support, launched an attack on Afghanistan. The goal was to oust its Islamist rulers, the Taliban. They had given safe haven to al-Qaeda and its leader, Osama bin Laden, who were behind the 9/11 attacks a few weeks before.

When the Taliban refused to hand over Bin Laden, the Allied attack began. Within a couple of months, the Taliban government had fallen. Then on 20 December 2001 the United Nations Security Council authorized the International Security Assistance Force (ISAF) to support Afghanistan's interim government.

On 11 August 2003 NATO took command of ISAF. Up to that point, ISAF had been under German and Dutch leadership. Since taking command of ISAF, the Alliance has expanded its mission's reach. Originally limited to Afghanistan's capital, Kabul, it now extends throughout the country. ISAF's troop strength has expanded from 5,000 at first to 50,000 in the summer of 2009. ISAF troops represent 42 countries, including all 28 NATO members.

fastFACT

ISAF counts Iceland as one of the NATO allies providing troops in Afghanistan. But Iceland has no armed forces. So who are these Icelandic troops? And how did a country with no armed forces ever become part of a military alliance in the first place? Iceland has contributed a handful of civilian emergency workers to ISAF. Their specialty is running airports. ISAF counts this as a troop contribution. Iceland was included in NATO from the beginning because its location well west of the European mainland made it a useful stopping point when crossing the Atlantic. It was especially useful in flight's early days.

The Importance of Trade With Europe to the US Economy

Besides military ties, the United States and Europe have economic bonds as well. In fact, the United States and the European Union as economic blocs are both so huge and so tightly connected to each other that their partnership dominates the world.

The Nature of US-EU Trade

You have read in this book about economies around the world. Some places export mostly raw materials and agricultural goods. If they want modern conveniences, they have to import them. As they try to climb up the economic ladder by producing more "value-added" goods, it's a struggle.

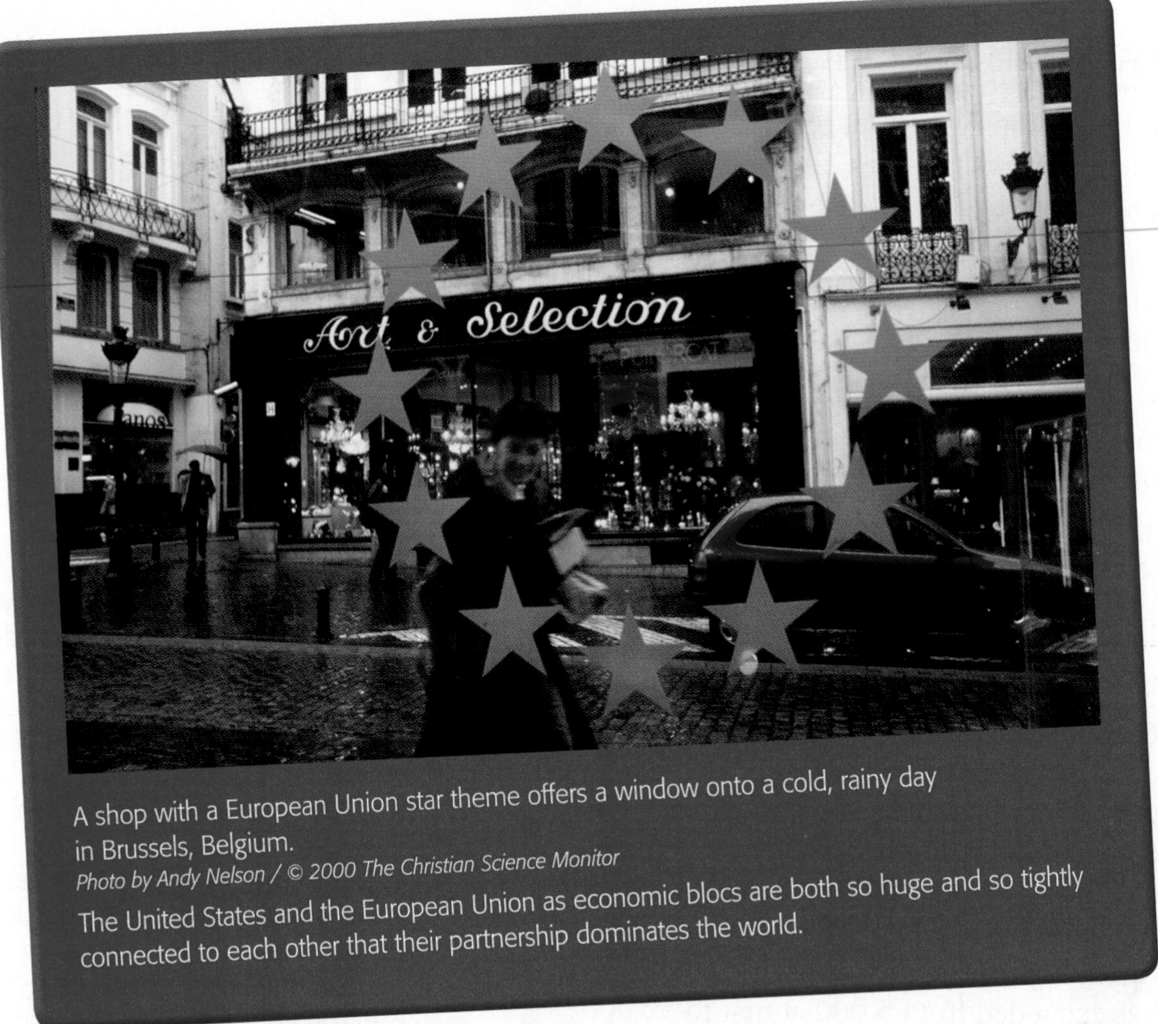

A shop with a European Union star theme offers a window onto a cold, rainy day in Brussels, Belgium.
Photo by Andy Nelson / © 2000 The Christian Science Monitor

The United States and the European Union as economic blocs are both so huge and so tightly connected to each other that their partnership dominates the world.

That's not what's going on in US-EU trade. The countries in these two blocs are at roughly equivalent stages of development. They are among the most advanced in the world. They include the world's wealthiest and best-educated populations. They produce advanced technologies and services.

Thus much of US-EU trade tends to be intra-industry—trade back and forth in similar products: cars and computers, for instance. The US and EU financial sectors are well integrated, too. This helps capital flow across the Atlantic almost as easily as jets fly.

Earlier in this lesson you read how the EU's membership overlaps with NATO's. Part of what makes NATO work is standardization of equipment. As Eastern European countries prepared to join NATO, for instance, they knew they had to make sure their radios could talk to NATO radios. From a trade perspective, NATO creates a large "common market" for defense and security technology. It's a significant factor in transatlantic trade.

The US-EU relationship dominates the larger world economic system, too. In the years since World War II, both partners have worked to create a more open global trading system.

The two sides do not always see eye to eye, however. Americans say the EU subsidizes its farmers unfairly. (US farm policy draws similar criticism at times, however.) The two sides have differing ideas about competition policy. And American policies often strike Europeans as "unilateralist"—one-sided. One sensitive example is the Helms-Burton Act passed in 1996. It prevents investors in Cuba from doing business in the United States.

The Importance of European Investment in the United States

In 2005 the EU had €808 billion—roughly $1.15 trillion—invested in the United States. This continued a well-established pattern of Europeans as major investors on this side of the Atlantic.

During the 1980s and early 1990s investors from Asia and the Middle East seemed to be on a real buying spree in the United States. They weren't shopping just for the kinds of goodies they could carry aboard their return flights in fancy tote bags. They were buying up whole buildings, including some famous American cityscape icons. This trend's peak came in 1989 when a group of Japanese investors bought Rockefeller Center in New York.

Weekend shoppers visit a downtown mall in Liverpool, England.

Photo by Robert Harbison / © 1997 The Christian Science Monitor

The US and EU financial sectors are well integrated. This helps capital flow across the Atlantic almost as easily as jets fly.

But Europeans have long been the real investors in the United States. One analyst has found that in the early 1990s, countries of the European Economic Community held about 57 percent of foreign direct investment in the United States. Britain accounted for nearly half of that. The Dutch were close behind. This pattern goes back to colonial times.

The Share of US Foreign Trade That Goes to Europe

The European Union as a whole is one of the largest merchandise trading partners of the United States. In 2008, for instance, the EU accounted for $272 billion of total US exports. Imports into the United States from Europe amounted to $368 billion. This means Americans buy more from Europeans than they sell to them.

The United States is also the largest non-EU trading partner of the EU as a whole. In 2007 EU exports to the United States were 21 percent of the EU's total sales abroad. EU imports from the United States that year were 13 percent of the total.

fastFACT

Among the top US exports to the EU are aircraft and machinery, including computers, integrated circuits, and office machine parts. Among US imports from the EU are passenger cars, machinery, including gas turbines, computers and components, office machinery, and parts and organic chemicals. Of EU members, Germany, Britain, and France are the leading US trade partners, followed by the Netherlands and Italy.

The trade deficit hasn't always been on the American side. For some years up until 1993 Americans ran a trade surplus with the EU. The United States sold more to Europe than it bought from there. But that ended during the boom years of the 1990s. Prosperity made Americans want to buy more German cars and French champagne. That burned off the trade surplus.

The Development of Human Rights and Democracy in Eastern Europe Following the Soviet Union's Collapse

While the United States and Western Europe were trading goods and services in the late twentieth century, Eastern Europe was having a tough time of it economically and politically. When the end of communism came, it came with stunning swiftness. Perhaps even more surprising was how little bloodshed was involved. In the fall of 1989 the Communist leaders of one country after another were just swept away like the autumn leaves.

All this was due partly to the Communists' deep unpopularity. It was due partly to changes Moscow was making as well. This was Gorbachev's perestroika at work. But it also had to do with how these countries had developed alternatives to communism. Some did better than others. On the whole, however, they did much better than their recent history might have predicted.

The Old City of Warsaw, Poland, boasts a wealth of historic architecture.

Photo by Robert Harbison / © 1993 The Christian Science Monitor

When Lech Walesa and his fellow-workers at Lenin Shipyard in Gdansk, Poland, signed the Gdansk Agreement guaranteeing them the right to form independent trade unions and to strike, it signaled the first big rip in the Iron Curtain.

The Solidarity Movement in Poland

On 31 August 1980 Lech Walesa and his fellow-workers at the Lenin Shipyard in the Polish city of Gdansk signed an agreement with their government. It ended a weeks-long strike. But its real importance was its guarantee of the right to form independent trade unions and to strike. You might call it the first big rip in the Iron Curtain.

During the 1970s the Polish government had borrowed lots of money from the West. The idea was to upgrade its factories that made goods for export. In theory, money earned from better production should have paid off the loans and given Poles a better standard of living. Businesses borrow like this all the time.

But the weaknesses and corruption of Communist planning and administration hobbled the Poles' efforts. A worldwide recession and a spike in oil prices didn't help either. By the mid-1970s Poland was crumpling under a crushing burden of debt.

Meanwhile, the Polish people were organizing. A coalition of trade unionists, intellectuals, Roman Catholic clergy, and ordinary citizens took shape. Activists learned to defend workers' interests and human rights. The moral leadership of Catholic Church officials was a great help. Two key figures were Cardinal Stefan Wyszynski and the archbishop of Krakow, Cardinal Karol Wojtyla. As Pope John Paul II, Wojtyla became the first non-Italian pope since the sixteenth century.

Solidarity was more than just a trade union. It became the unofficial opposition to the Communist Party. Poles saw the Gdansk Agreement as pointing the way to a better life. It let them bring about democratic change to the extent possible within the communist system.

In December 1981 the regime put Poland under martial law. But through the 1980s Poland made halting steps toward democratization. On 12 September 1989 its parliament approved Minister Tadeusz Mazowiecki and his cabinet. It was Poland's first noncommunist government in more than 40 years.

The Charter 77 Movement in the Former Czechoslovakia

Czechoslovakia was one of the states carved out of the Austro-Hungarian Empire after World War I. German occupation snuffed out its independence in 1938. And soon after the end of World War II, Czechoslovakia found itself behind the Iron Curtain (see Chapter 4, Lesson 4).

In 1968 Alexander Dubcek led the government. He was a devoted Communist. But he called for "socialism with a human face." He wanted, among other things, freedom of religion, press, assembly, speech, and travel. People called it the "Prague Spring." After years of soul-numbing communism, Czechs and Slovaks finally had a genuinely popular leader.

He was not at all popular with Moscow, however. On the night of 20 August 1968 Soviet and other Warsaw Pact troops invaded. They occupied Czechoslovakia. The Dubcek government made clear at once that no one had "invited" them in. What's more, it insisted that the invasion violated socialist principles, international law, and the UN Charter.

But the Soviets forced Czechoslovakia to accept their troops on its soil—"temporarily." Moscow also replaced Dubcek with a harder-line leader. A period of "normalization" followed. Normal, that is, by communist standards. Political, social, and economic life stagnated. The new leaders cowed the people into silence.

But the embers of democracy burst back into flame on New Year's Day 1977. More than 250 human rights activists signed a manifesto called Charter 77. It criticized the government for failing to honor human rights granted in documents it had willingly signed. These included their own constitution and various treaties. And there was one more: the Final Act of the Conference on Security and Cooperation in Europe, which had been signed in 1975.

This agreement, also known as the Helsinki Accords, pledged the West to acknowledge postwar borders in Europe. The United States and NATO countries still refused to recognize the Baltic states' forced inclusion in the Soviet Union, however.

More importantly, as it turned out, the Helsinki Accords also pledged the Soviet bloc nations to respect human rights in their countries. These rights were included in their constitutions. But they weren't observed.

Helsinki would change that, though. You read earlier how Poles used the rights granted in the Gdansk Agreement as a wedge to crack open Communist rule in their country. Activists throughout Eastern Europe used the Helsinki Accords in the same way.

The Charter 77 initiative was an example of this. Its supporters weren't organized. But they continued to agitate for human rights over the years. On 17 November 1989 Communist police in Czechoslovakia violently broke up a peaceful demonstration for democracy. They brutally beat up many students.

Days after, Charter 77 and other democratic groups joined to form the Civic Forum. It was rather like Solidarity in Poland. That is, it was an alternative to the Communist Party in a one-party state where "party" had become a dirty word. The Civic Forum soon had the support of millions of Czechs. Its Slovak counterpart, Public Against Violence, flourished as well.

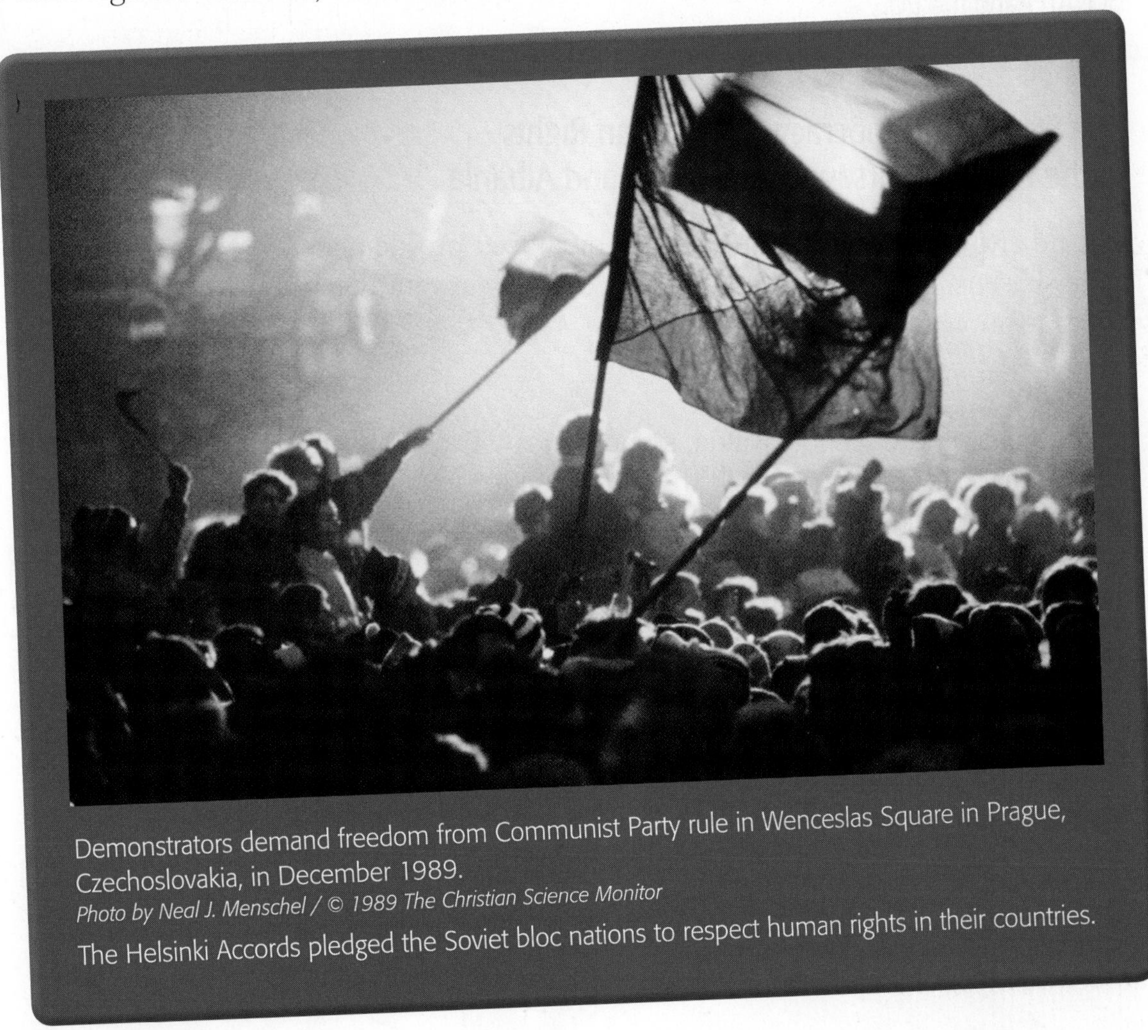

Demonstrators demand freedom from Communist Party rule in Wenceslas Square in Prague, Czechoslovakia, in December 1989.
Photo by Neal J. Menschel / © 1989 The Christian Science Monitor
The Helsinki Accords pledged the Soviet bloc nations to respect human rights in their countries.

The Czechoslovakian people had overwhelmingly turned against communism. In the face of this, the Party all but collapsed. Its leaders resigned. On 29 December 1989 the people of Czechoslovakia elected Vaclav Havel, a playwright and political activist, as their president.

By the end of 1990 Czechoslovakia had run free elections at the national, county, and local levels. It was no longer a communist country. It all happened so swiftly and so smoothly that people called it "the Velvet Revolution."

Slovakia

You may have noted that this book has sometimes referred to the Czech Republic and, in reference to different points in history, to Czechoslovakia. The difference is Slovakia.

The Czech lands and Slovakia were separate territories within the Austro-Hungarian Empire. They entered into a marriage of convenience to form Czechoslovakia after World War I. The union benefited both partners. But Slovakia was less affluent and advanced. Cultural differences separated the two regions, too. They never managed to bridge these gaps fully. After the "Velvet Revolution," Czechs and Slovaks finally chose to go their separate ways. On 1 January 1993 they established the Czech Republic and the Republic of Slovakia. People called it "the Velvet Divorce." The two countries get along well. Both are members of NATO and the EU.

The Status of Democracy and Human Rights in the Former Warsaw Pact Nations and Albania

Poland and Czechoslovakia had better organized pro-democracy forces than other Eastern European states. But that did not prevent the others from making the transition after communism fell.

Hungary

Like Poland and Czechoslovakia, some Warsaw Pact countries fostered the kind of political culture that allowed them to push for freedoms as well. For instance, soon after the establishment of the Warsaw Pact, Hungary tested the limits of Soviet control. A reformist leader, Imre Nagy, had come to power in 1953. He broke with the Stalinist policies of the prior regime.

But in the fall of 1956 the Soviets invaded Hungary. It was a much more brutal attack than the invasion that would end the Prague Spring in 1968. Some 200,000 Hungarians fled to the West. Nagy was arrested and, after a closed trial, executed in 1958. Hardliners took power again and carried out severe reprisals against the reformers.

Thirty years later, however, Hungary got another chance. It successfully changed to a Western-style parliamentary democracy. It was the first, and the smoothest, shift within the former Soviet bloc.

By 1987 activists within the Communist Party and among Budapest intellectuals were calling for change. In 1988 the parliament adopted a package of democratic reforms, including freedom of assembly and the press. A new electoral law and a radical revision of the constitution were other key features. In 1989 the Soviet Union promised to withdraw its troops from Hungary by June 1991.

Late in the summer of 1989 a national roundtable met. Made up of representatives of political parties of all persuasions, plus six social groups, it met to plan for free elections and a transition to democracy. Hungary held its first free parliamentary elections in 1990. It's repeated the process regularly ever since.

Romania

Romania's transition to democracy was less smooth. It followed the collapse of communism elsewhere in Eastern Europe in the late summer and fall of 1989. It all started with a mid-December protest in Timisoara, Romania's second-largest city. The immediate issue was the forced relocation of an ethnic Hungarian pastor. That protest grew into a countrywide uprising against Nicolae Ceausescu's regime. The crowd swept him from power. He and his wife were executed on 25 December 1989 after a cursory military trial. Confused street fighting killed about 1,500 people.

A time-exposure photo shows a stream of traffic flowing through a square in Bucharest, Romania.
Photo by Robert Harbison / © 1990 The Christian Science Monitor

Romania's transition to democracy was less smooth than elsewhere in Eastern Europe. President Nicolae Ceausescu and his wife were executed after an uprising in 1989; about 1,500 people died in confused street fighting.

A group calling itself the National Salvation Front set itself up as an impromptu governing coalition. It proclaimed the restoration of democracy and freedom. The group also dissolved the Communist Party and transferred its assets to the state.

Romania had not been home to much activism of the sort that helped the Poles and Czechs. That made Romania's swift progress after communism's fall all the more remarkable. However, there's also been troubling evidence of backsliding on democratic reforms since 2007. That's when Romania joined the EU. Critics fret that Romania "cleaned up its act" to get into NATO and the EU, but now is reverting to bad habits.

Bulgaria

Bulgaria's "Euro-Atlantic" path, by contrast, has been straighter and smoother. Bulgaria and Romania both joined NATO in 2004 and the EU in 2007.

Under the by-the-book Communist leadership of Todor Zhivkov, Bulgaria was a classic Soviet satellite. But its shift away from communism was similar to that of other countries. It had a serious economic crisis in 1996–97, which it worked through with international help. Today Bulgaria attracts American and European investment. It's also an active partner in US-led operations in Iraq and Afghanistan and in UN-led peacekeeping operations in the Balkans.

Albania

The last former communist nation to consider is Albania. Like Yugoslavia, it was never occupied by the Soviets during World War II. And it shared no border with the Soviet Union. That gave Albania, despite its poverty and general backwardness, some freedom to maneuver.

Also like Yugoslavia, Albania had one leader who ruled from World War II until his death in the 1980s. Albania's Tito was Enver Hoxha. He was an absolute dictator, but he managed to hold the country together.

When the Soviets broke with China in 1962, Albania sided with China. For years, China was Albania's only real ally. Albania pulled out of the Warsaw Pact in 1968. Ten years later, however, Albania broke with China, too.

Albania got its first democratically elected president in 1992. The country undertook major reform but then suffered some serious problems around 1997. A series of pyramid schemes defrauded investors all over the country. There was an infrastructure crisis as well. It led to people raiding public works for building materials. Things got so bad that armed revolts broke out all over. It took intense international mediation and a UN multinational protection force to restore order.

Albania is on a generally progressive path now, but it is still one of the poorest countries in Europe. Years of isolation have taken their toll. Albania joined NATO in 2009 and as of this writing has applied to join the EU.

Germany: East Meets West

As it left communism behind, East Germany had an advantage over the other former communist countries. West Germany simply absorbed it after the fall of the Berlin Wall.

On 7 October 1989 the leadership of East Berlin celebrated the fortieth anniversary of East Germany. It would be the country's last birthday. But Party leader Erich Honecker showed no signs he saw the end coming. Instead, in his speech for the East's anniversary, Honecker blasted West Germans. They were encouraging anticommunist protesters in the East, he said. "Socialism," he said, "will be halted in its course neither by ox, nor ass."

Mikhail Gorbachev was there, visiting from Moscow. He shot back a retort that has since become proverbial in Germany: *Wer zu spät kommt, den bestraft das Leben*. "Life punishes him who comes too late."

East Germany had the same kind of grassroots activists as the Poles and the Czechs. Two days after the fortieth birthday events, 70,000 protesters shouting "We are the people" demonstrated in Leipzig. Police held their fire. It was clear the regime's days were numbered. The Leipzig crowds reached 100,000 the following week. On 4 November more than 1 million Germans marched in East Berlin. They demanded democracy and free elections. On 7 November the East German government resigned. On 8 November the Politburo (leadership of the Communist Party) followed suit. The next day, on 9 November, officials opened the gates of the Berlin Wall. Anyone who wanted to could simply walk through. In less than a year, on 3 October 1990, Germany once again became a single country.

A man sits astride the Berlin Wall yelling *"Freiheit"* ("freedom") in 1989, only days after the first concrete slabs were wrenched from the famous barrier between East and West Germany.
Photo by R. Norman Matheny / © 1989 The Christian Science Monitor

Less than a year later, Germany once again became a single country.

New democracies and members in NATO and the EU expand the US roster of friends overseas. Despite wars between the United States and various countries in Europe, the United States and the Continent have grown into fast friends, strong trading partners, and even stronger allies over time. Both regions face numerous challenges in the decades ahead, ranging from common terrorist threats to mounting energy needs. Both also share the opportunity to more firmly guard long-held freedoms—from the liberty to express opinions; practice religion openly; publish newspapers, magazines, and books, both in print and online; and to freely assemble, among many other rights.

The United States and Europe will undoubtedly quarrel over many issues, as they have done all along. But common values and challenges, along with the strong historical, economic, cultural, and ethnic ties between the United States and Europe, promise close American-European relations and cooperation in the decades to come.

With this lesson, you've completed your introductory tour of the world's cultures, religions, languages, economic systems, and political structures. You've read a bit about the different ways people in various countries think and act, and why they often don't see things the way Americans do. You've studied some of the many environmental and economic challenges facing different regions of the world, and the role poverty often plays in those challenges.

Whether you go on to college after high school or enter the world of work, what you have learned in this course will benefit you as a citizen, manager, and employee. You'll have a deeper understanding of the forces affecting your country and the rest of the world today. You'll be better able to interpret the news reports you see and hear regarding events overseas. And you'll be more informed about the challenges your elected representatives face in dealing with them.

Of course, this course has only scratched the surface—there is so much more to learn about the rest of the world. All those involved in creating this book hope it whets your appetite to study even more about other countries—and the fascinating people who live in them.

Lesson 5 Review

Using complete sentences, answer the following questions on a sheet of paper.

1. The German chancellor was proved right in what prediction he made after his country decided to resume unrestricted submarine warfare in 1917?
2. How did George Washington figure into the debate on whether the United States should join the League of Nations?
3. Which mission change did NATO find itself in the midst of after the Soviet Union and the Warsaw Pact dissolved?
4. Which six members of the EU are not members of NATO?
5. Why is much of US-EU trade "intra-industry" trade?
6. What was the European Economic Community's share of foreign direct investment in the United States in the early 1990s? Which two European countries were the largest investors?
7. What did the Gdansk Agreement let Poles do?
8. What were the Helsinki Accords?

Applying Your Learning

9. Do you think the United States should intervene militarily overseas to protect human rights, as it did in the Balkans? Why or why not?

References

Introduction: What Is Global Awareness?

Ancient Egypt. (n.d.). The British Museum. Retrieved 7 January 2009 from http://www.britishmuseum.org/explore/world_cultures/africa/ancient_egypt.aspx

Ancient Greece. (n.d.). The British Museum. Retrieved 7 January 2009 from http://www.britishmuseum.org/explore/world_cultures/europe/ancient_greece.aspx

Ancient Rome. (n.d.). The British Museum. Retrieved 7 January 2009 from http://www.britishmuseum.org/explore/world_cultures/europe/ancient_rome.aspx

Glendon, M. A. (2001). *A world made new: Eleanor Roosevelt and the Universal Declaration of Human Rights*. New York: Random House.

Heatwole, C. A. (n.d.). *Culture: A geographical perspective*. Retrieved 7 January 2009 from http://www.emsc.nysed.gov/ciai/socst/grade3/geograph.html

Hirst, K. K. (2009). *Overview of the Inca*. About.com: Archaeology. Retrieved 15 January 2009 from http://archaeology.about.com/od/incaarchaeology/a/inca_empire.htm

Imperial China. (n.d.). The British Museum. Retrieved 7 January 2009 from http://www.britishmuseum.org/explore/world_cultures/asia/imperial_china.aspx

Jervis, N. (n.d.). *What is a culture?* Retrieved 7 January 2009 from http://www.emsc.nysed.gov/ciai/socst/grade3/whatisa.html

Literacy. (2009). *The World Factbook*. Retrieved 30 January 2009 from https://www.cia.gov/library/publications/the-world-factbook/fields/2103.html

The modern era. (n.d.). The British Museum. Retrieved 7 January 2009 from http://www.britishmuseum.org/explore/world_cultures/general/modern_era.aspx

Mughal India. (n.d.). The British Museum. Retrieved 7 January 2009 from http://www.britishmuseum.org/explore/world_cultures/asia/mughal_india.aspx

Native North America. (n.d.). The British Museum. Retrieved 7 January 2009 from http://www.britishmuseum.org/explore/world_cultures/the_americas/native_north_america.aspx

Origins of modern air pollution regulations. (2007, December 17). US Environmental Protection Agency. Retrieved 7 January 2009 from http://www.epa.gov/air/oaqps/eog/course422/apc1.html

Reynolds, A. (2002, September). A brief history of environmentalism. *Channel 4*. Retrieved 7 January 2009 from http://www.channel4.com/science/microsites/S/science/nature/environment.html

What is the WTO? (n.d.). World Trade Organization. Retrieved 20 April 2006 from http://www.wto.org/english/thewto_e/whatis_e/whatis_e.htm

World civilizations: An Internet classroom and anthology. (n.d.). Washington State University. Retrieved 15 January 2009 from http://www.wsu.edu/~dee/MESO/SUMER.HTM

Chapter 1, Lesson 1—The Middle East: An Introduction

Ancient Rome. (n.d.). The British Museum. Retrieved 20 January 2009 from http://www.britishmuseum.org/explore/world_cultures/europe/ancient_rome.aspx

The Balfour Declaration. (n.d.). Yale Law School. Retrieved 20 January 2009 from http://avalon.law.yale.edu/20th_century/balfour.asp

Bazzi, M. A. (2008, May 20). The heart of Lebanon's strife. *The Christian Science Monitor*. Retrieved 20 January 2009 from http://www.csmonitor.com/2008/0520/p09s02-coop.html

Carter, J. (1980, January 23). *State of the Union Address*. Retrieved 20 January 2009 from http://www.jimmycarterlibrary.org/documents/speeches/su80jec.phtml

Hemingway, C., & Hemingway, S. (2004). *The rise of Macedonia and the conquests of Alexander the Great*. Retrieved 20 January 2009 from http://www.metmuseum.org/TOAH/hd/alex/hd_alex.htm

Israel: Profile. (2007). US Department of State Background Notes. Retrieved 20 January 2009 from http://www.state.gov/r/pa/ei/bgn/3581.htm#history

Jordan: Transjordan. (1989). Library of Congress Country Studies. Retrieved 20 January 2009 from http://lcweb2.loc.gov/cgi-bin/query/r?frd/cstdy:@field(DOCID+jo0017)

Metz, H. C. (Ed.). (1989). *A country study: Jordan*. Washington, DC: Library of Congress. Retrieved 20 January 2009 from http://lcweb2.loc.gov/cgi-bin/query/r?frd/cstdy:@field(DOCID+jo0018)

Metz, H. C. (Ed.). (1990). *A country study: Egypt*. Washington, DC: Library of Congress. Retrieved 20 January 2009 from http://lcweb2.loc.gov/cgi-bin/query/r?frd/cstdy:@field(DOCID+eg0036)

Religion & ethics: Christianity. (n.d.). *British Broadcasting Corporation*. Retrieved 20 January 2009 from http://www.bbc.co.uk/religion/religions/christianity/

Religion & ethics: Islam. (n.d.). *British Broadcasting Corporation*. Retrieved 20 January 2009 from http://www.bbc.co.uk/religion/religions/islam/

Religion & ethics: Judaism. (n.d.). *British Broadcasting Corporation*. Retrieved 20 January 2009 from http://www.bbc.co.uk/religion/religions/judaism/

Roman Egypt. (2004). The Metropolitan Museum of Art. Retrieved 20 January 2009 from http://www.metmuseum.org/TOAH/hd/regy/hd_regy.htm

Syria: Profile. (2007). US Department of State Background Notes. Retrieved 20 January 2009 from http://www.state.gov/r/pa/ei/bgn/3580.htm#history

Thornton, T. (2008, December 9). *History of the Middle East database: World War I and the early mandate period*. Northfield Mount Hermon School. Retrieved 20 January 2009 from http://www.nmhschool.org/tthornton/mehistorydatabase/world_war_i_and_the_early_mandat.php

Turkey: The Ottoman Empire. (1995). Library of Congress Country Studies. Retrieved 20 January 2009 from http://lcweb2.loc.gov/frd/cs/trtoc.html

Who are the Kurds? (1999). *The Washington Post*. Retrieved 20 January 2009 from http://www.washingtonpost.com/wp-srv/inatl/daily/feb99/kurdprofile.htm

Who's Who in Iraq: Assyrians. (2004). *British Broadcasting Corporation*. Retrieved 20 January 2009 from http://news.bbc.co.uk/2/hi/middle_east/3770907.stm

Who's Who in Iraq: Turkmen. (2004). *British Broadcasting Corporation*. Retrieved 20 January 2009 from http://news.bbc.co.uk/1/hi/world/middle_east/3770923.stm

Chapter 1, Lesson 2—The Arab-Israeli Conflict

History of Middle East conflict. (2001, February 7). *British Broadcasting Corporation*. Retrieved 27 January 2009 from http://news.bbc.co.uk/1/hi/in_depth/middle_east/2001/israel_and_the_palestinians/340237.stm

Israel: Profile. (2007). US Department of State Background Notes. Retrieved 27 January 2009 from http://www.state.gov/r/pa/ei/bgn/3581.htm#history

Llewellyn, T. (1998, April 20). Israel builds a nation. *British Broadcasting Corporation*. Retrieved 27 January 2009 from http://news.bbc.co.uk/1/hi/events/israel_at_50/history/78608.stm

Llewellyn, T. (1998, April 20). Israel in war and peace. *British Broadcasting Corporation*. Retrieved 27 January 2009 from http://news.bbc.co.uk/1/hi/events/israel_at_50/history/78627.stm

Metz, H. C. (Ed.). (1990). *A country study: Egypt*. Washington, DC: Library of Congress. Retrieved 27 January 2009 from http://lcweb2.loc.gov/cgi-bin/query/r?frd/cstdy:@field(DOCID+eg0036)

Metz, H. C. (Ed.). (1990). *A country study: Israel*. Washington, DC: Library of Congress. Retrieved 27 January 2009 from http://lcweb2.loc.gov/frd/cs/iltoc.html

Second Arab Oil Embargo, 1973–1974. (n.d.). US Department of State. Retrieved 27 January 2009 from http://www.state.gov/r/pa/ho/time/dr/96057.htm

Chapter 1, Lesson 3—The Persian Gulf Wars

Bush calls end to 'major combat' (speech transcript). (2003, May 2). *Cable News Network*. Retrieved 4 February 2009 from http://www.cnn.com/2003/WORLD/meast/05/01/sprj.irq.main/

Bush: 'Leave Iraq within 48 hours' (speech transcript). (2003, March 17). *Cable News Network*. Retrieved 4 February 2009 from http://www.cnn.com/2003/WORLD/meast/03/17/sprj.irq.bush.transcript/

Friedman, T. L. (1990, August 6). The Iraqi invasion: Bush, hinting force, declares Iraqi assault 'Will not stand'; Proxy in Kuwait issues threat. *The New York Times*. Retrieved 4 February 2009 from http://query.nytimes.com/gst/fullpage.html?res=9C0CE2DD1E30F935A3575BC0A966958260&sec=&spon=&pagewanted=all

Gunning for Saddam. (2001, October). *PBS Frontline*. Retrieved 4 February 2009 from http://www.pbs.org/wgbh/pages/frontline/shows/gunning/interviews/butler.html

Iraq: Profile. (2008). US Department of State Background Notes. Retrieved 4 February 2009 from http://www.state.gov/r/pa/ei/bgn/6804.htm

Kuwait: Profile. (2007). US Department of State Background Notes. Retrieved 4 February 2009 from http://www.state.gov/r/pa/ei/bgn/35876.htm

The long road to war: Chronology. (2005). *PBS Frontline*. Retrieved 4 February 2009 from http://www.pbs.org/wgbh/pages/frontline/shows/longroad/etc/cron.html

Miles, D. (2007, September 10). Petraeus: Surge in Iraq works; Reductions could begin by summer 2008. *American Forces Press Service*. Retrieved 4 February 2009 from http://www.globalsecurity.org/wmd/library/news/iraq/2007/09/iraq-070910-afps04.htm

On This Day 7 June 1981: Israel bombs Baghdad nuclear reactor. (2008). *British Broadcasting Corporation*. Retrieved 4 February 2009 from http://news.bbc.co.uk/onthisday/hi/dates/stories/june/7/newsid_3014000/3014623.stm

On This Day 2 August 1990: Iraq invades Kuwait. (2008). *British Broadcasting Corporation*. Retrieved 4 February 2009 from http://news.bbc.co.uk/onthisday/hi/dates/stories/august/2/newsid_2526000/2526937.stm

Operation Provide Comfort. (2005). GlobalSecurity.org. Retrieved 8 February 2009 from http://www.globalsecurity.org/military/ops/provide_comfort.htm

Padden, B. (2006, August 28). Kurds push to make strong legal case of genocide against Saddam. *Voice of America*. Retrieved 4 February 2009 from http://www.globalsecurity.org/wmd/library/news/iraq/2006/08/iraq-060828-voa01.htm

Pickering testifies on Gulf cease-fire implementation. (1991, July 18). GlobalSecurity.org. Retrieved 4 February 2009 from http://www.globalsecurity.org/wmd/library/news/iraq/1991/910718-190813.htm

Senanayake, S. (2006, November 2). Iraq: Ethnic tensions increasing in oil-rich city. *Radio Free Europe/Radio Liberty*. Retrieved 4 February 2009 from http://www.rferl.org/content/article/1072472.html

Susman, T. (2009, February 6). Maliki's bloc prevails in Iraq elections. *Los Angeles Times*. Retrieved 6 February 2009 from http://www.latimes.com/news/nationworld/world/la-fg-iraq-elections6-2009feb06,0,2550359.story

Timeline: Iraq. (2009). *British Broadcasting Corporation*. Retrieved 4 February 2009 from http://news.bbc.co.uk/1/hi/world/middle_east/737483.stm

UN Security Council Resolution 1441. (2003). US Department of State. Retrieved 4 February 2009 from http://2001-2009.state.gov/p/io/rls/fs/2003/17926.htm

Chapter 1, Lesson 4—Islamic Fundamentalism and Terrorism

The 9/11 Commission Report. (2004). National Commission on Terrorist Attacks Upon the United States. Retrieved 11 February 2009 from http://govinfo.library.unt.edu/911/report/911Report_Ch2.htm

Ahlers, M. M. (2009, January 2). AirTran apologizes to Muslim family removed from plane. *Cable News Network*. Retrieved 16 February 2009 from http://www.cnn.com/2009/US/01/02/family.grounded/index.html

Country reports on terrorism 2000. (2001). US State Department, Office of the Coordinator for Counterterrorism. Retrieved 11 February 2009 from http://www.state.gov/s/ct/rls/crt/2000/2419.htm

Country reports on terrorism 2007. (2008). US State Department, Office of the Coordinator for Counterterrorism. Retrieved 11 February 2009 from http://www.state.gov/s/ct/rls/crt/2007/103704.htm

On This Day 26 February 1993: World Trade Center bomb terrorises New York. (2008). *British Broadcasting Corporation*. Retrieved 11 February 2009 from http://news.bbc.co.uk/onthisday/hi/dates/stories/february/26/newsid_2516000/2516469.stm

President Bush: September 11, 2001 (speech transcript). (2001, September 11). *The NewsHour with Jim Lehrer*. Retrieved 11 February 2009 from http://www.pbs.org/newshour/bb/military/terroristattack/bush_speech.html

The terrorist enemy. (n.d.). US State Department, Office of the Coordinator for Counterterrorism. Retrieved 11 February 2009 from http://www.state.gov/s/ct/enemy/index.htm

Wahhabi. (2005). GlobalSecurity.org. Retrieved 11 February 2009 from http://www.globalsecurity.org/military/world/gulf/wahhabi.htm

Chapter 1, Lesson 5—US Interests and Regional Issues in the Middle East

Adams, P. (2000, January 9). Water wars and peace. *British Broadcasting Corporation*. Retrieved 18 February 2000 from http://news.bbc.co.uk/1/hi/programmes/from_our_own_correspondent/596039.stm

Allan, T. (1998, March). Watersheds and problemsheds: Explaining the absence of armed conflict over water in the Middle East. *Middle East Review of International Affairs*, 2(1). Retrieved 18 February 2009 from http://www.biu.ac.il/SOC/besa/meria/journal/1998/issue1/jv2n1a7.html#author

Brief history. (n.d.). The Organization of the Petroleum Exporting Countries. Retrieved 18 February 2009 from http://www.opec.org/aboutus/history/history.htm

Crude oil and total petroleum imports top 15 countries. (2009). Energy Information Administration, US Department of Energy. Retrieved 18 February 2009 from http://www.eia.doe.gov/pub/oil_gas/petroleum/data_publications/company_level_imports/current/import.html

ElBaradei, M. (2007, July 12). *The International Atomic Energy Agency: Fifty years of atoms for peace*. International Atomic Energy Agency. Retrieved 18 February 2009 from http://www.iaea.org/NewsCenter/Statements/2007/ebsp2007n009.html

Iran: Profile. (2008). US Department of State Background Notes. Retrieved 18 February 2009 from http://www.state.gov/r/pa/ei/bgn/5314.htm

Islam and human rights. (2004). NO to Political Islam Campaign. Retrieved 18 February 2009 from http://www.ntpi.org/html/humanrights1.html

Kirby, A. (2000, June 2). Dawn of a thirsty century. *British Broadcasting Corporation*. Retrieved 18 February 2009 from http://news.bbc.co.uk/1/hi/sci/tech/755497.stm

Muir, J. (2002, July 8). Iran court slaps ban on dancer. *British Broadcasting Corporation*. Retrieved 18 February 2009 from http://news.bbc.co.uk/1/hi/world/middle_east/2115973.stm

Muslims speak out: What Islam really says about violence, Islam, and other religions. (n.d.). The Pew Forum on Religion and Public Life. Retrieved 18 February 2009 from http://newsweek.washingtonpost.com/onfaith/muslims_speak_out/2007/07/muslims_views_of_human_rights.html

Reduce oil dependence costs. (n.d.). US Department of Energy. Retrieved 18 February 2009 from http://www.fueleconomy.gov/FEG/oildep.shtml

The religion-state relationship and the right to freedom of religion or belief: A comparative textual analysis of the constitutions of predominantly Muslim countries (Executive Summary). (2005, March). United States Commission on International Religious Freedom. Retrieved 18 February 2009 from http://www.uscirf.gov/index.php?option=com_content&task=view&id=1887&Itemid=1

Thornton, T. (2007, July 18). *History of the Middle East database: 'Water wars' in the Middle East*. Northfield Mount Hermon School. Retrieved 18 February 2009 from http://www.nmhschool.org/tthornton/mehistorydatabase/waterwars.php

Treaty on the Non-Proliferation of Nuclear Weapons (NPT). (n.d.). US State Department. Retrieved 18 February 2009 from http://www.state.gov/t/isn/trty/16281.htm

Turkey, Iraq, and Syria to form collaborative water institute. (2008, March 13). Water for the Ages. Retrieved 18 February 2009 from http://waterfortheages.org/2008/03/13/turkey-iraq-and-syria-to-form-collaborative-water-institute/

Water resources: General summary of the Near East region. (n.d.). Food and Agricultural Organization of the United Nations. Retrieved 18 February 2009 from http://www.fao.org/nr/water/aquastat/regions/neast/index3.stm

Weber, C. (n.d.). What is OPEC? A brief history of the organization that controls the world's oil. *CBS News*. Retrieved 18 February 2009 from http://www.cbsnews.com/stories/2001/01/17/world/main264972.shtml

Welsh, P. (2000, June 2). Water conflict in Middle East. *British Broadcasting Corporation*. Retrieved 18 February 2009 from http://news.bbc.co.uk/1/hi/world/middle_east/764142.stm

Where does my gasoline come from? (2008). Energy Information Administration, US Department of Energy. Retrieved 18 February 2009 from http://www.eia.doe.gov/bookshelf/brochures/gasoline/index.html

Wolf, A., & Newton, J. (n.d.). *Case study of transboundary dispute resolution: The Tigris-Euphrates basin*. Oregon State University: The Program in Water Conflict Management and Transformation. Retrieved 18 February 2009 from http://www.transboundarywaters.orst.edu/research/case_studies/Tigris-Euphrates_New.htm

Wood, R. (2009). *Persecution of religious minorities in Iran*. US State Department. Retrieved 18 February 2009 from http://www.state.gov/r/pa/prs/ps/2009/02/117332.htm

Chapter 2, Lesson 1–Asia: An Introduction

Chinese scientists unearth 4,000-year-old noodle dish (suggests pasta invented in China). (2005, October 13). *KTVU San Francisco/Free Republic*. Retrieved 27 February 2009 from http://www.freerepublic.com/focus/f-news/1503158/posts

Ford, P. (2008, December 18). Pastor's private worship puts him under public scrutiny. *The Christian Science Monitor*. Retrieved 25 February 2009 from http://www.csmonitor.com/2008/1218/p25s10-woap.html

Gordon, R. G., Jr. (Ed.). (2005). *Ethnologue: Languages of the world* (15th ed.). Dallas, Texas: SIL International. Retrieved 25 February 2009 from http://en.wikipedia.org/wiki/Ethnologue_list_of_most_spoken_languages

Huang, C. (2008, July 2). Christianity in a Chinese workplace? For some. *The Christian Science Monitor*. Retrieved 25 February 2009 from http://www.csmonitor.com/2008/0702/p01s05-woap.html

The mystery of the sweet potato. (2004, June 11). *British Broadcasting Corporation*. Retrieved 27 February 2009 from http://www.bbc.co.uk/dna/h2g2/A1984421

Religion & ethics—Buddhism. (n.d.). *British Broadcasting Corporation*. Retrieved 25 February 2009 from http://www.bbc.co.uk/religion/religions/buddhism/

Religion & ethics—Hinduism. (n.d.). *British Broadcasting Corporation*. Retrieved 25 February 2009 from http://www.bbc.co.uk/religion/religions/hinduism/

Religion & ethics—Shinto. (n.d.). *British Broadcasting Corporation*. Retrieved 25 February 2009 from http://www.bbc.co.uk/religion/religions/shinto/

Religion & ethics—Taoism. (n.d.). *British Broadcasting Corporation*. Retrieved 25 February 2009 from http://www.bbc.co.uk/religion/religions/taoism/

Religion & ethics—Zoroastrianism. (n.d.). *British Broadcasting Corporation*. Retrieved 25 February 2009 from http://www.bbc.co.uk/religion/religions/zoroastrianism/

Richey, J. (2006). Confucius (c. 551–479 BCE). In *The Internet Encyclopedia of Philosophy*. Retrieved 25 February 2009 from http://www.iep.utm.edu/c/confuciu.htm

Teachings: The Noble Eightfold Path. (n.d.). The Buddhist Society. Retrieved 4 March 2009 from http://www.thebuddhistsociety.org/resources/index.html

The World Factbook. (2009). Washington, DC: US Central Intelligence Agency. Retrieved 26 February 2009 from https://www.cia.gov/library/publications/the-world-factbook/index.html

Chapter 2, Lesson 2–Japan, Korea, and China

Branigan, T. (2009, July 13). Kim Jong-il 'has pancreatic cancer.' *The Guardian*. Retrieved 20 August 2009 from http://www.guardian.co.uk/world/2009/jul/13/kim-jong-il-cancer

China: Profile. (2009). US Department of State Background Notes. Retrieved 4 March 2009 from http://www.state.gov/r/pa/ei/bgn/18902.htm

Commodore Perry and the opening of Japan. (2002, November 25). Washington, DC: Department of the Navy—Naval Historical Center. Retrieved 4 March 2009 from http://www.history.navy.mil/branches/teach/ends/opening.htm

Dolan, R. E., & Worden, R. L. (Eds.). (1990). *A country study: Japan*. Washington, DC: Library of Congress. Retrieved 5 March 2009 from http://lcweb2.loc.gov/frd/cs/jptoc.html

Japan: Profile. (2008). US Department of State Background Notes. Retrieved 5 March 2009 from http://www.state.gov/r/pa/ei/bgn/4142.htm

Modern history sourcebook: Emperor Qian Long's letter to King George III, 1793. (n.d.). Wellesley College. Retrieved 5 March 2009 from http://www.wellesley.edu/Polisci/wj/China/208/READINGS/qianlong.html

North Korea: Profile. (2009). US Department of State Background Notes. Retrieved 5 March 2009 from http://www.state.gov/r/pa/ei/bgn/2792.htm

Savada, A. M. (Ed.). (1990). *A country study: North Korea*. Washington, DC: Library of Congress. Retrieved 5 March 2009 from http://lcweb2.loc.gov/frd/cs/kptoc.html

Savada, A. M., & Shaw, W. (Eds.). (1990). *A country study: South Korea*. Washington, DC: Library of Congress. Retrieved 5 March 2009 from http://lcweb2.loc.gov/frd/cs/krtoc.html

South Korea: Profile. (2008). US Department of State Background Notes. Retrieved 5 March 2009 from http://www.state.gov/r/pa/ei/bgn/2800.htm

Worden, R. L., Savada, A. M., & Dolan, R. E. (Eds.). (1987). *A country study: China*. Washington, DC: Library of Congress. Retrieved 5 March 2009 from http://lcweb2.loc.gov/frd/cs/cntoc.html

Chapter 2, Lesson 3–India, Pakistan, and Afghanistan

The adventures of Hamza. (2002). Smithsonian Institution, Freer Gallery of Art and Arthur M. Sackler Gallery. Retrieved 12 March 2009 from http://www.asia.si.edu/press/prhamza.htm

Afghanistan: Profile. (2008). US Department of State Background Notes. Retrieved 13 March 2009 from http://www.state.gov/r/pa/ei/bgn/5380.htm

The art of the Mughals before 1600. (n.d.). Department of Islamic Art, The Metropolitan Museum of Art. Retrieved 12 March 2009 from http://www.metmuseum.org/toah/hd/mugh/hd_mugh.htm

Baldauf, S. (2002, December 12). Hard-line pro-Hindu rhetoric colors Indian elections. *The Christian Science Monitor*. Retrieved 13 March 2009 from http://www.csmonitor.com/2002/1212/p07s02-wosc.html

Bangladesh: Profile. (2008). US Department of State Background Notes. Retrieved 11 March 2009 from http://www.state.gov/r/pa/ei/bgn/3452.htm

Blood, P. (Ed.). (1994). *A country study: Pakistan*. Washington DC: Library of Congress. Retrieved 9 March 2009 from http://lcweb2.loc.gov/frd/cs/pktoc.html

Blood, P. (Ed.). (1997). *A country study: Afghanistan*. Washington, DC: Library of Congress. Retrieved 13 March 2009 from http://lcweb2.loc.gov/frd/cs/aftoc.html

Heitzman, J., & Worden, R. L. (Eds.). (1988). *A country study: Bangladesh*. Washington, DC: Library of Congress. Retrieved 11 March 2009 from http://lcweb2.loc.gov/frd/cs/bdtoc.html

Heitzman, J., & Worden, R. L. (Eds.). (1995). *A country study: India*. Washington, DC: Library of Congress. Retrieved 9 March 2009 from http://lcweb2.loc.gov/frd/cs/intoc.html

India: Profile. (2009). US Department of State Background Notes. Retrieved 9 March 2009 from http://www.state.gov/r/pa/ei/bgn/3454.htm

Mohandas Gandhi. (1994, January 1). *Historic world leaders*. Gale Research. Retrieved 14 March 2009 from http://galenet.galegroup.com/servlet/BioRC?vrsn=149&OP=contains&locID=arl_remote&srchtp=name&ca=2&c=6&AI=U13034200&NA=gandhi&ste=12&tbst=prp&tab=1&docNum=K1616000227&bConts=59

Mohandas Karamchand Gandhi. (1998, December 12). In *Encyclopedia of World Biography* (2nd ed.). Gale Research. Retrieved 14 March 2009 from http://galenet.galegroup.com/servlet/BioRC?vrsn=149&OP=contains&locID=arl_remote&srchtp=name&ca=2&c=5&AI=U13034200&NA=gandhi&ste=12&tbst=prp&tab=1&docNum=K1631002423&bConts=59

Pakistan: Profile. (2008). US Department of State Background Notes. Retrieved 9 March 2009 from http://www.state.gov/r/pa/ei/bgn/3453.htm

Partition still casts shadow on India-Pakistan ties. (2008, December 17). *National Public Radio*. Retrieved 13 March 2009 from http://www.npr.org/templates/story/story.php?storyId=98357841

Ray, S. (2008, November 11). The rise of India's Saffro-Nazis. *Asia Sentinel*. Retrieved 12 March 2009 from http://www.asiasentinel.com/index.php?option=com_content&task=view&id=1537&Itemid=174

Sardar, M. (n.d.). *The art of the Mughals after 1600*. The Metropolitan Museum of Art. Retrieved 12 March 2009 from http://www.metmuseum.org/toah/hd/mugh_2/hd_mugh_2.htm

Sengupta, S., Worth, R. F., & McDonald, M. (2008, December 12). India calls on Pakistan to do more on terror. *The International Herald Tribune*. Retrieved 12 March 2009 from http://www.iht.com/articles/2008/12/11/asia/mumbai.php

Taj Mahal. (2008). University of California at Los Angeles. Retrieved 11 March 2009 from http://www.sscnet.ucla.edu/southasia/Culture/Archit/TajM.html

Wolpert, S. (1991). *India*. Berkeley, CA: University of California Press. Retrieved 9 March 2009 from http://books.google.com/books?id=HmkL1tp2Nl4C&pg=PA41&lpg=PA41&dq=Mughals+Christians+Muslims+Hindus+Wolpert&source=bl&ots=mH2PrW_JJ-&sig=0t6dTjHKEccqbjMr7E9tejLuHk8&hl=en&ei=SqpxSuL_NI3GMJqtkbEM&sa=X&oi=book_result&ct=result&resnum=1

Chapter 2, Lesson 4—Environmental and Social Issues in Asia

Afghanistan's maternal and child mortality rates soar. (2005, August 4). UNICEF. Retrieved 16 March 2009 from http://www.unicef.org/media/media_27853.html

Baldauf, S. (2004, February 10). India's new loos save lives. *The Christian Science Monitor*. Retrieved 17 March 2009 from http://www.csmonitor.com/2004/0210/p06s01-wosc.html

Beijing Olympics get big green tick. (2009, February 18). United Nations Environment Program. Retrieved 20 March 2009 from http://www.unep.org/Documents.Multilingual/Default.asp?DocumentID=562&ArticleID=6086&l=en&t=long

Blood, P. (Ed.). (1994). *A country study: Pakistan*. Washington, DC: Library of Congress. Retrieved 15 March 2009 from http://lcweb2.loc.gov/frd/cs/pktoc.html

Broughton, E. (2005, May 10). The Bhopal disaster and its aftermath: A review. *Environmental Health*. Retrieved 17 March 2009 from http://www.pubmedcentral.nih.gov/articlerender.fcgi?artid=1142333

China environment. (n.d.). The World Bank. Retrieved 15 March 2009 from http://web.worldbank.org/WBSITE/EXTERNAL/COUNTRIES/EASTASIAPACIFICEXT/EXTEAPREGTOPENVIRONMENT/0,,contentMDK:20266322~menuPK:537827~pagePK:34004173~piPK:34003707~theSitePK:502886,00.html

China: Profile. (2009, January). US Department of State Background Notes. Retrieved 19 March 2009 from http://www.state.gov/r/pa/ei/bgn/18902.htm

China's Three Gorges Dam. (2001). *Cable News Network*. Retrieved 17 March 2009 from http://www.cnn.com/SPECIALS/1999/china.50/asian.superpower/three.gorges/

Forstall, R. L., Greene, R. P., & Pick, J. B. (2004, July). *Which are the largest? Why published populations for major world urban areas vary so greatly*. University of Illinois at Chicago: City Futures Conference. Retrieved 22 March 2009 from http://www.uic.edu/cuppa/cityfutures/papers/webpapers/cityfuturespapers/session3_4/3_4whicharethe.pdf

Green, M. (1986, April 28). Is China looser about birth control? *The New York Times*. Retrieved 19 March 2009 from http://query.nytimes.com/gst/fullpage.html?sec=health&res=9A0DE5DC1E3EF93BA15757C0A960948260

India: Bureau of democracy, human rights, and labor. (2008, March 11). US Department of State. Retrieved 20 March 2009 from http://www.state.gov/g/drl/rls/hrrpt/2007/100614.htm

India: Water. (n.d.). The World Bank. Retrieved 15 March 2009 from http://www.worldbank.org.in/WBSITE/EXTERNAL/COUNTRIES/SOUTHASIAEXT/INDIAEXTN/0,,contentMDK:20668501~pagePK:141137~piPK:141127~theSitePK:295584,00.html

Kelso, P. (2008, August 6). Olympics: Pollution over Beijing? Don't worry, it's only mist, say officials. *The Guardian*. Retrieved 20 March 2009 from http://www.guardian.co.uk/sport/2008/aug/06/olympics2008.china

Khatoon, A. (2005, September 26). Women workforce on the increase. *Dawn*. Retrieved 19 March 2009 from http://www.dawn.com/2005/09/26/ebr16.htm

McElwee, C. R., II. (2008). Who's cleaning up this mess? Rising environmental awareness is affecting business in China. *The China Business Review Online*. Retrieved 17 March 2009 from http://www.chinabusinessreview.com/public/0801/mcelwee.html

Nair, S. (2007). Child sex tourism. Washington, DC: US Department of Justice, Child Exploitation and Obscenity Section. Retrieved 23 March 2009 from http://www.usdoj.gov/criminal/ceos/sextour.html.

Rosegrant, M. W., & Hazell, P. B. R. (2001). *Transforming the rural Asian economy: The unfinished revolution*. International Food Policy Research Institute. Retrieved 19 March 2009 from http://www.ifpri.org/2020/BRIEFS/number69.htm

Trafficking in persons report 2008. (2008). US Department of State. Retrieved 20 March 2009 from http://www.state.gov/g/tip/rls/tiprpt/2008/index.htm

Water pollution in China. (n.d.). Pacific Environment. Retrieved 17 March 2009 from http://www.pacificenvironment.org/article.php?id=1878

Wealth gap 'spreads across Asia.' (2007, August 8). *British Broadcasting Corporation*. Retrieved 19 March 2009 from http://news.bbc.co.uk/1/hi/business/6936525.stm

Chapter 2, Lesson 5—US Interests and Regional Issues in Asia

2007 country reports on human rights practices. (2008). US Department of State. Retrieved 26 March 2009 from http://www.state.gov/g/drl/rls/hrrpt/2007/index.htm

Alford, P. (2006, October 28). North Korean famine, refugees, and international aid. *The Asia Pacific Journal: Japan Focus*. Retrieved 23 March 2009 from http://japanfocus.org/-Peter-Alford/2259

Auto sales: Market data center. (2009, March 3). *Wall Street Journal*. Retrieved 31 March 2009 from http://online.wsj.com/mdc/public/page/2_3022-autosales.html

Bhaskar, U. (2008, December 7). *Amid India-Pakistan tensions, bilateral trade plans put on hold*. Livemint.com. Retrieved 30 March 2009 from http://www.livemint.com/2008/12/07215020/Amid-IndiaPakistan-tensions.html

Cooper, J. C. (2004, March 22). The price of efficiency. *BusinessWeek*. Retrieved 31 March 2009 from http://www.businessweek.com/magazine/content/04_12/b3875603.htm

Countries and issues: East Asia. (n.d.). US Commission on International Religious Freedom. Retrieved 26 March 2009 from http://www.uscirf.gov/index.php?option=com_content&task=view&id=1368&Itemid=1

Countries and issues: South Asia. (n.d.). US Commission on International Religious Freedom. Retrieved 26 March 2009 from http://www.uscirf.gov/index.php?option=com_content&task=view&id=1377&Itemid=1

Countries of particular concern: Democratic People's Republic of Korea. (n.d.). US Commission on International Religious Freedom. Retrieved 26 March 2009 from http://www.uscirf.gov/index.php?option=com_content&task=view&id=2102&Itemid=1

Country reports on terrorism. (2008, April 30). US Department of State. Retrieved 25 March 2009 from http://www.state.gov/s/ct/rls/crt/2007/103711.htm

Demick, B. (2008, November 9). Chronic food shortage shows despite efforts by N. Korea to hide it. *Los Angeles Times*. Retrieved 30 March 2009 from http://www.boston.com/news/world/asia/articles/2008/11/09/chronic_food_shortage_shows_despite_efforts_by_n_korea_to_hide_it/?page=1

Designation of A. Q. Khan and associates for nuclear proliferation activities. (2009, January 12). Office of the Spokesman, US Department of State. Retrieved 28 March 2009 from http://2001-2009.state.gov/r/pa/prs/ps/2009/01/113774.htm

EMC Corporation sets up first South Asia development laboratory outside the US. (2007, November 7). Singapore Economic Development Board. Retrieved 31 March 2009 from http://www.edb.gov.sg/edb/sg/en_uk/index/news/articles/emc_corporation_sets.html

Freedom in the world—Afghanistan (2005). (2004, December 20). Freedom House, Inc.: UNHCR Refworld. Retrieved 25 March 2009 from http://www.unhcr.org/refworld/docid/473c54d6c.html

Glassman, M. (2005, December 20). Another GM lowlight. *Smartmoney*. Retrieved 31 March 2009 from http://www.smartmoney.com/investing/stocks/another-gm-lowlight-18768

Groshen, E. L., Hobijn, B., & McConnell, M. M. (2005, August). *U.S. jobs gained and lost through trade: A net measure*. Federal Reserve Bank of New York: Current Issues in Economics and Finance, 11(8). Retrieved 31 March 2009 from http://www.ny.frb.org/research/current_issues/ci11-8/ci11-8.html

Human rights. (n.d.). US Department of State. Retrieved 26 March 2009 from http://www.state.gov/g/drl/hr/index.htm

India: Profile. (2009). US Department of State Background Notes. Retrieved 23 March 2009 from http://www.state.gov/r/pa/ei/bgn/3454.htm#foreign

Indian nuclear doctrine. (n.d.). GlobalSecurity.org. Retrieved 30 March 2009 from http://www.globalsecurity.org/wmd/world/india/doctrine.htm

Japanese automakers in America: New plants, new jobs, new vehicles. (2006). Japan Automobile Manufacturers Association (JAMA). Retrieved 31 March 2009 from http://www.jama.org/library/brochure_Sep2006.htm

Landay, J. S. (1998, May 12). India rattles nuke saber. *The Christian Science Monitor*. Retrieved 31 March 2009 from http://www.csmonitor.com/1998/0512/051298.us.us.1.html

North Korea: Profile. (2009). US Department of State Background Notes. Retrieved 28 March 2009 from http://www.state.gov/r/pa/ei/bgn/2792.htm

North Korea: 'Six-Party Talks are over.' (2009, July 23). *CBS News*. Retrieved 21 August 2009 from http://www.cbsnews.com/stories/2009/07/23/world/main5181673.shtml

North Korea's nuclear program. (2009, June 16). *The New York Times*. Retrieved 21 August 2009 from http://topics.nytimes.com/topics/news/international/countriesandterritories/northkorea/nuclear_program/index.html

Nuclear weapons doctrine (Pakistan). (n.d.). GlobalSecurity.org. Retrieved 30 March 2009 from http://www.globalsecurity.org/wmd/world/pakistan/doctrine.htm

Pakistan uneasy over Obama's plan. (2009, March 29). *National Public Radio: Weekend Edition Sunday*. Retrieved 30 March 2009 from http://www.npr.org/templates/story/story.php?storyId=102481037

Pan, E., & Bajoria, J. (2008, October 2). *The U.S.-India nuclear deal*. The Council on Foreign Relations. Retrieved 30 March 2009 from http://www.cfr.org/publication/9663/

Resources on India and Pakistan: Recent events leading to India's nuclear tests. (n.d.). Monterey, Calif.: James Martin Center for Nonproliferation Studies. Retrieved 31 March 2009 from http://cns.miis.edu/research/india/bjpchron.htm

Roberts, P. (2005, Fall). Book review of 'Outsourcing America' by Ron Hira and Anil Hira. *The Social Contract Journal, 16*(1). Retrieved 31 March 2009 from http://www.thesocialcontract.com/artman2/publish/tsc1601/article_1354.shtml

Rombel, A. (2003, April 1). United States: Wir[e]less technology provider tries to forge new market. *Global Finance*. Retrieved 30 March 2009 from http://www.allbusiness.com/technology/telecommunications-cell-phones-phone-services/1138781-1.html

Sanctuary, C. (2002, January 4). Contentious line of control. *British Broadcasting Corporation*. Retrieved 30 March 2009 from http://news.bbc.co.uk/2/hi/south_asia/377916.stm

Seok, K. (2008, April 14). *North Korea's transformation: Famine, aid, and markets*. Human Rights Watch. Retrieved 25 March 2009 from http://www.hrw.org/en/news/2008/04/14/north-korea-s-transformation-famine-aid-and-markets

Spire appoints UST Technology to target fast-growing Southeast Asia solar market. (2008, January 29). *Reuters*. Retrieved 31 March 2009 from http://www.reuters.com/article/pressRelease/idUS152811+29-Jan-2008+BW20080129

State sponsors of terrorism overview. (2008, April 30). US Department of State. Retrieved 26 March 2009 from http://www.state.gov/s/ct/rls/crt/2007/103711.htm

UC study assesses ferocious new wave of outsourcing of white-collar jobs. (2003). University of California, Berkeley. Retrieved 28 April 2009 from http://www.universityofcalifornia.edu/news/article/5873

The Universal Declaration of Human Rights. (n.d.). The United Nations. Retrieved 26 March 2009 from http://www.un.org/Overview/rights.html

US takes North Korea off terror list. (2008, October 11). *Cable News Network*. Retrieved 28 March 2009 from http://www.cnn.com/2008/WORLD/asiapcf/10/11/us.north.korea/index.html

U.S. Trade in goods (imports, exports and balance) by country. (2009). US Census Bureau, Foreign Trade Statistics. Retrieved 22 April 2009 from http://www.census.gov/foreign-trade/balance/index.html#C

Chapter 3, Lesson 1—Africa: An Introduction

2006 Minerals Yearbook. (2009). US Geological Survey. Retrieved 6 April 2009 from http://minerals.usgs.gov/minerals/pubs/country/2006/myb3-sum-2006-africa.pdf

Adinlofu, E. (2009, February 11). *Modernity and the 'extended family system.'* Nigerians in America. Retrieved 6 April 2009 from http://www.nigeriansinamerica.com/articles/3239/1/Modernity-and-the-Extended-Family-System/Page1.html

Adow, M. (2005, July 27). Polygamy no fun, admits Ethiopian. *British Broadcasting Corporation*. Retrieved 6 April 2009 from http://news.bbc.co.uk/1/hi/world/africa/4720457.stm

Africa. (2009). In *Microsoft Encarta Online Encyclopedia 2009*. Retrieved 9 April 2009 from http://encarta.msn.com/encyclopedia_761572628_22/africa.html

African languages. (2009). In *Microsoft Encarta Online Encyclopedia 2009*. Retrieved 8 April 2009 from http://encarta.msn.com/encyclopedia_761565449/African_Languages.html

Belief systems: Indigenous, Islamic, Christian. (1997). Africa World Press Guide. Retrieved 8 April 2009 from http://worldviews.igc.org/awpguide/relig.html

Campbell, G. (2006, December 11). The sordid history behind Africa's conflict diamonds. *The Christian Science Monitor*. Retrieved 6 April 2009 from http://www.csmonitor.com/2006/1211/p09s01-coop.html

Harsch, E. (2004, January). Agriculture: Africa's 'engine for growth.' *Africa Recovery, 17*(4). Retrieved 6 April 2009 from http://www.un.org/ecosocdev/geninfo/afrec/vol17no4/174ag.htm

Hunter-Gault, C. (2009, April 5). Treating victims and their rapists in South Africa. *National Public Radio*. Retrieved 6 April 2009 from http://www.npr.org/templates/story/story.php?storyId=102654478

Jenkins, P. (2002, October). The Next Christianity. *The Atlantic, 290*(3). Retrieved 8 April 2009 from http://www.catholiceducation.org/articles/facts/fm0018.html

Johnson, R. W. (2009, April 5). The rise of Jacob Zuma; polygamist, 'Zulu peasant' and president in waiting. *The Sunday Times*. Retrieved 6 April 2009 from http://www.timesonline.co.uk/tol/news/world/africa/article6035797.ece

Natural resources and conflict in Africa: Transforming a peace liability into a peace asset. (2006, June 17–19). United Nations. Retrieved 6 April 2009 from http://www.un.org/africa/osaa/reports/Natural%20Resources%20and%20Conflict%20in%20Africa_%20Cairo%20Conference%20ReportwAnnexes%20Nov%2017.pdf

Polygamy and the president. (2009, March 25). *News 24.com*. Retrieved 6 April 2009 from http://www.news24.com/News24/South_Africa/News/0,,2-7-1442_2491221,00.html

Rabach, N. (2009, January 17). *Are African extended families a blessing or a curse today?* Africa Files. Retrieved 6 April 2009 from http://www.africafiles.org/article.asp?ID=19905

The story of Africa. (n.d.). *British Broadcasting Corporation*. Retrieved 9 April 2009 from http://www.bbc.co.uk/worldservice/specials/1624_story_of_africa/page92.shtml

Tran, P. (2007, March 12). Acceptance of polygamy slowly changes in Muslim Africa. *Voice of America*. Retrieved 6 April 2009 from http://www.voanews.com/english/archive/2007-03/2007-03-12-voa14.cfm

World Bank assistance to agriculture in Sub-Saharan Africa. (2007). The World Bank. Retrieved 6 April 2009 from http://www-wds.worldbank.org/external/default/main?pagePK=64193027&piPK=64187937&theSitePK=523679&menuPK=64187510&searchMenuPK=64187283&theSitePK=523679&entityID=000020953_20071210140256&searchMenuPK=64187283&theSitePK=523679

Chapter 3, Lesson 2—The Shadow of Western Colonialism

Africa, 500–1500. (2001). In *The Encyclopedia of World History*. Retrieved 14 April 2009 from http://www.bartleby.com/67/343.html

Berry, L. (Ed.). (1994). *A country study: Ghana*. Washington, DC: Library of Congress. Retrieved 15 April 2009 from http://lcweb2.loc.gov/frd/cs/ghtoc.html

Byrnes, R. M. (Ed.). (1990). *A country study: Uganda*. Washington, DC: Library of Congress. Retrieved 15 April 2009 from http://lcweb2.loc.gov/frd/cs/ugtoc.html

Byrnes, R. M. (Ed.). (1996). *A country study: South Africa*. Washington, DC: Library of Congress. Retrieved 15 April 2009 from http://lcweb2.loc.gov/frd/cs/zatoc.html

Cameroon: Profile. (2009). US Department of State Background Notes. Retrieved 16 April 2009 from http://www.state.gov/r/pa/ei/bgn/26431.htm

Collelo, T. (Ed.). (1988). *A country study: Chad*. Washington, DC: Library of Congress. Retrieved 15 April from http://lcweb2.loc.gov/frd/cs/tdtoc.html

Country reports on terrorism 2005. (2006, April 28). US Department of State. Retrieved 15 April 2009 from http://www.state.gov/s/ct/rls/crt/2005/64337.htm

Handloff, R. E. (Ed.). (1988). *A country study: Mauritania*. Washington, DC: Library of Congress. Retrieved 15 April 2009 from http://lcweb2.loc.gov/frd/cs/mrtoc.html

Historic figures: Henry Stanley (1841–1904). (n.d.). *British Broadcasting Corporation*. Retrieved 16 April 2009 from http://www.bbc.co.uk/history/historic_figures/stanley_sir_henry_morton.shtml

Meditz, S. W., & Merrill, T. (Eds.). (1993). *A country study: Zaire*. Washington, DC: Library of Congress. Retrieved 15 April 2009 from http://lcweb2.loc.gov/frd/cs/zrtoc.html

Metz, H. C. (Ed.). (1990). *A country study: Egypt*. Washington, DC: Library of Congress. Retrieved 13 April 2009 from http://lcweb2.loc.gov/frd/cs/egtoc.html

Metz, H. C. (Ed.). (1991). *A country study: Libya*. Washington, DC: Library of Congress. Retrieved 15 April 2009 from http://lcweb2.loc.gov/frd/cs/lytoc.html

Metz, H. C. (Ed.). (1991). *A country study: Nigeria*. Washington, DC: Library of Congress. Retrieved 13 April 2009 from http://lcweb2.loc.gov/frd/cs/ngtoc.html#ng0000

Metz, H. C. (Ed.). (1991). *A country study: Sudan*. Washington, DC: Library of Congress. Retrieved 15 April from http://lcweb2.loc.gov/frd/cs/sdtoc.html

Metz, H. C. (Ed.). (1993). *A country study: Algeria*. Washington, DC: Library of Congress. Retrieved 13 April from http://lcweb2.loc.gov/frd/cs/dztoc.html

Namibia: Profile. (2009). US Department of State Background Notes. Retrieved 16 April 2009 from http://www.state.gov/r/pa/ei/bgn/5472.htm

Portugal: Profile. (2008). US Department of State Background Notes. Retrieved 15 April 2009 from http://www.state.gov/r/pa/ei/bgn/3208.htm#history

Slavery. (2009). Encyclopædia Britannica. In *Encyclopædia Britannica 2009 Deluxe Edition*. Chicago: Encyclopædia Britannica.

Stanley, Sir Henry Morton. (2009). Encyclopædia Britannica. In *Encyclopædia Britannica 2009 Deluxe Edition*. Chicago: Encyclopædia Britannica.

Tanzania: Profile. (2009). US Department of State Background Notes. Retrieved 16 April 2009 from http://www.state.gov/r/pa/ei/bgn/2843.htm

Uganda: Profile. (2009). US Department of State Background Notes. Retrieved 16 April 2009 from http://www.state.gov/r/pa/ei/bgn/2963.htm#history

West Central Africa, 500–1000. (2001). In *The Encyclopedia of World History*. Retrieved 14 April 2009 from http://www.bartleby.com/67/348.html

Chapter 3, Lesson 3—Dictators, Leadership Challenges, and Ethnic Clashes

Botswana: Profile. (2008). US Department of State Background Notes. Retrieved 20 April 2009 from http://www.state.gov/r/pa/ei/bgn/1830.htm

Byrnes, R. M. (Ed.). (1996). *A country study: South Africa*. Washington, DC: Library of Congress. Retrieved 20 April 2009 from http://lcweb2.loc.gov/frd/cs/zatoc.html

Democratic Republic of the Congo: Profile. (2009). US Department of State Background Notes. Retrieved 20 April 2009 from http://www.state.gov/r/pa/ei/bgn/2823.htm

The genocide in Rwanda: The difficulty of trying to stop it happening ever again. (2009, April 8). *The Economist*. Retrieved 20 April 2009 from http://www.economist.com/world/mideast-africa/displaystory.cfm?story_id=13447279

'I am prepared to die': Nelson Mandela's statement from the dock at the opening of the defence case in the Rivonia Trial. (1964, April 20). African National Congress. Retrieved 26 April 2009 from http://www.anc.org.za/ancdocs/history/mandela/1960s/rivonia.html

Liberia: Profile. (2009). US Department of State Background Notes. Retrieved 20 April 2009 from http://www.state.gov/r/pa/ei/bgn/6618.htm

Metz, H. C. (Ed.). (1991). *A country study: Sudan*. Washington, DC: Library of Congress. Retrieved 20 April 2009 from http://lcweb2.loc.gov/frd/cs/sdtoc.html

Profile: Liberia's 'Iron Lady.' (2005, November 23). *British Broadcast Corporation*. Retrieved 23 April 2009 from http://news.bbc.co.uk/2/hi/africa/4395978.stm

Republic of the Congo: Profile. (2008). US Department of State Background Notes. Retrieved 20 April 2009 from http://www.state.gov/r/pa/ei/bgn/2825.htm

Rwanda: How the genocide happened. (2008, December 18). *British Broadcasting Corporation*. Retrieved 20 April 2009 from http://news.bbc.co.uk/1/hi/world/africa/1288230.stm

Rwanda: Profile. (2009). US Department of State Background Notes. Retrieved 20 April 2009 from http://www.state.gov/r/pa/ei/bgn/2861.htm

The Sharpeville Massacre. (1960, April 4). *Time*. Retrieved 20 April 2009 from http://www.time.com/time/magazine/article/0,9171,869441,00.html

Sharpeville Massacre. (2009). Encyclopædia Britannica. In *Encyclopædia Britannica 2009 Deluxe Edition*. Chicago: Encyclopædia Britannica.

Sierra Leone: Profile. (2009). US Department of State Background Notes. Retrieved 20 April 2009 from http://www.state.gov/r/pa/ei/bgn/5475.htm

South Africa: Profile. (2008). US Department of State Background Notes. Retrieved 20 April 2009 from http://www.state.gov/r/pa/ei/bgn/2898.htm

Sudan—First civil war. (n.d.). GlobalSecurity.org. Retrieved 20 April 2009 from http://www.globalsecurity.org/military/world/war/sudan-civil-war1.htm

Sudan: Profile. (2009). US Department of State Background Notes. Retrieved 20 April 2009 from http://www.state.gov/r/pa/ei/bgn/5424.htm

Zimbabwe: Profile. (2008). US Department of State Background Notes. Retrieved 20 April 2009 from http://www.state.gov/r/pa/ei/bgn/5479.htm

Chapter 3, Lesson 4—AIDS, Health, Poverty, and Human Rights

2008 human rights report: Sudan. (2009). US State Department. Retrieved 30 April 2009 from http://www.state.gov/g/drl/rls/hrrpt/2008/af/119026.htm

2008 human rights report: Zimbabwe. (2009). US State Department. Retrieved 30 April 2009 from http://www.state.gov/g/drl/rls/hrrpt/2008/af/119032.htm

Adelaja, A. (2007, June 8). *Deforestation accelerating in Central Africa*. London: Science and Development Network. Retrieved 29 April 2009 from http://www.scidev.net/en/news/deforestation-accelerating-in-central-africa.html

Baldauf, S. (2009, April 7). Legacy of Rwanda's genocide: More assertive international justice. *The Christian Science Monitor*. Retrieved 30 April 2009 from http://www.csmonitor.com/2009/0407/p06s11-woaf.html

Beresford, B. (2001, June). AIDS takes an economic and social toll. *Africa Recovery, 15*(1–2). Retrieved 27 April 2009 from http://www.un.org/ecosocdev/geninfo/afrec/vol15no1/151aids9.htm

Clayton, J. (2008, November 27). Thabo Mbeki must answer for needless deaths of 365,000 Aids victims, says activist. *The Times*. Retrieved 27 April 2009 from http://www.timesonline.co.uk/tol/news/world/africa/article5240948.ece

Crilly, R. (2008, June 3). UN aid debate: Give cash, not food? *The Christian Science Monitor*. Retrieved 28 April 2009 from http://www.csmonitor.com/2008/0604/p01s02-woaf.html

De Capua, J. (2009, March 13). Sexually abused Congolese women subject of fact-finding mission. *Voice of America*. Retrieved 30 April 2009 from http://www.voanews.com/english/archive/2009-03/2009-03-13-voa25.cfm?CFID=189276618&CFTOKEN=84752513&jsessionid=6630255dbeab9ae1a37269776404c1536362

Dinan, S. (2009, April 7). Bush AIDS fight saved 1.1M, study says. *The Washington Times*. Retrieved 4 May 2009 from http://www.washingtontimes.com/news/2009/apr/07/bush-aids-fight-saved-11-million-study-says/

Doyle, A. (2008, June 10). Africa's deforestation twice world rate, says atlas. *Reuters*. Retrieved 29 April 2009 from http://www.reuters.com/article/environmentNews/idUSL1064180420080610

Eagle, W. (2009, March 26). African entrepreneurs pioneer new ways to improve sanitation. *Voice of America*. Retrieved 29 April 2009 from http://www.voanews.com/english/Africa/2009-03-26-voa40.cfm

Eritrea becoming 'a giant prison.' (2009, April 16). *British Broadcasting Corporation*. Retrieved 30 April 2009 from http://news.bbc.co.uk/1/hi/world/africa/8002178.stm

Eswaran, H., Almaraz, R., Reich, P., & Zdruli, P. (n.d.). *Soil quality and soil productivity in Africa*. US Department of Agriculture Natural Resources Conservation Service. Retrieved 29 April 2009 from http://soils.usda.gov/use/worldsoils/papers/africa3.html

Farnsworth, E. (2001, May 16). Fighting back in Botswana. *The NewsHour with Jim Lehrer*. Retrieved 27 April 2009 from http://www.pbs.org/newshour/bb/health/jan-june01/aids_5-16.html

Global Food Crisis. (2008). *The Christian Science Monitor*. Retrieved 9 September 2009 from http://www.csmonitor.com/specials/food-crisis/index.html

Global partnership to eliminate riverblindness. (n.d.). The World Bank Group. Retrieved 27 April 2009 from http://www.worldbank.org/afr/gper/

Hoban, R. (2009, April 17). Study rates Bush AIDS relief program major success. *Voice of America*. Retrieved 4 May 2009 from http://www.voanews.com/english/Science/2009-04-17-voa47.cfm

Initiative to End Hunger in Africa (IEHA). (n.d.). USAID. Retrieved 27 April 2009 from http://www.usaid.gov/locations/sub-saharan_africa/initiatives/ieha.html

International Criminal Tribunal for Rwanda. (n.d.). Washington, DC: US State Department. Retrieved 30 April 2009 from http://www.state.gov/s/wci/r/index.htm

Majtenyi, C. (2007, March 19). Kenya experiencing the effects of deforestation, climate change. *Voice of America*. Retrieved 29 April 2009 from http://www.voanews.com/english/archive/2007-03/2007-03-19-voa24.cfm?CFID=167173287&CFTOKEN=25805889&jsessionid=00309076d379637158b6643f2547a12981c7

Malaria deaths decline by 66% in Zambia. (2009, April 23). World Health Organization. Retrieved 27 April 2009 from http://www.who.int/mediacentre/news/releases/2009/malaria_deaths_zambia_20090423/en/index.html

Malaria: Overview. (n.d.). USAID. Retrieved 27 April 2009 from http://www.usaid.gov/our_work/global_health/id/malaria/index.html

Millions face starvation and disease as aid agencies are expelled from Darfur. (2009, March 5). Amnesty International. Retrieved 30 April 2009 from http://www.amnesty.org/en/news-and-updates/news/millions-face-starvation-disease-aid-agencies-expelled-from-darfur-20090305

Plaut, M. (2006, January 31). Africa's hunger—a systemic crisis. *British Broadcasting Corporation*. Retrieved 27 April 2009 from http://news.bbc.co.uk/1/hi/world/africa/4662232.stm

Sasman, C. (2008, April 25). Namibia: Tracking the trucking AIDS figures. *New Era*. Retrieved 27 April 2009 from http://allafrica.com/stories/200804250575.html

Sharp, J. (2007, February 14). Rwanda's Gacaca courts. *The World*. Retrieved 1 May 2009 from http://www.theworld.org/node/8032

Special Court for Sierra Leone. (n.d.). Washington, DC: US State Department. Retrieved 30 April 2009 from http://www.state.gov/s/wci/sierraleone/index.htm

Stearns, S. (2009, April 8). Sierra Leone rebel leaders sentenced for war crimes. *Voice of America*. Retrieved 30 April 2009 from http://www.voanews.com/english/2009-04-08-voa44.cfm

Tate, D. (2009, March 24). US lawmakers consider steps to ease world hunger. *Voice of America*. Retrieved 29 April 2009 from http://www.voanews.com/english/archive/2009-03/2009-03-24-voa69.cfm?CFID=179283463&CFTOKEN=71120970&jsessionid=8430474159498b90c7e42a3d706121375e12

Tjaronda, W. (2008, January 16). Namibia: Aids takes its toll on life expectancy. *New Era*. Retrieved 27 April 2009 from http://allafrica.com/stories/200801160344.html

Vorster, I., & van Rensburg, W. J. (2008, June 26). *The rediscovery of leafy vegetable boosts appreciation for diversity*. Bioversity International. Retrieved 29 April 2009 from http://www.bioversityinternational.org/index.php?id=21&tx_ttnews[tt_news]=501&tx_ttnews[backPID]={page:uid}&no_cache=1

Why biodiversity matters. (n.d.). Bioversity International. Retrieved 29 April 2009 from http://www.bioversityinternational.org/scientific_information/why_biodiversity_matters.html

World urbanization prospects: The 2007 revision population database. (2008). Population Division of the United Nations Department of Economic and Social Affairs. Retrieved 22 May 2009 from http://esa.un.org/unup/index.asp?panel=1

Zimbabwe government minister says will seize all land still in white hands. (2006, February 11). *Zim Online*. Retrieved 28 April 2009 from http://www.zimbabwesituation.com/feb11_2006.html

Chapter 3, Lesson 5—US Interests and Regional Issues in Africa

2008 comprehensive report on US trade and investment policy toward Sub-Saharan Africa and implementation of the African Growth and Opportunity Act. (2008). USAID. Retrieved 7 May 2009 from http://www.usaid.gov/locations/sub-saharan_africa/initiatives/2008_agoa_ustr_report.pdf

African immigration. (2005). US Library of Congress. Retrieved 6 May 2009 from http://lcweb2.loc.gov/learn/features/immig/african10.html

Beehner, L. (2005, June 8). *Africa: Debt-relief proposals*. Council on Foreign Relations. Retrieved 6 May 2009 from http://www.cfr.org/publication/8167/#8

Carter, P., III. (2009, February 9). *U.S. policy in Africa in the 21st century*. US Department of State. Retrieved 8 May 2009 from http://www.state.gov/p/af/rls/rm/2009/117326.htm

Clinton, H. R. (2009, April 15). *Announcement of counter-piracy initiatives*. US Department of State. Retrieved 7 May 2009 from http://www.state.gov/secretary/rm/2009a/04/121758.htm

Cruise ship fires on pirates to fend off attack. (2009, April 26). *The Associated Press*. Retrieved 7 May 2009 from http://wbztv.com/national/Msc.Melody.pirate.2.994779.html

Da Costa, G. (2009, March 3). Oil thieves destroy Shell pipeline in Southern Nigeria. *Voice of America*. Retrieved 8 May 2009 from http://www.voanews.com/english/archive/2009-03/2009-03-03-voa38.cfm

Debt relief under the Heavily Indebted Poor Countries Initiative. (2009, March). International Monetary Fund. Retrieved 6 May 2009 from http://www.imf.org/external/np/exr/facts/hipc.htm

Durkin, E. (2009, April 27). Captain Richard Phillips heard shots and ducked when rescued from pirates. *The Daily News*. Retrieved 7 May 2009 from http://www.nydailynews.com/news/us_world/2009/04/27/2009-04-27_freed_capt_heard_shots_and_ducked.html

Erixon, F. (2005, September 11). Why aid doesn't work. *British Broadcasting Corporation*. Retrieved 7 May 2009 from http://news.bbc.co.uk/1/hi/sci/tech/4209956.stm

Espejo, A., & Unigovskaya, A. (2008, February 25). Debt relief bringing benefits to Africa. International Monetary Fund. Retrieved 6 May 2009 from http://www.imf.org/external/pubs/ft/survey/so/2008/CAR022508A.htm

Faris, S. (2004, October 3). Can Africa get out of debt? *Time*. Retrieved 5 May 2009 from http://www.time.com/time/magazine/article/0,9171,901041011-708965,00.html

Fletcher, M. (2006, December 31). Bush has quietly tripled aid to Africa. *The Washington Post*. Retrieved 7 May 2009 from http://www.washingtonpost.com/wp-dyn/content/article/2006/12/30/AR2006123000941.html

Gaskell, S. (2009, April 14). Three Navy SEALS freed Capt. Phillips from pirates with simultaneous shots from 100 feet away. *The Daily News*. Retrieved 6 May 2009 from http://www.nydailynews.com/news/us_world/2009/04/14/2009-04-14_seals_freed_phillips_with_simultaneous_shots.html

Harman, D. (2007, August 23). Is Western aid making a difference in Africa? *The Christian Science Monitor*. Retrieved 7 May 2009 from http://www.csmonitor.com/2007/0823/p12s01-woaf.html?page=1

Harwood, M. (2007, September). *Perils amid profits in the Niger Delta*. Security Management. Retrieved 6 May 2009 http://www.securitymanagement.com/article/perils-amid-profits-niger-delta

Millennium Development Goals. (2008). United Nations. Retrieved 7 May 2009 from http://www.un.org/millenniumgoals

Mutume, G. (2003, July). Reversing Africa's 'brain drain.' *Africa Recovery, 17*(2). Retrieved 6 May 2009 from http://www.un.org/ecosocdev/geninfo/afrec/vol17no2/172brain.htm

Nigeria: Profile. (2009). US Department of State Background Notes. Retrieved 5 May 2009 from http://www.state.gov/r/pa/ei/bgn/2836.htm

Roberts, S. (2005, February 21). More Africans enter U.S. than in days of slavery. *The New York Times*. Retrieved 5 May 2009 from http://www.nytimes.com/2005/02/21/nyregion/21africa.html?_r=3&sq=Sam%20Roberts%20African%20immigrate&st=cse&adxnnl=1&scp=1&pagewanted=1&adxnnlx=1241719655-h+OasU0xlJSGAE68l/qFUw

Security Council adopts new resolution against piracy off Somalia. (2008, October 7). *United Nations Radio*. Retrieved 7 May 2009 from http://www.unmultimedia.org/radio/english/detail/35759.html

Sub-Saharan Africa: Africa Education Initiative (AEI). (2008). USAID. Retrieved 7 May 2009 from http://www.usaid.gov/locations/sub-saharan_africa/initiatives/aei.html

Sub-Saharan Africa: Initiative to End Hunger in Africa (IEHA). (2008). USAID. Retrieved 7 May 2009 from http://www.usaid.gov/locations/sub-saharan_africa/initiatives/ieha.html

Tebeje, A. (2005, February 22). *Brain drain and capacity building in Africa*. The International Development Research Centre. Retrieved 6 May 2009 from http://www.idrc.ca/en/ev-71249-201-1-DO_TOPIC.html

Chapter 4, Lesson 1—Russia and the Former Soviet Republics: An Introduction

Carvounis, C. C., & Carvounis, B. Z. (1989). U.S. commercial opportunities in the Soviet Union. *Review of Business, 11*. Retrieved 14 May 2009 from http://www.questia.com/googleScholar.qst;jsessionid=KR6TKs1y2CvQyNm10KV19hk7ysbXGgzZ78PqGtQjGtMWzMP1QCR6!1919953439!1173087732?docId=5000120383

Curtis, G. E. (Ed.). (1996). *A country study: Kazakhstan*. Washington, DC: Library of Congress. Retrieved 13 May 2009 from http://memory.loc.gov/frd/cs/kztoc.html

Curtis, G. E. (Ed.). (1996). *A country study: Kyrgyzstan*. Washington, DC: Library of Congress. Retrieved 13 May 2009 from http://memory.loc.gov/frd/cs/kgtoc.html

Curtis, G. E. (Ed.). (1996). *A country study: Russia*. Washington, DC: Library of Congress. Retrieved 13 May 2009 from http://memory.loc.gov/frd/cs/rutoc.html

Curtis, G. E. (Ed.). (1996). *A country study: Tajikistan*. Washington, DC: Library of Congress. Retrieved 13 May 2009 from http://memory.loc.gov/frd/cs/tjtoc.html

Curtis, G. E. (Ed.). (1996). *A country study: Turkmenistan*. Washington, DC: Library of Congress. Retrieved 13 May 2009 from http://memory.loc.gov/frd/cs/tmtoc.html

Dreifelds, J. (1995). *A country study: Latvia*. Washington, DC: Library of Congress. Retrieved 13 May 2009 from http://memory.loc.gov/frd/cs/eetoc.html

Fedor, H. (Ed.). (1995). *A country study: Belarus*. Washington, DC: Library of Congress. Retrieved 13 May 2009 from http://memory.loc.gov/frd/cs/bytoc.html

Iwaskiw, W. R. (Ed.). (1995). *A country study: Estonia*. Washington, DC: Library of Congress. Retrieved 13 May 2009 from http://memory.loc.gov/frd/cs/eetoc.html

On This Day 19 August 1991: Hardliners stage coup against Gorbachev. (n.d.). *British Broadcasting Corporation*. Retrieved 15 May 2009 from http://news.bbc.co.uk/onthisday/hi/dates/stories/august/19/newsid_2499000/2499453.stm

Russia: Profile. (2009). US Department of State Background Notes. Retrieved 13 May 2009 from http://www.state.gov/r/pa/ei/bgn/3183.htm

Ukraine: Profile. (2008). US Department of State Background Notes. Retrieved 13 May 2009 from http://www.state.gov/r/pa/ei/bgn/3211.htm

Vardys, V. S., & Slaven, W. A. (1995). *A country study: Lithuania*. Washington, DC: Library of Congress. Retrieved 13 May 2009 from http://memory.loc.gov/frd/cs/lttoc.html#lt0006

Zickel, R. E. (Ed.). (1989). *A country study: Soviet Union (former)*. Washington, DC: Library of Congress. Retrieved 13 May 2009 from http://memory.loc.gov/frd/cs/sutoc.html

Chapter 4, Lesson 2—Economic Restructuring: Communism and Capitalism

Curtis, G. E. (Ed.). (1996). *A country study: Russia*. Washington, DC: Library of Congress. Retrieved 20 May 2009 from http://memory.loc.gov/frd/cs/rutoc.html

Faulconbridge, G. (2007, October 31). No one can limit Russian arms exports: Putin. *Reuters*. Retrieved 20 May 2009 from http://www.reuters.com/article/worldNews/idUSL31836083 20071031

Russia: Overview of economy. (2008). In *Encyclopedia of the Nations*. Retrieved 20 May 2009 from http://www.nationsencyclopedia.com/economies/Europe/Russia-OVERVIEW-OF-ECONOMY.html

Russia: Profile. (2009). US Department of State Background Notes. Retrieved 20 May 2009 from http://www.state.gov/r/pa/ei/bgn/3183.htm

Russia reports $27 bln in arms export orders. (2009, March 2). *RIA Novosti*. Retrieved 20 May 2009 from http://en.rian.ru/russia/20090302/120376218.html

Soviet economic growth. (2004). In *Encyclopedia of Russian History*. The Gale Group. Retrieved 20 May 2009 from http://www.answers.com/topic/soviet-economic-growth

Zickel, R. E. (Ed.). (1989). *A country study: Soviet Union (former)*. Washington, DC: Library of Congress. Retrieved 20 May 2009 from http://memory.loc.gov/frd/cs/sutoc.html

Chapter 4, Lesson 3—Russia and the Republics

Agg, A. (2009, January 20). Ukrainian President Viktor Yushchenko's ugly poison scars have disappeared. *The Daily Mail*. Retrieved 28 May 2009 from http://www.dailymail.co.uk/news/worldnews/article-1123026/Ukrainian-president-Victor-Yushchenkos-ugly-poison-scars-disappear.html

Armenia: Profile. (2009). US Department of State Background Notes. Retrieved 27 May 2009 from http://www.state.gov/r/pa/ei/bgn/5275.htm

Azerbaijan: Profile. (2009). US Department of State Background Notes. Retrieved 27 May 2009 from http://www.state.gov/r/pa/ei/bgn/2909.htm

Belarus: Profile. (2008). US Department of State Background Notes. Retrieved 27 May 2009 from http://www.state.gov/r/pa/ei/bgn/5371.htm

CIS member states to speed up creation of customs union. (2009, May 22). *RIA Novosti*. Retrieved 25 May 2009 from http://en.rian.ru/world/20090522/155065095.html

Conflict history: Nagorno-Karabakh (Azerbaijan). (2004, September 22). International Crisis Group. Retrieved 29 May 2009 from http://www.crisisgroup.org/home/index.cfm?action=conflict_search&l=1&t=1&c_country=77

Curtis, G. E. (Ed.). (1994). *A country study: Armenia*. Washington, DC: Library of Congress. Retrieved 27 May 2009 from http://memory.loc.gov/frd/cs/amtoc.html

Curtis, G. E. (Ed.). (1994). *A country study: Azerbaijan*. Washington, DC: Library of Congress. Retrieved 27 May 2009 from http://memory.loc.gov/frd/cs/aztoc.html

Curtis, G. E. (Ed.). (1994). *A country study: Georgia*. Washington, DC: Library of Congress. Retrieved 27 May 2009 from http://memory.loc.gov/frd/cs/getoc.html

Curtis, G. E. (Ed.). (1996). *A country study: Kazakhstan*. Washington, DC: Library of Congress. Retrieved 27 May 2009 from http://memory.loc.gov/frd/cs/kztoc.html

Curtis, G. E. (Ed.). (1996). *A country study: Kyrgyzstan*. Washington, DC: Library of Congress. Retrieved 27 May 2009 from http://memory.loc.gov/frd/cs/kgtoc.html

Curtis, G. E. (Ed.). (1996). *A country study: Russia*. Washington, DC: Library of Congress. Retrieved 27 May 2009 from http://memory.loc.gov/frd/cs/rutoc.html

Curtis, G. E. (Ed.). (1996). *A country study: Tajikistan*. Washington, DC: Library of Congress. Retrieved 27 May 2009 from http://memory.loc.gov/frd/cs/tjtoc.html

Curtis, G. E. (Ed.). (1996). *A country study: Turkmenistan*. Washington, DC: Library of Congress. Retrieved 27 May 2009 from http://memory.loc.gov/frd/cs/tmtoc.html

Curtis, G. E. (Ed.). (1996). *A country study: Uzbekistan*. Washington, DC: Library of Congress. Retrieved 27 May 2009 from http://memory.loc.gov/frd/cs/uztoc.html

Dniester conflict frozen after 15 years. (2007, July 21). *British Broadcasting Corporation*. Retrieved 29 May 2009 from http://news.bbc.co.uk/1/hi/world/europe/6909192.stm

East: Frozen conflicts not so 'frozen' after all. (2006, November 10). *Radio Free Europe/Radio Liberty*. Retrieved 29 May 2009 from http://www.rferl.org/content/Article/1072643.html

Estonia names American as military chief, but U.S. objects. (1993, May 6). *The New York Times*. Retrieved 28 May 2009 from http://www.nytimes.com/1993/|05/06/world/estonia-names-american-as-military-chief-but-us-objects.html?scp=1&sq=einseln&st=cse

Estonia: Profile. (2009). US Department of State Background Notes. Retrieved 27 May 2009 from http://www.state.gov/r/pa/ei/bgn/5377.htm

Fedor, H. (Ed.). (1995). *A country study: Belarus*. Washington, DC: Library of Congress. Retrieved 27 May 2009 from http://memory.loc.gov/frd/cs/bytoc.html

Fedor, H. (Ed.). (1995). *A country study: Moldova*. Washington, DC: Library of Congress. Retrieved 27 May 2009 from http://memory.loc.gov/frd/cs/mdtoc.html

Georgia: Profile. (2009). US Department of State Background Notes. Retrieved 27 May 2009 from http://www.state.gov/r/pa/ei/bgn/5253.htm

Halpin, T. (2007, September 11). Viktor Yushchenko points finger at Russia over poison that scarred him. *The Times*. Retrieved 28 May 2009 from http://www.timesonline.co.uk/tol/news/world/europe/article2426190.ece

Iwaskiw, W. R. (Ed.). (1995). *A country study: Estonia*. Washington, DC: Library of Congress. Retrieved 27 May 2009 from http://memory.loc.gov/frd/cs/eetoc.html

Kazakhstan: Profile. (2009). US Department of State Background Notes. Retrieved 27 May 2009 from http://www.state.gov/r/pa/ei/bgn/5487.htm

Kramer, A. (2009, January 19). Russia and Ukraine sign agreement on gas. *The New York Times*. Retrieved 25 May 2009 from http://www.nytimes.com/2009/01/20/world/europe/20russia.html

Kyrgyzstan: Profile. (2009). US Department of State Background Notes. Retrieved 27 May 2009 from http://www.state.gov/r/pa/ei/bgn/5755.htm

Latvia: Profile. (2009). US Department of State Background Notes. Retrieved 27 May 2009 from http://www.state.gov/r/pa/ei/bgn/5378.htm

Lithuania: Profile. (2008). US Department of State Background Notes. Retrieved 27 May 2009 from http://www.state.gov/r/pa/ei/bgn/5379.htm

Moldova: Profile. (2009). US Department of State Background Notes. Retrieved 27 May 2009 from http://www.state.gov/r/pa/ei/bgn/5357.htm

Moldova uncorks its secret weapon. (2002, October 16). *British Broadcasting Corporation*. Retrieved 25 May 2009 from http://news.bbc.co.uk/1/hi/world/europe/2331261.stm

Page, J. (2004, December 8). Who poisoned Yushchenko? *The Times*. Retrieved 28 May 2009 from http://www.timesonline.co.uk/tol/news/world/article400357.ece

Q&A: Conflict in Georgia. (2008, November 11). *British Broadcasting Corporation*. Retrieved 29 May 2009 from http://news.bbc.co.uk/1/hi/world/europe/7549736.stm

Rimple, P. (2008, October 20). After summer war, identity crisis grips Abkhazia. *The Christian Science Monitor*. Retrieved 1 June 2009 from http://www.csmonitor.com/2008/1020/p04s01-woeu.html

Role of Russia in foreign trade of Latvia. (2006). Lettia.lv. Retrieved 27 May 2009 from http://www.lettia.lv/en_a_latvija-krievija-tirdznieciba.html

Russia: Profile. (2009). US Department of State Background Notes. Retrieved 27 May 2009 from http://www.state.gov/r/pa/ei/bgn/3183.htm

Russia urges Estonia to probe vandalism of Soviet war memorial. (2009, May 25). *RIA Novosti*. Retrieved 25 May 2009 from http://en.rian.ru/russia/20090525/155082978.html

Russian ends trade ban on Moldova. (2006, November 29). *British Broadcasting Corporation*. Retrieved 25 May 2009 from http://news.bbc.co.uk/1/hi/world/europe/6194072.stm

Russian forces battle Georgians. (2008, August 8). *British Broadcasting Corporation*. Retrieved 29 May 2009 from http://news.bbc.co.uk/1/hi/world/europe/7550354.stm

Sheeter, L. (2007, March 27). Latvia, Russia sign border deal. *British Broadcasting Corporation*. Retrieved 27 May 2009 from http://news.bbc.co.uk/1/hi/world/europe/6498049.stm

Tajikistan: International trade. (2008). In *Encyclopedia of the Nations*. Retrieved 28 May 2009 from http://www.nationsencyclopedia.com/economies/Asia-and-the-Pacific/Tajikistan-INTERNATIONAL-TRADE.html

Tajikistan: Profile. (2009). US Department of State Background Notes. Retrieved 27 May 2009 from http://www.state.gov/r/pa/ei/bgn/5775.htm

Tajikistan: Reconsidering Russia. (2008, August 29). *Stratfor Global Intelligence*. Retrieved 28 May 2009 from http://www.stratfor.com/analysis/tajikistan_reconsidering_russia

Trade and customs. (2009). Investment and Development Agency of Latvia. Retrieved 29 May 2009 from http://www.liaa.gov.lv/?object_id=1916

Turkmenistan: Profile. (2008). US Department of State Background Notes. Retrieved 27 May 2009 from http://www.state.gov/r/pa/ei/bgn/35884.htm

Ukraine: Profile. (2009). US Department of State Background Notes. Retrieved 27 May 2009 from http://www.state.gov/r/pa/ei/bgn/3211.htm

Uzbekistan: Profile. (2008). US Department of State Background Notes. Retrieved 27 May 2009 from http://www.state.gov/r/pa/ei/bgn/2924.htm

Walker, R. (2007, May 17). At CGIS, attorney Amsterdam blasts Russian Federation, others. *The Harvard Gazette*. Retrieved 25 May 2009 from http://www.news.harvard.edu/gazette/2007/05.17/09-russian.html

Chapter 4, Lesson 4—Russia and World Relationships

The Berlin Airlift: June 27, 1948 to May 12, 1949. (n.d.). The Truman Library. Retrieved 1 June 2009 from http://www.trumanlibrary.org/teacher/berlin.htm

China-Russia oil pipeline serves strategic goals of both sides. (2009, May 11). *Xinhua News Agency*. Retrieved 31 May 2009 from http://www.china.org.cn/international/2009-05/11/content_17754499.htm

Cole, J. (1984, December 17). *TV interview for BBC (Gorbachev: 'We can do business together')*. Margaret Thatcher Foundation. Retrieved 1 June 2009 from http://www.margaretthatcher.org/speeches/displaydocument.asp?docid=105592

Curtis, G. E. (Ed.). (1996). *A country study: Russia*. Washington, DC: Library of Congress. Retrieved 31 May 2009 from http://memory.loc.gov/frd/cs/rutoc.html

Intermediate-Range Nuclear Forces Treaty (INF Treaty), 1987. (n.d.). US Department of State, Office of the Historian. Retrieved 1 June 2009 from http://history.state.gov/milestones/1981-1989/INF

Japan: Profile. (2009). US Department of State Background Notes. Retrieved 31 May 2009 from http://www.state.gov/r/pa/ei/bgn/4142.htm

Kafala, T. (2003, September 17). The veto and how to use it. *British Broadcasting Corporation*. Retrieved 30 May 2009 from http://news.bbc.co.uk/1/hi/world/middle_east/2828985.stm

Kramer, A. E. (2005, December 1). For oil fields, Soviet-era secrecy. *The New York Times*. Retrieved 3 June 2009 from http://www.nytimes.com/2005/12/01/business/worldbusiness/01iht-maps.html?_r=2

Monroe Doctrine. (2008). In *The Encyclopedia of American Foreign Policy*. Retrieved 31 May 2009 from http://www.americanforeignrelations.com/A-D/Doctrines-The-monroe-doctrine.html

North Korea: Profile. (2009). US Department of State Background Notes. Retrieved 31 May 2009 from http://www.state.gov/r/pa/ei/bgn/2792.htm

O'Neill, M. (2000, Spring). Soviet involvement in the Korean War: A new view from the Soviet-era archives. *OAH Magazine of History, 14*(3). Retrieved 31 May 2009 from http://oah.org/pubs/magazine/korea/oneill.html

Russia: Profile. (2009). US Department of State Background Notes. Retrieved 31 May 2009 from http://www.state.gov/r/pa/ei/bgn/3183.htm

Russian arms sales to China down. (2009, April 11). *United Press International*. Retrieved 31 May 2009 from http://www.upi.com/Top_News/2009/04/11/Russian-arms-sales-to-China-down/UPI-83641239486214/

Russian-Japanese economic relations. (2009, May 8). *RIA Novosti*. Retrieved 31 May 2009 from http://en.rian.ru/infographics/20090508/121510421.html

The United States and the founding of the United Nations, August 1941–October 1945. (2005). US State Department. Retrieved 30 May 2009 from http://www.state.gov/r/pa/ho/pubs/fs/55407.htm

The United States, the Soviet Union, and the end of World War II: Historical background. (2005). US State Department. Retrieved 1 June 2009 from http://www.state.gov/r/pa/ho/pubs/fs/46345.htm

Winston Churchill's Iron Curtain Speech (transcript). (1946). About.com: 20th Century History. Retrieved 30 May 2009 from http://history1900s.about.com/library/weekly/aa082400a.htm

Worden, R. L., Savada, A. M., & Dolan, R. E. (Eds.). (1987). *A country study: China*. Washington, DC: Library of Congress. Retrieved 31 May 2009 from http://memory.loc.gov/frd/cs/cntoc.html

Yu Bin. (2008, June 18). China has an 'old friend' in Medvedev. *Asia Times Online*. Retrieved 31 May 2009 from http://www.atimes.com/atimes/Central_Asia/JF18Ag03.html

Zickel, R. E. (Ed.). (1989). *A country study: Soviet Union (former)*. Washington, DC: Library of Congress. Retrieved 31 May 2009 from http://memory.loc.gov/frd/cs/sutoc.html

Chapter 4, Lesson 5–US Interests and Regional Issues in Russia and the Former Soviet Republics

Abaca, R. (2009, January 25). Peak oil production in Russia suggests worldwide supplies on the brink. *Market Rap*. Retrieved 9 June 2009 from http://www.marketrap.com/article/view_article/9147/peak-oil-production-in-russia-suggests-worldwide-supplies-on-the-brink

Brooke, J. (1989, January 11). Cuba pulls 450 soldiers out of Angola. *The New York Times*. Retrieved 2 June 2009 from http://www.nytimes.com/1989/01/11/world/cuba-pulls-450-soldiers-out-of-angola.html

Clines, F. X. (1990, January 9). Upheaval in the East: Trade Bloc; Soviets and partners say Comecon needs repair. *The New York Times*. Retrieved 5 June 2009 from http://www.nytimes.com/1990/01/09/world/upheaval-in-the-east-trade-bloc-soviets-and-partners-say-comecon-needs-repair.html

Expedition One crew. (2003, April 22). National Aeronautics and Space Administration. Retrieved 8 June 2009 from http://spaceflight.nasa.gov/station/crew/exp1/index.html

The Global Initiative to Combat Nuclear Terrorism. (2006, July 15). US Department of State. Retrieved 7 June 2009 from http://www.state.gov/t/isn/c18406.htm

Harding, L. (2007, April 11). Russia threatening new cold war over missile defence. *The Guardian*. Retrieved 7 June 2009 from http://www.guardian.co.uk/world/2007/apr/11/usa.topstories3

Iran & Russia lead oil price hawks; IRGC says it's taking control of Hormuz traffic. (2008, November 3). *Entrepreneur*. Retrieved 7 June 2009 from http://www.entrepreneur.com/tradejournals/article/188379603.html

New global survey data available: Freedom gains amid global threats. (2003, May 8). Freedom House. Retrieved 8 June 2009 from http://www.freedomhouse.org/template.cfm?page=70&release=122

The Nunn-Lugar Cooperative Threat Reduction (CTR) Program. (2005, January 20). NTI. Retrieved 7 June 2009 from http://www.nti.org/db/nisprofs/russia/forasst/nunn_lug/overview.htm

Pellerin, C. (2007, February 21). *Space cooperation highlights 200 years of U.S.-Russia relations*. US Department of State. Retrieved 8 June 2009 from http://www.america.gov/st/washfile-english/2007/February/20070221131459lcnirellep0.7167169.html#ixzz0HwYu2PUK&C

Profile: Mercosur—Common Market of the South. (2008, September 18). *British Broadcasting Corporation*. Retrieved 5 June 2009 from http://news.bbc.co.uk/1/hi/world/americas/5195834.stm

Russia: Profile. (2009). US Department of State Background Notes. Retrieved 1 June 2009 from http://www.state.gov/r/pa/ei/bgn/3183.htm

Shuttle-Mir overview. (2007, November 23). National Aeronautics and Space Administration. Retrieved 8 June 2009 from http://www.nasa.gov/mission_pages/shuttle-mir/

Spotts, P. N. (2008, August 20). Will US-Russia tensions extend to space? *The Christian Science Monitor*. Retrieved 8 June 2009 from http://features.csmonitor.com/innovation/2008/08/20/will-us-russia-tensions-extend-to-space/

Text of Mahmoud Ahmadinejad's speech. (2005, October 30). *The New York Times*. Retrieved 7 June 2009 from http://www.nytimes.com/2005/10/30/weekinreview/30iran.html

Zickel, R. E. (Ed.). (1989). *A country study: Soviet Union (former)*. Retrieved 2 June 2009 from http://lcweb2.loc.gov/frd/cs/sutoc.html

Chapter 5, Lesson 1—Latin America: An Introduction

The Bay of Pigs and the Cuban Missile Crisis, 1961–1962. (n.d.). US State Department: Timeline of US Diplomatic History. Retrieved 26 June 2009 from http://www.state.gov/r/pa/ho/time/ea/17739.htm

Biography: Bernardo O'Higgins. (n.d.). Answers.com. Retrieved 26 June 2009 from http://www.answers.com/topic/bernardo-o-higgins

Bolivia: Profile. (2008). US Department of State Background Notes. Retrieved 25 June 2009 from http://www.state.gov/r/pa/ei/bgn/35751.htm#foreign

Botton, Alain de. (2009, April 18). French Guiana—Out of this world. *The Independent*. Retrieved 24 June 2009 from http://www.independent.co.uk/travel/americas/french-guiana--out-of-this-world-1670291.html

Brazil. (2009, June). *The World Factbook*. Retrieved 29 June 2009 from https://www.cia.gov/library/publications/the-world-factbook/geos/BR.html

Cuba: Profile. (2008). US Department of State Background Notes. Retrieved 26 June 2009 from http://www.state.gov/r/pa/ei/bgn/2886.htm

Cuba rejects OAS membership, official says. (2009, June 4). *Cable News Network*. Retrieved 30 June 2009 from http://www.cnn.com/2009/WORLD/americas/06/04/cuba.oas/

Diamond, J. (1998). *Guns, germs, and steel: The fates of human societies*. New York: W. W. Norton & Co.

French Guiana (including Inini). (n.d.). Infoplease. Retrieved 24 June 2009 from http://www.infoplease.com/ipa/A0107544.html

Haggerty, R. A. (Ed.). (1989). *A country study: Haiti*. Washington, DC: Library of Congress. Retrieved 25 June 2009 from http://lcweb2.loc.gov/frd/cs/httoc.html

Hanratty, D. M., & Meditz, S. W. (Eds.). (1988). *A country study: Colombia*. Washington, DC: Library of Congress. Retrieved 23 June 2009 from http://lcweb2.loc.gov/frd/cs/cotoc.html

Hudson, R. A. (Ed.). (1997). *A country study: Brazil*. Washington, DC: Library of Congress. Retrieved 26 June 2009 from http://lcweb2.loc.gov/frd/cs/brtoc.html

The indigenous languages of Latin America. (n.d.). The Archive of the Indigenous Languages of Latin America: University of Texas at Austin. Retrieved 26 June 2009 from http://www.ailla.utexas.org/site/la_langs.html

José de San Martín. (n.d.). In *Microsoft Encarta Online Encyclopedia 2009*. Retrieved 25 June 2009 from http://encarta.msn.com/encyclopedia_761574866/jose_de_san_martin.html

Launch a 'rocket' from a spinning 'planet.' (2005, September 8). NASA. Retrieved 26 June 2009 from http://spaceplace.nasa.gov/en/kids/ds1_mgr.shtml

Meditz, S. W., & Hanratty, D. M. (Eds.). (1997). *A country study: Panama*. Washington, DC: Library of Congress. Retrieved 26 June 2009 from http://lcweb2.loc.gov/frd/cs/patoc.html

Member states and permanent missions. (2009). Organization of American States. Retrieved 30 June 2009 from http://www.oas.org/documents/eng/memberstates.asp

Merrill, T. L., & Miró, R. (Eds.). (1996). *A country study: Mexico*. Washington, DC: Library of Congress. Retrieved 23 June 2009 from http://lcweb2.loc.gov/frd/cs/mxtoc.html

Miguel Hidalgo y Costilla. (2008). In *The Columbia Encyclopedia* (6th ed.). Retrieved 26 June 2009 from http://www.encyclopedia.com/doc/1E1-Hidalgoy.html

Monroe Doctrine, 1823. (n.d.). US State Department: Timeline of US Diplomatic History. Retrieved 25 June 2009 from http://www.state.gov/r/pa/ho/time/jd/16321.htm

Panama. (n.d.). Infoplease. Retrieved 25 June 2009 from http://www.infoplease.com/ipa/A0107870.html

Religion and ethics: Santeria. (n.d.). *British Broadcasting Corporation*. Retrieved 24 June 2009 from http://www.bbc.co.uk/religion/religions/santeria/

South America. (2009). Encyclopædia Britannica. In *Encyclopædia Britannica 2009 Deluxe Edition*. Chicago: Encyclopædia Britannica.

The Spanish-American War, 1898. (n.d.). US State Department: Timeline of US Diplomatic History. Retrieved 26 June 2009 from http://www.state.gov/r/pa/ho/time/gp/90609.htm

Suriname: Profile. (2009). US Department of State Background Notes. Retrieved 24 June 2009 from http://www.state.gov/r/pa/ei/bgn/1893.htm

Treaty of Tordesillas. (2009). About.com: Geography. Retrieved 25 June 2009 from http://geography.about.com/library/weekly/aa112999a.htm

Chapter 5, Lesson 2—Economic Reform, Leadership, and the Political Pendulum

Argentina: Profile. (2008). US Department of State Background Notes. Retrieved 1 July 2009 from http://www.state.gov/r/pa/ei/bgn/26516.htm

CAFTA-DR (Dominican Republic-Central America FTA). (2009, May 31). Office of the United States Trade Representative. Retrieved 3 July 2009 from http://www.ustr.gov/trade-agreements/free-trade-agreements/cafta-dr-dominican-republic-central-america-fta

Colombia: Profile. (2009). US Department of State Background Notes. Retrieved 1 July 2009 from http://www.state.gov/r/pa/ei/bgn/35754.htm

Cuba: Profile. (2008). US Department of State Background Notes. Retrieved 1 July 2009 from http://www.state.gov/r/pa/ei/bgn/2886.htm

De Ferranti, D., Perry, G. E., Ferreira, F. H. G., Walton, M., Coady, D., & Cunningham, W., et al. (2003). *Inequality in Latin America and the Caribbean: Breaking with history?* The World Bank. Retrieved 3 July 2009 from http://siteresources.worldbank.org/BRAZILINPOREXTN/Resources/3817166-1185895645304/4044168-1186325351029/10Full.pdf

El Salvador: Profile. (2009). US Department of State Background Notes. Retrieved 1 July 2009 from http://www.state.gov/r/pa/ei/bgn/2033.htm

Free trade agreements. (n.d.). US Department of State. Retrieved 3 July 2009 from http://www.state.gov/e/eeb/tpp/bta/fta/index.htm

Friedman, G. (2008, May 13). Mexico: On the road to a failed state? *Stratfor Global Intelligence*. Retrieved 2 July 2009 from http://www.stratfor.com/weekly/mexico_road_failed_state

Gibb, T. (2002, March 24). US role in Salvador's brutal war. *British Broadcasting Corporation*. Retrieved 1 July 2009 from http://news.bbc.co.uk/2/hi/americas/1891145.stm

Haggerty, R. A. (Ed.). (1990). *A country study: Venezuela*. Washington, DC: Library of Congress. Retrieved 1 July 2009 from http://lcweb2.loc.gov/frd/cs/vetoc.html

Hanratty, D. M., & Meditz, S. W. (Eds.). (1988). *A country study: Colombia*. Washington, DC: Library of Congress. Retrieved 1 July 2009 from http://lcweb2.loc.gov/frd/cs/cotoc.html

Hanratty, D. M., & Meditz, S. W. (Eds.). (1988). *A country study: Paraguay*. Washington, DC: Library of Congress. Retrieved 1 July 2009 from http://lcweb2.loc.gov/frd/cs/pytoc.html

Hudson, R. A. (Ed.). (1997). *A country study: Brazil*. Washington, DC: Library of Congress. Retrieved 1 July 2009 from http://lcweb2.loc.gov/frd/cs/brtoc.html

Inequality in Latin America & the Caribbean: Breaking with history? (2003, October 7). The World Bank. Retrieved 30 June 2009 from http://web.worldbank.org/WBSITE/EXTERNAL/COUNTRIES/LACEXT/0,,contentMDK:20384897~pagePK:146736~piPK:146830~theSitePK:258554,00.html

Lopez, J. H., & Perry, G. (2008). *Inequality in Latin America: Determinants and consequences.* The World Bank, Latin America and the Caribbean Region, Office of the Regional Chief Economist. Retrieved 30 June 2009 from http://www-wds.worldbank.org/servlet/WDSContentServer/WDSP/IB/2008/02/01/000158349_20080201123241/Rendered/PDF/wps4504.pdf

Merrill, T. (Ed.). (1993). *A country study: Nicaragua.* Washington, DC: Library of Congress. Retrieved 1 July 2009 from http://lcweb2.loc.gov/frd/cs/nitoc.html

Merrill, T. L., & Miró, R. (Eds.). (1996). *A country study: Mexico.* Washington, DC: Library of Congress. Retrieved 29 June 2009 from http://lcweb2.loc.gov/frd/cs/mxtoc.html

Nicaragua: Profile. (2008). US Department of State Background Notes. Retrieved 1 July 2009 from http://www.state.gov/r/pa/ei/bgn/1850.htm

North American Free Trade Agreement (NAFTA). (2009, May 11). Office of the United States Trade Representative. Retrieved 3 July 2009 from http://www.ustr.gov/trade-agreements/free-trade-agreements/north-american-free-trade-agreement-nafta

Venezuela: Profile. (2009). US Department of State Background Notes. Retrieved 1 July 2009 from http://www.state.gov/r/pa/ei/bgn/35766.htm

Chapter 5, Lesson 3—Cartels and the Growing Drug Trade

Hanratty, D. M., & Meditz, S. W. (Eds.). (1988). *A country study: Colombia.* Washington, DC: Library of Congress. Retrieved 1 July 2009 from http://lcweb2.loc.gov/frd/cs/cotoc.html

Managua meeting strengthens regional response to drugs and crime in Central America. (2009, July 2). United Nations Office on Drugs and Crime. Retrieved 6 July 2009 from http://www.unodc.org/unodc/en/frontpage/2009/June/ministers-commit-to-fight-illicit-drugs-and-crime-in-central-america.html

Minster, C. (2009). Biography of Pablo Escobar: Colombia's drug kingpin. About.com: Latin American History. Retrieved 5 July 2009 from http://latinamericanhistory.about.com/od/20thcenturylatinamerica/a/bioescobar.htm

Padgett, T. (2008, July 2). Colombia's stunning hostage rescue. *Time.* Retrieved 7 July 2009 from http://www.time.com/time/world/article/0,8599,1819862,00.html

Rebuilding the state to repel the threat of drug trafficking. (2008, Second Quarter). CICAD *Observer*, (2, Year 6). Retrieved 5 July 2009 from http://www.cicad.oas.org/oid/NEW/Information/Observer/08_02/caputo.asp

Southern border violence: Homeland security threats, vulnerabilities, and responsibilities. (2009, March 30). US Justice Department. Retrieved 3 July 2009 from http://www.usdoj.gov/dea/pubs/cngrtest/ct032709.pdf

Chapter 5, Lesson 4—Poverty, Educational Limitations, and Environmental Challenges

Barclay, E. (2007, June 23). *Clearing the smog: Fighting air pollution in Mexico City, Mexico, and São Paulo, Brazil.* Disease Control Priorities Project. Retrieved 10 July 2009 from http://www.dcp2.org/features/47

Bradley, T. (2008, December 26). Once world's smoggiest, Mexico City now a model for improving air quality. *The Associated Press.* Retrieved 10 July 2009 from http://green.sympatico.msn.ca/canadianpressarticle.aspx?cp-documentid=811045

Budget: Latin America and the Caribbean. (2005, June 14). USAID. Retrieved 9 July 2009 from http://www.usaid.gov/policy/budget/cbj2006/lac/

Country comparison: Population growth rate. (n.d.). *The World Factbook.* Retrieved 10 July 2009 from https://www.cia.gov/library/publications/the-world-factbook/rankorder/2002rank.html

Education statistics: Average years of schooling of adults (most recent) by country. (n.d.). UNESCO. Retrieved 10 July 2009 from http://www.nationmaster.com/graph/edu_ave_yea_of_sch_of_adu-education-average-years-schooling-adults

Equality with dignity: Towards indigenous rights in Latin America. (2004, October 18). United Nations Children's Fund. Retrieved 9 July 2009 from http://www.unicef.org/media/media_23644.html

Fay, M. (Ed.). (2005). *The urban poor in Latin America*. The World Bank. Retrieved 10 July 2009 from http://siteresources.worldbank.org/INTLACREGTOPURBDEV/Home/20843636/UrbanPoorinLA.pdf

Focus on global warming and air quality in Latin America: New Clean Air Institute established. (2006, July 13). The World Bank. Retrieved 10 July 2009 from http://web.worldbank.org/WBSITE/EXTERNAL/COUNTRIES/LACEXT/0,,contentMDK:20993269~menuPK:258568~pagePK:2865106~piPK:2865128~theSitePK:258554,00.html

Global Environment Outlook GEO4: Environment for development. (2007). United Nations Environment Program.

Hanratty, D. M., & Meditz, S. W. (Eds.). (1988). *A country study: Colombia*. Washington, DC: Library of Congress. Retrieved 1 July 2009 from http://lcweb2.loc.gov/frd/cs/cotoc.html

Honduras. (2008, April 2). In *New World Encyclopedia*. Retrieved 9 July 2009 from http://www.newworldencyclopedia.org/entry/Honduras?oldid=680318

Honduras: Profile. (2009). US Department of State Background Notes. Retrieved 7 July 2009 from http://www.state.gov/r/pa/ei/bgn/1922.htm#econ

Hudson, R. A. (Ed.). (1997). *A country study: Brazil*. Washington, DC: Library of Congress. Retrieved 6 July 2009 from http://lcweb2.loc.gov/frd/cs/brtoc.html

Latin America must fight discrimination against indigenous people—UNICEF. (2005, July 8). UN News Centre. Retrieved 9 July 2009 from http://www.un.org/apps/news/story.asp?NewsID=14935&Cr=indigenous&Cr1=people

Merrill, T. L., & Miró, R. (Eds.). (1996). *A country study: Mexico*. Washington, DC: Library of Congress. Retrieved 6 July 2009 from http://lcweb2.loc.gov/frd/cs/mxtoc.html

Portillo, Z. (1999, April 8). Latin America gets poor marks. *InterPress Third World News Agency (IPS)*. Retrieved 10 July 2009 from http://www.converge.org.nz/lac/articles/news990408a.htm

Vietnam's coffee farmers in crisis. (2002, September 18). *British Broadcasting Corporation*. Retrieved 7 July 2009 from http://news.bbc.co.uk/2/hi/asia-pacific/2265410.stm

World Bank calls for more family planning. (2008, July 11). People and the Planet. Retrieved 10 July 2009 from http://www.peopleandplanet.net/doc.php?id=3332

Chapter 5, Lesson 5—US Interests and Regional Issues in Latin America

Archibold, R. C. (2009, March 22). Mexican drug cartel violence spills over, alarming US. *The New York Times*. Retrieved 16 July 2009 from http://www.nytimes.com/2009/03/23/us/23border.html?_r=1

Barshefsky, C., Hill, J. T., & O'Neil, S. K. (2008). *U.S.-Latin America relations: A new direction for a new reality*. Council on Foreign Relations, Independent Task Force Report No. 60. Retrieved 16 July 2009 from http://www.cfr.org/content/publications/attachments/LatinAmerica_TF.pdf

The Bay of Pigs and the Cuban Missile Crisis, 1961–1962. (n.d.). US State Department: Timeline of US Diplomatic History. Retrieved 16 July 2009 from http://www.state.gov/r/pa/ho/time/ea/17739.htm

Belsie, L, & Axtman, K. (2006, June 12). Post-Katrina, New Orleans coming back more Hispanic. *The Christian Science Monitor*. Retrieved 16 July 2009 from http://www.csmonitor.com/2006/0612/p01s03-ussc.html

Bethell, J. T. (n.d.). 'A splendid little war': Harvard and the commencement of a new world order. *Harvard Magazine*. Retrieved 16 July 2009 from http://harvardmagazine.com/1998/11/war.html

Cave, D. (2008, June 9). States take new tack on illegal immigration. *The New York Times*. Retrieved 16 July 2009 from http://www.nytimes.com/2008/06/09/us/09panhandle.html?_r=1&pagewanted=1&sq=illegal%20immigration&st=cse&scp=8

Cuba: Profile. (2008). US Department of State Background Notes. Retrieved 13 July 2009 from http://www.state.gov/r/pa/ei/bgn/2886.htm

Davidson, A. (2006, March 30). Q&A: Illegal immigrants and the US economy. *National Public Radio*. Retrieved 16 July 2009 from http://www.npr.org/templates/story/story.php?storyId=5312900

The Destruction of the USS Maine. (2003). Department of the Navy, Naval Historical Center. Retrieved 16 July 2009 from http://www.history.navy.mil/faqs/faq71-1.htm

Haggerty, R. A. (Ed.). (1989). *A country study: Haiti*. Washington, DC: Library of Congress. Retrieved 13 July 2009 from http://lcweb2.loc.gov/frd/cs/httoc.html

Immigration and emigration. (2009, June 26). *The New York Times*. Retrieved 16 July 2009 from http://topics.nytimes.com/top/reference/timestopics/subjects/i/immigration_and_refugees/index.html?inline=nyt-classifier

Kandaswamy, P. (2009, July 14). Latin American remittances heavily impacted by global economy. *Honduras This Week Online*. Retrieved 16 July 2009 from http://www.hondurasthisweek.com/business/1341-latin-american-remittances-heavily-impacted-by-global-economy

Mariel boatlift. (n.d.). GlobalSecurity.org. Retrieved 16 July 2009 from http://www.globalsecurity.org/military/ops/mariel-boatlift.htm

Operation Mongoose. (n.d.). GlobalSecurity.org. Retrieved 16 July 2009 from http://www.globalsecurity.org/intell/ops/mongoose.htm

Perez, E., & Dade, C. (2007, January 17). An immigration raid aids blacks for a time. *The Wall Street Journal*. Retrieved 16 July 2009 from http://www.post-gazette.com/pg/07017/754517-28.stm

Porter, E. (2005, April 5). Illegal immigrants are bolstering Social Security with billions. *The New York Times*. Retrieved 16 July 2009 from http://www.nytimes.com/2005/04/05/business/05immigration.html?_r=3&scp=10&sq=illegal%20immigration&st=cse

Preston, J. (2008, May 1). Fewer Latino immigrants sending money home. *The New York Times*. Retrieved 15 July 2009 from http://www.nytimes.com/2008/05/01/us/01immigration.html?_r=1&scp=9&sq=remittances%20to%20Latin%20America%20and%20impact%20on%20United%20States&st=cse

Refugees and the Cold War. (n.d.). In *Encyclopedia of American Foreign Policy*. Retrieved 16 July 2009 from http://www.americanforeignrelations.com/O-W/Refugee-Policies-Refugees-and-the-cold-war.html

Roberts, S. (2008, February 11). Proportion of immigrants in US rises. *The New York Times*. Retrieved 16 July 2009 from http://www.nytimes.com/2008/02/11/us/11cnd-immig.html?_r=1

Rough Rider Colonel Roosevelt. (n.d.). Theodore Roosevelt Association. Retrieved 16 July 2009 from http://www.theodoreroosevelt.org/life/Rough_riders.htm

Semple, K. (2009, May 27). Haitians in US illegally look for signs of a deporting reprieve. *The New York Times*. Retrieved 16 July 2009 from http://www.nytimes.com/2009/05/28/nyregion/28haitians.html?_r=1

The United States, Cuba, and the Platt Amendment, 1901. (n.d.). US State Department: Timeline of US Diplomatic History. Retrieved 16 July 2009 from http://www.state.gov/r/pa/ho/time/ip/86557.htm

Who's coming to America: Today's immigrants come from different places, but their reasons are similar to those that motivated earlier immigrants. (n.d.). Retrieved 16 July 2009 from http://www.thefreelibrary.com/Who%27s+coming+to+America:+today%27s+immigrants+come+from+different...-a0197233239

Chapter 6, Lesson 1—Europe: An Introduction

Alchin, L. K. (n.d.). *The Great Schism.* Middle Ages. Retrieved 24 July 2009 from http://www.middle-ages.org.uk/the-great-schism.htm

Brodman, J. W. (1986). *Ransoming captives in Crusader Spain: The Order of Merced on the Christian-Islamic frontier.* University of Central Arkansas: The Library of Iberian Resources Online. Retrieved 22 July 2009 from http://libro.uca.edu/rc/rc1.htm

Canossa. (2008). In *The Columbia Encyclopedia* (6th ed.). Retrieved 20 July 2009 from http://www.encyclopedia.com/doc/1E1-Canossa.html

The centuries of al-Andalus. (1999, December 23). *The Economist.* Retrieved 24 July 2009 from http://www.economist.com/world/europe/displaystory.cfm?story_id=346770

Crawford, P. (1997). Crusades. The ORB: The Online Reference Book for Medieval Studies. Retrieved 24 July 2009 from http://www.the-orb.net/encyclop/religion/crusades/crusade_intro.html

Crusades. (2009). Encyclopædia Britannica. In *Encyclopædia Britannica 2009 Deluxe Edition.* Chicago: Encyclopædia Britannica.

Curtis, G. E. (Ed.). (1992). *A country study: Poland.* Washington, DC: Library of Congress. Retrieved 24 July 2009 from http://memory.loc.gov/frd/cs/pltoc.html#pl0000

Curtis, G. E. (Ed.). (1996). *A country study: Russia.* Washington, DC: Library of Congress. Retrieved 24 July 2009 from http://memory.loc.gov/frd/cs/rutoc.html

Dunn, J. C., Jr. (n.d.). The Parthenon and the Acropolis. How stuff works. Retrieved 24 July 2009 from http://adventure.howstuffworks.com/parthenon-and-the-acropolis-landmark.htm/printable

Europe: Bulgaria. (2009). *The World Factbook.* Retrieved 24 July 2009 from https://www.cia.gov/library/publications/the-world-factbook/geos/bu.html

Europe: Romania. (2009). *The World Factbook.* Retrieved 24 July 2009 from https://www.cia.gov/library/publications/the-world-factbook/geos/ro.html

Greco-Roman origin myths: Art discussion: The fall of Phaëton. (n.d.). The National Gallery of Art. Retrieved 24 July 2009 from http://www.nga.gov/education/classroom/origin_myths/art_phaeton.shtm

Heilbrunn timeline of art history: The Crusades (1095–1291). (n.d.). The Metropolitan Museum of Art. Retrieved 24 July 2009 from http://www.metmuseum.org/toah/hd/crus/hd_crus.htm

Hickman, K. (2008). *Muslim invasions: Martel triumphs at Tours.* About.com: Military History. Retrieved 24 July 2009 from http://militaryhistory.about.com/b/2008/10/10/muslim-invasions-martel-triumphs-at-tours.htm

Holy Roman Empire. (2009). In *Microsoft Encarta Online Encyclopedia 2009.* Retrieved 24 July 2009 from http://encarta.msn.com/encyclopedia_761558731/holy_roman_empire.html

The Jewish Virtual Library. (n.d.). Retrieved 24 July 2009 from http://www.jewishvirtuallibrary.org/index.html

Lewis, R. (n.d.). Introduction to *Cato, a tragedy in five acts.* Constitution Society. Retrieved 24 July 2009 from http://www.constitution.org/addison/cato_play.htm

Metz, H. C. (Ed.). (1995). *A country study: Turkey.* Washington, DC: Library of Congress. Retrieved 24 July 2009 from http://memory.loc.gov/frd/cs/trtoc.html

Nationalism as a destructive force. (n.d.). Oswego City School District Regents Exam Prep Center. Retrieved 24 July 2009 from http://regentsprep.org/Regents/global/themes/nationalism/division.cfm

Ortner, M. J. (2001). Captain Nathan Hale (1755–1776). The Connecticut Society of the Sons of the American Revolution. Retrieved 24 July 2009 from http://www.connecticutsar.org/patriots/hale_nathan_2.htm

Richman, S. (2008). Fascism. In *The Concise Encyclopedia of Economics.* Library of Economics and Liberty. Retrieved 24 July 2009 from http://www.econlib.org/library/Enc/Fascism.html

Roman Empire, Eastern. (2009). Encyclopædia Britannica. In *Encyclopædia Britannica 2009 Deluxe Edition*. Chicago: Encyclopædia Britannica.
Solsten, E. (Ed.). (1993). *A country study: Austria*. Washington, DC: Library of Congress. Retrieved 24 July 2009 from http://memory.loc.gov/frd/cs/attoc.html#at0037
Solsten, E., & Meditz, S. W. (Eds.). (1988). *A country study: Finland*. Washington, DC: Library of Congress. Retrieved 24 July 2009 from http://memory.loc.gov/frd/cs/fitoc.html
Solsten, E., & Meditz, S. W. (Eds.). (1988). *A country study: Spain*. Washington, DC: Library of Congress. Retrieved 24 July 2009 from http://memory.loc.gov/frd/cs/estoc.html#es0000
Timeline: Finland. (2009, January 21). *British Broadcasting Corporation*. Retrieved 24 July 2009 from http://news.bbc.co.uk/2/hi/europe/1032683.stm

Chapter 6, Lesson 2—The European Union

Austria. (2009). Encyclopædia Britannica. In *Encyclopædia Britannica 2009 Deluxe Edition*. Chicago: Encyclopædia Britannica.
Battles: The Battle of Verdun, 1916. (2003, October 4). First World War: The War to End All Wars. Retrieved 27 July 2009 from http://www.firstworldwar.com/battles/verdun.htm
Drozdiak, W. (1998, September 28). Kohl's place in history is secure. *The Washington Post*. Retrieved 27 July 2009 from http://community.seattletimes.nwsource.com/archive/?date=19980928&slug=2774661
The Euro. (n.d.). European Commission: Economic and Financial Affairs. Retrieved 27 July 2009 from http://ec.europa.eu/economy_finance/the_euro/index_en.htm?cs_mid=2946
Europa: The history of the European Union. (n.d.). Europa: Gateway to the European Union. Retrieved 27 July 2009 from http://europa.eu/abc/history/index_en.htm
European Atomic Energy Community (Euratom). (2009). Encyclopædia Britannica. In *Encyclopædia Britannica 2009 Deluxe Edition*. Chicago: Encyclopædia Britannica.
European Coal and Steel Community. (2009). In *Microsoft Encarta Online Encyclopedia 2009*. Retrieved 27 July 2009 from http://encarta.msn.com/encyclopedia_761589431/european_coal_and_steel_community.html
Fear of floating. (2009, June 11). *The Economist*. Retrieved 27 July 2009 from http://www.economist.com/specialreports/displaystory.cfm?story_id=13767437
Gross, D. (2004, December 28). Euro trash: Even drug dealers are giving up on the dollar. *Slate*. Retrieved 27 July 2009 from http://slate.msn.com/id/2111504/
Münchau, W. (2008, April 4). *Euro to replace dollar as world's reserve currency*. EuroIntelligence. Retrieved 27 July 2009 from http://www.euractiv.com/en/euro/euro-replace-dollar-world-reserve-currency/article-171351
Paul, R. (2007, January 1). The world's reserve currency. *Hawaii Reporter*. Retrieved 27 July 2009 from http://www.hawaiireporter.com/story.aspx?d80229ff-1011-45fd-919b-004f6b0ebd33
Porter, R. D., & Judson, R. A. (1996, October). The location of US currency: How much is abroad? *The Federal Reserve Bulletin*. Retrieved 27 July 2009 from http://findarticles.com/p/articles/mi_m4126/is_n10_v82/ai_18786211/?tag=content;col1
Q&A: The Lisbon Treaty. (2009, June 30). *British Broadcasting Corporation*. Retrieved 27 July 2009 from http://news.bbc.co.uk/2/hi/europe/6901353.stm
Q+A - Replacing the dollar as reserve currency. (2009, July 8). *Reuters*. Retrieved 27 July 2009 from http://www.reuters.com/article/usDollarRpt/idUSN0627861320090708

Chapter 6, Lesson 3—Immigration, Terrorist Cells, and Ethnic Strife

The 3/11 Madrid bombings: An assessment after 5 years. (2009). Woodrow Wilson International Center for Scholars: International Security Studies. Retrieved 1 August 2009 from http://www.wilsoncenter.org/index.cfm?topic_id=1416&fuseaction=topics.item&news_id=518495
2008 human rights report: France. (2009). US Department of State. Retrieved 3 August 2009 from http://www.state.gov/g/drl/rls/hrrpt/2008/eur/119079.htm

2008 human rights report: Germany. (2009). US Department of State. Retrieved 3 August 2009 from http://www.state.gov/g/drl/rls/hrrpt/2008/eur/119081.htm

2008 human rights report: United Kingdom. (2009). US Department of State. Retrieved 3 August 2009 from http://www.state.gov/g/drl/rls/hrrpt/2008/eur/119111.htm

Al-Qaeda 'claims Madrid bombings.' (2004, March 14). *British Broadcasting Corporation*. Retrieved 3 August 2009 from http://news.bbc.co.uk/2/hi/europe/3509426.stm

Al-Qa'ida (the base). (2009). Federation of American Scientists. Retrieved 31 July 2009 from http://www.fas.org/irp/world/para/ladin.htm

Ammitzbøll, P., & Vidino, L. (2007, Winter). After the Danish cartoon controversy. *Middle East Quarterly, 14*(1), 3–11. Retrieved 3 August from http://www.meforum.org/1437/after-the-danish-cartoon-controversy

Asylum in the EU in 2008. (2009). European Union. Retrieved 3 August 2009 from http://europa.eu/rapid/pressReleasesAction.do?reference=STAT/09/66&format=HT

Ben-David, E. (2009, Spring). Europe's shifting immigration dynamic. *Middle East Quarterly, 16*(2), 5–24. Retrieved 3 August 2009 from http://www.meforum.org/2107/europe-shifting-immigration-dynamic

Caulcutt, C. (2007, November 28). No change in the 'banlieues' since 2005. *France 24*. Retrieved 3 August 2009 from http://www.france24.com/france24Public/en/special-reports/20071127-banlieues-riots-france-villiers-le-bel/20071127-france-economy-unemployment-suburbs-riots-government-change.php

Council split on Turkey. (2007, June 1). EurActiv.com. Retrieved 3 August 2009 from http://www.euractiv.com/en/enlargement/council-split-turkey/article-159645

Cyprus: Profile. (2009). US Department of State Background Notes. Retrieved 2 August 2009 from http://www.state.gov/r/pa/ei/bgn/5376.htm

European arrest warrant. (2006). European Union. Retrieved 1 August 2009 from http://europa.eu/legislation_summaries/justice_freedom_security/judicial_cooperation_in_criminal_matters/l33167_en.htm

France: Profile. (2009). US Department of State Background Notes. Retrieved 3 August 2009 from http://www.state.gov/r/pa/ei/bgn/3842.htm

France to let in eastern workers. (2008, May 28). *British Broadcasting Corporation*. Retrieved 3 August 2009 from http://news.bbc.co.uk/2/hi/europe/7424096.stm

Graff, J. (2005, November 2). Why Paris is burning. *Time*. Retrieved 3 August 2009 from http://www.time.com/time/world/article/0,8599,1125401,00.html

Hall, B. (2000, June). Immigration in the European Union: Problem or solution? *Prospect Magazine*. Retrieved 3 August 2009 from http://www.oecdobserver.org/news/fullstory.php/aid/337/

Homeland Security: Hamburg Cell. (2006). GlobalSecurity.org. Retrieved 31 July 2009 from http://www.globalsecurity.org/security/profiles/hamburg_cell.htm

Ireland: Profile. (2009). US Department of State Background Notes. Retrieved 3 August 2009 from http://www.state.gov/r/pa/ei/bgn/3180.htm

Kulish, N. (2009, April 26). As economic turmoil mounts, so do attacks on Hungary's gypsies. *The New York Times*. Retrieved 3 August 2009 from http://www.nytimes.com/2009/04/27/world/europe/27hungary.html?_r=2&hp

Lawless, J. (2003, February 4). Radical Muslim cleric barred from North London mosque. *The Associated Press*. Retrieved 1 August 2009 from http://www.independent.co.uk/news/uk/home-news/radical-muslim-cleric-barred-from-north-london-mosque-745800.html

Leiken, R. S. (2005, July/August). Europe's angry Muslims. *Foreign Affairs*. Retrieved 3 August 2009 from http://www.cfr.org/publication/8218/

Lives lost to the Troubles. (2009, January 28). *British Broadcasting Corporation*. Retrieved 3 August 2009 from http://news.bbc.co.uk/2/hi/uk_news/northern_ireland/7853266.stm

MacAskill, E., Laville, S., & Harding, L. (2006, February 4). Cartoon controversy spreads throughout Muslim world. *The Guardian*. Retrieved 3 August 2009 from http://www.guardian.co.uk/world/2006/feb/04/muhammadcartoons.pressandpublishing

Madrid bombing probe finds no al-Qaida link. (2006, March 9). *The Associated Press*. Retrieved 31 July 2009 from http://www.msnbc.msn.com/id/11753547/

Milne, S. (2008, July 10). This persecution of Gypsies is now the shame of Europe. *The Guardian*. Retrieved 3 August 2009 from http://www.guardian.co.uk/commentisfree/2008/jul/10/race.humanrights

Murder raises ethnic tension higher. (2009, April 30). *British Broadcasting Corporation*. Retrieved 3 August 2009 from http://news.bbc.co.uk/2/hi/europe/8026722.stm

The new al-Qaeda: Madrid bombings. (2005, July 21). *British Broadcasting Corporation*. Retrieved 3 August 2009 from http://news.bbc.co.uk/2/hi/programmes/4697707.stm

Noble, R. K. (2004). *Secretary General's keynote address on 'Terrorism and the law: The global challenge.'* INTERPOL. Retrieved 1 August 2009 from http://www.interpol.int/public/ICPO/speeches/SG20040604.asp

Perera, R. (2002, July 2). Germany tries to make itself foreigner-friendly. *The Chronicle of Higher Education*. Retrieved 3 August 2009 from http://chora.virtualave.net/germany-immigration.htm

Phillips, J. (2006). *The evolving al-Qaeda threat*. The Heritage Foundation. Retrieved 31 July 2009 from http://www.heritage.org/research/homelandsecurity/hl928.cfm

Right of Union citizens and their family members to move and reside freely within the territory of the member states. (2007). The European Union. Retrieved 3 August 2009 from http://europa.eu/legislation_summaries/justice_freedom_security/free_movement_of_persons_asylum_immigration/l33152_en.htm

Solsten, E. (Ed.). (1995). *A country study: Germany*. Washington, DC: Library of Congress. Retrieved 3 August 2009 from http://memory.loc.gov/frd/cs/detoc.html

Strieff, D. (2006, July 5). Terror-tinged U.K. mosque gets a makeover. *MSNBC*. Retrieved 3 August 2009 from http://www.msnbc.msn.com/id/13501930/ns/world_news-islam_in_europe/

United Kingdom: Profile. (2009). US Department of State Background Notes. Retrieved 3 August 2009 from http://www.state.gov/r/pa/ei/bgn/3846.htm

The West at war: Transatlantic cooperation in the fight against terrorism (Part II). (2006). The Washington Institute for Near East Policy. Retrieved 1 August 2009 from http://www.washingtoninstitute.org/templateC05.php?CID=2518

World directory of minorities and indigenous peoples—Germany: Turks and Kurds. (2008). Minority Rights Group International. Retrieved 3 August 2009 from http://www.unhcr.org/refworld/topic,463af2212,488edfe22,49749d1a41,0.html

Chapter 6, Lesson 4—The Creation and Collapse of Yugoslavia

Bosnia and Herzegovina: Profile. (2009). US Department of State Background Notes. Retrieved 6 August 2009 from http://www.state.gov/r/pa/ei/bgn/2868.htm

Croatia: Profile. (2008). US Department of State Background Notes. Retrieved 6 August 2009 from http://www.state.gov/r/pa/ei/bgn/3166.htm

Curtis, G. E. (Ed.). (1990). *A country study: Yugoslavia*. Washington, DC: Library of Congress. Retrieved 27 January 2009 from http://lcweb2.loc.gov/frd/cs/yutoc.html

Fineman, M. (1999, June 24). The night is long when you're afraid. *Los Angeles Times*. Retrieved 5 August 2009 from http://latimes.perfectmarket.com/1999/jun/24/news/mn-49678

Kosovo: Profile. (2009). US Department of State Background Notes. Retrieved 3 August 2009 from http://www.state.gov/r/pa/ei/bgn/100931.htm

Macedonia: Profile. (2009). US Department of State Background Notes. Retrieved 6 August 2009 from http://www.state.gov/r/pa/ei/bgn/26759.htm

The Milosevic indictment. (2001, June 29). *The Guardian*. Retrieved 6 August 2009 from http://www.guardian.co.uk/world/2001/jun/29/warcrimes

Milosevic's Yugoslavia. (n.d.). *British Broadcasting Corporation*. Retrieved 6 August 2009 from http://news.bbc.co.uk/hi/english/static/in_depth/europe/2000/milosevic_yugoslavia/default.stm

Montenegro: Profile. (2009). US Department of State Background Notes. Retrieved 6 August 2009 from http://www.state.gov/r/pa/ei/bgn/70949

Peter II. (2009). Encyclopædia Britannica. In *Encyclopædia Britannica 2009 Deluxe Edition*. Chicago: Encyclopædia Britannica.

Russo-Turkish wars. (2009). Encyclopædia Britannica. In *Encyclopædia Britannica 2009 Deluxe Edition*. Chicago: Encyclopædia Britannica.

Serbia: Profile. (2009). US Department of State Background Notes. Retrieved 6 August 2009 from http://www.state.gov/r/pa/ei/bgn/5388.htm

Slovenia: Profile. (2009). US Department of State Background Notes. Retrieved 6 August 2009 from http://www.state.gov/r/pa/ei/bgn/3407.htm

Van Hook, L. W. (2001). *Ethnicity in exile: Coping with the Yugoslavs in World War II*. Woodrow Wilson International Center for Scholars. Retrieved 3 August 2009 from http://www.wilsoncenter.org/index.cfm?topic_id=1422&fuseaction=topics.publications&doc_id=8402&group_id=7427

Walker, R. (2007, September 27). Serbian foreign minister talks about Kosovo, other issues. *The Harvard Gazette*. Retrieved 6 August 2009 from http://www.news.harvard.edu/gazette/2007/09.27/09-serbia.html

Chapter 6, Lesson 5–US Interests and Regional Issues in Europe

Albania and Croatia join NATO. (2009). US Department of State. Retrieved 10 August 2009 from http://www.america.gov/st/peacesec-english/2009/April/20090401130205dmslahrellek0.6114008.html

Albania: Profile. (2009). US Department of State Background Notes. Retrieved 11 August 2009 from http://www.state.gov/r/pa/ei/bgn/3235.htm

American entry into World War I, 1917. (n.d.). US State Department: Timeline of US Diplomatic History. Retrieved 9 August 2009 from http://www.state.gov/r/pa/ho/time/wwi/82205.htm

The Atlantic Conference & Charter, 1941. (n.d.). US State Department: Timeline of US Diplomatic History. Retrieved 9 August 2009 from http://www.state.gov/r/pa/ho/time/wwii/86559.htm

The Berlin Airlift. (n.d.). *PBS: The American Experience*. Retrieved 13 August 2009 from http://www.pbs.org/wgbh/amex/airlift/timeline/timeline2.html

Bosnia buries Srebrenica victims. (2009, July 9). *British Broadcasting Corporation*. Retrieved 10 August 2009 from http://news.bbc.co.uk/2/hi/europe/8146182.stm

Bulgaria: Profile. (2009). US Department of State Background Notes. Retrieved 11 August 2009 from http://www.state.gov/r/pa/ei/bgn/3236.htm

Curtis, G. E. (Ed.). (1992). *A country study: Poland*. Washington, DC: Library of Congress. Retrieved 27 January 2009 from http://memory.loc.gov/frd/cs/pltoc.html

Czech Republic: Profile. (2009). US Department of State Background Notes. Retrieved 11 August 2009 from http://www.state.gov/r/pa/ei/bgn/3237.htm

EU-U.S. economic ties: Framework, scope, and magnitude. (2006). Washington DC: Library of Congress—Congressional Research Service. Retrieved 13 August 2009 from http://fpc.state.gov/documents/organization/62662.pdf

Fast facts about NATO. (2009). *Canadian Broadcasting Corporation*. Retrieved 10 August 2009 from http://www.cbc.ca/world/story/2009/04/03/f-nato-fast-facts.html

Germany: Profile. (2009). US Department of State Background Notes. Retrieved 11 August 2009 from http://www.state.gov/r/pa/ei/bgn/3997.htm

Henry Luce and 20th century U.S. internationalism. (n.d.). US State Department: Timeline of US Diplomatic History. Retrieved 9 August 2009 from http://www.state.gov/r/pa/ho/time/wwii/100929.htm

Hungary: Profile. (2009). US Department of State Background Notes. Retrieved 11 August 2009 from http://www.state.gov/r/pa/ei/bgn/26566.htm

Implementation Force (IFOR) in Bosnia and Herzegovina (1995–1996). (2007). North Atlantic Treaty Organization. Retrieved 10 August 2009 from http://www.nato.int/issues/ifor/index.html

The League of Nations, 1920. (n.d.). US State Department: Timeline of US Diplomatic History. Retrieved 9 August 2009 from http://www.state.gov/r/pa/ho/time/wwi/99150.htm

The list: Who's left in Afghanistan? (2008, March). *Foreign Policy*. Retrieved 10 August 2009 from http://www.foreignpolicy.com/story/cms.php?story_id=4235&print=1

Meier, A. (2008, August 20). Let Russia join NATO. *Los Angeles Times*. Retrieved 10 August 2009 from http://www.latimes.com/news/opinion/la-oe-meier20-2008aug20,0,1714241.story

NATO to assume command of ISAF in Kabul August 11. (2003). US Department of State. Retrieved 10 August 2009 from http://www.america.gov/st/washfile-english/2003/August/20030808154539renneflO.4603083.html

NATO's 60th Anniversary—1949–2009. (2009). North Atlantic Treaty Organization. Retrieved 10 August 2009 from http://www.nato.int/60years/anecdotes.html

NATO's role in Afghanistan. (2009). North Atlantic Treaty Organization. Retrieved 10 August 2009 from http://www.nato.int/cps/en/natolive/topics_8189.htm

NATO's role in Kosovo. (2007). North Atlantic Treaty Organization. Retrieved 10 August 2009 from http://www.nato.int/koSovo/kosovo.htm

Ott, M. (1993). Foreign investment in the United States. In *The Concise Encyclopedia of Economics*. Library of Economics and Liberty. Retrieved 11 August 2009 from http://www.econlib.org/library/Enc1/ForeignInvestmentintheUnitedStates.html

The Paris Peace Conference and the Treaty of Versailles. (n.d.). US State Department: Timeline of US Diplomatic History. Retrieved 9 August 2009 from http://www.state.gov/r/pa/ho/time/wwi/89875.htm

Peace support operations in Bosnia and Herzegovina. (2009). North Atlantic Treaty Organization. Retrieved 10 August 2009 from http://www.nato.int/issues/sfor/index.html

Poland: Profile. (2009). US Department of State Background Notes. Retrieved 11 August 2009 from http://www.state.gov/r/pa/ei/bgn/2875.htm

Romania: Profile. (2009). US Department of State Background Notes. Retrieved 11 August 2009 from http://www.state.gov/r/pa/ei/bgn/35722.htm

Slovakia: Profile. (2008). US Department of State Background Notes. Retrieved 11 August 2009 from http://www.state.gov/r/pa/ei/bgn/3430.htm

Solsten, E. (Ed.). (1995). *A country study: Germany*. Washington, DC: Library of Congress. Retrieved 27 January 2009 from http://memory.loc.gov/frd/cs/detoc.html

Sound recording of President Truman talking about the Berlin Airlift. (1964). Harry S. Truman Library. Retrieved 13 August 2009 from http://www.presidentialtimeline.org

US barriers to trade and investment report for 2006. (2007). The European Commission. Retrieved 11 August 2009 from http://trade.ec.europa.eu/doclib/docs/2007/february/tradoc_133290.pdf

Wilson's Fourteen Points, 1918. (n.d.). US State Department: Timeline of US Diplomatic History. Retrieved 9 August 2009 from http://www.state.gov/r/pa/ho/time/wwi/17688.htm

Woodrow Wilson's speech notes, in shorthand, for his 'Fourteen Points' address, [8 January 1918]. (1918). Washington, DC: The Library of Congress. Retrieved 8 August 2009 from http://memory.loc.gov/cgi-bin/query/r?ammem/mcc:@field(DOCID+@lit(mcc/057))

Glossary

abdicate—to give up the throne. (p. 377)
affirmative action—a government policy that enforces hiring and other goals to combat discrimination. (p. 208)
agenda—a set of goals to achieve. (p. 95)
amnesty—a pardon for crimes (p. 308); forgiveness or pardon. (p. 587)
analects—fragments or literary excerpts. (p. 134)
anarchy—a situation that's out of control with, in effect, no one in charge. (p. 171)
annex—to take over. (p. 53)
anticlericalism—opposition to the involvement of the clergy in secular affairs. (p. 527)
anti-Semitism—prejudice against Jewish people. (p. 370)
apartheid—racial segregation. (p. 279)
arable—able to be farmed. (p. 172)
archipelago—a large group of islands spread across the sea. (p. 149)
aristocrat—the nobles or "top class." (p. 179)
assimilate—to become like one's environment; to blend or fit in; to make (something or someone) similar, to absorb, to take in. (p. 653)
atheistic—believing God doesn't exist. (p. 369)
authoritarian—requiring absolute obedience. (p. 393)
autocratic—where total power rests in one person. (p. 396)
autonomous—independent. (p. 29)

bilateral—between two individual parties. (p. 412)
biodiversity—the number and variety of plant and animal species of a place, or of the world as a whole. (p. 329)
brain drain—the loss of skills and knowledge from a place when its educated people leave. (p. 348)
British raj—British rule in India. (p. 184)
burqa—a full-body covering for women. (p. 118)

caliph—a universal Muslim ruler. (p. 26)
caliphate—the Arab political unity of Islam's golden age, centered in Baghdad. (p. 99)
capital—money and resources available to invest. (p. 231)
capitalism—an economic system in which the means of production are privately owned. (p. 12)
cartel—a group of independent entities that band together to control the price of a commodity. (p. 114)
caste—hereditary social class. (p. 179)

central bank—a government body that issues currency, regulates the supply of credit, and holds the reserves of other banks. (p. 640)
civil service—government employees and institutions. (p. 154)
clandestine—secret. (p. 53)
class struggle—the working classes locked in conflict with the "oppressive" property—owning classes. (p. 393)
collective farm—a farm or a group of farms organized as a unit and managed and worked cooperatively by a group of laborers under state supervision. (p. 379)
collectivization—the process of putting something under the ownership or control of the "collective"—a group of people. (p. 390)
collusion—a secret agreement. (p. 343)
commonwealth—a self-governing territory voluntarily associated with the United States. (p. 479)
communal—shared. (p. 169)
communism—an economic system in which property belongs to everyone and work is organized for the benefit of everyone. (p. 12)
concession—a contract granting the right to operate something (p. 54); a land area under the control of a foreign power. (p. 156)
condominium—a territory subject to joint rule by two or more powers. (p. 292)
confessionalism—a system of allocating offices among different religious and ethnic groups. (p. 40)
conquistadores—conquerors. (p. 487)
conscripts—draftees. (p. 61)
constitutional monarchy—a government by a king or queen whose powers are limited by the constitution and laws of the country. (p. 73)
contraceptives—birth control pills and devices. (p. 213)
co-opt—to exploit for one's own purposes. (p. 517)
coup d'état—a sudden takeover of a government. (p. 74)
covert—hidden or secret. (p. 575)
creoles—people born in Latin America of European parentage. (p. 498)
crude—another name for oil, especially in its raw or unprocessed state. (p. 111)
Crusades—a series of wars (1095 to 1291) intended to liberate Jerusalem from Muslim rule. (p. 609)
cult of personality—an unhealthy intense personal focus on a leader. (p. 380)
culture—includes language, ideas, beliefs, customs, codes, institutions, tools, techniques, works of art, rituals, and ceremonies, among other elements. (p. 4)
customs union—an association of nations to promote free trade within the union and set common tariffs for nations that are not members. (p. 633)

de facto—accepted as fact even if not based on law. (p. 188)
deforestation—the removal of trees. (p. 329)
defraud—to deprive someone of something by lying or cheating. (p. 215)
demobilize—to take out of military service. (p. 307)
demographics—a population's makeup in race, ethnicity, and culture, among other characteristics. (p. 659)

desertification—the process whereby land becomes desert. (p. 330)
détente—relaxation of international tension. (p. 453)
dialectical materialism—the process by which the class struggle leads to the dictatorship of the proletariat, socialism, and then communism. (p. 393)
Diaspora—the scattering of Jews far from their traditional homeland. (p. 61)
dictatorship of the proletariat—an early stage of socialism, marked by the workers' dominance in putting down the resistance of the property-owning classes. (p. 393)
disenfranchise—to deprive people of their vote. (p. 288)
doctrine—a body of principles. (p. 227)
dual-use technology—technology that can be used for civilian or military purposes. (p. 227)

economics—the study of the production and distribution of goods and services, and their management. (p. 10)
edicts—proclamations or commands. (p. 155)
egalitarian—without class divisions. (p. 389)
embargo—ban on trade. (p. 65)
emigrant—someone who travels out of one place to settle in another. (p. 42)
émigré—someone who leaves his country, especially during war. (p. 417)
epidemic—the sudden and rapid spread of a disease. (p. 317)
equatorial—set along the equator. (p. 249)
established church—a church officially favored by the state and supported by tax revenues. (p. 664)
ethnic cleansing—the organized elimination of an ethnic group or groups from a region or society by deportation, forced emigration, or genocide. (p. 616)
ethno-linguistic group—a group of people who share a common language and culture. (p. 257)
Eurasia—the landmass that includes Europe and Asia. (p. 131)
Euroskeptics—people who oppose further EU integration. (p. 639)
evangelizing—recruiting. (p. 485)
expropriation—seizure of a foreign firm's assets, with no compensation paid. (p. 591)
extradition—the legal process by which one country surrenders a criminal or criminal suspect to another for punishment or trial. (p. 545)

faction—group. (p. 253)
famine—a drastic, wide-ranging food shortage. (p. 323)
fertile crescent—a crescent-shaped area reaching from the Nile Valley through the eastern shore of the Mediterranean to Mesopotamia. (p. 27)
feudalism—the political, economic, and social system that prevailed in medieval Europe and relied on a relationship among lords, vassals, and serfs. (p. 11)
figurehead—a person supposedly in charge. (p. 96)
fissionable—can be split to make nuclear explosions. (p. 251)

foreign direct investment—what occurs when a company establishes a physical presence in a foreign country. (p. 342)
forfeiture—the government's seizure of property involved in criminal activity. (p. 546)
free enterprise—private companies owned by individuals. (p. 391)

genocide—the mass killing of one kind of people. (p. 295)
geopolitical—how a country's geography—as well as its natural resources—affects its relations with other nations. (p. 467)
glasnost—open public discussion of problems. (p. 382)
graft—the illegal use of power to get more power, money, and property. (p. 539)
griot—an African storyteller, especially one from West Africa. (p. 256)
gross national product—the sum total of a country's output of goods and services. (p. 64)
guest worker—a migrant worker who works abroad temporarily and then returns home. (p. 587)
gunboat diplomacy—the threat, or limited use, of naval force to reach a foreign policy goal. (p. 161)
guru—teacher or priest. (p. 139)

habitat—a creature's natural home. (p. 331)
hacienda—an estate. (p. 511)
hard currency—money that can be converted to other currencies. (p. 224)
hereditary rule—passing down titles, like chief or king, and genes from family member to family member. (p. 282)
homogeneous—to be of one kind, to be similar. (p. 143)
human trafficking—forcing, defrauding, or coercing someone into labor or sexual exploitation. (p. 215)

ideology—a core shared belief. (p. 154)
Indian subcontinent—a term used to refer to India, Pakistan, Bangladesh, and Sri Lanka. (p. 177)
indigenous—native. (p. 261)
industrialize—to develop and build a modern manufacturing base (factories) in a country or region. (p. 201)
infidels—nonbelievers. (p. 484)
infrastructure—roads, rail lines, power lines, communications cables, and water and sewer lines. (p. 192)
insurgency—an organized rebellion trying to overthrow a government. (p. 105)
interim—temporary. (p. 187)
international terrorism—terrorism that involves the citizens or territory of more than one country. (p. 95)
intifada—uprising. (p. 70)
irrigate—water. (p. 253)

isolationism—a policy of avoiding alliances and other forms of international relations. (p. 709)
isthmus—a narrow strip of land, with water on either side, that connects two larger bodies of land. (p. 479)

junta—a group of military officers ruling a country after seizing power. (p. 519)

karma—the total effect of someone's actions and conduct throughout his or her life. (p. 137)
Knesset—the Israeli parliament. (p. 67)
Koran—the holy book of Islam. (p. 36)

liberation theology—an activist movement of Roman Catholic priests who make direct efforts to improve the lot of the poor. (p. 528)
lingua franca—a common language used by the speakers of other languages. (p. 149)
linguist—someone who studies languages. (p. 260)

madrassa—religious schools. (p. 197)
mandate—a commission, or an assignment, from the League of Nations authorizing a member nation to administer a territory. (p. 38)
maquiladoras—export-reprocessing centers. (p. 554)
maritime—of or relating to the sea. (p. 351)
market share—the percentage, or amount, of overall sales of any particular product a company controls. (p. 235)
martial law—military rule. (p. 166)
Marxism—the political and economic theories of Karl Marx, a founder of socialism and communism. (p. 379)
mercantilism—the doctrine that the government of a nation can strengthen its economic interests by protecting its home industries, increasing foreign trade, and ensuring that the nation exports more than it imports. (p. 11)
metropolitan—a church leader, like an archbishop in the West. (p. 369)
monotheistic—to adhere to the idea of one God. (p. 34)
muster out—to discharge. (p. 306)

narcotic—an addictive drug that alters mood or behavior and usually induces sleep. (p. 545)
nascent—developing. (p. 49)
nationalize—to put under state control. (p. 55)
nation-state—an autonomous political entity that is home to a more or less homogeneous group of people. (p. 617)
navigable—capable of carrying ships or boats. (p. 479)
normalization—a return to normal relations without tensions. (p. 465)
nuclear nonproliferation—preventing the spread and increase of nuclear weapons. (p. 120)

offshoring—moving factories or work from the United States to other countries. (p. 231)
oil reserves—the supply of crude oil that a country can retrieve. (p. 111)
onus—the burden, or the responsibility. (p. 353)
outsourcing—the procurement of goods and services from an outside supplier. (p. 22)

pan-Arabism—a movement for greater cooperation among Arab states. (p. 75)
pandemic—a widespread or even global disease, affecting high numbers of people worldwide. (p. 316)
parasite—a creature that grows and feeds off another organism without contributing to the well-being of the host. (p. 314)
parastatal—owned partly or wholly by the government. (p.325)
partition—to divide (p. 41)
perestroika—restructuring of the economy. (p. 383)
plebiscite—a direct vote of the entire electorate. (p. 226)
pogrom—organized persecutions or massacres. (p. 61)
polities—organized political units. (p. 271)
polygamy—having more than one spouse at a time. (p. 255)
polytheistic—worshipping many gods. (p. 489)
primogeniture—the right of first-born sons to inherit all their fathers' property. (p. 374)
principality—a territory ruled by a prince. (p. 373)
proletariat—the working classes. (p. 393)
proselytizing—efforts to win converts to a religion. (p. 485)
protectionism—the policy or practice of restricting imports to protect home industries. (p. 13)
protectorate—a relationship of protection and partial control that a superior power assumes over a dependent country or region. (p. 37)
provisional—temporary. (p. 157)
proxy—a stand-in. (p. 96)
purdah—the veiling and seclusion of married women. (p. 210)

quisling—a traitor who serves as the puppet of the enemy occupying his or her country. (p. 627)
quotas—limits. (p. 114)

reactionary—opposed to progress. (p. 106)
reconciliation—an end to disagreement. (p. 293)
referendum—a vote by the people. (p. 637)
regent—one who rules for a lawful monarch who is too young for the throne. (p. 374)
rehabilitation—restoring one's good reputation. (p. 443)

remittance—a sum of money a worker abroad sends back home to his or her family. (p. 586)
renounce—to give up or turn away from. (p. 240)
reparation—the act of making amends for an injury, often through payments to the injured party. (p. 688)
repatriated—returned to their homeland. (p. 281)
republic—a form of government run by the people generally through elected representatives. (p. 157)
reserve currency—a currency that governments keep on hand to pay international debts. (p. 645)
resource nationalism—policies or efforts to nationalize a country's natural resources. (p. 591)

sabotage—acts of deliberate destruction to hinder an operation or cause. (p. 340)
sacraments—religious rites. (p. 612)
safe haven—a space that provides a secure base for extremist action. (p. 107)
samurai—the warrior aristocrats of Japan. (p. 161)
savanna—a flat grassland of tropical or subtropical regions. (p. 250)
scapegoat—one who is forced to take the blame for others' failings. (p. 618)
schism—a break or split within a group. (p. 610)
secretariat—the offices that manage a country's or an organization's affairs. (p. 428)
sectarian—relating to religious or other strongly held beliefs. (p. 288)
secularization—a movement away from religion in general. (p. 484)
sedition—words or deeds meant to stir up rebellion against the government. (p. 679)
self-determination—the principle that the people of a particular territory should decide how it is to be governed. (p. 19)
separatist—a member of a movement to break away from a larger body. (p. 415)
sharia—Islamic religious law. (p. 98)
shoguns—military governors. (p. 160)
simony—the practice of buying and selling church offices. (p. 612)
social mobility—the ability of individuals or groups to move up or down within a class structure according to changes in income, education, or occupation. (p. 557)
social stratification—division of a society into layers. (p. 271)
socialism—a form of rule in which the government controls everything from businesses to how much land people may own. (p. 377)
soviet—a Russian word that means council. (p. 377)
status quo antebellum—the state of things before the war. (p. 75)
steppes—vast treeless grass-covered plains. (p. 364)
stigma—symbol of disgrace. (p. 321)
subjugate—to conquer or subdue. (p. 296)
sub-Saharan Africa—that part of Africa south of the Sahara Desert. (p. 257)
subsidy—government money used to keep prices artificially low for goods such as food and oil. (p. 414)

subsistence farming—a type of farming in which the farmers and their families eat most of what they produce and sell very little. (p. 556)
sultan—a ruler. (p. 32)
superpowers—militarily superior countries. (p. 121)
sustainable development—economic progress that doesn't harm the environment. (p. 354)
syncretism—a combination of different forms of religious belief or practice. (p. 486)

taiga—coniferous (cone-bearing) forest. (p. 364)
Taliban—an Islamic fundamentalist militia that governed Afghanistan for several years. (p. 197)
terrorism—premeditated, politically motivated violence against noncombatants by subnational groups or clandestine agents, generally to influence an audience. (p. 94)
terrorist cell—a small group of usually three to five terrorists who work together, separate from other groups nearby. (p. 663)
terrorist group—any group that practices terrorism or has a subgroup that does. (p. 95)
theory of comparative advantage—holds that countries should specialize in the goods and services where they have a relative edge. (p. 13)
totalitarian—featuring absolute government control of every aspect of life. (p. 392)
trade—the buying and selling of goods and services. (p. 13)
transatlantic—crossing the Atlantic Ocean. (p. 271)
transcendental—a supernatural world beyond the human "here and now." (p. 136)
transnational—to be active across international borders. (p. 105)
tribute—a tax. (p. 373)
trusteeship—an arrangement for one country to govern another under international control. (p. 164)
tundra—a vast treeless area between the tree line and the Arctic icecap, with permanently frozen subsoil. (p. 364)

universal franchise—when everyone gets to vote, particularly when all races and ethnicities get to vote. (p. 279)
urbanization—the movement of population from rural areas into cities. (p. 205)

vernacular—the language people actually speak. (p. 612)
viable—able to survive. (p. 52)
vicious circle—a situation where one trouble leads to another that aggravates the original problem. (p. 315)
visa—a document that gives the bearer permission to travel to a particular country. (p. 584)

Wahhabism—an austere form of Sunni Islam, a so-called reform movement that began 200 years ago to rid Islamic societies of practices and teaching acquired over the centuries. (p. 98)

warlords—rulers who exercise both military and civil authority in the absence of a strong central government. (p. 158)

warm-water port—a port that does not ice up during the winter. (p. 448)

weapons of mass destruction (WMD)—chemical, biological, or nuclear weapons that can kill large numbers of people in one use. (p. 84)

white paper—a statement of government policy. (p. 51)

Yishuv—the Jewish community in Palestine before statehood. (p. 53)

Zionism—a movement to establish a home in Palestine for the world's Jews. (p. 41)

Index

A

B

C

D

E

J

N

O

P

Q

R

S

T

U

V

W

Y

Z